Semantic Knowledge Management:
An Ontology-Based Framework

Antonio Zilli
University of Salento, Italy

Ernesto Damiani
University of Milan, Italy

Paolo Ceravolo
University of Milan, Italy

Angelo Corallo
University of Salento, Italy

Gianluca Elia
University of Salento, Italy

Information Science REFERENCE

INFORMATION SCIENCE REFERENCE

Hershey · New York

Director of Editorial Content: Kristin Klinger
Senior Managing Editor: Jennifer Neidig
Managing Editor: Jamie Snavely
Assistant Managing Editor: Carole Coulson
Typesetter: Amanda Appicello
Cover Design: Lisa Tosheff
Printed at: Yurchak Printing Inc.

Published in the United States of America by
Information Science Reference (an imprint of IGI Global)
701 E. Chocolate Avenue, Suite 200
Hershey PA 17033
Tel: 717-533-8845
Fax: 717-533-8661
E-mail: cust@igi-global.com
Web site: http://www.igi-global.com

and in the United Kingdom by
Information Science Reference (an imprint of IGI Global)
3 Henrietta Street
Covent Garden
London WC2E 8LU
Tel: 44 20 7240 0856
Fax: 44 20 7379 0609
Web site: http://www.eurospanbookstore.com

Library of Congress Cataloging-in-Publication Data

Semantic knowledge management : an ontology-based framework / Antonio Zilli ... [et al.], editor.

p. cm.

Summary: "This book addresses the Semantic Web from an operative point of view using theoretical approaches, methodologies, and software applications as innovative solutions to true knowledge management"--Provided by publisher.

Includes bibliographical references and index.

ISBN 978-1-60566-034-9 (hardcover) -- ISBN 978-1-60566-035-6 (ebook)

1. Knowledge management. 2. Semantic Web. 3. Semantic networks (Information theory) I. Zilli, Antonio.

HD30.2.S457 2009

658.4'038--dc22

2008009117

British Cataloguing in Publication Data
A Cataloguing in Publication record for this book is available from the British Library.

Editorial Advisory Board

Table of Contents

Detailed Table of Contents

This chapter provides an introduction to ontology engineering discussing the role of ontologies in informative systems, presenting a methodology for ontology design, and introducing ontology languages. The chapter starts by explaining why ontology is needed in informative system, then it introduces the reader to ontologies by leading the reader in a stepwise guide to ontology design. It concludes by introducing ontology languages and standards. This is a primer reading aimed at preparing novice readers of this book to understanding more complex dissertations, for this reason it can be avoided by expert readers.

This chapter introduces OntoExtractor, a tool for semi-automatic generation of taxonomy from a set of documents or data sources. The tool generates the taxonomy in a bottom-up fashion: starting from structural analysis of the documents, it generates a set of clusters, which can be refined by a further grouping generated by content analysis. Metadata describing the content of each cluster is automatically generated and analysed by the tool for generating the final taxonomy. A simulation of a tool, based on implicit and explicit voting mechanism, for the maintenance of the taxonomy is also described. The author describes a system that can be used to generate taxonomy from a heterogeneous source of information, using wrappers for converting the original format of the document to a structured one. This way OntoExtractor can virtually generate taxonomy from any source of information just adding the proper wrapper. Moreover, the trust mechanism allows a reliable method for maintaining the taxonomy and for overcoming the unavoidable generation of wrong classes in the taxonomy.

This chapter summarizes technologies and approaches that permit to search information in a knowledge base. The chapter suggests that the search based on both keywords and ontology allows a more effective search, which understands the semantic of the information in a variety of data. The chapter starts with the presentation of current methods to build taxonomy, fill the taxonomy with documents, and search documents. Then, we describe our experience related to the creation of an informal taxonomy, the automatic classification and the validation of search results with traditional measures, which are precision, recall and f-measure. We intend to show that the use of ontology for domain representation and knowledge search offers a more efficient approach for knowledge management. This approach focuses on the meaning of the word, and thus becoming an important element in the building of the Semantic Web.

Peer-to-peer (P2P) systems represent nowadays a large portion of Internet traffic, and are fundamental data sources. In a pure P2P system, since no peer has the power or responsibility to monitor and restrain others behaviours, there is no method to verify the trustworthiness of shared resources, and malicious peers can spread untrustworthy data objects to the system. Furthermore, data descriptions are often simple features directly connected to data or annotations based on heterogeneous schemas, a fact that makes difficult to obtain a single coherent trust value on a resource. This chapter describes techniques where the combination of Semantic Web and peer-to-peer technologies is used for expressing the knowledge shared by peers in a well-defined and formal way. Finally, dealing with Semantic-based P2P networks, the chapter suggests a research effort in this direction, where the association between cluster-based overlay networks and reputation systems based on numerical approaches seems to be promising.

This chapter presents a prototypal e-Learning system based on the Semantic Web paradigm, called SWELS (Semantic Web E-Learning System). The chapter starts by introducing e-Learning as an efficient and just-in-time tool supporting the learning processes; then a brief description of the evolution of distance learning technologies will be provided, starting from first generation e-Learning systems until the current Virtual Learning Environments and Managed Learning Environments, by underling the main differences between them and the need to introduce standards for e-Learning with which to manage and overcome problems related to learning content personalization and updating. Furthermore, some limits of the traditional approaches and technologies for e-Learning will be provided by proposing the Semantic Web as an efficient and effective tool for implementing new generation e-Learning systems. In the last section of the chapter the SWELS system is proposed, by describing the methodology adopted for organizing and modelling its knowledge base, by illustrating its main functionalities, and by providing the design of the tool together with the implementation choices. Finally, future developments of SWELS will be presented, together with some remarks regarding the benefits for the final user in using such system.

There are different approaches to modelling a computational system, each providing a different semantics. We present a comparison between different approaches to semantics and aim at identifying which peculiarities are needed to provide a system with a uniquely interpretable semantics. We discuss different approaches, namely, description logics, artificial neural networks, and relational database management systems. We identify classification (the process of building a taxonomy) as common trait. However, in this paper we also argue that classification is not enough to provide a system with a Semantics, which

opment of knowledge management systems and knowledge sharing. Activity theory as a philosophical and cross disciplinary framework for studying different forms of human practices is well suited for study research within a community of practice such as knowledge management in collaborative research. This paper shows how activity theory can be used as a kernel theory for the development of a knowledge management design theory for collaborative work.

This chapter provides a classification of virtual communities of practice according to methods and tools offered to virtual community's members for knowledge management and for the interaction process. It underlines how these methods and tools support users during the exchange of knowledge, enable learning, and increase user ability to achieve individual and collective goals. In this chapter virtual communities are classified in virtual knowledge-sharing communities of practice and virtual learning communities of practice according to the collaboration strategy. A further classification defines three kinds of virtual communities according to the knowledge structure: ontology-based VCoP; digital library-based VCoP; and knowledge map-based VCoP. This chapter describes also strategies of interaction used to improve the knowledge sharing and learning in groups and organization. It shows how agent-based method supports interaction among community's members, improves the achievement of knowledge and encourages the level of participation of users. Finally this chapter describes the system's functionalities that support browsing and searching processes in collaborative knowledge environments.

Knowledge Management (KM) is considered by many organizations to be a key aspect in sustaining competitive advantage. In the mechanical design domain, the KM facilitates the design of routine product and brings a saving time for innovation. This chapter describes the specification of a project memory as an organizational memory to specify knowledge to capitalize all along project in order to be reuse. Afterwards it presents the design of a domain ontology and a multi agent system to manage project memories all along professional activities. As a matter of fact, these activities require that engineers with different specialities collaborate to carry out the same goal. Inside professional activities, they use their know-how and knowledge in order to achieve the laid down goals. The professional actors competences and knowledge modelling allows the design and the description of agents' know-how. Furthermore, the paper describes the design of our agent model based on an organisational approach and the role of a domain ontology called OntoDesign to manage heterogeneous and distributed knowledge.

Section III
Semantic-Based Applications

This chapter introduces a distributed framework for OKM (Organizational Knowledge Management) which allows IKWs (Individual Knowledge Workers) to build virtual communities that manage and share knowledge within workspaces. The proposed framework, called K-link+, supports the emergent way of doing business of IKWs, which require allows work at any time from everywhere, by exploiting the VO (Virtual Office) model. Moreover, since semantic aspects represent a key point in dealing with organizational knowledge, K-link+ is supported by an ontological framework composed of: (i) an UO (Upper Ontology), which defines a shared common background on organizational knowledge domains; (ii) a set of UO specializations, namely workspace ontologies or personal ontologies, that can be used to manage and search content; (iii) a set of COKE (Core Organizational Knowledge Entities) which provide a shared definition of human resources, technological resources, knowledge objects, services and (iv) an annotation mechanism that allows one to create associations between ontology concepts and knowledge objects. K-link+ features a hybrid (partly centralized and partly distributed) protocol to guarantee the consistency of shared knowledge and a distributed voting mechanism to foster the evolution of ontologies on the basis of user needs.

This chapter proposes an agent-based architecture for home care support whose main capability is to continuously admit and apply new medical knowledge, entered into the system, capturing and codifying implicit knowledge deriving from the medical staff. Knowledge is the fundamental catalyst in all application domains and this is particularly true especially for the medical context. Knowledge formalization, representation, exploitation, creation and sharing are some of the most complex issues related to Knowledge Management. Moreover, Artificial Intelligence techniques and Multi-Agent System (MAS) in health care are increasingly justifying the large demand for their application since traditional techniques are often not suitable to manage complex tasks or to adapt to unexpected events. The manuscript presents also a methodology for approaching medical knowledge management, from its representation symbolism to the implementation details. The codification of health care treatments, as well as the formalization of domain knowledge, serves as an explicit, a priori asset for the agent platform implementation. The system has the capability of applying new, implicit knowledge emerging from physicians.

KM has become an important strategy for improving organisational competitiveness and performance. Organisations can certainly benefit from the lessons learnt and insights gained from those that have adopted it. This chapter presents the results of a case study conducted in a consultancy firm and the major aim is to identify how KM has been developed and implemented. Specifically, the elements investigated in the case study include the following KM aspects: strategies and activities; leadership and coordination; systems and tools; training; culture and motivation; outcomes and measurement; and implementation approach. Hopefully, the information extracted from this study will be beneficial to other organisations that are embarking on the KM journey.

In this chapter we present StockWatcher, an OWL-based Web application that enables the extraction of relevant news items from RSS feeds concerning the NASDAQ-100 listed companies. The application's goal is to present a customized, aggregated view of the news categorized by different topics. We distinguish between four relevant news categories: i) news regarding the company itself; ii) news regarding direct competitors of the company; iii) news regarding important people of the company; and iv) news regarding the industry in which the company is active. At the same time, the system presented in this chapter is able to rate these news items based on their relevance. We identify three possible effects that a news message can have on the company, and thus on the stock price of that company: i) positive; ii) negative; and iii) neutral. Currently, StockWatcher provides support for the NASDAQ-100 companies. The selection of the relevant news items is based on a customizable user portfolio that may consist of one or more of these companies.

Preface

In the last few years, many international organizations and enterprises have designed, developed, and deployed advanced knowledge management systems that are now vital for their daily operations. Multi-faceted, complex content is increasingly important for companies and organizations' successful operation and competitiveness.

The Semantic Web perspective has added to knowledge management systems a new capability-- reasoning on ontology-based metadata. In many application fields, however, data semantics is getting more and more context- and time-dependent, and cannot be fixed once and for all at design time.

Recently, some novel knowledge generation and access paradigms such as augmented cognition, case-study-based reasoning, and episodic games have shown the capability of accelerating the kinetics of ideas and competence transmission in creative communities, allowing organizations to exploit the high interactive potential of broadband and mobile network access.

In this new scenario, traditional design-time data semantics frozen in database schemata or other metadata is only a starting point. Online, emergent semantics are playing an increasingly important role. The supply of semantics is twofold: firstly, human designers are responsible for providing initial semantic mappings between information and its environment used for context-aware access. Secondly, the meaning of data is dynamically augmented and adapted taking into account organizational processes and, in general, human cognition.

The Semantic Web paradigm was proposed to tackle some of the problems related to implicit representation of data semantics affecting Web-related data items (e.g., email messages or HTML pages), providing the capability of updating and modifying ontology-based semantic annotations. Today, advanced knowledge management platforms incorporate on-demand production of Semantic-Web style metadata based on explicit, shared reference systems such as ontology vocabularies, which consist of explicit though partial definitions of the intended meaning for a domain of discourse. However, providing a consistent Semantic-Web style explicit representation of an organization's data semantics is only a first step for leveraging organizational knowledge.

It is widely recognized that business ontologies can be unstable and that managing ontology evolution and alignment is a constant challenge, as well as a heavy computational burden. Indeed, this problem cannot be tackled without realizing that integrating initial, design-time semantics with emergent, interaction-time semantics is as much an organizational, business-related process as a technology-based one.

THE KIWI VISION

The KIWI (Knowledge-based Innovation for the Web Infrastructure) vision was born out of an interdisciplinary research project involving a computer science research group, SESAR lab (http://ra.crema.unimi.it)

and eBMS, an advanced business school working in the e-business management area (http://www.ebms.unile.it). The project was funded by the Italian Ministry of Research - Basic Research Fund (FIRB).

KIWI envisioned a distributed community composed of information agents sharing content, for example, in advanced knowledge management platforms, corporate universities or peer-to-peer multimedia content sharing systems. In this community, agents and human actors are able to cooperate in building new semantics based on their interaction and adding it to content, irrespective of the source (and vocabulary) of the initial semantics of the information.

The KIWI vision considers emergent semantics constructed incrementally in this way as a powerful tool for increasing content validity and impact.

The observation that emergent semantics result from a self-organizing process has also some interesting consequences on the stability of the content from the business management and social sciences point of view. Also, this perspective promises to address some of the inherently hard problems of classical ways of building semantics in information systems. Emergent semantics provides a natural solution as its definition is based on a process of finding stable agreements; constant evolution is part of the model and stable states, provided they exist, are autonomously detected. Also, emergent semantics techniques can be applied to detect and even predict changes and evolution in the state of an organization or a community.

THIS BOOK'S STRUCTURE

This book contains a number of contributions from well-recognized international researchers who, although working independently, share at least some of the aims and the interdisciplinary approach of the original KIWI project.

The contents are structured in three sections. The first one is completely related to the KIWI project; the activities, the theoretical results, and the prototypes developed are presented and discussed. The work was developed in a methodological framework that represents the phases and the tools for an effective introduction of a semantic-based knowledge management platform in a community. The second one presents other theoretical works related to the introduction of the semantic description of knowledge resource in organization or in technological environment. The third section instead is devoted to the description of technological systems and applications that are planned and developed for improving with the semantic aspect the management of knowledge resources.

More in particular, Chapter I, "KIWI: A Framework for Enabling Semantic Knowledge Management," by Paolo Ceravolo, Angelo Corallo, Ernesto Damiani, Gianluca Elia, and Antonio Zilli, provides a general overview of the KIWI vision and approach, while Chapter II, "Introduction to Ontology Engineering," written by Paolo Ceravolo and Ernesto Damiani, provides a no-prerequisites introduction to Semantic-Web style explicit representation of data semantics. Thanks to these introductory chapters the reader will be able to understand the basic techniques of data annotation by means of ontology-based vocabularies. Semantic-Web style annotations give an explicit representation of the data semantics as perceived at design-time by the data owners and creators. However, in many cases semantic annotations are not created manually, but extracted from existing data.

Chapter III, "OntoExtractor: A Tool for Semi-Automatic Generation and Maintenance of Taxonomies from Semi-Structured Documents," by Marcello Leida, and Chapter IV, "Search Engine: Approaches and Performance" written by Eliana Campi and Gianluca Lorenzo, respectively discuss semi-automatic techniques and tools for generating semantic annotations, and the performance of classic (as opposed to semantics-aware) access and search techniques. These chapters identify many potential advantages and pitfalls of a "straightforward" application of Semantic Web techniques to add semantics-aware annotations to business data.

Then, the scope of the book broadens, taking into account later additions to annotations expressing data semantics due to interactions. Chapter V"Toward Semantic-based P2P Reputation Systems," by Ernesto Damiani and Marco Viviani, shows how peer-to-peer interaction at different levels of anonymity can be used to superimpose new annotations to existing metadata, assessing their reliability and trustworthiness. An important field for exploiting online, emergent semantics based on interactions is Web-based e-learning, where the learner patterns of behavior when interacting with content can be captured and transformed into additional annotations to the content itself or to its original metadata.

Chapter VI, "SWELS: A Semantic Web System Supporting e-Learning," by Gianluca Elia, Giustina Secundo, and Cesare Taurino, explores this semantics-aware perspective on e-learning, while Chapter VII, "Approaches to Semantics in Knowledge Management," by Cristiano Fugazza, Stefano David, Anna Montesanto, and Cesare Rocchi, discusses some fundamental problems raised by the adoption of explicit semantics representation techniques as the basis of knowledge management systems.

The next two chapters deal with the relation between design-time and emergent data semantics on one side and the definition of the business processes where data are used on the other side. Namely, Chapter VIII, "A Workflow Management System for Ontology Engineering," by Alessandra Carcagnì, Angelo Corallo, Antonio Zilli, Nunzio Ingraffia, and Silvio Sorace, describes a methodology and its implementation in a workflow management system for producing ontology-based representations. Chapter IX, "Activity Theory for Knowledge Management in Organizations," by Lorna Uden, proposes a theoretical foundation to workflows for generating knowledge.

The following chapters discuss in detail the application of the KIWI vision to specific business-related scenarios. Namely, Chapter X, "Knowledge Management and Interaction in Virtual Communities," by Maria Chiara Caschera, Arianna D'Ulizia, Fernando Ferri, and Patrizia Grifoni, is about the practical integration of design-time and emergent semantics in the context of the highly dynamic virtual communities of Web 2.0. Chapter XI, "An Ontological Approach to Manage Project Memories in Organizations," by Davy Monticalo, Vincent Hilaire, Samuel Gomes, and Abderrafiaa Koukam, goes back to organizational knowledge management, elaborating on the specific problems posed by managing semantically rich content such as project memories. Chapter XII "*K-link+*: A P2P Semantic Virtual Office for Organizational Knowledge Management," by Carlo Mastroianni, Giuseppe Pirrò, and Domenico Talia describes a practical solution relying on peer-to-peer technology and protocols supporting different levels of anonymity.

The book's concluding chapters contain highly interesting and practical case-studies. Namely, Chapter XIII, "Formalizing and Leveraging Domain Knowledge in the K4CARE Home Care Platform," by Ákos Hajnal, Antonio Moreno, Gianfranco Pedone and David Riaño, deals with the increasingly important scenario of knowledge management supporting healthcare and assisted living environments. Chapter XIV, "Knowledge Management Implementation in a Consultancy Firm", by Kuan Yew Wong and Wai Peng Wong, presents a case study related to managing the information produced in a consultancy activity, which present interesting problems related to intellectual rights management. Chapter XV, "Financial News Analysis Using a Semantic Web Approach," by Alex Micu, Laurens Mast, Viorel Milea, Flavius Frasincar, and Uzay Kaymak, discusses the user centered extraction of semantics from financial newsfeeds.

In Chapter XVI, "Enhancing E-Business on the Semantic Web through Automatic Multimedia Representation," by Manjeet Rege, Ming Dong, and Farshad Fotouhi, a Semantic Web automatic data description process is applied to multimedia content; the system is aimed at improving electronic collaboration between firms and customers.

Chapter XVII, "Utilizing Semantic Web and Software Agents in a Travel Support System," by Maria Ganzha, Maciej Gawinecki, Marcin Paprzycki, Rafal Gasiorowski, Szymon Pisarek, and Wawrzyniec Hyska, presents an ontology based e-business application: ontologies are used to make functioning an agent-based travel support system, the ontology , used to demarcate data, enable to manage user profiles. In the end, Chapter XVIII, "Personalized Information Retrieval in a Semantic-based Learning Environment," by Antonella Carbonaro and Rodolfo Ferrini, discusses a learning system able to arrange course using an ontological description of contents and users.

CONCLUSION

With the rapid emergence of social applications on the Web, self-organization effects have once again proven their interest as a way to add semantics to existing business knowledge.
This book discusses how identifying emerging relationships among previously unrelated content items (e.g., based on user and community interaction) may dramatically increase the content's business value. ES (Emergent Semantics) techniques enrich content via a self-organizing process performed by distributed agents adaptively developing the proper interpretation via multi-party cooperation and conflict resolution. Emergent content semantics is dynamically dependent on the collective behavior of communities of agents, which may have different and even conflicting interests and agendas.

According to the KIWI overall vision, a new generation of content will self-organize around end-users semantic input, increasing its business value and timeliness. The KIWI approach envisions a more decentralized, user-driven "imperfect," time-variant Web of semantics that self-organizes dynamically, tolerating conflicts.

Prof. Ernesto Damiani, University of Milan, Italy
Prof. Giuseppina Passiante, University of Salento, Italy

Acknowledgment

We would like to thank the team that worked at the KIWI project, some of whom contributed chapters to this book. In particular, we would like to thank Prof. E. Damiani (Università degli Studi di Milano, Milano, Italia) and Prof. Passiante (Università del Salento, Lecce, Italia) who coordinated the two research units involved in the KIWI project. The KIWI project was funded by the Italian Minister for Scientific Research (MIUR) through the Basic Research Fund (FIRB).

Special thanks to Dott Cristina Monteverdi (Università degli Studi di Milano, Milano, Italia) for her effective and energetic help in revising the English spelling of this book.

We would like to express our gratitude to all authors of this book, to all reviewers who participated in the process to improve the contents, and to all those who gave us the possibility to publish this book.

The Editors
P. Ceravolo, A. Corallo, E. Damiani, G. Elia, A. Zilli

Section I
Knowledge-Based Innovations for the Web Infrastructure

Chapter I
KIWI:
A Framework for Enabling Semantic Knowledge Management

Ernesto Damiani
University of Milan, Italy

Paolo Ceravolo
University of Milan, Italy

Angelo Corallo
University of Salento, Italy

Gianluca Elia
University of Salento, Italy

Antonio Zilli
University of Salento, Italy

ABSTRACT

Research on semantic-aware knowledge management provides new solutions, technologies, and methods to manage organizational knowledge. These solutions open new opportunities to "virtual challenges" as e-collaboration, e-business, e-learning and e-government. The research carried out for the KIWI (Knowledge-based Innovation for the Web Infrastructure) project is focused on the strategies for the current Web evolution in the more powerful Semantic Web, where formal semantic representation of resources enables a more effective knowledge sharing. The first pillar of the KIWI framework concerns development of ontologies as a metadata layer. Resources can be formally and semantically annotated with these metadata, while search engines or software agents can use them for retrieving the right information item or applying their reasoning capabilities. The second pillar of the KIWI framework is focused on the semantic search engine. Their capabilities and functionalities have to be improved in order to take advantage of the new semantic descriptions. A set of prototypal tools that enable knowledge experts to produce a semantic knowledge management system was delivered by the project. The KIWI framework and tools are applied in some projects for designing and developing knowledge-based platforms with positive results.

INTRODUCTION AND MOTIVATIONS

The widespread diffusion of Internet, broadband availability and accessing devices have changed the way human beings develop their professional lives, the way people work and look for information, the way people book and have entertainment, and the way people live their personal relationships. This new "hardware" context (i.e., cabled and wireless networks) has opened the doors to a new way of content diffusion and to a new generation of applications, called generally Web 2.0, which is enabling Web surfers to be direct protagonists of the content creation (Anderson, 2007).

This powerful technological context and this wider and wider content availability have put a new question: how can we use them? This is the context the project "KIWI" tried to face. The strategy and the solutions provided by the research carried out for this project contribute to the "Semantic Web" research stream (Berners-Lee et al., 2001).

While the new "hardware" conditions enable new software capabilities, society and all its business processes require users to exploit them to obtain new and more powerful results. Technological innovations enable Web surfers to put into practice their creativity and imagination. In the end, all aspects of the everyday life are nicked by this technological trend. "Knowledge workers" (Drucker, 1994) have now an extremely powerful tool for their work. Being information reachable in a few clicks, the knowledge worker can focus on its more valuable activities: extracting knowledge from the information space, creating new knowledge from the assembled information, planning and carrying out knowledge-based projects, configuring connections among data and information. That is, the knowledge worker can be focused more on reasoning and applying knowledge than looking for data and information.

Another important aspect of the life of organizations which changed with Internet concerns team management and the collaborative behaviour in a team and among teams. Today, people can collaborate on a global scale, expert communities have emerged and are glued together using Internet-based collaboration; networks of practitioners meet on virtual squares (Gloor, 2006). Wider teams and communities mean more (tacit and explicit) knowledge, more perspectives, more expertise, and then more creative capabilities (Nonaka & Takeuchi, 1995). Being so, organizations started to use Web to improve collaboration in their teams, and as a by-product, even free interests-based communities emerged, generally called CoP (Wenger, 1999).

The Web is a platform even for other types of social networks: user and consumer communities that are communities that have as main aim the exchange of knowledge on specific topics, as the performance and the usability of a software or the behaviour of firms. In the end, people are experiencing a new way of collaborating, sharing knowledge, obtaining helps and suggestions, so that today very few questions cannot be answered via Internet.

From an organizational point of view, projects can be carried out without any regional limits in this way organizations are transforming themselves from being "multinational" to being really "global," from a stage where each factory builds its relations and partnerships on a local or national level to a stage where supply chains connect actors from many nations. From this point of view, the Internet is the infrastructure on which globalization spreads over, while communication is cheaper, simpler and more complete day by day; working side by side is not a location problem but a band problem and this makes the "global company" real (Malone, 2004; Tapscott & Williams, 2006).

At the same time (and substantially for the same reasons), directors, managers, workers, all people need more and more information and knowledge, and they need them "now." But while the Web contains quite surely the needed information, the question to answer is: where is it? It might be already organized in a Web page (then the problem is to find this page), or it must be assembled by aggregating data and information from different sources (then the problem is even more complex: recognizing the elements composing the answers, finding each of them and aggregating them together). Perhaps it is in an official Web site, or it is in a forum of experts or in a blog, and so on; in other words, is it trustful? The knowledge worker does not have to work hard in looking for knowledge, but he has to work hard for recognizing and extracting the right knowledge in the ocean of overflowing information.

The evolution of Web applications in its firsts 15 years proposes this wide range of issues. Web users live in a closed loop of needs and solutions. Web developers propose each day a huge quantity of applications under any type of licenses for the most diverse problems. The researcher and practitioner communities are defining standards for data and applications, and a new horizon for the future.

The KIWI project is aimed at participating at this research stream by facing the semantic aspects of data and information, that is, how to build a metadata layer that formalizes semantic descriptions of the resources useful for improving the managing capabilities of resources themselves.

SEMANTIC WEB: PROBLEMS AND SOLUTIONS

The concept of "Semantic Web" was introduced by Tim Berners-Lee in 2001 with a pioneering paper on Scientific American (Berners-Lee et al., 2001). After this publication the "Semantic Web" concept was applied to quite all the different aspects of the Web, from information management to Web services. The W3C (World Wide Web Consortium) is facing the topic and some standards were already suggested as RDF (Recourse Description Framework) or OWL (Ontology Web Language). These are descriptive languages for building semantic schemas to which data and information resources can refer. But many different approaches are continuously tested with the aim of improving the machine capabilities. The obvious limits the Web had in 2001 concern the capability of surfing automatically through Web pages and Web services, and to manage personal and public data. The Semantic Web is the possible answer to the need of a fast interaction among human users who have the personal goal of browsing the Web, and Internet as a whole composed of many actors (Web sites) and services (Web services) . As stated in (Berners-Lee et al., 2001), the Semantic Web is a place in which users have to think, and applications have to act.

The Semantic Web approach is applied in many business sectors but no clear results are available. One of the most appealing applicative contexts is the tourist sector; many projects are on going for developing technological systems based on ontologies, (see www.teschet.net.). From a technological point of view, this applicative context shows interesting challenges: many actors and services to coordinate (housing service, transportation service, cultural services, payment services); a huge amount of data (user personal and private data, payment data, timing data, etc.); many services to distribute (information service, booking services and ticketing service, etc.). From the business point of view, the innovation

Figure 1. Total sites across all domains December 1995–September 2007, source: (Netcraft, 2007)

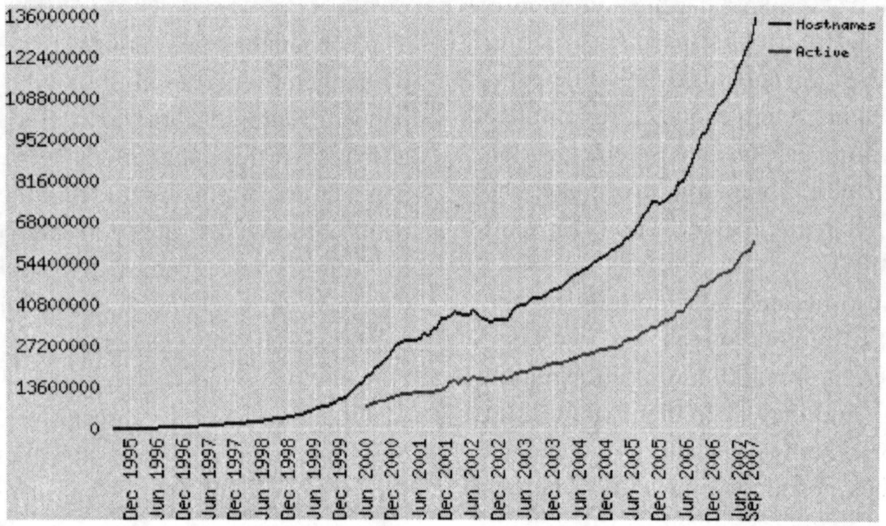

introduced by semantic technologies changed the way organizations (especially tourist firms) interact with customers, and, mainly, customers take significant advantages of these technological innovations. Anyway, the lacking of globally accepted standards reduces the range of technological innovations.

The other most important applicative context is Web itself, that is the "Semantic Web" should be a Web where reaching the right information is simpler. The Web is growing at exponential rate. Figure 1 shows the number of the hostnames from 1995 to early 2007 (Netcraft, 2007). A similar trend is recognizable for the number of pages for a Web site (Huberman & Adamic, 1999). It is obvious that each Web surfer knows only an extremely low percentage of the Web, and search engines are his compass. A lot of search engines are available on the Web. They differ in many features. The two most important elements are the algorithm for indexing and ranking pages and the presentation of query's results.

Search engines designed in the '90s indexed Web pages using keywords extracted from documents while the ranking (the importance of document with respect to each keyword) was built on the number of similar words it contains, the distance among them, and other topological data of the resource.

The first revolutionary search engine was (or is) Google[a]. Its indexing and ranking process is managed by the software PageRank™, the most important innovation it introduced concerns the page ranking. It assumes a link from the page A to the page B as a "vote" for the page B, so the page B is more important and trustful, and its rank is higher.

Another interesting search engine is Vivisimo[b]; its power lies in the capability of clustering in real time the query results: they are aggregated at query time according to their keywords, and the user can browse the cluster structure refining the query's terms.

A fascinating search engine is Kartoo[c] for its graphical interface. Results are showed in maps. Each Web page (the query result) is a node in the map, and, what is more interesting, nodes are connected by "labelled links" that reflect the connection semantic between the two Web sites. Then, users can browse the map and after each action the search engine refine the query and then the map.

While Google is the most powerful and used search engine, the other two engines mentioned above underline what it totally missing--the capability of showing connections among the query results. Vivisimo and Kartoo use the keywords provided by the user for extracting a Web section, then they point out connections among Web pages and make them usable for a more aware analysis of the results.

THE KIWI PROJECT

The KIWI project was aimed to study the possibilities to manage huge amounts of data and information through ontologies, that is, through their semantic descriptions.

An ontology is an "explicit specification of a conceptualization" (Gruber, 1993). Ontologies have to be public and reachable by users (explicit); they represent a formal and logical description (specification) of a view of the world (conceptualization) that users are committed to. Ontologies are schemas of the world in which every items (class, relationship, attribute) are described using a natural language vocabulary, the explicit and formal triple composed of a class, a relationship and another class (as relationship value) or composed of a class, attribute and value (of the attribute) are expressed by a declarative language like RDF (Beckett, D. 2004) or OWL (Smith et al., 2004).

The first problem that comes to mind is related to the definition of the ontology. To be useful, an ontology needs to represent a shared conceptualization of the knowledge domain, that is, users recognize the interpretation of the world the ontology states.

Ontologies show their power in two main applicative contexts: (a) in managing data by different application exchanging and processing them, that is, when many applications are (or might be) integrated in a technological platform or system; and (b) in searching data, information and knowledge on the Web.

In the first case, ontologies may be treated as a general standard to which data and applications are adapted. Currently, quite all applications have their specific database, call data with application-specific name, use application-specific standards, and so on. If two applications or Web services (that is the most frequent case) have to exchange automatically data, integration must be organized by hand with a lot of development efforts. Instead, if shared ontologies were used for referencing data during the application's development phase, data could retain the same name and the same relations and attributes for every application and could be exchanged without effort.

The Semantic Web is not only ontology. Data, information and service and whatever type of resources should be indexed using metadata extracted from the ontology to be manageable through their semantics. This is the most complex task for Semantic Web researchers. While automatic indexing tools are quick but do not guarantee precision (it depends on the number of resources to be processed), manual indexing tools can be very precise but they are so extremely time consuming that only a small quantity of resources can be processed.

Furthermore, indexed documents must be opportunely managed. A semantic-based data structure needs right tools to be accessed and made usable by users. Search engines should access and manage new forms of data embedded in (Web) documents, generally RDF-based tags and their values; databases should represent not only a simple and unlabeled relationship but labeled, structured, and directed connections among resources. Moreover, the representation of the metadata structure and ontological concepts and their relationship need to be effective to improve the user experience. Search engines are trying many different approaches to this last topic as already explained for the examples about Vivisimo.com and Kartoo.com.

The main research questions pursued for the KIWI project are listed below:

1. Are there any methodologies for developing and maintaining ontologies? Are there any useful tools to this aim?
2. Which are the best strategies for indexing resources? And in which context?
3. How semantic search functionalities can be presented to users?

These research questions are clearly connected in a workflow that starts from non-digital knowledge about a specific domain and aims at providing to users a "semantic search" interface where looking for knowledge resources in a wide pool of documents and services.

Applications and methodologies developed for the KIWI project are conceived to be integrated in a knowledge management platform in order to introduce a semantic layer between knowledge resources and applications. In this way, resources can be managed (by push or pull engine) automatically respect their effective contents.

THE AIM OF KIWI

Today, communities and organizations need technological systems and internet connections in order to manage their documents, their processes, and their knowledge archives (goods, services, customers, etc.). Even collaborations and interactions among project teams can be mediated by Web applications that enable synchronous and asynchronous communications. Moreover, the latest Web applications, generally called Web 2.0 (Anderson, 2007), try to promote and sustain individual creativity and to encourage a virtual meeting and social network among users based on their individual interests and jobs.

Technological platforms are used as medium on which communication flows and knowledge is stored; they may be simply a passive system that users manage, or active systems that support users in their "on line life." The innovations connected with the Semantic Web research are focused on the development of active technological platforms. The assumption at the base of the Semantic Web research is if a clear, standardized and semantic-based description of resources and users is available, then it is possible to automate "reasoning," to aggregate data and information resources and to provide the right resource to the right user.

This assumption is very simple and reasonable, but it is not straightforward, it needs to develop a complex system of components:

1. a description of knowledge domain: the development of ontologies is a complex and time consuming activity, moreover today there are not any clear standard for the user description while ontologies that describe knowledge domains are extremely "application focused," that is not reusable out of the its specific context;
2. a standardized, semantic-based and clear description of the resources (data and information):
   a. "standardized" means that the description must be developed using a standard language (RDF, OWL, etc.) in order to be accessible by any "reader,"
   b. "semantic-based" means that the description must be referred to an ontol-

ogy (or at least a taxonomy), a world statement able to define elements and relationships among them, then to define a semantic for each term,

c. "clear" means that the description must be unambiguous. Logical properties of the language and the ontological description of the knowledge domain can help in achieving a high level of clearness;

3. then it is possible "to reason": the "artificial intelligence" research stream has a long history on this issue but no human like "reasoning" capability has been obtained.

The KIWI project is focused principally on the issues of defining ontologies and on developing a semantic search engine able to access the ontology itself and to extract resources described with semantic metadata. Any study on descriptive languages is devoted only to acquiring their structure as we assume the importance to use a widespread standard that only international bodies like the W3C can guarantee.

The final aim of the project is to sketch a methodology for developing ontology and describing knowledge resources and to develop an integrated set of tools for enabling users without deep technological skills to use them for building their semantic knowledge base. The strategy that is pursued is based on the awareness that the Semantic Web needs two types of skills: a technical expertise for using languages, tools and systems and knowledge expertise in order to develop effective ontologies.

THE APPLICATIVE CONTEXTS

Two major applicative contexts of the project are "local business districts" and "public administration and decision makers."

In business districts built by several actors (firms, associations, workers, etc.) working in the same industry or in a supply chain it is extremely important to have a knowledge platform on which to share insights, business strategies, technological trends, opportunities, and, at the same time, on which to debate about productive strategies and techniques, marketing solutions, customer care, political strategies, and similar issues. Actors involved in a supply chain can improve their productive coordination if they share information about warehouse, forecasts and limits. Moreover in the knowledge society these issues concern not only business actors but even public administrations and then decision makers, so they should be involved as users of the platform in order to be aware about needs, trends, and opportunities on going. In this context, the speed in recognizing information is a determinant performance factor for the network as whole.

Actually, people to whom we are referring as possible users of our technological system prefer direct face to face contacts for building their information network and avoid wasting time in looking for data and information.

A semantic knowledge platform should reduce difficulties in sharing information and knowledge through an exact description of the resource meaning. Actors of the district, as users of the platform, can browse the ontology for reaching the resources they are interested in. The ontology, the language spoken by the platform, will make the information system more familiar, while the simplicity of searching, retrieving, recognizing, and accessing the information will make the system more appealing for busy people.

The most important platform aspects are the quality of the ontology and the capability to browse it, that is, the same as browsing the knowledge base.

The KIWI project wants to provide knowledge domain experts with simple and user friendly tools to build ontologies implemented in the RDF language. This language was chosen for its simplicity and its diffusion on the Web (even in the form of "dialect" as RSS), so the future inclusion of a new type of resources for extending the knowledge base of the system will be easy to execute. The ontologies are stored in databases that represent the "triplet" structure of the RDF and are accessed by a tool (Assertion Maker) for describing the knowledge resources. The Assertion Maker is able to open an ontology and a document (in a "xml" format), the user can associate to each section of the document (title, paragraphs or others) a concept or a triple (subject-predicate-object) extracted from the ontology. In this way, a set of "semantic keywords" (simple assertion) or complex assertions are stored in the database for each document. The ontology and the assertions the knowledge experts created are used by the "Semantic Navigator," a semantic search engine. The Semantic Navigator proposes the ontology in two views. The first shows the taxonomy based on the relation "Is_A" as an indented list of concepts, and the second one enables user to build on line assertions from the ones already available in the RDF implementation of the ontology.

The described process is not feasible as stated. The indexing phase as described before is a very long hand-made process and it could be performed only on a limited set of resources. A necessary improvement is to introduce a semiautomatic system for pre-processing information resources. Specifically it is possible to assign them to one or more concepts of the "Is_A" taxonomy extracted from the ontology, and in a second phase expert users can improve assertions associated to the resources. In this way, a wide pool of documents can be indexed with semantic keywords (that are triples such as "document," "speak of," "concept/instance"), while a reduced number of resources (that need it) are indexed with the more detailed complex assertions ("document," "speak of," "concept/instance," "relation/attribute," "concept/instance/value").

This strategy was applied to the Virtual eBMS[d] experiment and it will be discussed in the Chapter 5 of this book.

Semantic Navigator, at the top of the presented process, empowers the search and retrieval capabilities. Users can be quite sure that the results' list contains documents related to the assertion built. The assurance is based on the preciseness of the classification process. But our system can be further improved.

A "trust evaluation" component is planned to be added in the Semantic Navigator. It is expected that users that retrieve a knowledge resource with Semantic Navigator will assign a vote to the sentences the resources is indexed by. So, time after time, the assertion's base may be extended and

Figure 2. Structure of the tools developed for the KIWI projects and their inputs and outputs

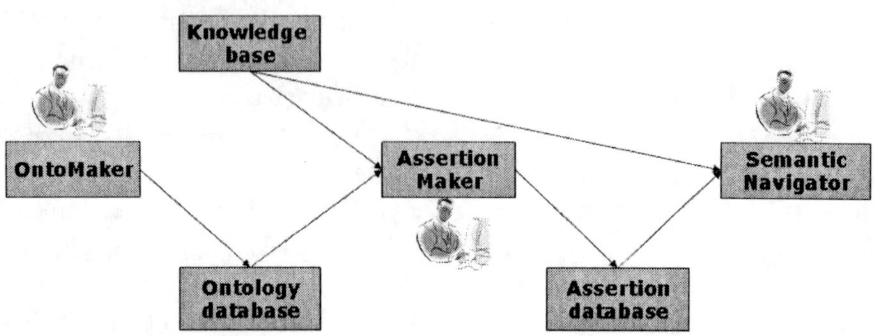

refined directly by knowledge domain experts (users of the platform that hosts the KIWI tools). In the end, Semantic Navigator gives as result of a query a list of knowledge items built on the ontological representation of their contents and ranked respect to the votes users gave to all the assertions associated to each of them.

This strategy is well suited for the knowledge society. The quick changes of the cultural and scientific background of people and the application of existing concepts and theory to new and different cases need dynamic knowledge bases, and the descriptive layer (ontology and resource metadata) is an integral part of it. Knowledge workers have to evolve their skills and competences day by day. Their daily work is a constant application of knowledge to new problems through a focused learning process. In the first case, experiences improve the worker's understanding and it is fundamentally peer-recognized, while in the second case there is a formal evaluation (the exam) and the profile of the worker can be officially extended.

Similarly, innovations emerge from the application of old knowledge items to new applicative contexts, or from the creation of new knowledge items for solving new problems (Afuah, 2002). Innovations change the view of the world, or, in the Semantic Web words, change ontologies, and then resources' metadata. To apply these changes we need to update ontologies and metadata, but this task need strong efforts and in a knowledge-based platform each change generally impacts on a wide part of the knowledge base. Instead, if an evolutionary approach is used, as we described before, the evolution of the knowledge base is managed by the user community itself: experts introduce simple changes (new concepts or new relations) and start to update metadata of resources and readers assign trust values to them. In this way, the knowledge base (ontologies and metadata) is updated, but old versions are not deleted. Therefore, structural updates of the knowledge bases rarely are necessary.

In the following sections, a deeper description of the framework developed for the KIWI project is presented. Methodologies and tools are discussed from the conceptual and usability point of view. The developing of ontologies is only partially a technological task. The most important phase of this task is the conceptualization of the world the ontology is going to represent, the definition of the context in which the ontology will be used, the user needs, and technological context in which it will be inserted. All these issues will define the characteristic the ontology should show. The technological application details are discussed in other chapters of this book.

The same approach is used for the other tools that compose the KIWI framework: the Assertion Maker and the Semantic Navigator.

At the end of this chapter, the main applications of the KIWI framework we are working on are discussed. The framework is applied in three projects of technological and Web-based innovation in communities of experts. In these cases, the Semantic Web approach to knowledge sharing was chosen and the KIWI framework is effective in helping them to design by themselves their knowledge base.

TOOLS AND METHODOLOGIES

Internet is used as the technological infrastructure by worldwide communities and organizational teams. The "geographical proximity" that was necessary until a few years ago is substituted with "relational proximity" that can span the whole Web space. Some most recent Web platforms show how near could become people who simply share information resources, hind-sights or pleasures. "Social software" is the name that represents this category of Web systems where users are invited to present themselves, to share something of them and to "connect" with other users. The Internet is the technical infrastructure while Web platforms are the technological systems on which knowledge and collaboration flow at higher and higher speed.

The KIWI project is focused on the development of a framework and an integrated application set for enabling a Semantic Web-based knowledge management strategy. The framework and applications are enough flexible to be inserted in any specific knowledge-based platform in order to make the knowledge base more structured and the searching and retrieving of right resources simpler.

The framework is structured in three different phases; the first one is the definition and implementation of the ontology that represents the shared conceptualization of the knowledge domain the community is faced to. The ontology is a valid filter for managing the knowledge resource base with respect to its meaning.

Having the ontology, resources need to be indexed or annotated using the ontology's concepts. Resource indexing is the second step.

The last phase is the every day usage of the knowledge resources. The user can search and retrieve the right resource browsing the ontology and, if any user description is available, access his/her recommendations.

HOW TO DEVELOP ONTOLOGIES

The issue of "ontology developing" is a time-honored one. The concept of ontology came from the artificial intelligence (Bennett, et al., 2006), but it seems to be very interesting in the Semantic Web movement as a semantic layer between data (resources) and users (human or intelligent agents).

In order to be useful, ontology has to be shared. In an international community of users who start interacting each other the first difficulty comes from languages. The same things can be called with different names in different local areas. Ontology can help the community to define and explicit a common language and to strengthen the efficacy of direct interactions. Moreover, ontology enables one to understand simply and effectively the world as it is seen by the community; this aspect is extremely useful in the process of entering a community, as well as an organizational intranet.

The process of developing an ontology might be quite different depending on the level of user involvement. It can be developed by a limited group of experts (belonging or not to the user community) and then imposed to the community's members, or it can be developed collectively in order to improve immediately the collaborative definition of the world (Corallo et al., 2005).

In the first case, many topics have to be explicitly defined in order to build an ontology that operates correctly in the technological platform in which it will be inserted in. The methodology we have defined is long and complex as problems are to be foreseen and solved. Ontology has to be usable even by applications that are not yet developed; the balance between the explicit and the implicit knowledge has to be monitored and that means meta-properties have to be defined and introduced, and applications using the ontology have to be able to reason on meta-properties. Perspective users (human being or intelligent agents) and the usage (cataloguing, searching, exchanging information) have to be well-understood as they pose limits on the logical layer of the explicit statements.

Implementation can start only when all these issues are solved. The first step is the creation of a vocabulary where concepts and relations are explained; then concepts can be structured in an "Is_A" taxonomy, and in the end relations among concepts can complete ontology. This methodology is described in depth in Chapter 9.

This top-down approach imposes to deal with all issues related to the ontology usage is clearly defined before the ontology is really developed and used, so even if the knowledge expert is very smart, some more limits could appear when users use it in the technological platform.

If this top-down approach is followed, a simple "KIWI" tool for ontology implementing is available "OntoMaker" (see Figure 4). It permits to build graphically concepts and relations among them, to translate the structure in the RDF language and to build a database (MS-Access) to store the ontology. The value of this tool is that the data it produces are in a format readable by other tools that follow the ontology building step in the KIWI framework.

In a specific application of the KIWI framework at the knowledge-based collaborative platform called Virtual eBMS and developed at eBMS-S. S. ISUFI, University of Salento (Italy), a second bottom-up approach was followed.

The Virtual eBMS is a platform for knowledge resource sharing and for project management and integrates e-lerning components. Ontology is used for cataloguing and searching information items in the wide pool of resources. It was possible to experiment the bottom-up approach as users belong to a very defined and high experienced community: the researchers and students of the eBusiness Management School. They were involved directly in the building of the vocabulary. Following this approach (Corallo et al., 2005), the most important issues are collectively discussed in a starting phase while the ontology development is mandated to the "collective intelligence." According to this approach, basic requirement in the ontology building phase but it should not overcome the world and applicative context definition that is necessary detailed in the top-down approach.

In other cases, a fully automatic approach is more useful for the ontology development. Tools for the automatic clustering of documents are already available, but their usage with a semantic aim needs further work. Moreover documents have a structure composed of different sections to be treated differently and generally automatic clustering tools are not able to distinguish these components. On the "Semantic Web" documents will not be text blobs, but they will be available as "structured content," that is, text introduced and followed by explicative tags. Under this as-

Figure 3. Schematic view of the methodology for ontology developing (see Chapter 9)

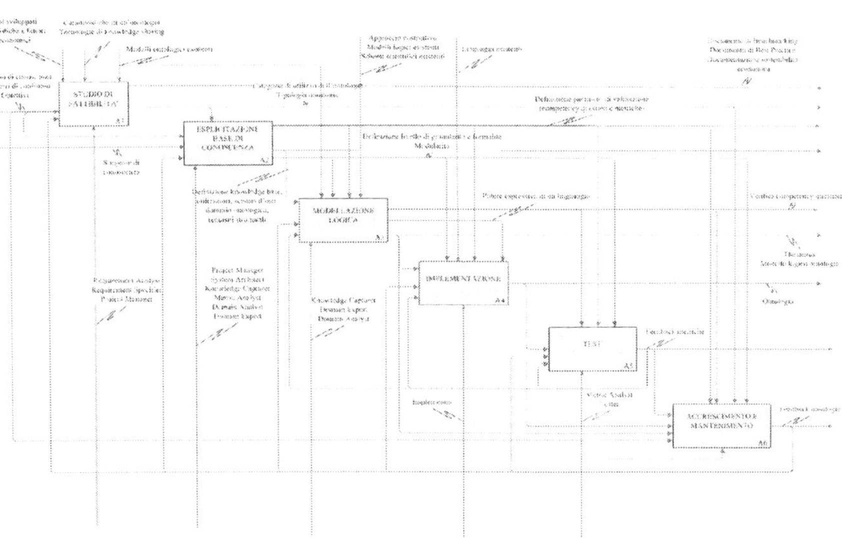

sumption, it is possible to build document clusters and successively to analyze ontology, both the document structure and the tag value. OntoExtractor, the topic of Chapter 4, is the application that clusters documents with respect to their structure and builds an ontology starting from the tag value of each document.

OntoExtractor contains a module for translating standard textual document formats (as pdf, doc, or html) in XML format and it was chosen as the widely used metadata standard for Web contents. A matching algorithm discovers regular patterns of text in the original document and assigns the recognized section to the right "tag" in the new xml version of the document. The algorithm is able to recognize documents that have a clear and well formatted structure as this chapter has, so documents that are composed

Figure 4. A screenshot of OntoMaker

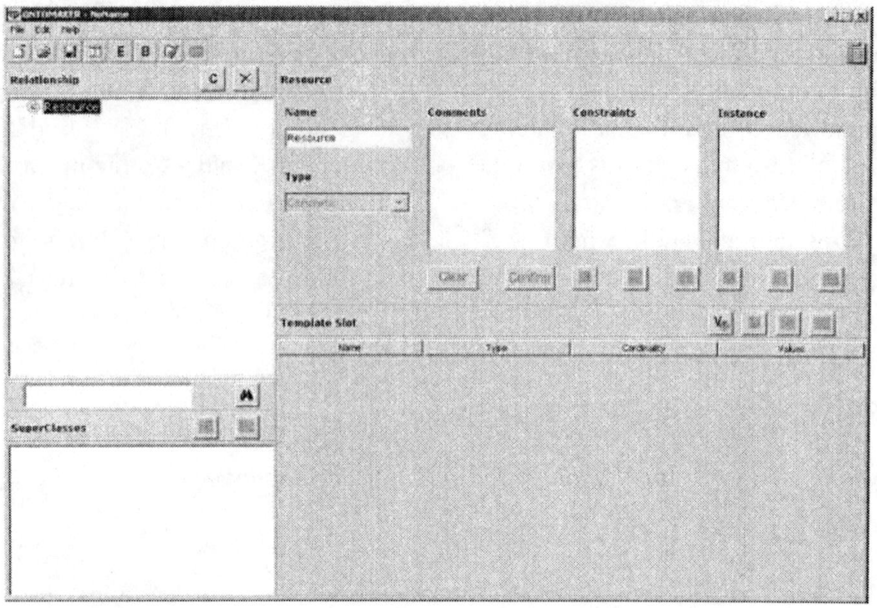

Figure 5. Relations among clusters and documents

	S1	S2	S3
d1		x	
d2	x		
d3		x	
d4			x

	C1	C2	C3
d1	x		
d2	x		
d3		x	
d4		x	

of different sections, as papers and technical books, can be functional documents. In the next step, OntoExtractor recognizes the document tag structure and evaluates the similarity among them using a similarity measure like the Jaccard norm (for more details on the technical description of OntoExtractor see Chapter 4). The outputs of this process are document clusters with a similar structure.

In a second step, documents are processed for clustering on tag values. Thus, a document can be assigned to two different clusters: one encoding a structural feature, the other one encoding a set of typical values. The structural feature is determined by the tags belonging to the documents and their position. Sets of tag' values encode other clusters. Now having this distribution of documents we can organize then into a hierarchy. This can be done using FCA (Formal Concept Analysis), a method for conceptually analyzing data and knowledge, which supports the construction of concept hierarchies (Ganter & Wille, 1999).

Informally speaking, FCA groups all the documents belonging to a same set of clusters into a same concept, having as super concepts the concepts containing a super set of documents, and as sub concepts the concepts containing a sub set of documents. As shown in Figure 5, these relations can be described in a tabular format. Using well-known algorithms, the tabular format can be seen as a hierarchy, as shown in Figure 6. This hierarchy provides the backbone of an ontology to be extended manually.

Figure 6. A hierarchy of clusters

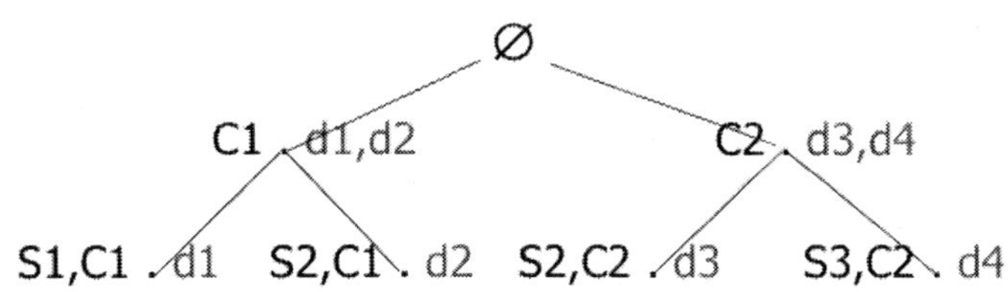

Figure 7. Evolution of total assertion trust in a complex community (see Chapter 4)

This approach to ontology building produces a more effective indexing, but it keeps having a precision problem. A "trust evaluating" function will be therefore introduced in order to enable users to give a vote to the association of resources to concepts. In this way, "trusted" indexes emerge. Moreover, it is possible to weight opportunely the judge in order to manage communities with different levels of cultural backgrounds. It seems obvious that the trust judgment of a "senior" is more valuable than a judgment of a "junior." Some simulations (see Figure 7) show that the algorithm implemented with the OntoExtractor works better with complex communities (different background levels).

This "semi-automatic evaluation" approach to ontology building is very useful if the resource's base is composed of well-structured documents and the community is positively involved in the evaluation process.

EVALUATING THE ONTOLOGY: ONTOMETER

As stated before, ontologies are a representation of the world. This implies that ontology has to change as new knowledge becomes available, new requests come from the business environment, and improvement in the technological system enables new functionalities and applications. Three main types of evolutions can affect ontologies knowledge domain's evolution, conceptualization's evolution, specification's evolution (Noy & Klein, 2002).

Figure 8. Screenshot of the application Ontometer. A set of metrics is evaluated on an RDF implementation of ontology.

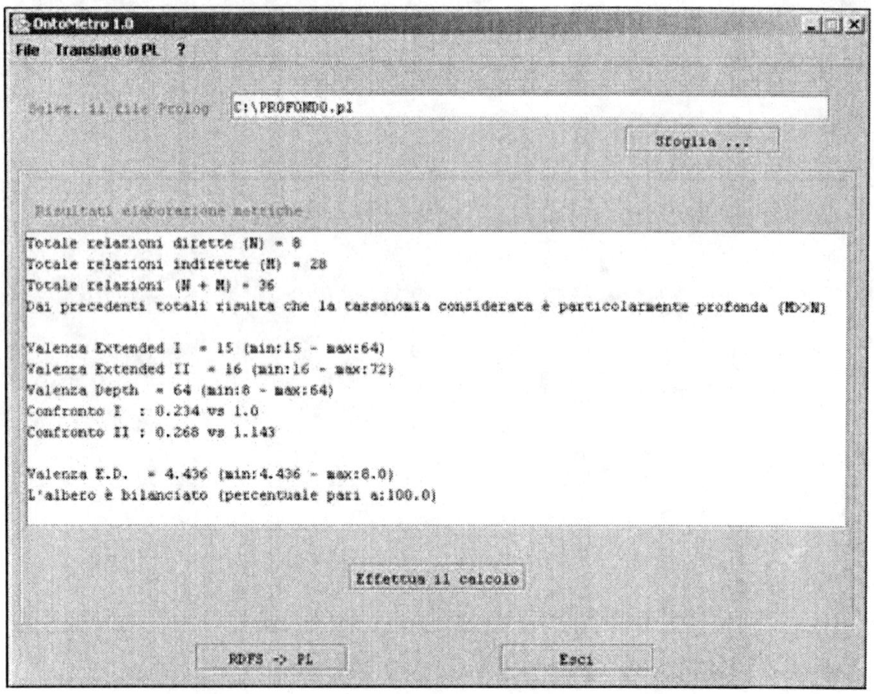

The first one is related to direct changes in the knowledge base of the community as it is the case when a big department is split into two smaller ones. The second evolution of ontologies is related to changes in the aim with which users look at the world. A user can see his/her computer from the hardware point of view or from the software point of view; the object is the same, but the properties he/she will underline are completely different. Changes in the specification are related to a new implementation in different languages of the same ontology; it could be necessary for improving the reasoning capability of the system in which the ontology is deployed.

When changes in the ontology produce a new structure, then it will be opportune to monitor this evolution in order to have a well-organized ontology. Ontometer (see Figure 8) is a tool aimed at evaluating some metrics on an ontology implemented in the RDF language. In the KIWI project we focused our attention to the taxonomy extracted from the ontology as it strikes the user firstly.

Three metrics were defined as depth, extension, and balance (Za, 2004). Depth is a measure of the number of concepts from the "root" concept to the most specific one; we think that this is a measure connected to the details of the world the taxonomy is able to represent. If you accept that users do not want to click to many times before reaching the right concept, a high value of depth means that (probably) you can break up the ontology into many more focused ontologies in order to improve the user's experience.

Figure 9. A screenshot of the Indexer. On the left the taxonomy extracted from the ontology, on top-right the xml structure of the document, on bottom-down the assertion associated to the document.

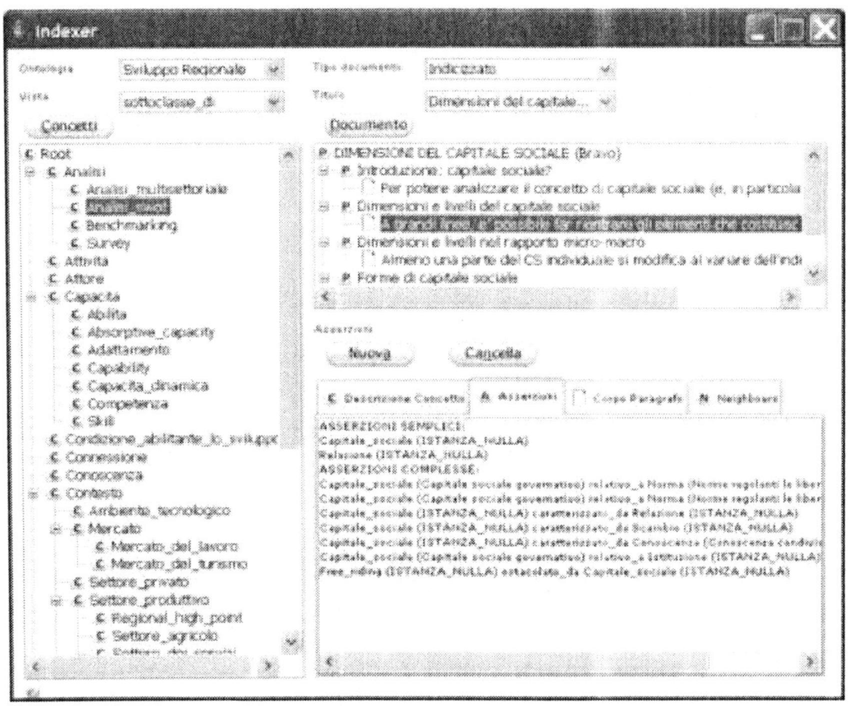

Extension is a parameter that evaluates the number of children-nodes; if a concept has only one sub-concept (probably) it means that the ontological difference among them is not so significant, and we should re-think the necessity to distinct the classes. At the same time, if a concept has many (10 or more) subclasses, it could be more useful to regroup them in order to simplify the taxonomy browsing.

Balance tells us if the different branches of the taxonomy are developed coherently at a similar level of depth. This metric helps us in monitoring the continuous adding of details and specific classes. Moreover, a poor detailed branch of a taxonomy could be a symptom of a not so important section of the knowledge domain or of a not good expertise available for designing the ontology itself.

The Ontometer is able to evaluate these metrics on an RDF ontology (but even on a general xml file). The RDF structure is translated in a Prolog knowledge base because it is simpler to manage. With a set of direct Prolog queries metrics are evaluated, a screenshot of the Ontometer results panel is reported in Figure 8.

INDEXING RESOURCES

If an "automatic ontology building" approach is chosen, the association among concepts and resources (the semantic assertions) is created automatically.

If the other two proposed approaches (top-down or bottom-up) are followed, another phase is necessary: resources have to be indexed respected to the ontology (or taxonomy). Only after this activity, knowledge resources become retrievable.

In the KIWI project, this phase can be managed through the application "Assertion Maker". It was developed for helping knowledge domain experts to create assertions on resources.

Assertion Maker is able to open at the same time a document and an ontology, so users can create a direct association among a section of the document (title or paragraphs) and concepts of the ontology (simple assertion) or, that is the best, between a section of the document and a triple (assertion) subject-relation-object available in the ontology (complex assertion). Assertions are implemented in the RDF language or they can be stored directly in a database. Both these outputs are accessible to the Semantic Navigator, the tool for searching and retrieving documents starting from the semantic metadata, that is their related ontological assertions.

SEMANTIC NAVIGATOR

The Semantic Web is thought for extending the capabilities of users in managing resources, the most important step of this job is accessing the right knowledge resource. The only method to look for anything on the Web is utilizing a search engine. Today there are a lot of search engines (as already stated in this chapter) that try to help users in recognizing the structure that connects the Web sites of a query's answer list. In particular, the primary or secondary page is differentiated (indented on goggle as example) or some general relations among them are highlighted (as vivisimo.com or kartoo.com do). No commercial search engine is able to search information resources for ontological assertions. The first reason is the missing database of semantic assertion on Web resources.

In the KIWI framework, this task is accomplished by Semantic Navigator.

This tool is the interface between users and the knowledge base composed by both the ontology and documents. It is thought for multiple knowledge domains, that is multiple ontologies. A user can select the ontology she is interested in when accessing the service. In this way, wide and complex organizations composed of different departments can manage many knowledge bases (at departmental level in example) through only one access point. The next step for the user is the definition of the relation through which the Navigator extracts the taxonomy. Ontological concepts generally are all connected through some special relations via "Is_A" (subclass_of) or "Part_Of" links. These relations then can be used to build a special view of the taxonomical structure that holds the ontology. At this point, the user can start the direct search activity: clicking on a concept she obtains all resources that are in some way associated to it (see Figure 10). The user can further refine the search concept by selecting a specific instance of it (this function is not available in the implementation presented in Figure 10). In this modality, the Semantic Navigator is working like a normal search engine with a simple categorization, but the Semantic Navigator goes in the next step: using special functionalities user can select a relation from those that come out from the concept, and then she can select a concept among the "object" concepts. The instance can be specified even for the object concept. At each step of this refining action, the answer's list is updated purging items not related to the updated assertion.

A more appealing version of the Semantic Navigator was implemented for an e-learning environment called SWELS - Semantic Web E-Learning System, (see Figure 11 and chapter 7). With this prototypal implementation, the KIWI project tried to face two types of problems: the first one is in regard to the representation of the

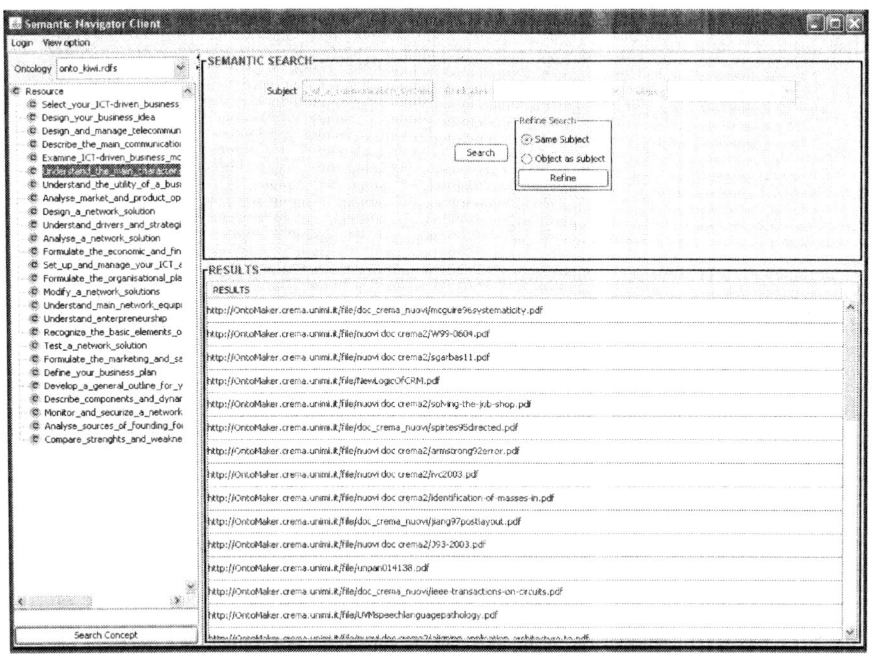

Figure 10. Screenshot of the Semantic Navigator. The concept's list is on the left, the "assertion refining" module is on the top, and in the bottom the resources associated with the selected concept are retrieved (prototypal implementation).

ontology, and the second one is in regard to the user-centred provision of contents.

In the SWEL version of the Semantic Navigator a graphical tab is available. The ontology is presented as an oriented graph where concepts are represented by a labeled square and the relations by a labeled and directed (from the subject to the object) arrows. Clicking on a box, a contextual menu appears and the "retrieve documents" is among the available options.

The SWELS platform introduces a user-centred e-learning module delivery: if content are semantically described, even with a "difficulty level" attribute, and if user profile is built using the same ontology then the delivery of the content can be focused on the specific background level and curriculum of a learner.

The KIWI framework has been applied to several technological innovation projects characterized by the needs of a knowledge management system including semantic-based functionalities.

The most important cases to which the framework has been applied needed a knowledge platform providing a semantic description of resources and enabling innovative search techniques.

Some general properties of these projects follow: (1) knowledge domains are well-focused and well known by users, and that (2) user communities are composed of people with a high level of technological skills. These two features guarantee that community members are able to develop an adequate and well structured ontology, and to take advantage of new application functionalities.

APPLICATIONS OF THE KIWI FRAMEWORK

The BT-Exact Case

BT-Exact runs a research centre investing high efforts in knowledge management applications.

Figure 11. SWELS (Semantic Web E-Learning System) (prototypal implementation)

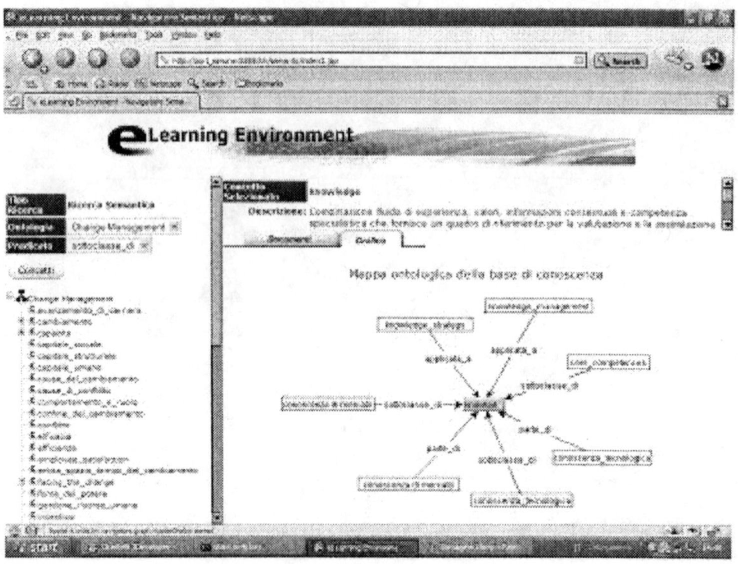

One of the main projects concerns the development of an intelligent platform for business analysis, capable of modelling complete customer lifecycles including the customer lifetime value. The system learns from previous events to predict the future events a customer might experience. These predictions can be used for pro-active customer care initiatives, such as complaint prevention or directed marketing.

There are a number of obstacles to introducing open e-commerce on the Internet. One major problem is the semantic interoperability.

Interoperability problems among interacting computer systems have been well-documented. In the past, these problems have been addressed using technologies such as CORBA, DCOM and various middleware products. Later, XML has gained acceptance as a way of providing a common syntax for exchanging information. A number of schema-level specifications (usually as a Document Type Definition or an XML Schema) have recently been proposed as standards to use in e-commerce, including ebXML.

A solution to semantic heterogeneity problems should provide heterogeneous software systems with the ability to share and exchange information in a semantically consistent way. For this reason, the system must be equipped with intermediate terminologies using formal ontologies and must specify the translation among them using ontology mappings. But the cost of manual mapping is not sustainable. Rather, this mapping must be generated automatically using matching operators that can discover semantics relations among elements of the system.

Matching operators are known to be data dependent, because different operators are tailored to different data, and no generic matching function can be designed. For this reason, the only way for implementing a generic Data Integration algorithm is to support different matching operators. OntoExtractor provides a rich palette of matching operators to be integrated in the BT-Exact applications.

The Engineering Institute Case

In Puglia, a region in Southern Italy, the local Association of Engineers is going to implement a new technological platform for improving knowledge diffusion and sharing, supporting collaborative behaviour, and access to official documentation as laws, announcements, work opportunities, and so on. The institute case provides an opportunity for investigating the applicability of the KIWI framework.

Using innovative search engines, the association wants to reduce the time to reach information items, regardless of the professional experience of the person doing the query. Their specific domain knowledge is laws on house constitutions, a field where laws and regulations are very complex.

In Italy there are three public administrations that are empowered to rule on this topic: the government gives general rules on building security and construction sites; the regional administration specifies building characteristics and typologies for different areas; and local administrations produce specific rules about dimensions and services. The goal which the association would like to reach is identifying the right rule(s) for the specific case each construction engineer is dealing with.

The KIWI framework appears very useful in this case because:

- the knowledge base, laws, is wide but finite,
- manual indexing process is feasible as high level knowledge experts are available,
- changes in the rule base are numerable (they change one by one),
- users know quite well their specific case (their project), so the search can be quite exact in an ontological environment.

The methodology specified for this case starts from the developing of a simple ontology in the

RDF language, indexing manually resources (laws) and implementing a customized Semantic Navigator. Thanks to the granular format of the laws (articles, paragraphs, and numbered lists), the indexing process can associate a complete RDF triple (subject–predicate–object) to each elementary item.

In order to achieve this goal, a specific strategy for developing the ontology was used (a variation of the bottom-up approach); a subset of the laws that compose the knowledge base were selected and accurately read by knowledge experts in order to extract and associate concept(s) or triple(s) (concept–predicate–concept) to each meaningful elementary item. At the end of this activity, a set of "draft assertions" was available for each knowledge item; ontology was built by refining and integrating in a coherent meaning the concepts and relations that compose all triples. This phase of the process was executed principally by the knowledge experts but with a continuous collaboration with the KIWI partnership in order to reduce difficulties of integrating the knowledge base in the KIWI system.

The second step was to annotate formally the knowledge base (laws). Substantially this job is the semiautomatic translation of the annotations created in the previous phase in the RDF language using the Assertion Maker. KIWI Semantic Navigator has been implemented in a custom version in order to be integrated in the platform of the Engineering Institute.

In order to carry out this application, a team composed of researchers from the KIWI partnership and system architects and software developers was composed. The team met regularly with both the aim of completing system development through the customization of the KIWI tools and transferring the knowledge defined during the project from the university to the firm.

T results of this application of the KIWI project framework include the diffusion of the concepts, approaches, methodologies, and applications developed in the research project to SMEs.

The Virtual eBMS Case

Another application of the KIWI knowledge focused on a semiautomatic approach to annotating knowledge bases.

Virtual eBMS (http://virtual.ebms.it) is a platform for knowledge management, e-learning, and e-business. It was implemented for eBMS researchers, its network of collaborators, firms, and research centres with which there is a form of collaboration.

This platform enables Master and PhD students of eBMS to perform many tasks of their daily work, such as accessing scientific documents and distributing their reports to themselves and to their tutors. Through the Virtual eBMS, they can also access e-learning courses created by eBMS research staff.

The project management section proposes functionalities for organizing projects, managing people involved in projects, their deliverables and deadlines, expected results, and so on. Also it permits to browse the knowledge base looking for resources able to help staff members in completing their task.

In the Virtual eBMS platform the knowledge base is composed of the internally produced documentation (project reports, scientific paper, books, and so on) and external resources downloaded periodically from scientific or specialized Web sites selected by researches. The standard tool for the user to interact with the knowledge base is based on the IBM Verity search engine (now a product of Autonomy Group). It can be used as a standard Web search engine, searching resources with keywords, and as a sort of semantic search engine. In fact Verity is able to search for keywords in selected classes of one or two taxonomies (see Figure 13).

In this context, since information resources are so numerous, it is not possible to add annotations by hand. An automatic or, at least, a semiautomatic strategy is necessary. In fact, Verity is complemented with an Intelligent Classifier tool

Figure 12. The home page of the Virtual eBMS for logged users

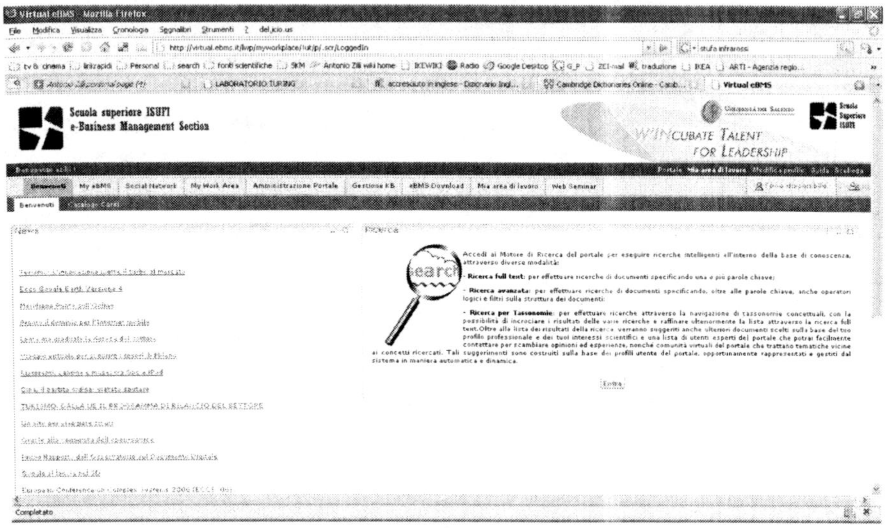

Figure 13. A screenshot of the Verity search engine integrated in the Virtual eBMS. From top to bottom: the keyword-based search functionality, the taxonomy search refinement functions, the answer list

Figure 14. The workflow for the document classification

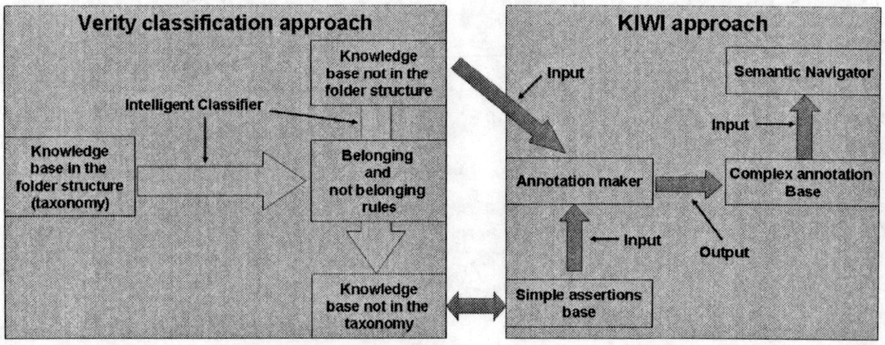

that permits to transform a "folder-based" organization of documents in "association rules." The document base is organized as a structured tree of folders, so the Intelligent Classifier can extract rules based on document keywords. These rules are used for the classification of new documents during updates phase to the document base.

If "association rules" are forgotten, documents are simply associated to a taxonomy concept; in other words, documents are annotated with a "simple assertions" using the KIWI framework language. If the taxonomy is an "Is_A" view of an ontology, we can extend these simple assertions to complex assertions using KIWI Assertion Maker. In order to carry out this semantic extension of the Virtual eBMS, we implemented this process: "assertions" produced by the intelligent classifier were translated in the RDF language (a simple application was developed with this aim), so they are accessible by the Assertion Maker. At the same time, documents used in this experimentation were translated into xml format to make them readable by the Assertion Maker too. At this point, the knowledge base can be completely browsed by the Semantic Navigator that will access an RDF version of the ontology according to which documents are classified.

THE EVOLUTION OF THE KIWI FRAMEWORK

If managing huge quantities of data and services was a problem in 2001, when Berners-Lee proposed his "Semantic Web," today the situation is even worse.

In the last few years, Web 2.0 technological innovations simplified the data publication and information and knowledge resources. The quantity of information on the Web increased more quickly in the past 2 or 3 years as these services are widely used by Web surfers.

In the last few years, these applications (blog and wikies in particular) have been introduced even at the organization level.

eBMS is studying an evolution of the KIWI framework called SIMS (Semantic Information Management System), a knowledge and collaborative platform we are developing for the DISCoRSO (Distributed Information Systems for CooRdinated Service Oriented interoperability) project (Corallo et al., 2007).

The focus of this platform is extending the Semantic Web approach in order to manage coherently many different information resources. Documents, wiki articles, blog posts, and so on

Figure 15. The SIMS architecture (Corallo et al., 2007)

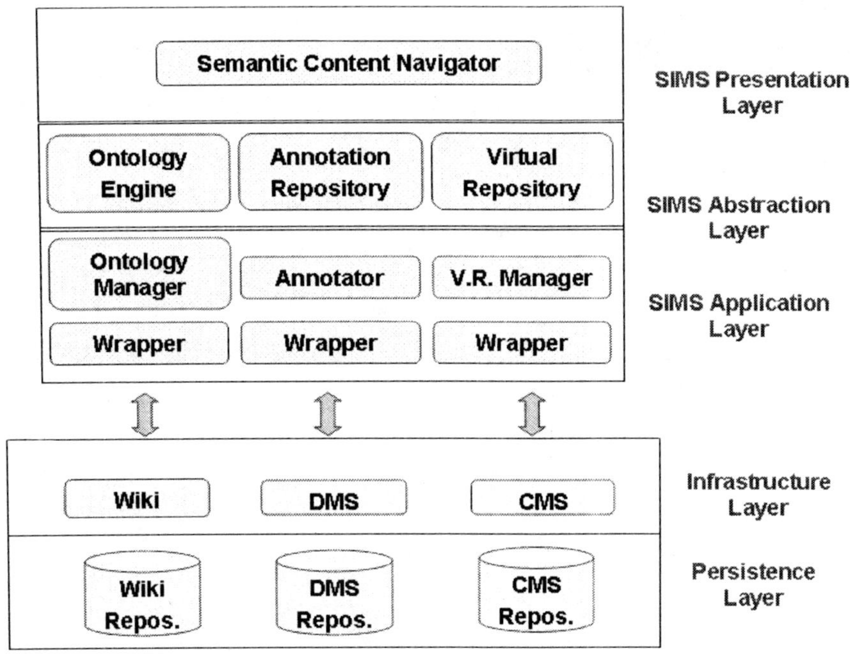

are described semantically respect to a domain ontology. The Virtual Repository (see Figure 15) was implemented via a Jackrabbit data manager that enables to describe (evolving) resource attributes. The Semantic Content Navigator will be able to access simultaneously the ontology stored in the Ontology Manager database, the semantic annotations stored in the Annotation Repository database, and the documents stored in the Virtual Repository database.

REFERENCES

Afuah, A. (2002). *Innovation management: Strategies, implementation, and profits.* Oxford University Press, USA.

Anderson, P. (2007). What is Web 2.0? Ideas, technologies and implications for education. *JISC Technology and Standards Watch*, Feb. 2007.

Beckett, D. (2004). RDF/XML Syntax Specification, Retrieved on January, 2007, from http://www.w3.org/TR/rdf-syntax-grammar/

Berners-Lee, T., Hendler, J., & Lassila, O., (May 2001). The Semantic Web. *Scientific American,* 34–43.

Carcagnì, A., *Metodologia e sviluppo di un workflow per la definizione di ontologie.* Unpublished degree dissertation, University of Salento, Italy.

Corallo, A., Elia, G., & Zilli, A. (2005). *Enhancing communities of practice: an ontological approach.* Paper presented at 11th International

Conference on Industrial Engineering and Engineering Management, Shenyang, China.

Corallo, A., Ingraffia, N., Vicari, C., & Zilli, A. (2007). *SIMS: An ontology-based multi-source knowledge management system*. Paper presented at the 11th Multi-Conference on Systemics, Cybernetics and Informatics (MSCI 2007), Orlando, Florida, USA.

Drucker, P. F. (1994). *Post-capitalist society*. Collins.

Ganter, B., & Wille, R. (1999). *Formal concept analysis: Mathematical foundations* (translated from B. Ganter, R. Wille: Formale Begriffsanalyse - Mathematische Grundlagen. Springer, Heidelberg 1996) Springer-Verlag, Berlin-Heidelberg.

Gloor, P. A. (2006). *Swarm creativity : Competitive advantage through collaborative innovation networks*. Oxford University Press, USA.

Gruber, T. R. (1993). Towards principles for the design of ontologies used for knowledge sharing. In N. Guarino & R. Poli (Eds.), *Formal ontology in conceptual analysis and knowledge representation*. Deventer, The Netherlands. Kluwer Academic Publishers.

Huberman, B. A., & Adamic, L. A. (1999). *Internet: Growth dynamics of the world-wide web. Nature*, 401(6749):131-131.

Netcraft (2007). September 2007 Web Server Survey, Retrieved on September 2007, from http://news.netcraft.com/archives/web_server_survey.html

Malone, T. W. (2004). *The future of work: How the new order of business will shape your organization, your managementsStyle and yourlLife*. Harvard Business School Press.

Nonaka, I., & Takeuchi, H. (1995). *The knowledge-creating Company : How Japanese companies create the dynamics of innovation*. Oxford University Press.

Noy, N. F., & Klein, M. (2002). *Ontology evolution: Not the same as schema evolution*. (Tech. Rep. SMI-2002-0926). Stanford University.

Secundo, G., Corallo, A., Elia, G., & Passiante G. (2004). *An e-learning system based on Semantic Web supporting a learning in doing environment*, Paper presented at the International Conference on Information Technology Based Higher Education and Training, Istanbul, Turkey.

Smith, M. K., Welty, C., McGuinness, & Deborah L. (2004). *OWL Web ontology language guide*, Retrieved on January 2007, from http://www.w3.org/TR/owl-guide/

Tapscott, D. & Williams, A. D. (2006). *Wikinomics: How mass collaboration changes everything*. Portfolio Hardcover.

Wenger, E. (1999). *Communities of practice: Learning, meaning, and identity*. Cambridge University Press.

Bennett, B. & Fellbaum, C. (Eds.), (2006). *Formal ontology in information systems*. In *Proceedings of the4th International Conference* (FOIS 2006), Volume 150, Frontiers in Artificial Intelligence and Applications. IOS Press.

ENDNOTES

[a] http://www.google.com/technology/

[b] http://search.vivisimo.com/

[c] http://www.kartoo.com/. Kartoo is a meta-search engine, the query is launched on a set of other search engine, their results are connected and processed for the visualization.

[d] http://virtual.ebms.it

Chapter II
Introduction to Ontology Engineering

Paolo Ceravolo
University of Milan, Italy

Ernesto Damiani
University of Milan, Italy

ABSTRACT

This chapter provides an introduction to ontology engineering discussing the role of ontologies in informative systems, presenting a methodology for ontology design, and introducing ontology languages. The chapter starts by explaining why ontologies are needed in informative systems, then it introduces the reader to ontologies by leading him/her in a stepwise guide to ontology design. It concludes by introducing ontology languages and standards. This is a primer reading aimed at preparing novice readers of this book to understanding more complex dissertations; for this reason it can be avoided by expert readers.

CHAPTER SUMMARY

In this chapter, we introduce the fundamental notions of *ontology* and *ontology engineering* and explain why they turned out to be of paramount importance in the development of the new generation of Web-based systems that will compose the Semantic Web (Berners-Lee, 2001). Then, we focus on the emerging discipline of *ontology design*, which considers the design of ontologies for specific application *domains*. Our aim is to give some simple, yet general guidelines toward designing ontologies and managing their entire life cycle, including their design, validation, and deployment.

WHAT IS WRONG WITH INFORMATIVE SYSTEMS?

The ideas that we shall discuss in this chapter do require a bit of intellectual effort, so it makes sense to try to build some motivation before delving into them. In order to convince the reader that this effort is actually worth making, let us informally consider some unexpected consequences of the Internet-based information explosion.

The availability of a pervasive, global infrastructure for information distribution such as the World Wide Web, together with the dramatic decline in communication and storage costs per information unit, has greatly encouraged information production.

Government agencies, corporations, consortia, and a host of other organizations keep themselves busy producing all sorts of documents, databases, and spreadsheets, not to mention computer programs and their documentation.

Then, they publish their efforts on internal Intranets or on the global Net and wait for their employees, customers or someone else to take advantage of them.

Well-intentioned as these organizations may be when producing information, the sheer size of the data they publish every day may make those data practically useless.

Internet technology has been successful in boosting productivity; inasmuch it provided the means for information to reach its intended destinations quite easily, but processing such information (and deciding if it is relevant) is becoming more and more of a chore for the recipients. As a result, organizations around the world are discovering that using the Web or e-mail for knowledge distribution has become a rather unreliable and time-consuming process.

Few people nowadays bother to read unsolicited e-mail messages, even if the message's sender belongs to their organization and has a legitimate motive for sending it. Referring people to information posted on internal or public Web sites turned out to be also not very effective, as few users have enough time for checking the sites that might contain useful information regularly.

On the other hand, the very same people that eschew dealing with information directed at them may well later be found using search engines to look for information they need on the Web, often without much success.

The development of hypermedia has made Web search an intermediate situation between information seeking and content learning, where specific abilities are needed to obtain even modest results.

As expert users of Web-based search engines know very well, attempts at indexing and retrieving information using keyword-based indexing techniques have met only with partial success, and WWW content location is still more an art than a science.

In order to convince ourselves of the drawbacks of keyword-based indexing of network resources, we shall use an example.

Suppose that you are a masters student of modern literature searching the Web for information on the making of the Romantic novel in 19th-century Europe. For some reason, you ignored the lecture notes that were produced by your lecturer and sent to you weeks before via e-mail. Tomorrow, you are supposed to give a talk on this subject and the course Web site is down. So, conventional *direct* inquiry to someone else (either synchronously via a phone call, or asynchronously via an e-mail message) is out of the question; all you can do is to adopt a marketplace style of inquiry, and look for the information yourself.

Soon, you discover that feeding the keywords "romantic" and "novel" into a keyword-based WWW search engine will not solve your problem.

- First of all, while the search is likely to produce many results, not all of them will be relevant to your query. In other words, the *precision* of the search result, that is, the ratio between the number of relevant results and the total number of retrieved pages will be substantially lower than one. This should not be unexpected; after all, the English term "novel" is both a noun and an adjective, and can be used with very different meanings.

- Secondly, you will notice that some potentially useful Web pages you heard of from other students will not show up in the result of your search. The *recall* of the search result, that is, the ratio between the number of retrieved pages and the total number of relevant pages on the WWW will be substantially lower than one. Once again, this is hardly surprising. Not all Web pages about the making of the romantic novel are written in English. Even if one is, it does not necessarily contain the words "romantic" or "novel."

Also, Web pages dealing with related topics such as romantic short stories or poems, though potentially useful, will not be retrieved by your keyword-based search simply because they do not contain the keywords you specified in your query.

It would seem that while precision could be improved by filtering results, increasing recall would involve some query extension/reformulation; but how?

In order to avoid a slow and costly trial-and-error procedure, it is better to avoid augmenting the query with additional keywords at random; you could apply some simple theoretical notions.

Here is a simple theory consisting of two statements:

- "The word 'novel' refers to the concept of a literary composition."
- "Novels, tales and poems are all literary compositions."

Equipped with such a theory, you will be able to:

1. Apply *filtering* and increase your own search precision by disregarding pages where the term "novel" is an adjective rather than a noun.
2. *Expand* your query, manually feeding the words "poems" and "short stories" (in addition to "novel") into the engine, in order to increase the search recall.

You might ask yourself whether it is really necessary to carry out this procedure manually. Could some sophisticated Web search engine carry out this simple procedure automatically, increasing precision and recall accordingly? The answer to this question, of course, is "yes," provided that someone (most likely, the people managing the search engine) is able to:

1. Develop and maintain some theoretical background for all domains targeted by user searches
2. Associate concepts like "novel" with the corresponding real-world object instances, that is, network resources

A *semantics-aware search engine* of this kind is a good example of a *Semantic Web application*, that is, *an application whose searching, retrieving, and processing decisions about resources are based on data semantics represented via their association with concepts.*

Most of today's Web pages carry little background information besides their contents[a]; even when some background information is there, it seldom refers to some independently defined and shared vocabulary or body of knowledge.

Nonetheless, it is widely acknowledged that difficulties arising when Web applications need to meaningfully share information are now the main hurdle to unraveling the full potential of Web-based communication[b].

What is somewhat more surprising is that the same remark we just made about the global Web can be made of many corporate-wide repositories of business information. In the past, organization-wide efforts at knowledge sharing nearly always produced document-based KMS (Knowledge Management Systems), that is, collections of documents internally maintained by organizations and focused on particular domains.

The role of shared knowledge in e-business is also important, though somewhat less certain. Sharing some document definitions (e.g., having the same notion of "invoice") certainly provides an effective framework for specifying the actions that must take place on each end of a business transaction. The information sharing may be obtained simply by defining a common invoice format, or, alternatively by sharing background knowledge including all the higher level concepts (e.g., customer or item) that invoices refer to.

DISCUSSING STATES OF AFFAIRS

Before attempting a definition of ontology and explaining why it is becoming increasingly important for software engineers and developers of Web-based applications, we need to clarify some preliminary notions.

All human activities, computer-assisted or not, introduce their own peculiar point of view from which the universe of available information is examined and interpreted by practitioners.

For instance, a house building plan will be read differently by electricians and plumbers, each group easily selecting facts pertaining to their field of interest from the totality of information available from the plan.

Architects or engineers who author house plans often try and make this information selection process easier, for example, by adding to the plan suitable *description labels* that point out specific fields to which information items are related.

In general, however, craftsmen's own knowledge and common sense suffice to distinguish what is relevant from what is not from the point of view of their trade.

Sometimes this *domain knowledge* can be applied directly: *trained and licensed* electrician *is required to* straightforwardly identify the *meaning* of instances of a graphical symbol in the house plan associating them with the concept of a power outlet[c]. In our example the knowledge universe (the house plan) is small and unambiguous, so that ⚡-shaped symbols are readily understood

Figure 1. The meaning triangle (Ogden & Richards, 1923)

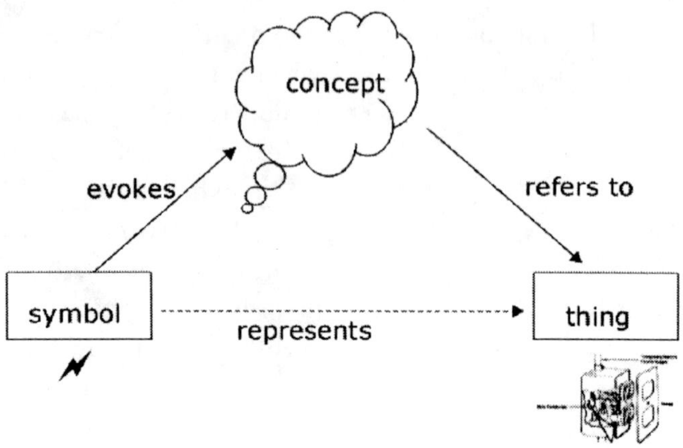

(see Figure 1) to be pointers to the power outlets' locations. Other times, however, some sort of *reasoning* must be applied, for example, in order to recognize that an empty light bulb socket can be used as a temporary power outlet for small appliances.

It is not difficult to understand that the electrician reading the house plan, though probably regarding himself or herself as a very practical person, is in fact applying some sort of *theory* about the *state of affairs* expressed by the house plan itself.

In the first case, the electrician's theory is merely stating a fact about some of the house plan data, associating a *symbol* with a *concept* and the *concept* with a *thing* (a ≁ -shaped symbol indicates a power outlet). In the second case, the theory needs to provide support for some sort of reasoning (e.g.,, if *x* is the symbol designating an outlet, then the figure under *x* specifies the maximum power that can be supplied through the device).

Note that an electrician's theory cannot (neither is it expected to) account for all information in the house plan, as the latter will contain data related to concepts that are interesting, say, for plumbers and irrelevant for electricians. Limited and vaguely stated as it is, however, the theory is undeniably important for the electrician's work.[d]

Figure 2. Intelligent communication via shared ontology

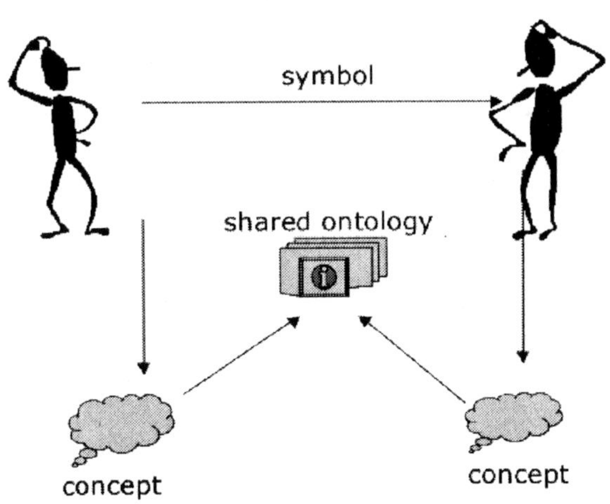

Practitioners have been traditionally communicating among themselves such "theories of the state of affairs" as a part of their training; to do so, they use plain natural language and, when possible, practical examples. Sharing such theories is indeed a prerequisite of what we call *intelligent communication*, involving the successful transmission of a symbol together with its association, on the part of the recipient, with the same concept it was associated with on the sender's side (Figure 2).

This is exactly the type of communication that took place in our example between the architect and the electrician, when the latter read the ≁ -shaped symbol.

On the other hand, philosophers and mathematicians have always been interested in investigating how theories of states of affairs could be expressed formally, for instance using the language of logic, as well as in the properties they should have.

The traditional name for the investigation of the formal properties of theories of states of affairs is "ontology," referring to the area of philosophy that studies theories of *being*[e]--that is, theories of what there is in the world (from a given point of view).

Of course, here it is not our intention to adopt the traditional philosophical definition of ontology as the "discipline dealing with theories of being." Rather, we will use the slightly different notion proposed, among others, by Grüber. While ontology seen *as a philosophical discipline* investigates all common problems posed by the activity of modeling (i.e., describing) state of affairs, a specific ontology seen *as a model* can be defined as "the explicit specification of an abstract, simplified view of a world we desire to represent" (Grüber, 1995).

In this narrower sense, ontology specifications being "explicit," means that all concepts and relationships that compose worldviews must be given explicit terms and definitions.

It is important to point out that this kind of specification is hardly possible using natural language.

In plain English, terms and concepts have a *many-to-many relationship*: the same word can refer to multiple concepts, and the same concept can be associated with many terms. In other words, terms in natural language very seldom possess a single undisputed meaning. Rather, their meaning is determined by the past experiences of speakers. Misunderstandings, therefore, may result from speakers having different references for the same term.

Also, using natural language for defining concepts makes it much easier to confuse the "symbols" or "terms" used in communication with the things or objects in reality.[f]

For this reason, concept definitions will have to be given in a restricted formal language, allowing for automatic ontology processing and checking.[g]

On the other hand, good ontology formalization is just the beginning. Indeed, there are several issues about ontologies and ontology design that can only be resolved empirically, usually through a good deal of domain knowledge and some common sense. Ontology may have wonderful formal properties, but it will be of limited use if it does not capture the intended semantics of the user's terminology.[h]

ONTOLOGY DESIGN 101

Before elaborating further on the general issues about ontologies introduced in the previous section, we shall try to get at least the flavor of the concrete ontology design activity by applying some basic notions. We shall start by designing a simple ontology from scratch; the basic steps

Figure 3. Stepwise ontology design

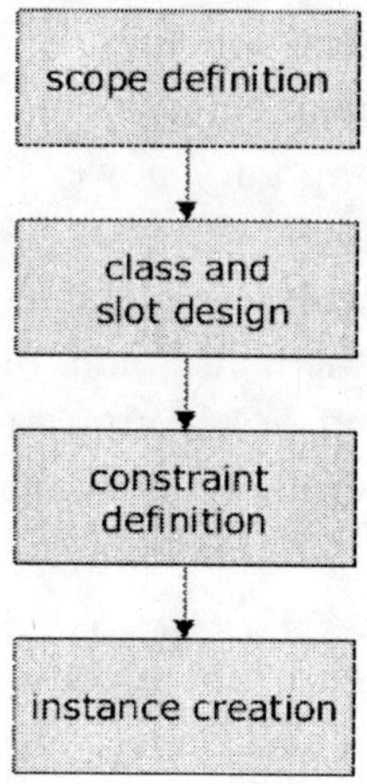

of our ontology design (see Figure 3) will later be extended and enriched to become general design guidelines.

Several computer-based tools are available to help people in ontology design (in the rest of this chapter, we shall use OntoMaker). OntoMaker is an implementation highly inspired from Protégé-2000, a free tool developed at Stanford University (Noy, 2001) which supports users in constructing domain ontologies, customizing knowledge-acquisition forms, and entering domain knowledge[i]. Our own open source re-implementation of Protégé, including some support for modular ontologies and useful templates, is available at http://ra.crema.unimi.it/ontology. Of course, the result of our interaction with Protégé's user interface will be some sort of internal image of the ontology structure (the formal language representation we hinted at above). It is worth mentioning that designing ontologies from scratch is seldom a good idea. Reusing design efforts made by others allows for using ontologies that have been already validated through use in other applications. [j]

A STEPWISE GUIDE TO ONTOLOGY DESIGN

The four consecutive steps we shall follow in designing our ontology are shown in Figure3. Now, we are ready to discuss the purpose of each step and the activities associated with it.

Step 1: Scope Definition

In this preliminary step, we need to decide what will be the boundaries of our domain. What is the state of affair, that is, the portion of the world that our ontology will model? What types of questions should the ontology enable us to answer?

Our example will deal with a single, special-purpose ontology, partially covering the domain of emergency health care. When performing the scope definition step, it is often a good idea to provide an *application scenario*, clarifying who will be the parties that will share the ontology and which questions the ontology should help to answer. For instance, our sample ontology could be used for ensuring intelligent communication between people working at a remote location (say, an oil-drilling offshore platform) and physicians with whom the paramedics may get in touch via a teletype device connected to long-distance communication link in case of an emergency. When sending a message to the physicians providing remote support, the paramedic on the oil-drilling platform will use a vocabulary that will be used also in the responses traveling in the opposite direction. Besides ensuring that both sides of the communication line will employ the same set of symbols, [k] we need to make sure that both sides of the communication will associate those symbols with the same concepts. To achieve this both parties must be agree on a *shared ontology*.

As we discussed in the previous section, in the real world, the development of such ontology is the result of a complex social process rather than the outcome of design. In fact, ontology sharing is achieved by exposing physicians, nurses and, to some extent, paramedics to the same set of notions and ideas during their training. Here, though, we are willing to try and put this shared knowledge in writing.

Of course, modeling the entire domain of emergency health care would require a whole book; therefore, for the sake of conciseness, we shall limit ourselves to a simplified version of an interesting sub-domain, the one of emergency blood transfusions.

We shall assume sets of transfusion kits to be available on the platform and that they have already been pre-selected in order to match the blood types of the people working there. Our ontology is aimed at ensuring that the paramedic and the remote support will "speak the same language" should a transfusion need to be administered. Ontology scope is therefore restricted to the communication that may take place while administering an emergency transfusion and does not support, say, discussion about the opportunity of blood transfusion in general.

After having delimited our ontology's *scope*, we may ask ourselves what precisely will be its *purpose*. A good way to clarify an ontology's purpose is listing some questions the ontology should help to understand (and, therefore, to answer correctly and unambiguously). In our case, these questions are the ones that will be asked via the Teletype by the remote physician to our paramedic (or vice versa) in the framework of the medical supervision required for a blood transfusion to take place.

Here are some examples:

1. Is the transfusion kit you are using compatible with the patient?
2. Have you checked that the transfusion kit has not expired yet?
3. Have you disposed of the empty blood pack?

Step 2: Class and Slot Design

This step is probably the most important phase of ontology design, and therefore deserves some introductory definitions. Computer programmers who are well versant in object-oriented languages know very well that a *class* is a collection of elements with similar properties; here, a class corresponds to a *concept* in the application domain that needs to be represented in the ontology[l]. Obviously, we must include all concepts one is likely to need to answer the questions listed above; but before doing so, we should provide a more precise definition of class.

Luckily enough, we can refer to an elementary set theory: classes can be seen as *sets*, as they have *instances* like sets have elements. An instance of a class is a real-world object falling under the concept corresponding to the class. So, a specific transfusion kit stored in a refrigerator is an instance of the class of all transfusion kits. [m]. We expect to use the classes of our ontology to define the main concepts shared by paramedics and physicians about blood transfusion. Class and property names will build up our domain vocabulary, but classes are much more than "names for sets:" in fact, they describe the internal structure of their instances[n] identifying their internal parts that we call *slots*. Slots describe parts or attributes of the class instances and may themselves belong to other classes. We call *domain* of a slot the class (or classes) whose instances can have the slot, while the *range* of a slot contains the class (or classes) to which slot values belong.

Each time an instance of the domain is created, instances of all the slots in its range are also generated.

Here are some of the classes we will include in our domain analysis:

- *Blood packs*, that is, the sterile containers normally used for transfusions and the blood component (plasma, whole blood or other) they contain
- *Filters*, to be placed between the blood pack and the needle when administering the transfusion
- *Needles* to be inserted in the patient's vein when administering the transfusion
- *Compatibility labels*, showing the ABO group and Rh factor data of a blood component, as well as the results of tests performed on it to determine the antigens it contains
- *Transfusion kits* composed of a pack, plus a needle, a filter and a compatibility label

Figure 4. The communication setting

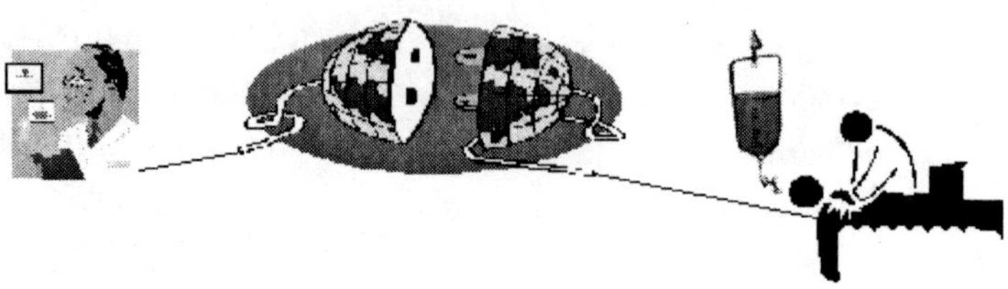

A pack's properties include its capacity (usually around 300 ml.) and the material it is made of(usually, PVC plastics). The blood component's properties include its expiry date and anti-coagulant additives, while the compatibility label's properties hold the values it shows--the associated component's blood type, Rh factor and, possibly, the results of various tests performed on it. Finally, the filter and the needle included in the kit will have many properties, some of them being codes specified by their supplier (such as the supplier's code and model number), and others being numbers expressing their dimensions and physical characteristics.

Note that ontology classes' slots are very versatile. They can be used to denote "intrinsic" properties of a class, whose values cannot be changed for a given instance (e.g., the ABO group of a blood unit or the diameter of a needle). Also, they may contain "extrinsic" properties that, at least in principle, could be changed at will by an external authority (e.g., a blood unit's expiry date). A class' slots may also denote the smaller parts that, when put together, constitute the class' instances, such as the blood component and pack slots of a transfusion kit. Finally, the slots may model a class' relations to other classes.

Class slots may be simple or complex. Simple slots contain primitive values (such as strings or numbers), while complex ones contain (or point to) instances of other classes. Of course, nothing prevents these other classes to have complex slots of their own: for example, the class Transfusion Kit includes a complex slot that holds an instance of the Blood Pack class (Figure 5); the latter, in turn, contains a Blood Component slot (Figure 6).

The class-slot relation models very naturally the inclusion hierarchy, which is often called the ontologies' PART-OF hierarchy. The PART-OF hierarchy is very important in domain modeling,

Figure 5. The slots of the transfusion kit class, including a blood pack instrance

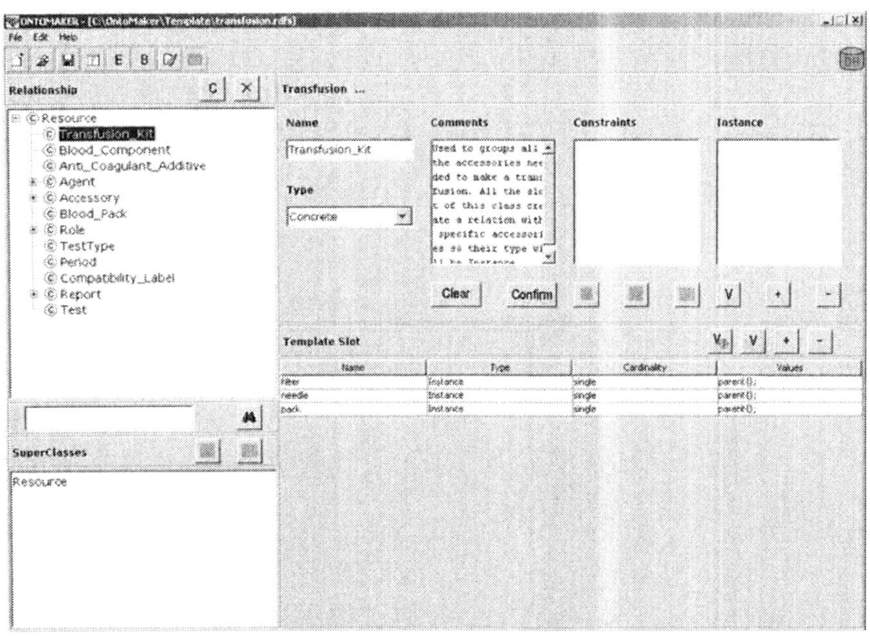

but slots can be used to model many other types of relationships than physical inclusion, including loose association. Beside static links such as PART-OF and IS-A, relationships to be modeled may include *dynamic semantic links* (expressing shorter-term relationships such as *x influences y*, or *x leads to y*) or *physical relationships* (such as *close to*, *under* or *near*).

Depending on the specific application, *temporal* (like *precede*, *follow*) and *logical* relationships (e.g., *cause*, *product*) could also be included.[o]

For instance, the class of Patients of our blood transfusion example might include a GP slot, representing the General Practitioner physician that looks after the patient while he/she is at home.

However, the GP in charge of the Patient is not in any way "a part" of it. Rather, the GP slot models a dynamic *association relationship* that may be severed at will by either party.

This difference also influences the graphical representation of such relationships. In technical terms, the PART-OF hierarchy is a *forest*, i.e. a set of taxonomic tree-shaped graphs, [p] while the GP-relation may well include cycles, as nothing prevents a GP from having another GP among her/his patients. In other words, while no object can contain an instance of itself, nothing prevents a GP to look after another.

Besides the PART-OF hierarchy and other named relationships modeled by their complex slots, ontology classes constitute another taxonomic hierarchy (also called the subclass-superclass, inheritance or IS-A hierarchy[q]). If you think of a class as a set of elements, a subclass is simply a subset: an instance of a subclass is also an instance of its superclass.[r] A subclass inherits all the slots from its superclass. Inheritance is not mandatory: a subclass can always *override* the

Figure 6. The blood pack class contains a complex blood component slot

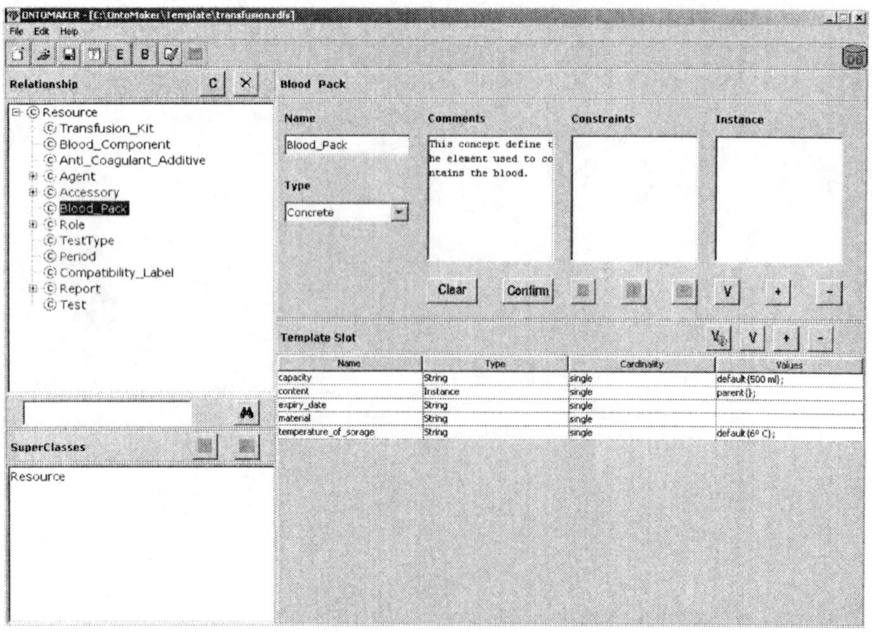

facets of its superclass in order to "narrow" the list of allowed values.

There are two basic techniques for designing IS-A hierarchies: the top-down approach, that defines the most general concepts first and then specialize them, and the bottom-up one, that defines the most specific concepts and then organize them in more general classes.

These two techniques are convenient for description purposes, but as such are seldom adopted in practice: experienced domain modelers usually adopt a combination of the two. Namely, they first define the most salient domain concepts via a set of classes (often called the domain's *core classes*) and then go on generalizing and specializing the core classes until they obtain a complete domain model.

Proceeding bottom-up in our ontology design, Filters and Needles included in transfusion kits can be regarded as specialization of the more general concept of an Accessory. From Accessory, Filters and Needles inherit a supplier code and a model number slot; each subclass will then add its own specific slots, such as the needle's diameter.

Another important class in our domain analysis is *Patients*, that is, people to whom emergency blood transfusion can be administered. Their properties, besides name, gender, age and the like, include a compatibility label specifying their blood compatibility data, such as blood type, Rh factor and the antibodies found in their blood. Such label is usually worn around the wrist (see Figure 10).

Following the bottom-up design approach, our atients class could be defined as a subclass of a more general class like Employees. This is rather tempting, as the Employees class is likely to have been modeled in other business ontologies (e.g., in a "Payroll and Personnel" ontology), and reusing it would allow the Patients class to inherit all slots that may already be defined for Employees. However, this temptation should be resisted due to a main limitation of inheritance hierarchies--their inability to handle *exceptions*. In other words, if we made Patients a subclass of an Employees class, our model would assume all patients treated on the offshore platform to be employees of the oil-drilling company. Our ontology would not be able to handle the entirely possible case when a person under treatment on the platform is not an employee, but a person coming, say, from a nearby vessel or helicopter. Therefore, we define an ad-hoc class called Role as a superclass of Patients.[5] In general, there is a fundamental question to ask oneself when designing an IS-A class hierarchy:

Figure 7. Our ontology's classes IS-A structure

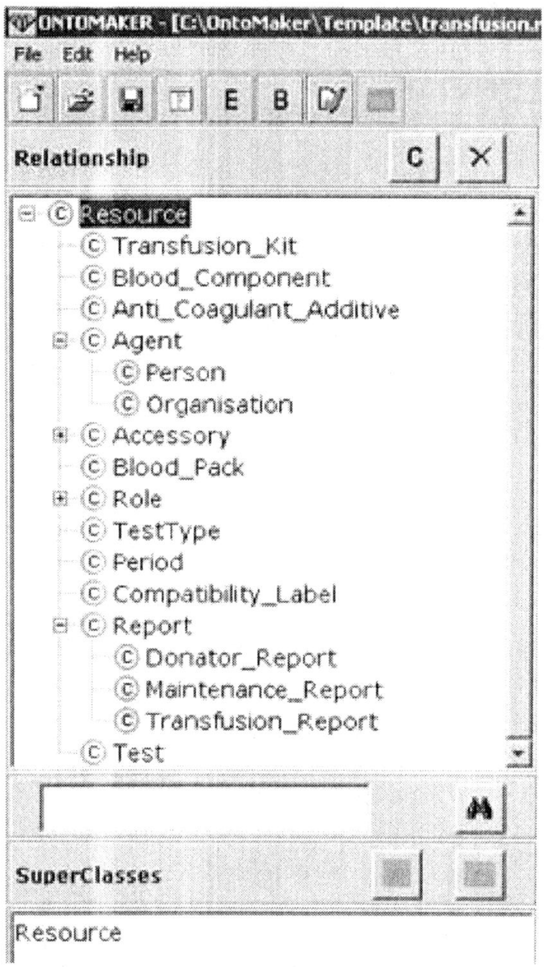

"Is each instance of the subclass also an instance of its superclass?"

It is easy to see that the answer is "yes" if we take Role as a superclass of Patients, while it would be "no" if we made Patients a subclass of the Employees class.

Figure 7 shows the overall IS-A class hierarchy represented by using the Protégé tool.

By the way, our discussion has shown that the IS-A relationship is *transitive*: if B is a subclass of A, and C is a subclass of B, then C is a subclass of A.

The "A" symbol next to a class name indicates it is an *abstract* class, that is, a class that will have no instances: its only role is to be an inheritance repository for its sub-classes. In other words, abstract classes allow for factoring out common characteristics that are shared by other classes that are derived from them. A domain's core classes are usually modeled as abstract classes.

Note that if a class has multiple superclasses (*multiple inheritance*), it inherits slots from all of them. Multiple inheritance is a powerful modeling tool, but introduces two serious problems.

- *Inheritance conflicts* arise when two superclasses of the same subclass have slots with the same name but different types: which one should the subclass actually inherit? There is no general answer to this question, as different systems resolve conflicts differently. Many *static conflict resolution* techniques have been proposed, for instance using the order in which classes are defined in order to establish their priority as far as transmitting their slots to descendants is concerned[1] (the interested reader is referred to (Masini, 1991)). However, few ontology designers would leave the decision "from which of its superclasses should this class inherit a given slot?" to an automatic procedure; this kind of ambiguity is explicitly tackled by enforcing naming conventions in the design phase, that is, employing different names for the slots of different superclasses.
- *Inheritance cycles* arise when a class comes to inherit from another class that is its descendant via a different inheritance path. Cycles are usually prevented at definition time. Figure 8 shows a Protegè window where the version our class hierarchy is updated. A class Employees has been introduced between People and Patients. Then, Patients have been inserted among People superclasses. The error message points out that an inheritance cycle has been detected.

Figure 8

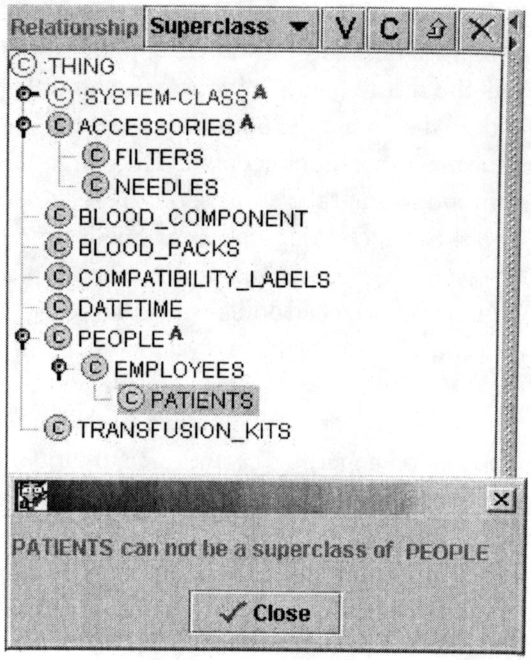

Step 3: Constraints' Enforcement

Once all classes and slots have been defined, the third phase of ontology design deals with fine-tuning the concepts of our ontology in order to make them a more precise description of their instances. In this phase, we will also need to provide documentation for both classes and slots, describing them in natural language, compiling a Thesaurus based on the ontology's vocabulary (including *synonyms*) and listing all the implicit assumptions that were relevant to class definitions.

An important by-product of our ontology design will be a domain's *vocabulary* including all terms we used for classes and properties names.

"Fine-tuning" an ontology concept involves two distinct operations:

1. Adjusting the cardinality ranges of its simple slots
2. Replacing whenever possible classes with their subclasses as types of its complex slots

These two operations amount to stating a set of *constraints* (also called *facets*) that describe or limit the set of possible values a slot can hold. There are two basic flavors of slot constraints: *cardinality constraints* restrict the number of values a slot can have, while *type constraints* specify the internal structure that is allowed for slot values. Cardinality constraints are simple to understand: a maximum cardinality of one means that the slot can have at most one value (single-valued slot), while a maximum cardinality greater than one means that the slot can have multiple-values.

Type constraints are somewhat more complex, and their careful design is crucial for our ontology to be applicable in real situations. On complex slots, type constraints simply amount to specifying the type to which the slot values will belong. The type can be either elementary or complex.

Figure 9. Imposing constraints on capacity slot's facets

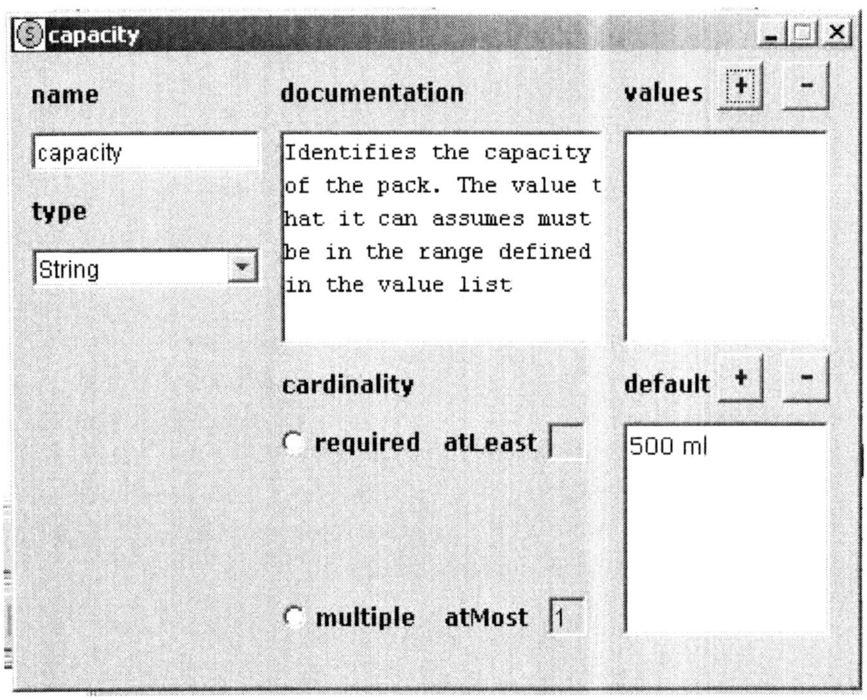

Elementary types are common built-in data types, such as a string of characters ("F239"), integer or floating-point numbers (42, 3.5), a Boolean value or an enumerated type (i.e. a list of allowed values like high, medium, low). Complex types are instances of other classes. For instance, in our sample ontology, the slot COMP_BRACELET of the Patients class and the slot LABEL of Transfusion kit will belong to the same class COMP_LABELS. On simple slots, which belong to an elementary type such as String or Integer, type constraints identify sub-ranges or enumeration, that is, lists of elementary-typed values. Figure 9 shows how range constraints can be defined for the capacity slot of our Blood Pack class.

Another activity involving slot values relates to inverse slots, that is, slots that allow following the PART-OF hierarchy (or other relations) in both directions.

For instance, suppose that we add a class Supplier to our hierarchy and provide it with a slot called "produces" holding multiple instances of the Accessories class. Indeed, adding to the Accessories class a "Produced_by" slot whose values is an instance of the Supplier class does not add to the information provided by our model, but makes the model itself much easier and faster to navigate.

Step 4: Instance Creation

This step involves creating class instances by assigning slot values for the instance frames. Of course, instances' slot values must conform to the facet constraints defined in the previous step; knowledge-acquisition tools like Protégé often enforce such constraints as a form of input validation. Figure10 shows the creation of an instance of the Patients class, a fictitious patient whose name is Alexander McDonald.[u] Near the right lower corner of the window, a smaller form shows our patient's instance of the compatibility label.

Putting Ontologies to Work

Now that we have completed the steps to create our first ontology, we may briefly comment on how it relates to the application scenario we identified in the first step. Our ontology was designed as a common conceptual framework to be used when the oil-drilling platform paramedic and the remote support physician need to communicate. Basically, what the physician needs to do is to supervise the compatibility check between the transfusion kit being used on a patient and the patient herself/himself.

Thanks to the blood transfusion ontology, the compatibility check can be precisely defined in terms of the slots of the involved instances of the Transfusion Kit and Patients classes, even if the paramedic and the physician have never met before and were trained in different environments. Let us consider a pair formed by a Patients class' instance (patient) requiring the transfusion and a candidate Transfusion kit class' instance (kit). Checking compatibility means that the (distinct) instances of the Compatibility Label class contained respectively in the Label slot of the patient and in the Comp_Label slot of the kit must contain the same values of blood group, Rh factor and antibodies.

A looser version of this constraint could also be added, requiring that the Comp_Label slot of the kit to hold value 0 for the blood group and value '+' for the Rh factor, regardless of the Patients instance's Label slot.

At this point, the first question listed in the scope definition phase of our ontology has been given a precise definition in terms of the shared ontology.[v] The fact that the supervision procedure for the transfusion is clearly expressed in terms of the ontology ensures that the paramedic and the remote physician will actually mean the same thing.

Figure 10. An inverse slot

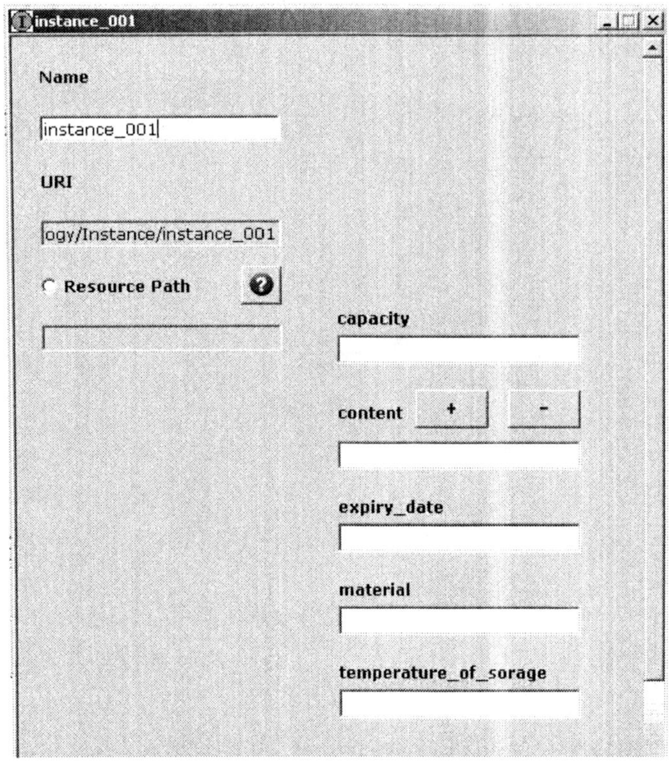

Figure 11. An instance creation

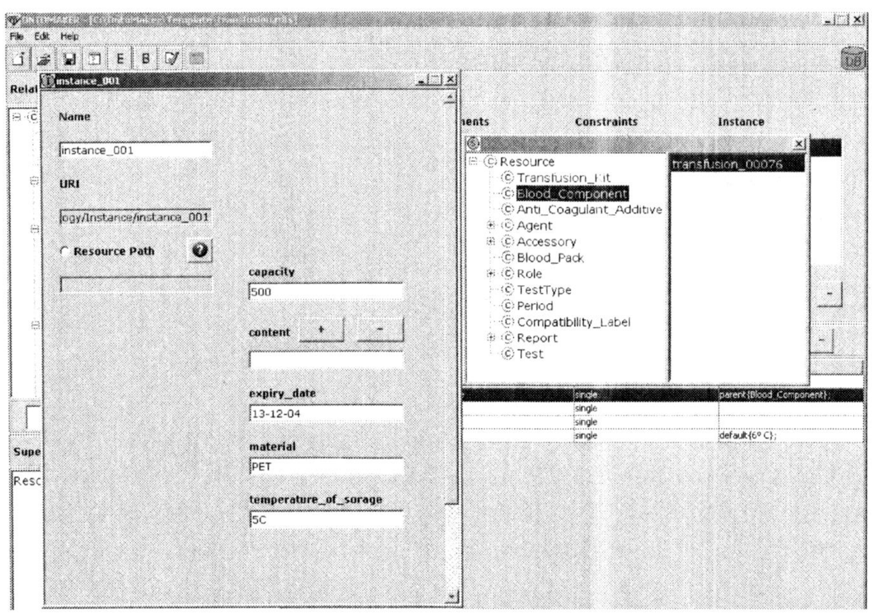

Figure 12. The compatibility check

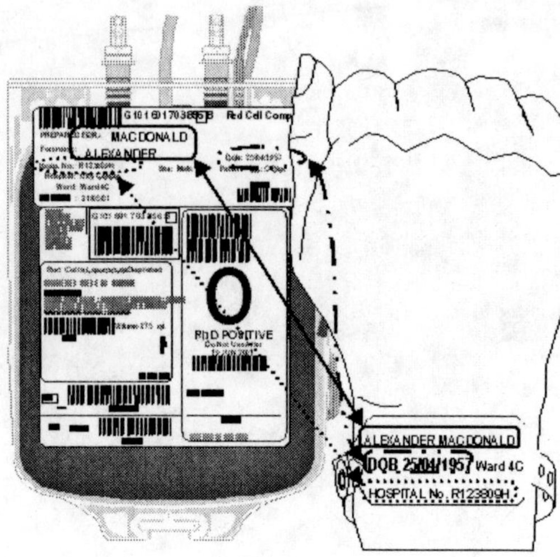

WHAT IS ONTOLOGICAL ENGINEERING?

Ontological engineering (Fernandez, 1997) is the activity of *ontology* development and maintenance; as such, it is a discipline of *knowledge management.*

As with other knowledge engineering artifacts, the lifecycle of ontologies may be depicted as a *waterfall* composed by consecutive phases, namely *design*, *validation*, and *deployment*, *mapping* and *sharing* (Figure13).

While the ontology design phase has been covered in the previous section, the other phases of our waterfall model of the ontologies' lifecycle deserve a brief comment.

- *Validation* phase consists in evaluating the ontology quality from the point of view of its completeness. Common questions to be answered in this phase are the following: Are the ontology's hierarchies correct (free of cycles), well-balanced trees? Does the ontology capture all the concepts of interest? Is it cluttered up with unnecessary concepts? While difficult to *resolve by* simply inspecting the ontology, empirical criteria exist that may be used to answer *such questions*: for instance, if a class has only one child, there may be a modeling problem.
- *Deployment* phase consists in expressing the ontology in a suitable formal, machine-readable syntax.
- *Mapping* phase, also called *indexing*, consists in the association of the ontology concepts to the instances (or to the resource identifiers) they are related to. It is tempting to elaborate further and say that the notion of resource should be itself part of a shared ontology. Indeed, many "Web ontologies" including the concepts relevant to the WWW domain have been proposed in the literature

Figure 13. Waterfall ontology lifecycle

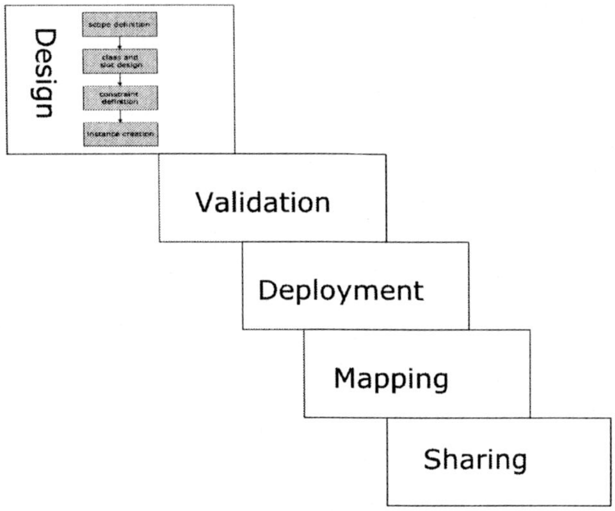

to that effect. A natural language definition of resource has even been standardized by the IETF (Internet Engineering Task Force) and can be found in RFC 2396. That document defines (in plain English) a resource as "anything that has identity". Examples of resources include electronic documents, images, services (e.g., "today's weather report for Rome"), and a collection of other resources, identified by unique URL (Uniform Resource Locators).

- Not all resources are network "retrievable"; for example, human beings (equipped with a SSN number) and bound books in a library (equipped by ISBN codes) can also be considered resources.
- Of course, the effectiveness of the Semantic Web approach heavily relies on the quality of ontology based modeling of the corresponding domain. For this reason, the next sections are devoted to developing the subject of ontological engineering in some detail.
- *Sharing* consists in publishing the ontology and its resource mappings in order to foster cooperative processing of the resources according to the corresponding ontology concepts.

A waterfall model has some obvious drawbacks, the main one being that it can hardly accommodate change.

In practice, when developing an ontology (as any other domain model) several iterations involving the ontology users and the application scenario may be necessary.

The purpose of these multiple iterations is to evolve and fine-tune the ontology on the basis of the results of its application in a real world scenario. This involves adding new concepts when needed, purging the ontology of unnecessary ones and refining the IS-A and PART-OF hierarchies to

Figure 14. Iterative ontology lifecycle

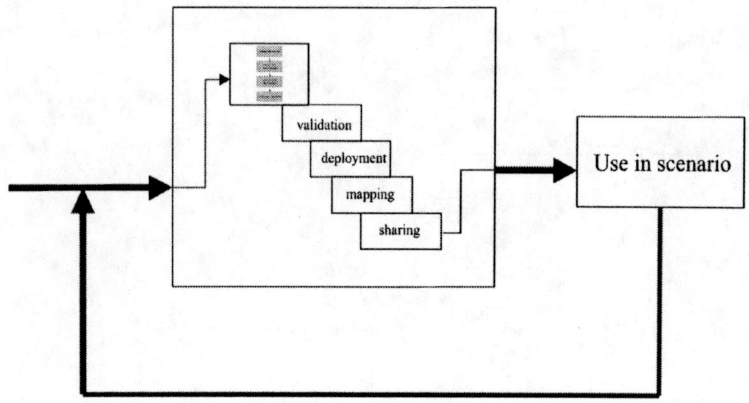

the desired level of detail. This filtering operation mentioned here should not be confused with the validation step in the design phase. Inspecting the topology of the class hierarchy does it on the basis of the users' feedback: ontology development iterations will incorporate a restricted version of the waterfall cycle.

Before going on to introduce more advanced techniques for ontology design, a word of caution is of order: ontology building may be a complex, time-consuming, and expensive process.

Being a formal encoding of a point of view on a domain's state of affairs, ontology requires wide consensus across a community whose members may have very different visions of the domain under consideration. Also, it may be difficult for users to identify what implicit assumptions have been made and to understand the key distinctions within the ontology. In practice, consensus can be obtained in two basic ways: a top-down process, where huge "heavyweight" ontologies are developed by consortia and standards organizations, and a bottom-up one, where small "lightweight" ontologies are developed by large numbers of people and then merged.

ONTOLOGY CATEGORIES

Unless we limit ontology application to very narrow scenario (as we did in our blood transfusion example), ontologies cannot be designed as monolithic structures, as this would mean to redefine each time some basic general concepts (e.g., Person, Organization, Blood_Pack, and the like) that are bound to appear in most ontologies. Indeed, a careful analysis of ontology properties allows for decomposing a generic ontology into modular components. While this analysis could be carried out by defining an "ontology of ontologies,"[w] that is, defining the concept of ontology and modeling its IS-A and PART-OF hierarchies, we shall informally refer to the decomposition of Figure15.

- *Top-level* ontologies contain general concepts that are used in most applications, such as a date, the time of the day or a person's identification data. One would expect a general agreement and perhaps an international and very stable standard to exist on the structure of such widespread concepts.

Figure 15. Ontology categories

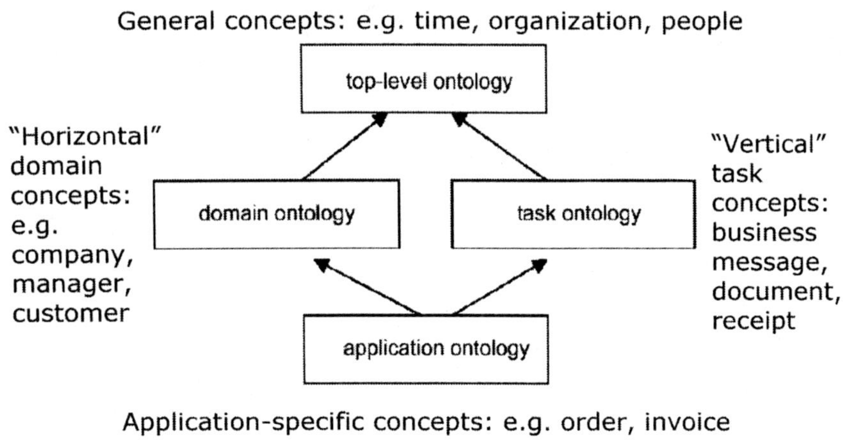

Indeed, such standards are numerous and their number is always growing: top-level ontologies built on them should be developed by consortia rather than by single organizations.

- *Domain* ontologies contain the main concepts of a restricted domain of interest, like Patients in health care or Novels in modern literature. Domain ontologies are developed without reference to any specific problem: they constitute their developer's (an individual or, more frequently, an organization) view of the environment it operates in. For this reason, they tend to change slowly and are usually developed as a part of corporate- or organization-wide projects.
- *Task* ontologies are composed of special-purpose concepts needed to solve a particular class of problems: the Compatibility Label, encoding a number of hematological information for each patient, will be part of a task ontology for hematological health care. The change rate of a task ontology is variable and depends on how dynamic its context is.
- *Application* ontologies exhibit the fastest rate of change as they comprise concepts dealing with the problem at hand, such as the Transfusion kit concept when administering a transfusion. Such ontologies have the fastest obsolescence and need frequent revision.

Even the most detailed application ontology will not entirely capture a context's *implicit knowledge*.

It is therefore important to keep the following distinction: on one hand, there is the ontology itself, which specifies concepts used by definition or convention in a domain. On the other hand, there is the (implicit) knowledge of empirical facts about the ontology's concepts and relationships. This additional, accessory knowledge may change rapidly and is not explicitly represented in the ontology. In the domain of emergency health care, for example, concepts such as patient transfusion and blood pack are parts of the ontology. The fact that scissors are needed to make a blood pack ready for transfusion is an example of empirical, implicit knowledge that is not part of the ontology, whose validity can be assessed, and which can be modified.

INTRODUCTION TO ONTOLOGY LANGUAGES

A number of technological problems must be solved before an ontology like the one described in the previous section can actually be deployed and used.

There is a problem that comes immediately to mind: ontologies and associations between resources and ontology concepts should be expressed using a standard formal language.

Two main ingredients of a formal language are *lexicon* and *syntax*. A lexicon is the *vocabulary* of symbols we are allowed to use when defining ontology and associating concepts to resources. In our case, the lexicon we use for defining ontologies will have to include all classes' and relationships' names, plus additional keywords (i.e., reserved terms that cannot be used as classes' or relationships' names) like "class" and "relationship." One might observe, not without reason, that choosing a lexicon is a major part of the total effort of writing an ontology, as lexical relations such *hyperonymy* (a.k.a. *broader term relationship*) and *hyponymy* (*narrower term relationship*) already describe the structure of the IS-A relationship. This observation is at the basis of WordNet, a widespread linguistic support tool for ontology designers.

Using Thesauri for Ontology Design

Wordnet is an online, free-of-charge lexical reference system developed at Princeton University (http://www.cogsci.princeton.edu/~wn) that organizes English nouns, adjectives and adverbs into synonym sets, each representing a lexical concept. The WordNet system explicitly represents hyperonymy and hyponymy as well as other relationships such as *meronymy* (i.e., PART-OF).

The vocabulary to be used for classes' and relationships' names depends on the human language the designer employs for domain modeling; for this reason, a multilingual European version of WordNet has also been developed in the framework of the EuroWordNet project, aimed at developing a multilingual database with basic semantic relationships among words for several European languages (Dutch, Italian and Spanish). These WordNets will be linked to the English version via a shared top-level ontology.

As a matter of fact, linguistic tools have been around for a long time, under the time-honored name of *Thesaur.i*[x] According to the International Standard Organization, a Thesaurus is a "vocabulary of a controlled indexing language, formally organized so that the a priori relationships among concepts (for example as "broader" and "narrower") are made explicit" (ISO 2788, 1986:2), or "A controlled set of terms selected from natural language and used to represent, in abstract form, the subjects of documents" (ISO 2788, 1986:2).

When the ontology designer is choosing the names for classes and relations in a domain ontology, using WordNet and/or a Thesaurus as a starting point is nearly always a good idea.[y] Linguistic tools suggest correct language usage and often point out possible related concepts; also, visual presentation favors better interaction between users and the information systems and reinforces the understanding of a Thesaurus. On the other hand, general-purpose Thesauri rarely contain a detailed model of a specific domain, so most of the application-specific work is left to the ontology designer.[z]

For example, searching WordNet for hyponyms (i.e., narrower terms), of noun "blood transfusion," defined by the system as "the introduction of blood or blood plasma into a vein or artery" will give us the result: *transfusion, exchange transfusion, blood transfusion (the introduction of blood or blood plasma into a vein or artery).*

WordNet's answer points out the existence of the narrower concept of exchange transfusion, which is a special kind of transfusion[aa] that might have been (and in fact was) overlooked by the ontology designer.

Ontology Languages' Syntax

The ontology language's syntax is the *grammar* we use to construct (either visually or textually) sentences like 'class Patient is in relation IS-A with class Person' or 'instance ID00001 belongs to class Patient'. Syntax specification must allow for ontology parsing, i.e. for automatically filtering out definitions that are not well formed, such as 'class Patient is in relation IS-A.'[ab]

Language definitions used in practice also specify one or more *low-level data formats* that software applications can use internally to represent the language definition itself (i.e., lexicon plus syntax) and, more importantly, the sentences belonging to the language.

A low-level data format should be platform-independent and preferably text-based. Binary formats are less interchangeable and usually exhibit a faster obsolescence.

What are the formal languages commonly used to encode and exchange ontologies? In other words, which are the lexicon, syntax and low-level data format that Protégé or our Ontomaker tool use when saving an ontology that we designed via their graphic user interface? A look at Protégé's Select Format window (Figure 16) hints to a text-based format, but it does not say much about the syntax of the language that will be used.

We shall develop a checklist and describe some basic requirements that ontology languages should satisfy. Our list of requirements comes rather straightforwardly from the discussion in the previous sections.

1. *Human and machine readability:* ontology specifications need to be readable by human users as well as by software programs.
2. *Well defined syntax:* ontology specifications need to be automatically parsed, i.e. checked by programs for lexical and syntactical correctness. Also, an ontology specification language should include a definition of the corresponding instances' encoding, in a form that allows instance parsing.[ac]

Figure 16. Saving an ontology in Protege

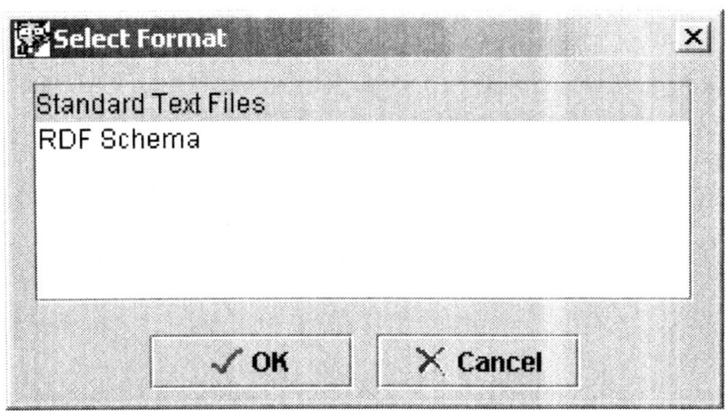

3. *Expressive power:* an ontology language should be expressive enough to describe most domains. At the very least, the language should allow for unambiguously expressing PART-OF and IS-A hierarchies, as well as other relationships among concepts.
4. *Well defined semantics:* ontology specifications should be associated with a clearly understood model, allowing for automatic checking of their consistency.
5. *Efficient support for reasoning:* Ontology specifications should support a number of advanced features, such as following relationships when navigating instances, establishing new inter-ontology relationships on the fly and discovering (unexpected) relationships spontaneously arising from existing ones.

Ontological Languages

In the last 10 years, a variety of ontological languages have been developed. Different languages can have different perspectives but for the most part *are* rooted in FOL (First Order Logic). Three main features differencing ontological languages among them: (i) the syntax; (ii) the expressivity power; (iii) the software support. LP (Logic Programs)[ad] is the family of languages that have the longest tradition in Computer Science. Prolog, Datalog, RuleML are some examples of such kind of languages. Languages, such as Ontolingua, F-Logic and OCML, are based on the Frame Theory while others, such as LOOM, OIL, and OWL, are based on DL (Description Logic). [ae] One of the most important standards is OWL (Ontology Web Language). This is a Web-based language for defining DL ontologies. OWL is a language that is designed to be strong on the formal specification as well as on the architectural side. OWL uses URI for naming elements and the structure of the ontology (the set of relation connecting elements) is provided according to the RDF standard, that is, an XML serialization describing assertions in terms of triples composed of a subject, a predicate and an object. The structure *is* based on *a* triple. *Information can be added by constructing* a triple *related* to *the* other *items* by selecting a common subject or object. This provides the maximum scalability; while the XML serialization guarantees the interoperability with other Web standards.

A current research issue is related to the problem of *reconciliating* DL and LP. The main difference between these tow families of languages is that the first one is monotonic while the other is not. A formal language is monotonic if the addition of new assertions in a knowledge base *K* cannot invalidate the deductions obtained in *K*. This is a very important feature for representing knowledge in distributed systems because the assertion forming a knowledge base can derive from different sources. DL guaranties this property but in order to maintain the computational complexity under control other limitations are imposed. For example, DL limits to two the number of arguments that a predicate can support. But combining DL and LP the computational complexity can be maintained under control extending, in the same time, the expressivity power. For example, W3C working group called *Rules Working Group* is developing this research issue.

CONCLUSION

In this chapter, we described what an ontology is and outlined some of the basic principles and techniques (including a simple stepwise methodology) that designers should follow when building one.

It is difficult to overestimate the potential of ontology-based domain modeling toward the (much-needed) general improvement of WWW information organization and access.

At its simplest, ontology-based indexing of digital resources amounts to a huge effort towards a re-organization (and, hopefully, a fuller comprehension) of the huge body of knowledge currently available on corporate Intranets and/or on the global Net. This re-organization will make navigation easier and search engines' result more accurate, because users will be able to state or select concept names out of a *shared controlled vocabulary* rather than trying to invent their own keywords.

However, indexing existing resources *a posteriori* is just a small part of the picture: the "Semantic Web" strategy of the World Wide Web Consortium (http://www.w3.org/) envisions *apriori* concept-based indexing as an integral part of the production, marketing and commercialization of digital content.

Finally, it is important to underline once again that designing an ontology from scratch is seldom a good idea. Various types of ontologies already exist, aimed at different domains and tasks; many of them are organized in publicly available libraries. Also, several good software tools (including Protégé 2000 and our own OntoMaker) support the process of re-using and developing existing ontologies in addition to helping in creating new ones.

REFERENCES

Berners-Lee, T., Hendler, J., & Lassila, O. (2001). The Semantic Web. *Scientific American, 284* (5) 34–43.

Brachman, R.J. (1983). *What IS-A is and isn't: An analysis of taxonomiclLinks in semantic networks.*

Fernandez, M., Gomez-Perez, A., & Juristo, N. (1997). Meta-ontology. *From ontological art toward ontological engineering. In Spring Symposium Series, Stanford University. Stanford, CA.*

Gruniger, M. & Lee J. (2002). *Ontology applications anddDesign.* Comm. of the ACM, *45*(2), 39-41.

Gruber, T.R. (1995). *Toward principles for the design of ontologies used for knowledge sharing.* Int. J. Hum. Comput. Stud *43,* (5/6), 907–928.

Ogden, C. K. & Richards, I. A. (1923). *The meaning of meaning.* 8th Ed. New York, Harcourt, Brace & World, Inc.

Noy N. F., Sintek M., Decker S., Crubezy M., Fergerson R. W., & Musen M. A. (2001). *Creating Semantic WebcContents with Protégé 2000.* IEEE Intelligent Systems 16(2), 60-71.

Masini G., Napoli A., Colnet D. & Leonard D. (1991). *Object-Oriented Languages.* A.P.I.C. Series, No. 34.

Holsapple C. W. & Joshi K. D. (2001). *A collaborative approach to ontology design.* Communications of the ACM. *45* (2), Welbourne, M. Knowledge, Acumen Publishing.

ENDNOTES

[a] The closest approximation being the keyword contained in the <META> tags contained in the <HEAD> portion of HTML pages to facilitate indexing by search engines' spiders.

[b] The negative impact of knowledge sharing unsolved problems on the effectiveness of Web information searches is comparable to the one of the Internet's initial lack of reliability or security

[c] These will be determined, in most countries by national or regional standards.

[d] Note that here we are not concerned with *models* of the electrician's theory, i.e. with its being true or false in a real situation (although the house owner should probably be).

[e] The Greek prefix "onto" refers to the present participle of the verb "to be", while the suffix "logia" means, as usual, "discipline".

f In their 1923 book (Ogden, 1923), philosophers Ogden and Richards argued that a major problem in human communication is some speakers' habit of treating words as if they were things in reality. As we shall see, this subtle difference may become even more difficult to remember when both words and the things they refer exist as digital encoding in a computer's memory or on a communication channel.

g For instance, giving the specification of ontology as a set of axioms in a logical language (see chapter two) it would be possible to list the models of the ontology's axioms (i.e., list all their possible truth-values). This enables comparing models to the ones intended by the designer (i.e., his/her beliefs about the world).

h Philosophers often refer to this distinction when characterizing knowledge as needing support of some sort of justification in term of a state of affairs.

i Protégé (http://protege.stanford.edu/) is a complete software platform which can be extended with graphical widgets to access other knowledge-based systems. It also includes a library which other applications can use to access and display knowledge bases.

j Several libraries of ontologies are currently available on the Web, including the DAML and Ontolingua libraries (respectively located at www.daml.org/ontologies and at www.ksl.stanford.edu/software/ontolingua/) as well as Protégé's own ontology library (http://protege.stanford.edu/plugins.html).

k Choosing these symbols amounts to defining the *application-level protocol* used for communicating.

l There is however an important difference: an O-O programming language class' structure defines the dynamic behavior of objects via the classes' methods and the physical representation of the objects' data. On the other hand, ontology is about the structure of concepts that model a domain, and does not deal with actual physical representation.

m As the reader may have guessed, things can get much more complicated should the context of the communication be unknown *a priori*. In fact, a real object can be classified under the umbrella of multiple concepts, depending on the situation. In our setting, for instance, a needle will naturally fall under the concept of blood transfusion accessory; for a police officer investigating drug abuse, the concept of "crime evidence" may be more appropriate for the same object.

n Technically speaking, classes provide an *intensional* description of their instances, i.e. give us the criteria we need to identify and generate instances themselves. Common sets, on the other hand, can also be defined via *extension*, i.e. simply by listing their elements.

o Instructional ontology traditionally includes the so-called instructional links (such as analogy and example).

p The forest can be easily turned into a single tree by providing a common root, that is, a UNIVERSE class including all the others as its slots.

q Once again, this hierarchy is a forest that can be turned into a tree by providing an undescribed concept like THING as its common root.

r Actually, the one given here is only one of the many possible interpretations of the inheritance relationship; finding new ones has been for a while a favorite topic of artificial intelligence research. As early as 1983, Ronald Brachman (1983) gave more than 10 different definitions of inheritance, each carrying a somewhat different semantics. We adopted the set-oriented interpretation for modelling as it is readily understood and clearly underlines the distinction between superclass-subclass relationship (the inclusion set operator $\subset$) and the class-instance one (the set membership $\in$)

s Of course there is much to be said against inserting a general-purpose class like People in a special purpose ontology like the one we are designing. Indeed, one would better refer to an external, general-purpose ontology for this type of concepts. We shall elaborate on this idea on the next sections.

t Dynamic techniques for inheritance conflict resolution delay the decision about multiple slot inheritance to the moment of instance creation. It is interesting to observe that humans naturally rely on this kind of techniques. For instance, consider a "Repro" class composed of printed reproductions of famous pictures. Repro will inherit from "Pictures" and "Prints" superclasses, both having an "author" slot. In turn, these two "author" slots belong respectively to a "Painter" and a "Printer" class. Which slot should be inherited when processing a specific instance of Repro in a specific situation? This is a problem very easy to solve for humans and much harder for machines. For this reason, dynamic conflict resolutions techniques are seldom used in software applications, due to the additional performance burden they impose.

u Of course, as our example shows, instance creation does not amount to producing the physical objects associated with the ontology concepts; rather, we obtain a computer-based digital *encoding* of them. This distinction can sometimes be blurred or dropped altogether when the instance objects are themselves digital, so that the digital encoding of the object and the object do coincide.

v Definition of the other two questions is left to the interested reader as an exercise.

w This "ontology of ontologies" is an example of a "meta-model", and is therefore sometimes called a "meta-ontology" by computer scientists, though it is very close to the original idea of ontology as "theory of theories of state of affairs".

x This observation remains true even if we only consider Thesauri in their electronic form: the ISO 2788 standard containing guidelines for the establishment and development of monolingual thesauri dates as far back as 1986.

y This is especially true if the ontology designer happens not to be a native speaker of the natural language from which the ontology's terms must be extracted.

z Of course, this work involves looking around for standard specific Thesauri in his/her domain of interest. In the case of our example, for instance, the Agency for Health Care Policy and Research (AHCPR) and the American Medical Informatics Association are promoting vocabulary standards for coding primary care data. In collecting health services research data, AHCPR relies on documentation provided by primary care practitioners. According to the agency (http://www.ahcpr.gov/), "Without data standards and vocabulary, researchers will not be able to capture the content of primary care practice".

aa Exchange transfusions involve slow removal of a person's blood and its replacement with equal amounts of a donor's blood.

ab The visual counterpart of this incorrect sentence would be a dangling IS-A slot. Protégé displays an error message when we try and save an ontology that is not well formed.

ac Of course, instance parsing is only possible on the instances' digital representations.

ad In a broad sense, Logic Programing is a term used for referring to programs rooted in mathematical logic. In the everyday use this terms is limited to languages adopting the negation as faillure.

ae Description Logic is a family of logic-based knowledge representation formalism included in a decidable fragment of First Order Logic.

Chapter III
OntoExtractor:
A Tool for Semi-Automatic Generation and Maintenance of Taxonomies from Semi-Structured Documents

Marcello Leida
University of Milan, Italy

ABSTRACT

This chapter introduces OntoExtractor, a tool for the semi-automatic generation of the taxonomy from a set of documents or data sources. The tool generates the taxonomy in a bottom-up fashion. Starting from structural analysis of the documents, it produces a set of clusters, which can be refined by a further grouping created by content analysis. Metadata describing the content of each cluster is automatically generated and analysed by the tool for producing the final taxonomy. A simulation of a tool, based on an implicit and explicit voting mechanism, for the maintenance of the taxonomy is also described. The author depicts a system that can be used to generate the taxonomy from a heterogeneous source of information, using wrappers for converting the original format of the document to a structured one. This way, OntoExtractor can virtually generate the taxonomy from any source of information just adding the proper wrapper. Moreover, the trust mechanism allows a reliable method for maintaining the taxonomy and for overcoming the unavoidable generation of wrong classes in the taxonomy.

INTRODUCTION

Nowadays, people can easily access virtually infinite sources of information. This unlimited supply of knowledge is potentially useful in a number of application scenarios; on the other hand, information needs to be organized and structured to become a robust and trusted source of knowledge. *CoP (Communities of Practise)* (Lave et al., 1991) are forming spontaneously, for example, among people sharing same interests, or according to an organization model, for instance among people working on the same project. Members of those communities interact and share information. The need for an organized and common structure that describes shared information is then evident. In the last few years, business ontology has been recognized as the most promising way to describe shared knowledge in a business environment. Shared information often can be redundant, incomplete, or subject to different interpretations. Therefore, we must be able to deal with different levels of uncertainty. Recent studies (Fagin, 1998; Fagin, 1999, & Fagin, 2002) propose using Soft Computer Techniques as a promising approach to handle uncertainty. *The Knowledge Management Group* of the University of Milan, during the collaboration with BT Intelligent Systems Research Centre, has developed and, in part, implemented a fuzzy-based approach to extract metadata and description knowledge from heterogeneous information sources. Moreover, a fuzzy-based trust system for the maintenance of the generated hierarchy has been proposed. The following sections briefly present the theories behind this approach and the demo software developed on the basis of those theories. Section 2 is a general overview of the construction of the hierarchy; the original approach is intended to build classes of ontology from the knowledge base in a bottom-up fashion. The section is focused on presenting the techniques implemented in the *On-*

Figure 1. Overall structure of the process

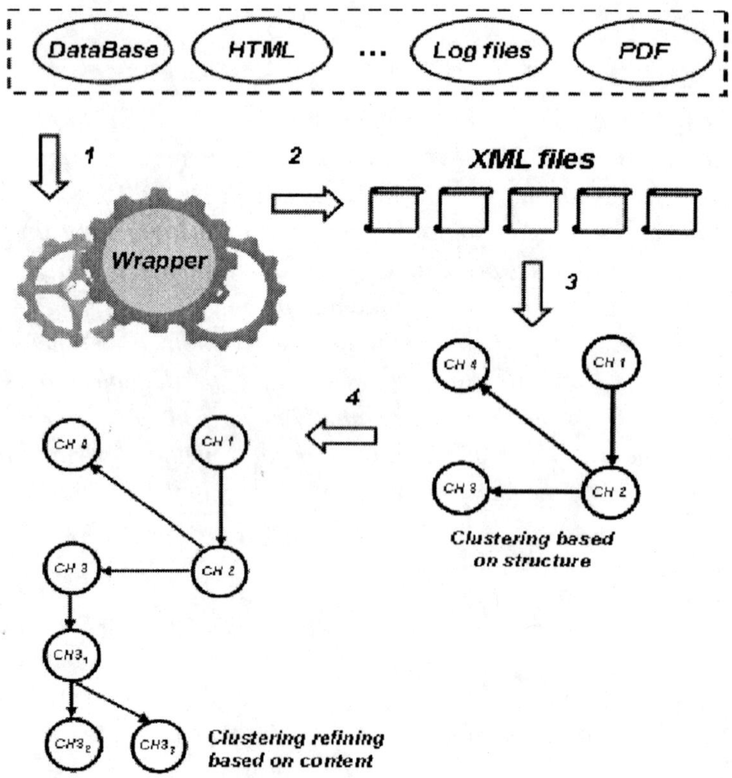

toExtractor software--a tool that clusters different types of documents with respect to their structure and their content. Section 3 describes a technique for automatic validation of the generated assertions, by explicit vote, or by considering implicit information that a user produces browsing the hierarchy; the community is described as a Fuzzy Set that depicts the distribution of the expertise in relation to the weight of their behaviours. This section is followed by a brief description of the simulator software used to test the algorithms illustrated. Last section regards the future directions of this approach and some important results and conclusions are presented.

ONTOEXTRACTOR: CONSTRUCTION OF THE HIERARCHY

OntoExtractor (Cui et al., 2005) is a tool, developed by the *Knowledge Management Group* of the University of Milan, which extracts metadata from heterogeneous information, producing a "quick-and-dirty" hierarchy of knowledge. This tool implements most of the techniques described in this section. The construction of the hierarchy occurs in a bottom-up fashion. Starting from heterogeneous documents, we use the clustering process to group the documents in meaningful clusters. These clusters identify classes in the ontology or, like in the current version of the *OntoExtractor* tool, extensions of *iPhi* categories (Martin et al., 2003).

The construction of the hierarchy is a three-step process:

1. Normalizing the incoming documents in XML format (Salton et al., 1996)
2. (Optional) Clustering the documents according to their structure using a Fuzzy Bag representation of the XML tree (Ceravolo et al., 2004; Damiani et al., 2004)
3. Refining the structural clustering analyzing the content of the documents, producing a semantic clustering of the documents

In addition, it is possible to analyze the produced hierarchy in order to discover *is-a* and *part-of* relations among the cluster representative documents (ClusterHeads) (Ceravolo et al., 2006).

NORMALIZING THE KNOWLEDGE BASE USING A COMMON DATA REPRESENTATION (XML)

This first step in the process of building a hierarchy is choosing a common representation for the information to be managed. The data may come from different and heterogeneous sources--from unstructured to semi-structured or structured information, such as textual documents, HTML files, XML files, or records in a database. We choose XML as a target representation, as it is a *de-facto* standard for metadata and data representation.

The wrapping process is shown in Figure 2; for semi-structured and structured sources the wrapper does not have much to do. All it has to perform is applying a mapping between the original data and elements in the target XML tree. Unstructured sources of information need additional processing aimed at extracting the hidden structure of documents. This phase uses well-known text-segmentation techniques (Salton et al., 1996) in order to find relations among parts of a text. It is an iterative process that takes as input a text blob (which is a continuous flow of characters representing the whole content of a document) and gives as output a set of text-segments identified by the text segmentation process. The process stops when no text blob can be further segmented. At this point, a post-processing phase analyzes the resulting tree structure and generates the corresponding XML document.

Figure 2. Wrapping process

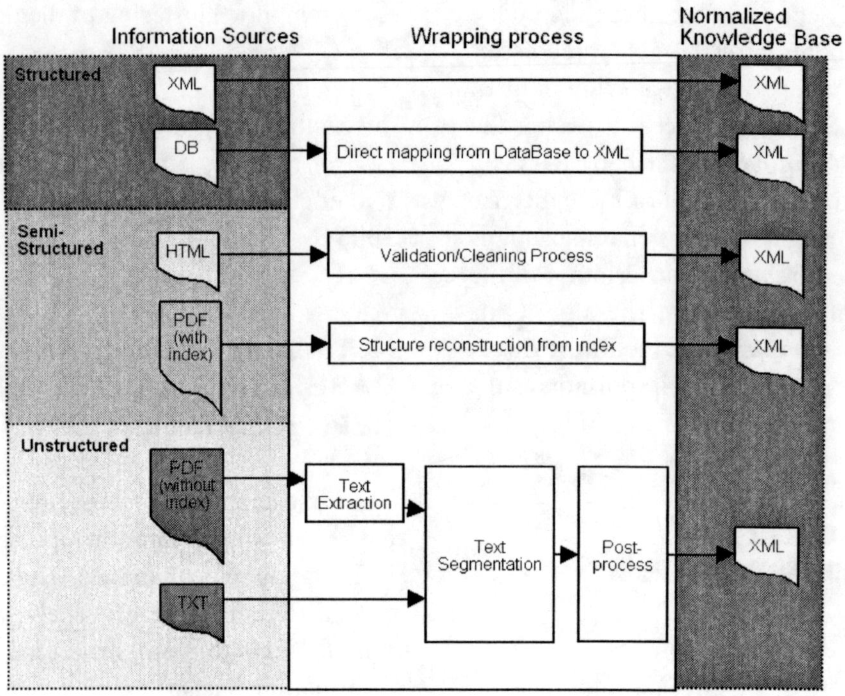

In the current version of the *OntoExtractor* software, a Regular Expressions matching approach is also available in order to discover regular patterns like titles of sections in the documents, helping controlling the text segmentation process. This is a preliminary approach that compares each row of the document with the regular expression (i.e., {[0-9]+(([.]?)|([.]?[0-9]+))*(\s+\w+)+}; we used this expression to match chapters, sections and paragraph headlines, which are usually preceded by numbers separated by a "."). We will employ the regular expressions to assist the segmentation process to recognize headlines.

CLUSTERING BY STRUCTURE

The *OntoExtractor* tool uses a flat encoding for the internal representation of XML documents for processing and analysis processes. Documents are represented as Fuzzy Bags, so elements can be repeated.

Due to the fact that the importance of tags can differ, it is possible to assign a different weight ($0 \leq X \leq 1$) to each tag in the document. In other words, for each element in the XML document *d*, the Fuzzy Bag encoding *d* contains a Fuzzy Element whose membership value is determined by the position of the tag in the document's structure and by other topological properties.

The *OntoExtractor* tool currently provides two different methods to calculate the membership function of a Fuzzy Element:

1. Nesting: this is a "lossy" representation of the original document topology, because this membership value does not keep track of which is the parent tag of the current tag, as shown in Figure 3. Giving a vocabulary *V*= {R/1, *a*/0.9, *b*/0.8, *d*/0.6, *e*/0.4}, applying (1) to the tree representation of a generic XML document *A*.xml or *B*.xml, we obtain the fuzzy bag *A* = *B* = {R/1, *a*/0.3, *a*/0.225, *b*/0.2, *d*/0.3, *e*/0.2}
2. The membership value for each element is:

$$\mathbf{M = Ve / L} \qquad (1)$$

Where:
M: membership value
Ve: weight of the tag in the vocabulary
L: nesting level of the tag with **Lroot** = 0

3. MV: this is an experimental representation introduced by our group, which keeps memory of the parent tag. The membership value for each element is:

$$\mathbf{M = (Ve + Mp) / L} \qquad (2)$$

Where:
M: membership value
Mp: membership value of the parent tag with **Mroot** = 0
Ve: weight of the tag in the vocabulary
L: nesting level of the tag with **Lroot** = 0

The MV membership value helps, in certain cases, to keep memory of the tree structure of the original document, referring to Figure 3: using the same vocabulary V, applying (2) to the tree representation of the two XML documents *A.xml* and *B.xml* we obtain A = {R/1, *a*/0.53, *a*/0.36, *b*/0.33, *d*/0.8, *e*/0.7} and B = {R/1, a/0.56, a/0.37, b/0.34, d/0.8, e/0.7} which are different.

Given a XML document coming from Amazon and processed with our *OntoExtractor* giving the same weight 1 (vocabulary weight) to all the tags: we obtain the Fuzzy Bags (see Example 1).

In order to compare the XML documents modeled as fuzzy bags we have chosen between the measures of comparison studied in Bouchon-Meunier et al. (1996) and Bocs et al. (2001). We privileged measures giving a higher similarity weight to the bags where elements (tags) belonging to the intersection are less nested. This is motivated by the fact that, if a tag is nearer to the root than another one, it seems reasonable to assume that it has a higher semantic value.

Figure 3. Two generic XML documents A.xml and B.xml

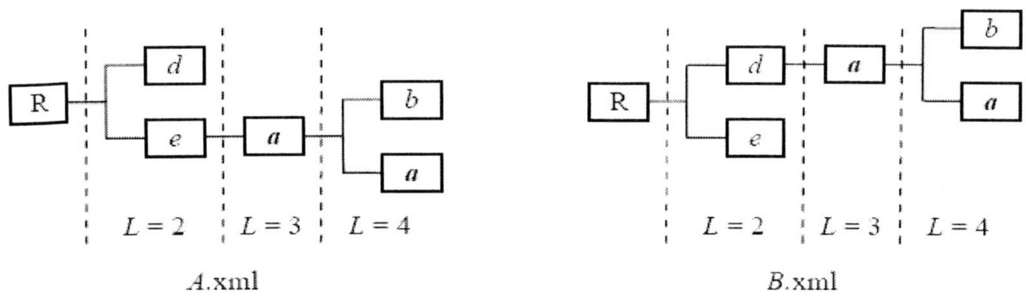

Example 1

```
<Item>
        <ASIN>0060009357</ASIN>
        <Category>Food, Drink</Category>
        <CustomerReviews>
                <AverageRating>5.0</AverageRating>
                <TotalReviews>2</TotalReviews>
                <TotalReviewPages>1</TotalReviewPages>
                <Review>
                        <ASIN>0060009357</ASIN>
                        <Rating>5</Rating>
                        <HelpfulVotes>17</HelpfulVotes>
                        <CustomerId>A1ZCYC0RHTRMZF</CustomerId>
                        <TotalVotes>18</TotalVotes>
                        <Date>2004-10-25</Date>
                        <Summary>Reach your RealAge and eat well too</Summary>
                        <Content>Dr. Phil does a ...</Content>
                </Review>
                <Review>
                        <ASIN>0060009357</ASIN>
                        <Rating>5</Rating>
                        <HelpfulVotes>52</HelpfulVotes>
                        <CustomerId>A1FYZ9WKLY4CPJ</CustomerId>
                        <TotalVotes>54</TotalVotes>
                        <Date>2003-11-21</Date>
                        <Summary>Best healthy cookbook on the market!</Summary>
                        <Content>I love this book! ...</Content>
                </Review>
        </CustomerReviews>
                        </Item>
```

In *OntoExtractor*, the comparison between two Fuzzy Bags is computed using *Jaccard* norm: The formula to compute this norm is:

$$S(B1,B2) = Approx(|Bag1 \cap Bag2| / |Bag1 \cup Bag2|)$$

Where:

B1 and **B2** are the input fuzzy bags

$\cap$ Is the intersection operator

$\cup$ Is the union operator

$| |$ Is the cardinality operator

Approx ( ) is the approximation operator

S is the *Jaccard* similarity value between B1 and B2

For more theoretical information about this norm and how the union, intersection, approximation and cardinality operations are expressed, please refer to Ceravolo et al. 2004; Damiani et al. 2004, and Cui et al. 2005.

Using this norm, the tool can perform a partitioned clustering technique that is a hybrid

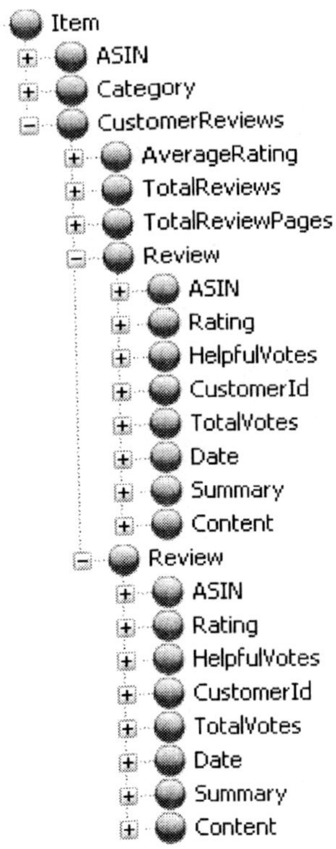

Figure 4a. The document tree

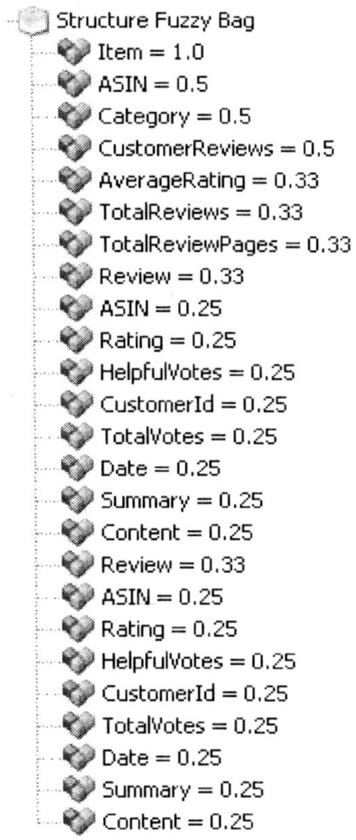

Figure 4b. Fuzzy Bag generated with Nesting membership

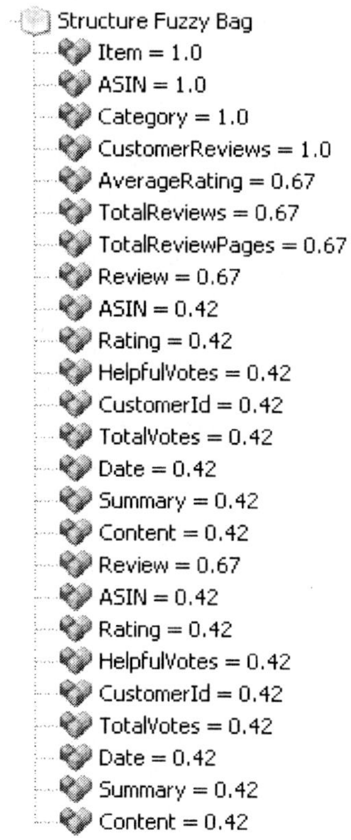

Figure 4c. Fuzzy Bag generated with MV membership

version between *K-means* and *K-NN* clustering algorithms.

OntoExtractor uses an *alpha-cut* value as a threshold for the clustering process, in order to avoid suggesting the initial number of clusters (k) and avoiding this way some clustering problems of the *k-means* algorithm.

The clustering algorithm compares all documents with the centroid of each cluster, considering only the bigger resemblance value. If this value is bigger than the given *alpha,* the document is inserted in the cluster; otherwise, a new empty cluster is generated and the document is inserted in it.

The OntoExtractor tool offers two different ways to calculate the centroid of each cluster: one method chooses the document that has the smaller representative Fuzzy Bag. In this method, the centroid always corresponds to a real document. The other method generates a new Fuzzy Bag that is the union of all the Fuzzy Bags in the cluster. This way, the generated Fuzzy Bag does not have a compulsory correspondence with a real document.

The tool offers the possibility to select the value for *alpha* and the number of samples to consider in the interval, in order to give the user the possibility of choosing between different

Figure 5a. Clustering using Min size centroid (in green)

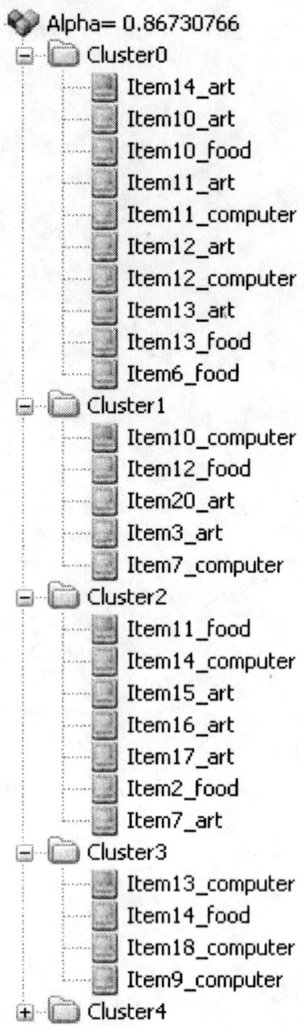

Figure 5b. Clustering using general centroid (in green)

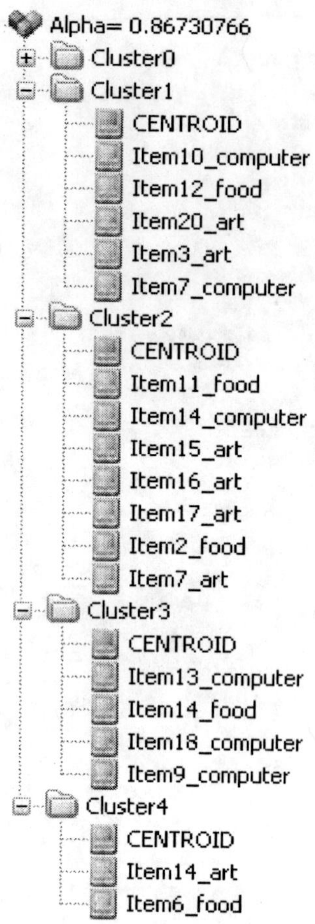

clustering techniques. The difference between the two clustering techniques is that the Min size centroid represents the intersection of the Fuzzy Bags representing the documents in the cluster, and general centroid is the union of all the Fuzzy Bags representing the documents in the cluster. The choice of one technique or the other depends on how we want to choose the Fuzzy Bag that will represent the cluster in the metadata ontology building process.

CLUSTERING BY CONTENT

The second clustering process that we propose is clustering by content of the tags. Content-based clustering is independent for each selected structural cluster, so that it is possible to give different clustering criteria for each generated structural cluster, as shown in Figure 6. Note that users can select which clustering process to perform; for instance, if there is no need of structural

Figure 6. Domain class subdivision based on structure (a) and refinement based on content (b)

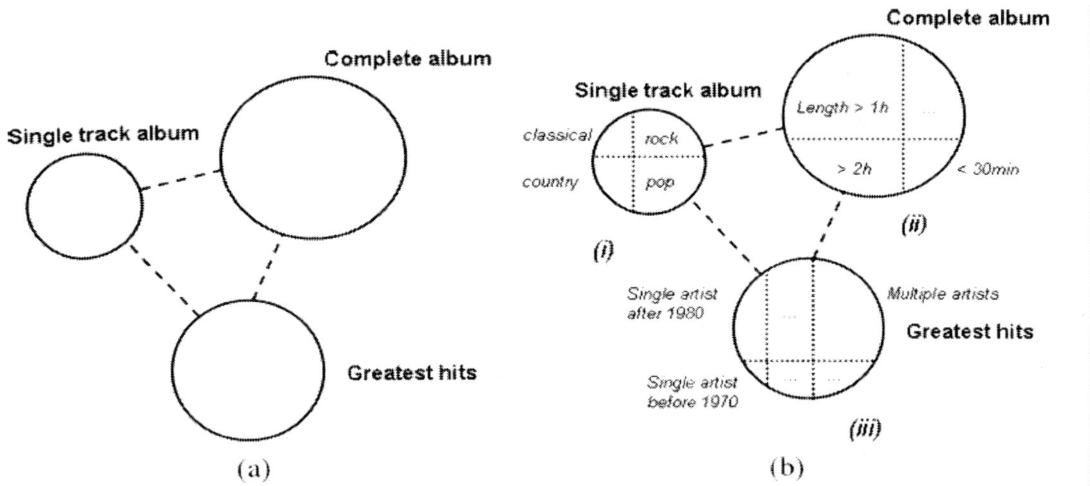

Figure 7. Ttag-level comparison between data belonging to the same tag in different documents

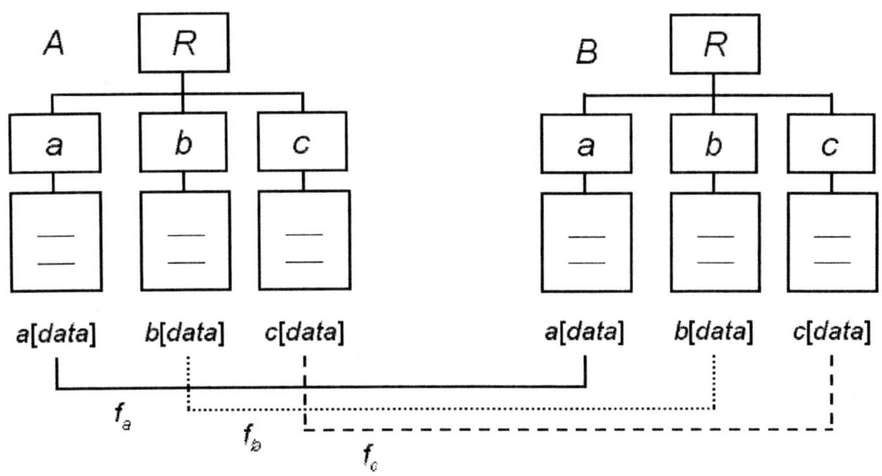

clustering, then only content-based clustering is performed.

It is important to remember that our clustering technique works on XML documents that are somehow structured. Therefore, we compute content-based similarity at *tag level*, comparing content of the same tag among different documents. Then we compute content-based similarity at *document level* by aggregating tag level similarity values.

Referring to Figure 7 it is necessary to choose two different functions: a function *f* to compare data belonging to tags with the same name in different documents:

$$f_a(\{a[data]\}_A, \{a[data]\}_B) \ ,$$

$$f_b(\{b[data]\}_A, \{b[data]\}_B) \ ,$$

$$f_c(\{c[data]\}_A, \{c[data]\}_B) \qquad (3)$$

where:

$\mathbf{f_i}$: function used to compare the content *f* with the selected tag;

$\mathbf{\{x[data]\}_Y}$: the data in the tag x of document y;

and a function ***F*** to aggregate the individual ***f*s**:

$$F(f_a, f_b, f_c) \qquad (4)$$

We have two possibilities for choosing the **F** function:

- ***F*** is a *t-norm*: conjunction of the single values ($fa \wedge fb \wedge fc$)
- ***F*** is a *t-conorm*: disjunction of the single values ($fa \vee fb \vee fc$)

Referring to Figure 8, it is evident that we need to consider also cases where documents have multiple instances of the same tag at different nesting levels and documents where the tag is not present. So in the first case we have:

$$f_b(null, b[data]_B) = 0$$

and in the second case we evaluate the distance between the tags using the formula:

$$f_x = \max_{p,k} \frac{1}{1+\Delta_{p,k}} f_{x_{p,k}}(\{x_p[data]\}_{D_1}, \{x_k[data]\}_{D_2})$$

$$\Delta = |\mu(x_p) - \mu(x_k)|$$

Figure 8. Example of comparison with null values and nested values

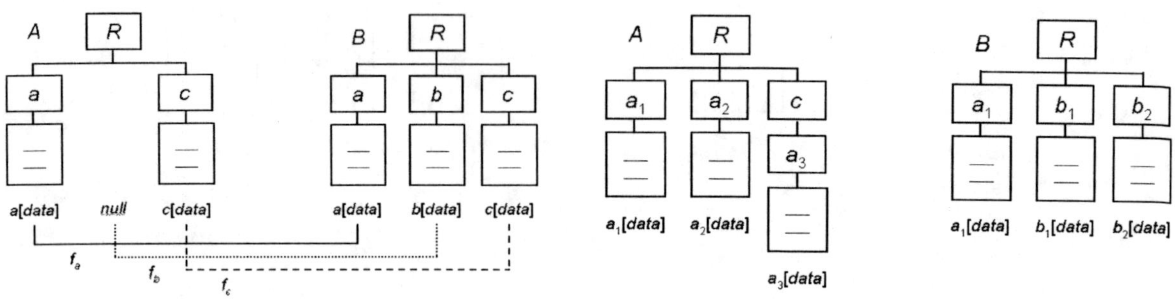

Occurrences of terms have distinct informative roles depending on the tags they belong to. So, it is possible either to define a different function *f* for each group of data of the same tag in different documents, or choosing a function considering the membership value □*(xi)* associated to the *i*th tag.

We represent the content of each tag (A_n*[data]*, B_n*[data,]* C_n*[data],...* in (2)) with the well-known *VSM (Vector Space Model)* widely used in the modern information retrieval system. The VSM is an algebraic model used for information filtering and retrieval. It represents natural language documents in a formal manner by the use of vectors in a multi-dimensional space.

The VSM usually builds a *documents-terms* matrix and processes it to generate the *document-terms* vectors. Our approach is similar but we create one matrix for each tag in the document; correspondingly, we create a *tags-terms* vector.

There are several methods to generate the tags-terms vector; including *LSA* (*Latent Semantic Analysis)* (Landauer et al., 1998)) by *SVD* (*Singular Value Decomposition*), a well-known method of matrix reduction that adds latent semantic meaning to vectors.

Using *LSI,* producing tags-terms vectors is a three-step process:

Producing tags-terms matrix: for each tag in the document, a documents-terms matrix is produced. It is important to remember that we do not consider the document as a unique text-blob, but we build the documents-terms matrix at the tag level. We shall have as many documents-terms matrix as there are tags. If a tag is not present in a document, a row of zeros is added to the matrix. Each entry in the matrix can be computed in several ways as well. We use the *tf-idf* weight (Salton et al. 1987):

$$\mathrm{tf} = \frac{n_i}{\sum_k n_k}$$

with:

$\mathbf{n}_i$ number of occurrences of the considered term;

$\sum_k \mathbf{n}_k$: number of occurrences of all terms.

$$\mathrm{tfidf} = \mathrm{tf} \cdot \log\left(\frac{|D|}{|(d_j \supset t_i)|}\right)$$

with:

tf: term frequency

|D|: total number of document in the corpus

$|(d_j \supset t_j)|$: number of documents where the term t_j appears (that is *nj≠ 0*).

Computing SVD: once the matrix has been generated, we process it by SVD. SVD is a factorization method used in linear algebra for matrix reduction. It relies on the assumption that any *m* x *n* matrix **a** (*m* >= *n*) can be written as the product of an *m* x *n* column-orthogonal matrix **u**, an *n* x *n* diagonal matrix with positive or zero elements, and the transpose of an *n* x *n* orthogonal matrix **v**.

Suppose *M* is an *m*-by-*n* matrix whose entries come from the field *K*, which is either the field of real numbers or the field of complex numbers. Then there exists a factorization of the form:

$$M = U\Sigma V^*,$$

where *U* is an *m*-by-*m* unitary matrix over *K*, the matrix ∑ is *m*-by-*n* with nonnegative numbers on the diagonal and zeros off the diagonal, and V^* denotes the conjugate transpose of *V*, an *n*-by-*n* unitary matrix over *K*. Such a factorization is called a *singular-value decomposition* of *M*.

The matrix *V* thus contains a set of orthogonal "input" or "analysing" base-vector directions for *M*.

The matrix *U* contains a set of orthogonal "output" base-vector directions for *M*.

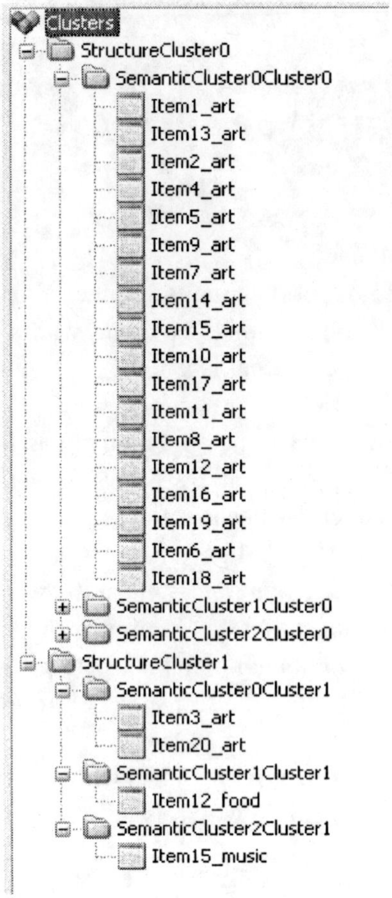

Figure 9. Example of content clustering based on category

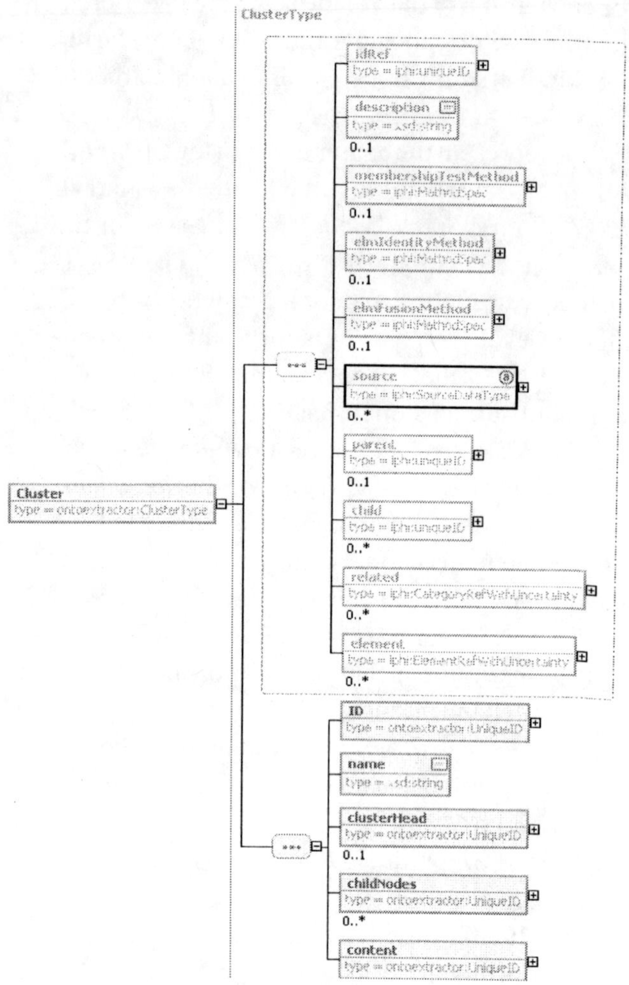

Figure 10. XSD schema representation of the cluster element type

The matrix Σ contains the singular values, which can be thought of as scalar "gain controls" by which each corresponding input is multiplied to give a corresponding output.

One commonly insists that the values $\Sigma_{i,i}$ be ordered in non-increasing fashion. In this case, the diagonal matrix Σ is uniquely determined by M (though the matrices U and V are not).

Generating vectors: After the matrix decomposition, we generate a new *m-by-n* matrix using an *r-reduction* of the original SVD decomposition.

$$M = U_r \Sigma_r V_r^*$$

Only the r column vectors of U and r row vectors of V^* corresponding to the non-zero singular

Figure 11. XSD schema representation of the document element type

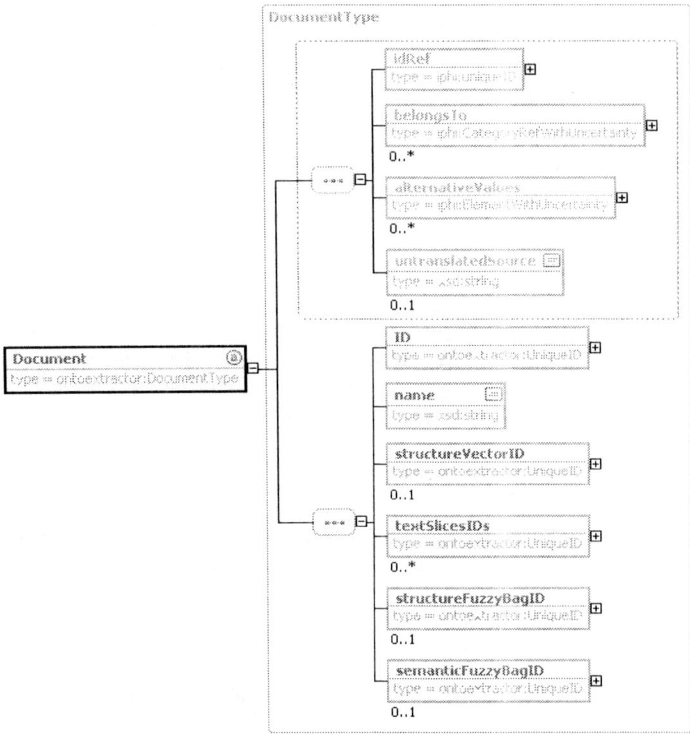

values $\sum_r$ are calculated. The remaining vectors of U and V^* are not calculated.

The resulting new matrix is not a sparse matrix anymore, but it is densely populated by values, with hidden semantic meaning. Then the matrix is normalized in the range [0,1].

Each row in the matrix is stored in the associated tag in the document model as a new Fuzzy Bag with the terms as the element and the entry in the vector as membership value.

Now tag contents are represented by Fuzzy Bags and we can compare them by means of different distance measures (f in (2)(3)): we can use traditional Euclidean distances such as the Cosine distance, considering the Fuzzy Bags as normal vectors, or we can use Jaccard norm to measure the similarity between two fuzzy bags. The similarity between two documents is the result of F.

Using F as a comparison measure, we can perform the clustering process employing the same algorithms utilized for the structural clustering, on the content of the selected cluster to refine.

In *OntoExtractor*, for each tag it will be possible to choose the algorithm used to generate the Fuzzy Bag, the distance function f, and aggregation function F.

The image refers to a clustering process performed on a dataset of Amazon reviews of various items. We considered the tag <Category> as discriminator for the clustering process and clustered the content of StructureCluster0 and

StructureClusterl using the well-known Cosine Distance on the term-vector as comparing measure *f* and a standard T-norm as aggregation function *F*. The resulting clustering has been converted to a *iPhi* hierarchy by extending cluster classes with *iPhi* categories and extending document representation with *iPhi* elements, including the *iPhi* JAXB schema in the *OntoExtractor* JAXB schema file.

In Figure 10 and Figure 11 the XSD schema used to represent the document and the clusters in relation to *iPhi* hierarchy schema are represented. The elements and attributes inherited from the *iPhi* schema are coloured in white.

BOTTOM-UP ONTOLOGY GENERATION

Once the clustering process is completed, we obtain a hierarchy of semantic clusters, possibly refined using content-driven clustering. As explained previously, for each cluster we generate a centroid, which is the most representative element of the cluster, and we call it *clusterHead*. This *clusterHead*, even if it does not refers to a real document, is a Fuzzy Bag.

OntoExtractor takes as input the *clusterHeads* resulting from the structural clustering process and organizes them into a hierarchy, expressed according to a standard Semantic Web format, which can be used as it is or added to an existing ontology of the application domain. This hierarchy is the basis for identifying a set of candidate classes to be verified in the Trust Layer.

In order to build the ontology, structural *clusterHeads* must be organized by setting up ontological relations among them. While traditional ontology learning approaches focus on hyperonomic and association relations, our technique can take advantage of structural information including elements' cardinality. Taking this information into account, we can extract several types of relations. In particular, our approach is aimed at detecting four ontological relations: (*i*) subclass-of; (*ii*) value restriction; (*iii*) cardinality restriction; (*iv*) associated-to.

These relations are typical of a number of knowledge representation languages, and are usually denoted via DL *(Description Logics)* formalisms used for setting up the Semantic Web knowledge representation standards.

The basic idea we rely on for identifying candidate classes is organizing *clusterHeads* in a hierarchy. A typical technique adopted to organize sets of objects composed of attributes is to build the lattice of their intersection. The technique adopted in order to build the lattice of binary relations over a pair of sets is an extension to *FCA (Formal Concept Analysis)* by Fuzzy Bags developed by our group.

Table 1. Tthe context of the Fuzzy Bags of the resulting clusterHeads

	Volume	Title	Author	Journal	Proceedings
CH1	0.3/4	0.8/4	0.8/4	0.5/4	0
CH2	0.5/19	0.8/19	0.8/19	0.5/19	0
CH3	0.5/1	1/1, 0.5/5	0.5/5	0	1/1
CH4	0.5/1	0.5/1	0.5/1	0.5/1	0.5/1
CH5	0.5/1	1/1, 0.5/12	0.5/23	1/1	0.5/6

ClusterHeads are used to define the initial context of our *FCA* analysis. Being fuzzy bags, *clusterHeads* are composed of *term / gradual-integer* pairs.

Our extension to FCA was experimented with a dataset selected from the XML Data Repository of the University of Washington. This repository hosts entries belonging to different digital archives of research publications, and therefore needs little pre-processing in terms of stop-words filtering besides disregarding connective particles such as prepositions and articles. Also, it is a typical example of heterogeneous data in semi-structured format.

After the generation of the hierarchy, we obtain the *clusterHeads* in Table 1.

This table can be summarized by two functions: *f* and *g*, defined as follows: the function *f* maps a set ***X*** of *clusterHeads* into a set ***Y*** of common attributes (tag elements in the Fuzzy-Bags), while *g* is the dual for the attribute sets. Operating with gradual integer we can not use binary relations between the set of *clusterHeads* and the set of attributes. In FCA the co-domain of function *f*, i.e. the set of attributes common to a given set of documents X, is equivalent to the intersection of the documents in X, and identifies a set of common attributes Y. Hence, in our extension, the function has to return the intersection among the fuzzy bags associated to the documents in X, and the fuzzy bag obtained by this intersection must be included by all the fuzzy bags of X, as follows:

$$\Omega_{A \cap B}(x) = min(\Omega_A(x), \Omega_B(x))$$

According to this definition, we can now define the new functions *f* and *g* and build the lattice of concepts from them.

As shown in Figure 12, the lattice generated from the original clusterHeads discovers new concepts (cl, c2, c3 and c4). FCA allows us to compute a concept lattice on the cluster-heads. The rationale of this step is to identify abstract classes describing general concepts shared by several *clusterHeads*. Note that hierarchy isolated cl as the subset of the attributes common to all documents in our context. In c2 we have documents published in proceedings, in c3 documents published in journals, and in c4 documents published both in proceedings and journals. The

Figure 12. Lattice of concepts (Cn) generated from Table 1 with the related FuzzyBag

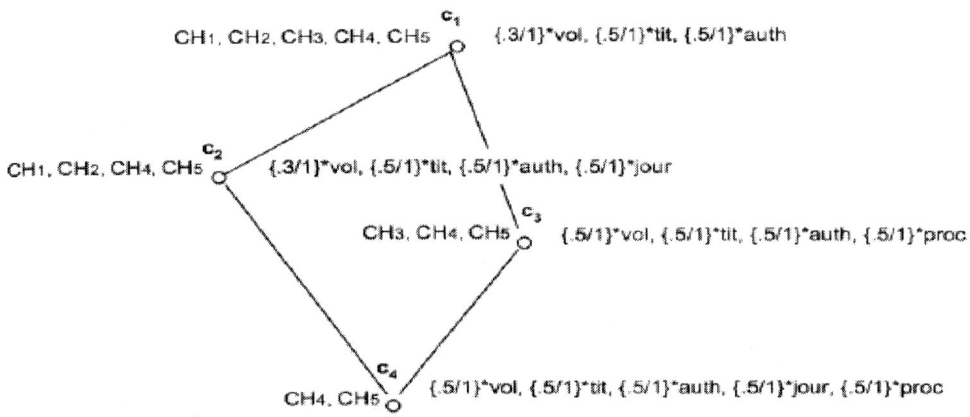

difference between concepts c2 and c3 is due to attributes journals and proceedings. Journals are in c2 but not in c3, proceedings is in c3 but not in c2. These new concepts are defined as intersections between Fuzzy Bags and hence they are Fuzzy Bags as well.

In our extension to FCA, gradual integers encode information about term relevance and cardinality. The peculiarity of our extension consists in encoding information about relevance and cardinality of terms by means of gradual integers. This information will allow us to produce metadata assertions associating concepts of the hierarchy with the documents that are classified according to a reliability degree. A document classified in a *clusterHead* can be associated to the ontology class generated from the *clusterHead* and with all its super-classes, according to the *subclass-of* hierarchy. For instance, a document D belonging to CH2 will be associated with class c4, and therefore to c2, c3, and c1.

The coverage of these associations is not equivalent in all assertions because we can use the fuzzy bag associated to class representation in order to define a degree of coverage between the document and the class. In general, the fuzzy bags associated with classes toward the top of the hierarchy are lower than those in the bottom. We can obtain the similarity between two Fuzzy Bags using *Jaccard* norm. The value obtained computing this similarity measure can be used for setting an initial trust value to be refined in the Trust Layer.

Once the lattice has been build by exploiting term relevance, we can try to discover new concepts by extending concepts already discovered using a discriminative process based on term cardinality: *clusterHeads* with a strong cardinality difference with respect to the formal concept they belong to, are used to form a new formal concept. According to the traditional definition of similarity, we can define dissimilarity as follows:

D(CHa,CHb) = 1 - S(CHa,CHb)
D(CHa,CHb) = 1 - Approx(|CHa ∩ CHb | / | CHa ∪ CHb |)

Figure 13. The lattice with new concepts (C5, C6) and cut down from irrelevant attributes using a threshold of 0.4 (vol. in Figure 12)

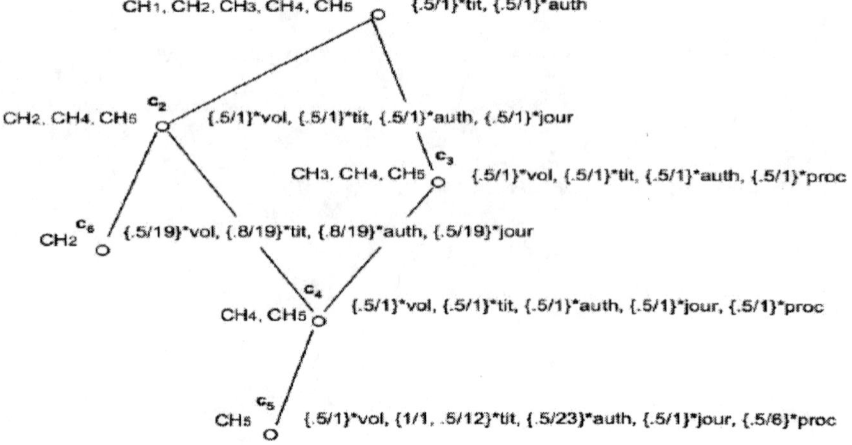

ClusterHeads with a dissimilarity measure higher than a given threshold will form new formal concepts.

A precaution in order to avoid discovering irrelevant concepts is to cut down the hierarchy deleting attributes whose relevance value lies below a given threshold.*OntoExtractor* uses the hierarchy obtained by our FCA extension to generate subclass-of relations.

Attributes belonging to the classes of the hierarchy are used in order to generate part-of relations. The data-type to be associated to part-of relations is defined on the basis of the results of the content-based clustering. Also, value restriction relations are added to the hierarchy on the basis of the blocks composing the content-based partition of each cluster.

Cardinality restriction relations can be set if the *clusterHeads* member of a candidate class shows relevant differences in cardinality.

The role of cardinality restrictions is very important in our approach; therefore, the minimum language expressiveness we need for expressing the hierarchy is a first order language restricted to formulas with two variables, allowing qualified restriction on roles. Fortunately *OWL* satisfies these expressiveness requirements (Horrocks et al. 1999). Indeed, *OWL* is even more expressive than we need for our automatic construction process. However, the adoption of *OWL* as the target language for *OntoExtractor's* output is justified because it is a standard and because we offer to the knowledge engineer a way to extend the representation extracted from the system.

MAINTENANCE AND EVOLUTION OF THE HIERARCHY

In this section, we illustrate the use of trustworthiness to improve the overall quality of the assertions produced by *OntoExtractor.* Automatically generated assertions like "class *B* is a subclass of class *A*" or "instance *X* belongs to class *A*" may turn out to be debatable or plainly wrong when checked by human experts. In our approach, we do not require human inspection for all automatically generated assertions, as this would require an effort comparable to manually writing them from scratch.

Rather, we leave it to community members to express their views on the trustworthiness of each assertion. We start from all assertions about data produced by *OntoExtractor.* While interacting with documents, users can provide important feedback on metadata trustworthiness. This information is captured and transformed in a second metadata layer composed by *trust assertions* expressing the level of trust of the assertions in the first layer. This second layer can be computed by a central server or by distributed clients; in both cases, the trust degree associated with each trust assertion must be aggregated and the result provided to all interested clients. On the basis of this aggregated trust degree, clients can compute their *custom views* on the original metadata base, using a customizable threshold to discard untrusted assertions. The architecture of our *Trust Layer* is composed of a centralized *Publication Center* that collects and displays metadata assertions manually added by the ontology engineer or produced by the *OntoExtractor.*

Of course, our Center will assign different trust values to assertions depending on their origin: assertions written by a domain expert are much more reliable than those automatically generated by *OntoExtractor.* All assertions in the Publication Center are indexed and a group of clients interacts with them by navigating them and providing implicitly (with their behavior) or explicitly (by means of an explicit vote) an evaluation about assertion trustworthiness. This trust-related information is passed by the Publication Center on to the Trust Manager in the form of new assertions of a special type. These *trust assertions* are built using the well-known technique of *reification* (the act of building a data model for a previously abstract concept). Reification allows a computer to process an abstraction as if it were any other data.

Let us now examine the process in more detail. In a first phase, clients navigate the collection of metadata by selecting a single assertion (or an *assertion pattern*). This returns a set of documents indexed by the assertion.

According to their evaluation of results, clients may explicitly (e.g. by clicking on a Confirm association button) assign a rating to the quality of the link, that is, to the underlying assertion. More frequently, a non-intrusive technique is used: when users click on a document they are interested in, in order to display it, the system considers this action an implicit vote confirming the quality of the association between document and metadata (after all, it was the metadata that allowed the user to reach the document).

Of course, explicit votes count more than implicit ones; also, aggregation should be performed by taking into account voters' profiles (when available). Once enough votes have been collected and aggregated, our Trust Manager will associate community-wide *trust values* to trust assertions. A suitable *aggregation function* is used to collect votes and update trust values during the whole system life cycle. Then, trust values are made available to all interested parties and clients can compute different views on the original metadata based on them (e.g., filtering out all metadata whose trust value Tv satisfies $Tv \leq x$ where x is a given threshold).

The main problem to solve is how to aggregate trust values. Once the values are collected they need to be aggregated.

When users have an identity, ratings have to be aggregated initially at user level, and then at global level. Several techniques for computing reputation and trust measures in non-anonymous environments have been proposed in Jøsang et al.

Figure 14. Tthe architecture of the Trust Layer

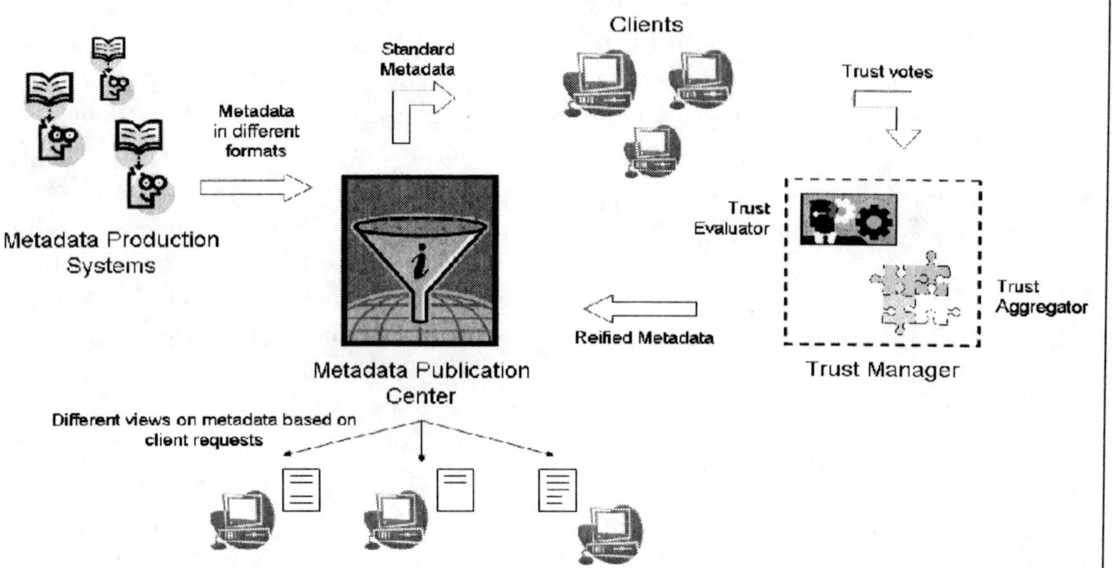

(2005). Our approach assumes that the level of trust for an assertion is the result of the aggregation of *fuzzy values* representing human interactions with the original metadata. Choosing the aggregation operator, however, is by no means straightforward. Arithmetic average performs a rough compensation and assumes that the level of trust for an assertion is the result of the aggregation of *fuzzy values* representing human interactions with the original metadata.

The weighted means allows the system to compute and aggregate values from the ones coming from several sources, taking into account the reliability of each information source.

The *OWA* (*Ordered Weighted Averaging operator*) (Fodor et al., 1995): In an OWA-based solution is compared with a probabilistic approach, where a reputation is defined as a probability and can be computed by an event-driven method using a Bayesian interpretation. This operator is a weighted average that acts on an ordered list of arguments and applies a set of weights to tune their impact on the final result: it allows the user to weight the values supplied in relation to their relative ordering. In our case, we start with a set of ratings *{rti}*, where *ti* is the rating timestamp,

$$f_{OWA} = \frac{\sum_{k=1}^{n} w_k r_{t_k}}{\sum_{k=1}^{n} w_k}$$

where **n** is the number of reputations $\mathbf{r}_t$ to aggregate and **w** is a weighting vector.

In our recent works (Aringhieri et al., 2006), OWA aggregator has been successfully compared to other aggregators. Unfortunately, OWA aggregator works well only in a community where all users have the same expertise level and their votes have the same relevance. To model more complex situations we use *WOWA* (*Weighted OWA*) (Torra, 1997) which combines the advantages of OWA with the *weighted mean*. WOWA uses two sets of weights: **p** corresponding to the *relevance of the sources*, and **a** corresponding to the *users' votes (implicit/explicit)*.

Let *p* and *w* be two weight vectors of dimension *n* (p = [*p*1, *p*2, …, *pn*], w = [*w*1, *w*2, …., *wn*]) such that: *i*) *pi* ∈ [0; 1] and ∑*i pi* = 1; *ii*) *wi* ∈ [0; 1] and ∑*i wi* = 1. A mapping *f*WOWA : R*n* ⊠ R is a *WOWA (Weighted Ordered Weighted Averaging)* operator of dimension *n* if:

$$f_{WOWA}(a_1, a_2, \dots, a_n) = \sum_i \omega_i a_{\sigma(i)}$$

where *{σ(1), σ(2), ..., σ(n) }* is a permutation of *{1, 2, ..., n}* such that $a_{\sigma(I-1)} \leq a_{\sigma(i)}$, $i = 2, \dots, n$, weight ω*i* is defined as:

$$\omega_i = w^*\left(\sum_{j\leq i} p_{\sigma(j)}\right) - w^*\left(\sum_{j<i} p_{\sigma(j)}\right)$$

TRUST SIMULATOR

Our group developed a Trust Layer simulator in order to test aggregation algorithms such as WOWA. The simulator can model implicit and explicit voting behaviour of a defined community of different expertise levels.

Over a defined number of iterations, a population composed of three types of user--(*i*) *Senior*, (*ii*) *Junior* and (*iii*) *Employee*--interacts with metadata produced semi-automatically and modifies their visibility voting on them depending on the different *expertise* of each group of users. We decide to assign a high expertise value to the first group of users (that we consider well reputed) and, on the opposite, a low expertise one to the last group (considered unknown). So the level of expertise corresponds to the "relevance of the sources vector" **p**. The "vector containing users (explicit/implicit) votes" **a** is composed at every iteration (for every assertion) of the votes generated depending on the user *skills*, that represent the probability to vote "correctly" on an assertion.

Table 2

Vector p:	0.9 for Senior	0.5 for Junior	0.3 for Employee
Vector W:	wi = 0:8 if ai > 0:5	wi = 0:2 if ai ≤ 0:5	0.1 ≤ ai < 1
Vector a1:	ai(explicit) = $0{:}82^{d}$	ai(implicit) = $0{:}82^{(1/d)}$	d = 0.2
Vector a2:	ai(explicit) = $0{:}82^{d}$	ai(implicit) = $0{:}82^{(1/d)}$	d = 0.3
Skills:	0.9 for Senior	0.5 for Junior	0.3 for Employee

Figure 15. Tthe results of the simulation on the first composition of the population

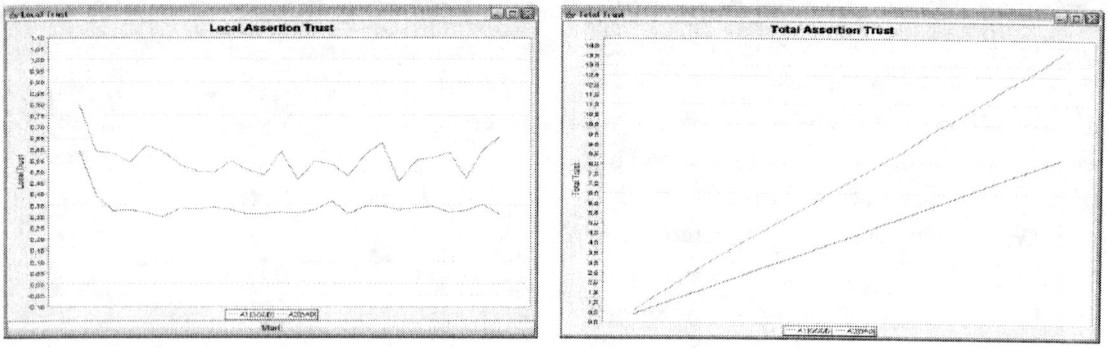

Figure 16. Tthe results of the simulation on the second composition of the population

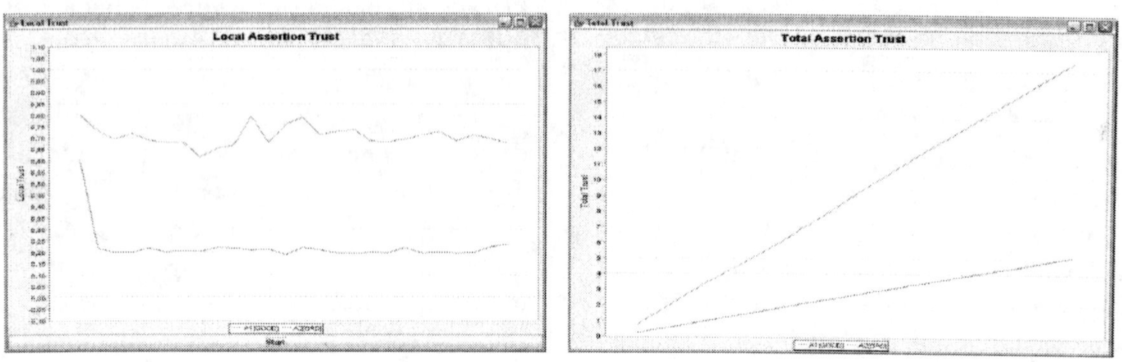

Since we are dealing with a simulation, we assume to know a priori the goodness of an assertion; in this way we can model user skills such as the "correct" assertions receive higher votes respect to the "incorrect" ones. High and low values that users can assign are established at the simulation start, and they are based on the initial trust value connected to the metadata in exam.

The final vector that has to be defined is the "relevance of the value vector" w. Its values are generated directly from the vector a, depending on the approach (optimistic or pessimistic) one decides to follow.

We tested the WOWA algorithm on our simulator comparing two simulations, differing for the composition of the population:

1. SENIOR = 20% JUNIOR = 30% EMPLOYEE = 50%
2. SENIOR = 60% JUNIOR = 20% EMPLOYEE = 20%

We assume other parameters equal for both simulations:

POPULATION: 50 users
NUMBER OF ITERATIONS: 50
ASSERTIONS:

- *A1* – Trust Initial Value = 0.82 (considered as a good assertion)
- *A2* – Trust Initial Value = 0.75 (considered as a not good assertion)

The result of our two simulations on the given assertions are shown in Figure 15 and 16, the left graph shows the result of the WOWA aggregation for each iteration and the right one shows the global level of trust for each assertion. As you can see from differences between Figure 15 and 16, using a composition of the population with bigger *Senior* expertise component, the difference between the level of trust between the two assertions rapidly increases, confirming that the WOWA aggregator well models different compositions of the community.

CONCLUSIONS AND FURTHER WORK

The Knowledge Management Group at the University of Milan has described his bottom-up, semi-automatic fuzzy technique for metadata generation from heterogeneous data sources.

The preliminary phase of the process consists in converting data coming from the heterogeneous data sources in a common format, such as XML. The homogeneous set of documents is converted in fuzzy bags and processed in order to generate the first level of the final taxonomy, which refers to the structure of the document. In a similar fashion, the documents inside a structure cluster are processed for generating the contextual classification. The taxonomy created this way is a metadata describing classes of documents, which is automatically generated and thus it is errors prone.

Nevertheless, this approach relies on the user community's feedback for assessing metadata correctness, following the evolution of the community view of the domain. Our assertions are associated with a *trust level*, which is updated according to the community views throughout the ontology life-cycle by means of suitable voting algorithms (Damiani et al., 2003).

Future developments of this work include a complete framework for community-based representation and update trust-related assertions expressing a community view over an automatically constructed ontology.

REFERENCES

Aringhieri, R., Damiani, E., De Capitani di Vimercati, S., Paraboschi, S., & Samarati, P.

(2006). *Fuzzy Techniques for Trust and Reputation Management in Anonymous Peer-to-Peer Systems,* JASIST.

Bosc, P., & Damiani E. (2001). Fuzzy service selection in a distributed object-oriented environment, *IEEE Transactions on Fussy Systems, 9* (5), 682-698.

Bouchon-Meunier, B., Rifqi, M., Bothorel S. (1996). Towards general measures of comparison of objects, *Fuzzy Sets and Systems, 84,* 143-153.

Ceravolo, P., Nocerino, M. C., & Viviani, M. (2004). Knowledge extraction from semi-structured data based on fuzzy techniques, *Knowledge-Based Intelligent Information and Engineering Systems,* In *Proceedings of the 8th International Conference,* KES 2004, Part III, pp. 328-334.

Ceravolo, P., Corallo, A., Damiani, E., Elia, E., Viviani, M., & Zilli, A. (2006). Bottom-up extraction and maintenance of ontology-based metadata, *Fuzzy Logic and the Semantic Web,* Computer Intelligence, Elsevier.

Cui, Z., Damiani, E., Leida, M., & Viviani M.(2005). OntoExtractor: A fuzzy-based approach in clustering semi-structured data sources and metadata generation, *Knowledge-Based Intelligent Information and Engineering Systems, 9th International Conference, KES 2005,* Melbourne, Australia, September 14-16, 2005, Proceedings, Part I, ser. Lecture Notes in Computer Science, vol. 3681. Springer, pp. 112-118.

Damiani, E., De Capitani di Vimercati, S., Paraboschi, S., & Samarati, P. (2003). Managing and sharing servents' reputations in p2p systems. *IEEE Transactions on Knowledge and Data Engineering, 15* (4), 840-854.

Damiani, E., Nocerino, M. C., & Viviani, M. (2004). Knowledge extraction from an XML data flow: building a taxonomy based on clustering technique, *Current Issues in Data and Knowledge Engineering,* In *Proceedings of EUROFUSE 2004: 8th Meeting of the EURO Working Group on Fuzzy Sets,* 133-142.

Fagin, R. (1998). Fuzzy Queries in Multimedia Database Systems, *ACM Sigact Sigmod Sigart Symposium on Principles of Database Systems,* 17, pp. 1-10.

Fagin, R. (1999). Combining fuzzy information from multiple systems. *Journal of Computer and System Sciences, 58* (1), 83-99.

Fagin, R. (2002). Combining fuzzy information: An overview, *Sigmod Record, 31* (2),109-118.

Fodor,J., Marichal, J. L. & Roubens, M. (1995). Characterization of the ordered weighted averaging operators, *IEEE Trans. on Fuzzy Systems, 3* (2), 236-240.

Horrocks, I., Sattler, U., & Tobies S. (1999). Practical reasoning for expressive description logics. In *Proceedings of the 6th International Conference on Logic Programming and Automated Reasoning LPAR '99,* , (pp. 161-180). London, UK: Springer-Verlag

Jøsang, A., Ismail, R., & Boyd, C. (2005). A survey of trust and reputation systems for online service provision. *Decision Support Systems.*

Landauer, T. K., Foltz, P. W., & Laham, D. (1998). Introduction to latent semantic analysis. *Discourse Processes, 25,* 259-284.

Lave, J., & Wenger, E. (1991). *Situated learning: Legitimate peripheral participation,* Cambridge University Press.

Martin, T. P., & Azvine, B. (2003). Acquisition of soft taxonomies for intelligent personal hierarchies and the soft Semantic Web. *BT Technology Journal, 21,* 113-122.

Salton, G., , Singhal, A., Buckley, C., & Mitra M. (1996). Automatic Text Decomposition Using Text Segments and Text Themes, *Conference on Hypertext,* pp.53-65.

Salton, G., & Buckley, C. (1987). *Term weighting approaches in automatic text retrieval* (Tech. Rep. UMI Order Number: TR87-881). Cornell University.

Torra, V. (1997), The weighted OWA operator. *International Journal of Intelligent Systems, 12* (2), 153-166.

University of Washington, *XML Data Repository*, Retrieved on from, http://www.cs.washington.edu/research/xmldatasets, 2005

World Wide Web Consourtium. *OWL Web Ontology Language*--Overview, December 2003. http://www.w3.org/TR/owl-features/

Chapter IV
Search Engine:
Approaches and Performance

Eliana Campi
University of Salento, Italy

Gianluca Lorenzo
University of Salento, Italy

ABSTRACT

This chapter presents technologies and approaches for information retrieval in a knowledge base. We intend to show that the use of ontology for domain representation and knowledge search offers a more efficient approach for knowledge management. This approach focuses on the meaning of the word, thus becoming an important element in the building of the Semantic Web. The search based on both keywords and ontology allows more effective information retrieval exploiting the Semantic of the information in a variety of data. We present a method for taxonomy building, annotating, and searching documents with taxonomy concepts. We also describe our experience in the creation of an informal taxonomy, the automatic classification, and the validation of search results with traditional measures, such as precision, recall and f-measure.

INTRODUCTION

The rapid increase of the information amount in an organization or in a distributed environment in general, makes difficult to find, organise, classify, access, and use this information. Therefore, as the number of documents used by an organization increases, the need to classify them into an intuitive and meaningful hierarchical structure becomes a challenge in order to facilitate the retrieval and the use of information.

The main problem in information retrieval is to provide the user with a concise and significant set of documents as a result for a specific query on a large set of information. The result depends on the terms the user specifies in the query and the quality of the result depends on the quality of the query.

Relevance of particular information is subjective to the individual, and the context of this information is the determining factor. If the search is bound to a particular context, it produces a poorer but more precise and effective set of results.

A survey of Delphy Group demonstrates that the categories and the hierarchical structure of information are able to narrow the search area and find relevant information faster (Delphy Group, 2002).

Therefore, a major challenge is how to create a hierarchy without examining each document, especially when there are thousands of documents to classify, and how to execute a semantic indexing of the information to achieve effectiveness in the information retrieval. We adopted an approach based on Semantic Web technology in the area of knowledge management.

This chapter describes the various methodologies to create taxonomy and fill it with documents, through indexing of information sources. We describe how to create "informal taxonomy," classify documents into taxonomy categories, and evaluate performances of this classification. We show how taxonomy represents an efficient way to organize a specific domain of an organization. In particular, we present our methods related to KIWI (Knowledge-based Innovation for the Web Infrastructure) project and applied in the Virtual eBMS platform (Virtual platform of eBusiness Management school). Then, existing technologies for searching documents in a knowledge repository are considered and the results of these different technologies are evaluated through three measures of performance: precision, recall, F-measure.

KNOWLEDGE MANAGEMENT IN THE KIWI PROJECT

The KIWI project aims at representing and managing organizational knowledge using technologies and methodologies based on Semantic technologies. Taxonomy and/or more complex structures, like ontologies, are key elements to structure the knowledge base of an organization. The KIWI project develops a set of open source tools, which allow for a formal domain representation and enable creative cooperation among users and interaction with the knowledge base:

- OntoMaker, an ontology editor;
- OntoMeter, a tool to evaluate the quality of a formal representation;
- OntoAssistant, a tool for semiautomatic document annotations;
- Semantic Navigator, a tool to browse ontology and knowledge base.

We have proposed a methodology to provide a more effective automatic document classification process. In particular, the methodology comprises four steps:

1. Developing a conceptual structure (an informal taxonomy) that presents the knowledge domain of the eBMS-ISUFI;
2. Defining rules for each category through positive and negative training set;
3. Filling the hierarchical structure with documents through semi-automatic classification;
4. Testing the quality of the classification rules, through precision, recall and F-measure, refining of the classification rules and periodic taxonomy maintenance.

This methodology has been applied to the Virtual eBMS knowledge management system.

This technological platform, developed by ISUFI-eBMS University of Lecce, provides numerous tools for organizational knowledge management.

TAXONOMY AS DOMAIN REPRESENTATION

The lack of time to search, analyze, classify, and structure information is an important problem within an organization. Professionals spend more than 25% of the day in searching for information: the ability to create knowledge surpasses the ability to retrieve relevant information (Delphy Group, 2002).

The challenge of an organization is how to find the relevant and pertinent information; retrieval of relevant information quicker is the key benefit, which gives immediate access to the right information and allows the user to satisfy his/her request. Taxonomy provides a valid support in the retrieval of information (Thomson Scientific, 2004).

With the term taxonomy we mean a non-formal taxonomy, that is a hierarchical structure of concepts, not strictly related by "is-a" relation. The concepts, that represent a specific domain, are organized in an intuitive way, including not only "is-a" relations, but also "part-of" or "include" relations. Taxonomy helps to organise the information and explain the conceptual relationships within and among various concepts with these benefits:

- Providing an overview of the structure of the domain;
- Retrieving relevant information for user needs;
- Reducing the time of the search;
- Improving the effectiveness of the research.

Taxonomy is the key element to structure the knowledge of an organization. It allows one to organise the domain of interest, to classify documents in categories, and to limit the search to a subset of specific categories.

Therefore, the building of taxonomy is the first step to obtain an optimal classification and efficient retrieval in the interest domain.

There are four steps in the process of building and using taxonomy (Verity Group, 2004):

1. Developing a taxonomy;
2. Defining model of rules for the taxonomy categories;
3. Filling the taxonomy with documents;
4. Navigating the taxonomy.

In particular, it is possible to detail these four steps in (Delphy Group, 2002):

- Select data to use as basis of taxonomy structure;
- Spider data to extract concepts of the domain representing by taxonomy;
- Process concepts to develop cluster of related concepts or documents;
- Develop taxonomy structure, a hierarchical organization of concepts;
- Develop and submit training sets to the taxonomy structure, in order to define the rules that describe the taxonomy categories;
- Classify corpus of data to fill the taxonomy structure and provide links and pointers to data;
- Display hierarchical structure in an intuitive or graphical way;
- Administration for modifying structure, renaming and linking to maintain the taxonomy and the knowledge base.

It is possible to leave out steps or add other steps in depending on the design approach and technologies of the platform used to represent the knowledge, to classify source of information and to retrieve the documents.

DEVELOPING A TAXONOMY

The propagation of unstructured data has increased the difficulty to find relevant information about a particular subject. Taxonomy facilitates the search and the retrieval of the information. In order to structure information into a hierarchy of categories, it is necessary to organise the domain to represent. The result of this stage is a hierarchical structure of categories and the technique for building taxonomy can be:

- *manual*, using a human domain expert: the domain expert organizes the domain with a hierarchical structure and assigns names to its categories;
- *semiautomatic*, using the competence of the human domain expert in addition to the automatic generation of taxonomy;
- *automatic*, using concept mapping, extraction and naming: a software automatically extracts key concepts contained in a set of documents and organizes them into a hierarchy; automatic naming generates labels for these categories.

Manual Taxonomy Building

The taxonomy development process is a human intensive process and requires huge resources in terms of cost and time. If the domain to model has precise and limited borderline and its structure is unambiguous, it is possible to organise the domain using human domain experts. According to this approach, the expert builds a hierarchical structure of concepts that represent the specific thematic of the domain identifying and selecting the key concepts. Each concept identifies a taxonomy category, in which a set of documents is placed in relation to the matching between the concepts and the topic of the document.

The formal taxonomy is a hierarchical organization of concepts structured according to "is-a" relation. The taxonomy is the base of a more complex structure of concepts and relationships of a domain: the ontology. In fact, the ontology is "a specification of a conceptualization" (Gruber, 1993). A conceptualization is an abstract, simplified view of the domain that we wish to represent. Therefore, the methodologies ideated to build ontologies can be used to build taxonomies and although the methodologies proposed are specific for the ontology creation, they can be applied to the taxonomy. For this reason, for the definition of our informal taxonomy, we consider various methodologies planned to create the ontology.

There are several methodologies for building ontology suing different approaches. Some of them describe how to build an ontology from scratch or reusing other ontologies, such as Cyc approach,[2] Uschold and King's proposal 0(Uschold & Gruninger, 1996), METHONTOLOGY (Corcho et al., 2003), On-To-Knowledge[3] 0(Sure & Studer, 2002); other approaches describe how to build an ontology through the transformation of other ontologies, for example using reengineering or ontology merging.

The characteristics of these different methodologies for the ontology development process can be grouped in this way according to the OntoWeb study (OntoWeb, 2000):

1. Proposed construction strategy, including:
    - life cycle proposal that identifies the set of stages through which the ontology moves during its life time;
    - strategy according to the application that uses the ontology and the methodologies;
    - a core ontology as a starting point in the development of the domain ontology;
    - strategy to identify concepts from the most concrete to the most abstract (bottom-up), from the most abstract to the most concrete (top-down), or from the most relevant to the most abstract and most concrete (middle-out).

2. Proposed ontology development process, that is divided in other processes and these processes are made by activities. The processes are:
    - project management process to create the framework for the project and to ensure the right level of management throughout the entire product life cycle,;
    - ontology development-oriented process, that includes pre-development processes related to the study of the ontology installation environment, development processes to build the ontology, post-development processes related to the installation, operation, support, maintenance and retirement of an ontology;
    - integral process to ensure the completion and quality of project functions and cover the processes of knowledge acquisition, verification and validation, ontology configuration management, documentation development and training.
3. Methodologies' use refers to the use of the methodology or method in projects, the acceptation of the methodology by other groups.
4. Technological support refers to the tools that provide full or partial support to the methodology or method.

Semi-Automatic Taxonomy Building

Semi-automatic generation of taxonomy utilises a combination of these approaches:

- supervised machine learning approach that requires a collection of training examples;
- NLP (Natural Language Processing) approach for generating taxonomic concepts and relationships between them;
- clustering and data mining approach to facilitate search, categorization and visualization of data.

An example of semiautomatic taxonomy is TaxaMiner (Kashyap et al., 2005), a framework for building taxonomy aimed at minimizing human contribution. This framework consists of:

- combination of clustering, NLP and various customized techniques for taxonomy generation;
- identification of statistical parameters computed during the clustering process that characterizes the differentiation in the taxonomic structure;
- techniques for extraction of a taxonomy from the cluster hierarchy;
- techniques for automatic generation and refinement of labels for nodes in the ultimate taxonomy;
- metrics for evaluating the quality of the taxonomy.

The components of the framework generate taxonomic structures from textual documents.

Automatic Taxonomy Building

The aim of ATG (Automated Taxonomy Generation) is to hierarchically cluster the document set and extract a sequence of clusters. This sequence captures all the levels of specificity/generality in the set and it is ordered by the value of the specificity/generality measure. Then each cluster in the sequence is analysed to extract from it a set of labels that best captures the topic of documents. At the end, this set of labels is reduced to decrease the number of potential labels for the taxonomy nodes (Sheth, Ramakrishnan, & Thomas, 2005).

Thematic Mapping (Chunget et al., 2002; Verity Group, 2004) is an example of a system that utilises automatic taxonomy building. It is a key component of VIC (Verity Intelligent Classifier), a tool of Verity's enterprise content organization tool suite.

It automatically identifies significant concepts in a set of unstructured documents and extracts key terms (nouns or noun phrases) from the documents. Intelligent Classifier uses one of the following three possible criteria to measure the importance of a term (Verity Group, 2004):

- *Term Frequency*: the total number of times a term occurs in the document set;
- *Document Frequency*: the number of documents in the set in which the term occurs;
- *TFIDF*: Term Frequency divided by the Document Frequency.

The concepts are organised in a tree hierarchy to reflect general-to-specific relation and meaningful names are assigned to concepts.

Thematic Mapping only generates one possible concept hierarchy out of the many possible concept hierarchies for the document set.

TAXONOMY BUILDING FOR THE KIWI KNOWLEDGE BASE

For the organization of KIWI knowledge base, domain experts manually structure the domain accordingly to the specific knowledge and the organizational requirement of the eBMS.

The result of such activity is a set of categories opportunely correlated with hierarchical relations and that reassumes and organizes the knowledge of the domain.

DEFINING MODEL OF RULES FOR THE CATEGORIES OF THE TAXONOMY

After creating the taxonomy, the next step is to associate "category definition" to each category of the taxonomy.

The Definition of the Model of Rules

Each "category definition" consists of a rule against which each document can be evaluated.

There are several ways for building rules:

- expert-defined model of rules: a domain expert defines and maintains a rule for each category;
- semiautomatic model of rule creation: automatic rule creation algorithm is combined with the contribution of a domain expert;
- automatic model of rule creation: an automatic algorithm creates the rules.

Which method to use for defining the model of rules depends on different factors, such as the accuracy required for the rules, the amount of time and effort available, the level of contribution of human expertise, and the quantity of positive and negative training data available (Forman, 2002). If sufficient human expertise and time are available, it is possible to manually create the initial model of rules and then, if necessary, enhance these rules with automatic rule creation using some positive and negative sample documents. If, instead, a large amount of positive and negative training data is available, rules can be automatically generated. Such rules can also be further refined by domain experts. When both human expertise, time, and positive and negative training data are not sufficient, it is preferable to start with automatic model of rule creation, and then to select rules that are relevant and to manually enhance them.

The methodologies used for the rule creation in a taxonomy use various and different algorithms.

Statistical Text Analysis and Clustering

Clustering is a form of "unsupervised learning" and it is a process of grouping similar entities or objects together in-group based on some notion of similarity. Clustering uses a given similarity metric and, as a result of the grouping of data into clusters, attempts to use this information to learn something about the interactions between the clustered entities (Verity Group, 2004).

This technology analyses and measures the co-occurrence of words and the relative placement of words is relevant; words in the fist line or in the title are more likely important than words in the copyright section. In addition, clustering looks for frequency, placement, grouping, and distance among words in a document.

Pattern Matching

This is the process of looking for groups of words; other recognized patterns include frequency, placement of words in a document, proximity of words to each other, and cluster of related words. This process supports decision in ambiguous or multiple cases 0(Delphi Group, 2002).

Bayesian Probability

The Bayesian method tries to derive the probability of words for a particular category by analyzing terms and phrases within the documents. The Bayesian probability uses statistical models from words in training sets and uses pattern analysis to associate the probability of correlation (Delphi Group, 2002).

The basic idea of this approach is to use the joint probability to estimate the probabilities of words and categories given a document.

Semantic and Linguistic Clustering

Documents are clustered or grouped in relation to the meaning of words using Thesauri, dictionaries, probabilistic grammars, idioms, verb chains, and noun phrases. A linguistic application analyses the sentence structure identifying the parts of the speech (subjects, verbs, and objects) and using them to extract the sentence meaning. (Delphi Group, 2002).

Taxonomy-by-Example

This methodology builds the taxonomy from a training set of documents that well represent a domain. Building a taxonomy from the training set can be an automatic or supervised algorithm. Such an algorithm analyses new documents in comparison to the training set and searches for similar concepts. This approach is also referred as "machine learning" (Delphi Group, 2002).

Support Vector Machine

SVM (Support Vector Machine) is a supervised learning method, based on the concept of distance in a linear space.

With this method, a vector can represent a document; the vector direction is determined by the words it spans and the vector scale is determined by how many times each word occurs in the document. The method analyses new documents and separates the relevant documents from the irrelevant ones in relation to the vector (rules) associated to each category. (Delphi Group, 2002).

K-Nearest Neighbours

The k-nearest neighbour method classifies an unknown document among its neighbours within the training data, assuming that all the documents correspond to points in an n-dimensional space. A neighbour is deemed nearest if it has the smallest Euclidian distance, in the n-dimensional feature space. When $k = 1$, the unknown document is classified into the class of its closest neighbour in the training set 0(An, 2001).

Performances of these methodologies depend on the domain to which they are applied. A more efficient solution is usually to combine two or more methods to define rules in order to increase the accuracy and the relevance of grouping similar documents.

RULES DEFINITION IN KIWI

Our research group applied an enhanced automatic rule creation algorithm (LRC, Logistic Regression Classifier) in order to define the rule set for the KIWI taxonomy categories (Verity Group, 2004). LRC is a machine-learning algorithm that automatically creates the rules from a set of positive and optionally negative documents called *training documents*. Positive documents refer to documents that are relevant to the category and negative documents are documents irrelevant to the category of interest. Therefore, positive documents determine inclusion in the category, while negative documents determine exclusion. Positive documents are inserted into the leaf node of the taxonomy, and then the LRC algorithm is executed. LRC automatically learns a classification rule for each category. During the training process, for each category, LRC automatically identifies important positive and negative relevant terms and computes a numerical weight for each term. The weight value is positive for positive terms and negative for negative terms; the absolute value of a weight indicates the relevance of the corresponding term to the category (In Verity, categories are also named topics).

LRC uses various parameters to refine the extracted rules, such as document frequency, maximum number of topic relevance, maximum number of LRC iterations, LRC misclassification penalty, stemming, data path, LCR log, collection field, field delimiter.

At the end of the process, each category is uniquely defined by a rule that is represented by a vector of terms and relative weights.

FILLING THE TAXONOMY WITH DOCUMENTS

After creating the taxonomy and defining the model of rules associated to each category, the next step is to fill the taxonomy with category documents; this step can be:

- *manual*: for each document, a domain expert determines the categories that should

Figure 1. Filling taxonomy with documents

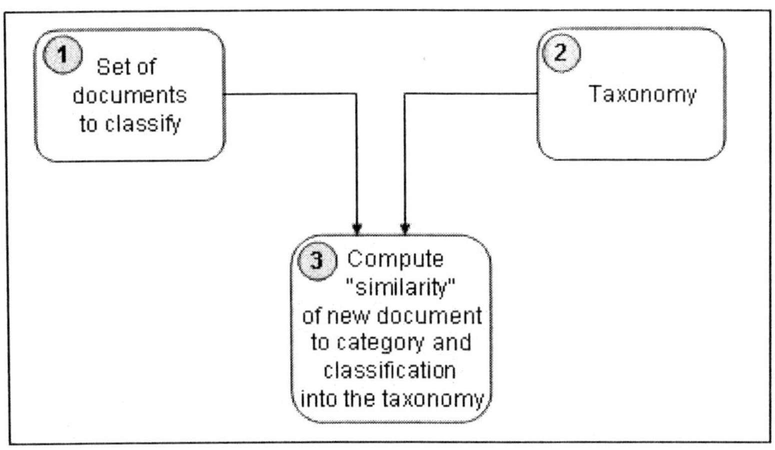

be filled and explicitly fills those categories with appropriate documents;

- *automatic*: the system evaluates new documents against each category rule and assigns the documents to the appropriate categories in the taxonomy;
- *both automatic and manual*: the association of the document to the categories is executed automatically by some algorithm and manually with the contribution of a domain expert.

Figure 1 represents the general diagram of the process to fill the taxonomy. A set of documents to be classified is retrieved in different ways (for example, from Web sites or from local organization databases), each document is manually or automatically evaluated against the rules and then it is classified into one or more categories.

Due to the importance of the different techniques for filling the taxonomy, each methodology will be explained in more detail and some technological applications are supplied as examples for the different approaches.

Manual Classification

This approach is often used in library and technical collections, and requires individuals to assign each document to one or more categories of taxonomy. These individuals are usually domain experts, who have a deep knowledge of the domain represented by the taxonomy. Manual classification can achieve a high degree of accuracy, but is more labour-intensive and more costly than automated techniques (Blumberg & Atre, 2003).

Automatic-Manual Combination

This approach combines automatic and manual technologies and exploits both the advantages of the low costs in term of time from the automatic classification and the advantages of a high control of the document manual indexing.

Automatic Classification

Numerous algorithms are available to classify automatically a set of documents and two approaches can be used: supervised classification using machine learning techniques and unsupervised classification (clustering) (Denoue & Vignollet, 2001).

Supervised classification requires a set of pre-classified documents where each document is associated to a predefined category. This classification system first analyses the occurrences of each concept in the sample documents and then constructs a model for each category using a machine algorithm (such as LRC described above). This model of rules is used to classify automatically subsequent documents in the categories. The system refines its model, "learning" the category as new documents are processed. Examples of this approach are: Autonomy[4] and Stratify[5] that use Bayesian algorithms, Verity that uses a form of SVM (Support Vector Machine) approach, Microsoft that uses SVM in its SharePoint portal (Blumberg & Atre, 2003).

Unsupervised classification does not require a set of pre-classified documents. Documents are compared to each other and the algorithm tries to structure them, and this structure depends on the nature of the algorithm. Some of them produce a flat classification of the documents, others a hierarchy of classes, such as HAC (Hierarchical Agglomerative Clustering) (Denoue & Vignollet, 2001).

The Verity System uses an automatic classification. Verity automatically fills the taxonomy with documents during the indexing process, using VIC (Verity Intelligent Classifier) (Verity Group, 2004), a tool to build and fill taxonomies. Verity System uses positive and negative sample documents to automatically generate the rules that define the categories and on which the new documents are valuated. The technology used by VIC is the Verity's LRC (Logistic Regression Classification). LRC defines a rule (vector of words and relative weights) associated to each category and a new document is evaluated against that rule; a score is assigned to each document evaluated based on the category rule.

It is important to choose a classification threshold for each category to limit the number of categories assigned to each document. Threshold is a numeric value (from 0 to 1) assigned to each category; the score assigned to a new document in relation to the rule of a category is evaluated with the score of that category. The thresholds should be set high enough that only those documents with "significant" scores are assigned to the categories.

Therefore, the classification of a new document depends on its score, that is compared with the score-threshold decided for a specific category; if the score of the document is higher then the threshold assigned to a particular category, the document is inserted in that category, otherwise the document is rejected, and so on for all categories of the taxonomy.

Each document is evaluated by two parameters: the rule and the score-threshold associated to each category of the taxonomy. The score-threshold can be set for the entire taxonomy, a category and all of its subcategories, or a single subcategory at any level of the taxonomy 0(Verity Group, 2004).

According to the model in Figure 1, Figure 2 represents the classification with the Verity System:

FILLING TAXONOMY IN THE KIWI SYSTEM

In the KIWI project, the automatic-manual approach is implemented for inserting documents into the categories. The approach focuses on the development of a set of tools (eBMS, 2005) which allow the users to represent a specific domain through taxonomy or ontology to index documents and to browse the taxonomy/ontology for document retrieval.

Users can formalize the conceptualization of the domain of interest using the OntoMaker tool, a taxonomy and ontology editor, and obtaining the implementation of it in taxonomy. Ontometer

Figure 2. Filling taxonomy with documents in the Verity System

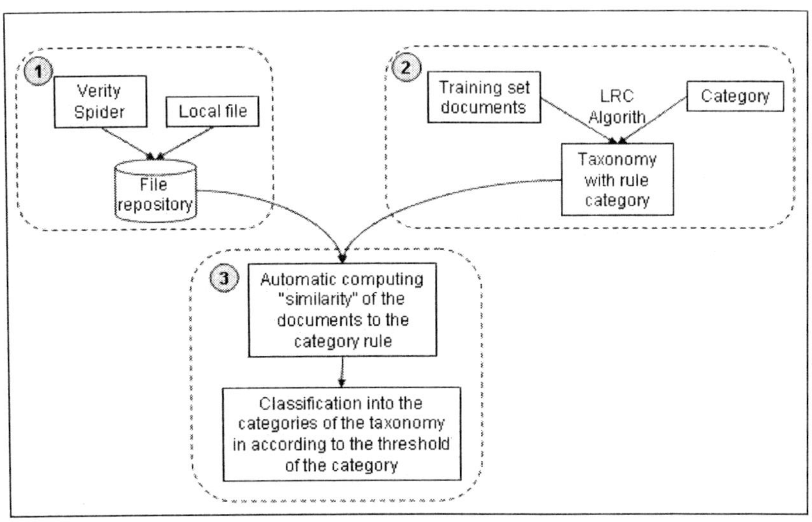

is a tool for quality evaluation of the representation. It evaluates some metrics on a model and assists the ontology developer in building a homogeneous model. After this, it is possible to insert the documents into the categories of the taxonomy (or ontology).

The knowledge base that includes the documents to index is built both with the internal organizational knowledge and with external sources by semantic spider.

The approach used in KIWI combines two steps: the automatic classification by VIC and the manual classification by KIWI's OntoAssistant tool.

In the "automatic classification" step, VIC uses the taxonomy implemented with Ontomaker, and indexes automatically the documents in the taxonomy. As described above, VIC uses LRC to define a rule associated to each category of the taxonomy, so a new document is evaluated against this rule and it is assigned into the appropriate category. Therefore, LRC creates a simplex semantic assertion between a document and a category (concept) of the taxonomy. A simplex semantic assertion is an association between a concept and a document and explains that the document topic is represented by the meaning of the associated concept (Chekuri et al., 1997).

In the "manual classification" step, the VIC's concept-document association can be used by the OntoAssistant to be translated in a complex semantic assertion. A complex semantic assertion is an association between a triples, such as Subject-Relation-Objec,t and a document, that explains the semantics of the document (Chekuri et al., 1997).

Since the OntoAssistant uses RDFS file, Verity2RDF tool can be used to translate the VIC's

Figure 3. Filling taxonomy with manual and automatic approaches in the KIWI system

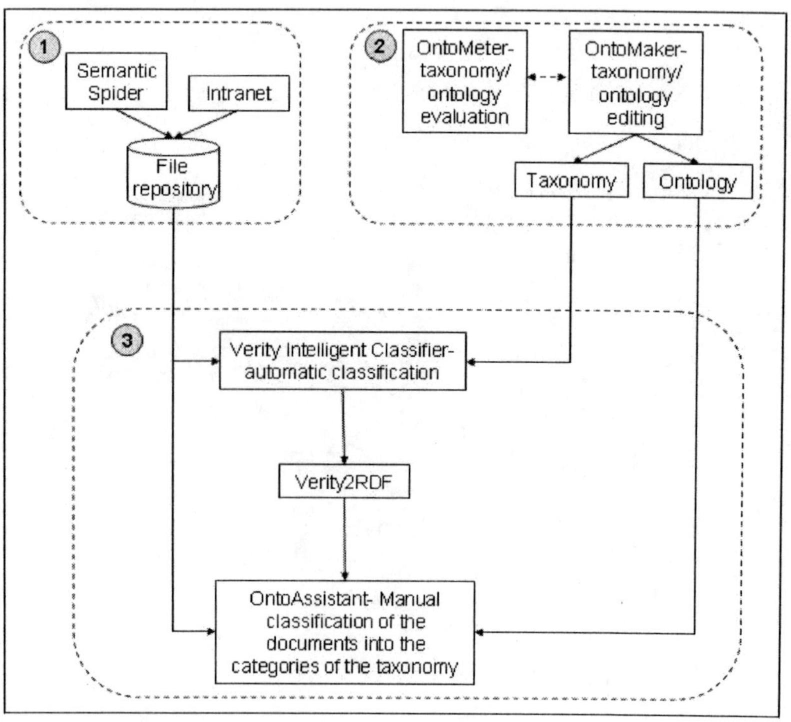

assertions in RDFS format, in order to be valid input for the OntoAssistant. OntoAssistant uses this RDFS file and transforms simplex semantic assertions in complex semantic assertions.

In addition, the implemented ontology is the input for the OntoAssistant for the manual creation of simplex and complex assertions. The domain expert indexes manually a selected section of a document with the exact concept (category) of the ontology (simplex semantic assertion) or with triples (complex semantic assertion) extracted from the ontology.

SEARCH ENGINE TECHNIQUES

The objective of a search in a knowledge base is to satisfy the user requests and his/her information needs. According to Broder (2002), this required information can be informational (concepts and information about a particular topic), navigational (the site to reach) or transactional (site where it is possible to perform a certain transaction, such as download a file, access to database, shop) (Broder, 2002).

The currently available technologies for searching information in a knowledge repository can classified in three categories:

- *keyword-based search*: the user enters one or more search terms and the search engine returns a lists of document summaries;
- *linguistic search*: the user enters a query and the search engine uses some linguistic analysis to reduce ambiguities improving relevance of the returned results;
- *directory-based search*: a hierarchal structure of categories organizes the information space which the user can browse starting from broader categories and navigating through the hierarchy to more specific one; in this approach, there is not query formulation required.

Most search technologies combine more than one of these approaches.

Keyword-Based Search

This process of identifying the relevant documents involves matching the keywords of the user query with the documents of the repository.

The weakness of these search engines is that they only support keyword-oriented search and the result of the search is a set of pages that include a given set of keywords. In fact, most queries return either no page or a long list of pages, which include the given keywords, but most of them are irrelevant. Although some search engines offer "advanced" search features, as Boolean combinations of terms and word stemming (stemming is the process of extracting the roof of the word and ignoring plural versions or other modifications of the word; for example, the roof of jumped, jumping and jumps is jump), the search and retrieval methodologies without a classification solution present many limitations:

- they do not distinguish the topic of the keywords in the queries and so all documents in which those keywords appear are considered relevant and presented to the users;
- they cannot distinguish the different interpretations of a word in a given context and so the returned results might contain a mix of uses of the word.

Some advanced keyword-based search engines look for the keyword in the title, in the abstract, in the body of a document or in the metadata section. An application crawls through the subject document and each instance of a keyword is put into an indexing database that describes its occurrences and where that word was located within the paragraph, page or document.

Figure 4 shows a representation of a keyword-based search.

Figure 4. Search model for a keyword-based search

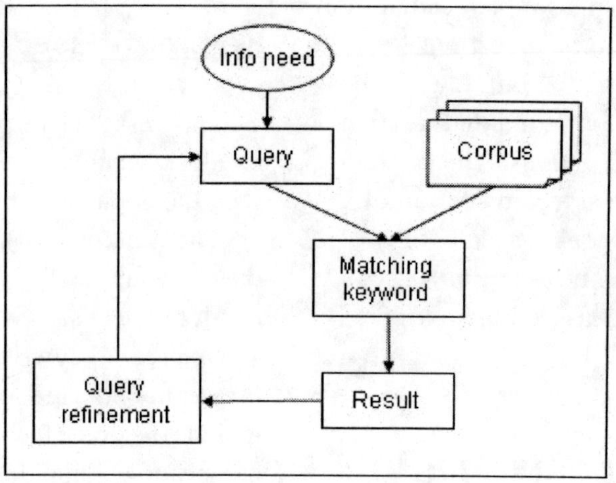

Linguistic Search

The performance of search engines depends on their ability to capture the meaning of a query most likely intended by the users.

A variety of approaches and methodologies are used to resolve ambiguities, to extract the semantics within natural language text, and to capture the intended meaning of a search query. The common types of language ambiguities (Ntoulas et al., 2005) that search engines try to resolve are:

- *part-of-speech*: a phrase may have multiple interpretations depending on the context; POS (Part-Of-Speech) disambiguation is the process of assigning a part-of-speech tag, such as noun or verb or adjective to each word in a sentence determining how the word functions within the context;
- *word sense*: a word takes on a multiple of different meanings or senses. The WSD (Word Sense Disambiguation) () allows to search for a specific sense of a word eliminating documents which contained the same word but they are semantically irrelevant;
- *phrase identification*: multiple words can be grouped into phrases to describe a concept more precisely; in order to properly identify phrases it is necessary to perform a linguistic analysis at a broader context;
- *named entity recognition*: named entities can refer to names of people, companies, locations, date and other; NER is used to search specifically for a particular entity of interest for the users;
- *full sentential parsing*: parsing is the process of decomposing a sentence into smaller units, as well as identifying the grammatical role of each unit and its relationship with other units.

An example of search engine that uses a linguistic analysis is Infocious Web Search Engine (Ntoulas et al., 2005).

The goal of Infocious Web Search Engine is to improve the way users find information on the Web by resolving ambiguities in natural language.

This is achieved by performing the linguistic analysis on the content of the indexed Web pages. This additional step of linguistic processing gives Infocious a deeper understanding of the content of web pages so it can better match user queries and can improve relevance of the returned results. In order to understand the content of Web pages, Infocious focuses on three types of ambiguity: part-of-speech ambiguity, phrasal ambiguity, and topical ambiguity.

The architecture of Infocious contains a crawler that downloads pages from the Web and gives them to Linguistic Analysis algorithms; the output is sent out to various indexes that can handle and store efficiently the specialized information generated by the Linguistic Analysis algorithms. These indexes are used during query time to answer the user requests, organise the results in intuitive ways and present related topics, key phrases and suggestions (Ntoulas et al., 2005).

Directory-Based Search

Net directories such as Yahoo! (Chekuri et al., 1997) provide a hierarchical document classification; each document in the directory is associated with a node of the tree. Moving along the tree, a user can access a set of pages that have been manually pre-classified and placed in the tree. Search in a directory is convenient and leads the user to the set of documents he/she is searching, but it leads to only a part of domain indexed in that directory.

Combination of Directory-Based Search and Keyword-Based Search

Some search engines use a combination of keyword-based search and context-sensitive search based on classification. This approach offers the advantages of these two types of search:

- the traditional approach by keyword-based search, in which a query containing keywords is used to narrow the results of the search only to the documents of interest;
- the directory-based search, in which a taxonomy or an ontology is used to limit the search on few categories.

Figure 5. Search model for Yahoo

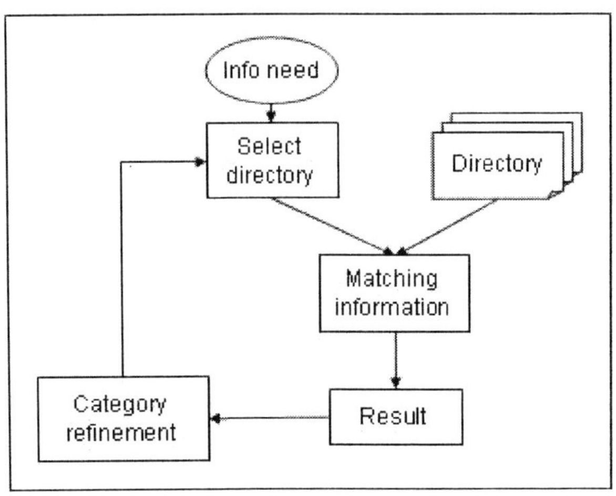

This approach uses a hierarchical structure (taxonomy or ontology) of the domain that limits the search only to the part of the domain of interest, because it involves the concepts and the relations of a particular context. Once the Semantic search engine determines the context (concepts) of the required information, it can explore related entities through associations (relations with another concept).

Then, the results of the Semantic search can be restricted using the keyword-based search that improves the precision of search engines while it excludes the documents that do not contain the keywords in the queries.

Virtual eBMS uses this kind of approach. The platform supports three types of search:

- *keyword-based search*, specifying one or more keywords in a query;
- *advanced search*, specifying one or more keywords in a query and detailing some logic operators and other filters on the document, such as the file format, the title, the author or the date of creation;
- *taxonomy-based search*, selecting the category of interest in which the user wants to search a document.

With a basic search (keyword-based search), the user can search documents into the Virtual eBMS Knowledge Repository that contains one or more keywords or a selected phrase. The system finds a list of documents that contain the keywords or the phrase required by the user.

The advanced search allows the user to define a query for the keyword-based search using a set of advanced operators and parametric filters.

In the search section, two taxonomies are visualized and they can be browsed by the user to find a list of documents catalogued in a particular knowledge category. The nodes of the selected relational taxonomy have one or more sub categories and the nodes selected from the two taxonomies have common documents that satisfy the search

Figure 6. Combination of search models in the Virtual eBMS

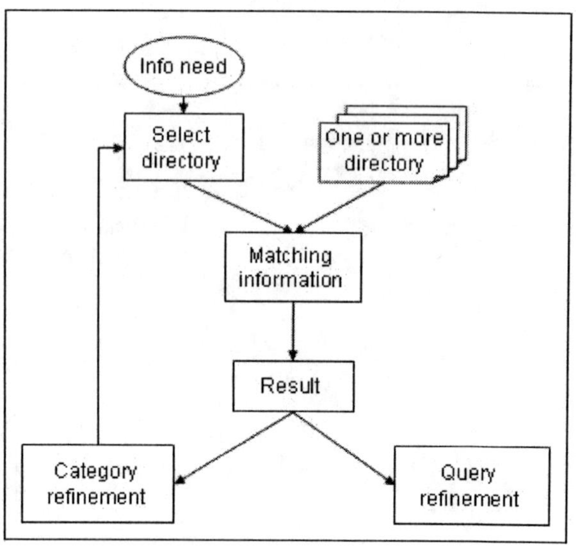

query. To obtain a further precise result, the user can also edit a query in the search text field and execute it over the selected categories.

In addition, it is possible to navigate into a Visual Knowledge Tree that can help user to understand the available domain representation, switching to a dynamic visual representation of the current taxonomy: inserting a term in the corresponding text field, the node becomes the centre of the graphical knowledge tree representation. For each category, the graph shows the number of documents contained in it and the number of sub categories.

THE EVOLUTION OF WEB SEARCH ENGINES

As stated before user queries can be classified into navigational, informational and transactional. Moreover, it is possible to identify three stages in the evolution of Web search (Broder, 2002; Guozhen et al., 2001):

1. First generation: search engines use mostly on-page data (text and formatting), they are close to classic IR (Information Retrieval) and support mostly informational queries. They analyse the location and frequency of words in web pages to determine ranking and pages are processed by classic IR techniques such as (TF*IDF). TF(i) is simply the Frequency of Term *i* in the document, and IDF is the Inverse Document Frequency, given by *(N/n(i))* where *N* is the total number of documents, and *n(i)* is the number of documents in which word *i* occurs. This was the state-of-the art around 1995-1997 and AltaVista, Excite, WebCrawler are examples of this generation.
2. Second generation: search engines use Web-specific data such as link analysis and anchor-text to evaluate page quality and take it into consideration while ranking. The quality of each page does not rely on its neighbouring pages, but on the global topology: this global mutual dependence of page quality is computed through iteration. This technique improves the quality search and uses both informational and navigational queries. This generation started in 1998-1999, and Google is a successful case.
3. Third generation: search engines attempt to unite data from multiple sources in order to try to answer "the need behind the query," going beyond the limitation of a fixed corpus, via semantic analysis, context determination, dynamic data base selection, and so forth. The aim is to support informational, navigational and transactional queries.

Third generation search engines go well beyond the Google model, using intelligent clustering of results, natural language processing and more human contribution to improve search results. An example is Clusty, which tries to cluster results into categories. This is helpful when a search query includes results from more than one topic area and so a user can quickly pick the appropriate cluster (Guozhen et al., 2001).

Third-generation search technologies are designed to combine the scalability of existing Internet search engines with new and improved relevancy models. This will include contextual relevance, allowing searches to be performed across any type of content and any type and number of sources.

Emerging innovative search engines can help make search more meaningful, subjective and task-based. While traditional search engine is good for finding information, the new search engine is good for discovering information at a rapid rate.

Current search technologies do not replace traditional search engines; they rather work in conjunction with traditional search engines to provide a more powerful search.

The new search engines are included in the Web 2.0 vision, in which people collaborate and share information online in new ways, which include social networking, wikis, communication tools and social book marking.

Web 2.0 is the term used to describe the practice of using the Web to communicate by requesting, obtaining, and sharing relevant information. It is characterized by online social networks such as MySpace, blogs, automatic information feeds, information pull rather than push and the sharing of user generated content.

SEARCH ENGINES PERFORMANCE

Numerous methods to evaluate the performance of information retrieval have been developed. The most used methods are: Precision, Recall and F-measure (Maynard et al., 2006; Song et al., 2005).

The Precision is defined as the probability that an item is correctly identified in a category. It measures the number of correctly identified items as a percentage of the number of the identified items. In other words, it measures how many items that the system identifies actually belong to a specific category against all items identified into that category.

The Recall, defined as the probability that an item belonging to a specific category, is actually inserted into that category by the system. In other words, it expresses the percentage of items correctly identified into a category against all the items that would have to be inserted correctly in that category.

The F-measure is often used in conjunction with the Precision and the Recall, as a weighted average of the two. The F-measure is the harmonic mean of recall and precision. Using a harmonic mean helps minimize the influence of any variable, while at the same time penalizing uneven contribution. In term of measuring search performance, this means that a highly performing search system returns a high percentage of relevant documents, with minimized noise.

According to:

- TP – True Positive as a document correctly classified in a specific category;
- FP – False Positive as a document incorrectly classified in a specific category;
- FN – False Negative as a document incorrectly non classified in a specific category;
- TN – True Negative as a document correctly non classified in a specific category,

the metrics are formally defined as:

Figure 7. Nature of documents

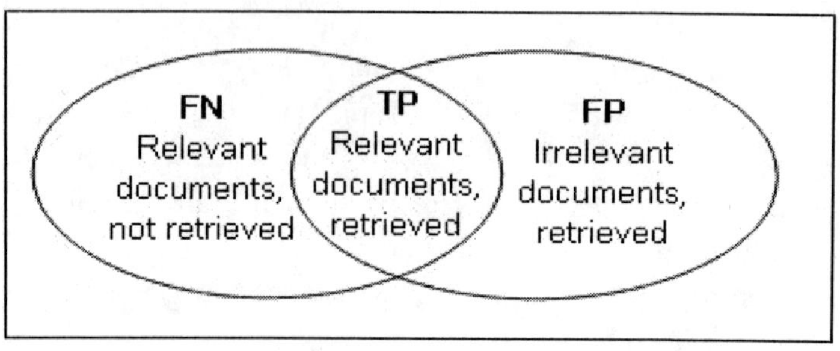

- Precision $P = TP / (TP + FP)$
- Recall $R = TP / (TP + FN)$
- F-measure $F1 = 2/((1/Precision) + (1/Recall))$

The Recall and the Precision are inversely related; for an increase in precision, there is a decrease in recall and vice versa. Typically, Web search engines tend to have great recall, but poor precision, whereas, a good medical search application should return fewer results related to the specific patient.

Much of this relationship has to do with the language. If the goal of a search is ample retrieval, the searcher must include synonyms, related terms, broad or general terms for each concept. Consequently, precision will suffer, because the probability of retrieving irrelevant material increases.

In other words, the need to access all relevant information implies large volume of data: improving completeness of catalogued information (recall), the purity (precision) of the results decreases in proportion.

These measures of performance are efficient if they are used in a limited domain with a well defined document repository. Used in the Web, they have some limitations. In this case, for instance, the recall is impossible to measure; in addition, most searches on the Web are not concerned with finding all the relevant material. In this case, it is opportune to choose a measure of the quality of the documents, in term of the relevance of the document according to the satisfaction of the user information need (Dennis et al., 2002). Obviously, this measure depends on the evaluator's or domain expert's judgment and the specific context of the search.

Figure 8. Trade-off between precision and recall

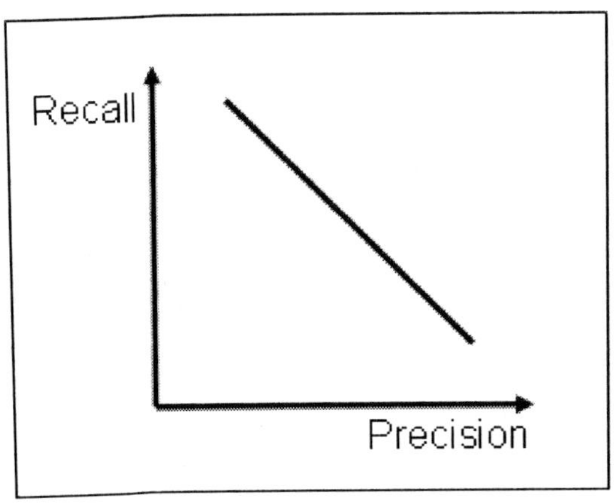

In the following section we show the experimental result of three different studies:

1. Performance Results of Web-based search engine ;
2. Experimental Results of Ontology Driven Semantic Search;
3. Performance of KIWI Categories.

Performance Results of Web-Based Search Engine

We consider an experimental research on search engine performance carried out by Department of Library and Information Science, University of Kashmir, Srinagar-India (Safi & Rather, 2005).

The method includes three stages:

1. collection of related available material (in print and electronic format) for the study and selection of search engines and search terms;
2. test of search engines;
3. analysis of the results for estimation of precision and recall.

The search engines investigated for retrieval scholarly information are:

- AltaVista
- Google
- HotBot

- Scirus
- Bioweb

AltaVista, Google, and HotBot are general search engines, Scirus is a specific search engine about Science&Technology, Bioweb is specific search engine related to Biotechnology.

The selected search engines offer two modes of searching--simple and advanced. The study has chosen the advanced one, using available features for refining and producing precise numbers of results.

Twenty search terms were drawn and classified under three groups: single (for example, antibiotics, cloning); compound (for example, "enzyme technology," "molecular cloning"); and complex terms (e.g.,, biotechnological AND "process control," "genetically modified" OR "engineered foods") for investigating how search engines control and handle single and phrase terms. Single terms were submitted in natural form, compound terms as suggested by respective search engines and complex terms with suitable Boolean operators AND and OR between the terms to perform special searches. Five separate queries were constructed for each term in accordance with the syntax of the select search engine.

Each query was submitted to the selected engines, which retrieved many results. Only the first 10 results were evaluated to limit the study in view of the fact that most of the users usually look up under the first ten hits of a query. So search engines were evaluated taking the first 10 results pertaining to scholarly information for estimation of precision and recall.

The system utilises precision and recall measure to evaluate the performance of the chosen search engines.

In the experiment, Precision is defined as the fraction of a search output that is relevant for a particular query and its measurement requires knowledge about the relevant and non-relevant hits in the evaluated set of documents. Thus, it is possible to calculate absolute precision of search engine, which provides an indication of the relevance of the system. In the context of the considered study, the definition of precision is:

$$\text{Precision} = \frac{\text{Sum of the scores of scholarly documents retrieved by a search}}{\text{Total number of evaluated results}}$$

To determinate the relevance of each page, a four-point scale was used to calculate precision. The criteria employed for the purpose were:

- a page representing the full text of research paper, seminar/conference proceedings or a patent was given a score of three;
- a page corresponding to an abstract of a research paper, seminar/conference proceedings or a patent was given a score of two;
- a page corresponding to a book or a database was given a score of one;
- a page representing other than the above (i.e., company Web pages, dictionaries, encyclopedia, organization, etc.) was given a score of zero;
- a page occurring more than once under different URLs was assigned a score of zero;
- a non response of the server for subsequent three searches was assigned a score of zero.

The recall is defined as the ability of a retrieval system to obtain all or most of the relevant documents in the collection. There is no correct method of calculating absolute recall of search engines, as it is impossible to know the total number of relevant results in enormous databases. This study was carried out by grouping the relevant results (corresponding to scholarly documents) of individual searches to form the denominator of the calculations. The relative recall value is thus defined as:

$$\text{Relative recall} = \frac{\text{Total number of scholarly documents retrieved by a search}}{\text{Sum of scholarly documents retrieved by all five search engines}}$$

Table 1 presents the main precision and relative recall of selected search engines for scholarly information retrieval.

Two search engines, "AltaVista" and "HotBot," were revisited during June 2005 to investigate the effect of their algorithm policy on precision and recall; the mean precision and recall of the observation in AltaVista show an increase while HotBot shows marginal increase in precision and decrease in its recall value, as shown in Table 2.

The main precision obtained for single, compound and complex queries of the respective search engines show Scirus as having the highest precision (0.83) for complex queries followed by compound queries (0.63). AltaVista scored the highest precision (0.50) for complex queries followed by compound queries (0.24). Google and HotBot performed better with complex and compound queries, while Bioweb performed better with single queries, as shown in Figure 9.

Comparing the corresponding mean relative recall values, Scirus has the highest recall (0.32) followed by HotBot (0.29) and Google (0.20). AltaVista scored a relative recall of 0.18 and Bioweb the last (0.05). Scirus performed better on complex queries (0.39) followed by compound queries (0.37). HotBot did better in single and compound queries (0.31). Google attained highest recall on compound queries (0.22) followed by complex queries (0.21). AltaVista's performance is better on complex queries (0.28) where as Bioweb performed better on single queries (0.11) (Figure 10).

The results describe better performance of Scirus in retrieving scholarly documents, and it was the best choice for those who have access to various online journals or databases like Biomed-

Table 1. Mean precision and relative recall of search engines during 2004

	AltaVista	**Google**	**HotBot**	**Scirus**	**Bioweb**
Precision	0.27	0.29	0.28	0.57	0.14
Recall	0.18	0.20	0.29	0.32	0.05

Table 2. Comparison of mean precision and mean recall of AltaVista and HotBot search engines between 2004 and 2005

	Mean Precision 2004	**Mean Precision 2005**	**Mean Recall 2004**	**Mean Recall 2005**
AltaVista	0.27	0.29	0.18	0.21
HotBot	0.28	0.33	0.29	0.27

Figure 9. Precision of five search engines for single, compound, and complex terms

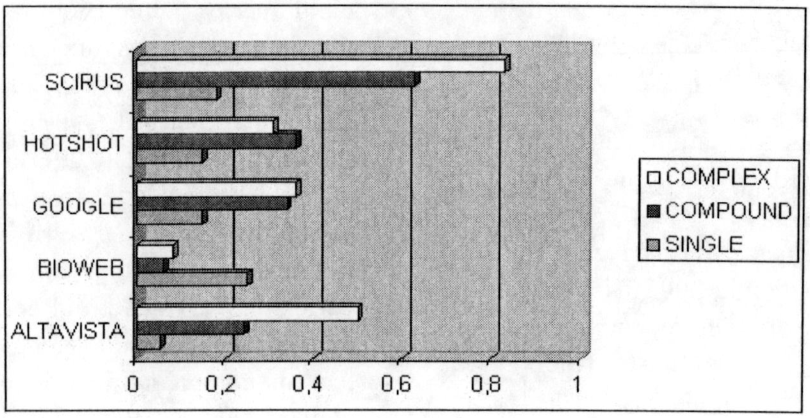

Figure 10. Relative recall of search engines for single, compound, and complex terms

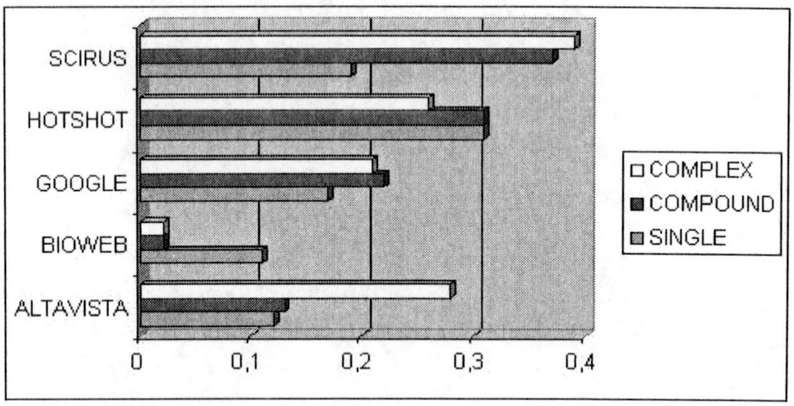

net, Medline plus, and so forth. HotBot offered a good combination of recall and precision but had a larger overlap with other search engines, which enhanced its relative recall over Google search engine. AltaVista once prominent on the Web has lagged behind and the Bioweb is the weakest among the selected search engines. Further, the results reveal that structured queries (phrased and Boolean) contribute in achieving better precision and recall. The results also establish that precision is inversely proportional to recall.

Experimental Results of Ontology Driven Semantic Search

For the evaluation of semantic search engines we consider an approach based on the ontology navigation carried out by Department of Automatics and Informatics, Polytechnic of Torino 0 (Bonino et al., 2004).

The search engine consists of an automatic detection mechanism that is able to trigger appropriate navigation on the concepts hierarchy defined by domain ontology. The key points for the refinement process of the semantic search are the availability of domain ontology and the ability to understand semantic relationships among ontology concepts. When an application requires retrieval, this must specify three parameters:

- the relevance threshold: this discriminates relevant documents from non relevant ones;
- the number of relevant documents to be retrieved;
- the conceptual query: this is composed by a sequence of concepts and related weights.

The system utilized is DOSE, a Distributed Open Semantic Elaboration platform based on a modular multilingual architecture, which includes ontology, annotations, lexical entities and search functions. In this system, two modules are defined: "Basic Search" that implements the (TF*IDF) vector space model at the semantic level and "Clever Search" that provides smart functionality for query refinement based on ontology navigation.

Two experiments were carried out in order to assess value of the approach and improvements between a common IR technique applied to semantic annotations and the ontology driven search engine.

Starting from this great amount of data, a set of queries and correspondent relevant pages were defined. Therefore, two different queries have been issued both to the Basic Search module and to the Clever Search and results have been compared by means of precision-recall graphs.

This test illustrates that the documents judged as relevant by a human expert were not annotated by concepts specified in the query. Since the Clever Search engine performs a query expansion, new concepts were introduced into the query allowing the retrieval of previously "uncoverable" documents.

In both cases, the ontology powered search provided better results in terms of precision and recall. Although the results are not yet competitive from the point of view of precision and recall since the Basic Search module is not optimized, however they show that an ontology based query expansion process is able to provide improvements to search result relevance by retrieving quickly relevant documents and by discovering knowledge not explicitly expressed in the user query.

Performance of KIWI Categories

We used precision and recall measures to evaluate the quality of the document classification, testing the result of the retrieved documents in order to refine classification rules and optimize the values of precision and recall.

If the values of precision and recall are not satisfactory, we perform some action to enhance the quality of the classification:

- reconsider the documents of the training set for the categories whose values of precision and recall are decidedly under the average, verifying that the documents used for the training are meant for the category
- modify manually the rules of the categories whose precision is small
- lower the threshold of the categories whose value of recall is not satisfactory, in order to improve this value.

We decided to have good recall rather than good precision; in fact, although in this way we

Table 3. Average values of precision, recall and F-measure of some categories of taxonomy

Category	Precision	Recall	F-Measure
Technology Management	57%	77.1%	64%
Innovation	18.8%	51.7%	25.35%
Marketing	54%	60%	55%
Leadership	29.75%	60%	39.33%
Global Business	21.04%	52%	29.16%
General management	13.9%	68.3%	21.82%

Figure 11. Performance of information retrieval approaches

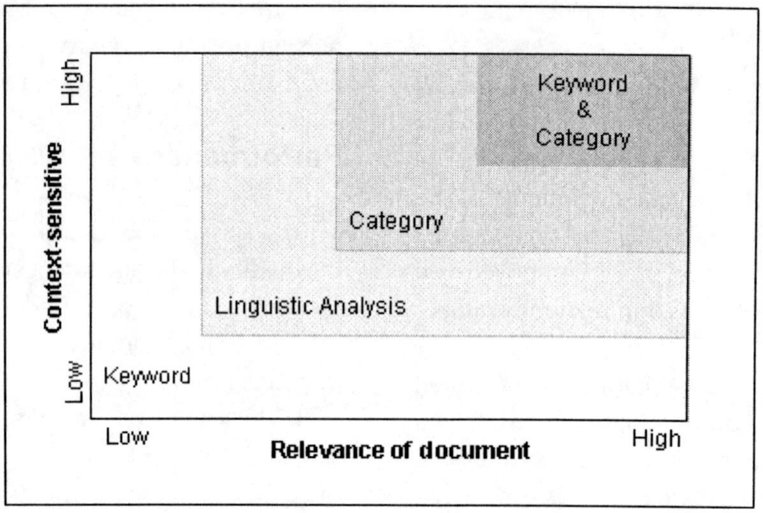

can increase False Positive, we increase True Positive as well and the consequent diminution of precision can be compensated by the possibility to refine the result using textual search.

We carried out eight tests, in which we evaluate the precision and recall measures of the classification in all categories of our hierarchical structure. If these measures are under an established value, we take one or more actions described in order to enhance that value (eBMS, 2006). In Table 3, we show the average values of precision, recall and F-measure of some categories of taxonomy, which are obtained after the improvements in order to enhance the performance.

Relevance of Search Approaches

Considering the methodologies for information retrieval explained above, it is possible to evaluate these approaches in relation to the level of context-sensitiveness and relevance of documents.

The keyword-based search presents low results in terms of context-sensitiveness and relevance of documents. In fact, this search delivers results in the form of a long undifferentiated list of documents that contain given words used in the query. The search engine performs a simple match between the given words and all words contained in the documents of the knowledge base. An enhancement of the keyword-based search is the linguistic search. The result is still a set of pages including given words used for the search, but the search engine uses some techniques of linguistic analysis in order to capture the real meaning of the word intended by user.

The search for category, instead, guarantees that the documents present in that category reflect a specific topic. Therefore, the user can search documents in a specific part of knowledge base that corresponds to the interest topic and has high level of context-sensitive documents.

The search for category can be improved if it is used with the keyword-based search. In this way, once the category of interest is defined, it is possible to restrict the number of the documents of the category performing the usual keyword-based search and limiting the result only to the documents that contained specific keywords.

Therefore, searches based on category or category with more precise and efficient keyword results compared with other kinds of search.

The test in Virtual eBMS confirms this result. In our test, we propose to retrieve a particular document in the knowledge base of Virtual eBMS that speeches about ontology, using three modalities of search:

- first search: we suppose the user is not expert in the topics of the knowledge base, and so he/she utilises a generic keyword-based search and looks for all the documents that contain the word "ontology;"
- second search: we suppose the user is expert in the topics of the domain and knows that the searched document is probably contained in a specific category; so he/she looks for the document in a particular category. In our example the category is "Topics/Technology Management/Semantic Web;"
- third search: the user is a domain expert and knows exactly the category that con-

Table 4. Results of different searches in Virtual eBMS

	Number of retrieved document	Position of the particular document in the list of retrieved documents
Keyword-based search, searching "ontology" word	1.048	1.026
Category search in the "Semantic Web" category	27.365	14
Keyword & Category search in the "Semantic Web" category and with "ontology" word	27	11

tains the specific document; once user individuates the category, he/she wants to restrict the number of the documents of the category, considering only the documents that contain the word "ontology," so he/she uses the category search in conjunction with keyword-based search.

Table 4 summarizes the results obtained for the different kinds of search, considering the number of documents retrieved by the search engine and the position of the specific document in the list of all retrieved documents.

We note that, in the keyword-based search, the search engine retrieves 1.048 documents containing the "ontology" word and, in particular, the document we want to find is at position 1.026. That means we find a great number of documents, and the document of interest is at a low position in the list. Therefore, the search of this document has a low level of relevance.

With the search in a specific category, we consider all documents of that category (27.365 documents in the "Semantic Web" category) and we find the specific document at position 14. Therefore, we have good level of context-sensitiveness because all considered documents belong to a specific topic (category) and a good level of relevance because it is at high location in the list.

If, after a category search, we use a keyword-based search with "ontology" word, we enhance significantly the result, because we restrict the list of documents to 27 documents, and the particular document is the 11th document in the list; so we obtain high level of context-sensitiveness and relevance of documents.

If we had optimized the search engine to obtain high precision, we would have achieved best results and so the specific document to a higher relevant position. Instead, we prefer getting high recall, first because the user is usually an expert and so he/she knows the category in which performing the search, and then because there is the opportunity to optimize the results of an initial search with a successive keyword-based search.

CONCLUSION

As more information is made available in a knowledge base, the need to organise and structure this knowledge in an easy way to access and use becomes essential. Particularly, a solution for an efficient information retrieval is crucial to satisfy user information needs. The approach that results efficient to the challenge of successful search is based on taxonomy as method to structure the interest domain and to help user to find information more easily and precisely.

This chapter presents different methodologies to organise a domain through taxonomy, to define the model of rules accordingly to the meaning of the taxonomy categories, to classify the documents in the taxonomy and to retrieve information.

All approaches present a different level of automation, depending on the contribution of the domain expert and the adopted algorithm. The method based on expert contributions presents high levels of accuracy and precision but it is not appropriate in large domains with many documents. The automatic method, instead, is able to manage more information, but it often does not present a high level of performance. However, the performance of the system depends on the domain where these technologies and methods are applied.

In addition, the use of ontology can improve the effectiveness of the representation, organization and retrieval of information, because the concepts and the relations expressed in the ontology enhance the context-sensitiveness level in all the phases of the information workflow (organisation, structuring, representation, visualization, access, retrieval, use). The advantages of an ontology-based approach are the nature of the relational structure of the ontology, which provides a mechanism to enable machine reasoning. The conceptual instances within an ontology are not only a set of keywords but they have inherent semantics and the relationships with the classes represent the classification structure.

Therefore, the application based on ontology or taxonomy becomes an important feature in the building of the Semantic Web, making it easier for machines to automatically process and integrate the data information on the Web.

REFERENCES

An, A. (2005). Classification methods. In J. Wang (Ed.), *Encyclopedia of Data Warehousing and Mining* (pp. 144-149). New York: Idea Group Inc.

Blumberg, R., & Atre S. (2003). Automatic classification: Moving to the mainstream. *DR Review Magazine 13*(4), 12-19.

Bonino, D., Corno, F., Farinetti, L., & Bosca A. (2004). Ontology driven semantic search. *WSEAS Transaction on Information Science and Application, 1*(6), 1597-1605.

Broder, A. (2002). A taxonomy of Web search. In *ACM SIGIR Forum* (pp. 3-10). New York, USA: ACM.

Chekuri C., Goldwasser, M., Ragavan, P., & Upfal, E. (1997). *Web search using automatic classification.* Paper presented at 6th International World Wide Web Conference, Santa Clara, California USA.

Chung, C. Y., Lieu, R., Liu, J., Mao, J., & Raghavan, P. (2002). Thematic mapping--From unstructured documents to taxonomies. In *Proceedings of the 11th Iinternational Conference on Information and Knowledge Management 2002* (pp. 608-610). Virginia, USA: ACM.

Corcho, O., & Lopez, M. F., Perez, A. G., (2003). Methodologies, tools and languages for building ontologies. Where is their meeting point? *Data & Knowledge Engineering,* 46 (2003), 41–64.

Delphi Group. (2002). *Taxonomy & content classification,* Retrieved on March, 2007, from http://lsdis.cs.uga.edu/SemanticEnterprise/Delphi_LingoMotorfinal.pdf

Dennis, S., & Bruza, P., McArtur, R. (2002). Web searching: A process-oriented experimental study of three interactive search paradigms. *Journal of the American Society for Information Science and Technology, 53*(2),120-133.

Denoue, L., & Vignollet, L. (2001, January). *Personal Information Organization using Web Annotation.* Paper presented at the *WebNet 2001 World Conference on the WWW and Internet, Orlando, FL.*

eBMS. (2005). *KIWI--Ontology for knowledge mapping* (Project Deliverable). Lecce, Italy: University of Lecce

eBMS. (2005). *KIWI--Application Context* (Project Deliverable). Lecce, Italy: University of Lecce

eBMS. (2006). *Test Verity in the Virtual eBMS project* (Project Deliverable). Lecce, Italy: University of Lecce

Ezzy, E. (2006). Search 2.0 vs Traditional search. Retrieved on September, 2007, from http://www.readwriteweb.com/archives/search_20_vs_tr.php

Forman, G. (2002). Incremental machine learning to reduce biochemistry lab costs in the search for drug discovery. In *Proceedings of the 2nd ACM SIGKDD Workshop on Data Mining in Bioinformatics.* Edmonton, Alberta, Canada.

Guozhen, F., Xueqi, C., & Shuo, B. (2001). SAInSE: An intelligent search engine based on

WWW structure analysis. In *Proceedings of the 15th International Parallel & Distributed Processing Symposium* (p. 168). Washington, DC, USA: IEEE Computer Society.

Gruber, T. R. (1993). *What is an ontology?* Retrieved on July 2007, from http://www-ksl.stanford.edu/kst/what-is-an-ontology.html

Kashyap, V., Ramakrishnan, C., Thomas, C., Bassu, D., Rindflesch, T.C., & Sheth, A. (2005). TaxaMiner: An experiment framework for automated taxonomy bootstrapping. *International Journal of Web and Grid Services, Special Issue on Semantic Web and Mining Reasoning.*

Maynard, D., Peters, W., & Li, Y. (2006, May). *Metrics for evaluation of ontology-based information extraction.* Paper presented at WWW2006, Edinburgh, UK.

Ntoulas, A., Chao, G. & Cho, J. (2005). *The infocious Web search engine: Improving Web searching through linguistic analysis.* Paper presented at International World Wide Web Conference Committee (IW3C2), Beijing, China.

Safi, S.M., & Rather, R.A. (2005). Precision and recall of five search engines for retrieval of scholarly information in the field of biotechnology. *Webology,* 2(2), Article 12.

Sheth, A., Ramakrishnan, C., & Thomas, C. (2005). Semantics for the Semantic Web: The implicit, the formal and the powerful. *International Journal on Semantic Web & Information Systems, 1*(1), 1-18.

Song, M., Lim, S., Park, S., Kang, D., & Lee, S. (2005). Automatic classification of Web pages based on the concept of domain ontology. In *Proceedings of the 12th Asia-Pacific Software Engineering Conference (APSEC'05)* (pp. 645-651). IEEE.

Sure, Y., & Studer, R., (1999). *On-to-knowledge methodology* (Final Version, Project Deliverable D18). Germany: University of Karlsruhe.

Thomson Scientific. (2004). *Getting just what you need: strategies for search, taxonomy and classification*". Retrieved on July, 2007, from http://scientific.thomson.com/free/ipmatters/infosearch/8228762/search_tax_class.pdf

Uschold, M., & Gruninger, M. (1996). *Ontologies: Principles, methods and applications.* Scotland, United Kingdom: University of Edinburgh.

Verity Inc. (2004). *Verity Collaborative Classifier.* Verity Inc.

Verity Inc. (2004). *Verity Intelligent Classification Guide.* Verity Inc.

ENDNOTES

1 Web page: http://ra.crema.unimi.it/
2 Web page: http://www.cyc.com
3 Web page: http://www.ontoknowledge.org
4 Web page: http://www.autonomy.com
5 Web page: http://www.stratify.com/
6 Web page: http://www.microsoft.com/office/sharepoint/prodinfo/default.mspx
7 Web page: http://www.infocious.com
8 Web page: http://www.yahoo.com
9 Web page: http://virtual.ebms.it
10 Web page: http://clusty.com/
11 Web page: http://www.altavista.com/
12 Web page: http://www.altavista.com/
13 Web page: http://www.google.it/
14 Web page: http://www.hotbot.lycos.it/
15 Web page: http://www.scirus.com/
16 Web page: http://www.bioweb.dk/

Chapter V
Towards Semantic-Based P2P Reputation Systems

Ernesto Damiani
University of Milan, Italy

Marco Viviani
University of Milan, Italy

ABSTRACT

Peer-to-peer (P2P) systems represent nowadays a large portion of Internet traffic, and are fundamental data sources. In a pure P2P system, since no peer has the power or responsibility to monitor and restrain others behaviours, there is no method to verify the trustworthiness of shared resources, and malicious peers can spread untrustworthy data objects to the system. Furthermore, data descriptions are often simple features directly connected to data or annotations based on heterogeneous schemas, a fact that makes difficult to obtain a single coherent trust value on a resource. This chapter describes techniques where the combination of Semantic Web and peer-to-peer technologies is used for expressing the knowledge shared by peers in a well-defined and formal way. Finally, dealing with Semantic-based P2P networks, the chapter suggests a research effort in this direction, where the association between cluster-based overlay networks and reputation systems based on numerical approaches seems to be promising.

INTRODUCTION

Nowadays P2P (Peer-to-Peer) systems represent a large portion of Internet traffic, and are fundamental data sources. They are characterized by their heterogeneity and their dynamic and autonomic nature. In essence, a P2P system is viewed as a distributed network system composed of participants (peers) with similar resource capabilities. In a pure P2P system, since no peer has the power or responsibility to monitor and restrain the others behaviours, there is no method to verify the trustworthiness of shared resources, and malicious peers can spread untrustworthy data objects to the system. Furthermore, data descriptions are often simple features directly connected to data or annotations based on heterogeneous schemas, a fact that makes difficult to obtain a single coherent trust value on a resource. The combination of Semantic Web and peer-to-peer technologies can be used for expressing the knowledge shared by peers in a well-defined and formal way: metadata are absolutely crucial in order to describe the resources managed by the peers. Moreover, Semantic-based peer-to-peer networks have a number of important advantages over previous simpler peer-to-peer networks. Over the years, efforts have been done to refine topologies of P2P networks, modern routing protocols like Chord (Stoica et al., 2001), CAN (Ratnasamy et al., 2001) are based on the idea of (DHT) (Distributed Hash Tables) for efficient query routing, but they not address more complex metadata sets. Only in the last few years, the Semantic-based networks --the Edutella project (Nejdl et al., 2003)--combines Semantic Web and peer-to-peer technologies in order to make distributed learning repositories possible and useful. In this chapter, we provide a brief overview of trust research field and reputation systems and we investigate in particular P2P-based ones. We describe their evolution over the years, their different topologies, and the advantages of using metadata connected to resources and Semantic-based networks in order to build Semantic-based P2P reputation systems.

TRUST AND REPUTATION SYSTEMS: AN OVERVIEW

The increasingly electronic commerce transactions, Web-based access to information, interpersonal interactions via electronic means, have led to a growing interest and study about trustworthiness of these services, since it is often hard to assess the trustworthiness of remote entities. In particular what is difficult is to collect evidence about unknown transaction partners, and that makes it hard to distinguish between high and low quality service providers in a computer network.

Trust is not a new research topic in computer science, and depending on the area where the concept of trust is used--security and access control in computer networks, reliability in distributed systems, game theory and agent systems, and policies for decision making under uncertainty--it varies in these different communities in how it is represented, computed, and used.

In this section, according in particular to (Jösang, Ismail, & Boyd, 2007) (Artz & Gil, 2007) (Ramchurn, Huynh, & Jennings, 2004) (Grandison & Sloman, 2000) we will give an overview of trust research in computer science, describing how different areas define and use trust in a variety of contexts. The various definitions of trust will be reviewed and classified, with particular reference to collaborative sanctioning systems, known as *reputation systems*.

Reasoning about Trust

Trust is a complex subject related to belief in the honesty, truthfulness, competence, reliability, and so forth, of the trusted person or service. There is no general consensus in the literature on what trust is and on what constitutes trust management, because the term trust is being used with a variety of meanings (McKnight & Chervany, 1996), but many have recognized the value of modeling and reasoning about trust computationally. In (Jösang et al., 2007) two definitions of trust are introduced: *reliability trust* and *decision trust*, respectively. The first one is introduced by means of the Gambetta definition of trust (Gambetta, 1988) as "the subjective probability by which an individual, *A*, expects that another individual, *B*, performs a given action on which its welfare depends." This definition includes the concept of *dependence* on the trusted party, and the *reliability* (probability) of the trusted party as seen by the trusting party.

However, having high (reliability) trust in a person in general is not necessarily enough to decide to enter into a situation of dependence on that person (Falcone & Castelfranchi, 2001). So Jösang et al. introduce the definition inspired by (McKnight & Chervany, 1996) where "decision trust" is "the extent to which one party is willing to depend on something or somebody in a given situation with a feeling of relative security, even though negative consequences are possible.

A definition given in (Mui, Mohtashemi, & Halberstadt, 2002), refers to past encounters, and may be thought as *reputation-based* trust, described as "a subjective expectation an agent has about another's future behaviour based on the history of their encounters."

Another formal definition given in (Grandison & Sloman, 2000), affirms that trust is "the firm belief in the competence of an entity to act dependably, securely, and reliably within a specified context" (assuming dependability covers reliability and timeliness).

The last definition we will provide, from Olmedilla et al. (Olmedilla, Rana, Matthews, & Nejdl, 2006), refers to actions and not competence like the previous one: "trust of a party A to a party B for a service X is the measurable belief of A in that B behaves dependably for a specified period within a specified context (in relation to service X)."

As shown by previous definitions, trust is a composition of many different attributes: reliability, dependability, honesty, truthfulness, security, competence, timeliness, risk. Depending on the environment in which we are operating, the suitable definition of trust for that environment can comprise different sets of attributes.

Modeling Trust

Definitions of trust given in the previous section, and its context-dependent attributes, show to us that trust is a fundamental concept in distributed systems (where individual components interact to achieve some overall objective).[a] In this kind of systems (open and large scale) trust can be explicitly represented and reasoned about by the components in the system, that can be modeled as an *open multi-agent system* that is composed of autonomous *agents* that interact with one another using particular mechanisms and protocols (Ramchurn et al., 2004). Two common ways of determining trust are through using (*i*) *policies* or (*ii*) *reputation* (Bonatti & Olmedilla, 2005). The definitions of "hard evidence" used in policies opposed to the estimation of trust used in reputation systems, as appear in (Artz & Gil, 2007), reflect the difference between the term *hard security* used for traditional mechanisms like authentication and access control, and *soft security* for social control mechanisms in general, of which trust and reputation systems are examples. The difference between these two approaches was first described in (Rasmusson & Jansson, 1996).

Policies describe the conditions necessary to obtain trust, and can also prescribe actions and outcomes if certain conditions are met. Policies frequently involve the exchange or verification of credentials, which are information issued (and sometimes endorsed using a digital signature) by one entity, and may describe qualities or features of another entity. In this field, the terms authorization and authentication are often connected to trust. *Authorization* can be seen as the outcome of the refinement of a more abstract trust relationship. We define authorization as a policy decision assigning access control rights for a subject to perform specific actions on a specific target with defined constraints. *Authentication* is the verification of an identity of an entity, which may be performed by means of a password, a trusted authentication service, or using certificates. There is then an issue of the degree of trust in the entity that issued the certificate. Note that authorization may not be necessarily specified in terms of an identity. Anonymous authorization can be implemented using capabilities or certificates.

Reputation is an assessment based on the history of interactions with or observations of an entity, either directly with the evaluator (personal experience) or as reported by others (recommendations or third party verification).

How these histories are combined can vary, and recursive problems of trust can occur when using information from others (i.e., can I trust an entity's recommendation about another entity?).

At a basic level, both credentials and reputation involve the transfer of trust from one entity to another, but each approach has its own unique problems which have motivated much of the existing work in trust.

Reputation-Based Trust

After having briefly analyzed in the previous sections the areas where the concept of trust can be investigated, now our attention will be specially focused on trust in reputation-based models. Nowadays, the study and modeling of reputation have attracted the interest of scientists from different fields (Mui et al., 2002, Sabater & Sierra, 2002) such as: sociology, economics, psychology, and computer science. In a multi-agent system, reputation refers to a perception that an agent has of another's intentions.

The computational models of reputation consider different sources: the direct interactions, the information provided by other members of the society about experiences they had in the past (Sabater & Sierra, 2001; Zacharia, Moukas, & Maes, 2000), and the different types of social relations among their members (Sabater & Sierra, 2002).

The concept of *reputation* is closely linked to the one of trustworthiness (Jösang et al., 2007), it refers to a perception that an agent has of another's intentions and norms (Mui et al., 2002). It is very relevant to systems where there is information asymmetry about quality and trust, due to the large number of players involved and their anonymity/pseudonymity.

Reputation can be considered as a *collective measure of trustworthiness* (in the sense of reliability) based on the *referrals* or *ratings* from members in a community; it is a *social* notion generally built by combining trust assessments given by a group or agents to obtain a single value representing an estimate of reputation.

Computing Trust

Trust scores can be computed based on own experience (normally considered more reliable than public information such as ratings from third parties), on second hand referrals, or on a combination of both. As introduced before, reputation can be defined as a measure of trust, and each entity maintains reputation information on other entities. A trust decision can be a transitive process; a party who relies on the reputation score of some remote party is in fact trusting that party through trust transitivity (Jösang & Pope, 2005).

Marsh was the first, in his doctorate thesis (Marsh, 1994), to introduce a computational model for trust. His model is quite simple, based on a scalar value of trust, and does not discuss reputation. Over the years, other several methods for computing trust have been proposed. This section, according to (Griffiths, 2005; Jösang et al., 2007;), shortly describes various principles for trust computation.

Numerical/Threshold-Based Models

They are the most commonly used when agents represent the trustworthiness of others in numeric intervals, typically [-1, +1] or [0, 1]. The lower bound corresponds to complete distrust and the upper bound to blind trust. The numerical value representing the reputation of an agent is updated by some function after each interaction, and usually these methods tend to use a threshold to define different levels of trustworthiness.

The eBay.com reputation system, for example, sums the number of positive ratings and negative ratings separately, and keeps the total score as the positive score minus the negative one. Amazon.com, Epinions.com and other auction sites feature reputation systems like eBay's, with variations such as a rating scale from 1 – 5, use slightly more advance schemes, or several measures (friendliness, prompt response, quality product, etc.).

Probabilistic Models

They are a subset of numerical approaches in which trust is represented in the interval [0, 1] and this number represents a probability with a clear semantics associated with it. Among many probabilistic approaches there are those based on Bayesian probability distributions.

Bayesian systems take binary ratings as input and are based on computing reputation scores by statistical updating of beta PDF (Probability Density Functions). They are particularly used in *recommender systems* (Adomavicius & Tuzhilin, 2005).

Belief Models

Belief theory is a framework related to probability theory, but where the sum of beliefs over all possible outcomes does not necessarily add up to one. The missing part is interpreted as uncertainty. In Yu & Singh (2002) the authors have proposed to use belief theory to represent reputation scores: the ratings provided by individual agents are belief measures determined as a function of an agent's past history of behaviours with individual agents as trustworthy or not trustworthy using predefined threshold values for what constitutes trustworthy and untrustworthy behaviour.

Discrete Trust Models

They rely on human verbal statements to rate assertions (Ex. *Very Trustworthy, Trustworthy, Untrustworthy, Very Untrustworthy*) (Abdul-Rahman & Hailes, 2000). Using discrete measures, they have the disadvantage that it is not simple to use computational principles that are substituted by heuristic mechanisms.

Fuzzy Models

In these kinds of models linguistic variables are used to represent trust; in this case, membership functions describe to what degree an assertion can be described as trustworthy or not trustworthy.

In (Falcone & Castelfranchi, 2001) *Fuzzy Cognitive Maps* (FCM) (Kosko, 1986) are used to model the relevance of the system inputs before their aggregation.

A distinct approach was taken by the REGRET system (Sabater & Sierra, 2001; Sabater & Sierra, 2002), where fuzzy concepts are integrated into the analysis of social networks in electronic marketplaces.

In (Aringhieri et al., 2006) fuzzy aggregation operators have been used for the synthesis of opinions expressed by peers in a P2P distributed reputation system. The behaviour of fuzzy aggregation was assessed by comparison with other approaches like Eigentrust (Kamvar, Schlosser, & Garcia-Molina, 2003).

In Griffiths (2006) the author proposes the notion of undistrust and incorporates it in his system based on flexible fuzzy rules: they are specifiable by a system designer, and agents are able to scale inputs according to their current preferences regarding the relative importance of the trust dimensions.

Flow Models

Flow models are called those systems that compute trust or reputation by transitive iteration through looped or arbitrarily long chains. Examples of flow models are the PageRank (Brin & Page, 1998) algorithm used by Google (ranking a page according to how many other pages are pointing at it) and the Advogato's reputation scheme (Levien, 1995) (where members rank each other according to how skilled they perceive each other to be using Advogato's trust scheme, essentially a centralized reputation system based on the flow model).

Reputation Network Architectures

In a reputation system, how ratings and reputation scores are communicated among participants determines the *network architecture*. The two main types are *centralized* and *distributed* architectures.

Centralized Reputation Systems

Information is collected as ratings from members in the community in *centralized reputation systems*. A *central authority* collects all the ratings (*reputation centre*) and typically derives a reputation score for every participant and makes all scores publicly available.

Participants can then use each other's scores (for example when deciding whether or not to transact with a particular party). Ratings from all the agents are collected by the reputation centre that continuously updates each agent's reputation score as a function of the received ratings. Updated reputation scores are provided online for all the agents to see, and can be used by the agents to decide whether or not to transact with a particular agent.

Distributed Reputation Systems

Scores are not submitted to a central location in a *distributed reputation system* for obtaining reputation scores of others. Instead, there can be distributed stores where ratings can be submitted, or each participant simply records the opinion about each experience with other parties and provides this information on request from relying parties. A relying party who considers transacting with a given target party must find the distributed stores, or try to obtain ratings from as many community members as possible who have had any experience with that target party.

The relying party computes the reputation score based on the received ratings. In case the relying party has had direct experience with the target party, the experience from that encounter can be taken into account as private information, possibly carrying a higher weight than the received ratings.

In a distributed environment, every participant is responsible for collecting and combining ratings from other participants. Because of the distributed environment it is often impossible or too costly to obtain ratings resulting from all interactions with a given agent. Instead the reputation score is based on a subset of ratings, usually from the relying party's "neighbourhood."

Peer-to-Peer Environments

Peer-to-peer networks represent nowadays an environment well suited for distributed reputation management. In P2P networks, every node plays the role of both client and server, and is therefore sometimes called a *servent*. This allows the users to overcome their passive role typical of Web navigation, and to engage in an active role by providing their own resources.

In the wake of the *PageRank* algorithm (Brin & Page, 1998) for ranking Web sites by authority, the *EigenTrust* algorithm (Kamvar et al., 2003) computes a global reputation value (using PageRank) for each entity. Reputation in this work is the quality of a peer's uploads within a peer-to-peer network.

The *P2PRep* system (Cornelli et al., 2002) gives protocols and an algorithm for sharing reputation information with peers in a peer-to-peer network. This work also uses the idea of referral trust in its approach.

The Aberer and Despotovic (2001) approach uses statistical analysis to characterize trust and reputation so that the computation remains scalable.

Embracing qualities of a peer-to-peer network to provide a more robust method of reputation management, Damiani et al. (2002) present the *XRep* protocol, which allows for an automatic vote using user's feedback for the best host for a given resource.

In Olmedilla et al. (2006) the authors describe the requirements in supporting trust in "virtual organizations of shared resources," discuss the limitations of existing work on trust in the context of grid computing, and argue that semantic representations can address the requirements outlined.

P2P SYSTEMS: AN OVERVIEW

The term "peer-to-peer" refers to a class of systems and applications that employ distributed resources to perform a function in a decentralized manner. Some of the benefits of a P2P approach include: improving scalability by avoiding dependency on centralized points; eliminating the need for costly infrastructure by enabling direct communication among clients; and enabling resource aggregation.

P2P is frequently confused with other terms, such as traditional distributed computing (Coulouris & Dollimore, 1988), grid computing (Foster & Kesselman, 1998), and ad-hoc networking (Perkins, 2001). To better define P2P, in the next sections we will introduce the comparisons between P2P and its alternatives, and P2P goals, terminology, and taxonomies.

A Taxonomy of Computer Systems

A taxonomy of computer systems based on topology classifies them into *centralized* and *distributed* systems (Milojicic et al., 2003).

Centralized systems represent single-unit solutions, including single- and multi-processor machines, as well as high-end machines, such as supercomputers and mainframes.

Distributed systems are those in which components located at networked computers com-

Figure 1. A taxonomy of computer systems architectures

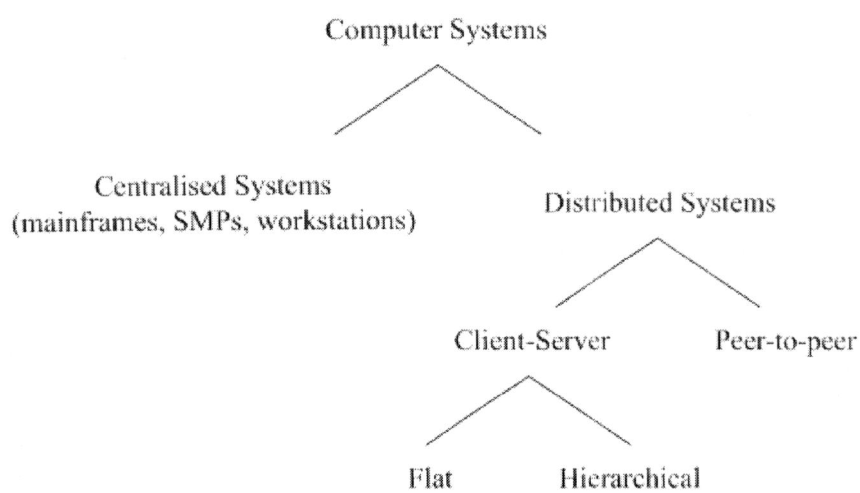

municate and coordinate their actions only by passing messages (Coulouris & Dollimore, 1988). Distributed systems can be further classified into the *client-server* model and the *peer-to-peer* model.

Client-Server model[b] represents the execution of entities with the roles of clients and servers. Any entity in a system can play both roles but for a different purpose, that is, server and client functionality residing on separate nodes. Similarly, an entity can be a server for one kind of request and client for others.

The client-server model can be *flat* or *hierarchical*. In the flat model, all clients communicate with a single server, while in the hierarchical model the servers of one level are acting as clients to higher level servers.

P2P model[c] enables peers to share their resources (information, processing, presence, etc.) with at most a limited interaction with a centralized server. Peers may have to handle a limited connectivity (wireless, unreliable modem links, etc.), support possibly independent naming, and be able to share the role of the server (Oram, 2001). It is equivalent to having all entities being clients and servers for the same purpose.

A Taxonomy of Peer-to-Peer Systems

One possible classification of peer-to-peer networks is according to their degree of centralization (Yang & Garcia-Molina, 2003). The peer-to-peer model can be *pure*, *hybrid* or *super-peer*.

In *pure peer-to-peer systems*, such as Gnutella (http://www.gnutella.com) and Freenet (http://www.freenet.com), a centralized server does not exist, but all peers have equal roles and responsibilities.

In a *hybrid model,* such as Napster (http://free.napster.com/), a centralized server and clients exist: search is performed on a centralized directory, but download still occurs in a P2P fashion – hence, peers are equal in download only.

The *super-peer model* is an intermediate solution, in which super-peer nodes act like peers of pure peer-to-peer systems, but also they are connected with clients in a centralized way (such as KaZaA (http://www.kazaa.com), one of the most popular file-sharing system today).

Pure P2P Networks

In pure peer-to-peer systems, all peers are equivalent: they have the same role and responsibilities. A centralized server and clients do not exist; on the contrary, each peer is both a server and a client: it is a *servent*. All nodes have the same responsibilities in terms of publish, download, query and communicate with any other connected node.

The Gnutella network belongs to the category of pure peer-to-peer systems. By means of its protocol, users are able to search for and retrieve files from other users connected to Internet using a *flooding* protocol.

Hybrid P2P Networks

In hybrid peer-to-peer systems there is distinction among peers. Peers are not equivalent; they have different roles and responsibilities. In a hybrid peer-to-peer model there are one or several index servers and clients that are directly connected to a server. A server obtains meta-information, such as the identity of the peers on which some information is stored. Client peers connect to a server to publish information about the contents they offer for sharing and to search for files. A popular hybrid peer-to-peer system is Napster.

Super-Peer P2P Networks

The super-peer peer-to-peer model represents an intermediate solution between pure and hybrid peer-to-peer models. A *super-peer* is a node of the network that acts as a server to a subset of clients and it is also equivalent to other peers in a network that consists only of super-peers. The query process is more efficient than the one in Gnutella, because in Gnutella all peers of the network should handle queries, unlike in super-peer networks only super-peers handle this process. Client-peers are connected to a super-peer, in a client-server way and they send their requests to it.

KaZaA is a well-known super-peer system; it is another file sharing system that is used to exchange multimedia files. It uses the FastTrack protocol *(http://developer.berlios.de/projects/gift-fasttrack/).*

P2P Overlay Networks

As introduced in the previous sections, P2P networks are an efficient mechanism for sharing information among large numbers of users. However, query processing still remains in current P2P systems quite inefficient, because most of these systems create a random *application-level overlay network*[d]. The P2P overlay network consists of all the participating peers as network nodes. The search technique functionalities rely on the underlying P2P overlay infrastructure.

Based on how nodes are linked to each other in the overlay network, we can classify P2P networks as *unstructured* or *structured.*

Unstructured P2P Overlay Networks

Unstructured P2P overlay networks organize peers in a random graph that may be flat and all participant peers have the same functionalities, or hierarchical using super peers that have additional functionalities for special purposes. Current search techniques in unstructured P2P overlay networks can be categorized as *blind* or *informed techniques.* In a blind search, peers have no information about object locations, while the informed search uses a central or distributed index service containing related information to object locations to manage the search process.

Structured P2P Overlay Networks

In structured P2P overlay networks, the topology is tightly controlled and contents are placed not at random peers but at specified locations that will make subsequent queries more efficient.

Such structured P2P systems use the *Distributed Hash Table* (DHT) (Balakrishnan et al., 2003; Castro et al., 2002; Keong Lua et al., 2005) as a substrate, in which data object (or value) location information is placed deterministically, at the peers with identifiers corresponding to the data object's unique *key*, making it easier to locate content later on.

DHT-based systems have a property that consistently assigns uniform random *NodeIDs* to the set of peers. Data objects are assigned unique identifiers called *keys*, chosen from the same identifier space. Keys are mapped by the overlay network protocol to a unique live peer in the overlay network. P2P overlay networks support the scalable storage and retrieval of {*key*, *value*} pairs on the overlay network. Given a key, a store operation (*put*(*key*, *value*)) and a lookup retrieval operation (*value* = *get*(*key*)) can be invoked to store and retrieve the data object corresponding to the key, which involves routing requests to the peer corresponding to the key. Each peer maintains a small routing table consisting of its neighbouring peers' *NodeIDs* and IP addresses. Lookup queries or message routing are forwarded across overlay paths to peers in a progressive manner, with the *NodeIDs* that are closer to the key in the identifier space.

Different DHT-based systems will have different organization schemes for data objects and key space and routing strategies.

In this way, the DHT-based search technique used by structured networks is efficient for exact match queries, but cannot be easily extended to key with approximate values. Furthermore, in general, nodes may not be willing to accept arbitrary content nor arbitrary connections from others.

Well-known protocols implementing the DHT abstraction, are Chord (Stoica et al., 2001), Pastry (Rowstron & Druschel, 2001), Tapestry (Zhao et al., 2004), Kademlia (Maymounkov & Mazières, 2002) and CAN (Ratnasamy et al., 2001).

A key difference in the algorithms is the data structure that they use as a routing table. Chord maintains a data structure that resembles a *skiplist*.

Each node in Kademlia, Pastry, and Tapestry maintains a *tree-like* data structure. CAN uses a *d*-dimensional Cartesian coordinate space to implement the DHT abstraction. The coordinate space is partitioned into *hyper-rectangles*, called *zones*.

THE USE OF SEMANTICS IN P2P NETWORKS

In the last years, in order to solve the problem of the scalability of P2P designs connected to unstructured systems, and the problem of the impoverished query languages connected to structured ones, several hybrid techniques has been proposed. In Harren et al. (2002) for example, the authors outline a research agenda for building complex query facilities on top of DHT-based P2P systems.

These techniques combine the characteristics of structured overlay networks and/or super-peer networks to provide an efficient similarity search in P2P networks organizing data in *feature spaces*, describing their content to provide an efficient processing of complex queries and organizing peers in the same feature spaces to limit the flooding overhead over the network.

Li et al. in (2004) present the design of an overlay network, namely *SSW (Semantic Small World)*, that facilitates an efficient Semantic-based search in P2P systems. This overlay network, during peer joins and leaves, dynamically groups peers with semantically similar data closer to each other and maps these clusters in a high-dimensional *semantic space* into a one-dimensional small world network that has an attractive trade-off between search path length and maintenance costs. Further, SSW dynamically updates the overlay to take advantage of query locality and data distribution characteristics.

In Hu, Ardon, & Sereviratne (2004) the authors proposed a service directory that groups service entities of the same category together; this is achieved by dedicating part of the node identifiers to correspond to their service category semantic. Using *Chord* as the peer-to-peer substrate, this scheme logically divides the Chord circle into equidistant arcs; each arc is called an *island*. This scheme will result in the formation of islands of varying population, and thus changing the uniformly spread topology of the original Chord. Simulations are used to investigate the path length and message load of the changed topology. An additional routing scheme is also proposed and simulated to exploit the new topology to gain better path length.

PARIS (Comito, Patarin, & Talia, 2006) proposes an integrated approach in which semantic data integration, based on schema mapping, and peer-to-peer topology are tightly bound to each other. In PARIS, the combination of decentralized semantic data integration with gossip-based (unstructured) overlay topology management and (structured) distributed hash tables provides the required level of flexibility, adaptability and scalability, and still allows one to perform rich queries on a number of autonomous data sources. PARIS uses a hybrid topology that mixes structured and unstructured overlays. More precisely, *local groups* are organized in *unstructured overlays*, while *peers* are also part of a *DHT*. All peers in the same local group share the same schema, and all peers with the same schema are in the same group. In parallel, peers also participate in a DHT. From the way authors construct peer identifiers (i.e., prefixed by the schema identifier), all peers sharing the same schema will be contiguous in the identifier space. In the paper authors make use of the routing interface of the DHT, ignoring its storage capacities. They use Chord to implement this DHT.

Cluster-Based P2P Networks

According to Kacimi et al. (2005), P2P networks taking into consideration the content similarity among peers and using clustering techniques involving the creation of links on top of the unstructured P2P overlay network to group peers with similar content are called *cluster-based P2P networks*. They impose a *graph structure* on the underlying overlay, obtained capturing and exploiting *context-based* or *content-based* proximity among peers.

Context-Based Clustering

Peers in a P2P network can be clustered according to different context-based information, such as IP address, network distance, application needs, and so forth.

Krishnamurthy et al. (2001) define a cluster-based P2P architecture, called CAP (Cluster-based Architecture for P2P), by assigning peers which share IP address prefixes to the same cluster.

In the same way in Bestavros & Mehrotra (2001) authors use DNS (Domain Name Server) information to group Web clients served by the same DNS.

In Löser et al. (2003), the authors use static or dynamic peer properties, where static properties can be a query or result schema or IP domain shared by the member peers, while dynamic properties can be the types and number of resources of a peer.

Content-Based Clustering

Content-based clustering exploits similarities among the resources held by peers, evaluating semantic descriptions associated with peers (keyword-based annotations, schema or ontologies) or low level features.

In Crespo & Garcia-Molina (2002) *SONs (Semantic Overlay Networks)* are proposed, that is, a flexible network organization that improves query performance while maintaining a high degree of node autonomy. With SON, nodes with semantically similar content are clustered together. In a SON system, queries are processed by identifying which SON (or SONs) are better suited to answer it. Then the query is sent to a node in those SONs and the query is forwarded only to the other members of that SON.

In Nejdl et al. (2003) the use of a *super-peer topology* for schema-based networks is suggested: each peer connects to one super-peer only. A super-peer then connects to other super-peers and builds up the backbone of the super-peer network (Figure 2).

In schema-based networks, super-peers manage routing indices and determine which query is forwarded to which peer or to which super-peer.

The concept of *SOC (Semantic Overlay Clusters)* for super-peer networks enabling a controlled distribution of peers to clusters is introduced in Löser et al. (2003). In a super-peer network, a set of clients together with their super-peer form a cluster. Intra-cluster data communication takes place via direct peer-to-peer links among clients, and inter-cluster communication takes place via links among super-peers. So far all the above described methods do not illustrate the cluster structure semantically. For enabling SOC as logical layers above the physical network topology we need a clustering method suitable to match semantically information provider peers to super-peer based clusters. Similar to the definition for Semantic overlay networks by Crespo & Garcia-Molina (2002) the authors assume existing information provider peers and existing super-peers as nodes in a physical network. Both can exchange messages within the network.

Figure 2. Peers connected to the super-peer backbone

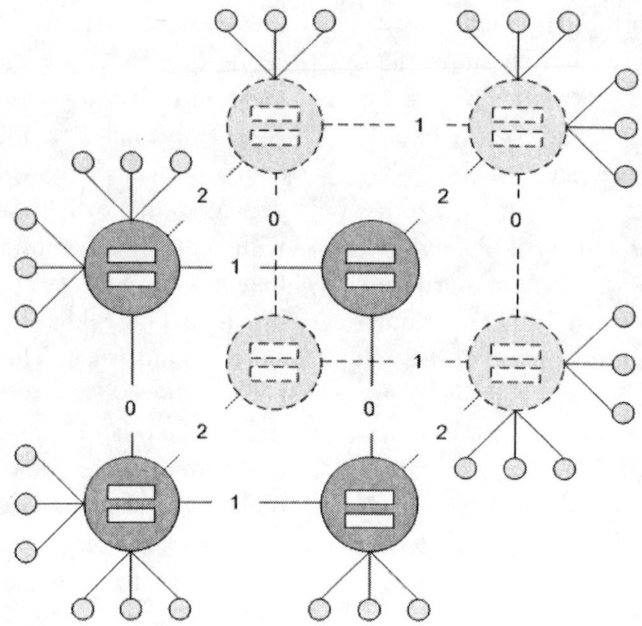

The Piazza project (Tatarinov et al., 2003) is a PDMS (Peer Data Management System) aimed at sharing semantically heterogeneous data and schemas. Clusters are built by creating mappings among semantically similar peers.

HON-P2P is a Hybrid Overlay Network P2P architecture described in (Kacimi et al., 2005) for sharing multimedia content. Using low level feature-based and semantic characteristics, peers are grouped in clusters based on the similarity of their contents. The architecture allows two types of structured overlays: *semantic overlays* (based on ontologies or concept classification hierarchies) and *feature-based overlays* (built on multimedia content features).

The cluster architecture is a two level hierarchy consisting of super peers (responsible for the cluster management) and simple peers. A peer can join different clusters in different overlays.

PeerCluster (Huang & Chang, 2006) is a cluster-based peer-to-peer system, for sharing data over Internet. It logically groups the computers of users/computers interested in similar topics (*interest clusters*), increasing the query efficiency. Intra-cluster and inter-cluster broadcasting are the two major operations used to resolve queries, over a *hypercube topology* used to carry out the system.

CONCLUSIONS AND FURTHER RESEARCH

Several methods have been proposed to manage trust, in particular in unstructured systems. These ones are not suitable for efficiently querying and retrieving information among entities, especially in presence of decentralized systems as P2P ones.

Today P2P is one of the most widespread and realistic model to exchange data and/or information among agents belonging to a network. So, over the years, structured overlay networks have been developed in order to improve efficiency in P2P systems.

Different methods have been offered to compute trustworthiness making use of DHT-based (or structure-based) techniques (Lee, Kwon, Kim, & Hong, 2005) (Zhou & Hwang, 2006). In Fedotova, Bertucci, & Veltri (2007), the authors analyzed the possibility of applying these techniques in Trust and Reputation environments. In all these cases, the application of structured-based models has the aim of providing fast trust aggregation and secure message transmission, exploiting the self-organization properties of these techniques in the process of peer join and leave.

In the above described techniques, semantics plays an irrelevant role in the computation of reputation values, due to the fact that pure DHT techniques organize peers and data in a keyword-based manner, supporting only exact match queries based on key-based searches. Compared with other techniques for computing trust in unstructured P2P systems, DHT-based ones have the already mentioned advantages of efficiency.

New and different techniques have been developed in order to take into consideration semantics connected to data in the construction of a "semantic overlay network," in particular to enrich P2P systems by the employment of *content/semantic-based searches*.

Up to this time, none of these techniques have been used to enrich Trust & Reputation Systems with semantics, while we think it could be extremely promising the use of numeric approaches for computing reputation values (Ceravolo, Damiani, & Viviani, 2006;

Damiani et al.,2006; Damiani, Ceravolo, & Viviani, 2007) in association with semantic-based P2P networks, in particular the ones based on clustering techniques.

Towards Cluster-Based P2P Reputation Systems

Cluster-based P2P networks, using an overlay network on top of the unstructured P2P one, organize peers in *clusters* by the analysis of their common properties or interests. Over the years reputation has been used in particular to estimate the trustworthiness of servents, so it could be possible to organize peers in clusters based on low-level peer characteristics (Löser et al., 2003), but it is becoming clearer and clearer that in a dynamic scenario servent reputation is insufficient to reduce malicious behaviours. Both servent and *resource* reputation must be used in modern P2P reputation systems. So, dealing with cluster-based ones, peers have to be organized in groups considering similarity among their contents (Crespo & Garcia-Molina, 2002; Jin et al., 2005; Löser et al., 2003; Nejdl et al., 2003). This researches associate peers with a semantic description based on keyword-based annotations, schema or ontologies.

Cluster-based P2P systems have been studied in order to limit the scope of flooding to members of a cluster. It is our opinion that, having at our disposal such a peer and data organization, an improved query processing it is not the only advantage we can obtain.

At this level we are not interested in the underlying architecture that supports and maintains the cluster-based structure; it can be obtained by the use of a DHT-technique, a super-peer network and so on. What we are interested in is that, regardless of the chosen typology, it is possible to obtain and maintain (semantic) *distances* between peers and data, in order to take into consideration this piece of information during the process of reputation computation.

In a "classic" unstructured P2P Reputation System, each node in the worst case has to evaluate the level of trustworthiness of every other node in the network. In our hypothesis nodes belonging to the same cluster are semantically closer,

Figure 3. A cluster-based overlay network on top of the underlying P2P network

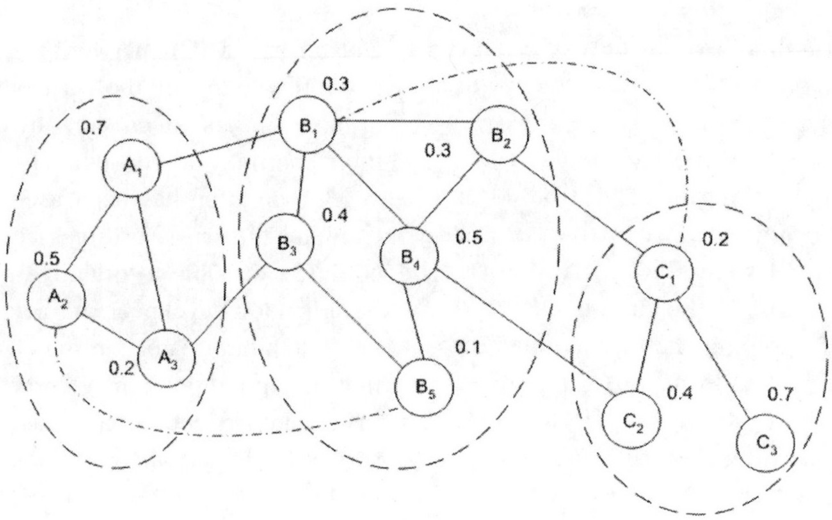

and have the possibility to express a meaningful judgment on their neighbours. The concept of *distance* between the given resource, who asks for it, and the entity providing a judgment on that resource, become fundamental in such a scenario. Other possible information about the trustworthiness of a peer or a resource is obviously taken into consideration in the process of aggregation of trust values, for example as illustrated in (Damiani et al., 2007).

Figure 3 shows a possible clustering configuration in a Semantic-based network. For the sake of simplicity, here we will not explain the clustering process and the feature selection phase; we will only show the final scenario, where peers have been divided according to their semantically closeness, and the numbers associated to them indicate the trust value of nodes. Each peer maintains a table where the list of its resources is maintained and updated: for each resource is stored its reputation value and foreign indexes (dashed line between B_1 and C_1 for example) are maintained to indicate that a resource physically stored in a peer belonging to a certain cluster, would be semantically belonging to another one.

In the aggregation phase among trustworthiness values, several aggregation operators can be considered; we suggested in Damiani et al. (2006) the WOWA aggregation operator (Torra, 1997) because of its properties, but it is our purpose the study of other ones, exploiting the possibility to take into account in the aggregation process the semantic distance among peers and resources.

REFERENCES

Abdul-Rahman, A., & Hailes, S. (2000). Supporting trust in virtual communities. In *Hicss '00: Proceedings of the 33rd hawaii international conference on system sciences-volume 6* (p. 6007). Washington, DC, USA: IEEE Computer Society.

Aberer, K., & Despotovic, Z. (2001). Managing trust in a peer-2-peer information system. In *Cikm '01: Proceedings of the tenth international conference on information and knowledge management* (pp. 310-317). New York, NY, USA: ACM Press.

Adomavicius, G., & Tuzhilin, A. (2005, June). Toward the next generation of recommender systems: A survey of the state-of-the-art and possible extensions. *IEEE Transactions on Knowledge and Data Engineering, 17* (6), 734-749.

Aringhieri, R., Damiani, E., De Capitani di Vimercati, S., Paraboschi, S., & Samarati, P. (2006). Fuzzy techniques for trust and reputation management in anonymous peer-to-peer systems: Special topic section on soft approaches to information retrieval and information access on the web. *Journal of the American Society for Information Science and Technology (JASIST), 57* (4), 528-537.

Artz, D., & Gil, Y. (2007). *A survey of trust in computer science and the semantic web.* (To appear in Journal of Web Semantics, 2007).

Balakrishnan, H., Kaashoek, F. M., Karger, D., Morris, R., & Stoica, I. (2003, February). Looking up data in P2P systems. *Commun. ACM, 46* (2), 43-48.

Bestavros, A., & Mehrotra, S. (2001). *DNS-based internet client clustering and characterization* (Tech. Rep.). Boston, MA, USA: Boston University.

Bonatti, P., & Olmedilla, D. (2005). Driving and monitoring provisional trust negotiation with metapolicies. In *Proceedings of the 6th IEEE International Workshop on Policies for Distributed Systems and Networks (POLICY'05)* (pp. 14-23). Washington, DC, USA: IEEE Computer Society.

Brin, S., & Page, L. (1998). The anatomy of a large-scale hypertextual web search engine. In *Proceedings of the 7th Iinternational Conference on World Wide Web 7 (Www7)* (pp. 107-117). Amsterdam, The Netherlands: Elsevier Science Publishers B. V.

Castro, M., Druschel, P., Hu, Y. C., & Rowstron, A. (2002). *Topology-aware routing in structured peer-to-peer overlay networks* (Tech. Rep. No. MSR-TR-2002-82). Microsoft Research, One Microsoft Way.

Ceravolo, P., Damiani, E., & Viviani, M. (2006). Adding a trust layer to Semantic Web metadata. In F. C. Enrique Herrera-Viedma Gabriella Pasi (Ed.), *Soft computing in web information retrieval: models and applications* (Vol. 197). New York, NY, USA: Springer.

Comito, C., Patarin, S., & Talia, D. (2006). A semantic overlay network for p2p schema-based data integration. In *Proceedings of the 11th IEEE symposium on computers and communications (ISCC '06)* (pp. 88-94). Washington, DC, USA: IEEE Computer Society.

Cornelli, F., Damiani, E., Vimercati, S. D. C. di, Paraboschi, S., & Samarati, P. (2002). Choosing reputable servents in a p2p network. In*: Proceedings of the 11th international conference on world wide web (Www '02)* (pp. 376-386). New York, NY, USA: ACM Press.

Coulouris, G. F., & Dollimore, J. (1988). *Distributed systems: concepts and design.* Boston, MA, USA: Addison-Wesley Longman Publishing Co., Inc.

Crespo, A., & Garcia-Molina, H. (2002). *Semantic overlay networks for P2P systems* (Tech. Rep.). Computer Science Department, Stanford University.

Damiani, E., Ceravolo, P., & Viviani, M. (2007). Bottom-up extraction and trust-based refinement of ontology metadata. *IEEE Transactions on Knowledge and Data Engineering, 19* (2), 149-163.

Damiani, E., De Capitani di Vimercati, S., Samarati, P., & Viviani, M. (2006). A WOWA-based aggregation technique on trust values connected to metadata. *Electronic Notes in Theoretical Computer Science*, *157* (3), 131-142.

Damiani, E., Vimercati, De Capitani di Vimercati, S, Paraboschi, S., Samarati, P., & Violante, F. (2002). A reputation-based approach for choosing reliable resources in peer-to-peer networks. In *Proceedings of the 9th ACM conference on computer and communications security (CCS '02)* (pp. 207-216). New York, NY, USA: ACM Press.

Falcone, R., & Castelfranchi, C. (2001). Social trust: A cognitive approach. In *Trust and deception in virtual societies* (pp. 55-90). Norwell, MA, USA: Kluwer Academic Publishers.

Fedotova, N., Bertucci, M., & Veltri, L. (2007). Reputation management techniques in dht-based peer-to-peer networks. *Second International Conference on Internet and Web Applications and Services (ICIW'07).*

Foster, I., & Kesselman, C. (1998). *The grid: Blueprint for a new computing infrastructure.* San Francisco, CA, USA: Morgan Kaufmann Publishers Inc.

Gambetta, D. (1988). Can we trust trust? In *Trust: Making and breaking cooperative relations.* Basil Blackwell. (Reprinted in electronic edition from Department of Sociology, University of Oxford, chapter 13, pp. 213-237).

Grandison, T., & Sloman, M. (2000, September). A Survey of Trust in Internet Applications. *IEEE Communications Surveys and Tutorials, 3* (4). (http://www.comsoc.org/livepubs/surveys/public/2000/dec/index.html)

Griffiths, N. (2005). Trust: Challenges and opportunities. In *Agentlink News, 19*, 9-11.

Griffiths, N. (2006, September 11-13). A fuzzy approach to reasoning with trust, distrust and insufficient trust. In M. Klusch, M. Rovatsos, & T. R. Payne (Eds.), In *Proceedings of the Cooperative information agents x, 10th International Workshop, cia2006,* Edinburgh, UK (p. pp. 360-374). Springer.

Harren, M., Hellerstein, J. M., Huebsch, R., Loo, B. T., Shenker, S., & Stoica, I. (2002). Complex queries in DHT-based Peer-to-Peer Networks. In *Revised papers from the first international workshop on peer-to-peer systems (Iptps '01)* (pp. 242-259). London, UK: Springer-Verlag.

Hu, T. H. ting, Ardon, S., & Sereviratne, A. (2004). Semantic-laden peer-to-peer service directory. In *Proceedings of the 4th International Conference on Peer-toPpeer Computing (P2p '04)* (pp. 184-191). Washington, DC, USA: IEEE Computer Society.

Huang, X.-M., & Chang, C.-Y. (2006). PeerCluster: A cluster-based peer-to-peer system. *IEEE Trans. Parallel Distrib. Syst., 17* (10), 1110-1123.

Jin, S., Park, C., Choi, D., Chung, K., & Yoon, H. (2005). Cluster-based trust evaluation scheme in an ad hoc network. *ETRI Journal, 27* (4), 465-468.

Jösang, A., Ismail, R., & Boyd, C. (2007). A survey of trust and reputation systems for online service provision. *Decis. Support Syst., 43* (2), 618-644.

Jösang, A., & Pope, S. (2005). Semantic constraints for trust transitivity. In *Proceedings of the 2nd asia-pacific conference on conceptual modelling (Apccm '05):* (pp. 59-68). Darlinghurst, Australia: Australian Computer Society, Inc.

Kacimi, M., Yetongnon, K., Ma, Y., & Chbeir, R. (2005). HON-P2P: A Cluster-based Hybrid Overlay Network for Multimedia Object Management. In *Proceedings of the 11th international conference on parallel and distributed systems (Icpads'05)* (pp. 578-584). Washington, DC, USA: IEEE Computer Society.

Kamvar, S. D., Schlosser, M. T., & Garcia-Molina, H. (2003). The EigenTrust algorithm for reputation management in P2P networks. In *Proceedings of the 12th international conference on world wide web (Www'03)* (pp. 640-651). New York, NY, USA: ACM Press.

Keong Lua, E., Crowcroft, J., Pias, M., Sharma, R., & Lim, S. (2005). A survey and comparison of peer-to-peer overlay network schemes. *Communications Surveys & Tutorials, IEEE*, 72-93.

Kosko, B. (1986). Fuzzy Cognitive Maps. *International Journal of Man-Machine Studies, 24* (1), 65-75.

Krishnamurthy, B., Wang, J., & Xie, Y. (2001). Early measurements of a cluster-based architecture for p2p systems. In *Proceedings of the 1st acm sigcomm workshop on internet measurement (Imw '01)* (pp. 105-109). New York, NY, USA: ACM Press.

Lee, S. Y., Kwon, O.-H., Kim, J., & Hong, S. J. (2005). A reputation management system in structured peer-to-peer networks. In *Proceedings of the 14th IEEE international workshops on enabling technologies: Infrastructure for collaborative enterprise (Wetice'05)* (pp. 362-367). Washington, DC, USA: IEEE Computer Society.

Levien, R. L. (1995). *Attack resistant trust metrics.* Unpublished doctoral dissertation, University of California at Berkeley.

Li, M., Lee, W.-C., & Sivasubramaniam, A. (2004). Semantic small world: An overlay network for peer-to-peer search. In *Proceedings of the Network Protocols, 12th IEEE international conference on (Icnp'04)* (pp. 228{238). Washington, DC, USA: IEEE Computer Society.

Löser, A., Naumann, F., Siberski, W., Nejdl, W., & Thaden, U. (2003). Semantic overlay clusters within super-peer networks. In K. Aberer, V. Kalogeraki, & M. Koubarakis (Eds.), *Databases, information systems, and peer-to-peer computing, first international workshop, dbisp2p, Berlin, Germany, September 7-8, 2003, revised papers* (p. 33-47). Springer.

Löser, A., Siberski, W., Wolpers, M., & Nejdl, W. (2003). Information integration in schema-based peer-to-peer networks. In J. Eder & M. Missiko® (Eds.), In *Proceedings of the Conference on Advanced Information Systems Engineering* (Vol. 2681, p. 258-272). Springer.

Marsh, S. P. (1994). *Formalising trust as a computational concept.* Unpublished doctoral dissertation, Department of Computing Science and Mathematics, University of Stirling.

Maymounkov, P., & Mazières, D. (2002). Kademlia: A peer-to-peer information system based on the XOR Metric. In *Revised papers from the1stt International Workshop onPpeer-to-Peer Systems (Iptps '01)* (pp. 53-65). London, UK: Springer-Verlag.

McKnight, D. H., & Chervany, N. L. (1996). *The meanings of trust* (Tech. Rep. No. WP 96-04). University of Minnesota, Carlson School of Management.

Milojicic, D. S., Kalogeraki, V., Lukose, R., Nagaraja, K., Pruyne, J., Richard, B., et al., (2003, July). *Peer-to-peer computing* (Tech. Rep. No. HPL-2002-57R1). Hewlett Packard Laboratories.

Mui, L., Mohtashemi, M., & Halberstadt, A. (2002). Notions of reputation in multi-agents systems: a review. In *Proceedings of the1stt International Joint Conference on Autonomous Agents and Multiagent Systems (Aamas '02)* (pp. 280-287). New York, NY, USA: ACM Press.

Nejdl, W., Wolpers, M., Siberski, W., Schmitz, C., Schlosser, M., Brunkhorst, I., et al. (2003). Superpeer-based routing and clustering strategies for rdf-based peer-to-peer networks. In *Proceedings of the 12th International Conference on World Wide Web (Www '03)* (pp. 536-543). New York, NY, USA: ACM Press.

Olmedilla, D., Rana, O. F., Matthews, B., & Nejdl, W. (2006). Security and trust issues in semantic grids. In C. Goble, C. Kesselman, & Y. Sure (Eds.), *Semantic grid: The convergence of technologies.* Internationales Begegnungs- und Forschungszentrum fuer Informatik (IBFI), Schloss Dagstuhl, Germany.

Oram, A. (2001). *Peer-to-Peer: Harnessing the Power of Disruptive Technologies.* Sebastopol, CA, USA: O'Reilly & Associates, Inc.

Perkins, C. E. (2001). Ad hoc networking: An introduction. In *Ad hoc networking* (pp. 1-28). Boston, MA, USA: Addison-Wesley Longman Publishing Co., Inc.

Ramchurn, S. D., Huynh, D., & Jennings, N. R. (2004). Trust in multi-agent systems. *Knowl. Eng. Rev., 19* (1), 1-25.

Rasmusson, L., & Jansson, S. (1996). Simulated social control for secure internet commerce. In *Nspw '96: Proceedings of the 1996 workshop on new security paradigms* (pp. 18-25). New York, NY, USA: ACM Press.

Ratnasamy, S., Francis, P., Handley, M., Karp, R., & Schenker, S. (2001, October). A scalable content-addressable network. In*Proceedings of the 2001 Conference on Applications, Technologies, Architectures, and Protocols for Computer Communications* (*Sigcomm '01*) (pp. 161-172). New York, NY, USA: ACM Press.

Rowstron, A., & Druschel, P. (2001, November). Pastry: Scalable, distributed object location and routing for large-scale peer-to-peer systems. In *Proceedings of the 18th ifip/acm International Conference on Distributed Systems Platforms (middleware 2001)* (p. 329-350).

Sabater, J., & Sierra, C. (2001). REGRET: reputation in gregarious societies. In *Proceedings of the fifth international conference on autonomous agents* (*Agents '01)* (pp. 194-195). New York, NY, USA: ACM Press.

Sabater, J., & Sierra, C. (2002). Reputation and social network analysis in multi-agent systems. In *Proceedings of the first international joint conference on autonomous agents and multi-agent systems* (*Aamas '02)* (pp. 475-482). New York, NY, USA: ACM Press.

Stoica, I., Morris, R., Karger, D., Kaashoek, F., & Balakrishnan, H. (2001). Chord: A scalable peer-to-peer lookup service for internet applications. In *Proceedings of the 2001 acm Sigcomm Conference* (pp. 149-160).

Tatarinov, I., Ives, Z., Madhavan, J., Halevy, A., Suciu, D., Dalvi, N., et al. (2003). The piazza peer data management project. *SIGMOD Rec., 32* (3), 47-52.

Torra, V. (1997). The weighted owa operator. *International Journal of Intelligent Systems, 12* (2), 153-166.

Yang, B., & Garcia-Molina, H. (2003, March 5-8). Designing a Super-Peer Network. In U. Dayal, K. Ramamritham, & T. M. Vijayaraman (Eds.), In *Proceedings of the 19t International Conference on Data Engineering,*Bangalore, India (p. 49-). IEEE Computer Society.

Yu, B., & Singh, M. P. (2002). An evidential model of distributed reputation management. In *Proceedings of the first international joint conference on autonomous agents and multiagent systems* (*Aamas '02)* (pp. 294-301). New York, NY, USA: ACM Press.

Zacharia, G., Moukas, A., & Maes, P. (2000). Collaborative reputation mechanisms for electronic marketplaces. *Decis. Support Syst., 29* (4), 371-388.

Zhao, B. Y., Huang, L., Stribling, J., Rhea, S. C., Joseph, A. D., & Kubiatowicz, J. D. (2004). Tapestry: A resilient global-scale overlay for service deployment. *Selected Areas in Communications, IEEE Journal on, 22* (1), 41-53.

Zhou, R., & Hwang, K. (2006). Trust overlay networks for global reputation aggregation in p2p grid computing. In *20th international parallel and distributed processing symposium (ipdps 2006), proceedings, 25-29 April 2006, Rhodes island, Greece*. IEEE.

ENDNOTES

[a] In small-scale or closed systems this trust can be implicit, imbued to the individual components and the system overall by its designers and implementers.

[b] *Client* is informally defined as an entity (node, program, module, etc.) that initiates requests but is not able to serve requests. If the client also serves the request, then it plays the role of a server. Server is informally defined as an entity that serves requests from other entities, but does not initiate requests. If the server does initiate requests, then it plays the role of a client. Typically, there are one or a few servers versus many clients.

[c] *Peer* is informally defined as an entity with capabilities similar to other entities in the system.

[d] An overlay network is a computer network which is built on top of another network. Nodes in the overlay can be thought of as being connected by virtual or logical links, each of which corresponds to a path, perhaps through many physical links, in the underlying network. For example, many peer-to-peer networks are overlay networks because they run on top of the Internet. Dial-up Internet is an overlay upon the telephone network.

Chapter VI
SWELS:
A Semantic Web System Supporting E-Learning

Gianluca Elia
University of Salento, Italy

Giustina Secundo
University of Salento, Italy

Cesare Taurino
University of Salento, Italy

ABSTRACT

This chapter presents a prototypal e-learning system based on the Semantic Web paradigm, called SWELS (Semantic Web E-Learning System). The chapter starts by introducing e-learning as an efficient and just-in-time tool supporting the learning processes. Then a brief description of the evolution of distance learning technologies will be provided, starting from first generation e-learning systems through the current Virtual Learning Environments and Managed Learning Environments, by underling the main differences between them and the need to introduce standards for e-learning with which to manage and overcome problems related to learning content personalization and updating. Furthermore, some limits of the traditional approaches and technologies for e-learning will be provided, by proposing the Semantic Web as an efficient and effective tool for implementing new generation e-Learning systems. In the last section of the chapter, the SWELS system is proposed by describing the methodology adopted for organizing and modeling its knowledge base, by illustrating its main functionalities, and by providing the design of the tool followed by the implementation choices. Finally, future developments of SWELS will be presented, together with some remarks regarding the benefits for the final user in using such system.

INTRODUCTION

In a context of rapid environmental and technological change, characterized by an increasing obsolescence of knowledge, organizations need to accelerate the renewal and to increase the effectiveness of their managerial competences. Such continuous change is a determinant of continuous learning processes that calls for the capacity to organize at all levels of the organization new working processes that have to be more knowledge intensive, multidisciplinary, and collaborative.

This requires a profound rethinking of the processes supporting the design, development, and delivery of learning (McCrea et al., 2000) in a way that the learning process becomes more effective, just-in-time, and customized.

As a consequence, learning should not be a passive activity which is only done when people are in the educational institutions without knowing how the knowledge is used in the real world. It should be a continuous and active process performed under a specified goal and situation where the knowledge is really needed. Moreover, as huge amount of knowledge becomes available through Internet in the information society, it becomes possible for people to access the knowledge they need when necessary. In such a circumstance, the most important thing about having a lot of knowledge is to know how to find the knowledge, to be ready to understand and master the new knowledge, and to create knowledge for future use to close the loop of knowledge production and consumption. For these reasons, the goal of education and learning should be augmented to include training of learning capability and creativity of the learners (Mizoguchi, 2000).

Such considerations are some prominent drivers of the e-learning. Since e-learning applications are accessible from anywhere at any time, ICT-based learning environment has been gaining increasing attention from the research community.

In this context, the recently emerged (VLE) Virtual Learning Environments revealed themselves very effective from the pedagogical point of view, especially if they are compared with the previous (CBT) Computer Based Training and (WBT) Web Based Training systems.

However, VLE did not completely solve the problems related to the organization and navigation of the learning materials. Indeed, most of the current Web-based learning solutions show some limits in accessing the right knowledge, as well as in the learning pattern navigation process (given that they do not allow a complete and multidimensional vision of the knowledge available, therefore users are obliged to follow the learning modules according to a linear path designed for a generic learner). In addition, there is the need to optimize the processes related to learning resource organization and aggregation, and the subsequent access and reuse of such resources with respect to a not scheduled learner profile.

Our focus here is on the creation of a Web-based learning environment that enables fast, just-in-time and relevant learning. Indeed, current Web-based solutions do not meet the above mentioned requirements, and some pitfalls are for example information overload, lack of accurate information, and content that is not machine-understandable.

These limits suggest the application of Semantic Web technologies (Barnes-Lee, 2000) to e-learning as means for implementing new generation e-learning systems. The Semantic Web technologies support the innovation process in a learning environment, exploiting the opportunity to create and manage data that are *machine understandable* and not *only machine readable* (Secundo et al., 2004).

An effective way to apply the Semantic Web approach to e-learning could be the use of the ontology backbone, which allows the *ontology-based* description of the learning materials (knowledge base), adding small semantic annotations to each learning object created (Nejdl, 2001). By using an ontology-based approach, learning resources can be easily organized into customized learning patterns and delivered on demand to the learner, according to her/his profile and knowledge needs.

Moreover, such an approach allows to virtuously combine the content description process with the content navigation one: content description to easily identify the learning resources required to achieve the desired learning goals; content navigation to minimize the required time for accessing the learning resources by adopting the right approach of exploring the learning space.

Therefore, according to this approach and to the alignment between e-learning and Knowledge Management we present an application of the KIWI approach called SWELS (Semantic Web E-Learning System). This tool is a prototypal e-learning system based on the Semantic Web paradigm which main functionalities are:

- The creation of an ontology-based view;
- The semantic representation and visualization of learning modules (knowledge base);
- Learning modules (knowledge base) accessing;
- The visualization of the structure of the ontology.

Moreover, SWELS provides an innovative functionality to learners--the opportunity to navigate a domain ontology explicitly. By explicitly navigating the domain ontology, learners not only have the direct access to the knowledge they need inside the knowledge base, but also they are empowered in reaching the following goals (Secundo et al., 2004):

1. The complete exploration of the knowledge base, keeping the awareness and the visibility of the learning path performed to reach the extracted knowledge;
2. The gradual, but deep, understanding of the semantic structure of the knowledge domain they are exploring, through the comprehension of the meanings of concepts and relations of the ontology.

The chapter starts by introducing e-learning as an efficient and just-in-time tool supporting the learning processes, arisen from the learning requirements of the new, dynamically changing knowledge society. Then a brief description of the evolution of distance learning technologies will be provided, starting from first generation of e-learning systems (CBT) through the current Virtual Learning Environments and MLEs (Managed Learning Environments), by underling the main differences between them and the need to introduce standards for e-learning with which to manage and overcome problems related to learning content personalization and updating. Furthermore, some limits of the traditional approaches and technologies for e-learning will be provided, especially referring to the knowledge organization and access as well as to the learning content navigation. At this point, the Semantic Web will be proposed as an efficient and effective tool for implementing new generation e-learning systems, since that the application of such technology to e-learning provides an ontology-based description and organization of learning materials around small pieces of semantically annotated learning objects. In the last section of the chapter the SWELS e-learning system is proposed. The description of such an innovative solution starts with some insights on the methodology adopted for organizing and modeling the Knowledge Base of SWELS, then the main functionalities of the e-learning system will be illustrated; following, the design of the tool together with the implementation choices will be provided; finally, future developments and some remarks will be presented regarding the benefits for the final user (the learner) in using such system.

E-LEARNING: A TECHNOLOGY FACILITATING THE LEARNING PROCESSES

Learning is a critical support mechanism for organizations to compete, not only from the point of view of education, but also from the point of view of the New Economy (Drucker, 2000). The incredible velocity and volatility of today's markets require just-in-time methods for supporting the need-to-know of employees, partners, and distribution paths.

Time, or the lack of it, is the reason given by most businesses for failing to invest in learning. Therefore, learning processes need to be fast and just-in-time. Speed requires not only a suitable content of the learning material (highly specified, not too general), but also a powerful mechanism for organizing such material. Also, learning must be a customized on-line service, initiated by user profiles and business demands. In addition, it must be integrated into day-to-day work patterns and needs to represent a clear competitive edge for the business. In a few words, learning needs to

Table 1. Summary of problems and needs in education (Adapted from: Koper, 2004)

Dimension	*Problems/Needs*
I. Changes in Societal Demands	1. Current higher education infrastructure cannot accommodate the growing college-aged population and life-long learning enrolments, making more distance education programs necessary. 2. Knowledge and information are growing exponentially and Lifelong learning is becoming a competitive necessity. 3. Education is becoming more seamless between high school, college, and further studies.
II. Changes in Learning Teaching process	4. Instruction is becoming more learner-centred, non-linear, and self-directed. 5. There is an increasing need for new learning and teaching strategies that a) is grounded in new instructional design research and b) exploit the capabilities of technology. 6. Learning is most effective when learners are engaged in solving real-world problems; learning environments need to be designed to support this problem-centred approach. 7. Students demand more flexibility; they are shopping for courses that meet their schedules and circumstances. 8. Higher-education learner profiles, including online, information-age, and adult learners, are changing. 9. Academic emphasis is shifting from course-completion to competency. 10. The need for faculty development, support, and training is growing. 11. Instructors of distance courses can feel isolated.
III. Changes in Organization of Educational Institutions	12. There is a shift in organizational structure toward decentralization. 13. Higher education outsourcing and partnerships are increasing. 14. Retention rates and length of time taken to completion concern administrators, faculty members, students and tax payers. 15. The distinction between distance and local education is disappearing. 16. Faculty members demand reduced workload and increased compensation for distance courses. 17. Traditional faculty roles are shifting or unbundling.

be relevant to the (semantic) context of the business of people and organizations (Adelsberger et al., 2001).

In this scenario, Web-based learning environments have been gaining increasing attention from the research community, since e-learning applications can represent real facilitator of the learning processes both in business and in academic contexts. The following table (Table 1) underlines some problems and needs that can be effectively overcome with e-learning; such problems and needs are summarized and grouped on several e-learning domain dimensions (Koper, 2004):

But, what does e-learning mean? E-learning is the use of Internet technologies to create and deliver a rich learning environment that includes a broad array of instruction and information resources and solutions, the goal of which is to enhance individual and organizational performance (Rosenberg, 2006). E-learning is not just concerned with providing easy access to learning resources, anytime, anywhere, via a repository of learning resources, but is also concerned with supporting such features as the personal definition of learning goals, and the synchronous and asynchronous communication, and collaboration, between learners and between learners and instructors (Kolovski et al., 2003). It aims at replacing old-fashioned time/place/content predetermined learning with a just-in-time/at work-place/customized/on-demand process of learning (Stojanovic et al., 2001).

Traditional learning process could be characterised by centralised authority (content is selected by the educator), strong push delivery (instructors push knowledge to students), lack of a personalisation (content must satisfy the needs of many), and the linear/static learning process (unchanged content). The consequences of such organisation on the learning are expensive, slow and too unfocused (problem-independent) learning process.

But dynamically changed business environment puts completely different challenges on learning process--fast, just-in-time (cheap) and relevant (problem-dependent) learning, as mentioned above. This can be solved with the distributed, student-oriented, personalised, non-linear/dynamic learning process--e-learning. The principle behind e-learning is that the tools and knowledge needed to perform work are moved to the knowledge workers--wherever and whoever they are.

In the recent years, new breeds of IS (Information System) () known as LMS (Learning Management Systems) and LCMS (Learning Content Management Systems) are evolving to enable learning in organisations (Brennan et al., 2001). In essence, LMS replace isolated and fragmented learning programmes with a systematic means of assessing and raising competency and performance levels throughout the organisation, by offering a strategic IS solution for planning, delivering, and managing all learning events, including both online and classroom-based learning (Greenberg, 2002). LMS are often coupled with LCMS which facilitate the management and administration of the learning content for the online learning prgrammes in the form of learning objects (Brennan et al., 2001).

E-LEARNING SYSTEMS: FROM VIRTUAL LEARNING ENVIRONMENTS TO MANAGED LEARNING ENVIRONMENTS

In the 90s the primary impact of the Internet technologies on distance learning was mainly on the possibility of having different ways for aggregating and delivering learning content. Indeed, the application of such technologies to the learning processes has introduced a set of opportunities and advantages: the possibility to generate and transport on the Web multimedia audio/video flows at low costs (therefore promoting the diffusion of synchronous learning environments on asynchronous ones); the use of standard technologies for information exchange that allow to dynamically and effectively structure and navigate learning content; the possibility for learners to acquire knowledge and to continuously revise and update it by adapting the learning environment to their needs. In other words, Web-based learning environments shifted from stand-alone technologies towards highly integrated e-learning and knowledge management infrastructures and tools enabling the creation of learning communities and supporting the collaboration between members and organizations. However, in the last years Internet technologies failed in the process of creating and managing learning contents in a way that they could be easily and dynamically reused and updated. This because of the inability of trainers and learning managers to create learning materials that could be fast and easily adapted to the learning needs of learners as well as to the new ways of content delivery. Such considerations have been driven the shift from first generation e-learning systems, based on the delivery of Web-based learning content and on the basic Internet standards, towards second generation ones, based on "ad-hoc" e-learning standards (Damiani et al., 2002).

Second generation e-learning systems are based on the creation of VLEs that have risen from the integration between e-learning and knowledge management solutions. The primary aim of VLEs is to allow people to share knowledge, interests and experiences, thereby encouraging the creation of Virtual Learning Communities based on blended learning solutions in which face-to-face and virtual classroom meetings are combined with Web-based learning patterns to provide to learners a complete, interactive and effective learning experience. Nevertheless, if from one side VLEs revealed themselves very effective from the pedagogical point of view (especially if considered in relation to the e-learning platform of first generation), from the other side they showed some limits as regards to the problem of learning content aggregation and organization, and the subsequent access and reuse by learners with a non scheduled user profile. The classification and management of contents are the strength points of the so-called MLE. MLEs privilege the content design, creation, and management in respect to the content delivery infrastructure, considered as an element with which the content has to interoperate. The main goal of MLEs is to manage in an integrated way a complete system for analyzing, developing, and evaluating competences, for scheduling and organizing learning patterns, for managing roles and virtual classrooms, for tracking the learners and for final evaluation of the competences reached (Secundo et al., 2004). The complete separation proposed by MLEs between the management infrastructure and the final output of the learning material is enabling the development and the diffusion of standards for e-learning in several applicative contexts (Lockwood et al., 2001):

- DRM (Digital Right Management) and privacy management;
- Low level formats for learning content;
- Metadata for content description
- Personalization of content according to the learner profile and to the linguistic/social/cultural environment;
- XML-based models and languages for structuring and describing dynamic learning patterns (i.e., Educational Modeling Language);
- Technologies and methodologies for interoperability with Internet/Intranet delivery infrastructures.

Nowadays there are several key international players (including IEEE, IMS, ARIADNE, ADL and AICC) that are focusing their efforts on the issues of interoperability and reuse, resulting in a multitude of standards that can be used for building interoperable learning systems. These attempts at building learning platforms for interoperability are mainly targeted to ease the need of LMSs for adaptation to standards, but as a consequence, learners can be expected to gain more freedom. For example, the goal of SCORM (Sharable Content Object Reference Model) is to provide a reference model for content that is durable (survives system changes), interoperable (between systems), accessible (indexed and searchable) and reusable (able to be modified in different contexts and by different tools). This will hopefully allow students to move more freely between LMSs and even to combine several services from different LMSs.

SOME LIMITS OF TRADITIONAL APPROACHES AND TECHNOLOGIES FOR E-LEARNING

Current approaches, models and technologies for e-learning introduce, on the other hand, several problems. First, most content providers have large monolithic systems where adaptation to standards will not significantly change the underlying teacher-learner model. Students will be presented with material in a context often leading up to some form of (standardized) test. New and more interesting methods for learning--such as techniques for collaboration, annotation, conceptual modeling, and so forth.--will not profit from such adaptation. Second, even though monolithic, closed or proprietary systems will be able to exchange learning resources, course-like structures and keep track of students with the help of those standards, they will need to go through yet another process of adaptation to the next big batch of agreements on learning technologies, such as e.g. profiling and tracking of student performance. Third, the current perspective on metadata is too limited. Anyone who has something to say about a learning resource should be able to do so. This includes learners, teachers and content contributors such as authors and providers. Communicating this metadata is equally important as it can help, direct or encourage others to actively participate and learn. Proposed solutions, such as the adoption of SCORM, will result in learning resources (and their metadata) that will reappear in different versions and formats rather than dynamically evolve and improve (Naeve et al., 2001).

In a few words, today many of the e-learning systems available on market lack in specific functionalities for the creation and delivery of dynamic, modular learning paths that match the knowledge needs in a contextualized (according to learner's current activities) and individualized (according to learner's experiences, competences profiles, learning history and personal preferences) way.

This suggests a strong integration among e-learning and knowledge management functionalities to define a rich learning environment with wealth and variety of resources available just-in-time to learners, both through structured and unstructured knowledge objects through interaction with other people (Elia et al., 2006). The key to success is therefore the ability to reduce the cycle time for learning and to adapt "content, size and style" of learning to the learner and to the business. Therefore, to overcome such problems, a new learning framework is required, based on the key points mentioned above and opened to a multitude of new services. In order to be effective, it needs a powerful language for expressing facts about resources and schemas that will allow machines as well as humans to understand how these facts are related without relying on heuristics. Moreover, there is a need for expressing facts about remote (identifiable) objects without accessing remote data stores.

EMERGING PERSPECTIVES OF E-LEARNING IN THE SEMANTIC AGE

In an e-learning environment, the learning content should be oriented around small modules (the so called learning objects) coupled with associated semantics (the metadata) so that learners are able to find what they need in a specific moment and context. Furthermore, these modules should be related by a "dependency network" or "conceptual Web" to allow individualised learning. Such a dependency network permits, for example, the learning objects to be presented to the learner in an orderly manner, with prerequisite material being presented first. Additionally, in an e-learning environment, the learner should be able to add extra material and links (i.e., annotate) to the learning objects for their own benefit or for that of later students. This framework lends itself to an implementation based on the Semantic Web, incorporating cooperating software agents, which additionally make use of appropriate Web services to provide the functionality. The facilities the applications based on these technologies can provide, include allowing e-learning content to be created, annotated, shared, and discussed, together with supplying resources such lecture notes, student portfolios, group projects, information pages, discussion forums, and question-and-answer bulletin boards. Moreover, such applications allow students to benefit from more interaction with their peers (for example, sharing resources found on the Web), as well as with the instructors and tutors, by also providing an easy way for sharing and archiving information, whether of general interest or specific to a group project they are involved in (Kolovski et al., 2003).

T first generation WWW was a powerful tool for research and education, but its utility is hampered by the inability of the users to navigate easily the huge amount of sources for the information they require. The Semantic Web is a vision to solve this problem. It is proposed that a new WWW architecture will support not only Web content, but also associated formal semantics (Barnes-Lee, 1998). The idea is that the Web content and the related semantics (or metadata) will be accessed by Web agents, allowing these agents to reason about the content and produce intelligent answers to user queries. The Semantic Web, in practice, comprises a layered framework: an XML layer for expressing the Web content (the structure of data); a RDF (Resource Description Framework) layer for representing the semantics of the content (the meaning of data); an ontology layer for describing the vocabulary of the domain; and a logic layer to enable intelligent reasoning with meaningful data (Stojanovic et al., 2001).

Within an e-learning framework, the Semantic Web provides the technology that allows a learning object to be (Naeve et al., 2001):

- **Described with metadata.** Since a resource can have uses outside the domains foreseen by the provider, any given description (metadata instance) is bound to be incomplete. Because of the distributed structure of RDF, a description can be expanded or new descriptions following new formats (schemas) can be added. This allows for creative uses of content in new and unforeseen ways. Hence, one of the most important features of the current Web - the fact that anyone can link anything to anything--has been carried over into RDF.
- **Annotated.** Every resource identifiable by an URI can be annotated, with personal notes and links by anyone.
- **Extended.** In terms of content (structured, by means of XML descriptors), permitting multiple versions to exist. Indeed, successive editing of the content can be done via special RDF-schemas allowing private, group consensus or author-specific versions of a common base document. The versioning history will be a tree with known and unknown branches, which can be traversed with the help of appropriate versioning tools.
- **Shared by, and communicated to, anyone** who has expressed an interest in such content. RDF is application independent. Since the metadata is expressed in a standard format, which is independent of the underlying schemas, even simplistic applications can understand parts of complex RDF graphs.

If the learner's favourite tool does not support the corresponding schemas, it can at least present them in a rough graph, table or whatever standard form it has for describing resources and their properties. If more advanced processing software is available (such as logic engines), more advanced treatment of the RDF descriptions is possible.

- **Certified**. There is no reason why only big organizations should certify learning resources. Individuals, such as teachers, may want to certify certain content as a quality learning resource that is well suited for specific learning tasks.

Apart from these uses, it is possible to invent new schemas describing structures, personalization, results from monitoring and tracking, processes and interactions that can enrich the learning environment in various ways.

The key property of the Semantic Web architecture (common-shared-meaning, machine-processable metadata), enabled by a set of suitable agents, establishes a powerful approach to satisfy the e-learning requirements: efficient, just-in-time, and task relevant learning. Learning material is semantically annotated and for a new learning demand it may be easily combined in a new learning course. According to his/her preferences, a learner can find useful learning material very easily. The process is based on semantic querying and navigation through learning materials, enabled by the ontological background. So, the Semantic Web can be exploited as a very suitable platform for implementing an e-learning system, because it provides all means for the ontology development, the ontology-based annotation of learning materials, as well as their composition in learning modules and proactive delivery of the learning materials through e-Learning portals.

In the following table (Table 2), the most important characteristics (or pitfalls) of the traditional learning and improvements achieved using the e-learning environment are showed; furthermore, a summary view of the possibility to use the Semantic Web for realizing the e-learning requirements is presented (Drucker, 2000; Stojanovic et al., 2001).

An important aspect related to the use of Semantic Web in educational contexts is how to represent a course in a formal, semantic way so that it can be interpreted and manipulated by computers as well as humans (i.e., the creation and management of data that are machine understandable and not only machine readable). This process is known in the literature as "educational modeling." A semantic model is developed using a variety of methods: literature research, expert group discussions, validation sessions, and so forth, and the result is described with a formal modeling language, like UML. The UML class diagrams can be translated to RDF-Schema and/or OWL Web Ontology Language, depending on the richness of the model. XML-Schema's (XSD) and other semantic bindings like Topic Maps can also be generated from the UML models (Koper, 2004). A semantic representation of learning content provides efficient solutions to the following problems (Koper, 2004):

- The development of Web-based courses that are flexible, problem-based, non-linear, incorporate multimedia and are adaptive to learner characteristics, is expensive and extremely time-consuming. A semantic framework can help the course developers in the structuring and integration of the development work. In addiction, authoring and design support agents and tools could be created to help the developers to do their jobs more effectively and efficiently.
- An explicit notation of learning content can preserve and share knowledge about effective learning designs. It gives the possibility to build and share catalogues of effective learning patterns that can be communicated very precisely and can be adapted to other contexts, problems, and content.

Table 2. Differences between training and e-learning and main benefits of applying Semantic Web technologies to e-learning (Adapted from Drucker, 2000; Stojanovic et al., 2001)

Dimension	Training	e-Learning	Semantic Web
Delivery	Push--Instructor determines agenda	Pull--Learner determines agenda	Knowledge items (learning materials) are distributed on the Web, but they are linked to commonly agreed ontologies. This enables the creation of user-specific learning patterns, by semantic querying for topics of interest.
Responsiveness	Anticipatory--Assumes to know the problem	Reactionary --Responds to problem at hand	Software agents on the Semantic Web may use commonly agreed service language, which enables coordination between agents and proactive delivery of learning materials in the context of actual problems. The vision is that each user has his/her own personalised agent that communicates with other agents.
Access	Linear-- Pre-defined progression of knowledge	Non-linear --Allows direct access to knowledge in whatever sequence makes sense to the situation at hand	User can describe situation at hand (goal of learning, previous knowledge) and perform semantic querying for the suitable learning material. The user profile is also accounted for. Access to knowledge can be expanded by semantically defined navigation.
Symmetry	Asymmetric -- Training occurs as a separate activity	Symmetric -- Learning occurs as an integrated activity	The Semantic Web offers the potential to become an integration platform for all business processes in an organisation, including learning activities.
Modality	Discrete-- Training takes place in dedicated chunks with defined starts and stop	Continuous -- Learning runs in the parallel loops and never stops	Active delivery of information (based on personalised agents) creates a dynamic virtual learning environment.
Authority	Centralized --Content is selected from a library of materials developed by the educator	Distributed -- Content comes from the interaction of the participants and the educators	The Semantic Web will be as decentralised as possible. This enables an effective co-operative content management.
Personalization	Mass produced- - Content must satisfy the needs of many	Personalized-- Content is determined by the individual user's needs and aims to satisfy the needs of every user	A user (using personalised agent) searches for learning material customised for her/his needs. The ontology is the link between user profile and needs, and characteristics of the learning material.
Adaptiveness	Static-- Content and organization/taxonomy remains in their original authored form without regard to environmental changes	Dynamic-- Content changes constantly through user input, experiences, new practices, business rules and heuristics	The Semantic Web enables the use of knowledge provided in various forms, by semantic annotation of content. Distributed nature of the Semantic Web enables continuous improvement of learning materials.

- Instantiation of an e-learning course in current LMSs (Learning Management Systems) can be a time-consuming job that has to be repeated for every new run of the course. One has to assign users, create groups, but also has to set-up the communication and collaboration services (e.g., discussion forums, workspaces, etc.) mostly by hand. A representation of a course that includes a specification of the set-up of the services enables the automation of this instantiation process.
- When the representation of the learning material includes a semantic, higher level description of the interactive processes that occur during the learning process, software agents can interpret these to support learners and staff in managing the workflow of activities in learning. These agents can also support the filtering of the appropriate resources to be used during the performance of an activity.
- Adaptation to individual learner characteristics (i.e., his/her learner profile) is highly desirable, since learners have not the same learning pre-requisites, skills, aptitudes or motivations. However, such adaptation can only be done realistically when the adaptation is wholly or at least partially automated (therefore, including descriptions of the conditions for adaptation). Otherwise, it becomes a very demanding work for the learner and/or his/her learning manager.
- A semantic annotation of learning content enables and facilitates sharing and re-use of learning objects (that is one of the major objectives in the field of e-learning). This sharing and re-use is needed to make the content development process more efficient. On the contrary, if learning objects are not semantically represented, it might be hard to find them on local or remote repositories, hard to integrate them into new contexts and--relating to the problem of interoperability and learning object exchange among different LMSs--hard to interpret and structure them in the correct way.
- An explicit semantic representation can serve as a means to create more advanced and complex, but consistent learning designs than is possible without such a representation. This is a characteristic of any language with semantic that enables one to write, read, rewrite and share meaning (e.g., natural language).

SWELS: AN E-LEARNING SYSTEM BASED ON SEMANTIC WEB TECHNOLOGIES

According to the alignment between e-learning and knowledge management approaches, a prototypal e-learning system based on the Semantic Web paradigm has been implemented called SWELS. Such system has been designed and developed at the eBMS (e-Business Management Section) () of the Scuola Superiore ISUFI, University of Lecce (Italy) and it is the result of a research activity under the KIWI project.

This paper represents an extended version of a previous publication that the authors G. Secundo, A. Corallo, G. Elia G. Passiante (2004) published in the proceedings of the International Conference on Information Technology Based Higher Education and Training, May 29th--June 2th, 2004 Istanbul, Turkey.

The SWELS system is intended to be an innovative tool for knowledge acquisition and competence development of learners and knowledge workers that exploits Semantic Web technologies in order to provide an effective and useful support to online learning processes. The system, indeed, is conceived as a tool with which to potentially overcome the limits of the current e-learning applications in terms of learning content creation and delivery, that is, the inability of existing tools to create dynamics and adaptive learning paths that match the learning profile of learners as well as their knowledge needs. SWELS points out a proactive behaviour based on a matching process among the profile of the user, his/her interests as well as his/her just-in-time choices during the learning activities, and the learning content available in the knowledge base; as a consequence learning resources can be easily organized into customized learning patterns and delivered on demand to the user.

Learning materials which SWELS refers to are focused on "Change Management and Leadership" knowledge domain, that has been modeled through a domain ontology. Such an ontology contains the list of concepts and semantic relations with which to provide a semantic description of the learning objects (text files, images, graphs, as well as multimedia audio-video files) of the domain.

KNOWLEDGE BASE ORGANIZATION AND MODELING

Learning materials (i.e., the knowledge base) are described by means of a domain ontology that provides a semantic representation of content, adding small semantic annotations to each learning resource. In particular, the knowledge base modeling process can be organized in two main steps:

1. Definition of the knowledge base ontology. The ontology definition consists in identify-

Figure 1. A representation of knowledge base flexibility

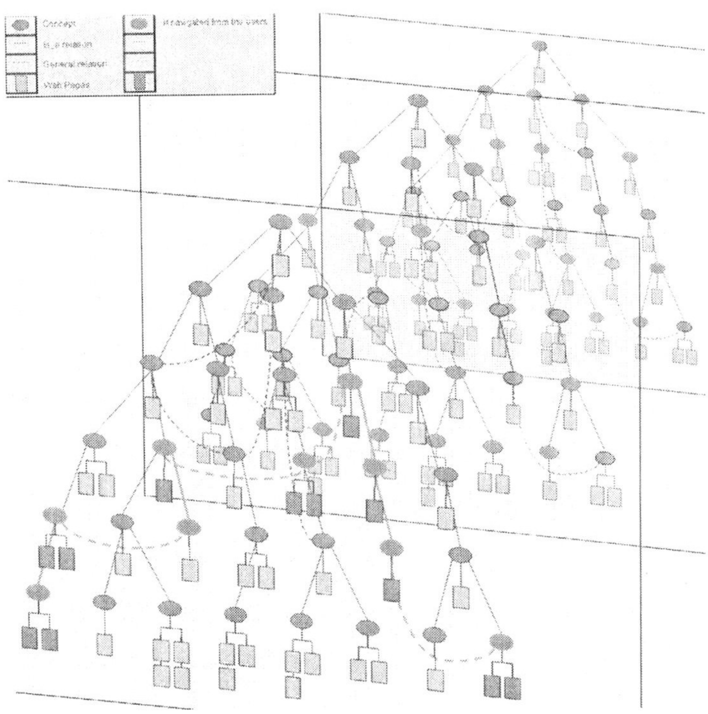

ing the learning module structure and defines the abstract notions and vocabulary that will be available for the learner to conceptualize the learning modules.
2. Description of the knowledge resources. Knowledge items are tagged with one concept belonging to the ontology. In this way, learner can identify each resource and, using the ontological relationships, he/she can explore new resources tagged by different domain concepts.

Such a description of learning content allows an effective organization of them in the knowledge base, therefore providing to learners the possibility to have an explicit navigation of the domain ontology.

The two main advantages for the final users are, from one hand a complete exploration of the modeled knowledge base, which allows them to have a total awareness of the available content, as well as the visibility of the performed learning path to reach the required knowledge. So, learners are conscious both of the total amount of knowledge present in the knowledge base, and of the knowledge extracted till then and of knowledge heritage to explore in the future. From the other hand, learners can understand, step by step, the semantic structure of the knowledge domain they're exploring by surfing the ontology, by gradually being aware of the meanings of ontology's concepts and relations.

This approach to the knowledge base organization and modeling provides more flexibility for learners as regard to the learning content access, since that they can explicitly browse the knowledge base and dynamically configure their learning patterns (Figure 1).

FUNCTIONAL DESCRIPTION OF SWELS

The interaction between the learner and the system can be represented through a use case

Figure 2. Use case diagram

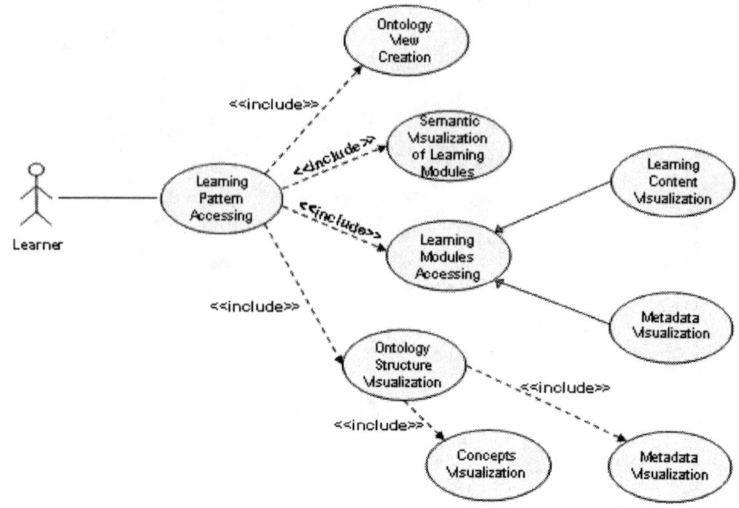

Figure 3. State chart diagram

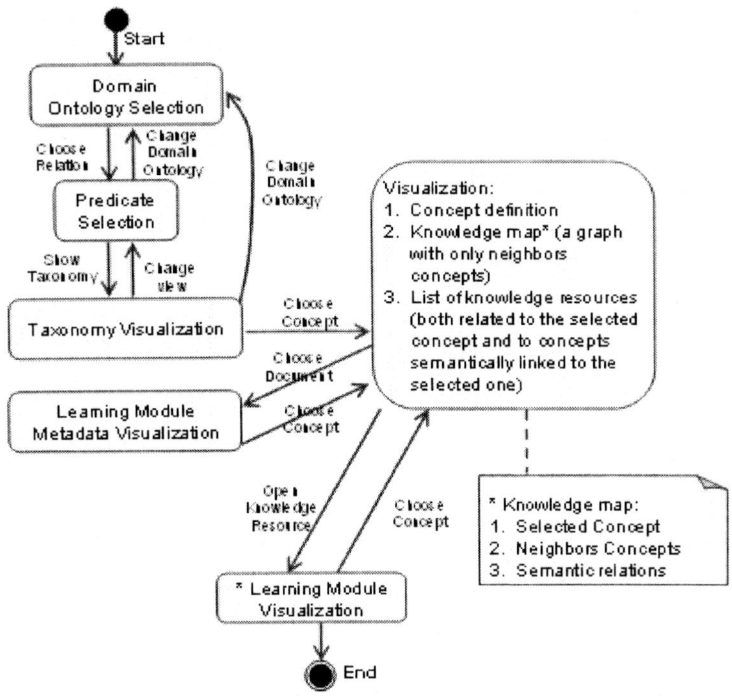

diagram that shows the main functionalities of the tool (Figure 2).

As the use cases show, in order to have access to the dynamically created learning patterns, learners have to perform a set of different steps.

The following state chart diagram describes the overall behaviour of the system by underling the logic sequence of the states and the list of the state transitions related to the user events according to interaction between learner and system described before (see Figure 3).

CREATION OF THE ONTOLOGY-BASED VIEW

When a learner accesses the SWELS, he/she has to select the domain ontology and the relation by which creating the ontology view. When predicate is chosen, the tool generates the taxonomic representation of the ontology, through a tree-structure (Figure 4).

Figure 4. Ontology view creation

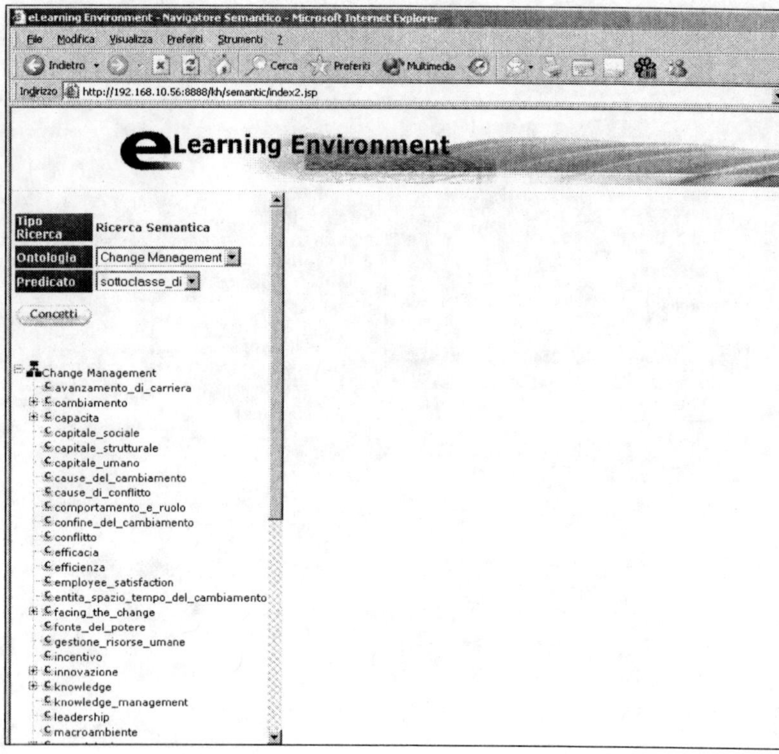

SEMANTIC REPRESENTATION AND VISUALIZATION OF LEARNING MODULES

After the ontology view creation, the learner can generate his/her own personalized learning pattern by browsing the concepts of the ontology. By clicking on each concept, a list of elements will be shown:

- Concept definition (top of the page);
- List of knowledge resources indexed on the selected concept (body of the page--with blank relation);
- List of knowledge resources indexed on concepts linked to the selected concept through one of the ontology relationships (body of the page – with specified relation).

Such information is organized in the tab "Documenti" (Knowledge Resources) as follows (Figure 5).

ONTOLOGY STRUCTURE VISUALIZATION

When a learner selects the specific concept which he/she is interested to, together with the semantic visualization of the learning modules, SWELS generates also a knowledge map containing both the selected concept and the neighbour concepts.

Figure 5. Semantic representation and visualization of learning modules

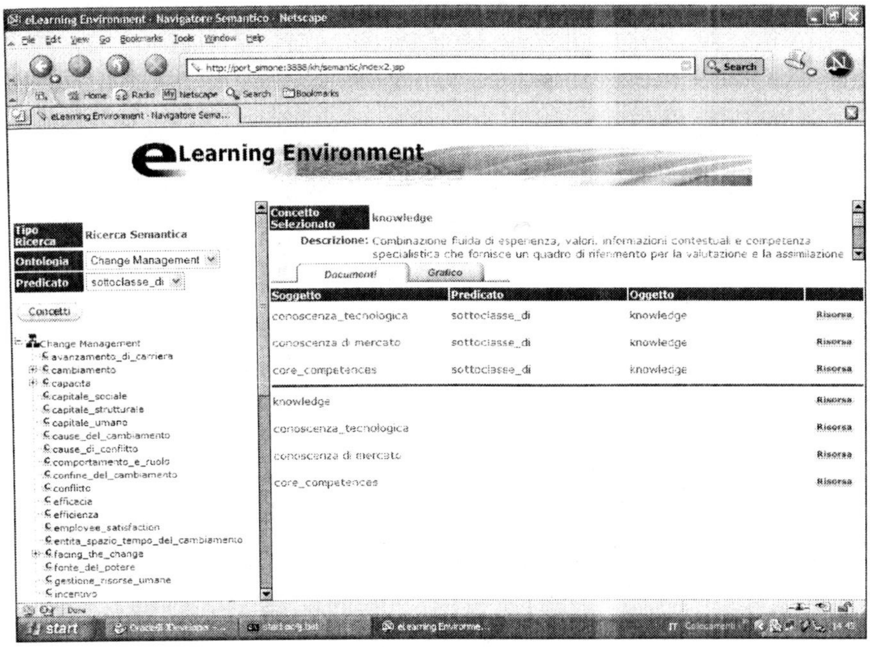

Figure 6. Ontology structure visualization

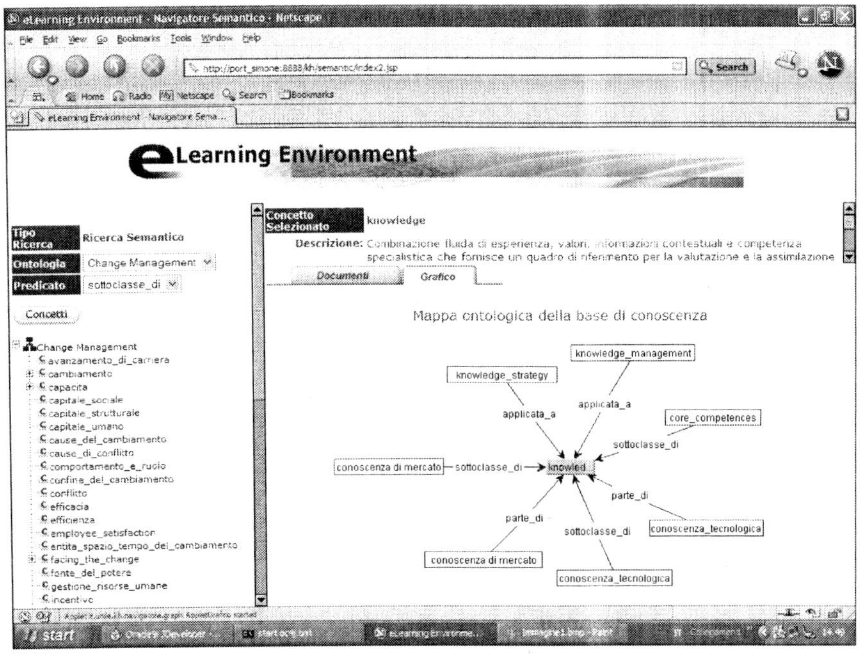

Such a graph is organized in the tab "Grafico" (Graph) of the application, and represents the semantic boundary of the concept (specifying the neighbour concepts, the semantic connections and the direction of these connections). The semantic boundary is illustrated through a radial layout (neighbourhood view) --as TGViz one (a Plug-in of Protégé) and Visualizer one (a Plug-in of OntoEdit)--to give to the learner an explicit and immediate representation of the ontology structure (Figure 6). It is important to note that, referring to each triple (subject, predicate, object), the direction of the arrows connecting two concepts goes from the subject to the object of the triple; this allows the learner to have a unique interpretation of the semantic map.

In this way, two different and complementary representations of the domain ontology are available: the tree-structure (on the left of the page) and the graph-structure (on the right). This choice allows a better understanding of the knowledge domain (since that it provides two different ways for representing the knowledge available in the domain) and gives the learner the opportunity to select and extract the right learning resources according to his/her "learning profile."

LEARNING MODULE ACCESSING

By clicking on the button "Risorsa" (Resource), in the list of the knowledge resources indexed in

Figure 7. Learning module accessing

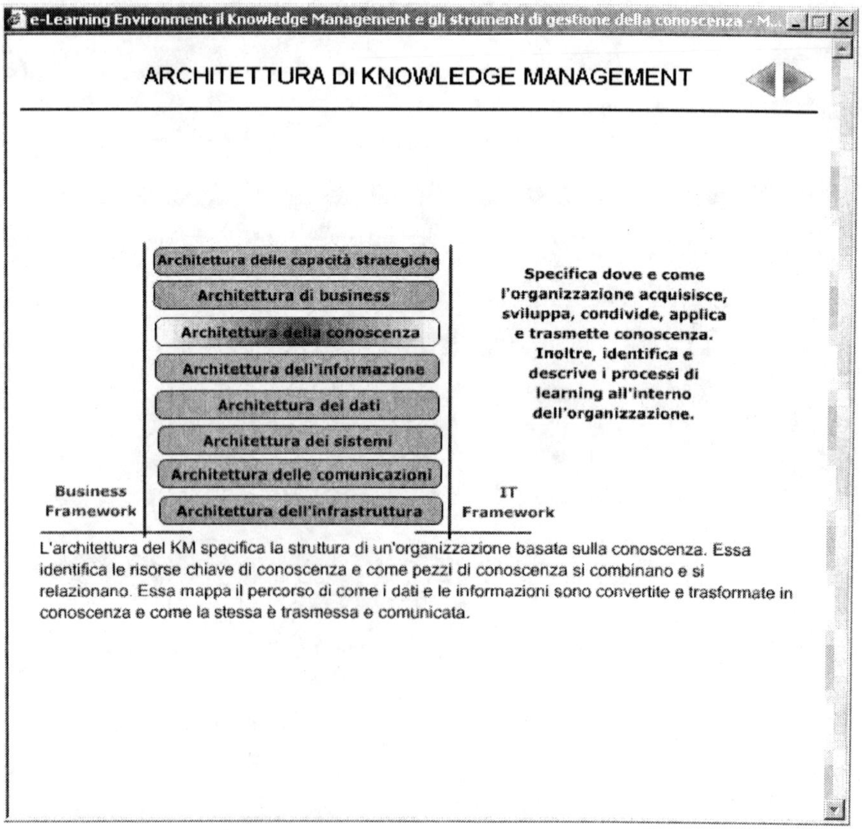

Figure 8. E-learning metadata

the tab "Documenti" (Figure 5), the learner has the direct access to the chosen learning module; in this way, the selected learning module will be launched in a new browser window and he/she can attend it autonomously (Figure 7).

Moreover, the learner can also access metadata describing knowledge resources, by clicking on resource name. In this way, Dublin Core metadata (Dublin Core Metadata Initiative, 2006) will be shown (Figure 8).

DESIGN OF THE TOOL

Concerning the design of SWELS, we decided to adopt the MVC (Model-View-Controller) design

Figure 9. The MVC (Model-View-Controller) design pattern

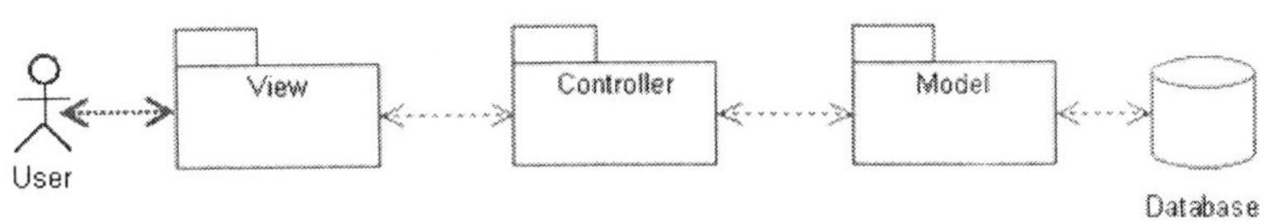

Figure 10. Package diagram

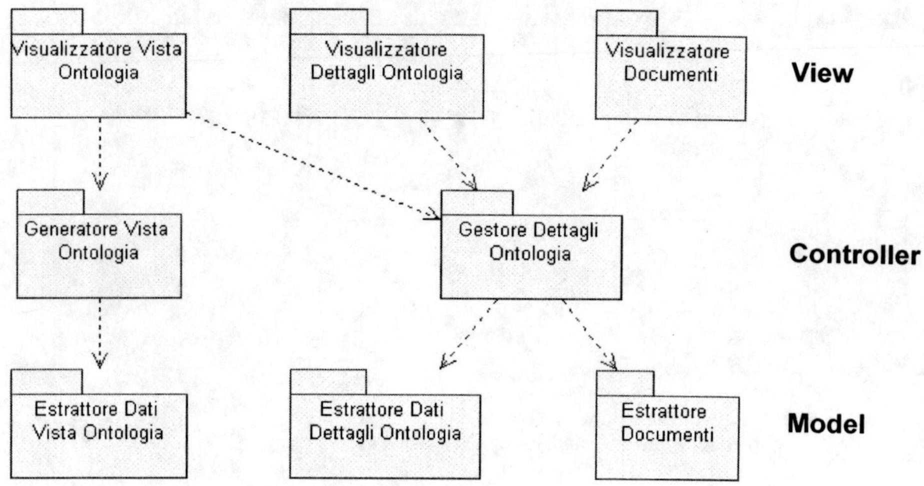

Figure 11. Class diagram for the ontology view creation

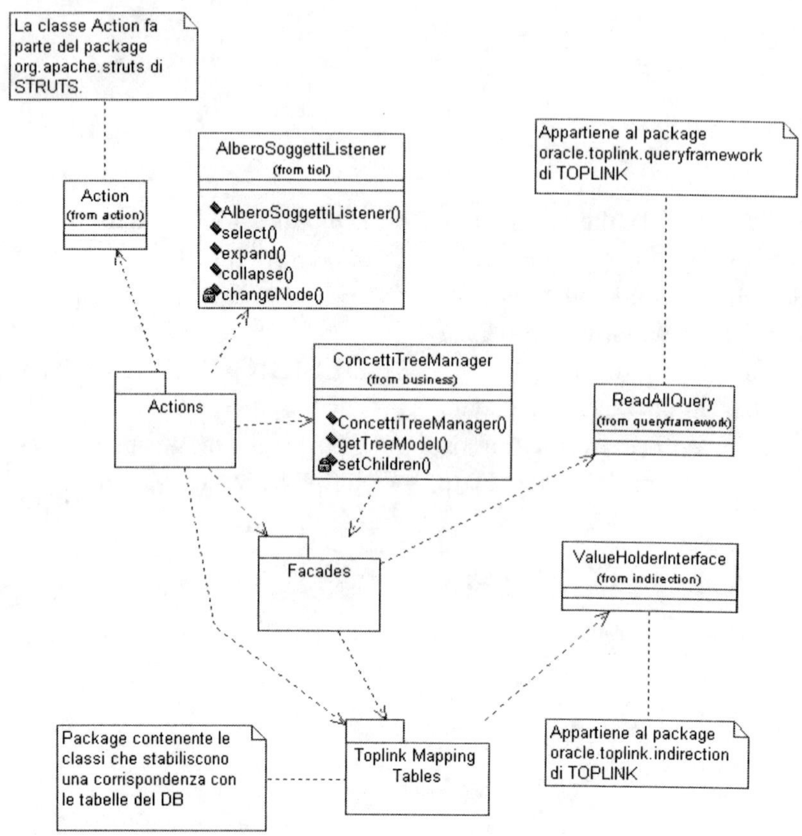

pattern (Figure 9) since that it allows enterprise applications to support multiple types of users with multiple types of interfaces. By representing the logic architecture of the system with such a "Three Tier" model, it is possible to keep separated core business model functionalities from the presentation and the control logic that uses those functionalities. Such separation permits multiple views to share the same enterprise data model, which makes supporting multiple clients easier to implement, test, and maintain (Sun Microsystems, Inc., 2002).

According to the Three Tier model adopted for the SWELS design , the first diagram proposed is the package diagram that shows developed class packages and the dependencies among them (Fowler et al., 1999) (Figure 10).

Going on in the description of the SWELS design, following are shown the class diagrams describing the types of the objects in the system and the various kinds of static relationships that exist among them. In particular, we propose the class diagram related to the ontology view creation (Figure 11), the class diagram related to the semantic visualization of the learning modules (Figure 12), and the class diagram related to the ontology structure visualization (Figure 13).

Figure 12. Class diagram for the semantic visualization of the learning modules

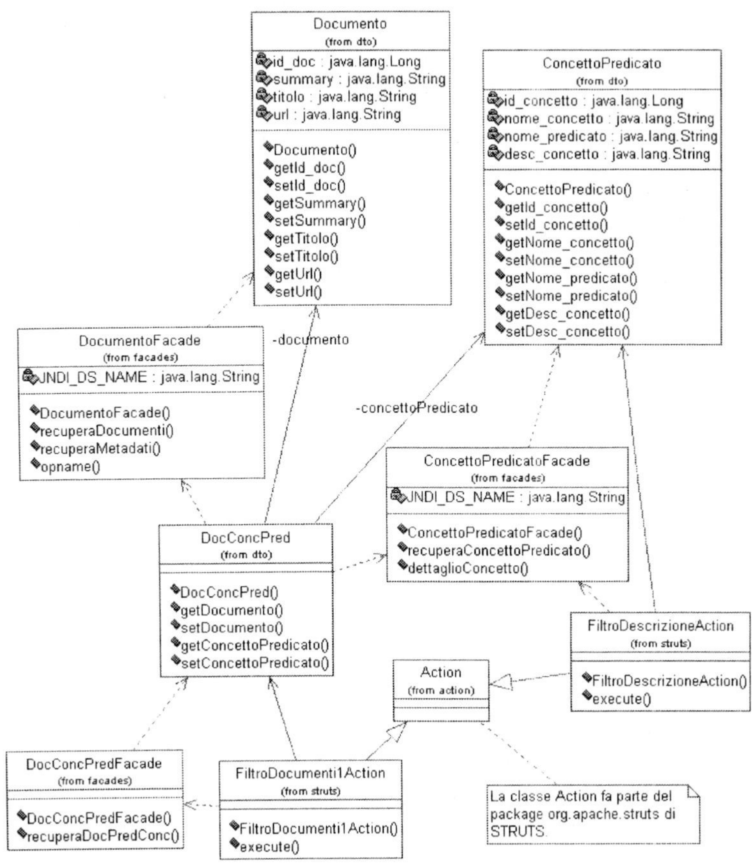

Figure 13. Class diagram for the ontology structure visualization

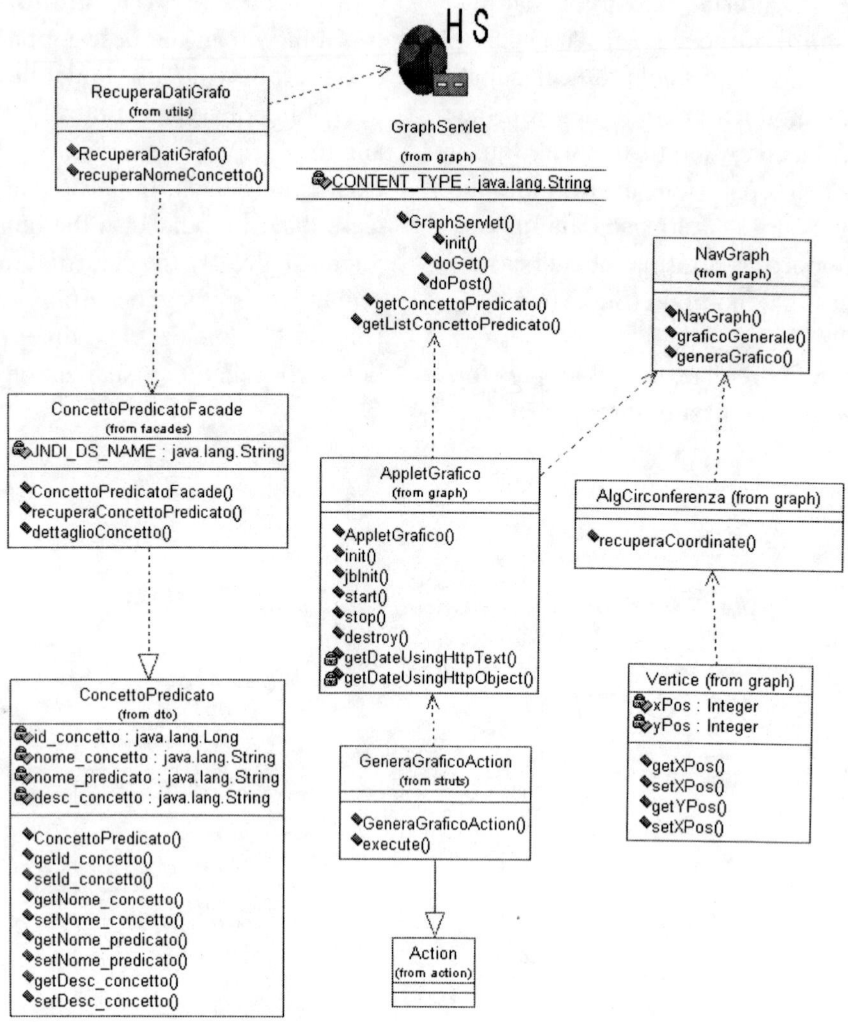

TECHNOLOGICAL ISSUES

With regard to implementation choices, SWELS is a J2EE Web-based application, developed according to the MVC (Model-View-Control) pattern (which implies together the use of Servlets as well as JSPs technologies), by using two suitable frameworks:

- *Jakarta Struts*, an open source framework for creating Java Web applications that utilize a MVC architecture. The framework gives three key components: a "request" handler provided by the application developer that is mapped to a standard URI, a "response" handler that transfers control to another resource which completes the response, a

Figure 14. Integrating struts framework in MVC architectures

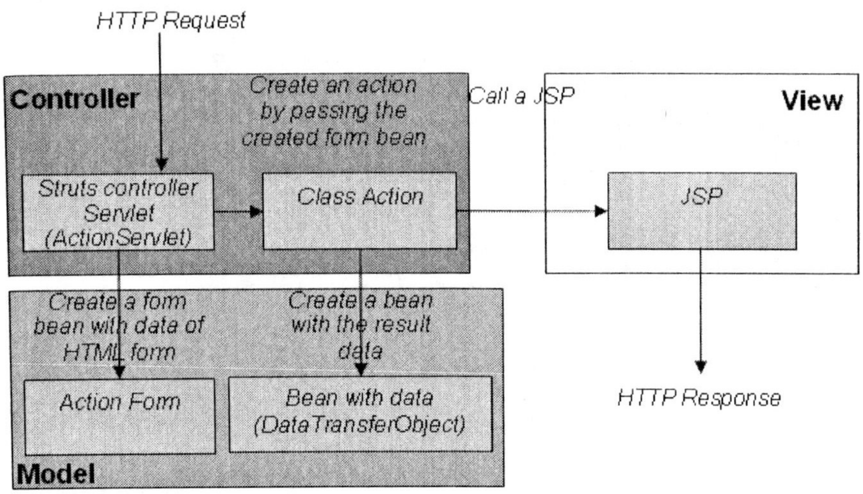

tag library that helps developers create interactive form-based applications with server pages (The Apache Software Foundation, 2006).

- *Oracle9iAS Toplink*, an ORM (Object Relational Mapping) framework for implementing the 'Model' layer that is free only for non-commercial applications.

Furthermore, the ontology is codified in RDFS and is stored in a relational database. The DBMS is Oracle 9i; the relational database schema for the application is the following (Figure 15):

Finally, the standard for e-learning metadata is Dublin Core; the implementation of SCORM 1.2 is a work-in-progress.

These implementation choices give the tool a high level of flexibility and scalability; indeed, it can be used on several knowledge bases by developing a specified domain ontology and by exploiting the potentialities of ORM framework.

EMPIRICAL EVIDENCE

During the exciting experience of conceptualization, design and implementation phases of SWELS, some attempts to validate the effectiveness of the whole approach were made. Specifically, we refer to a process realized on empirical evidence basis to acquire some insights for improving the overall system. This process is articulated in two test phases--the 'alpha test' phase and the 'beta test' phase.

The "Alpha test" phase was performed by the team involved in the implementation of the system itself. From one side, software developers tested many times and under different conditions each functionality of the system. They also executed a general test for the overall system to evaluate its robustness and the coherence of data management and tracking systems. From the other side, the subject matter experts, after the design phase and the coordination of teams involved into the

Figure 15. Relational schema of the database implemented

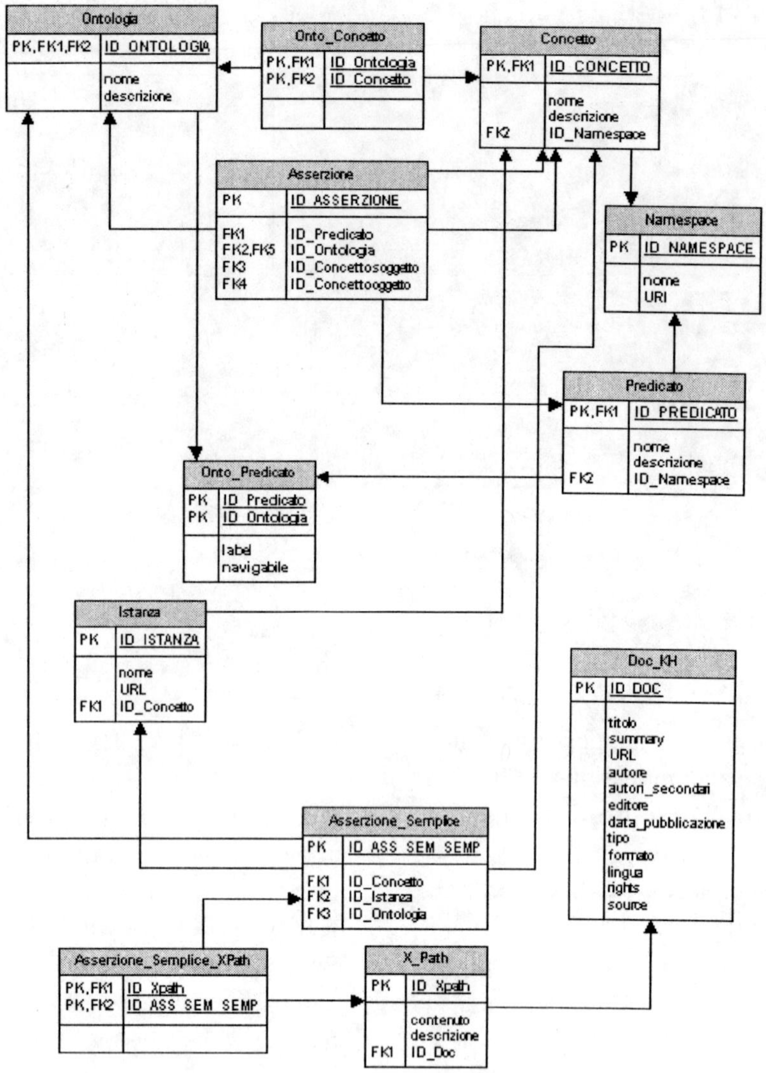

content creation process, executed a double-layer control: one for the exactness of how each topic was expressed, and one for the semantic link about different topics. Both tests revealed a set of enhancements that have been implemented in the new version of SWELS.

The "Beta test phase" was performed by involving a group of 20 students attending an International master program at the eBMS of Scuola Superiore ISUFI,. They used SWELS (platform and contents) as an additional learning tool during the attendance of the module on

"Change Management and Leadership." After one week, at the end of this module, a face-to-face discussion meeting was organized with the participation of an outstanding professor in this field. Final impressions of master participants about SWELS were extremely positive, because they represented a sort of personal assistant to deepen and clarify some difficult concepts of the module and, above all, to have a systemic vision of the general topic.

FUTURE DEVELOPMENTS OF SWELS

The next steps that we aim to develop in the future are:

- The implementation of an interactive radial layout layer (i.e., an interactive graphical interface to activate the "conceptual semantic boundary"). In our opinion, this improvement could make SWELS more effective, since that learners can immediately access learning modules, by directly clicking on the concepts shown in the radial graph.
- The ontological representation of two further learning dimensions: the typology and characteristics of the learning resource (i.e., assessment, difficulty level, etc.) and the learner profile expressed in terms of interests and knowledge gaps (by tracking the learning pattern dynamically created by learners).
- The integration of SWELS into a LMS, that means the development of a personal learning agent integrated into a LMS that proactively configures and recommends personalized learning paths to the learners according to their learning profile.

Finally, a large scale experimentation of the system should be organized in order to evaluate the effectiveness of SWELS and, more in general, of the learning approach embedded in SWELS.

CONCLUSIONS

SWELS platform is the result of applying Semantic Web technologies to e-learning. Such a strategic choice allows learners and knowledge workers to increase the effectiveness of their learning process since it enables a personalized access to learning materials as well as a complete and deep understanding of the knowledge domain.

Indeed, from the point of view of the final users, the main benefits of using SWELS are:

- The explicitation of tacit knowledge contained in the knowledge base conceptualization process and held in the minds of subject matter experts as well as domain designers;
- The systematization of knowledge through an explicit indexing of knowledge resources through simple and complex semantic assertions;
- A more direct access to the knowledge domain by explicitly navigating and browsing the ontology map;
- A more flexible structure of the learning materials that can be easily recombined and described for other purposes and learning goals in other knowledge domains.

In our beliefs, this approach could provide a new way in which students learn, since it is based on a learner-centric strategy characterized by:

- The role of personal tacit knowledge and learning experiences as the starting point and the knowledge background of future learning patterns;
- A solution-oriented approach for creating just-in-time new learning patterns;

- The possibility to fulfill the personal skill gap by actively participating and self-exploring the knowledge base;
- A stimulus to the "knowledge curiosity" of learners in deepening specific knowledge domains;
- The development of knowledge, skills and attitudes conceived as capacity for effective actions and problem solving;
- A set of customized training curricula consistent to learners' needs, their own time and place, without compromising its effectiveness (Keegan, 2000);
- A dynamic creation of learning paths, starting from different knowledge resources semantically annotated, according to the learner interests and knowledge needs, expressed by them in real time.

REFERENCES

Adelsberger, H., Bick, M., Körner, F., & Pawlowski, J.M. (2001). Virtual education in business information systems (VAWI)--Facilitating collaborative development processes using the Essen learning model. In H. Hoyer (Ed.), *20th ICDE World Conference on Open Learning and Distance Education. The Future of Learning – Learning for the Future: Shaping the Transition.*

Barnes-Lee, T. (2000). What the Semantic Web can represent. Retrieved on September 22, 2006, from http://www.w3.org/DesignIssues/RDFnot.html

Barnes-Lee, T. (1998), Semantic Web Roadmap. *W3C Design Issues.* Retrieved on April 12, 2005, from http://www.w3.org/DesignIssues/Semantic.html

Brennan, M., Funke, S., & Andersen, C. (2001). The learning content management system--a new e-Learning market segment emerges. *IDC White Paper.* , Retrieved on September 25, 2006, from http://www.internettime.com/Learning/lcms/IDCLCMSWhitePaper.pdf

Dublin Core Metadata Initiative (2006). Dublin Core Metadata Terms., Retrieved on May 26, 2003, from http://dublincore.org

Damiani, E., Corallo, A., Elia, G., & Ceravolo, P. (2002, November). *Standard per i learning objects: Interoperabilità ed integrazione nella didattica a distanza.* Paper presented at the International Workshop eLearning: una sfida per l'Università - Strategie Metodi Prospettive, Milan, Italy.

Drucker, P. (2000). Need to know: Integrating e-learning with high velocity value chains. *Delphi Group White Paper.* Retrieved on September 22, 2006, from www.delphigroup.com

Elia , G., Secundo, G., and Taurino, C. (2006), Towards unstructured and just-in-time learning: The "Virtual eBMS" e-Learning system. In A Méndez-Vilas, A. Solano-Martin, J. Mesa González, & J.A. Mesa González (Eds.), *m-ICTE2006: Vol. 2. Current Developments in Technology-Assisted Education* (pp. 1067-1072). FORMATEX, Badajoz, Spain.

Fowler, M. & Scott, K. (Eds.). (1999). *UML Distilled Second Edition--A Brief Guide to the Standard Object Modelling Language.* A. Wesley.

Greenberg, L. (2002). LMS and LCMS: What's the Difference? *Learning Circuits, ASTD.* Retrieved September on 25, 2006, from http://www.learningcircuits.org/2002/dec2002/greenberg.htm

Keegan, M. (Ed.). (2000). *e-Learning, The engine of the knowledge economy.* Morgan Keegan & Co.

Kolovski, V., & Galletly, J. (2003). Towards e-learning via the Semantic Web. In B. Rachev, & A. Smrikarov (Eds.), In *Proceedings of the 4th*

International Conference on Computer Systems and Technologies--CompSysTech'2003 (pp. 591 - 596). ACM New York, NY, USA.

Koper R. (2004). Use of the Semantic Web to solve some basic problems in education. *Journal of Interactive Media in Education.* 2004(6), pp.1-23.

Lockwood, F., & Gooley, A. (Eds.). (2001). *Innovation in open and distance learning - successful development of online and Web-based learning.* London, Kogan Page.

McCrea, F., Gay, R. K., & Bacon, R. (2000). *Riding the big waves: a white paper on the B2B e-Learning Industry.* San Francisco/Boston/New York/London: Thomas Weisel Partners LLC.

Mizoguchi, R. (2000). IT revolution in learning technology, In *Proceedings of SchoolNet 2000,* Pusan, Korea (pp. 46-55).

Naeve, A., Nilsson, M., & Palmer, M. (2001), E-learning in the semantic age. CID, Centre For User Oriented It Design. Stockhom, Sweden. Retrieved on September 30, 2006

Nejdl, W. (2001). Learning repositories--Technology and context. In A. Risk (Ed.), *ED-Media 2001 World Conference on education multimedia, Hypermedia and Telecommunications: Vol. 2001, N. 1.*

Rosenberg, M. J. (Ed.). (2006). *Beyond E-Learning: Approaches and technologies to enhance knowledge, learning and performance.* Pfeiffer.

Secundo, G., Corallo, A., Elia, G., and Passiante, G. (2004). An e-Learning system based on semantic Web supporting a Learning in Doing Environment. In *Proceedings of International Conference on Information Technology Based Higher Education and Training--ITHET 2004.* IEEE XPlore, available at http://ieeexplore.ieee.org/iel5/9391/29802/01358145.pdf

Stojanovic, L., Staab, S., & Studer, R. (2001,October 23-27). eLearning based on the Semantic Web. In W. A. Lawrence-Fowler & J. Hasebrook (Eds.), In *Proceedings of WebNet 2001--World Conference on the WWW and Internet,* Orlando, Florida. (pp.1174-1183). AACE.

Sun Microsystems, Inc. (2002). Java Blueprints--Model-view-controller. Retrieved on July 15, 2003, from http://dublincore.org http://java.sun.com/blueprints/patterns/MVC-detailed.html

The Apache Software Foundation, (2006). Apache Struts. Retrieved on September 22, 2006, from http://struts.apache.org/

Chapter VII
Approaches to Semantics in Knowledge Management

Cristiano Fugazza
University of Milan, Italy

Stefano David
Polytechnic University of Marche, Italy

Anna Montesanto
Polytechnic University of Marche, Italy

Cesare Rocchi
Polytechnic University of Marche, Italy

ABSTRACT

There are different approaches to modeling a computational system, each providing different semantics. We present a comparison among different approaches to semantics and we aim at identifying which peculiarities are needed to provide a system with uniquely interpretable semantics. We discuss different approaches, namely, Description Logics, Artificial Neural Networks, and relational database management systems. We identify classification (the process of building a taxonomy) as common trait. However, in this chapter we also argue that classification is not enough to provide a system with a Semantics, which emerges only when relations among classes are established and used among instances. Our contribution also analyses additional features of the formalisms that distinguish the approaches: closed versus. open world assumption, dynamic versus. static nature of knowledge, the management of knowledge, and the learning process.

INTRODUCTION

The growing demand for information and knowledge management is pushing research efforts in computer science towards the development of technologies that allow massive amounts of data to be automatically processed and stored, for the user to dispose of them. In areas like SW (Semantic Web) applications, KR (Knowledge Representation), RDBMS (Relational Database Management Systems), and logic-based systems, research has led, during the last decade, to impressive advances in the creation and the implementation of applications that facilitate the management of knowledge. The availability of such an enormous amount of information also resulted in the necessity to develop systems with the ability to integrate information that originate from heterogeneous sources and organize them into a single source.[1]

On the one hand, these systems allow for not only data storage and retrieval, but also additional logic-based processing, like checking consistency of data; on the other hand, they require to combine different data storage systems (e.g., different database instances) or even different interpretation paradigms (e.g., relational calculus, logical formalisms, or the structure underlying neural networks). Particularly, the integration of heterogeneous data sources poses challenges when their storage systems differ in their underlying semantics, that is, when their logical interpretations do not adhere to the same paradigm. As an example, consider independent organizations collaborating in the EE (Extended Enterprise): the capability of combining into a single data source the data stored in a relational database and the axioms that constitute a *KB (Knowledge Base)* may represent a striking advantage on the market or industry. In this situation, before starting the integration process, it is necessary to have a clear sense of how to correctly join the semantics of the different sources.

The purpose of this chapter is to introduce three popular approaches to knowledge representation, underpinned by different semantics, to show in what they differ, and to present two alternative approaches to the problem of information integration. Particularly, we will focus on the notion of semantics and on the different features that contribute to the notion of semantics for each of the approaches described in this chapter. A good explanation of the concept of semantics in the various approaches requires some introductory knowledge of basic logical formalisms, like propositional and predicate logics. In order to explain how different can result the representation of the same domain and data in different formalisms, we define a sample scenario that will be developed and represented in the distinct formalisms in the next sections.

This chapter is organized as follows. First, we describe a sample scenario that we will use to show differences among the chosen formalisms; then we present the formalisms, starting with elementary notions of propositional and predicate logic and, continuing with the introduction of some concepts in RDBMS, ANNs, and DLs theories. We accompany the theories with explanations on how to consider the features of each formalism and how they lead to different interpretations of the scenario. Finally, we describe two popular integration efforts among different formalisms, namely optimization of query answering in DLs, exploiting RDBMS storage with DL-Lite and OWA/CWA integration with hybrid reasoning.

A SAMPLE SCENARIO

The scenario we will illustrate is the trading of goods; it involves companies, products, articles, markets, and consumers. We introduce these concepts in order to sketch our sample scenario; they will be represented in the different approaches with the addition of instance data to populate the schema.

The main categorization defined by the example is the one distinguishing among different kinds of enterprises. A *company* is a generic entity that provides something (e.g., a service, a product, or another type of goods). *Manufacturer*, *distributor*, and *reseller* are further categorizations of company, while the concept *suppliers* denote the union of distributors and resellers. A *product* is produced by a manufacturer, is sold by a reseller, and is distributed in a specific *market* by a distributor. An *article* is a product which is made by the business entity under consideration (e.g., the manufacturer owning the knowledge base), as opposed to a generic, possibly competing, company. As for a generic product, an article has a *name*, a *sale price*, and it is distributed in a *target market*, a further categorization of market. Finally, a *consumer* is someone who buys an article.

In the following of this chapter, it will be clear that not all approaches to data modeling can express these entities in such a way that, when executing queries over the KB, the result can be expected as correct. This is primarily due to the fact that traditional data structures (e.g., those expressed by relational databases all around the world) typically represent entities that can be exhaustively described and enumerated by the business entity hosting the system. Instead, wherever external data structures defined by third parties are instantiated in the KB, relational databases may fall short of expressing incomplete data structures in a consistent way.

A PRIMER ON SEMANTICS OF DATA STRUCTURES

Recently, there has been a growing interest in the notion of semantics. Probably pushed forward by the development of the SW, many researchers in computer science have (re)started investigating the field of semantics. Such a notion has been already widely investigated in many fields like linguistics, philosophy, and logic. Following the analytic stream as conceived in Russell (1908) and Frege (1918), the concept of semantics in philosophy evolved in formal terms until Montague provided a formalization (Montague, 1974), which is broadly accepted in the field of logic-based linguistic studies. In philosophy, a less formal trend brought to the definition of semantics in terms of "correspondence to the world" (Wittgenstein), an approach influenced by the formal work of Tarsky about the notion of truth. Meanwhile, the work in cognitive psychology explored the human process of categorization and classification, which led to the development of models, inspired by formal models in logic, but more focused on representational issues (frames, etc.).

In Balkenius and Gärdenfors (1991), the authors show that, by developing a high-level description of the properties of neural networks, it is possible to bridge the gap between the symbolic and the subsymbolic levels (Smolensky, 1993). We can make the connection between the approaches closer by providing a different interpretation of the structure of a neural network. Balkenius and Gärdenfors introduce the notion of *schema* as the key concept for this construction. A schema is neutral with respect to the different views of cognition and have been used in both fields (Balkenius, 1993). Moreover, Balkenius uses the term "schema" as a collective name for the structure used in the works of Piaget (1952), Piaget and Inhelder (1973), Rumelhart and McClelland (1986), and Arbib and Hanson, (1987), also including concepts such as Frames (Minsky, 1986) and Scripts (Schank & Abelson, 1977).

Nowadays, the concept of semantics is involved in many research fields: natural language processing, Semantic Web, knowledge representation, and medical informatics. Our purpose is to analyse the notion of semantics in different approaches adopted in the design and implementation of computer systems. We consider three approaches to domain modeling: RDBMS, ANNs (Artificial

Neural Networks), and DLs (Description Logic). RDBMS and DLs are grounded in the theory of propositional logic and its connectives: AND, OR, and NOT, with the addition of universal ($\forall x$) and existential ($\exists x$) quantification of variables from predicate logic, while some particular type of ANNs (McCulloch and Pitts, 1943) can express connectives of propositional logic. However, despite their common groundwork, these approaches have evolved in different directions and are usually employed in fairly different application fields and with heterogeneous purposes. Research and discussion in the fields of RDBMS, ANN, and DL cannot abstract from the diverse notions of semantics they express. In this chapter, we closely look at each approach, highlighting peculiarities and common traits.

After a brief introduction to the theoretical background of propositional and predicate logic, we first consider the relational approach of RDBMS , which allows fast retrieval of structured data via queries over tables. This approach, where data are organized in terms of homogeneous *tuples* (i.e., records with the same number and type of attributes), is by far the most widely adopted architecture for data storage. The second approach we consider is represented by ANN, which has a fairly different and peculiar approach to the modeling of a domain, exploiting a necessary initial learning phase in order to train the ability of the ANN to classify input data. Finally, DL is a well-known approach in the knowledge representation field and uses logic tools (subsumption, consistency, and satisfiability) to implement reasoning over structured data. Such an approach finds its roots in logical formalisms and exploits a clear definition of semantics, often expressed in terms of model theory.

In order to compare the several approaches, we identified a small number of features that unequivocally determine the semantics conveyed by a specific representation formalism; specifically:

- static versus. dynamic nature of the structural description of data items (e.g., the relational schema in RDBMS);
- closed versus. open world assumption when answering queries (i.e., considering the knowledge conveyed by the system as, respectively, complete or incomplete);
- management of implicit knowledge (i.e., whether the system comprises knowledge not explicitly stated in its memory configurations);
- need for a learning phase;
- classification.

After introducing the distinct notions of semantics suggested by RDBMS, ANN, and DL, we will look at two examples of integration efforts between distinct approaches. Firstly, we claim that, in particular situations, even a well-designed RDBMS may fail to retrieve all the correct answers to a query. This happens because the semantics of the relational model is only capable of expressing complete (i.e., exhaustive) knowledge while some data structures are to be considered incomplete. On the other hand, the unparalleled performance of RDBMS when answering queries makes it difficult to implement DL systems that are equally fast. Trying to bridge this gap, *we* introduce a very simple DL that allows for taking advantage of RDBMS as the storage facilities, for instance data while retaining the open-world approach of DL to express incomplete data structures.

Moreover, we will show that modern computer applications (especially those intended to manage data in the EE) quite often need to integrate the different interpretations of a knowledge base. Specifically, proprietary data structures that may be correctly expressed with RDBMS schemata are often extended with data structures defined and populated by third parties (e.g., individual companies in the EE scenario) that cannot be expressed by the relational model; on the contrary, only applications complying with the model-theoretic approach of DL (e.g., DL reasoners) can process this category of data structures correctly. Consequently, *we* tackle the problem of integrating distinct approaches into a hybrid system that is capable of processing both complete and incomplete knowledge.

KNOWLEDGE REPRESENTATION PARADIGMS AND ASSOCIATED SEMANTICS

Basic Logic Formalism

We introduce here some basic notion of logic formalisms. For more advanced reading, please refer to (Kelly, 1997).

Propositional Logic. Propositional logic is a formalism that allows one to assign a truth value to formulæ, that are structures composed of atomic propositions and connectives. An atomic proposition is basically a sentence, considered as a whole and not dividable, which we want to assign a truth value to. For example:

ACME Corp. is a manufacturer.
All products are sold in some market.

Connectives are symbols that allow to link propositions to build formulæ. The basic connectives are conjunction (AND) and disjunction (OR), which are binary operators, and negation (NOT), which is a unary operator. There are additional connectives in the theory of propositional logic (implication and equivalence), but since they are expressible by means of the three basic connectives, we do not consider them here.

A truth value is an assignment of truth, either "true"(T) or "false" (F) to an atomic proposition, that is, a declaration that a proposition is true or false. In order to evaluate the truth value of a formula, all statements and connectives must be evaluated. The NOT inverts the truth value of the statement it is applied to, but how to determine the truth value of a formula containing AND or OR connectives? The former assigns to the formula a value of "true" if all propositions are true, and the latter if at least one of the propositions is true.

Propositional logic also allows for a basic reasoning service, called *entailment* or *logical implication*, which amounts to answering the following question: Given a knowledge base Σ, which is a set of atomic propositions and/or formulæ, can a proposition α be derived by the knowledge base? If this happens, then Σ is also called model of α, i.e., a model is an interpretation that is always true. Moreover, if the knowledge base logically implies true, then it is said to be *satisfiable*. In order to avoid that reasoning produces wrong results, reasoning should satisfy two properties:

1. **Soundness**: All propositions derived are true and no false proposition can be derived.
2. **Completeness**: All possible propositions that can be derived are given in output.

There are two main possibilities to check if entailment (and, in general, any reasoning service,) is sound and complete: 1) enumerating and evaluating all possible truth assignments of the knowledge base and of the derived statements; and 2) using *tableaux calculus*, a procedure that helps constructively to build a model for the knowledge base. The enumeration of all truth assignments of a knowledge base can become very long and complex if there are many statements: a single proposition can have two truth assignments; two propositions can have four truth assignments, and so on. In a generic knowledge base with *n* statements, there are 2^n possible truth assignments. On the other side, tableaux calculus is based on the idea of incrementally building a model for the knowledge base, using rules to decompose formulæ into their components and to create a tree-like structure whose branches either end with a clash, which indicates that such a truth assignment contains contradictory statements (therefore it is not a model for the knowledge base), or are closed, meaning that the truth assignment is a model for the knowledge base.

Predicate Logic. In propositional logic it is possible to state whether an atomic proposition or a formula is true or false, but there is no possibility, neither to state the truth value of a set of statements, nor to describe the internal structure of an atomic proposition. In predicate logic, atomic propositions are expressed by means of relationships among objects of the domain, raising new possibilities to describe the internal structure of an element and to describe a set of elements by means of a common characteristic. In order to clearly introduce some notion of predicate logic, consider the first statement in the example of the previous section, which can be expressed as:

Manufacturer(acme_corp)

There is no sentence here and the atomic statement, which we want to state the truth of, is composed of a predicate (*Manufacturer*), which denotes sets of elements of the domain with the same characteristics, and a constant (*acme_corp*), which is a real element in the domain. Predicates and constants are two of the symbols that help building statements in predicate logic. Additional symbols are required in order to translate the second statement into a logic-based formalism:

$$\forall x.Product(x)\exists y.(Market(y) \wedge isDistributedIn(x,y)$$

Note the writing conventions that we use: concept and property names are, respectively, capitalized and non-capitalized, with composite names rendered with medial capitals (*Product, isDistributedIn*). Individuals are always written lowercase, with an underscore in composite names (*acme_corp*).

Unlike in propositional logic, the structure of the statement is less easy to follow. This formula should be read "All x which are known to be products are distributed in some y which is a market." This example introduces variables (x, y), which act as placeholders for elements of the domain, and quantifiers. Existential quantification ($\exists y$) expresses the existence of at least one element of the domain that satisfies a constraint: "There is at least one y that is a market." Universal quantification ($\forall x$) identifies a set of elements of the domain that belong to one or more predicates, according to some properties: "All x that are products."

Note also that we have found two types of predicates: unary (i.e., with one argument in parenthesis) like *Product(x)*, *Manufacturer(acme_corp)* and binary (i.e., with two arguments in parenthesis) like *isDistributedIn(x, y)*. The former type denotes *concepts*, that is, sets of constants that share some characteristic, while the latter denotes *roles*, that is, relationships between two constants. Predicates with higher arity, that is, that express a relationship among three or more constants, are also possible. Hence, besides the connectives available in propositional logic (AND, OR, and NOT), predicate logic has a richer palette of operators for describing the entities populating a domain.

As in propositional logic, there are some available reasoning services, which allow one to decide the truth of a formula or a set of formulæ. Before introducing reasoning services, it is necessary to define the semantics underlying predicate logic, which is based on the concept of *interpretation*. Intuitively, an interpretation is an assignment of {T, F} to each formula in a set of formulæ, or in a complex formula, that permits the evaluation of the whole (complex) formula. Moreover, the same complex formula should be understood in the same way by different people or automatic systems, avoiding misinterpretations. Formally, given a non-empty set Δ, an interpretation I is defined as a pair $I = (\Delta^I, \cdot^I)$, where Δ^I is a non-empty set called domain and $\cdot^I$ is a function mapping:

- Constants to elements of the domain: $a^I \in \Delta$;

- n-ary predicate symbols to relations over the domain: $P^I \subseteq \Delta^n$.

Introduction to Relational Databases

The *relational model* constitutes the theoretical background underlying RDBMS, representing the most widely implemented technology for data storage and retrieval. The relational model was formalized by Edgar Codd in 1969; the interested reader may refer to a revised version of this work (Codd, 1990) for a thorough description of the model. In a nutshell, a relation is defined by a set of typed attributes and a set of attribute values, grouped as tuples that are consistent with the attribute types. According to the set-theoretic interpretation of the relational model, a relation can be seen as a subset of the Cartesian product of the domains indicated by the attributes; on the other hand, the relational model can be seen as a two-valued propositional logic (i.e., whose variables evaluate to either true or false). Relations can be manipulated and combined by means of the set of operators constituting *relational algebra*. Basic operators are *projection* on the instance values of a subset of attributes ($\pi_{a1,\ldots,an}$) and *selection* of tuples on the basis of a condition (σ_c). As an example, in order to retrieve the name and price of products that are of type "refrigerator," we may write the following formula:

$$\pi_{name,price}(\sigma_{type='refrigerator'}(products)) \qquad (1)$$

The basic pool of operators is completed by set operators, *union* ($\cup$), *difference* ($\setminus$), *Cartesian product* ($\times$) of two relations, and the *rename* operator ($\rho_{a1/a2}$), that is a necessary formal means to execute the Cartesian product on relations whose attribute names are not disjoint. The basic set can be used to define a large number of *join* operations, simplifying practical applications of relational algebra.

Instead of relations and tuples, database administrators are more comfortable with terms like *table* and *row*; the difference in not purely lexical because all RDBMS implementations divert from the relational model in the operational semantics they convey. As an example, table attributes in RDBMS may evaluate to NULL, a special value which indicates missing information and is handled by the system differently from traditional algebraic evaluation. Rather than relying on relational algebra, RDBMS admit the SQL (Structured Query Language) (Abiteboul, Hull, & Vianu, 1995) as the interface language for querying data base instances. SQL also extends the capabilities of the language with commands for schema creation (e.g., for creating and modifying tables), data manipulation (e.g., inserting rows), access control (i.e., specifying access rights on users), and transaction control (i.e., defining sequences of operations that allow for compensation of failures through rollback). As an example, the formula in 1 can be translated into the following SQL statement:

```
SELECT name, price FROM products
WHERE type = 'refrigerator;'
```

The database system engineering also takes advantage of ER (Entity-Relation) diagrams (Chen, 1976) for structuring data according to abstractions such as generalization and aggregation. Unfortunately, these constructs (as well as n-ary relations) may not be directly translated into a relational schema that can be expressed by RDBMS; instead, a preemptive phase in database implementation takes care of restructuring the input schema, so it complies with a normal form that can be directly implemented by existing applications. In this work, we investigate the practical application semantics of knowledge base management; consequently, we drain concepts and terminology from SQL systems. Similarly, in the evaluation of the expressiveness the different formalisms allow for, we will take into account the practical capabilities of implementations. As an example, the handling of generalization hierarchies is not considered a feature of RDBMS because such hierarchies are flattened during normalization. To the extent of this work, we think a database as a structured pool of data. We do not go into details of database theory, so we point the reader to (Abiteboul et al., 1995) for a comprehensive introduction to the topic. A database relies on a schema, which describes the 'things' which are stored in the database.

Among different approaches to the structure of a schema, the most commonly known and commercially adopted is the relational schema, which allows one to define information in terms of multi-related records (tables). Alternative (but less used) approaches are the hierarchical one (e.g., the one used in LDAP), the network model (which permits multiple inheritance via lattice structures) the object-oriented model, and the XML-based model. The representational tool in relational databases is the *table*, which allows the representation of instances and relations among instances. For example, a manufacturer can be represented as in Table 1, which is an abstraction of the database table defining the manufacturer concept in order to store instance data.

The first row represents the schema of the table. The database table is named *Manufacturer* and has three attributes: *name*, *address*, and *state*. The second row represents a tuple in the table. A tuple is the generic name for an *n*-ary relation (i.e., the relation between the concept and its attributes, where *n* is the number of attributes) and represents in practice one line of a table. Table 1 describes a particular instance of manufacturer, whose name is 'Clocks Inc.,' whose office is on the '5th Avenue' in the 'New York' State. More formally, both a definition and an instance can be expressed as a tuple. For example, the following is a tuple representing the manufacturer definition[2]:

Manufacturer: name, address, state

whereas the Clocks Inc. instance can be expressed as:

Manufacturer(Clocks Inc., 5th Avenue, New York)

Table 1. Definition of manufacturer

Manufacturer	name	address	state
	Clocks Inc.	5th Avenue	New York

Table 2. Definition and instantiation of relation 'provides.'

provides	Manufacturer	Product
	Clocks Inc.	Digital Watch

In the definition of the concept, it is possible to specify the type of an attribute (e.g., integer, string, etc.) and whether it is mandatory or not. Attributes' fillers (namely, column values) have to be of the same type. For example, the address of a manufacturer has to be a string; the state has to be a string as well or constrained to belong to a list, and so forth. A table can also express a relationship. Consider Table 2: the first row defines relation 'provides,' which can hold between a manufacturer and a product. Assuming 'Digital Watch' is an instance of product, the second row states the fact that the manufacturer named 'Clock Inc.' provides the product named 'Digital Watch.' In the real world, in order to avoid the problems related to multiple tuples with the same value (say, 'Clocks Inc.') for a given attribute, tuples are univocally identified within a table by *keys*, that is, typically numeric attributes whose values are kept unique within a table instance. Relationships between tuples from distinct tables can then be expressed by referring these attribute values as *foreign keys*.

It is important to notice that Table 2 states a relation between two tuples, the 'Clocks Inc.' instance and the 'Digital Watch' instance. This simple database allows one to make queries, for example, to retrieve all products of a given manufacturer, retrieve all manufacturers in the state of New York, and so forth. The purpose of a relational database, especially in commercial applications, is fast querying, supported by views that are built during batch procedures. A view is a sort of virtual table containing tuples of some particular table column, with pointers to the row associated with the value, usually built to quickly locate some tuples (rows) in a table. Views simply quicken the retrieval but the application works anyway, just slower. Views can be built on any combination of attributes, which are usually the most frequently queried.

We can distinguish three main actions which are performed on a database--schema construction, population, and querying. The first action is the definition of the tables and of the relations between them. During this phase some semantics is involved, especially during the establishment and statement of relations. For example, the definition of table 'provides' requires that the elements which populate it have to come from the manufacturer and the product table. More formally, in set theory terms, the pairs that populate the table have to be a subset of the Cartesian product obtained by coupling tuples of the manufacturer table and tuples of the product table. The same 'semantic requirement' will apply in the subsequent phases: population and querying. Population is the constructions of instances, tuples describing the objects which populate the database. During the population there will be a sort of type check, to control the type-correctness of the tuples populating table 'provides.' The querying phase involves also the specification of properties, which introduce additional semantic operations. For example, it is possible to retrieve all the Manufacturers in the New York state. In other words, the retrieval allows one to specify constraints on the values of the tuples to be searched in a specific table or in a set of tables.

OWA/CWA. The underlying assumption of RDBMS is that the world is closed. This means that, during the querying phase, if a table does not exist or is void, the result is an empty set of tuples.

Static/Dynamic system. Relational databases are static systems. In this case, static means that, unlike ANN approaches, there is no training phase required for the system to work. Once the schema has been declared and populated, the system is ready to be used.

Incomplete knowledge. The management of incomplete knowledge is not handled by RDBMS. A database must always be capable of retrieving the information that describes what one of its elements is; so it must have certainty about the data it stores and retrieves. It is important to notice that the main purpose of relational databases is fast querying of explicitly stated knowledge.

INTRODUCTION TO ARTIFICIAL NEURAL NETWORKS

The definition of an ANN could be seen as a system of programs and data structures that approximate the operations of the human brain. They involve a large number of processes operating in parallel, each with its own small "sphere of knowledge" and access to data in its local memory. The communication among physiological neurons is carried out through the exchange of neurotransmitters. These concur to activate the action potential; therefore, they activate or not neighbor neurons. We can represent the operation of neurons by means of a logical structure, like McCulloch and Pitts already formalized back in 1943. These kinds of neurons can be arranged in short temporal sequences. The answer of the only output neuron represents the value of truth of any represented binary logical operation on the input neurons. The weights and the thresholds are chosen so that, at every time step, a logical computation is carried out. This model of neural net allows the computation of propositional negation, conjunction (AND) and disjunction (OR). Using an identity function, a net of formal neurons computes exclusive OR (XOR) of two propositions.

The Perceptron of Rosenblatt (1962) is the natural extension of the formal neuron of McCulloch and Pitts. It has the ability to estimate in parallel a variety of predicates in input and the weighted sum of the output is compared with a threshold. An appropriate choice of the interconnection weights and of the thresholds will supply the output for the correct classifications of the input. Minsky and Papert (1969) pointed out that the Perceptron was limited in its possibility of classification. It is not able, in fact, to compute the XOR unless by the introduction of hidden layers of unit between the input and output layer. Minsky and Papert could not propose a learning rule to deal with the hidden units. A number of people have since independently discovered the learning rule for a multi-layered Perceptron net-

Figure 1. A high-level view on neural networks

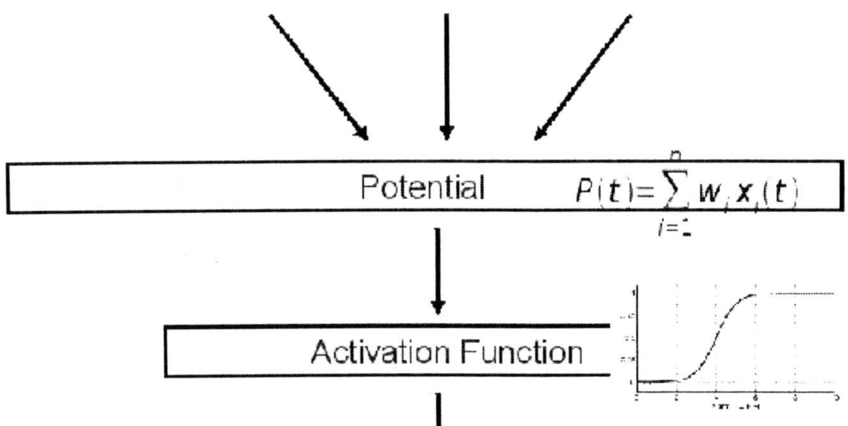

$$P(t)=\sum_{i=1}^{n} w_i x_i(t)$$

$$u(t+1)=\frac{1}{1+e^{-(P(t)-S)}}$$

work. The first one to discover the generalized delta rule, or back-propagation algorithm was Werbos in 1974 (Werbos, 1994). Consequently, this particular neural network becomes a dynamic system with feedback in which there are states that can be seen like binary words of *n* bits. These states are evoked from classes of stimuli and so they become the representation of these classes. Every state of the net (the dynamic system) is an instantaneous photo of such system. A dynamics sequence of the states of the net is a trajectory in the space to *n* dimensions of which the binary words (representatives the states of the net) are vertexes. Figure 1 shows how a generic neural network unit works.

In Balkenius and Gärdenfors (1991), an artificial neural network N is defined as a 4-tuple $<S, F, C, G>$. *S* is the space of all possible states of the neural network. The dimensionality of *S* corresponds to the number of parameters used to describe a state of the system. *F* is a set of state transition functions or activation functions. *C* is the set of possible configurations of the network. *G* is a set of learning functions that describe how the configurations develop as a result of various inputs to the network. Two interacting subsystems in a neural network: $<S, F>$ that governs the fast changes in the network, that is, the transient neural activity, and $<C, G>$ that controls the slower changes that correspond to the whole learning in the system. ANNs have a distributed representation of knowledge (Kurfess, 1999); an item is not represented by a single symbol or a sequence of symbols, but by the combination of many small representational entities, often referred to as microfeatures. We could say that a static schema is a stable pattern of activity in a neural network.

A schema α corresponds to a vector $< a_1, \ldots, a_n >$ in the state space *S*. A schema α is currently represented in a neural network with an activity vector $x = < x_1, \ldots, x_n >$ means that $x_i \leq a_i$ for all $1 \leq i \leq n$. Let α, β be two schemata. If $\alpha \leq \beta$, then β can be considered to be a more general schema than α, and α can thus be seen as an instantiation of schema β.

Semantics in ANN. According to Healy and Caudell (2006), concepts are symbolic descriptions of objects and events, observable or imagined, at any arbitrary level of generality or specificity. They are organized as a multi-threaded hierarchy ordered from the abstract to the specific. In this context, the semantics of a neural network can be expressed as an evolving representation of a distributed system of concepts, many of them learned from data via weight's adaptation. To build a class we usually use definitions or constraints, which are conditions to be satisfied, or better they are features and attributes of the same classes. Classes are composed of members representing a specific domain. ANNs create sub-symbolic class relations strongly related to the particular described domain. These kinds of relations are embedded into the dynamical system structure. This dynamical system architecture is a model of described and learned domain.

OWA/CWA. A clear distinction between closed world assumption and open world assumption in the field of ANN is not so easy. The standard models of neural networks are usually closed world systems. We could evaluate the "openness" of a neural network by first considering its physical structure: for example, if we need a variable number of nodes, we can apply a pruning approach that removes redundant units from a network (Wynne-Jones, 1991). On the other hand, we can use a fixed structure but change the amount of information in the training set. An example about learning the past tenses of English verbs can be found in Rumelhart and McClelland (1986). It is a simple Perceptron-based pattern associator interfaced with an input/output encoding/decoding network which allows the model to associate verb stems with their past tenses using a special phoneme-representation format.

Static/dynamic system (Learning and relational semantics). The process of learning modifies the structure of the weights in the neural network in order to maximize the number of constraints that are satisfied. In this way, ANNs catch the constraint structure of the particular modeled context, so we can say that it has "learned" the relational semantics of that domain. This point of view shows that semantics is a kind of *Gestalt* that organizes data into a coherent structure. The understanding of meaning could consist of the emergence of coherence starting from a chaotic initial state through a phase transition. Even Balkenius and Gärdenfors (1991) have shown that, by introducing an appropriate schema concept and exploiting the higher-level features of the resonance function in a neural network, it is possible to define a form of non-monotonic inference relation. So, "truth" in ANNs consists of the dynamic state in which a node is active or not, that is, the truth embedded into the knowledge state of the system.

The particular dynamic system represented by a specific ANN structure is the model of the learned domain. Typically, a neural network is initially "trained" with large amounts of data and rules about data relationships. One of the most important features of a neural network is its ability to adapt to new environments. Therefore, learning algorithms are critical for the study of neural networks. Learning is essential to most of these neural network architectures and hence the choice of the learning algorithm is a central issue in the development of an ANN. Learning implies that a processing unit can change its input/output behavior as a result of changes occurred in the environment. Since the activation functions are usually fixed when the network is constructed and the input/output vector cannot be changed, the weights corresponding to that input vector need to be adjusted in order to modify the input/output behavior.

A method is thus needed at least during a training stage, to modify weights in response to the input/output process. A number of such learning functions are available for neural network models. Learning can be either supervised, in which the network is provided with the correct answer for the output during training, or unsupervised, in which no external teacher is present. MLP (Multiple Layer Perceptron) training algorithms are examples of supervised learning using the EBP (Error BackPropagation) (Rumelhart & McClelland, 1986). EBP is a gradient descent algorithm that uses input vectors and the corresponding output vectors to train a multiple layer network until it can approximate a given function. It was proved that MLPs, which are networks with biases, a sigmoid layer, and a linear output layer, can approximate any function with a finite number of discontinuities.

Kohonen's Self-Organising Maps (Kohonen, 2000) are based on non-supervised learning. The preservation of neighborhood relations is a very useful property that has attracted a great interest, for which similar input patterns from the input space will be projected into neighboring nodes of the output map, and conversely, nodes that are adjacent in the output map will decode similar input patterns. All self-organizing networks have been generally considered as preserving the topology of the input space, and this is the consequence of the competitive learning. However, by following recent definitions of topology preservation, not all self-organising models have this peculiarity.

Incomplete knowledge. After learning, every input data given to the ANN is classified, even if it was never seen before or if there is no evident relation with already present elements. So, incomplete knowledge can not be discovered in ANNs. For example: if we want to build a suitable model of neural network that represents the concept of "Monopoly" within our sample scenario, we can choose among different neural network architectures. We decided to use a Multilayer Perceptron that models the relation among the different instances of article, products, Manufacturers, and so on. The learning algorithm of the

MLP is represented by Equation 2, as presented in Rumelhart and McClelland (1986).

$$\Delta w_{ij} = -\eta \frac{\partial E}{\partial w_{ij}} + \alpha \Delta w_{ij}(n-1) \quad (2)$$

The minimum error (E) obtained during the training depends on a suitable learning rate (η) and momentum (α). Once completed the training, it is necessary to test its effective ability to recognize concept *Monopoly*. The training set will be represented by all the instances of *TargetMarket* [Country code, Product Code, Manufacturer]. So, when we minimize the error on the association training set of *TargetMarket* and typology of monopoly, we will have a model of this kind of concept embedded in the Perceptron structure. Moreover, this model can associate, after the training phase, a new instance of *TargetMarket* (never seen before) to one of the class of *Monopoly*. In this way, a neural network is able to fill missing information.

INTRODUCTION TO DESCRIPTION LOGICS

DLs are a family of languages for knowledge representation and reasoning. Technically, they are defined as a decidable fragment of First Order Logic (Kelly, 1997), restricted to unary and binary predicates. We briefly introduce here the basic concepts underlying DLs: components, syntax, semantics, and reasoning. We point the interested reader to the Description Logic Handbook (Baader, Calvanese, McGuinness, Nardi, & Patel-Schneider, 2003) or to the bibliography for a deeper presentation.

*Components of a DLS (*Description Logic System). The three main components of a DLS are depicted in Figure 3. A KB is a set of *assertions* (also called *statements* or *axioms*) about a domain, defined by means of *concepts* (a.k.a. *classes*), *roles* (a.k.a. *properties*), and *relationships*; it can be described in DLs by means of a concept language. The axioms are written in a concept language, and are organized in a TBox and

Figure 2. Multilayers perception modelling the concept "monopoly"

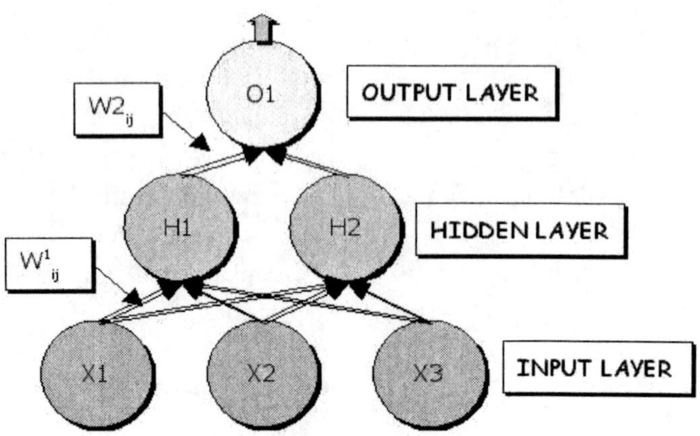

Figure 3. The components of a description logic system

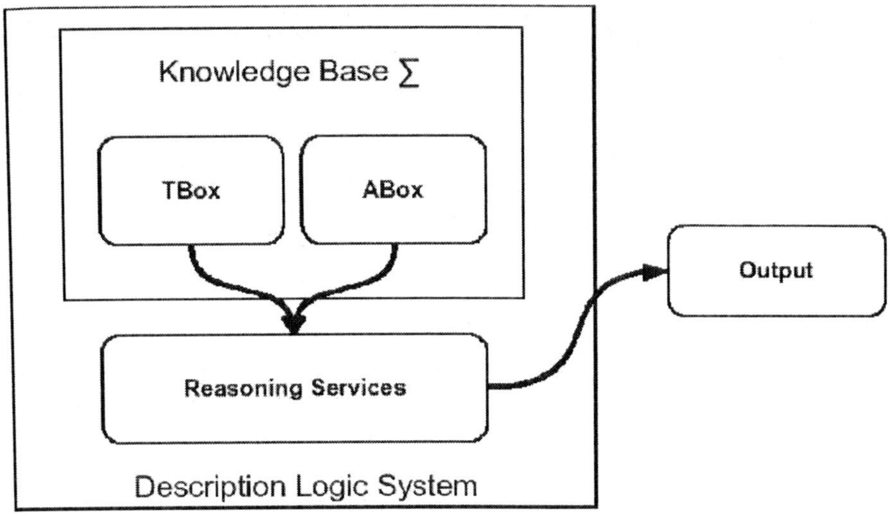

in an ABox, the former containing the described domain structure, and the latter containing real objects. Reasoning services allow one to deduce additional information from the knowledge stored in the KB. It is worth noting that the very core of a DLS is its ability to correctly reason over the data contained in the knowledge base.

Before describing the components of a DLS, we give an overview of concept languages.

Concept languages. Like every language, a concept language consists of a syntax, which encompasses constructors that allow to link elements or sets of elements in the domain. Concept languages allow to write axioms (assertions over elements or sets of elements in the domain) to define concepts and roles (i.e., properties of concepts and relationships among concepts), which are aggregates of elements in the domain, and to make assertions about single elements (called also *individuals* or *instances*) of the domain. Concepts are defined by unary predicates and roles by binary predicates and can be either atomic or complex. Here are some examples.

1. $TargetMarket \sqsubseteq Market$. "A target market is a particular type of market" or, more technically, "The set of all target markets is contained in the set of all markets."
2. $Article \equiv Product \sqcap \exists\, hasName \sqcap \exists\, hasSalePrice$. "An article is a kind of product, and it has a name and a sale price". Product is an atomic concept (i.e., it is not defined in terms of other concepts). Article is a complex concept, *hasName* and *hasSalePrice* are roles.
3. $isDistributedIn.Market$, $isDistributedIn^{-}.Article$. This is more subtle, but it basically says "An article is sold in a market". It expresses explicitly the *range* (*Market*) and *domain* (*Article*) of role *isDistributedIn*, although one would better write it as $Article \equiv \exists\, isDistributedIn.Market$. The value after

the," (e.g., in *isDistributedIn.Market* it would be *Market*) is called *filler* of the property. The superscript $^-$ denotes the inverse property. The DL syntax indeed only allows one to specify the filler (i.e., the range) of a property and not its domain.

4. *Product(cell_phone).* "Cell phone is a Product," or "Cell phone is an individual of type Product."
5. *isDistributedIn(cell_phone, italy).* "Cell phone is sold in Italy." Note the difference in the syntax between the definition of the role *isDistributedIn* above and its instantiation here.

TBox and ABox. The TBox contains the *intensional* knowledge, which is general knowledge concerning the domain of discourse, fixed in time and usually not subjected to changes. The TBox contains terminological axioms, that is, axioms that define concepts and roles, like in examples 1-3 above. The ABox contains the *extensional* knowledge, which concerns specific elements of the domain, and might change over time. The ABox contains assertional axioms, that is, that describe and represent assertions about individuals in the domain, like in examples 4-5 above. TBox and ABox form the KB, denoted by $\Sigma = (T, A)$, where T is the TBox and A the ABox. Although knowledge bases and databases may seem very similar from a structural point of view, with the tables of a RDBMS resembling the TBox and the tuples of each table resembling the actual data contained in the ABox, there are a lot of differences from a conceptual point of view that we will show with the following example.[3]

T = {***Article*** ≡ *Product* ⊓ *isProducedBy.Company* ⊓ *hasName* ⊓
⊓ *hasSalePrice* ⊓ ≥1 *isDistributedIn.TargetMarket*,
Product ≡ *isProducedBy.Manufacturer* ⊓ ≥1 *isReselledBy.Reseller* ⊓
⊓ ≥1 *isDistributedBy.Distributor* ⊓ ≥1 *isDistributedIn.Market*
Market ⊑ *Country*, ***TargetMarket*** ≡ *Market* ⊓ *hasCurrency*,
Consumer ≡ ∃ *buys.Article*, ***Company*** ≡ ∃ *Provides*}

A = {*provides(acme_corp, anvil), provides(acme_corp, rockets),*
provides(logistics_inc, transportation), Manufacturer(clocks_inc),
Supplier(logistics_inc), buys(will, anvil), buys(lisa, toaster),
buys(pauline, digital_watch), buys(john, chronograph)}

A KB also contains the so-called "implicit knowledge," information not explicitly stated, but that can be logically deduced by the existing knowledge. Implicit knowledge can be discovered with the help of *reasoning services*, for example in the answer to a query posed by a user to the system. A reasoning engine (called *reasoner*) also provides additional inference services: depending on the input and on the goal, the system carries out different processes. Hence, it is immediately seen that, unlike in RDBMS, it is not necessary to explicitly state neither that *anvil, toaster, digital watch, and chronograph* are articles, nor that *Will, Lisa, Pauline*, and *John* are consumers, since these conclusions are automatically derived from the definition *Consumer = buys.Article* ("A customer is someone who buys an article") relation: since the filler of role buys is *Article*, then every second argument of the relation buys is automatically derived to be an element of the set *Article*. The same applies to *Consumer*: since it is defined as someone who buys an article, then every first argument in the relation is derived to be an element of the set *Consumer*. Note also the difference in the definition of *Consumer* and *Company*: they are both valid, but the former represents someone who buys an article, whereas the latter represents an entity that provides something.

This causes the inability of deriving additional information on the filler of role *provides*. We know that a company provides something, but we do not know what. We might discover subsequently that a company provides *Good*s, so we can modify in our knowledge base the actual axiom to *Company* $\equiv \exists$ *provides.Good*.

Semantics of DL Languages. We will denote with Δ the domain of discourse, with $\times$ the Cartesian product of two generic sets and with $\sqsubseteq$ the subsumption relation (i.e., relations between super- and subclasses) between Concepts or Roles. The semantics of DL languages is given in terms of an *interpretation*, defined as a pair $I = (\Delta^I, \cdot^I)$, where Δ^I is a non-empty set called *domain* and the interpretation function $\cdot^I$ is a *mapping* from every Concept to a subset of Δ^I, from every Role to a subset of $\Delta^I \times \Delta^I$ and from every Individual to an element of Δ^I. An interpretation I is a *model* for a Concept C if the set C^I is non-empty.

Besides those presented in the beginning of this section, DLs provide many additional connectives, also called *constructors*, each of which has its own semantics, so that it can be uniquely interpreted. The basic constructors, AND, OR, and NOT have the same interpretation as in predicate logic: the conjunction of two or more concepts (i.e., concepts related by AND), evaluates to true if and only if all the concepts are true, and similar arguments apply to disjunction (OR) and negation (NOT).

Additional constructors provided by DLs include *inverse roles*, *(qualified) number restrictions*, and *functionality*. *Inverse roles* are roles with their arguments swapped, for example *producedBy* (like in "A product is produced by a manufacturer") and *produces* ("A manufacturer produces a product"). *Number restrictions* allow to specify how many values of a particular role can be specified for a concept, it is also called *cardinality restriction* and can be specified as an exact restriction, as an at-least restriction, or as an at-most restriction, meaning that the value allowed is either an exact value (i.e., the one given in the restriction), or it must be at least or at most equal to the given one.

- A national article is distributed in exactly one target market.
  NationalArticle $\equiv =1$ *isDistributedIn.TargetMarket*
- An article is distributed at least in ten target markets.
  Article $\equiv \geq 10$ *isDistributedIn.TargetMarket*
- An exclusive article is distributed in at most three target markets.
  ExclusiveArticle $\equiv \leq 3$ *isDistributedIn.TargetMarket*

Functionality is a particular characteristic of a role that allows one to uniquely identify the filler for that role when describing a given individual. Formally, given a functional role R and individuals x, y, z, if $R(x, y) \sqcap R(x, z)$, it follows necessarily that $y = z$. For example, you may want to constrain each company to have only one CEO (Chief Executive Officer), so that whenever you talk about this company, its CEO is uniquely identified. Now, suppose that role *hasCEO* is functional, and you have the following axioms.

hasCEO(acme_corp, john_smith)
hasCEO(acme_corp, john_h_smith)

There are two possibilities to read these two axioms: either John Smith and John H. Smith are the same person, or your knowledge base is inconsistent, since functionality forbids that ACME Corp. (and every other company) has more than one CEO.

Reasoning. A DL system provides many basic inference services. Here we present some of them, and we sketch out how they are used to build some more complex ones.

1. *Subsumption*: decide whether a concept is more general than another. Upon Subsump-

tion, the process of *Classification* is built, which is the process that builds the hierarchy of the concepts in the TBox T.

2. *Consistency Check*: decide if Σ is satisfiable, that is, if it is coherent and admits a model.
3. *Concept Satisfiability*: decide if a concept *C* is satisfiable in a KB Σ.
4. *Instance Checking*: decide if an instance *C(a)* is satisfied in every model of Σ. On Instance Checking in based the process of *Retrieval* or *Query Answering*: given a KBs Σ and a concept C, find the set of all instances C(a) in Σ.

Static and dynamic systems. We have already noted that a KB stores two types of knowledge: intensional and extensional. The former is also said *timeless*, since it is unlikely to be changed. DLs and KB are indeed suitable for describing domains that can evolve over time, but only at the ABox level, that is, assertions on individuals and not on the structure stored in the TBox: the TBox is designed in a way that it hardly can be changed. Description Logics Systems are therefore static systems: they can not automatically update the TBox, as this implies the redefinition of an existing concept (see (De Giacomo, Lenzerini, Poggi, & Rosati, 2006)): only the interaction of the user can modify a concept. Note also, that the literature about updates w.r.t. the ABox is very limited (investigated in (Liu, Lutz, Milicic, & Wolter, 2006)), and also ontology evolution (i.e., ontology update w.r.t. the TBox) is almost uninvestigated (an exception is (Haase & Stojanovic, 2005)).

Management of incomplete knowledge. We have already seen that in a RDBMS what is not explicitly stated in a table is considered false: true is only the knowledge carried by the tuples. For example, if there is no tuple in a table that states "ACME Corp. is a supplier," then no query for suppliers to the RDBMS will return ACME Corp. as a result. This is what is called Closed World Assumption. In KBs, however, the answer to the same query might have a result, as it could be inferred from other statements that ACME Corp. is in fact a supplier. The following statements can, in fact, do the job: "A supplier provides manufactured goods" and "ACME Corp. provides anvils". From them we can infer that ACME, Corp. is a supplier, and that anvils are a type of manufactured goods.

Another difference between KB and RDBMS is in the management of incomplete knowledge in a domain. To understand what it is intended with incomplete knowledge, suppose that in our database we already have three tables: Supplier, Manufacturer, and Reseller. Consider the following example, composed of two statements:

ACME Corp. is not a reseller.
ACME Corp. is a supplier or a manufacturer.

These statements clearly define the concept of ACME Corp. as being either a supplier or a manufacturer, but not a reseller, but it is not straightforward how to represent this in our RDBMS. We cannot insert a tuple in any of the three tables of our database: we have to deal with information that does not exhaustively specify what ACME Corp. actually is. To do so, it is necessary to define what ACME Corp. is. It can be possible to represent that ACME Corp. is not a reseller, for example creating a NotReseller table, with appropriate foreign keys and constraints that check for an element of this table not to be in the Reseller table. More complicated is to represent the concept of ACME Corp. being either a supplier or a manufacturer, for which an exact representation might be impossible.

However, statements like these are common in knowledge representation and the ability to deal with them is substantial: one should be able to express what an individual in the domain is not, rather than explicitly tell what it is. Hence, in a DL that allows for negation and disjunction, the two statements can easily be represented as:

$\neg$*Reseller(acme_corp)*
Supplier(acme_corp) $\sqcup$ *Manufacturer(acme_corp)*

In a Description Logic that has no support for negation or disjunction,[4] the two statements can not be represented either.

Open and Closed World Assumption. The Closed World Assumption and the Open World Assumption represent two different approaches in how to evaluate knowledge in a knowledge base. The difference in their behaviour is usually clarified by a comparison between the structure of a KB $\Sigma=(T, A)$, and a relational database, where the schema of the latter (i.e., its tables and structure) roughly corresponds to T and its tuples correspond to A. The difference is that, on the one side, we have a single RDBMS instance, which represents the only possible interpretation of the stored data, while on the other we have one out of all possible interpretations of Σ. Hence, while in a RDBMS if information is not explicitly stated in a tuple, it is interpreted as "negative" or false knowledge, in a knowledge base it is considered false only if it contradicts some other axioms in the domain. The difference between the two behaviours is better seen with the help of an example.

An example of OWA and incomplete knowledge. Suppose you want to model a very simple scenario, where companies are either manufacturers or suppliers, but not both, and nothing else can be a company. This situation is formalised in Description Logics with the formulæ:

$$T = \{\ Company \doteq (Manufacturer \sqcup Supplier),\ Manufacturer \sqcap Supplier \sqsubseteq \bot\}$$

At a first glance, it might seem straightforward to represent the same scenario in a RDBMS, for example, with a table Company with two columns, one with the name of the company and one that shows whether it is a manufacturer or a supplier with an appropriate flag. This table can be created with a SQL statement:

```
CREATE TABLE Company (
    name String NOT NULL PRIMARY
        KEY,
    type ENUM ('Manufacturer', 'Supplier')
        NOT NULL)
```

Even when we start populating both the KB and the RDBMS with the same complete data, for example, with the information that ACME Corp. is a Manufacturer, everything seems correct. The ABox of the KB will contain an axiom and the RDBMS will have a table.

$A = \{Manufacturer(acme\_corp)\}$

Company	
ACME Corp.	Manufacturer

However, a prominent difference is going to become apparent when we want to represent in both the KB and the RDBMS some particular kind of data. For example, suppose we know that ACME Corp. is a company, but we do not know whether it is a manufacturer or a supplier. In a KB, we need only to add to the ABox the statement Company(acme corp), but when we want to insert that information in the Data Base, the lack of knowledge about ACME Corp. being a manufacturer or a supplier forbids that tuple to be inserted in the table, since one of the mandatory attributes 'Man' or 'Sup" is missing.

INTEGRATION EFFORTS

Currently, data bases aggregated from heterogeneous data sources (such as those in the EE scenario) are typically stored into large RDBMS, which can store and retrieve data with extreme efficiency. However, a user or a manager in the EE is facing two challenging tasks when trying to access different data sources (e.g., RDBMS, KBs, or other structured data). On the one hand, keeping the integrity of data bases may result not a trivial process; on the other hand, querying data aggregated from different sources might be impossible. Since consistency and other reasoning services are tasks that in DLs come for free, and since storage and retrieval systems like RDBMS provide the best performances, many efforts have been devoted in the last few years to investigating frameworks that allow to use DLs KBs and RDBMS together, exploiting their strengths and reducing their weaknesses. In this section, we present two popular approaches to information integration: DL-Lite, a framework that helps using DLs reasoning services to query data stored into relational databases, and hybrid reasoning frameworks, combining closed world reasoning on top of knowledge bases with open world reasoning.

Expressiveness and Performance With DL-Lite

We have seen that both RDBMS and DLs have drawbacks in their use: RDBMS do not allow for reasoning, have a loose support for logical consistency, a basic form of which is obtained by means of (possibly complex) integrity constraints and triggers, and have low expressiveness. Nevertheless, DLs are not tailored to manage large ABoxes (i.e., large amounts of data) since this requires to reason also with concept definitions, that is, with the TBox, and may have an extremely high computational complexity, depending on the constructors used. Moreover, the understanding of the formalism can be challenging. In the last decade, investigation in the field of Description Logics has been developed in two main directions.

- Following the increasing demand for expressive languages in both KR and the SW, the limits of expressiveness and computational complexity were pushed forward to the definition of new algorithms for very complex DLs, like for example SROIQ (Horrocks, Kutz, & Sattler, 2006), which is the base of the proposed revision 1.1 of the Web Ontology Language (OWL[5]). We will not cover this development branch since we are more interested in the integration between RDBMS and DLs than in the investigation of very expressive languages.
- A lot of efforts have been devoted to identifying simpler languages that, although limited in expressiveness, are useful for some specific applications. In this section, we focus our attention on a family of DLs, called DL-Lite (Calvanese et al., 2005), which offers interesting characteristics for information integration, in order to tackle the drawbacks presented at the beginning of this section. In particular, DL-Lite has the ability to exploit RDBMS technologies for storing large amounts of data, to check the data consistency, provided by logical inference, and can express complex queries to the RDBMS, translating formal queries into SQL queries.

Especially in the Semantic Web community, KBs (commonly called *ontologies*) have been employed not only as a means for describing domains, but also as a conceptual view over data, that is, as an abstract means for interpreting the structure of the domain underlying instance data that are stored in a relational database. Semantic Web technologies are not yet widely used for storing axioms of knowledge bases, indeed, and developers tend to use RDBMS, which are more mature, as ontology repositories.

The use of ontologies as a conceptual view can also help addressing other issues that are related with the continuously rising needs for information integration and access. Suppose you have the necessity to merge distinct databases into a single one: obviously, you need to preserve data consistency. In order to avoid comparing the different schemata by hand, in order to check whether there are incoherent tables as well as misaligned tuples stored in the tables, it proves useful to exploit the representation provided by semantics-aware KBs, together with the inference services supplied by the underlying logical formalism, and let a description logics system carry out this work. If the response is positive, then the new database is logically consistent, otherwise it becomes necessary to modify the schema.

From a computational point of view, DL-Lite[6] is a very simple language, as the satisfiability of a KB can be computed in polynomial time. The grammar of DL-Lite is shown in Figure 4, where A, B, C denote concepts and R denotes a role. DL-Lite allows for existential quantification ($\exists R$), inverse roles ($\exists R^-$), negation of concepts ($\neg B$), and conjunction of concepts ($C_1 \cap C_2$). DL-Lite also permits to express inclusion assertion, $B \subseteq C$, e.g., assertion about hierarchy relations among concepts, and functionality assertions, (funct R), (funct R^-).

The expressiveness of DL-Lite is therefore limited, but it suffices to capture, for example, the semantics of UML class diagrams[7] and ER diagrams (Chen, 1976), i.e., DL-Lite has the same modeling capabilities of these two formalisms.

From this relation between DL-Lite and ER, it follows that DL-Lite can also capture the semantics of RDBMS, allowing the expression of the data carried by tuples in tables by means of DLs axioms. However, this is not enough to guarantee that the integration between DL-Lite and RDBMS is straightforward. Indeed, typical reasoning processes are different in the two formalisms: recalling the parallel between TBox and tables and between ABox and tuples, users of RDBMS are typically interested in querying instance data and not the structural properties of tables, that is, they are interested in data complexity. In DLs, querying the data (ABox) is generally more complex than querying the schema, since ABox reasoning also requires to consider, during the reasoning process, the definition of all concepts involved, and not only instance data. Hence, there are more axioms to be considered and reasoning is obviously influenced.

Moreover, a basic reasoning task in DLs is query answering, but the typical SQL query posed to a RDBMS is equivalent to what is called *conjunctive query answering* in DLs, which is a far more complex task than simple query answering, since it amounts to answering to many queries at the same time and then combining the results. There is an interesting implementation of DL-Lite, called QuOnto (Acciarri et al., 2005), which reflects all the features of DL-Lite. QuOnto indeed stores the data into a RDBMS, permitting the storage of large quantities of data and, moreover it allows a user to ask conjunctive queries to the knowledge base by transforming them into SQL queries, allowing the retrieval of results from the underlying RDBMS.

Figure 4. The grammar of DL-Lite

$$B ::= A \mid \exists R \mid \exists R^-$$
$$C ::= B \mid \neg B \mid C_1 \subseteq C_2$$

INTEGRATING CWA AND OWA WITH HYBRID REASONING

In the previous section, we presented a framework that is capable of integrating the richer palette of constructs provided by DLs with the RDBMS unparalleled performance. The purpose was to enable practical implementations of KBs that retain the open-world semantics of the former and take advantage of the inference techniques that were developed for DLs. Instead, in this section we introduce the issues related with the conjunct evaluation of open- and closed-world data structures, in order to retain the individual semantics. This sort of integration is becoming increasingly important because proprietary data structures, such as those stored by individual business subjects in their KBs, are frequently integrated with external data sources upon which traditional assumptions may no longer hold. Specifically, in many current scenarios it is not correct to consider a given piece of information as "false" only because a positive acknowledgment cannot be retrieved from the local system. In fact, such information may exist in the wider context of an extended enterprise, as the local system may be outdated or misaligned with the external contributions to the KB. In this case, the correct approach is to consider a statement as false only when the information actually stored by the system can rule out such possibility. On the contrary, mainstream data management facilities (e.g., RDBMS) rely on the assumption that everything not explicitly stated in the database can be automatically considered as false. Therefore, now we provide an example of how this difference is significant when applying inference techniques to derive information not explicitly stated in the KB. We then provide an overview of existing approaches to hybrid reasoning.

Throughout the chapter, we have highlighted the differences in expressiveness between the relational model, as implemented by RDBMS, and the ontology-based models that can be expressed as DL data structures. However, it should be pointed out that the semantics conveyed by RDBMS, as opposed to that of DLs, may sometimes provide the only correct interpretation on instance data. As an example, if we consider entity *Article* as the concept definition categorizing only those goods that are produced or distributed by the business subject under consideration (i.e., they are to be considered exhaustively detailed), then the query in (3) (expressed for convenience as natural language) amounts to verifying which instances of concept *Article* do not have two or more *TargetMarkets* associated with them.

retrieve articles that are distributed in at most one target market (3)

This can be straightforwardly implemented as a SQL query and we can be confident that the query a) will return all the results and b) does not contain false positives. Suppose now that we extend the KB with concept *Product* in order to express, other than goods produced by the business subject, also those goods that are produced by different business entities (e.g., competitors). This concept will typically be populated with instances by monitoring markets, executing surveys, and in general by collecting data sources that may not be complete or up-to-date. Moreover, members of concept *Product* can be related with the specific *Market*s they are distributed in[8], but we cannot be sure that a product is not distributed in a given market only because no such evidence can be retrieved from the knowledge base. The reformulation of (3) taking into account the new concept definition is the following:

retrieve products that are distributed in at most one market (4)

In this case, a SQL query may not retrieve the correct results, for instance false positives may be introduced because the system is not aware of all the markets products are distributed in. Instead, the approach provided by DL reasoners constitutes the correct interpretation of the data model[9]. The statement (4) can be easily translated into DL structures; specifically, the following DL axiom defines concept Query whose instances are those requested in (4):

$$Query \equiv Product \sqcap \leq 1\ isDistributedIn.Market \quad (5)$$

So far it seems that, once the correct semantics of the data structures to be modeled is clarified, it is possible to identify the category of applications that can execute a sound and complete inference on these data structures. Now, suppose that the definition in (6) is added to the knowledge base to express that a *TargetMarket* where no Product (i.e., goods produced by third parties) is distributed in is to be considered a *MonopolyMarket*:

a monopoly market is a target market where no product is distributed in (6)

On the one hand, listing *TargetMarkets* can be effectively achieved in the closed world by assuming that markets interested by articles are exhaustively described in the knowledge base. On the other hand, determining *MonopolyMarkets* amounts to determining, in the open world, which *TargetMarket* is featuring a competitor distributing his products in it. This is the typical situation in which choosing either of the interpretations presented in this chapter may produce unexpected results because it may fail to retrieve the correct answers to a query. Instead, it is necessary to combine both approaches into a hybrid knowledge base that may reflect the distinct semantics of data structures. As the closed-world component to be integrated with DL-based, open-world KBs, the best candidate is constituted by LP (Logic Programming) (Lloyd, 1987), the renown formalism grounding Prolog engines. Since the latter are not the only inference engines implementing this category of logic-based, closed-world reasoning (e.g., another outstanding example is constituted by the Jena framework[10]), we will generally refer to these applications as rule reasoners. In this section, we survey the main approaches to this kind of integration and the open issues related with them.

A rule is constituted by an antecedent (a.k.a., the rule body) containing the conjunctive pattern of atomic conditions that, when evaluating to true in the KB, triggers the insertion in the latter of the data structures contained in the consequent (a.k.a. the rule head):

$$A_1 \wedge \ldots \wedge A_n \rightarrow C \quad (7)$$

There is a general correspondence between constructs in rules and DL axioms; for example, implication ($\rightarrow$) can be modelled as subsumption ($\subseteq$), conjunction ($\wedge$) is semantically equivalent to intersection ($\cap$), etc. However, rules allow for more general structures with respect to DLs. As an example, atoms $A_1 \ldots A_n$ in (7) can contain n-ary relations, while DL is limited to expressing unary and binary relations. Consequently, a basic requirement for the integration of the two reasoning paradigms is a common language for interleaving DL-based class (concept) and property (role) definitions with general-purpose inference rules. The SWRL (Semantic Web Rule Language) (swrl, 2004) is the de-facto standard for embedding rule definitions into ontologies; more specifically, SWRL defines the structural components of rules (atoms, variables, etc.) as OWL classes and properties, so that rules can be introduced into ontologies by instantiating these entities.

Configuring a common representation framework can lead us not even half the way through the implementation of a hybrid system; in fact, SWRL at large is generally known to be undecidable. In order to discern which data structures are amenable to actual execution, we have to consider the theoretic aspects behind hybrid reasoning. Beside termination, it is also important to which extent hybrid reasoning can be sound and complete. As a straightforward example of how completeness of inference procedures may be in jeopardy by dividing a knowledge base into separated components, suppose that we further categorize concept *Reseller* into *ShopRetailer* and *Web-enabledRetailer,* as in the following DL axiom:

$$Reseller \equiv ShopRetailer \cup Web\text{-}enabledRetailer \quad (8)$$

Now, suppose that the following discount rates are defined:

shop retailers are applied a discount of 15%
Web-enabled retailers are applied a discount of 10%

The assignments of discount rates in 6 and 7 are then translated into rules and executed by the rule component of the knowledge base:

$$ShopRetailer(x) \rightarrow hasDiscount(x,' 15\%) \quad (9)$$

$$Web\text{-}enabledRetailer(x) \rightarrow hasDiscount(x, 10\%) \quad (10)$$

It is clear that conjunct evaluation of the two components cannot infer that a generic instance of class *Reseller* is a valid answer to the query 'retrieve resellers that has a discount associated with them.' Specifically, this happens because the multiple models computed by DL reasoners are incompatible with the closed-world inference implemented by rule reasoners. As a consequence, the possibilities examined by DL reasoning (that is, a *Retailer* being either a *ShopRetailer* or a *Web-enabledRetailer*) will not trigger any of the rules (9) and (10).

With regard to the separation between open- and closed-world components of a knowledge base, the background is multi-faceted because, as we have seen, combining decidable instances of both paradigms do not necessarily result into a decidable, sound, and complete system. A typical example of non-termination is constituted by cyclic definitions that may sometimes be the most intuitive way of expressing a concept, such as in the definition $Person \equiv \exists\ hasParent.Person$. Rule systems cannot wind the infinite chain that this simple definition can produce the way DL reasoners do. However, for the interesting properties acyclic terminologies are sharing with regard to complexity, cyclic definitions are typically ruled out in practical applications. Moreover, the example above shows that completeness of deductions cannot be granted unless particular care is taken in the interchange between structures from these distinct worlds, that is, the entities that are shared between the ontology and the rule base. Particularly, the interchange between the weaker form of negation-as-failure that is typically implemented by rule systems and the strong negation of DL systems may prevent inference from being complete (Damásio et al., 2005). Consequently, the state of the art is proposing competing views on how to implement hybrid systems. A first approach is constituted by bounding the expressiveness of the structural (i.e., DL-based) component to avoid "dangerous" constructs: AL-log (Donini et al., 1998) is an early example of hybrid system and integrates ALC knowledge bases with a relational component constituted by Datalog rules[11]; instead, the KAON2 framework (Motik et al., 2005) allows to cast the SHIQ fragment of a OWL DL KB into Description Logic Programs (Grosof et al., 2003), that can be executed by LP systems. Another approach is constituted by restricting the interaction of the structural and relational components, rather than the expressiveness of either. DL-safe rule bases (Motik et al., 2005) can be integrated with full SHOIN (D) but require variables to occur in a non-DL atom in the rule body. Specifically, non-DL literals of the form O*(x)* are added for each variable *x* in the rule body and a fact O*(a)* is added to the non-DL component of the knowledge base for each individual *a*. The most evident consequence of this is that rules only apply to existing individuals, a limitation that clearly does not exist in DL reasoners. Ontology editors can sometimes provide facilities for integrating the different aspects discussed so far: Protégé (Knublauch, Fergerson, Noy, & Musen, 2004) is featuring a plugin to edit SWRL rules and it is possible to alternatively process the knowledge base with either a DL reasoner or the Jess inference engine.[12] The Swoop editor[13] has an experimental development branch that allows for evaluating SWRL rules embedded in ontologies by means of SWI-Prolog. Finally, Hoolet[14] is a prototypical implementation of OWL-DL reasoner that uses the very efficient Vampire first order prover[15] for processing SWRL rules.

REFERENCES

Abiteboul, S., Hull, R., & Vianu, V. (1995). Foundations of Databases. Addison-Wesley.

Acciarri, A., Calvanese, D., De Giacomo, G., Lembo, D., Lenzerini, M., Palmieri, M., et al., (2005). Quonto: Querying ontologies. In *Proceedings of the 20th National Conference on Artificial Intelligence* (aaai 2005) (pp. 1670-1671).

Arbib, M. A., & Hanson, A. R. (Eds.). (1987). Vision, brain, and cooperative computation. Cambridge, MA, USA: MIT Press.

Baader, F., Calvanese, D., McGuinness, D., Nardi, D., & Patel-Schneider, P. F. (Eds.). (2003). Description logic handbook: Theory, implementation and applications. Cambridge University Press.

Balkenius, C. (1993). Some properties of neural representations. In M. Bodn & L. Niklasson, (Eds.), Selected readings of the Swedish conference on connectionism.

Balkenius, C., & Gärdenfors, P. (1991). Nonmonotonic inferences in neural networks. In Kr (pp. 32-39).

Boley, H., Dean, M., Grosof, B., Horrocks, I., Patel-Schneider, P. F., & Tabet, S. (2004). SWRL: A Semantic Web rule language combining OWL and RuleML.

Calvanese, D., De Giacomo, G., Lembo, D., Lenzerini, M., & Rosati, R. (2005). Tailoring OWL for data intensive ontologies. In *Proceedings of the Workshop on owl: Experiences and directions* (owled 2005).

Chen, P. P. (1976). The entity-relationship model--toward a unified view of data. ACM Trans. Database Syst., 1(1), pp.9-36.

Codd, E. F. (1990). The relational model for database management: version 2. Boston, MA, USA: Addison-Wesley Longman Publishing Co., Inc.

Damásio, C. V., Analytu, A., Antoniou, G., & Wagner, G. (2005, September 11-16). Supporting open and closed world reasoning on the Web. In *Proceedings of the Principles and Practice of Semantic Web Reasoning, 3rd International Workshop*, ppswr 2005, Dagstuhl castle, Germany. (Vol. 4187). Springer.

De Giacomo, G., Lenzerini, M., Poggi, A., & Rosati, R. (2006). On the update of description logic ontologies at the Instance Level. In Aaai 2006.

Donini, F. M., Lenzerini, M., Nardi, D., & Schaerf, A. (1998). AL-log: Integrating datalog and description logics. J. of Intelligent Information Systems, 10(3), 227-252.

Frege, G. (1918). Der Gedanke: Eine logische Untersuchung. Beiträge zur Philosophie des Deutschen Idealismus, I, pp.58-77.

Grosof, B. N., Horrocks, I., Volz, R., & Decker, S. (2003). Description logic programs: Combining logic programs with description logic. In *Proceedings of the 12th International. World Wide Web Conference* (www 2003) (pp. 48–57). ACM.

Haase, P., & Stojanovic, L. (2005). Consistent evolution of OWL ontologies. In ESWC (pp. 182-197).

Healy, M. J., & Caudell, T. P.(2006). Ontologies and worlds in category theory: Implications for neural systems. Axiomathes, 16(1-2), 165-214.

Horrocks, I., Kutz, O., & Sattler, U. (2006). The even more irresistible SROIQ. In *Proceedings of the 10th International Conference on Principles of Knowledge Representation and Reasoning* (kr 2006) (pp. 57–67). AAAI Press.

Kelly, J. J. (1997). The essence of logic. Upper Saddle River, NJ, USA: Prentice-Hall, Inc.

Knublauch, H., Fergerson, R. W., Noy, N. F., & Musen, M. A.(2004). The protégé owl plugin: An open development environment for Semantic Web applications. In International Semantic Web Conference (pp. 229-243).

Kohonen, T. (2000). Self-organizing maps. Springer.

Kurfess, F. J. (1999). Neural networks and structured knowledge: Knowledge representation and reasoning. *Applied intelligence*, 11(1), 5-13.

Liu, H., Lutz, C., Milicic, M., & Wolter, F. (2006). Updating Description Logic ABoxes. In Kr (pp. 46-56).

Lloyd, J. W. (1987). Foundations of logic programming; (2nd extended ed.). New York, NY, USA: Springer-Verlag New York, Inc.

Minsky, M. (1986). The society of mind. New York, NY, USA: Simon & Schuster, Inc.

Montague, R. (1974). Formal philosophy: Selected papers of Richard Montague. New Haven, Connecticut: Yale University Press. (Edited, with an introduction, by Richmond H. Thomason)

Motik, B., Sattler, U., & Studer, R. (2005). Query answering for OWL-DL with rules. *Journal of Web Semantics,* 3(1), pp.41-60.

Piaget, J. (1952). The origins of intelligence in children. New York, NY: Norton.

Piaget, J., & Inhelder, B.(1973). Memory and intelligence. Basic Books.

Rumelhart, D. E., & McClelland, J. L. (1986). Parallel distributed processing. Cambridge, MA, USA: MIT Press.

Russell, B.(1908). Mathematical logic as based on the theory of types. *American Journal of Mathematics, 30,* 222-262.

Schank, R. C., & Abelson, R. P. (1977). Scripts, plans, goals and understanding: an inquiry into human knowledge structures. Hillsdale, NJ: L. Erlbaum.

Smolensky, P. (1993). On the proper treatment of connectionism. In Readings in philosophy and cognitive science (pp.769–799). Cambridge, MA, USA: MIT Press.

Wynne-Jones, M. (1991). Constructive algorithms and pruning: Improving the multi layer perceptron. In Vichnevetsky, R. & Miller, J.J. (Ed.), 13th imacs world congress on computation and applied mathematics, (Vol. 2, pp. 747-750).

ENDNOTES

1. Knowledge can also be stored in distributed physical sources, that can be considered as a single logical one from the user's point of view. However, we will not cover these aspects here.
2. Note that attributes are written lowercase and fillers are capitalised.
3. Defined concept is written in boldface for the sake of readability.
4. Note that, since (A □ B) ≡ ¬(A □ B), a DL supporting negation and conjunction also supports disjunction.
5. http://webont.org/owl/1.1/index.html
6. We denote henceforth with DL-Lite the simplest language of the family, although our consideration is valid for other DL-Lite variants.
7. http://www.omg.org/uml/
8. Note that *Market* is defined as a superclass of *TargetMarket*, because *Products* are not necessarily distributed in *markets* where *Articles* are distributed in.
9. Note that, we have been using the term 'interpretation' in the broader sense of 'the act of interpreting' while in the DL jargon inspired by model theory it is intended as a 'mapping from the language to a world.'

10 http://jena.sourceforge.net/

11 Datalog programs do not feature negation and also comply with a safety condition according to which variables in the head of rules must also occur in the body.

12 http://herzberg.ca.sandia.gov/

13 http://code.google.com/p/swoop/

14 http://owl.man.ac.uk/hoolet/

15 http://reliant.teknowledge.com/cgi-bin/cvsweb.cgi/Vampire/

Chapter VIII
A Workflow Management System for Ontology Engineering

Alessandra Carcagnì
University of Salento, Italy

Angelo Corallo
University of Salento, Italy

Antonio Zilli
University of Salento, Italy

Nunzio Ingraffia
Engineering Ingegneria Informatica S.p.A., Italy

Silvio Sorace
Engineering Ingegneria Informatica S.p.A., Italy

ABSTRACT

The Semantic Web approach based on the ontological representation of knowledge domains seems very useful for improving document management practices, the formal and machine-mediated communication among people and work team and supports knowledge based productive processes. The effectiveness of a semantic information management system is set by the quality of the ontology. The development of ontologies requires experts on the application domain and on the technical issues as representation formalism, languages, and tools. In this chapter a methodology for ontology developing is presented. It is structured in six phases (feasibility study, expliciting of the knowledge base, logic modelling, implementation, test, extension, and maintaining) and highlights the flow of information among phases and activities, the external variables required for completing the project, the human and structural re-

sources involved in the process. The defined methodology is independent of any particular knowledge field, so it can be used whenever an ontology is required. The methodology for ontology developing was implemented in a prototypal workflow management system that will be deployed in the back office area of the SIMS (Semantic Information Management System), a technological platform that is going to be developed for the research project DISCoRSO founded by the Italian Minister of University and Research. The main components of the workflow management system are the editor and the runtime environment. The Enhydra JaWE and Enhydra Shark are well suited as they implement the workflow management standards (languages), they are able to manage complex projects (many tasks, activities, people) and they are open source.

INTRODUCTION

Knowledge has always been recognized as an important social resource, and its application and diffusion is a priority of all the evolved societies. Anyway, only in the last 30 years organizations have faced the knowledge management issue with a scientific approach, and only in the '90s the first results on the value of "intellectual capital" (Edvinsson & Malone, 1997) and on creation of organizational knowledge (Nonaka & Takeuchi, 1995) were published.

From a technological point of view, this issue impacts the applications for managing organizational knowledge resources, in more practical worlds: cataloguing, storing, searching, and accessing data, information, knowledge and even people. The application to the knowledge management systems of ontological descriptions and of the Semantic Web approach promises a more effective and knowledge focused environment.

An ontology is a vocabulary of concepts about a knowledge domain, where concepts are connected through relations. Concepts and relations represent items and their relations extracted from the real world. A particular relationship that connects items is the "Is_A" relation, through which a hierarchy of the elements, generally called taxonomy, can be arranged. Ontologies represent the real world as possible objective so they are able to embrace different views of the same context (Gruber, 1993). In this way, the same ontology could be used by users with different scientific and professional backgrounds. For these reasons, strong efforts need to develop ontologies; then usability and re-usability are important parameters for evaluating the developed ontology.

There are a few methodologies about how to develop ontologies (Uschold, 1996). In this chapter we will present a domain independent process. The defined methodology brakes down the process into different phases underlining the team involved, the inputs and outputs and the relations among phases. This methodology was defined with the aim to automating the process of ontology development in a workflow management environment. As creating an ontology is a complex project requiring people to collaborate, to exchange data and information related to the domain and to the technological platform in which the ontology is deployed, it is important that the interaction process will be codified and organized. Workflow management systems enable monitoring processes and permit people to be focused on their work and, at the same time, to be disinterested in process coordination issues, on the flow of documentation, and on the scheduling of all activities. These issues are the topics of the methodology for ontology development. In a workflow management system, each member of the team receives on his/her desktop the planned activities with the required input and resources without any needs to search for other important documents.

The developed methodology and the designed workflow have the following main properties:

- the methodology works well for both developing an ontology from scratch and for extending an already available one;
- the workflow system coordinates interactions among team members;
- the workflow system is a Web application so team can work on the same job without being co-located;
- the designed and developed workflow system is built with open source software.

In the following paragraph, an overview of the issues the ontology is able to simplify is presented in order to describe and understand the main characteristics which the methodology is focused on. Then, the methodology is presented and discussed. In the last section, the design and the implementation of the workflow management system implementing the methodology is discussed.

THE WEB

The Internet is a powerful backbone on which information and knowledge resources flow quite free among all connected users (Naughton, 2000). The World Wide Web (Berners-Lee, 1996) was born at the CERN[a] in 1989 by Tim Berners-Lee with the specific aim of helping members of the same work team to exchange data and other digital documents. The Web structures are based on the concept of hypertext: links from a page to another create a directed network of information and enable different topic paths.

In our language, each information item (being it a picture or a Web document) will be called "resource"; this uniform name reflects the uniformity with which they can be managed by users.

The growing number of Web resources makes indispensable to use a search engine for browsing contents of the Web. Search engines categorize Web contents respect to keywords they contain and for each keyword create a ranked list of Web resources (Gordon & Pathak, 1999). The most widely used search engines are Yahoo and Google; their specific tasks are the followings:

- *Browsing the Web.* All search engines use special tools (crawler[b]) for automatic analysis of the Web: they recognize in Web pages keywords and links to other pages, then do the same on the linked pages.
- *Cataloguing the resources.* The Web pages browsed by the crawler are indexed and partially stored for quicker answers.
- *Answering to queries.* When users search for specific keywords, the search engine proposes ranked lists of Web pages. The ranking algorithm is generally based on the number of times the keyword or similar terms are used in the page, or on how many links point to the page, or on the number of visitors of that page.

The most serious limit of Web search engines is that human user is compelled to access the resources and to verify directly the content as they are not able to recognize how formal, how official, how trustful the sites are. At the same time publishers can arrange Web pages in order to make them more searchable and valuable by the user. In the end, the Web is designed and implemented for human beings not for machines.

THE WEB 2.0

The Internet and the Web have changed the way people interact. From e-mail to chat, many systems were provided to users for collaborating in a knowledge-based framework (Alavi & Leidner, 2001). In recent years a technical revolution takes us at the Web 2.0 time an environment where

Table 1. Comparison between Web 1.0 and Web 2.0. based on information from Musser and Oreilly (2006)

Web 1.0	**Web 2.0**
DoubleClick	Google AdSense
Ofoto	Flickr
Akamai	BitTorrent
mp3.com	Napster
Britannica Online	Wikipedia
personal websites	blogging
evite	upcoming.org and EVDB
domain name speculation	search engine optimization
page views	cost per click
screen scraping	Web services
publishing	participation
content management systems	wikis
directories (taxonomy)	tagging ("folksonomy")
stickiness	syndication

there is not a clear distinction between content provider and user (Anderson, 2007).

In Table 1, the main differences between "Web 1.0" and "Web 2.0" are presented; the properties in the right column show that users of Web 2.0 sites are generally enabled to participate in the creation of the content itself, sometimes just by clicking (as with "google adsense"), sometimes directly by editing (as in "wikis").

Particular interest has a general type of Web 2.0 sites that provide features for a more effective virtual knowledge sharing. Social software enables users to publish personal contents, or bookmarks, or to aggregate contents already available, to tag these resources with individual keywords, to design a personal profile, and to enable people to network for improving the knowledge flow (examples of social software are http://www.myspace.com/, http://www.linkedin.com/, http://del.icio.us/, etc.). These types of platforms use individual keywords (or folksonomy) to organize contents; the assumption is that keywords create a "cloud of meaning" that helps users in browsing resources (Sinclair & Cardew-Hall, 2007). Folksonomy seems to be a shortcut for semantic description of resources (Specia & Motta, 2007).

At the same time an interesting technology that participates at the Web 2.0 evolution is "syndication." It is extremely useful for frequently updated contents. It is based on the description of contents through the RSS language,[c] a dialect of RDF (Resource Description Framework). The descriptions are available on-line and can be subscribed and opened by special "readers" on personal pages. In this way, information about a huge quantity of contents can be accessed directly on the user page (for example in the intranet) without browsing a lot of pages and without giving any personal data for receiving updates. Content aggregator sites (as http://www.netvibes.com, http://my.yahoo.com/ http://www.google.it/ig) are allowed by this strategy of content publication.

The evolution of the Web has extended the audience of content creator. While in '90s it was necessary to have some technical knowledge to create a Web page and publish contents, now a lot of platforms provide tools, services, and storage capability for publishing resources, including blog posts, wiki articles, etc.

THE SEMANTIC WEB

The exponential grow of the amount of data and information on the Web, caused even by the "Web 2.0" revolution on content publishing, makes it extremely difficult to maintain, search, find, and access information resources. While the content publishing was simplified so that a lot of people are able to produce Web contents, the search engines have not had any specific improvement. A strategy for solving this misalignment is the "Semantic Web." It is based on a new way to structure and catalogue Web contents. The HTML language uses tags to distinguish structural elements and their metadata (author, title, paragraph, content, etc.); the "Semantic Web" is based on the representation of the meaning (semantic) of the Web contents or of their structural elements.

The concept of Semantic Web was introduced in an article by Berners-Lee et al. (2001) and it is described as "... *an extension of the current one, in which information is given well-defined meaning, better enabling computers and people to work in cooperation.*" The Semantic Web is an environment where software agents can substitute human beings in a lot of mechanical activities leaving the user in defining the target. In a Semantic Web system software agents should be able to understand and process the semantic of contents, browsing autonomously Web sites in order to accomplish tasks and verify the trustfulness of the contents.

The Semantic Web concept is based on the availability of semantic metadata. Metadata describe special features of documents, but if expressed with a "descriptive" language, as RDF[d] or OWL[e] (Web Ontology Language), they can be referred to a common schema--an ontology. If the management system is enabled to access and process the schema, documents can be managed processing their metadata meaning. Similarly, software agents able to search and process data, information and services can be implemented referring their actions to semantic value of metadata.

So the Semantic Web is not only a new description of resources, but a new way of facing the contents diffused on the Internet infrastructure, and this issue concerns both the publication and the accessing resources. Semantic resource management is based on the direct management of schemas, the ontologies, that describe knowledge domains and that are the sources of the metadata values.

The schema structure gives to its elements (concepts and relations) a semantic value; reasoning on them is simpler and more effective than reasoning on individual resources. After six years from the introduction of the concept by T. Berners-Lee et al. (2001), a specific search engine for semantic schemas, semantic descriptions of documents and ontologies is available at http://swoogle.umbc.edu/. Many projects on ontology development were carried out, strong efforts are made for developing general and wide conceptualization of the human knowledge (the CYC[f] Knowledge Base™ or the WordNet®[g] are the most famous), some descriptive languages as RDF and OWL are in an advanced stage of development, but the Semantic Web approach is not diffused at all out of very narrow environments as intranets or very specialist platforms.

SEMANTIC WEB AND INTEROPERABILITY

The challenge of the Web at the knowledge society time is to make searchable, recognizable, and accessible resources (contents, services, goods) to the widest audience possible, even to non-experts and in a format compatible with the specific device. The pervasion of the Web-enabled interactions has extended the capabilities of both users and customers. Then searching contents, services, goods (the customer activity), describing them in a very accurate way (the provider activity), organizing items from different suppliers (the retailer activity) are tasks the Web is going to cope with. The strategy the search engines are following is based on the differentiation of content types, so while the Google search engine is focused on "standard" Web site, the "Google Product Search"[h] is focused on on-line shops' items; anyway this strategy is not so practical and the "Google Product Search" is in beta version.

If the organization of on-line retailer environment is a troubling issue, realizing a transaction is even more complex. Customers and sellers have to exchange a lot of data, and some of them are private; this action requires to share the description of data (are you paying with dollars or euro, or with credit card?), their format and, in the end, to trust them. Today, each e-shop or organization arranges a local technological system for selling its goods.

The technological aspect of this issue is the "interoperability," the capability of different technological systems (platforms, services, etc.) to exchange data. This aspect can be decoupled in two aspects: the technical one (two systems must be able "to talk" each other, they recognize themselves and have a protocol for communicating) and the semantic one (they use the same vocabulary and format).

The data management issue can be re-thought through the Semantic Web approach (Euzenat, 2001). Shared and public ontologies can be used to refer metadata of shop items, then applications that are going to manage them can use the same ontologies to recognize different names, unit of measure, completeness of data (for example, the "year" is composed of four or two numbers?), and so on. A Semantic Web-based approach to this issue should enable autonomous browsing of on-line shops by software agents targeted by users through ontologies (Obrst et al., 2007).

ONTOLOGY, THE HEART OF THE SEMANTIC WEB

As explained in the previous paragraphs, the Semantic Web improvements reside in "ontology," a conceptual schema that represents and interprets a knowledge domain reducing the misunderstandings. The clearest definition is "explicit specification of a conceptualization" (Gruber, 1993): it is explicit as it is coded and accessible by human-users and machines, it is specific as it represents the world as is because it is a conceptualization or an abstract representation of the world. The ontology, to be really useful, should be shared, accepted by the community of users since it should represent their view of the world.

Where Are Ontologies Useful?

The general applicative contexts for ontologies are: (a) communication among people, (b) interoperability among systems.

a. *Communication among people.* It is well known that when a new partnership for a specific project is built, partners need a long time (some months) for defining a common vocabulary, a shared meaning of the terms with which they talk about the world, in "Semantic Web" words, and the team need to define a shared ontology.
b. *Interoperability among applications.* The Web is an aggregation of microcosms of structured data and information which are described, built, and accessible by different applications. It seems quite natural because of the huge number of people that provide them autonomously. What seems

less obvious is that the same is valid for the technological system of organizations. Data, information, and documents have been developed in the last 20 years[i] by different applications (remember that MSOffice-2007 was commercialized in 2007, but all of us used some text editor before), using different databases (where businesses are represented and stored), for the realization of different productive processes, by different organizational structures and probably for different businesses.

The coherence and homogeneity of data became even more difficult to manage if we focus our attention on a whole supply chain, where different organizations and their technological systems have to interact.

Organizations have large document databases extremely focused on specific department processes and now are going to integrate them in one information system in order to sustain the reducing projecting, designing and producing time. The aggregation of data and information poses the question about the interoperability among applications: that is interoperability issues ontologies promise to solve. Ontologies are an intermediate layer between applications and data; they make the data produced in different ways and with different purposes homogeneous and augment the capability to automate the data exchange in workflows.

Ontologies have three main characteristics: (a) aim, (b) formality and (c) nature of the represented object.

a. With "aim" we intend the final purpose the ontology will accomplish; for example:
    - the knowledge sharing in a document management system: the human readability and comprehensibility will be taken more carefully in consideration
    - the automation of workflow: logical properties of the structure and precision will be taken more carefully in consideration.
b. An ontology can be extremely informal, as a natural language description of the world, or can be extremely formal, as a mathematical theory, but between these two possibilities there are many others:
    - strongly informal: the ontology is expressed in natural language,
    - structured: a subset of the natural language is used in order to reduce ambiguity and to improve the clarity,
    - semi-formal: the ontology is implemented in an artificial and well defined language,
    - rigorously formal: the ontology is implemented using a semantically defined language that is able to represent logical properties of world elements and of their relationship.
c. Ontologies could be aimed to illustrate different general levels of the world (Uschold, 1996); there are "top-level ontologies" that describe general concepts as "time," "object" and so on. These concepts are not domain dependent so they are well suited for defining a common conceptualization to which different domain ontologies used in a shared context refer.

Another type of ontologies are the "linguistic ontologies," structured vocabularies that try to formalize the human capability to group terms according to their semantic properties or other linguistic properties, (Wordnet[j] and Sensus[k] are examples of this type of ontologies). We have also the "scope ontologies" that present a description of the world for completing a specific task; they are strongly domain dependent. The "domain ontologies" describe completely a specific knowledge domain, (the Enterprise Ontology[l] is an example). Then we can classify the "general ontologies" that try to depict the whole world (the most important example is the CYC ontology[m]). The last type to be classified is the "meta-ontology" that represents primary representational concepts (as "class," "property," and others) used to define ontologies. The RDF Schema (Broekstra, Kampman & Van Harmelen, 2002) is a meta-ontology.

Ontology for Organizational Document Management

It is well known that the most of organizational information is not structured, so a lot of DMSs and DMSs (Document and Content Management Systems) are available on the market. DMSs or CMSs are well suited for managing document workflow, from the production of a piece of information to archiving and searching it, but this is not enough for arranging useful information base for the knowledge worker. Organizing, identifying, and sharing knowledge created by an organization is a complex task, and it needs a knowledge source to be interpreted respect to the semantic and the task the employee has to accomplish.

Ontologies are going to be used in this context in order to enable users to focus their attention on the semantic they are looking for and to extend the interoperability among different software systems. This approach to knowledge management needs a strong effort on knowledge modelling and designing phase as ontologies have to be readable both by human users that interact with a knowledge management system and by applications that process knowledge items automatically respect to the query.

The most effective use of the ontology is as an intermediate layer between the user and the entire organizational document base, so he/she can access all the available resources independently of their location and format from one access point (presumably a search engine).

Semantic Tools

Many tools are available for developing ontology. The most famous and effective is Protégé;[n] it is developed at Stanford University and presents a graphical and interactive interface. It is designed for knowledge experts that have to model a domain without having any specific competence on technical issues. Moreover, being distributed as open source there are many plug-ins and extensions that execute special visualizations and operations on ontologies.

Other important tools for the Semantic Web are Jena[o] (Java API for RDF) that makes RDF (but also OWL) models usable in Java programmes.

These tools are diffusing the usage of ontology in data and information management systems, especially in the free ones. Anyway, having a tool for implementing an ontology is not enough for realizing an effective ontology.

In the following paragraphs a methodology for designing a shared and effective ontology is presented. It is based on the assumption that the "ontology developing" project is not only a technical task but it must involve many competences, and sometimes the user community itself, in order to create a wide accepted ontological description of domain.

A METHODOLOGY FOR ONTOLOGY DEVELOPING

The KIWI project faced the relation between the technological issues and the ontology development process and a set of tools in a coherent framework was provided for sustaining the knowledge expert in translating tacit and unstructured domain knowledge in a formal codification. The KIWI project highlighted another issue, too. Ontology developing projects must be carried out by a complex team comprised of people with a subject matter knowledge and experience, people with technical background as some software related problems are to be solved and people with the skill for extracting, formalizing, and codifying knowledge as the most valuable source of the project is tacit knowledge impressed in worker brain, procedures, processes, or community habits. Any simple software tool could not fulfil this objective.

The research project DISCoRSO (Distribuited Information Systems for CooRdinated Service Oriented interoperability) founded by the Italian "Programma Operativo Nazionale Ricerca Scientifica, Sviluppo Tecnologico, Alta Formazione" 2000-2006 organized by the Italian Minister of Scientific Research tried to face this issue.

This project is focused on sustaining the technological innovation in organizations with a particular attention to the knowledge management practices in business districts. One of the objectives of this research project is to develop a semantic based knowledge management platform (SIMS--Semantic Information Management System (Corallo et al., 2007) characterized by the integration of different and innovative information sources (as documents, blog posts, wiki articles, multimedia files) in order to provide a single and ontology based access point to the whole knowledge base. The critical point of this project is not the technology (even if SIMS will implement not usual solutions), but the design of an effective knowledge base. In order to be effective users should have simple access to as many and right resources as possible, so different applications are aggregated (DMS, CMS, blog, wiki) to give the right application for updating knowledge resources but all different information items are managed via domain ontologies.

In this strategy the quality of the ontology determines the effectiveness of the platform so a strong attention was given to the ontology developing methodology. The framework defined for the KIWI project was further stressed in order to define more specific details (input and output of the phases), to identify roles and skills involved in the activities for having at the end of the process the best quality. The methodology was successively implemented in a workflow management environment where team members have a personal page where founding their open activities and the documents needed in order to carry them out.

Modelling the Methodology: The IDEF0 Technology

The methodology was represented through the IDEF0 (Integration DEFinition for function modelling) technology (Mayer, et al., 1992), which is well-suited for describing complex processes focusing not only on the timing management of the activities but even on the values added by each phase and on the knowledge flow among the phases and among the involved people. The IDEF0 was published in 1993 by the Computer System Laboratory of the National Institute of Standardization and Technology. It was developed for the US project ICAM (Integrated Computer Aided Manufacturing) aimed at improving productive processes toward their automation. A set of methodologies and languages were defined with the general goal of describing the whole productive process of an organization in a simple and global way, but with the possibility of focusing on detailed parts of the process related to a department or to a specific phase.

The specific objectives of the IDEF0 standard are:

- defining a set of tools for modelling functions, activities, processes and operations of an organization;
- defining a modelling technique that is independent from specific tools of CASE (Computer Aided Software Engineering) but that can be integrated with them.

The IDEF0 model of a process is a hierarchical structure composed of macro-processes at the top and then processes, phases, activities; each one of these can be represented at different detail levels. The syntactical elements of the IDEF0 language are the "functions," they are represented by a box, the data needed (input) and produced (output) by the functions are represented by entering and going out arrows (see Figure 1). Functions transform inputs in outputs, the process is performed by the mechanism (or the means) when the controls (requirements, conditions) are satisfied.

Figure 1. IDEF0 syntax

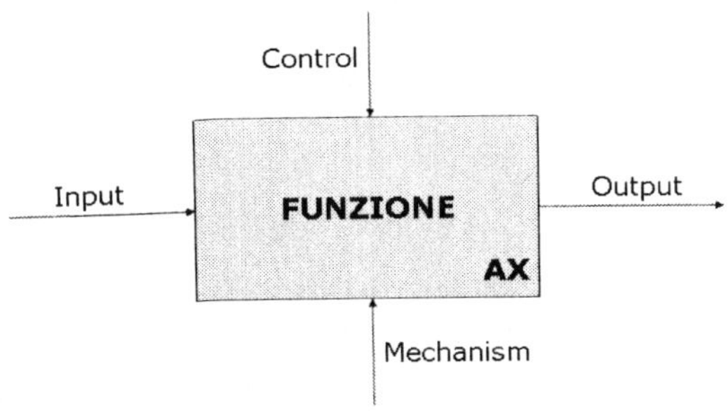

The Ontology Developing Process

The process of ontology developing is thought as a self-sufficient project. Generally it is a section of another technological project but we want to underline its complexity: a wide team is involved, different technologies are necessary, a lot of external factors (applicative context) are to be considered. The methodology and its workflow implementation help in carrying out this complex project and they are very powerful especially in non technological skilled environment.

The process of ontology developing is represented in Figure 2 as a macro-process and all the information (inputs, outputs, controls and mechanism) are represented. In order to make it actionable a more in depth description is necessary: in

Figure 2. IDEF0 representation of macro-process "ontology developing"

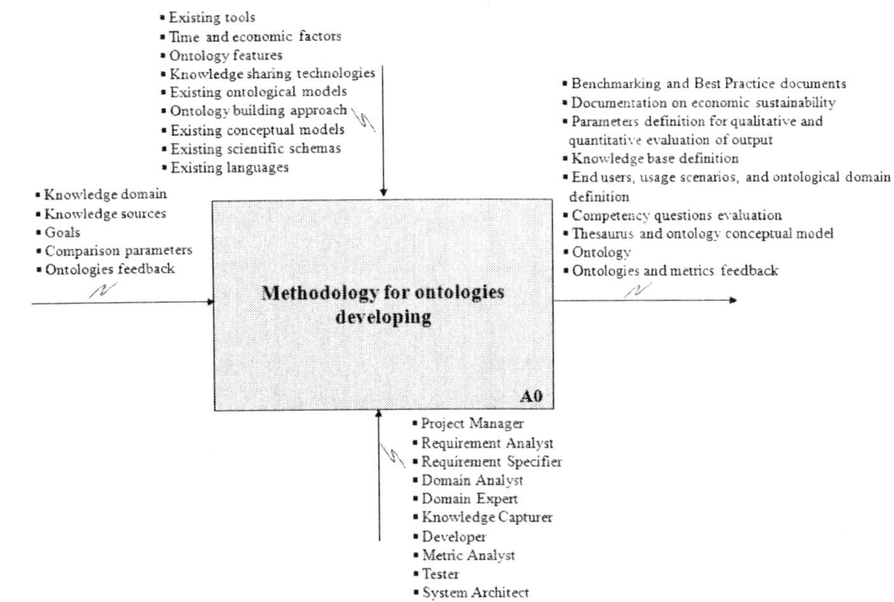

Figure 3. The main phases of the methodology for ontology developing represented with IDEF0 standards

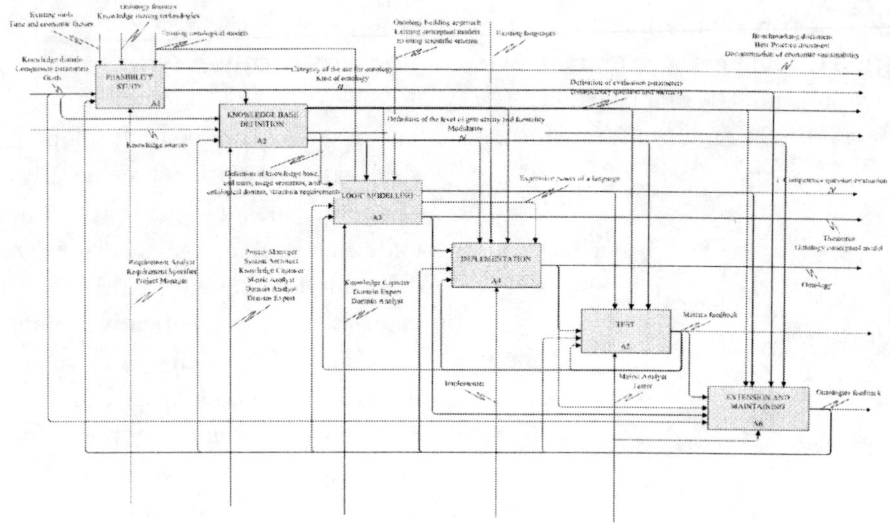

Table 2. Roles involved in the ontology development project

Project manager	He is responsible of the process; he coordinates the team.
Requirement analyst	He attends to pick up all necessary information to perform a benchmark analysis and supplies opportunity solution to critical points.
Requirement specifer	He translates the requirement in functionalities of the software product.
Metric analyst	He defines the evaluation metrics the product will satisfy.
Domain expert	He is the expert on the knowledge domain.
Knowledge capturer	He analyzes knowledge sources and extracts key concepts.
Domain analyst	He gives a mathematical representation of the knowledge domain
System architect	He is the software designer; he is responsible of the integration of the ontology with other applications.
Implementer	He develops the ontology code .
Tester	He takes care of ontology testing.
Metric analyst	He evaluates the developed ontology respect to the metrics that were defined.

Figure 3 the process is broken down in the main phases and their relationships are highlighted. The process implementing the methodology is composed of the following phases:

1. feasibility study;
2. knowledge base definition;
3. logic modelling;
4. implementation;

5. test
6. extension and maintaining.

Some of these phases are complex and will require another more detailed description.

Special attention must be focused on the involved team. The process consists of analytical activities, aimed at describing requirements and the applicative context of the ontology, technical activities, aimed at the ontology implementation in code through tools, and monitoring activities, monitoring both the project (so a project manager is necessary) and the product quality. Differently skilled people with different roles have to collaborate in order to produce an effective ontology. The present methodology defines a team for the ontology development project composed of the roles described in Table 2 (their specific involvement is described in the tables of each activity).

Feasibility Study

This activity is aimed at the definition of the knowledge domain the ontology has to represent in order to explicit the general elements, the issues to face, the objectives of the ontology itself and the effort needed. During this starting phase the real usage and the users of the ontology are

Table 3. Feasibility study

Feasibility Study	
Input	*Knowledge domain*: it is the knowledge field of applications (tourism, agriculture, biology, physics, services, etc.); here, both explicit and tacit knowledge is to be captured. *Goal*: an analysis of organizational processes should highlight the critical points. Goals for the ontology development project are the solutions of these critical points. *Comparison parameters*: parameters that will be used in performing benchmark analysis; the goal is to recognize the best practice among the compared ontologies.
Output	*Benchmarking document*: this document will define the best practice in the available semantic description of the knowledge domain. *Best practice document*: this document will describe the most efficient and effective methods and techniques of accomplishing tasks basing on the previous documented experiences. *Economic sustainability*: it is the planning of the organizational constraints on the project: deadlines, founds, efforts. *Ontology use category*: the description of the usage for which the ontology is going to be developed. *Kind of ontology*: the type of ontologies to be developed.
Control	*Existing tools*: software tools for the ontology implementation. *Time and economic factors*: definition of the economic constraints and deadlines. *Ontology features*: description of the ontology characteristics: the scope, the contest in which it will be used, the formality level, the nature of subject. *Knowledge sharing technologies*: the collaborative platform the team will use. *Existing ontological models*: reference to models of the already available ontologies.
Mechanism (Role)	Project manager Requirement analyst Requirement specifier

defined. Other already available ontologies can be selected for evaluation in order to not re-develop anything.

At the same time, all the applications of the technological platform that can be improved by the ontology are analyzed; this task is important for defining rightly and at the first attempts the logical and technical requirements of the ontology.

During this phase the schedule of the project, founds, involved team, and possible risks should be fixed.

Knowledge Base Definition

This phase of the methodology is aimed to define the domain, the aspects that will be represented, the knowledge base (people and documentation) that will be analyzed, the users of the ontology, and the business process or usage scenarios the ontology will be inserted in. At this point some general structural properties of the ontology can be defined, as the granularity (the elementary classes of the ontology), the formality of the rep-

Table 4. Knowledge base definition

Knowledge base definition	
Input	*Knowledge domain* *Goal* *Comparison parameters* *Knowledge sources:* the documentation or knowledge experts at disposal for analyzing the knowledge domain.
Output	*Knowledge base*: a selection of the resources that will be provided to the team involved in the Logic Modeling phase. *End users*: the ontology users; they can be human beings or intelligent agents (applications or software agents). *Usage scenario*: the type of business process the ontology will sustain (knowledge sharing, information retrieval, artificial reasoning). *Ontological domain*: the specific elements of the knowledge domain that will be represented by the ontology; *Structural requirements*: special constraints the concept structure must respect. *Competency questions and metrics*: qualitative and quantitative metrics that will be evaluated on the ontology before its deliver. *Granularity and formality level*: granularity is the detail level of the representation; formality regards the logical properties of the ontology. *Modularity*: the ontology can be an all-connected set of concepts (no modules) or a set of separated sub-sections (high modularity).
Control	*Ontology use category* *Kind of ontology*
Mechanism (Role)	*Project manager* *Metric analyst* *Knowledge capturer* *Domain analyst* *Domain expert* *System architect*

resentation (natural language or a strictly logical description of the world), the modularity structure (unified or independent multi-module structure). Being defined properties, some qualitative and quantitative metrics can be explicated; they will be evaluated at the end of the productive process. Some quantitative metrics can be found in Za (2004), while the qualitative metrics about the type of knowledge items should be found explicitly or implicitly in the ontology (Grüninger & Fox, 1995).

Logic Modeling

The knowledge domain, determined in the previous phase, is further divided in all the elementary items to which an explicitly defined concept or term is associated; moreover their relationships are explicitly defined. The Logic Modelling phase is constituted by three activities:

- *Definition of a vocabulary*: each term introduced for describing the domain has an

Table 5. Logic modeling

Logic Modelling	
Input	*Knowledge base* *End users* *Usage scenarios* *Ontological domain* *Structural requirements*
Output	*Thesaurus*: a list of worlds about the knowledge domain linked by meaning (synonymous or contrary) or other lessical relations. Each term is associated to a natural language definition. *Ontology conceptual model*: a graphic representation of vocabulary terms and all their semantic relations. *Language expressive power*: the effectiveness of the language to represent the requested formality; *Competency question evaluation*: the qualitative metrics could be evaluated before the finalization of the ontology.
Control	*Existing ontological models* *Competency questions and metrics* *Granularity and formality level* *Modularity* *Existing scientific schemes:* eventual other vocabularies on the same knowledge domain. *Ontology building approach*: the strategy with which finding out concepts and relations. It can be top-down, bottom-up, or middle-out. *Existing conceptual models*: general methodologies for representation of the concept and relation structure (semantic networks, frame, knowledge map)
Mechanism (Role)	*Knowledge capturer* *Domain analyst* *Domain expert*

unambiguous definition; it will be eventually accessible by the end users for understanding the intended meaning.

- *Definition of a thesaurus*: the vocabulary contains all the terms extracted from the knowledge base, these terms are aggregated for similarities or other linguistic properties to form the thesaurus. In this way it will be possible to select the right terms for identifying concepts (as bicycle) and contemporary to be able to manage other used terms associable to it (as tricycle). The thesaurus is extremely useful for improving the knowledge retrieval through search engines (Srinivasan, 1992).
- *Definition of a logic structure*: the terms selected in the previous sub-phase can be now semantically structured, that is concepts became classes and relationships became connections among them. Many strategies can be used for representing the logic structure, for example, semantic network, frames, and knowledge map.

Implementation

At the end of the previous phase the domain is already completely analyzed. All the elementary items and their relationships are recognized, described and defined in some natural language or graphical format. The ontology is ready to be implemented in a formal code written with a descriptive language as RDF or OWL in order to translate it in a machine-readable version. There are some graphical tools that help knowledge experts in implementing the ontology, so the knowledge of the language syntax is not so critical. The most effective tool is Protégé[P] (it is not alone, but we do not report others as they are not our focus); it is an old project of the Stanford University, it is distributed in open source version so there is a huge community of contributors that develop plug-in and extensions and that collaborate through mailing-list. Ontology implementing tools generally enable users to create classes, to build relationships and associate them to the right class, to link a definition to classes and

Table 6. Implementation

Implementation	
Input	*Thesaurus* *Ontology conceptual model*
Output	*Ontology*: the code that implements the ontology.
Control	*Granularity and formality level* *Modularity* *Competency questions and metrics* *Existing languages*: available ontology implementation languages (for example, RDF, OWL).
Mechanism (Role)	*Implementer*

relationships, to create instances of classes, and to define some logical restriction on values of the relationship. The code is subsequently produced at the "saving" time, and descriptions too much logically complex are usually purged if they are not supported by the chosen language.

Test

Now it is necessary to verify that the proposed requirements are satisfied. One of the outputs of the "expliciting of the knowledge base" phase was the (qualitative and quantitative) metrics; in this phase that metrics are evaluated on the ontology implemented. The result of this evaluation could be positive, so the ontology will be delivered and introduced in the platform, otherwise if the quality requirements are not satisfied it is necessary to come back at the right phase. There could be two conditions: a) requirements and metrics are too stringent, then it is opportune to reduce them; b) the developed ontology presents low quality in its

Table 7. Test

Test	
Input	*Ontology*
Output	*Metrics feedback*: report describing the evaluation process.
Control	*Granularity and formality level* *Modularity* *Competency questions and metrics* *Competency question evaluation*
Mechanism (Role)	*Tester* *Metric analyst*

Table 8. Extension and maintaining

Extension and Maintaining	
Input	*Ontology* *Metrics feedback*
Output	*Ontology feedback*: description of possible updates or extensions of the implemented ontology
Control	*Granularity and formality level* *Modularity* *Competency questions and metrics* *Competency question evaluation* *Ontology use category* *Kind of ontology*
Mechanism (Role)	*Tester* *Metric analyst*

structure, content, or logical description then it is opportune to came back at the "logic modelling" phase or "implementation" in dependence of the issue to face.

Extension and Maintaining

When the "test" phase validates the ontology, it is ready to be used in a knowledge management platform. This activity will be done by people who are not directly involved in the ontology developing project but who collaborate in the Knowledge Base Definition and Study Feasibility phases. Anyway, the project is not finished as the ontology has to evolve. The real usage will highlight the missing content, or a representation not aligned with the habits of the community using it. Moreover, in time new contents could be introduced, and there could be many reasons: the community changes its focus, innovations change the framework on which the community works, and so on. If the ontology is used by an indexer and by a search engine, the indexing process must be tuned, so it is opportune to take care of this activity.

The Main Properties of This Methodology

In the literature it is possible to find some methodologies (Maedche & Staab, 2001; Uschold & Grüninger, 1996) for ontology developing, so why another one? While they are generally aimed at giving to knowledge experts the right suggestions and hints in analysing the domain, in using an implementing tool, in understanding the main "logical" aspects of a specific implementation, we want to underline that it is quite impossible to isolate the implementation from the design. As the ontology will be used in a software application or, in general, in complex knowledge management systems, its main properties are defined by the usage and, manly, by the users it is planned for (two issues that are faced in the "Feasibility Study"). For developing an ontology, a certain knowledge about the domain has to be available (being it some domain experts or a document base); this knowledge will impact on the design of the ontology as some topic could be missing or a too much delimited perspective could be proposed, and these issues are discussed in the second phase (Knowledge Base Definition). Equivalently, knowledge about a domain improves very rapidly, the usage of the ontology can be changed or extended, the processes in which the ontology is used could change (for example, with the business process of the organization), so an "extension and maintaining" phase is necessary to evolve the ontology without disrupting its value in the system.

The proposed methodology describes and organizes explicitly all the activities that are to be realized for developing an ontology, listing data and information necessary to carry out the project. It is a guide that can be applied independently of the specific domain the ontology is focused on.

IMPLEMENTING THE METHODOLOGY

The DISCoRSO project aims to develop a Semantic-based Information Management System (Corallo et al., 2007). In this platform some domain ontologies are needed but they must respect some standards both qualitative (as the capability to involve the right experts) and quantitative (as the logical properties of the implementing language). The partnership decided to implement in the platform a WMS (Workflow Management System) to support the ontology development process that will be executed by the editorial board when the platform will be definitely distributed (Vanderaalst & Vanhee, 2004).

The implementation of the methodology is carried out through the XPDL (Extensible Process Definition Language) language (WfMC, 2002) that is a suggested as standard by the WfMC (Workflow Management Coalition)[q]. The XPDL language permits the representation of a workflow, an ordered set of activities that, following formal rules and involving different tools and resources, transform a defined set of inputs in a defined set of outputs. In the workflow it is essential to represent involved people and their role (owner, responsible, reviewer, etc.) in each activity, the flow of data and information, the tools with which completing tasks and the scheduling. The workflow runtime environment automates the flux of the data and information transferring them to the right people at the right time.

The workflow management system executing the ontology development process will be available in the "back office" area where the editorial units of the SIMS will monitor and sustain the knowledge base.

The value it introduces in the "back office" of the SIMS is related to:

- the simplification of the decision making process through its rationalization because all data and information necessary for taking a decision are recognized;
- the capability to monitor the process;
- the opportunity to forget all mechanical activities;
- the automatic and correct storage of the project documents and deliverables;
- the time and data management: all data and information are sent to the person involved in the activity when he/she can work on it;
- the reduction of costs by eliminating downtime.

The Workflow Management System

A workflow management system is a software environment where a process is modelled, implemented in a descriptive language and executed by a workflow engine.

The software environment is composed of two main components:

- a "modelling component," with which the analysts and process designers model processes, activities, tasks and assign to them people, effort, tools, and so on;
- a workflow execution component, the runtime environment of the WMS that interprets the process model (XPDL, BPEL (Arkin et al., 2005) or jPdl (Koenig, 2004), documents) and coordinates both the operations delegated to him/her and the delivery of documents and tasks to the right people.

The workflow engine manages automatically (following the project model) data and documents and has an interface to which each team member connects and finds his/her scheduled activity, its description and the related information, through the same interface he/she can upload deliverables or communicate the completion of the task (WfMS, 1996).

The Workflow Modelling Component

The BPMI (Business Process Management Initiative) published the BPMN (Business Process Modelling Notation) on May 2004 (White, 2004) that became OMG standard in 2005. This representation standard is the most comprehensible to business people, so they are enabled to model processes with a formal language and it is comprehensible to developers that can have an effective formal representation. The BPMN is a graphical language that represents activities, controls, their order and flux. The BPNM model is associated to the Business Execution Language in order to realize an executable description.

The first language produced by the WfMC was the WPDL (Workflow Process Definition Language) published in 1999 (Muehlen & Becker, 1999), it was successively improved by the quite contemporary research on XML and in 2002 the new version XPDL (XML Process Definition Language) was realised in 2002. The XPDL is a markup language able to describe a business process through a set of primitives described in a schema. The XPDL language permits to design a business process model in a machine readable version usable in an execution time. In our implementation the XPDL language was chosen because the designed workflow management system is compliant with it.

Enhydra Java Workflow Editor (JaWE)

Enhydra JaWE[r] is a workflow editor implemented in Java language compliant with the XPDL specific. This editor enables users to design the process in a graphical environment and to save the document in XPDL language, in this way it is executable in any workflow engine able to read this format. Moreover, if necessary the XML file is directly editable so some modification can be introduced by hand, anyway these types of modifications are advised against as they can introduce inconsistencies eventually recognized by an integrated validator. JAWE permits to define a Ldap repository[s] where project team members are classified, in this way it enables the engine to manage the task assigning activity.

The XPDL representation of a process contains three types of activities:

- "manual activities" accomplished by a user (as writing a report);
- "automatic activities" accomplished by the system (as sending a message)
- activities that are neither manual nor automatic, they are associate to a fictitious user called "arbitrary expression," in Figure 4 the "Route Activity" is used for synchronization and conditional branching.

The phases and activities of the methodology have to be mapped on this model, quite all the real activities will be "manual activities" associated to a team member, the coordination activities will be

Figure 4. Example of process represented in the graphical interface of JaWE. In red, the "arbitrary expression" user

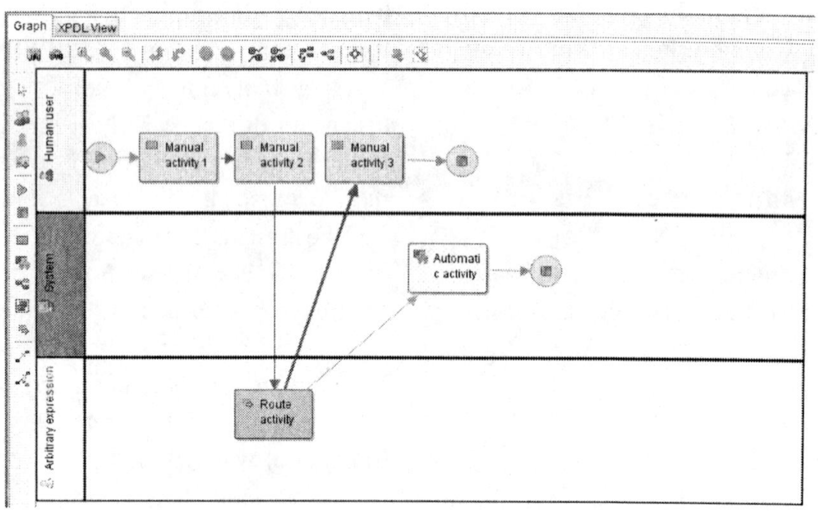

"automatic activities," but a couple of "arbitrary expression" is introduced for managing the not-completed phases.

Workflow Execution Component (Or Workflow Engine)

A workflow engine manages the execution of a workflow described in an opportune language and provides to the team members their tasks and the applications to complete it. In our implementation we chose as workflow engine Enhydra SHARK; it is based on the WfMC specifics (WfMC, 1998) and is effectively integrated with Enhydra JaWE.

Enhydra SHARK is able to manage the whole sequence of phases that determines the status of the process time after time: it stores information about involved people, the accomplished activities, when and how they were accomplished, and the produced deliverables. These data are used to monitor the status of the process.

The Implementation of the Methodology for Ontology Development

The methodology for ontology development was formalized in XPDL language through the JaWE editor. The whole process is divided in a set of activities at the same level (the multilevel description we executed with the IDEF0 language is not manageable in XPDL) associated to a member (in our case to a role). It is important to notice that representing all the activities at the same level does not introduce any distortion in our methodology.

In our formalization of the methodology we had to introduce a "system user," that represents the workflow engine itself, this virtual team member accomplishes all the automatic activities, while the "arbitrary expression" redirects to the right members the decisional activities. In the carried out model a team member is associated to each role,

Figure 5. Graphical representation of the process mapping the ontology development methodology

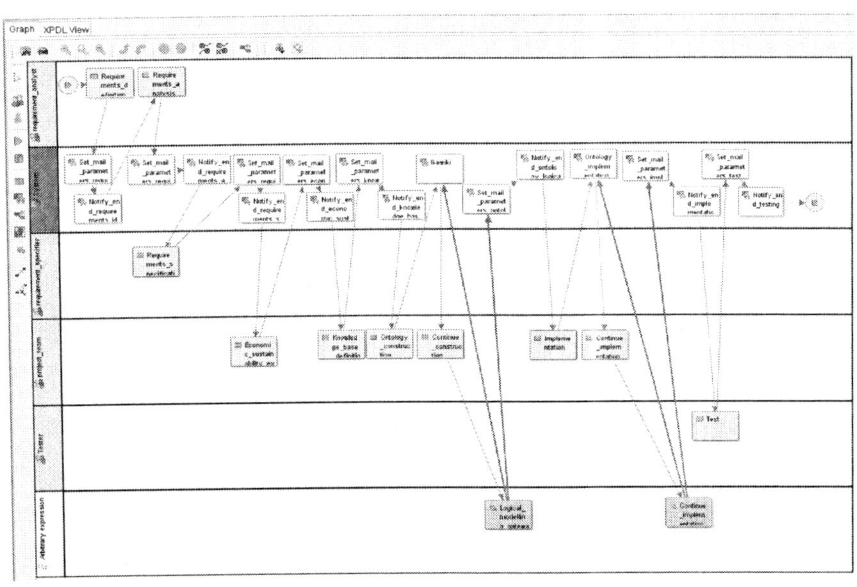

the Ldap system should manage cases in which the two or more members have the same role.

The methodology was translated into a process composed of the following activities:

- requirement collection;
- requirement analysis;
- requirement formalization;
- business sustainability;
- explicating knowledge base;
- building the ontology;
- rebuilding the ontology(this is a fictitious activity);
- implementing the ontology;
- re-implementing the ontology(this is a fictitious activity);
- test.

In Figure 5 the graphical model of this process is depicted. In this graphical model automatic activities of the "system user" as notifications about the completion of the activity are represented. We think that these notifications help the project manager in monitoring and coordinating the process. Two more types of automatic activities are in the model: the launch of the application to be used for accomplishing the "building the ontology" activity (a wiki application available in the SIMS platform is suggested for building collaboratively the vocabulary) and the tool Protégé for implementing the ontology for the "implementing the ontology" activity.

The two activities assigned to the "arbitrary expression" (see Figure 5) manage two activities that need more than one interaction between users and the system: the definition of the vocabulary is accomplished by many people so each time a team member connects to the system he/she is directed to the wiki application until he/she notifies the activity is accomplished, the same is valid for the implementation of the ontology.

The Shark Interfaces: XPL, eXtensible Presentation Language

As stated before, the Enhydra SHARK engine coordinates activities, teams, and documents. The interaction between the Enhydra SHARK engine and the team member is mediated by an application server that creates the delivered content in real time: when a user connect the engine recognizes the status of the project and presents his/her the right Web page.

A set of pre-arranged pages are developed and associated to the possible statuses of the project. They are developed with the XPL (eXtensible Presentation Language) language that the R&S Laboratory of Engineering Ingegneria Informatica S.p.A,[t] an Italian software firm involved in the research project DISCoRSO, is developing. Currently, it is at an experimentation phase. The development of XPL documents is achieved through an ad hoc plug-in of Eclipse[u] developed by the same laboratory.

The language XPL is a presentation language that enables the author to focus on the objects that will be displayed in the page, as tables, forms, menus, without taking care of their layout. It will be arranged by style sheets. Moreover, particular content will be inserted directly in the workflow engine.

The main properties of XPL language are:

- there are a lot of template graphical objects;
- it describes "general purpose" pages, that can be arranged opportunely just selecting the right style sheet; with this strategy contents can be simply delivered to different devices;
- it is based on XML syntax;
- the library of objects is simply extensible.

Limits of a Knowledge Management Workflow

The ontology development methodology we defined is characterized by strong knowledge based activities, but in this case the use of workflow engine modelling seems little effective. It results more incisive for business process delineation and automation.

To correctly define an ontology, a strong collaboration is required, the involved work groups have to evaluate information and to propose possible solutions. The output of these analyses is collected in reports. Modelling and executing this kind of processes through a workflow management system risks to harness the creativity of team members. Anyway, a methodology and its implementation in a WMS are useful if a virtual team is working on the same process and if a complex document base is going to be assembled.

THE ARCHITECTURE OF THE WORKFLOW MANAGEMENT SYSTEM

The software architecture of the workflow management system is represented in Figure 6. It is structured in 4 tiers:

- Data tier: the Ldap system manages team members, a DBMS manages documents and deliverables, an LKB (Local Knowledge Base) manages the process and activities;
- Application tier: the Profiling application manages members, their roles and rights, the workflow Engine (Enhydra SHARK) executes the process described by the model editor (Enhydra JaWE);
- Web tier: the MVC (Model View Controller) framework manages the knowledge flow between the connected user and the workflow engine;

Figure 6. The architecture of the implemented workflow management system

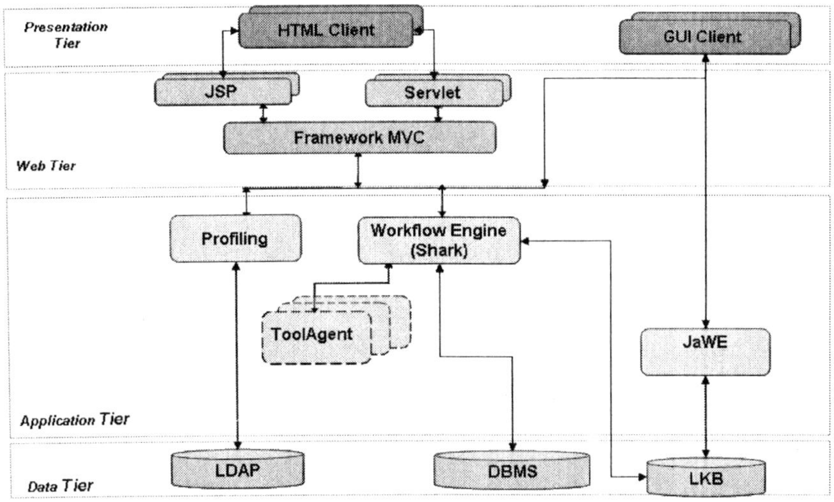

- Presentation tier: the applications providing the graphical interface of the WMS.

THE WORKFLOW MANAGEMENT SYSTEM

The Workflow Management System is based on an ecosystem of people and applications, in Figure 7 the main elements of our implementation is represented. It is composed of these main actors:

- The "process analyst" designs the process from its inputs to the final products, highlighting activities, outputs and their connections. In our implementation he/she uses the JaWE editor and produces the XPDL version of the process; the design is used both by the workflow interface developer ("developer") and directly by the Shark engine.
- The "developer" implements the design; he/she receives as inputs the description of the workflow and develops the objects (in XPL language) that will compose the web pages provided to the WMS users, he/she develops the infrastructure for managing the data, information and documentation related to the process.
- The users of the WMS, when they log in, the application server (Tomcat) queries to Enhydra SHARK (this connection is managed by a SharkAdapter Java class to be developed), the list of the open processes and the open activities the user is associated to, extract the web items (XPL resources) from the MVC framework and organize the user personal environment.

The WMS is designed as a back office environment of a knowledge management system (SIMS), and it will be accessible by the users of the platform involved in the ontology development process. The logged user access a personal home page where the activities he/she has to work on are

Figure 7. The workflow ecosystem, actors, roles, and applications

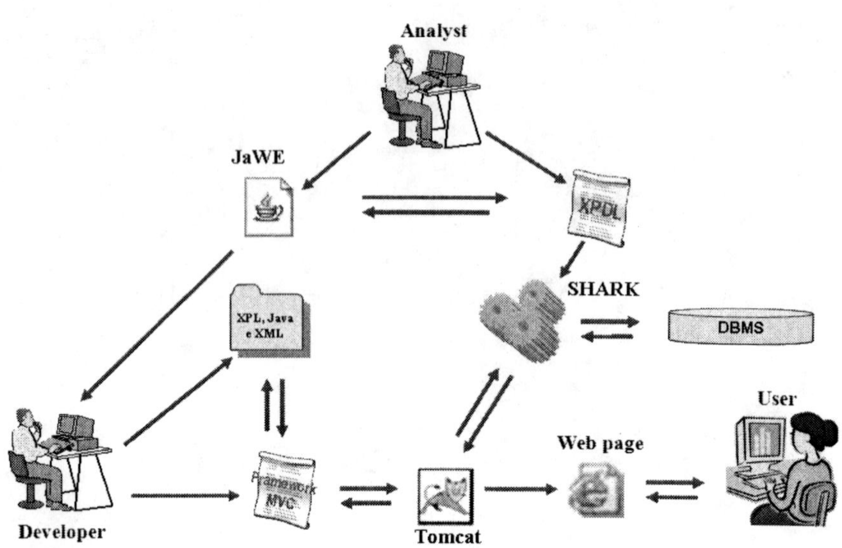

listed. Selecting one of these he/she accesses the "activity" page where the information, document, deadlines and other data are presented.

The "activity" page is composed of three main sections reflecting the properties of the "function" of the IDEF0 model (see Figure 1): inputs of the activity, all data and documents the user needs in order to accomplish it; controls on the realization of the activity (standards to respect, implementation characteristic and so on), outputs of the activity that will be developed and uploaded. In general the page presents a set of items to be downloaded (inputs and control documents) and a set of forms where new data and documents have to be uploaded (see Figure 7).

In the end of the page a set of buttons are available:

- Annul: the data provided for the activity realization are deleted;
- Suspend: the activity is interrupted, data and documents already uploaded are saved, the user will find the activity at the suspended status when he/she will connect again to the WMS;
- Confirm: the data and uploaded documents are stored in the database; the Enhydra SHARK engine registers the completion of the activity and updates the status of the process.

The most interesting activity of the process is the "logic modelling" ("building the ontology" in the workflow model): during this phase team members have to explicit concepts, their relationships and their definition, in other words all the items of the domain are highlighted. This activity will be executed by using the wiki application of the SIMS (Storelli, 2006), all team members involved in this activity will find in their personal page the

Figure 8. This Web page shows the activity of "Requirements analysis"

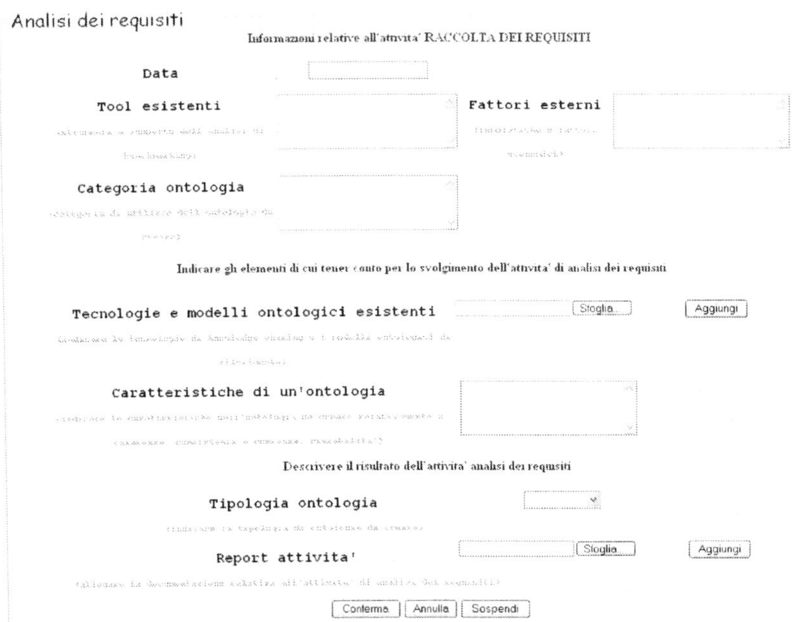

link to the wiki application. This activity page will be available until someone selects the "confirm" button; this special activity is managed by the "arbitrary expression" user who is introduced in the JaWE (and XPDL) process model.

The IkeWiki application was chosen for its semantic properties:

- its contents (wiki articles) are managed by specific ontologies (imported during the installation phase or created ad hoc);
- the wiki items (articles) are managed as elements of an ontology, so they can be defined as classes or relations; the relations can be used for connecting classes;
- the visualization of each article is composed of its definition (the wiki article itself) and of the relations that use the item as subject;
- the content of the application can be exported in RDF format.

The IkeWiki is extremely useful in the collaborative building of the ontology and the RDF produced exporting the contents can be used as a pre-implementation of the ontology itself that is the objective of the following "implementation" activity ("implementing the ontology" in the workflow model). The RDF version of the IkeWiki contents can be updated in a more formal language (OWL) using the Protégé tool suggested by this methodology. With this strategy the two activities, "logic modelling," and "implementation" that are the heart of the technical development of the ontology, are completely interconnected enabling a draft development of the ontology using a simple and widely used tool: the wiki.

FINAL CONSIDERATIONS

Today quite all the activities of the organizations are based on the exchange of knowledge and the flow happens through different communication channels, many of them are based on Web based systems. For managing the huge quantity of data, information and services the "Semantic Web" is based on the description of the meaning (the semantic) of the Web objects. The Semantic Web approach is based on the usage of ontologies, formal description of a knowledge domain, to which the resources' metadata are referred. So ontologies became the tools enabling the effective access to the knowledge distributed on the Web or in knowledge platforms.

The building of the ontologies is a critical task of a knowledge based platform. For the activities of the DISCoRSO research project (founded by the Italian Minister of University and Research), eBMS--S. S. ISUFI, University of Salento and Engineering Ingegneria Informatica defined a methodology for developing ontologies. The methodology is based on the recognition that the ontology development is a real project, characterized by an objective, a task structure, a team, a scheduling and so on.

The defined methodology implemented using the IDEF0 standard is composed of six phases- - feasibility study, knowledge base definition, logic modelling, implementation, test, extension and maintaining. This methodology should help organizations that are going to introduce a knowledge management platform to understand the properties of the ontology they need and then to develop it.

The methodology was moreover implemented in a Workflow Management System. Our aim is providing a back office area of the SIMS (Semantic Information Management System, the platform that we are developing for the DISCoRSO research project) where the team involved in the platform management is leaded in an ontology development project. In our implementation the Enhydra JaWE editor is used to translate the methodology in a formal and executable version implemented with the XPDL language and the Enhydra Shark engine is used as workflow runtime engine. The phases of the methodology were traduced in activities (XPL standard).

The implementation we realized is effective in sustaining a knowledge expert team in carrying out a technological project, in fact the WMS is able to provide to each member the information and the technical tools he/she needs for his/her activity.

Actually the research project considers the methodology of the completed work, while the implementation is under update as the general knowledge management platform (SIMS) is designed and developed.

REFERENCES

Alavi, M., & Leidner, D. E. (2001). Review: Knowledge management and knowledge management systems: Conceptual foundations and research issues. *MIS Quarterly*, 25(1), 107-136.

Anderson, P. (2007). What is Web 2.0? Ideas, technologies and implications for education. *JISC Technology and Standards Watch*, Feb. 2007

Arkin A., Askary S., Bloch B., Curbera F., Goland Y., Kartha N., Liu C., Thatte S., Yendluri P., Yiu A., editors, (2005). Web services business process execution language version 2.0. Working Draft, WS-BPEL TC OASIS.

Berners-Lee, T., (1996). Www: past, present, and future, *Computer,* 29(10), 69-77.

Berners-Lee, T., Hendler, J., & Lassila, O. (2001). The Semantic Web. *Scientific American* 34–43.

Broekstra, J., Kampman, A., van Harmelen, F. (2002). Sesame: A generic architecture for storing and querying rdf and rdf schema, pp. 54+.

Ceravolo, P., Corallo, A., Elia, G., and Zilli, A. (2004). Managing ontology evolution via relational constraints. In Mircea, Howlett, R. J., Jain, L. C., Mircea, Howlett, R. J., and Jain, L. C., (Eds.), KES, volume 3215 of Lecture Notes in Computer Science, pp. 335-341. Springer.

Corallo, A., Ingraffia, N., Vicari, C., Zilli, A. (2007). SIMS: An ontology-based multi-source knowledge management system. Paper presented at the 11th Multi-Conference on Systemics, Cybernetics and Informatics (MSCI 2007), Orlando, Florida, USA.

Edvinsson, L. & Malone, M. S. (1997). *Intellectual capital: Realizing your company's true value by finding its hidden brainpower.* Collins.

Euzenat, J. (2001). An infrastructure for formally ensuring interoperability in a heterogeneous Semantic Web, In *Proceeding of 1stInternational-Conference on Semantic Web Working Symposium (SWWS'01)* (pp. 345-360) Stanford, CA, USA.

Gordon, M., Pathak, P. (1999). Finding information on the World Wide Web: The retrieval effectiveness of search engines *Information Processing & Management*, 35(2), 141-180.

Gruber, T. R. (1993). Towards principles for the design of ontologies used for knowledge sharing. In Guarino, N. and Poli, R., (Eds.), *Formal ontology in conceptual analysis and knowledge representation*, Deventer, The Netherlands. Kluwer Academic Publishers.

Grüninger, M., Fox, M. (1995, April 13).Methodology for the design and evaluation of ontologies, In IJCAI'95, Workshop on Basic Ontological Issues in Knowledge Sharing.

Koenig, J. (2004), JBoss jBPM White Paper.

Maedche, A., Staab, S. (2001). Ontology learning for the Semantic Web. Intelligent Systems, IEEE [see also IEEE Intelligent Systems and Their Applications], 16(2), 72-79.

Mayer, R. J., et al., (1992), IDEF Family of Methods for Concurrent Engineering and Business Re-engineering Applications, Knowledge-Based Systems, Inc.

Muehlen, M. Z., Becker, J. (1999). Workflow process definition language - development and directions of a meta-language for wokflow processes, In Bading, L. et al., (Eds.) In *Proceedings of the 1st KnowTech Forum*, Potsdam.

Musser, J. & Oreilly, T. (2006). Web 2.0 Report. O'Reilly Media.

Naughton, J. (2000). A brief history of the future: Origins of the internet, Phoenix mass market p/bk.

Nonaka, I., & Takeuchi, H. (1995). The knowledge-creating company : How Japanese companies create the dynamics of innovation. Oxford University Press.

Obrst, L., Ceusters, W., Mani, I., Ray, S., & Smith, B. (2007). The evaluation of ontologies, pp. 139-158.

Sinclair, J. & Cardew-Hall, M. (2007). The folksonomy tag cloud: When is it useful? Journal of Information Science, pp. 0165551506078083v1.

Specia, L., & Motta, E. (2007). Integrating folksonomies with the Semantic Web, in The Semantic Web: Research and Applications, volume (4519/2007), pp. 624--639.

Srinivasan, P. (1992). Thesaurus construction, pp. 161-218.

Storelli, D. (2006). *Una piattaforma basata sulle ontologie per la gestione integrata di sorgenti di conoscenza eterogenee*. Unpublished degree dissertation, University of Salento, Italy.

Uschold, M. (1996). Building ontologies: Towards a unified methodology. In *Proceedings of the16th Annual Conference of the British Computer Society Specialist Group on Expert Systems,* Cambridge, UK.

Uschold, M., & Grüninger, M. (1996). Ontologies: principles, methods, and applications, *Knowledge Engineering Review*, 11(2), 93-155.

Vanderaalst, W., & Vanhee, K. (2004). Workflow management: Models, methods, and systems, (Cooperative Information Systems), The MIT Press.

WfMC (1996). The workflow management coalition specification (Feb 99), workflow management coalition terminology and glossary, Document Number WFMC-TC-1011, Document Status--Issue 3.0.

WfMC (1998). The workflow management coalition specification workflow management application programming interface (Interface 2&3) Specification, Document Number WFMC-TC-1009.

WfMC (2002). Workflow management coalition workflow standard: Workflow process definition interface--XML Process Definition Language (XPDL)--Document Number WFMC-TC-1025, Document Status –1.0 Final Draft October 25, 2002, Version 1.0, (WFMCTC-1025).

White, S. A. (2004). Business process modeling notation (BPMN) Version 1.0. Business Process Management Initiative, BPMI.org.

Za, D. (2004). *Una piattaforma basata sulle ontologie per la gestione integrata di sorgenti di conoscenza eterogenee*. Unpublished degree dissertation, University of Lecce, Italy.

ENDNOTES

[a] The CERN (**C**onseil **E**uropéen pour la **R**echerche **N**ucléaire) laboratory, an international laboratory for studies on physics of particles, is located on the border between France and Switzerland, near Geneva. Official web page http://public.web.cern.ch/Public/Welcome.html

[b] A crawler (know also as spider or robot) is a software for automated analysis of database; this is the activity of a search engine.

[c] For the specification of this language see: http://cyber.law.harvard.edu/rss/rss.html

d http://www.w3.org/RDF/

e http://www.w3.org/2004/OWL/

f http://www.cyc.com/cyc/cycrandd/technology/whatiscyc_dir/whatsincyc

g http://wordnet.princeton.edu/

h http://www.google.co.uk/products

i We are assuming that is this period the technology pervaded the organizations in all their activities, processes, departments, and so on.

j http://wordnet.princeton.edu/

k http://www.isi.edu/natural-language/projects/ONTOLOGIES.html

l http://www.aiai.ed.ac.uk/project/enterprise/enterprise/ontology.html

m http://www.cyc.com/

n http://protege.stanford.edu/

o http://jena.sourceforge.net/

p http://protege.stanford.edu/

q http://www.wfmc.org/

r http://www.enhydra.org/workflow/JaWE/index.html

s LDAP (Lightweight Directory Access Protocol) is a standard protocol to query and modify directory services

t http://eng.it/index.htm

u Eclipse is an open source project for defining a development platform. It is founded by a consortium of Ericsson, HP, IBM, Intel, MontaVista Software, QNX, SAP e Serena Software, called Eclipse Foundation. For more information: http://www.eclipse.org

Section II
Semantic in Organizational Knowledge Management

Chapter IX
Activity Theory for Knowledge Management in Organisations

Lorna Uden
Staffordshire University, UK

ABSTRACT

Current approaches to KMS (Knowledge Management Systems) tend to concentrate development mainly on technical aspects, but they ignore social organisational issues. Effective KMS design requires that the role of technologies is supporting business knowledge processes rather than storing data. CHAT (Cultural Historical Activity Theory) can be used as a theoretical model to analyse the development of knowledge management systems and knowledge sharing. Activity theory as a philosophical and cross-disciplinary framework for studying different forms of human practices is well suited for study research within a community of practice such as knowledge management in collaborative research. This chapter shows how activity theory can be used as a kernel theory for the development of a knowledge management design theory for collaborative work.

INTRODUCTION

The design and development of knowledge management systems is not trivial. Organisations are communities of people who compete among themselves for power and resources. There are differences of opinion and values, conflicts of priorities, and goals (Handy, 2005). Much of the research so far in KM (Knowledge Management) focuses on studying technological functionalities, but not the long-term impact of the system. Effective use of knowledge management system requires careful study of the continuous process of co-evolving complex social and technical systems. New tools lead to new practices and ways of working, which in turn lead to affordances for and constraints on technical innovation (Winograd, 1995). Knowledge management communities cannot be declared; they need to be allowed to grow over a long period of time (Wenger et al.,

2002). Instead of studying isolated relations between a particular innovation and an increase of effectiveness in a KM community, they should be examined as embedded in complex socio-technical systems, characterised by interdependence and long-term evolution (Moore, 2005). A way of conceptualising such systems, well-suited to the dynamic, evolving, and permeable nature is an activity system using activity theory. The traditional approach of developing such systems using the waterfall-based system development methods with their clear stages, deliverables and well-understood dependencies no longer suffices (Brooks, 1995). A more holistic approach is needed, particularly in the design stage. It is necessary to go beyond studying KM systems as change agents. Instead, to proactively improve specific ways of design that can contribute to desired changes in the environment. KM systems are complex and evolving socio-technological systems; they require a systematic and situated design approach. Each stakeholder in the system has unique design needs. The effects of conflicts need to be studied. They can only be studied in their interactions with other elements and systems in context. This requires that designers have understanding of this knowledge.

Activity theory not only provides an ideal candidate for understanding and helping with KM design, it can also be used as a kernel theory for the KM theory. This paper explores activity theory to help with knowledge management design in KMS. At the beginning there is a brief review of knowledge management; then design theories and their benefits for KM are given. This is followed by a short overview of activity theory. Some of the implications from activity theory for KMS kernel theory are proposed. The final section gives suggestions for further research.

The objectives of the paper are:

- A brief review of knowledge management
- A review of design theories for knowledge management
- A discussion of activity theory
- Description of how activity theory is used as a kernel theory for KMS
- Suggestions for future works

KNOWLEDGE MANAGEMENT

We are living in a knowledge economy. Knowledge is the whole body of cognition and skills that individuals use to solve problems. It includes theories and practical, everyday rules, and instruction for action (Probst et al., 2003). Knowledge has become the most important asset of an organization. Knowledge management is the process of identifying, capturing, organizing, and disseminating the intellectual assets that are critical to the organization long-term performance (Debowski, 2006). In order to survive in a knowledge society, organisations must learn to manage their intellectual assets. Knowledge is the only resource that increases with use. Knowledge management is referred to as the process for creating, codifying and disseminating knowledge for a wide range of knowledge intensive tasks. (Harris et al., 1998). These tasks can be decision support, computer assisted learning, research (e.g. hypothesis testing) or research support.

Knowledge management systems are tools to effect the management of knowledge and are manifested in a variety of implementations (Davenport et al., 1998) including document repositories, expertise databases, discussion lists, and context-specific retrieval systems incorporating collaborative filtering technologies. The purpose of KMS is to provide the technical support to enable knowledge capture and exchange among different users in organisations. It provides each user with a means to acquire, create, document, transfer, and apply knowledge to meet an organisation's needs. A KMS is a complete system because it comprises a number of sub-systems. Knowledge management is supported by a range of technologies, broadly grouped into four areas of activity:

business process management, content management, Web content management and knowledge application management.

KMS FAILURE

It is generally acknowledged that 80% of organisations have experienced failures in IT projects that should have enhanced organisational performance. The reason for these failures is that designers have emphasised the technical system instead of resolving issues relating to organisational context, managing the introduction of the system, recognising the needs and concerns of stakeholders, and involving managers and end users in the exchange process (Debowski, 2006).

KMS design and development is a complex process, particularly where the system affects a range of other organisational activities and systems. Successful KMS must address the following issues:

- The system must support corporate requirements;
- The designer must consider the social, cultural, organisational and political issues as well as the technical ones;
- The system should reflect knowledge management principles, particularly the encouragement of collaboration and communication;
- The system should be concerned for the individual.

THE DEVELOPMENT PROCESS OF KMS

According to Debowski (2006), the introduction of a complex technical system such as KMS, staged development must be carefully planned. Broadly, the stages are as follows:

- Justifying the need for KMS
- Identifying the system requirements
- Clarifying the system specifications
- Evaluating potential systems
- Selecting the system and/or its relevant components
- Implementing the system
- Evaluating the system acceptance and adoption.

Central to the development process is the identifying of the system requirements. Requirements analysis is an important stage in the development of a KMS. Current approaches do not provide the theoretical underpinnings to their design models. Ethnography is typically used to analyse human practice and its social relations. It is one of the most important methods for capturing software engineering requirements (Viller & Sommerville, 1999). Effective and efficient requirement elicitation is absolutely essential if software systems are to meet the expectations of their customers and users, and are to be delivered on time and within budget (Al-Rawas & Easterbrook, 1996; Loucopoulos & Karakostas, 1995).

Traditional approaches for requirement analysis cannot provide a theoretical basis for understanding 'regularly patterned' human activity (Probert, 1999). In order to overcome these problems, it is necessary to have a methodology and tools that can support the continuous evaluation of a statement of requirements as these evolve against a highly complex and dynamic problem situation. What is needed is to shift the focus from fixed and final requirements to those of a more dynamic nature. In particular, it is necessary to consider *human information* which, in social terms, does not have a physical reality and is not objective like physical information.

Instead, it is based on individual, group or organisational needs. Such information informs action in organisations and is thus closely related to organisational activity and organisational form. Organisational activity is itself a function of the social purposes of individuals, groups and organisations and is affected by issues outside the boundary of the organisation. Human information is subject to change and is ongoing (McGrath & Uden, 2000).

DESIGN THEORIES

Design is the use of scientific principles, technical information and imagination in the definition of a structure, machine or system to perform pre-specified functions with the maximum economy and efficiency (Fielden, 1975). It is vital to engineering, architectural and art disciplines. Design research is important for the information system disciplines such as knowledge management. Design is both a process (set of activities) and a product (artifactartifact)--a verb and a noun (Walls et al., 1992). It supports a problem solving paradigm that continuously shifts perspective between design process and design artifactartifacts for the same complex problem. According to Hevner and others (2004), the design process is a sequence of expert activities that produces an innovative product (i.e., the design artifact).

The design of knowledge management systems is complex, artificial and purposely designed. These systems are comprised of people, organizations, and technologies. Knowledge management, like information systems must address the interplay among business strategy, organisational infrastructure, IT strategy and IS infrastructure (Hevner et al., 2004).

Typically, the purpose of a theory is prediction and/or explanation of a phenomenon (Dubin, 1978). Natural science theories pertain to the physical or biological world and explain relationships among certain aspects of the natural world and/or predict the behavior of certain aspects of that world. Social science theories perform the same function for the behavior of people either individually or in groups. Design theory differs from explanatory and predictive theories found in the natural or physical sciences. It is a prescriptive theory based on theoretical underpinnings which says how a design process can be carried out in a way which is both effective and feasible (Walls et al., 1992). While science is concerned primarily with analysis, design is oriented toward synthesis.

Design theories refer to an integrated prescription consisting of a particular class of user requirements, a type of system solution, and a set of effective development practices (Walls et al., 1992). There are design theories for DSS, EIS and TPS. According to these authors, the main benefit of design theories is to articulate the boundaries within which particular design assumptions apply. Information design theories make the design process more tractable for developers by focusing their attention and restricting their options. They also inform researchers by suggesting testable research hypotheses (Markus et al., 2002).

An ISDT (Information System) Design Theory) is a package of three interrelated elements--a set of user requirements, a set of system features (or principles for selecting system features) and a set of principles deemed effective for guiding the process of development. These three elements can be used to guide designers facing particular sets of circumstances.

ISDTs have two distinctive characteristics. Firstly, they are based on theory and provide guidance to practitioners. The theory underlying ISDT is generally referred to as a kernel theory. It may be an academic theory (e.g., organisational psychology) or a practitioner theory in use. Kernel theory enables formulation of empirical testable predictions relating to the design theory outcomes such as system requirements fit. Conversely, ISDTs are also normative theories. They are prescriptive and evaluative rather than descriptive or predictive. Since ISDTs are intended to give guidance to developers, they must also pass the test of practices. They should also be able to answer questions such as, "Does the system work?"and "Does it do what it is supposed to do?" (Markus et al., 2002).

Benefits of Design Theories

The main benefits of design theories are (Markus et al., 2002):

- To formalise, justify and extend the traditional IS practice of labelling system types;
- To describe IS characteristic features and prescribe and effective developmental approach.

The value of this is to reduce developer uncertainty by restricting the range of allowable system features and development activities to a more manageable set, thereby increasing the development reliability and the success likelihood and to stimulate research.

Why KM Needs Design Theories

Current approaches to developing knowledge management systems typically are about formal modeling and analysis of formal knowledge requirements (Holsapple, 2003). Most of the tools are designed mainly to support acquisition and retrieval of codified knowledge in order to improve formal individual knowledge bases. There is little work being done to address the second generation of knowledge management where the focus is on informal emergent knowledge sharing within communities (Huysman & Wulf, 2006).

While traditional approaches are conducted to support work-related tasks of individuals or formal team work, they are not suitable for supporting informed knowledge sharing in CoP (Communities of Practice) that focus on emergent knowledge processes (Markus et al., 1992). This is because requirement analysis for knowledge sharing communities needs to take into account the social capital of the group (Huysman & Wulf, 2006).

According to Markus and others (2002), traditional ISDTs are not adequate for the design of a knowledge intensive-based system. The design of knowledge intensive systems require emergent processes characterised by highly unpredictable user types and work contexts as well as knowledge requirements for general and specific distributed expertise. These authors have proposed EKP (Emergent Knowledge Processes). EKPs are organisational activity patterns that exhibit three characteristics in combination: deliberations with no best structure or sequence; highly unpredictable potential users and work contexts; and information requirements that include general, specific and tacit knowledge distributed across experts and non experts. Examples of these systems include strategic business planning, new product development, basic research and organisational design. In discussing future research, Markus and others pose the question whether they might be alternatives to the kernel theory (Markus et al., 2002). This paper takes a different approach to the development of design principles for knowledge management system by adopting activity theory as our kernel theory and proposes a set of design principles (meta-requirements) for knowledge management systems.

OVERVIEW OF ACTIVITY THEORY

Activity theory is a socio-cultural, socio-historical lens through which we can analyse human activity systems. It focuses on the interaction of human activity and consciousness within its relevant environmental context (Leont'ev, 1981; Vygotsky 1978). The basic unit of analysis in activity theory is human activity. Human activities are driven by certain needs where people wish to achieve certain purposes. The activity is mediated by one or more instruments or tools. The basic principles of activity theory include object orientedness, internalisation/externalisation, mediation, hierarchical structure, and development. The most immediate benefit of activity theory is in providing a triangular template for describing these relationships and looking for points of tension as new goals, tools or organizational changes create stress with the current roles, rules and artifactartifacts.

An activity always contains various artifactartifacts (e.g., instruments, signs, procedures, machines, materials, laws, forms of work organisation). ArtifactArtifacts have a mediating role. Relations among elements of an activity are not directed, but mediated. For example, an instrument mediates between the subject and the object of doing. The object is seen and manipulated not 'as such,' but within the limitations set by the instrument (Kuutti, 1996). ArtifactArtifacts are created and transformed during the development of the activity itself and carry with them a particular culture--a historical remnant of that development. The relationship between subject and object of activity is mediated by a tool. A tool can be anything used in the transformation process, including both material tools and tools for thinking. The relationship between subject and the community is mediated by rules and the relationship between object and community is mediated by the division of labour--how the activity is distributed among the members of the community, that is, the role each individual in the community plays in the activity, the power each wields and the tasks each is held responsible for. Rules cover both implicit and explicit norms, conventions and social relations within a community as related to the transformation process of the object into an outcome. Each of the mediating terms is historically formed and open to further development (Kuutti, 1996). The basic structure of an activity can be illustrated as in Figure 1.

According to Kuutti (1996), activities can be considered as having three hierarchical levels--activity, action and operation, which can be

Figure 1. Basic structure of an activity

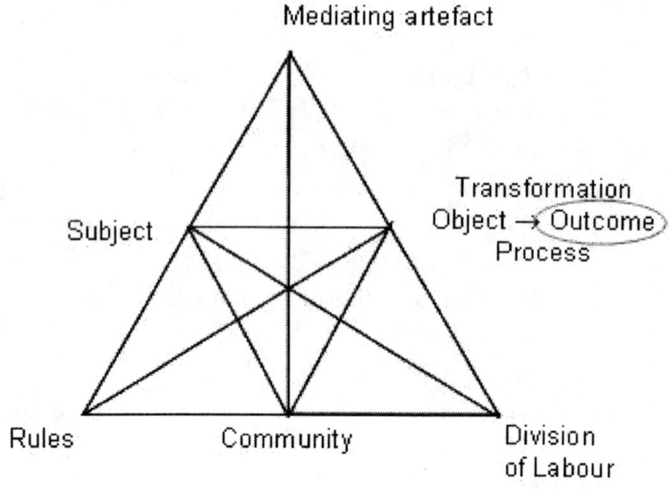

Figure 2. The three levels of activity

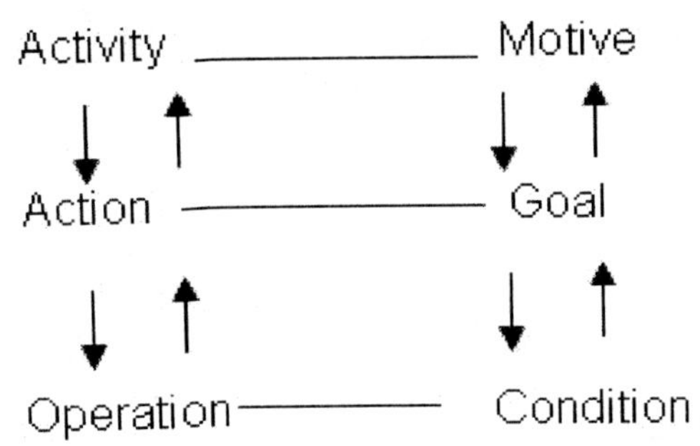

individual or cooperative. They can be considered as corresponding to motive, goal, and conditions. An activity (global) may be achieved through a variety of actions. The same action may be used as contribution to different activities. Similarly, operators may contribute to a variety of actions (see Figure 2). Kuutti uses a simple example of these levels to describe the activity (motive) of 'building a house' in which 'fixing the roof' and 'transporting bricks by truck' are at the action level and 'hammering' and 'changing gears when driving' are at the operation level. Every activity has an internal and external component with the subject and object existing as part of a dynamic and reciprocal relationship.

Why Activity Theory?

Nonaka and Takeuchi's (1995) model of knowledge creation describes a dynamic process in which explicit and tacit knowledge in organisations are exchanged and transformed through four modes. Knowledge creation in organisations is a process involving a continual interplay between explicit and tacit dimensions of knowledge.

Engeström (1999) argues that this approach to knowledge creation has several limitations. Firstly, this approach ignores the small cycles of team-based continuous improvements. Secondly, the model presents a rather deterministic order of events in the creation of knowledge. Thirdly, the four phases of the knowledge creation cycle are essentially different modes of representing knowledge: tacit-sympathised, explicit-conceptual, explicit-systemic, and tacit-operational. Fourthly, it does not seem to account effectively for sequences of formulating and debating a problem, in which knowledge is presented as an open multi-faceted problematic (Engeström, 1999). Finally, Nonaka & Takeuchi's model takes the initial existence of a fairly clear problem, task, or assignment as a given. It excludes the phases of goal and problem formation, delegating them to the management as an unexpected black box.

The author concurs with Engeström (1999) that activity theory offers benefits for the analysis of innovative learning at work (Engeström, 1999).

- Activity theory is deeply contextual and oriented at understanding historically-specific local practices, their objects, mediating artifactartifacts and social organisation (Cole & Engeström, 1993).
- Activity theory is based on a dialectical theory of knowledge and thinking, focused on the creative potential in human cognition.
- Activity theory is a developmental theory that tries to explain and influence qualitative changes in human practices over time.

In addition to these, there are some key principles from activity theory that are significant for knowledge management development (Hasan, 1999; Kuutti, 1999; McMichael, 1999).

- Activity theory provides a comprehensive unit of analysis.
- The use of mediating instruments. This mediating instrument makes it possible for an instrument to mediate and change a supporting activity as subjects invent their activities' context.

- The structure of the activity.
- Activity theory helps to maintain adequately the relationship between the individual and social levels in the objects to be studied, especially in situations where there is a need to grasp emergent features in individual and social transformation.
- Activity theory, by its nature, is multidisciplinary. Activities as a whole cannot be exhaustively studied by an individual discipline. Several disciplines should actually have the same context with respect to the research object, the context formed by activity. Despite focusing on different aspects of activity, all the other context-forming parts must be taken into account in order to preserve the validity of research.
- Activity theory enables the study and mastering of developmental processes. It regards contexts as dynamic systems mediated by cultural artifacts. In activity theory, contexts are seen as internally contradictory transformations, which imply transformations and discontinuous development.
- Activity theory is interventionist in its methodological approach.

Historical analyses in organisation theory are important in knowledge management. The structures and behaviour of today's organisation reflect culture and circumstance-specific historical development (McMichael, 1999). Historical analysis allows existing and emerging organisational structures to be examined as the result of their evolutionary development, sometimes intentional and others not.

ACTIVITY THEORY AS A KERNEL THEORY FOR KM DESIGN THEORY

The author's interest in design theory is the outcome of the increasing importance given by IS researchers to design research. Despite the great potential for enhancing the effectiveness of knowledge management system development, there is little theoretical work that can guide KM design requirements or process. This chapter argues that the underlying theoretical basis of KM can be addressed through a design theory of KMS. Many KMS methodologies have been advocated for KM development (Rubenstein-Montano et al., 2001; Schreiber et al., 1999; Wiig 1999). Although these methodologies have been useful to help in the development of KM Systems, there appears to be little evidence that their development processes and guidelines are well understood and supported by theoretical underpinnings. Good understanding of KMS design and use is still in its infancy.

Design is to be viewed as the process of problem understanding and problem solving with the aim of producing an artifact (Khushalani et al., 1994). The design of knowledge management systems involves knowledge sharing across groups and disciplines. Lanzara (1983) identifies several models of information system design, including:

- Design as functional analysis;
- Design as problem solving (Gasson, 2004);
- Design a problem setting;
- Design as situated, evolutionary learning (Gasson, 2004).

The author concurs with others (Glasser, 1966; Lave & Wenger, 1991) that design is situated in organisational contexts. Design is a dynamic process. Aspects of a solution are explored in conjunction with aspects of a problem understanding. Our understanding of organisational problems and appropriate design goals emerge as partial solutions are explored. Organisations are organised anarchies. People discover analysis and doing goals from what they are doing--the process of bargaining, learning, and adaptation (Clegg, 1994).

The creation of design science relies on existing kernel theories that are applied, tested, modified, and extended through the experience, creativity, intuition and problem-solving capabilities of the researcher (Markus et al., 2002). Activity theory has been successfully used as a framework for organisational theory (Blackler, 1993), organisational learning (Engeström, 1999), organisational sense making (Hasan, 2000), and organisational memory (Kuutti & Virkkunnen, 1995).

Design is Evolving

The design of a knowledge management system cannot be based solely on the systematic application of quantitative software measures, or any other methods from ideal natural science. It has to include an understanding of psychological, social, and cultural phenomena. It has to comprehend development as a basic feature. The design approach of KMS is concerned with making artifacts for human use. Design is a complex set of technical and social components and relationships that together constitute an activity system (Engeström, 1978). Activity theory tells us that we shall seek the design of our object not in our user's conscious and articulate interactions, but in their unconscious or partially conscious motives (Foot, 2002), which are best expressed in their activities rather than their explicit expressions of goals. Design in activity theory is not a conscious goal or aim. It is not even a single object, but an ensemble of elusive and constantly changing objects, both material and ideal (Zappen & Harrison, 2005).

The Hierarchy of Activity Structures Must be Understood

Activity should be the unit of analysis in the study of KMS. This is a conceptual level about the level at which most business analysis takes place, that is, at the level of action, which is undertaken towards specific goals (Hasan, 2000). Typically in most computer systems, actions which are routine and standardised can become automatic when driven to a lower level of operation under certain conditions.

Knowledge management may be the core business activity at the top level. This is where the knowledge is in the business. In activity theory, KM is not an end in itself, but more often, it is a support for other business activities at all three levels in the activity theory structure. Knowledge management as an explicit adjunct to core business activity, with value adding projects such as customer relation management is at the second level. These systems are viewed by activity theory as actions towards specific goals, but not as core business activities themselves. The third level in the activity theory hierarchy is that of operations where KM systems are seen as primary tools automating basic organisational knowledge management processes. Examples of tools include document management systems, data warehouses and performance scorecards.

Analyse Collective Activity

It is important in KM to use a collective activity system as the unit of analysis, giving context and meaning to seemingly random individual events. In activity theory, activity and context cannot be separated. The activity system itself is the context. What takes place in an activity system composed of object, actions and operations, is the context. Context is constituted through the enactment of an activity involving person (subject) and artifacts. Context is therefore the activity system and the activity system is connected to other activity systems. People consciously and deliberately generate contexts (activities) in part through their own objects. Context cannot be reduced to an enumeration of people and artifacts. In activity theory, context is not persistent and fixed information. Continuous construction is going on among the components of an activity system. Humans not only use tools, they also continuously renew and develop them either consciously or unconsciously. They not only use rules, but also transform them. It is generally acknowledged that understanding the social and organisational context is critical to the success of systems. The usability of a product depends on its context of use. Products should be designed for a specific context (Maguire, 2001). The role of context of use within usability is required by the International Standard ISO 13407 (ISO 1999).

Historically Analyze the Activity and Its Components

An activity system does not exist in a vacuum; it interacts with a network of other activity systems. For example, a project team (activity system) receives rules and instruments from business activity, its members are trained by educational activity, and it produces outcomes that are being used for activities in other organizational settings. An activity is also situated in time besides in a network of influencing activity systems. It is important to investigate its temporal interconnectedness (Pettigrew, 1990).

Secondly, historically analyse the activity and it constituent components and actions. History is the basis of classification. This means that the activity system and its components shall be understood historically. An activity is not a homogeneous entity. It is comprised of a variety of disparate elements, voices, and viewpoints (Engeström, 1990). The multiplicity can be understood in terms of historical layers. Activities are not static or rigid, they are constantly evolving. To understand a phenomenon means to know how it is developed into its existing form (Kaptelinin, 1996). This applies to all the elements of an activity. The current relationship between subject and object includes a condensation of the historical development of that relationship (Kuutti, 1996).

Analyze Contradictions of Activity System

Inner contradictions of the activity systems shall be analyzed as the source of disruption, innovation, change, and development of that system. Activities are not isolated units; they are like nodes in crossing hierarchies and networks. They are influenced by other activities and other changes in their environment. According to Kuutti (1996), external activities change some elements of activity, causing imbalances between them. Contradictions are used to indicate a misfit among elements, different activities or different development phases of the same activity. Contradictions manifest themselves as problems, ruptures, clashes and breakdown. Activity theory sees contradictions as a source of development. Activities are always in the process of working through some of these contradictions.

It is generally accepted that knowledge work is not an individual occupation, nor is it sufficient to say that knowledge work involves many people. On the contrary, knowledge work involves communication among loosely structured network communities of people. Understanding it involves identifying the social practices and relationships that are operative in a particular context. Lave and Wenger's (1991) notion of community of practice is a well-known example. A community of practice is defined by common tasks, methods, goals or approaches among a group of people (Thomas et al., 2001).

Knowledge Sharing Should Be Studied Within Context of Use

According to Boer and others (2000), knowledge sharing should be studied within context in which it is deployed. Knowledge sharing is defined as a set of behaviours involving exchange of knowledge or assistance to others. It has become an important issue in organisations that are keen to remain competitive. It is generally acknowledged that knowledge sharing does not take place in a vacuum--it takes place within an organisational context. Knowledge sharing is comprised of socio-technical, economic and historic facets. It should be studied within the context in which it is deployed (Boer et al., 2002). Activity theory is well suited for knowledge sharing because a knowledge sharing system can be described as an activity system using activity theory. Organizational settings (activities) should not be perceived as entities statically structured, but as a set of processes. Activity systems are best understood as disturbance producing systems.

Design as Mediated Activity

Design is a heteropraxial activity involving groups of people with different backgrounds and motivation in the process. During design, users and designers constituted a reified, implicit common understanding of the prototype.

In activity theory, all human endeavors are mediated by socially constituted artifacts (Engeström 1987; Leont'ev 1978). This means that KM design is mediated by artifacts. The designer (subject) shapes the design object by means of some design artifacts. The design object is the artifact produced in the design, the outcome the design activity is directed to. Design activity is mediated by design artifacts such as programming languages, methodologies, theories, technologies, and so forth.

The prototype in collaborative design serves two purposes. It is the continuously moving object of the design activity and is also a design artifact mediating the creation of insights and vision of the new system (Bertelsen, 2000).

Design Artifacts Mediate Across Heterogeneous Activities

Heterogeneous activities of different users contribute to design by tying together through their joint use of artifacts and their joint focus on the same object. Design artifacts tie different communities of practice together, maintaining meaning across groups, but by making senses in different ways to different groups. They not only take different shapes and serve different purposes to different groups; they also take different functions with one group across time, during use and design.

Design Artifacts Mediate Learning and Conception

Prototype mediates conception. Conception is about changing the existing *modus operandi*, both by identifying more suitable ways of realizing the established activity and by developing entirely new motives. It is concerned with understanding of the given and imagination of the better.

USES OF ACTIVITY THEORY FOR KNOWLEDGE MANAGEMENT

Hewlett-Packard uses activity theory to develop their knowledge management system.

According to Collins and others (2002), the Customer Support organization in HP is geographically distributed around the world, providing around-the-clock support to Hewlett-Packard customers who use the SMS (Systems Manager Suite) family of Hewlett-Packard software products. Knowledge authoring often takes place as a side effect of documenting the support cases in keeping with support-management. Collins and others (2002) report on a case study of the development of requirements for an evolving knowledge management software system in a customer support group within a large organization.

The study shows that using activity theory has led to the improvement of current work practices. The initial interviews with stakeholders improved their awareness of other members of the organization relevant to their work as well as improving their knowledge about mediating means at their disposal. There was also improved understanding between knowledge producers and consumers.

Besides the above example of Hewlett-Packard use of activity theory for knowledge management, there also several case studies of the use of activity theory for knowledge intensive systems. These include the work of Korpolla and others (2000) and (Crawford & Hasan, 2006). It is evidenced from these case studies that activity theory is appropriate for knowledge management research. These examples demonstrate that activity theory is eminently suitable as the underlying research framework for knowledge management.

FUTURE TRENDS

The use of activity theory as a kernel in design theory is still in its infancy. Further empirical studies would be needed to validate this. The author is currently working with our KMO partners to develop a KM design theory for collaborative research work. This new design theory will be developed based on activity theory as the kernel theory. The developed design theory will be empirically analysed through the development of artifacts. These artifacts will be validated according to the characteristics of design theory research.

CONCLUSION

The development of effective KM systems is a socio-cultural activity. A technical solution is not adequate to address the complexity of the system. Activity theory can be used to emphasise the importance of a systemic analysis of an organisational setting by considering it as a network of activities. Using the activity system as its unit of analysis, the activity theory avoids simple causal explanation of knowledge management analysis by describing an organisational setting as an ensemble of multiple systematically interacting elements including social rules, mediating artifacts and division of labour. It also explicitly perceives an activity as a dynamic phenomenon in which not only consensus and stability, but also conflicts, breakdown and discontinuities play a crucial role. Both the process of requirement analysis, knowledge sharing and the dynamic transformation of objects into artifacts and vice versa can be taken into account.

This paper gave only a glimpse of the use of activity theory as a kernel theory for the development of a KM design theory for collaborative research. Many issues need to be addressed before a design theory can be developed. KM communities are a special class of information system, both in terms of the artifacts and the methodologies used. Although there are several methodologies, and frameworks abound for the development of KM systems, most of those examples of methodological components are numerous design heuristics. However, there is still a lack of design theory in the KM Community for collaborative KM systems. Although the EKPs design theory addresses some of the issues of our collaboration, it does not meet our particular needs. Our design exhibits special characteristics: information requirements that include explicit and tacit knowledge for different groups of users; knowledge capture, creation and sharing that is distributed globally and virtual communities of practice from diverse cultures.

REFERENCES

Al-Rawas, A. & Easterbrook, S. (1996, February 1-2). Communications problems in requirements engineering: A field study.In *Proceedings of the 1st Westminster Conference on Professional Awareness in Software Engineering*, London, The Royal Society.

Bertelsen, O.W. (2000). *Scandinavian Journal of Information Systems 12,* pp. 15-27.

Blackler, F. (1993). Knowledge and the theory of organisation: Organisation as activity systems and reframing of management. *Journal of Management studies 30(6)*, 863-885.

Boer, N.I., van Baalen, P.J., & Kumar, K. (2002). An activity theory approach for studying the situatedness of knowledge sharing. In *Proceedings of the 35th Annual Hawaii International Conference on System Sciences* (HICSS 35.02)

Brooks, F. P. (1995). The mythical man-month: Essays on software engineering (anniversary ed.). Reading, MA: Addison-Wesley.

Clegg, C. (1994). Psychology and information technology: The study of cognition in organisations. *British Journal of Psyschology, 85*, 449-477.

Cole, H. & Engeström, Y. (1993). A cultural historical approach to distributed cognition. In G. Solomon (Ed.) *Psychological and educational considerations* (pp. 1-46). Cambridge, UK: Cambridge University Press

Collins, P., Shukla, S. & Redmiles, D. (2002). Activity theory and system design: A view from the trenches, Special Issue of CSCW on Activity Theory and the Practice of Design, Introduction to the Special Issue on Activity Theory and the Practice of Design , Computer Supported Cooperative Work (CSCW), Vol. 11, No 1-2/March , Springer, Netherlands.

Crawford, K. & Hasan. H. (2006). Demonstrations of the activity theory framework for research in information systems. *Australasian Journal of Information Systems Volume 13 Number 2, May 2006.*

Davenport, T.H., DeLong, D.W. & Beeres, M.C. (1998). Successful knowledge management Projects. *Sloan Management Review, Winter 1998,* pp 43-57.

Debowski, S. (2006). Knowledge management. John Wiley & Son, Australia.

Dubin, R., (1978). *Theory Building.* Free Press, New York.

Engeström, Y. (1987). Learning by expanding: An activity-theoretical approach to developmental research. Helsinki: Orienta-Konsultit, OY. Finland.

Engeström, Y. (1990). Developmental work: Research as activity theory in practice: Analysisng the work of general practitioners. In Y. Engeström, Learning, Working and Imaging: Twelve studies in activity theory, Orienta-Konsultit OY, Helsinki.

Engeström, Y. (1999). Innovative learning in work teams: analysing knowledge creation in practice. In Y. Engeström, R. Miettinen, & R-L Punamaki (Eds.), *Perspectives on activity theory: Learning in doing: Social, cognitive and computational perspectives.* (pp, 377-404) Cambridge University Press, UK.

Engeström, Y. (2005). Developmental work research: Expanding activity theory in practice, Vol. 12, ICHS, Berlin, 2005.

Fielden, (1975) G. D. R., *Engineering Design.* London: HMSO

Foot, K.A. (2001). Cultural historical activity theory as practical theory: Illuminating the development of a conflict monitoring network. *Communication Theory Vol.0 No.1. Feb 2001,* 56-83.

Gasson, S. (Working Paper) (2004). Organisational 'problem solving' and theories of social cognition. Available from http://www.cis.drexel.edu/faculty/gasson/research/problem-solving.html

Glasser, L. (1986). The Integration of Computing and Routine Work. *ACM Translation on Office Information Systems Vol. 4.* pp. 205-252.

Handy, C. (2005). Understanding Organisation. (4th Ed.) Penguin Global, 2005.

Harris K., Fleming M., Hunter R., Rosser B. & Cushman A. (1998). The knowledge management scenario: Trends and directions for 1998-2003. (Tech. Rep.*) Gartner Group.*

Hasan, H. (2000). The mediating role of technology in making sense of information in a knowledge intensive industry. *Knowledge and Process Management 6*(2*)* 72-82.

Hevner, A.R.., March, S.T., & Park, J. (2004) Design research in information systems research, *Mis Quarterly 28*(1), 75-105.

Holsapple, C.W. (2003). Handbook on knowledge management. Heidelberg: Springer.

Huysman, M. & Wulf, V. (2006). IT to support knowledge sharing in communities, towards a social capital analysis. *Journal of Information-Technology 2* (1),. 40 – 51.

ISO (1999). ISO 13407. Human centred design processes for interactive systems. International Standards Organisation.

Khushalani, A., Smith. R. & Howard, S. (1994). What happens when designers don't play by the rules: towards a model of opportunistic behavior in design. *Australian Journal of Information Systems, May,* 13-31.

Korpela, M., Soriyan, H. A., & Olufokunbi, K. C. (2000). Activity analysis as a method for information systems development: General introduction and experiments from Nigeria and Finland. *Scandinavian Journal of Information Systems,12,* 191-210.

Kuutti, K. & Vikkunen, J. (1995). Organisational memory and learning network organisation: The case of Finnish Labour Protection Inspectors. In *Proceedings of HICSS 28.*

Kuutti, K. (1996). Activity theory as a potential framework for human-computer interaction. In B. Nardi (Ed.), *Context and Consciousness* (pp.17-44). MIT Press.

Kuutti, K. (1999). Activity theory, transformation of work, and information system design. In Y. Engeström, R. Miettinen, & R-L Punamaki (Eds.), *Perspectives on activity theory: Learning in doing: Social, cognitive and computational perspectives.* (pp, 360-376). Cambridge University Press, UK.

Lanzara, G.F. (1983). The design process: Frames, metaphors and games. In U. Brefs, C. Ciborra, & L. Schneider (Eds), *System Design for, with and by The User.* North-Holland Publishing Company.

Leont'ev, A.N. (1978). Problems of the development of the mind. Moscow, Progress.

Lave, J. & Wenger, E. (1991). Situated learning: Legitimate peripheral participation. Cambridge University Press, Cambridge, UK.

Loucopoulos, P. & Karakostas, V. (1995). *Systems Engineering.* MCGraw-Hill, Maidenhead, UK,

MacGrath, M. & Uden, L. (2000, January) Modelling softer aspects of the software development process: An activity theory based approach. Thirty-third Hawaii International Conference on System Sciences. (HICSS-33) Wailea, Maui, Hawaii, USA - Software Process Improvement. IEEE Computer Society Press.

Maguire, M. (2000). Context with usability Actions. *International Journal of Human-Computer Studies 55,* 453-483.

Markus, M.L., Majchrzak, A., & Gasser, L. (2002). A design theory for systems that support emergent knowledge processes. *MIS Quarterly, 26*(3) 179-212.

McMichael, H. (1999). An activity based perspective for information system research. In *Proceedings of the 10th Amsterdam Conference on Information Systems.*

Moore, A. (2005, July 22-27) Towards a design theory for community information systems. In *Proceedings of the 11th International Conference on Human-Computer Interaction (HCII 2005)* Las Vegas, NV. Lawrence Erlbaum Associates, Mahwah, NJ.

Pettigrew, A. M. (1990). Longitudinal field research on change: Theory and practice. *Organization Science* 1(3), 267-292.

Pinch, T. J. & W. E. Bijker (1984). The social construction of facts and artifacts: Or how the sociology of science and the sociology of technology might benefit each other. In W. Bijker, T. Hughes and T. Pinch (Eds.), *The Social Construction of Technological Systems.* Cambridge, MA: MIT Press.

Probert, S.K. Requirements engineering, soft system methodology and workforce empowerment. *Requirements Engineering, 4,* (1999), Springer-Verlag, London, pp. 85-91.

Probst, G., Raub, S. & Romhardt, K. (2003). Managing knowledge: Building blocks for Success. John Wiley & Son, Chichester, UK.

Rubenstein-Mantano B., Liebowitz J., Buchwalter J., McCaw D., Newman B., & Rebeck K. (2001). SMARTVision: a knowledge-management methodology. *Journal of Knowledge Management, 5(4),* 300-310. MCB University Press.

Schreiber G., Akkermaus H., Anjewierden A., de Hoog R., Shadbolt N., van der Velde W., & Wielinga B. (1999). Knowledge engineering and management--The common KAD methodology. MIT press, Cambridge, MA.

Thomas, J.C., Kellogg, W.A., & Erickson, T. (2001). The knowledge management puzzle: Human and social factors in knowledge management. *IBM Systems Journal, 40*(4), 863-884.

Viller, S. & Sommerville, I. (1999). Social analysis in the requirement engineering process: From ethnology to method. *4th IEEE International Symposium on Requirement Engineering,* Limerick, Ireland. IEEE Computer Society Press, Los Alamitos, pp. 6-13.

Vygotsky, L.S. (1978). *Mind in society.* Harvard University Press, Cambridge, MA

Walls, J., Widmeyer, G., & El Sawy, O. (1992). Building an information system design theory for vigilant EIS, Information Systems Research **3**(1), 36 - 59.

Wenger, E., McDermott, R., & Snyder, W. (2002). Cultivating communities of practice. Cambridge, MA: Harvard Business School Press.

Wiig, K. (1999). Establish, govern and renew the enterprise's knowledge practices. Schema Press, Arlington, TX.

Winograd, T. (1995). From programming environments to environments for designing. *Communications of the ACM,* 38(6), 65-74.

Zappen J. P., & Harrison, M (2005). Intention and motive in information-system design: Towards a Theory and Method for Assessing Users' Needs. P. van den Basselaar & S. Koizumi (Eds.), Digital Cities 2003, LNCS 3081 pp. 354-368. Springer-Verlag, Berlin, Heidelberg, 2005.

Chapter X
Knowledge Management and Interaction in Virtual Communities

Maria Chiara Caschera
Institute for Research on Population and Social Policies, Italy

Arianna D'Ulizia
Institute for Research on Population and Social Policies, Italy

Fernando Ferri
Institute for Research on Population and Social Policies, Italy

Patrizia Grifoni
Institute for Research on Population and Social Policies, Italy

ABSTRACT

This chapter provides a classification of virtual communities of practice according to methods and tools offered to virtual community members for the knowledge management and the interaction process. It underlines how these methods and tools support users during the exchange of knowledge, enable learning, and increase the user ability to achieve individual and collective goals. In this chapter virtual communities are classified in virtual knowledge-sharing communities of practice and virtual learning communities of practice according to the collaboration strategy. A further classification defines three kinds of virtual communities according to the knowledge structure: ontology-based VCoP; digital library-based VCoP; and knowledge map-based VCoP. This chapter also describes strategies of interaction used to improve the knowledge sharing and learning in groups and organizations. It shows how agent-based method supports interaction among community members, improves the achievement of knowledge, and encourages the level of user participation. Finally, this chapter presents the system's functionalities that support browsing and searching processes in collaborative knowledge environments.

INTRODUCTION

The increasing achievement of the Web has led organizations to exploit collaborative technologies in order to cooperate in the generation of knowledge by developing new organizational capacities and encourage partnerships among different groups.

The cooperation can be achieved by a social-networking that improves and facilitates social interaction and enables one to remain in touch with friends exploiting the pervasive nature of information devices and services. In this context, an important role is performed by virtual communities.

A Virtual Community (VC) can be defined as an information source or the place of the knowledge creation (Kurabayashi et al., 2002) in which people share interests and information. The community participants have different knowledge or expertise and they can exchange useful information by communicating with each other.

VCs should be information rich, and they should allow information available for sets of people and not just for individuals. They aim to improve and encourage social processes allowing information sharing among colleagues, friends or people who share interests.

A virtual community aims to support shaping of a community memory and a knowledge base.

A particular kind of virtual communities are Virtual Communities of Practice (VCoPs) that represent just new organizational forms of cooperation using Information and Communication Technologies (ICTs) to carry out a collaborative environment. In 2002 Wenger (Wenger et al., 2002) defined the term Community of Practice (CoP) as a community that "binds together groups of people who share a concern, a set of problems, or a passion of the topic, and who deepen their knowledge and expertise by interacting on an ongoing basis."

In a CoP the communication among partners occurs through face-to-face meetings. However, nowadays organizations are geographically distributed so that their activities have to be coordinated and integrated using ICT. This has reduced the use of face-to-face meetings that are too expensive and time-consuming. It has also led to choose collaborative technologies facilitating communication, and do not impose spatial and temporal constraints. Therefore, CoPs have become increasingly VCoPs.

Consequently, ICT is a key element for the development of a VCoP because it enables individuals and organisations to virtually access and share their knowledge. In particular, two main ICT aspects are relevant for VCoPs: *knowledge management* and *interaction process*.

ICT support is required for a range of different tools and services necessary for *knowledge management*, which is used for sharing knowledge and increasing collaboration to achieve organizational purposes.

The most frequently used technologies are the Collaboration Technologies that allow synchronous, real time manipulation of common data (network chats). An example of a collaborative virtual environment is a Web-based virtual community (Bouras et al., 2005) that provides collaborative functionalities and synchronous and asynchronous interaction services.

This chapter provides taxonomy of virtual communities based on knowledge management and interaction strategies. With respect to knowledge management, we consider the main functions of knowledge management within VCoPs and we infer that it mainly allows the collaboration among community members and the organization of community knowledge. Consequently, we classify VCoPs according to collaboration strategies and the knowledge structure. We distinguish: between (i) virtual knowledge-sharing communities of practice and (ii) virtual learning communities of practice; and among (a) ontology-based VCoPs, (b) digital library-based VCoPs, and (c) knowledge map-based VCoPs, respectively.

With respect to interaction strategies, we identify two main methods to make the interaction among community members possible: (i) intelligent agents and (ii) collaborative knowledge.

KNOWLEDGE MANAGEMENT IN VCOPS

In literature different definitions of knowledge management and VCoPs can be found. Although these definitions refer to different contexts, they agree that knowledge management involves a set of procedures aimed at creating, organizing, sharing, and disseminating knowledge, making this knowledge more productive and producing significant benefits, such as shared intelligence and improved performance.

Knowledge management enables VCoP to make the collaboration and exchange of ideas among community members easier, and to preserve explicit as well as implicit (or tacit) knowledge that is created through the relationships among community members and would be lost without any form of management.

The distinction between explicit and tacit knowledge was introduced by Polanyi (1966). More specifically, the former is understood as the conscious knowledge that people hold explicitly and can be communicated to others. The latter refers to the intuitive, subconscious knowledge which people carry in their minds and which is difficult to communicate and disseminate to others. Explicit community knowledge is stored in the community repository and includes its documents, recorded discussions, conceptual models, and any kind of information readily available to community members. Tacit knowledge, instead, resides in the minds of community members and, therefore, it is intangible. Both kinds of knowledge have to be managed in order to preserve and organize information and improve the intellectual power of VCoP; however, the management of tacit knowledge is a crucial challenge due to its immaterial feature. Nokaka and Konno (1998) proposed the spiral model that explains how knowledge can be created and shared with others in a community using four modes of knowledge conversion: *socialization* (from tacit to tacit), that refers to the tacit knowledge transfer occurring through shared experiences, imitation and so on; *externalization* (from tacit to explicit), articulating tacit knowledge into explicit concepts; *combination* (from explicit to explicit), that occurs through the systematization of explicit knowledge concepts; *internalization* (from explicit to tacit) that occurs by applying explicit knowledge in real situations. This model highlights the dynamic nature of knowledge and can be considered as a basic model to understand how knowledge is created and transferred and how learning takes place in a VCoP.

VCoPs have a close association with knowledge management. VCoPs are generally not formal organizations whose members are geographically distributed and share interests, information needs, and problems. The use of knowledge management tools, in conjunction with ICT and the Internet, allows the support of geographically dispersed VCoPs members by performing two main functions. First, knowledge management enables the knowledge extension of a single member by providing tools for easily contacting and collaborating with other members and exchanging knowledge. Secondly, it allows the possibility of structuring knowledge and establishing a common knowledge base available to the community members.

We have started from these two features of knowledge management for classifying VCoPs. In fact, we propose a classification of VCoPs (see Table 1) according to:

- the collaboration strategy they adopt to enable the collaboration and sharing of knowledge

Table 1. A classification of VCoPs based on knowledge management strategies

	Collaboration Strategy	Knowledge Structure
Virtual Communities of Practice	Virtual knowledge-sharing communities of practice Virtual learning communities of practice	Ontology-based Virtual Communities of Practice Digital library-based Virtual Communities of Practice Knowledge map-based Virtual Communities of Practice

- the knowledge structure, that is the way in which they organize the community knowledge.

In particular, depending on the collaboration strategy, VCoPs can be broadly classified as:

- Virtual knowledge-sharing Communities of Practice;
- Virtual learning Communities of Practice.

Whereas according to the knowledge structure we can distinguish the following three kinds of VCoP:

- Ontology-based VCoP;
- Digital library-based VCoP;
- Knowledge map-based VCoP.

CLASSIFICATION OF VCOPS BASED ON COLLABORATION STRATEGIES

Virtual collaboration refers to the use of ICTs for supporting the collective interaction among multiple parties involved in (Hossain & Wigand, 2004). In the field of virtual communities, virtual collaboration is achieved through the use of collaborative knowledge management technologies that allow team members to collaborate on problems or projects, capture tacit knowledge of each member, and transform it into explicit knowledge of the community. In particular, these technologies enable VCoPs to help community members to share knowledge and learn. In the following, we classify VCoPs according to the collaborative knowledge management strategies they adopt, distinguishing between (i) virtual knowledge-sharing communities of practice and (ii) virtual learning communities of practice.

Virtual Knowledge-Sharing Community of Practice

Virtual knowledge-sharing communities of practice have as primary aim to allow socially distributed knowledge, sharing of problem definition and information transfer among community members. The most effective way for allowing knowledge-sharing is the conversation. It is through conversation that we learn how to learn together (Brown & Isaacs, 1996).

In a VCoP, conversations can occur through a shared space where community members can interact via email or discussion board, creating new knowledge and, mainly, sharing knowledge.

Therefore, common functionalities, provided by this kind of VCoP and aimed at sharing resources within the community, contain discussion

Figure 1. Main functionalities of a virtual knowledge-sharing communities of practice

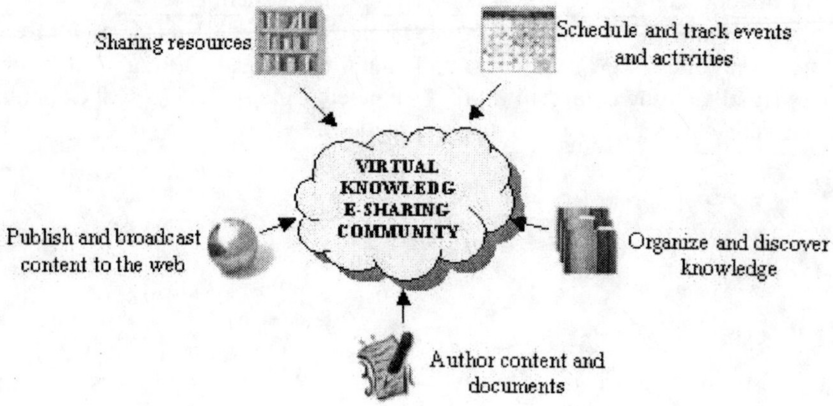

boards, which provide team members with the ability to post and reply to messages in a common area; a whiteboard, which allows dispersed users to brainstorm together, draw graphical objects into a shared window etc.; video/audio conferencing, which allows making virtual face-to-face meeting, and a shared notepad, which provides community members with the skill to create a document together.

Other functionalities concern the scheduling of common events and activities, the organization and retrieval of knowledge and the broadcast of shared documents to the Web (see Figure 1).

A particular communication tool for sharing knowledge is storytelling (Snowden, 1999). According to Sole and Wilson (2002), storytelling allows the sharing of knowledge and experiences through narrative and anecdotes in order to communicate lessons, complex ideas, concepts, and causal connections. Recently, this technique has been adopted within VCoPs with the aim of supporting and eliciting the cooperative work. In fact, through the active participation of community members to the story creation, it is possible to communicate embedded knowledge, resolve conflicts, simulate problem solving and, mainly, sharing tacit knowledge.

As in VCoPs most of knowledge to be managed is tacit, they need of appropriate tools and procedures that encourage the sharing of this kind of knowledge, such as social channels, interaction and collaboration activities. The System Dynamics CoP (Hafeez & Alghatas, 2007) is a specialist community which provides storytelling, discussion board and electronic newsletter for facilitating the processes of socialization, externalisation and combination and promoting events, courses, publications and stories within communities.

Com.ShareNet (Leal et al., 2006), a network tool for knowledge sharing activities of an innovative enterprise (Siemens), provides synchronous (network chats) and asynchronous (search machines, news, discussion forums, document management, urgent orders, etc.) collaboration technologies. Moreover, Siemens VCoP is supported by other two tools of knowledge management for e-learning and management of component networks.

To sum up, the process of knowledge sharing involves VCoPs to effectively convey what their members know, facilitating the creation of new knowledge and the resolution of common problems.

Virtual Learning Communities of Practice

Learning is a constructionist often social activity occurring through knowledge building (Vygotsky, 1962). It consists in a process whereby information is delivered from a knowledgeable source, such as a book or teacher, to recipients.

Some researchers argue that any VCoP has one or more elements of learning (Schwier, 2001). However, in Virtual learning Communities of Practice the focus is the education of community members, who are mainly students or trainees. Once the educational purpose is achieved, this kind of community aims at sustaining professional relationships and collaborations through time.

As depicted in Figure 2, the main functionalities available in a virtual learning CoP concern are: the consultation of educational material which comprises learning objects used by community members; the storage of learners' histories for recording their skills, needs and educational targets; a collaborative environment which makes group activities and communication easier.

Moreover, this kind of virtual community can offer community members several learning tools, such as surveys, tests, interactive lessons or researches on a digital library, or it can be used in order to design and teach a course and develop and integrate course materials.

In particular, there are three virtual learning tools: Wikis, Blogs, and Newsgroups (Xu et al., 2006).

A Wiki provides an effective virtual forum that allows users to add content and also to edit content supporting collaborative writing, opening discussions, interaction, and Web-authoring (Desitlets

Figure 2. Main functionalities of a virtual learning communities of practice

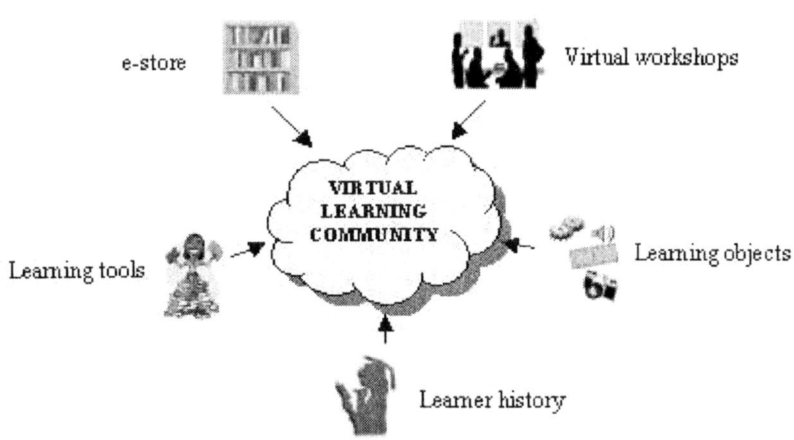

2005). Besides, it offers an asynchronous platform for VCoPs, and with its capacity to archive different page versions can act as repositories, thereby enabling effective knowledge management.

A Blog is a cooperation environment containing reverse chronologically ordered posts that are inserted in a common Web page.

A Newsgroup represents a repository of messages posted by many users from different locations. It can be considered as a virtual space where people exchange ideas, discuss, communicate, and even make friends (Roberts, 1998).

An example of virtual learning community is Educational MUVES (Cooper, 2003) giving community members several learning tools, such as synchronous chat rooms, threaded discussion boards, whiteboards, files, and public links sharing. Teachers can build chat rooms around specific topics, moderate, and participate in discussions. Threaded discussion boards can be used to collaborate with other students in problem solving activities.

The Virtual learning CoP proposed by Varlamis and Apostolakis (2006) provides a knowledge base for educational material, a profile base for the storage of learners' history and a collaboration environment for communication and participation in synchronous activities (see Figure 3).

CLASSIFICATION OF VCOPS BASED ON KNOWLEDGE STRUCTURES

Much of explicit community knowledge resides in documents, conceptual models, and discussions of its members. All this knowledge constitutes a community memory of past experiences and problem solutions that community members can reuse in their present experiences. Therefore, this community memory has to be maintained and retrieved in order to be useful and usable. An important aspect within VCoPs is thus represented by the methodology used to organize and structure community knowledge. In this section, we are proposing taxonomy of VCoPs, which groups them according to the technological solutions adopted to organize and share information, documents and services. That is, Semantic Web technology and ontologies represent a structured and directed

Figure 3. The virtual learning community proposed by Varlamis and Apostolakis

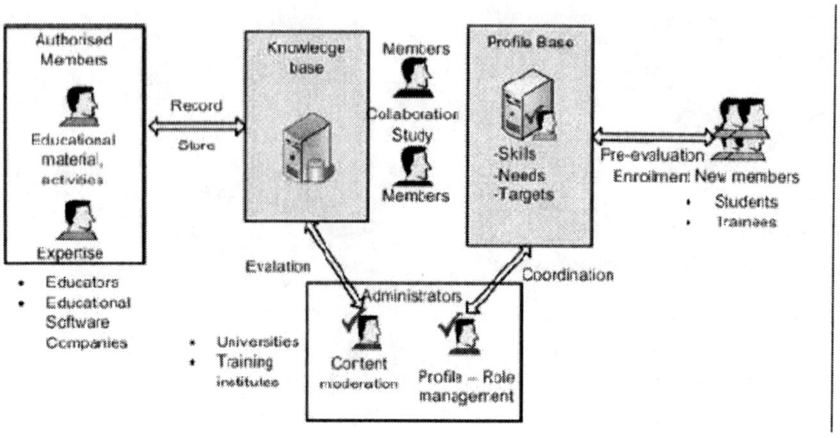

methodology for managing knowledge across the whole VCoP. Digital library and virtual communities are metaphors to share knowledge and can be used together providing another kind of VCoP knowledge organization model. Finally, a knowledge map management system is the third possible technological solution that can be adopted by a VCoP in order to organize, search and exchange community knowledge.

Therefore, in the following we distinguish among (i) ontology-based virtual communities of practice, (ii) digital library-based virtual communities of practice, and (iii) knowledge map-based virtual communities of practice.

Ontology-Based Virtual Communities of Practice

This kind of VCoPs relies on ontologies to structure community knowledge and to make this knowledge accessible by all members across the Web.

Semantic Web technologies are used within a VCoP as they allow one to give a well-defined meaning to information, better enabling knowledge acquisition, modelling, retrieval, reuse, publishing and preservation as well as people to work together. In particular, ontologies facilitate knowledge sharing as they offer a consensual and formal conceptualisation of a given domain. Ontologies improve knowledge management capabilities using a concept hierarchy to which community members can assign information.

Among tools which are used to share information within a VCoP and which can be brought into the Semantic Web, there are blogs that can be annotated for allowing information on bibliographies, reading lists and other interesting material to be searched, shared, and discussed in a more directed way.

In OntoShare (Davies et al., 2003), a knowledge resource annotated with metadata is provided in order to simplify information sharing within VCoPs. Ontologies are defined using RDFS (RDF Schema) and populated using the RDF (Resource Description Framework). This ontology-based system allows users to store, retrieve, and put community members in touch. Once a member

Figure 4. The service-oriented framework for distributed knowledge community management proposed by Chen et al.

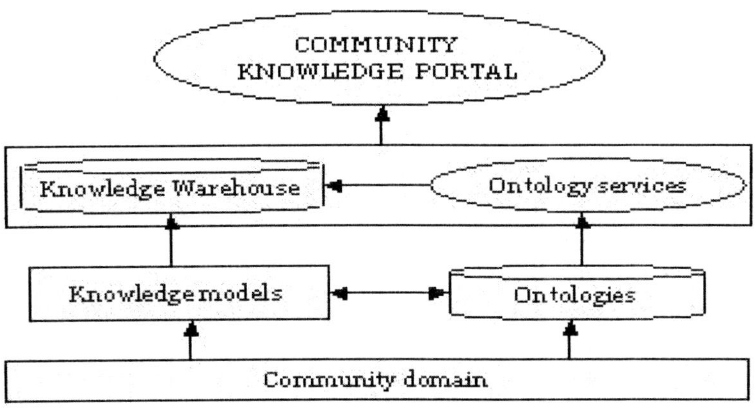

decides to share a piece of information, the system creates a new entry in the OntoShare system that represents effectively an ontology. Moreover, the OntoShare system permits to search and access the community store using a vector space matching and scoring algorithm to retrieve the pages which held in the OntoShare repository and which match most closely the query supplied by the user.

Another approach that applies Semantic Web technologies to enhance knowledge management and collaboration within VCoPs is proposed by Chen et al. (2002). They propose an integrated service-oriented framework for distributed knowledge management in a VCoP whose architecture is shown in Figure 4. In this framework, ontologies can be built from knowledge acquisition, and further used to create knowledge bases or to do semantic annotation. These knowledge bases can then be exploited by the services that provide mechanisms for querying or searching semantic content so as to facilitate knowledge publishing, use/reuse and maintenance.

Digital Library-Based Virtual Communities of Practice

This kind of VCoP uses digital libraries to support the preservation and access to community content and documents as well as resource sharing. Digital library-based VCoPs combine communication technologies and digital information storage in order to extend the basic functionalities provided by conventional libraries, such as the collection, cataloguing, searching, administration, and dissemination of bibliographic information.

Using digital libraries, users of a virtual community collaborate to share and evolve their knowledge in a domain of interest. In fact, members can actively discuss the community knowledge, use it and regularly update it. In particular, extended functionalities provided by digital libraries concern: adding multimedia contents and metadata to the digital library repository; adding hypermedia features (comments, links, etc.) to multimedia contents held in the digital library repository; discussing around a multimedia content (see Figure 5).

CKESS (Collaborative Knowledge Evolution Support System) (Bieber et al., 2002) offers an enhanced digital library that includes collaborative tools, such as computer-mediated communications, community process support, decision support, advanced hypermedia features, and conceptual knowledge structures. In particular, this system can be used in order to improve the process to locate articles more quickly. This process can be refined using a workflow diagram which explains the search path, helps users during the search, and guides them. The use of digital library can also support the learning process. In

Figure 5. A Digital library-based VCoP

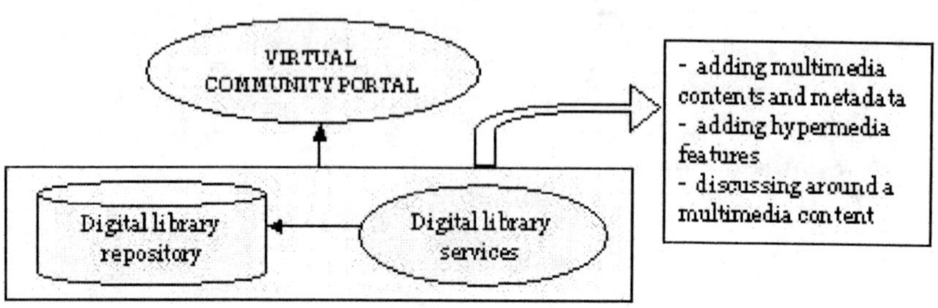

fact, learners have the opportunity to add links and annotations to various documents, interlink related documents and data, and add comments. The discussion environment offered by the digital library-based virtual community allows users to discuss aspects and to propose structures for developing curricula.

So the digital library-based virtual community supports its users, offering them workflow and decision analysis capabilities, conceptual knowledge structures, and allowing them to form a community memory and knowledge base.

These kinds of virtual communities can be improved using semantic digital libraries. These structures integrate information based on different metadata, such as user profiles, resources, taxonomies, and bookmarks. Moreover, semantic digital libraries use semantics in order to define more robust, adaptable and user-friendly search and browser interfaces. Finally, they improve the interoperability with other systems on metadata and communication level thanks to the use of semantics.

Knowledge Map-Based Virtual Communities of Practice

This kind of VCoP uses a knowledge map management system as a tool for structuring community knowledge, allowing knowledge navigation, seeking, and exchanging.

Adopting the definition provided by Lin and Hsueh (2003), the knowledge map consists in the categorization of documents characterized by concepts contributed to communities of practice (see Figure 6). Document categories are built in the knowledge map to represent concept hierarchy.

Within VCoPs, knowledge map techniques allow pointing both to people and documents helping to locate information of interest. In such a way community members can know who works/worked on a similar problem or if there are some documents/tools that help to solve their problem.

An approach based on knowledge map for content management in VCoPs is proposed by Lin et al. (2003). They adopt a bottom-up data categorization based on information extraction techniques for transforming unstructured contents into structured data, and data mining techniques for discovering relationships among contents. Moreover, they develop a procedure for updating the existing knowledge map when a community member allocates a new incoming content. In particular, their knowledge map management system is composed of: a knowledge map navigator for guiding knowledge object discovery; a knowledge seeker for identifying knowledge objects from the document base according to the user's request; a learning adviser for recommending necessary knowledge according to the learning history repository; a knowledge map manager

Figure 6. The knowledge map approach

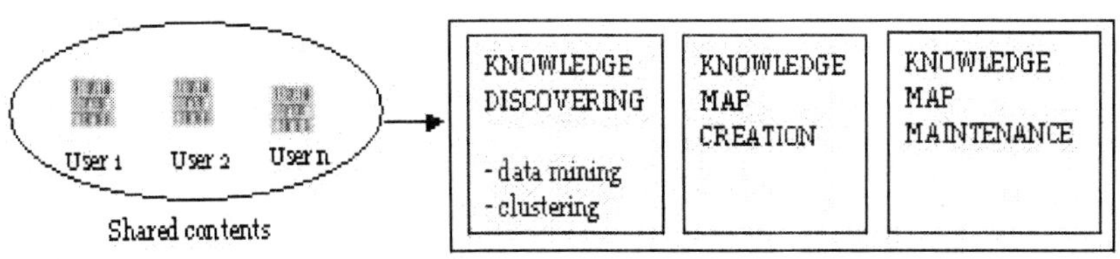

for coordinating the knowledge map navigation, seeking and learning.

Novak and Wurst (2004) propose a way for capturing, visualizing, and sharing implicit knowledge of a VCoP based on perceptual maps. These maps create personalized views on the unstructured community knowledge (e.g., mailing list archives, project descriptions, best-practices, and documents) as well as relate them to a shared conceptual structure. It is not a coincidence that these knowledge maps consists out of two main elements: the DocumentMap, that presents the information space into clusters of semantically related documents; and the ConceptMap, that provides a navigation structure of the information space. In order to construct these knowledge maps, the authors combine statistical text-analysis and clustering-based methods with methods based on the nearest neighbour algorithm.

INTERACTION PROCESS IN VCOPS

Virtual communities may be used to improve the knowledge circulation in organizations and groups. Important aspects in the design of a virtual community are to establish a sustainable level of participation and an efficient knowledge exchange process.

In order to achieve this purpose, the main feature to consider is the interaction process.

In fact, during this process, the key goal of the virtual community is to provide an easier and natural interaction with the medium Internet and with other environments.

Computer-mediated communication systems can be used to facilitate communication. These systems assist users to compose, store, deliver, and process communication (Reid, 1991). Computer-mediated communication refers to virtual environment which supports knowledge with functionalities for searching and browsing information. Moreover, this method assists users in sharing and exchanging their findings in virtual communities. In fact, some systems make available a repository of multimedia documents and the access can be controlled using computer-mediated communications (Gross, 2004).

The following different methods are proposed to make possible the interaction among community members:

- Agent-based interaction;
- Collaborative knowledge.

Furthermore, functionalities of a virtual community system can be broken up using the UML (Unified Modelling Language) through modeling techniques such as use cases, interaction diagrams, and class specifications (Kurabayashi et al., 2002). In this case, the environment consists of several autonomous and interoperable software components called services, which run on different machines in different locations.

INTERACTION IN VIRTUAL COMMUNITIES BASED ON AGENTS

The term "software agent" was defined by Etzioni and Weld (1995) as a computer program that behaves in a manner analogous to a human agent. They offer a social interface metaphor in a human-computer interaction and they own several qualities (Selker, 1994).

Considering the interaction process, intelligent agents can be used to support users in different ways. They can contribute to gradually improve the level of familiarity of each user with the system and the level of participation.

A further goal of intelligent agents in virtual communities is to encourage users to reflect in order to improve the achievement of knowledge connected to their interests, abilities and performance styles. Intelligent agents help users to plan their actions better and get closer to achieve their goals.

Figure 7. Goals of intelligent agents

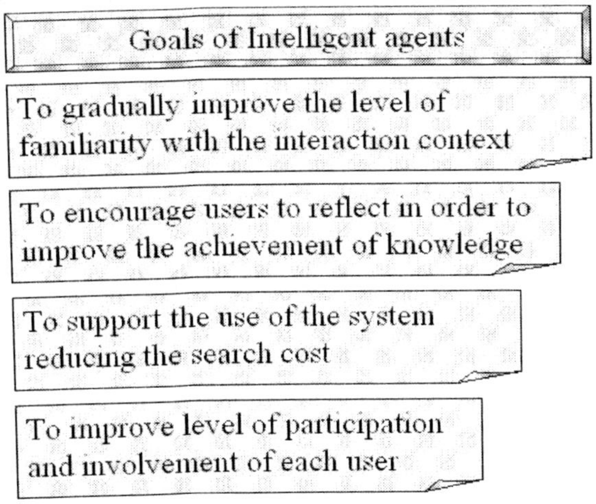

Moreover, they can be employed to support the use of the system reducing the search cost for value creation by locating and suggesting the system exploration. Figure 7 summarizes the main goals of intelligent agents in VCoPs.

First of all, an agent initiates and exercises control over its own actions according to user requests and determining how and when to satisfy these requests. Besides, it can modify requests asking clarification to the user. Considering temporal aspects, an agent is a continuously running process. An agent is able to automatically customize itself to its user preferences on the basis of user experience and its environment. Finally, an agent has a well-defined authentic personality that facilitates interaction with human users and allows obtaining information to accomplish its goals.

In virtual community environments, intelligent agents interact with users through an agent user interface using messages and suggestions. Users can directly request agent activity and agents can react to the user behaviour and system events.

Agents can be activated by events that are triggered by user commands, by states of the system or generated autonomously by the agent system (Angehrn, 2004). In this case, agents decide how to reach to the incoming events according to a specific logical module.

In virtual communities, agents are often used in order to:

- improve the learning process in on-line virtual communities;
- improve the level of participation and involvement of each user increasing the member familiarity and stimulating knowledge sharing and proactive behaviour.

Agent-Based Interaction in Virtual Learning Communities

Intelligent agent techniques can support networks of people who want to learn anywhere and anytime.

In Virtual learning communities, intelligent agents are programs that help and assist users during the learning process.

In particular, autonomous intelligent agents can improve the learning effectiveness and the learner satisfaction reducing costs (Thaiupathump et al., 1999). In fact, it is possible to observe how agents' activities during the online learning of students stimulate people for completing their works and improve the retention rate of students. The agents aid user enjoyment of the learning situation because a social relationship is established between user and pedagogical agent and this mechanism promotes learning in Web-based learning environment.

The agents can interact with users using text, graphics, speech and facial expressions, and users consider agents credible, useful and they internalize agents' suggestions (Jafari, 2002).

Moreover, in the context of learning communities, agent-based system supports cognitive

Figure 8. Basic agent architecture for teaching and learning

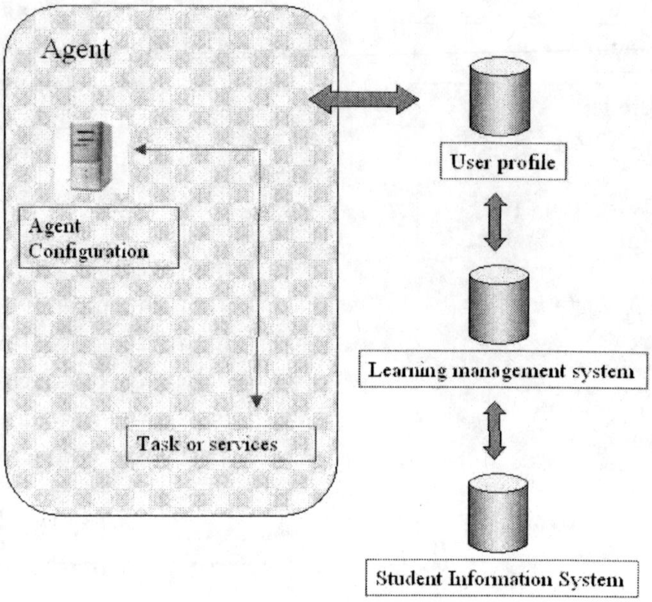

processes of Web-based learners during the learning process (Kinshuk and Lin, 2004). This type of system models the agent according to cognitive traits of students.

Students can configure the agent to perform specific tasks or services, and in the learning process the agent could be multipurpose or course specific. Figure 8 shows that the agent can access information about students and course, and according to this information the agent can perform intelligent actions.

Agent-Based Interaction in Virtual Knowledge-Sharing Communities of Practice

Within virtual communities of practice, the process of knowledge sharing can be usefully supported by systems based on intelligent agents.

Agent-based system based on cognitive agents can support the adoption of knowledge sharing practices within communities (Roda et al., 2003). To support the acquisition of information at the social and individual level, this framework identifies pedagogical strategies and activates personalised and contextualised intervention. Psycho-sociological theories are defined in (Beenen et al., 2004) for stimulating the participation in on-line communities.

Moreover, cognitive agents are used (Nabeth et al., 2005) to stimulate people participation using mechanisms to assist the community organizer. Cognitive agents are informed of social cognition theories, and they are able to infer the individual participatory profile of members from the observation of their online behaviours. The profile is built up considering events such as posting files, posting messages in bulletin boards, and answering to messages.

Diagnostic intelligent agents update the user model according to user actions and they deduce user characteristics. Furthermore, intelligent agents select the best proposal according to preference rules using the user model.

In Knowledge-sharing communities, agents communicate with the user and among each other by some communication protocols.

Interaction in Virtual Communities Based on Collaborative Knowledge

In other environments, the user is able to navigate through the system and she can access to a set of system functionalities, which are embedded in different interaction virtual Web spaces (Bouras et al., 2005). These Web spaces can cover different aspects of the virtual community knowledge.

The virtual community repository should be efficient and allow data entries that should be sufficient to support data queries. Moreover, the requests of community participants enable the repository growing because people improve knowledge adding information and cater to requests of other community members. So the interaction among community participants permits users to improve and update learning materials.

A virtual community can be used also to create an integrated Web-based learning environment that improves the knowledge creation process using participant experiences (Elia et al., 2006).

Besides, collaborative work services (Bieber et al., 2002) are used to provide a folder environment for managing records, queries, collections, documents, and annotations, and to support collaboration among users by folder sharing in communities and projects. This kind of systems is used also in learning communities, and offers an enhanced digital library functionality. In virtual community environments, these collaborative work services support the particular needs of online learning communities. Moreover, they allow an asynchronous interaction integrated with other common software tools, such as conferencing systems, discussions, forums, or bulletin boards.

Focal aspects which must be considered during the collaborative knowledge are the user requirements of social navigation, information about the context of a given virtual community and the target of the user group. It is hard to collect the user requirements on navigation because of the necessity to create questionnaires.

Furthermore, the social navigation is defined by the "navigation towards a cluster of people or navigation because other people have looked at something" (Dourish & Chalmers, 1994). In this environment, people are guided and informed by others and their actions, and information of interaction history, making explicit recommendations, and supporting are provided (Xu et al., 2006).

Social navigation can be direct or indirect (Dieberger et al., 2001). In the first approach, people directly give advices and guides each other, synchronously or asynchronously. While in indirect social navigation, people use navigation cues to be aware of other people actions or the traces of these actions.

CONCLUSION

This chapter has provided taxonomy of virtual communities considering tools and services offered to community members for knowledge management, and the interaction approaches used for the knowledge acquisition process.

The chapter has depicted knowledge management strategies that enable a VCoP to facilitate the collaboration and exchange of ideas among community members.

Virtual communities have been classified, according to the collaboration strategy, in virtual knowledge-sharing communities of practice and virtual learning communities of practice.

This chapter has also distinguished three kinds of virtual communities according to the knowledge structure: ontology-based VCoP; digital library-based VCoP; and knowledge map-based VCoP.

The second part of this chapter has dealt with interaction strategies used to improve the knowledge sharing in groups and organizations. It has shown virtual environments that support knowledge with functionalities for browsing and searching information.

In particular two main methods, which support interaction among community members, have been described: agent-based interaction and collaborative knowledge. A description of how intelligent agents support users in different environments and the main goals of intelligent agents during the improvement of the learning process and the sharing of knowledge are given.

Finally, system's functionalities that facilitate navigation in collaborative knowledge have been illustrated.

In summary, this chapter has proposed an overview of virtual communities underlying the main features to consider in the knowledge management and in the interaction process. It has also underlined the benefits bring about the knowledge sharing by the virtual communities. Moreover, the net of virtual communities can represent a benefit also for the electronic commerce (Kraft et al., 2000) because it creates strong consumer communities that share interests and they form informal groups with like-minded people.

REFERENCES

Angehrn, A.A. (2004). Designing intelligent agents for virtual communities. INSEAD CALT Report 11-2004.

Bieber, M., Engelbart, D., Furata, R., Hiltz, S. R., Noll, J., Preece, J., Stohr, E. A., Turoff, M., & Walle, B.V.D. (2002). Toward virtual community knowledge evolution. *Journal of Management Information Systems*, 18(4), 11-35.

Bouras, C., Igglesis, V., Kapoulas, V., & Tsiatsos, T. (2005). A Web-based virtual community. *Inernational. Journal of Web Based Communities, 1*(2), 127–139.

Brown, J. & Isaacs, D. (1996). Conversation as a core business process. *The Systems Thinker*, 7(10), 1-6.

Chen, L., Cox, S.J., Goble, C., Keane, A.J., Roberts, A., Shadbolt, N.R., Smart, P., & Tao, F. (2002). Engineering knowledge for engineering grid applications. In *Proceedings of the Euroweb 2002 Conference, The Web and the GRID: from e-science to e-business*, Oxford, UK, pp12-25.

Chinowsky, P. S. & Rojas, E. M. (2003). Virtual teams: Guide to successful implementation. *Journal of Management in Engineering*, July 2003, pp. 98-106.

Cooper, J. (2003). Educational MUVES: Virtual learning communities. *Journal of Education, Community and Values*, Volume 3, Issue 9.

Davies, J., Duke, A., & Sure Y. (2003). OntoShare: A knowledge management environment for virtual communities of practice. In *Proceedings of the 2nd International Conference on Knowledge Capture (K-CAP 2003)*, 20-27.

Desilets, A., Paquet, S., & Vinson, N. (2005). *Are wikis usable?* WikiSym 2005 Conference. San Diego, CA, USA, October 16-18.

Dieberger, A., Hook, K., Svensson, M., &Lonnqvist, P. (2001). *Social navigation researchagenda. In: CHI '01 extended abstracts on Human factors in computing systems, ACM Press (2001)*. pp.107–108.

Dourish, P. & Chalmers, M. (1994). Running out of space: Models of information navigation. (short paper). *HCI'94 (British Computer Society).*

Retrieved on from ftp://parcftp.xerox.com/pub/europarc/jpd/hci94-navigation.ps.

Elia, G., Secundo, G. & Taurino, C. (2006). A process-oriented and technology-based model of virtual communities of practices: Evidence from a case study in higher education. *m-ICTE2006--IV International Conference on Multimedia and Information and Communication Technologies in Education.*

Etzioni, O., & Weld, D. S. (1995). Intelligent agents on the Internet: Fact, fiction, and forecast. IEEE Expert, pp. 44-49.

Gross, T. (2004). Design, specification, and implementation of a distributed virtual community system. In *Proceedings of the Workshop on Parallel, Distributed and Network-Based Processing (PDP 2004)*, pp. 225-232.

Hafeez, K. & Alghatas, F. (2007). Knowledge management in a virtual community of practice using discourse analysis. *The Electronic Journal of Knowledge Management*, 5(1), 29-42.

Hossain, L. & Wigand, R. T. (2004). ICT enabled virtual collaboration through trust. *Journal of Computer-Mediated Communication JCMC, 10* (1), Article 8.

Jafari, A. (2002). Conceptualizing intelligent agents for teaching and learning. *Educause Quarterly, 3,* 28-34.

Kinshuk & Lin, T. (2004). Cognitive profiling towards formal adaptive technologies in Web-based learning communities, *International Journal of WWW-based Communities, 1,* 103-108.

Kraft, A., Vetter, M., & Pitsch, S.. (2000, January 4-7). Agent-driven online business in virtual communities. In *Proceedings of the 33rd Hawaii International Conference on System Sciences*, Volume 8, p.8033.

Kurabayashi, N., Yamazaki, T., Yuasa, T., & Hasuike, K. (2002). Proactive information supply for activating conversational interaction in virtual communities. *In the IEEE International Workshop on Knowledge Media Networking (KMN'02)* (pp.167-170).

Leal, W. L. M., & Coello Baêta, A. M. (2006). The contribution of communities of practice in an innovative enterprise. *Journal of Technology Management & Innovation, 1* (4).

Lin, F.-R., & Hsueh, C.-M. (2003). Knowledge map creation and maintenance for virtual communities of practice. In *Proceedings of the 36th Hawaii International Conference on System Sciences (HICSS'03)* (pp. 11-10) Big Island, Hawaii.

Ling, K., Beenen, G., Ludford, P., Wang, X., Chang, K., Cosley, D., Frankowski, D., Terveen, L., Rashid, A. M., Resnick, P., & Kraut, R. (2005). Using social psychology to motivate contributions to online communities. *Journal of Computer-Mediated Communication*, 10(4), article 10.

Nabeth, T., Angehrn, A.A., Mittal, P.K., & Roda, C. (2005). Using artificial agents to stimulate participation in virtual communities. CELDA 2005: 391-394.

Nonaka, I. & Konno, N. (1998). The concept of 'Ba': Building a foundation for knowledge creation. *California Management Review. 40*(3) Spring.

Novak, J. & Wurst, M. (2004). Supporting knowledge creation and sharing in communities based on mapping implicit knowledge. *Journal of Universal Computer Science, Special Issue on Communities of Practice*, *10*(3), 235-251.

Polanyi, M. (1966). *The tacit dimension*. London: Routledge & Kegan Paul.

Reid, E.M. (1991). Electropolis: Communication and community on Internet relay chat, electronic document of a B.A. Honors Thesis, University of Melbourne, Australia, also published in Intertek 3(3) (1992), pp. 7-15.

Roberts, T. (1998). Are newsgroups virtual communities? *In the SIGCHI conference on Human factors in computing systems,* ACM Press/Addison-Wesley Publishing Co. 360–367.

Roda, C., Angehrn, A., Nabeth, T. & Razmerita L. (2003). Using conversational agents to support the adoption of knowledge sharing Practices. Interacting with computers, elsevier, *15*(1), 57-89.

Schwier, R. A. (2001). Catalysts, emphases, and elements of virtual learning communities. Implication for research. *The Quarterly Review of Distance Education*, 2(1), 5-18.

Selker, T. (1994). COACH: A teaching agent that learns. Communications of the ACM, Vol. 37, No. 7, ACM Press. 92 – 99.

Snowden, S. (1999). The paradox of story. *Scenario and Strategy Planning,* 1(5).

Sole, D. & Wilson, D.G. (2002). Storytelling in organizations: The power and traps of using stories to share knowledge in organizations. *LILA Harvard University.*

Thaiupathump, C., Bourne, J., & Campbell, J. (1999). Intelligent agents for online learning. *Journal of Asynchronous Learning Networks, 3*(2). Retrieved on May 17, 2004, from http://www.sloan-c.org/publications/jaln/v3n2/pdf/v3n2_choon.pdf

Varlamis, I., & Apostolakis, I. (2006). A framework for building virtual communities for education. *EC-TEL 2006 Workshops Proceedings*, pp. 165-172.

Vygotsky, L. (1962). *Thought and language.* Cambridge, MA. MIT Press.

Wenger, E., McDermott, R., & Snyder, W. M. (2002). Cultivating communities of practice: A guide to managing knowledge. *Harvard Business School Press.*

Xu, W., Kreijns, K., & Hu, J.. (2006). Designing social navigation for a virtual community of practice. In Z. Pan, R. Aylett, H.Diener, & X. Jin, (Eds.), Edutainment: Technology and Application, proceedings of Edutainment 2006, *International Conference on E-learning and Games.* LNCS 3942, pp.27-38.

Chapter XI
An Ontological Approach to Managing Project Memories in Organizations

Davy Monticolo
SeT Laboratory, University of Technology UTBM, France

Vincent Hilaire
SeT Laboratory, University of Technology UTBM, France

Samuel Gomes
SeT Laboratory, University of Technology UTBM, France

Abderrafiaa Koukam
SeT Laboratory, University of Technology UTBM, France

ABSTRACT

Knowledge Management (KM) is considered by many organizations a key aspect in sustaining competitive advantage. In the mechanical design domain, the KM facilitates the design of routine product and brings a saving time for innovation. This chapter describes the specification of a project memory as an organizational memory to specify knowledge to capitalize all along project in order to be reuse. Afterwards it presents the design of a domain ontology and a multi agent system to manage project memories all along professional activities. As a matter of fact, these activities require that engineers, with different specialities, collaborate to carry out the same goal. Inside professional activities; they use their know-how and knowledge in order to achieve the laid down goals. The professional actors competences and knowledge modeling allows the design and the description of agents' know-how. Furthermore, the paper describes the design of our agent model based on an organisational approach and the role of a domain ontology called OntoDesign to manage heterogeneous and distributed knowledge.

INTRODUCTION

In today's challenging global market, companies have to innovate in order to improve competitiveness and business performance. They must bring innovative products to market more effectively and more quickly to maximize customer interest and sales. The pressure to reduce time, improve product quality, and lower costs have not gone away; they are being reaffirmed and folded into programs that focus on delivering the "right" product. Product leadership companies must continue to enter new markets with innovative products. This requires leveraging and reusing the product-related intellectual capital created by partners working together. Business innovation must occur in several dimensions including project organization, product definition, production engineering, ergonomics design, environmental impacts, and so forth.

In addition, the information technology explosion led to a shift in the economy and market rules forcing corporations to adapt their organization and management in order to improve their reaction and adaptation time. Information systems became backbones of organizations enabling project-oriented management and virtual teams, therefore the industrial interest in methodologies and tools enabling capitalization and management of organizational knowledge grew stronger. An organizational memory is "an explicit, disembodied and persistent representation of knowledge and information in an organization, in order to facilitate their access and reuse by members of the organization" (Gandon, 2002). The stake in building an organizational memory management system is the coherent integration of this dispersed knowledge in a corporation with the objective to promote knowledge growth, promote knowledge communication and in general preserve knowledge within an organization (Rabarijaona, 2001). This memory, explaining the organizational knowledge may be considered as a knowledge base of the organization. Such knowledge base can be restricted to the project world and so be called project memory. The project memory is a memory of knowledge and information acquired and produced during the realization of the projects (Matta, 2000). Thus, project memories constitute a basis for knowledge capitalization and reuse (Bekhti, 2003).

It is necessary to define the nature of this organizational knowledge before to present a knowledge management system. Starting from the bottom, we use the definition of knowledge information and data of Weggeman (1996) and Fukuda (1995):

- Data is a perception, a signal, a sign or a quantum of interaction (e.g., '200' or 'L' are data). Data is symbolic representation of numbers, fact, quantities; an item of data is what a natural or artificial sensor indicates about a variable;
- Information is data structured according to a convention (e.g., L=200mm). Information is the result of the comparison of data which are situationally structured in order to arrive at a message that is significant in a given context. Information is obtained from data which have been given significance and selected as useful.
- Knowledge is information with a context and value that make it usable (e.g., 'the shutter line out as a length L=200mm'). Knowledge is what places someone in the position to perform a particular task by selecting, interpreting and evaluation information depending on the context. Knowledge is an information which was interpreted (i.e., the intended meaning of which was decided) in context and which meaning was articulated with already acquired knowledge (Fukuda, 1995).

Consequently knowledge contained in the project memory is information located in a special context (the activities of the mechanical design process) and which is interpreted by professional actors. Thus the project memory model definition is related to the analysis of the professional activities.

Moreover we have to design and develop tools to assist engineers in building project memories. The first part of this work is to make understandable the project memory model by a knowledge management system. One solution is to conceptualize the knowledge elements described in the project memory, that is, to build a domain ontology.

To design the knowledge management system we have chosen to use the information agent paradigm. An information agent, is an agent providing at least one of the following services: information acquisition (to provide access to information sources and eventually some value-added services); information management (to update and maintain the content of an information source); information search (to find and contract the information services needed to answer a request); information integration (to merge heterogeneous information); information presentation (to format and present information in an adequate way) information adaptation (to adapt information services and results to the context and the users) (Gandon, 2002).

On the one hand the development of a product is realized by distributed heterogeneous entities one may call agents (human or not). On the other hand a multi agent system (MAS) is composed by distributed interacting agents trying to reach their goals. To successfully interact, agents will require the ability to cooperate, coordinate, and negotiate with each other, much as people do. Wooldridge and Jennings (1995) list qualities of an agent--autonomy, social ability, reactivity, and pro-activeness.

Thus we supplement an e-groupware with a MAS which provide the cognitive and social approach in modeling the intelligent collective and individual behaviors.

Among the traceability approaches we have chosen one which enable to capture explicit knowledge. Indeed we attempt to store Knowledge emerged during the collaborative activities. Our approach is based on the analyze of the cooperative and social aspects of the project organization in order to capitalize knowledge in a semi-transparent way for the professional actor and to propose a knowledge reuse from the knowledge needs of the actors during their activities. We use a project memory to store and organize this professional Knowledge. The issues addressed in this chapter are:

- How to define a project memory model from the professional activities modelling;
- How to specify a domain ontology to make understandable the project memory model to a knowledge management system;
- How to design a multi agent system to capitalize and reuse knowledge during the professional activities;
- How to manage project memories in using the domain ontology and the multi agent system;

The chapter is organized as follows: section one discusses the need of a organizational memory in companies; section two presents a related work focuses on project memories model and knowledge management systems based on MAS; section three describes the analysis of professional activities in order to identify knowledge to capitalize and based on a organizational approach; section four specifies the work on the knowledge resources in order to specify a project memory model; section five presents the design of a knowledge management system based on software agents in order to support the organizational KM settings; section six describes how the MAS with the domain ontology manage project memories and section seven presents the use of the knowledge management system and future directions of this work.

PROJECT MEMORY DEDICATED TO MECHANICAL DESIGN PROJECTS

Industrial Context

Our works are deployed in a company call Zurfluh-Feller of 400 employees in the domain activity of window rolling shutters. The research and development department is constituted by fifty technicians. The method department, laboratory department and the design and engineering department work together through a project organization in a concurrent engineering concept.

One of the problems we have tackled is to enable professional actors to reuse their collaborative professional experience from past projects. The direction of the company has decided to develop a knowledge engineering approach in building project memories to solve this problem.

Why to Build Project Memories

The aim of the knowledge management is to support the synergy between the professional actors and their information systems. This process is composed of activities such as the identification, the filing, the update until the destruction of knowledge became obsolete. Thus the knowledge management is an organisational process which aims at the optimization of the knowledge use in the company. This has an intellectual capital created by project teams when they develop new product. Indeed project teams use different professional specialities to design and develop new products. Each professional actor with his specialities brings several competences to jointly solve some tasks. Those competences use knowledge to realise activities. Knowledge engineering approaches model this type of knowledge to implement methods and classification technique to make this knowledge accessible in a form defined according to the context.

In an engineering context, it is difficult for professional actors to have an overview of a project or to remember the collaborative work of past projects. Only teams which have the practice to work together and enough experience, can define the fundamental knowledge to store. However, nowadays, project teams in companies are been formed the time of a project. This organisation implies a loss of collective knowledge and a difficult re-use of individual knowledge in a new project. The knowledge management could resolve this problem by capitalizing the past experiments and providing it to the other teams or to the future project teams. The difficulty of this work is to extract generic knowledge from the specific activities of the mechanical design process.

We have chosen to store this knowledge in the form of a project memory. The project memory contains knowledge acquired and produced during the realization of the projects. In an organisation of project and in a concurrent engineering context, project memories seem to be a good solution to capitalize knowledge. Indeed Project memories detain knowledge relative to the description of events (tasks, problems, success, etc.) encountered all along the project. Moreover it contains Knowledge associated to the results of the collaborative design activities.

RELATED WORK

Project Memories Models

The majority of the project memories models are focused on the presentation of the encountered problems and decision making. In all these works, the efforts are related to the traceability of the professional activities during the project and the acquisition of knowledge used and created by the actors.

The project memories focused on "decision making" model the problem resolution process. These models are based on the methods of design rationale such as QOC (Buckingham, 1997), DRCS (Klein, 1997), and IBIS (Conklin, 1998).

Other more recent methods improve the representation of the decision makings such as DIPA (Lewkowicz, 1999) and DyPKM (Bekhti, 2003). They capture the evolution of the decisions in the project, whereas others as INDIGO (Longueville, 2003) positions on the decision-making process. In addition Matta et al. (2000) propose a project memory model in building professional activities traces of the last projects. This model is based on two types of knowledge: the memory of the characteristics of project, and the memory of the rationale design. Other models present a different point of view, we can quote a model focus on cooperation (Golebiowska, 2002) and another related to the competences of the professional actors (Belkadi, 2007).

Multi Agent Systems to Manage Distributed and Heterogeneous Knowledge

Knowledge Engineering aims to collect, analyze, structure, and represent knowledge. Knowledge environments can be seen as distributed systems where actors with different specialities share their know-how in order to achieve their professional activities. In such environments the choice of multi agent systems is motivated by the following features: MAS can manage heterogeneous and distributed information, they can solve complex problems by splitting in simpler entities and they may act as assistants for professional actors in reusing knowledge.

Many knowledge management systems use the concept of personal assistant to interact with users. We can quote the research work of Paraiso and Barthès (2006), introducing a personal assistant to help the researchers in the projects of R & D. Stuber and Hassas (2003) conceive a personal assistant called 'alter ego' which must simultaneously assist the re-use of the individual experiment to facilitate the experience sharing. In addition, Guizzardi (2005) uses the concept of personal assistant to indicate to the users their profile and preferences in order to propose the good knowledge.

Agents have already been used in the Knowledge Engineering field in order to support and extend human interactions and capabilities, organize knowledge by facilitating information and documents classification and reuse. A new and very interesting research field recently growing is Agent-Mediated Knowledge Management (AMKM) whose intent is to link the Knowledge Engineering theories with agent-based models. Van Elst, Abecker, & Dignum (2004) argued that "the basic features of agents (social ability, autonomy, and proactiveness) can alleviate several of the drawbacks of the centralized technological approaches for KM". They proposed three dimensions to describe agent KM systems: the system development layer (from analysis to implementation of the system), the macro-level structure of the system, that is, the single agent and multi agent models and the KM applications area (share, learn, use, distribution, etc.). Taking into account the second dimension, they propose a classification of software or experimental models of agent systems that could support Knowledge Engineering. For example, agents whose task is to support knowledge workers in their daily work in a way to become "a personal assistant who is collaborating with the user in the same work environment" (Maes, 1994). Many different examples fall into this category, like Lieberman's Letizia (Lieberman, 1995) and the AACC project by Enembreck and Barthès (2002).

Agent-based systems have also been developed to support the creation of Organizational Memories; they are presented like "meta-information systems with tight integration into enterprise business processes rely on appropriate formal models and ontologies as a basis for common understanding and automatic processing capabilities" (Abecker, 2003). An example can be found in the FRODO project, a Distributed Organizational Memory System in which agents communicate with the FIPA ACL language. In this work, agents are not only described by their knowledge, goals and competencies, but also by their rights and obligations. Staab and Schnurr (2000) have developed the OntoBroker, a system based on assistant agent to manage organizational memories in order to help users in their project management. In addition Gandon (2002) develops a MAS using semantic Web technologies to manage organizational memories called corporate memories.

MODELLING PROFESSIONAL ACTIVITIES IN ORDER TO IDENTIFY KNOWLEDGE TO CAPITALIZE

An Organisational Approach to Model the Mechanical Design Process: The RIOCK Formalism

The first step of your work is to understand, analyze, and model the product development lifecycle used in the SME. Thus we have followed several engineering projects inside an experiment of knowledge management deployment during more than one year. With regard to this experience, we have analyzed design activities and validate the product development lifecycle with four phases: feasibility study; preliminary study; detailed stud; and manufacturing engineering. Each phase is structured according to some usual recurring usual stages for all projects. These stages can be processed simultaneously or sequentially. In the centre lifecycle we have a multi-disciplinary team. Indeed each phase requires professional actors from different specialities and each stage can be carried out simultaneously. The product design process is similar to the Gomes's lifecycle (Gomes, 2000) (Fig. 1).

In order to understand and to model the lifecycle, we used the formalism RIO. It is based on three concepts--roles, interaction, and organization. We consider the project and its stages like RIO organizations (Hilaire, 2000). Inside, roles are generic behaviours. These behaviours can interact mutually according to interaction pattern. Such a pattern which groups generic behaviours and theirs interactions constitutes an organization. Indeed agents (human in this case) instantiate an organization (roles and interactions) when they exhibit behaviours defined by the organization's roles and when they interact following the organization interactions (Castelfranchi, 2000). Moreover the RIO formalism proposes a heritage of roles and organizations. Indeed an organization can also be seen like a participant of an interaction using others entities. Anderson (2004) and Singh (1992) suggest to abstract an organization and to consider it like a role in another organization.

The project with its lifecycle is seen like an organization contained several sub organizations called phases and stages. Thus sub organizations are dependent with each other since they belong to the same organization. Consequently each lifecycle stage is an organization being able to be divided into under organizations. Figure 2 showed the organization 'feasibility study' with three roles which represent tree organizations. The role 'to write the schedule of conditions' is itemized in Figure 1.

As we have seen previously, the design process is a system inside which exist numerous processes. Indeed in a concurrent engineering context, projects are led by several professional actors with different professional fields. For each of them we observe some specifies professional process. On the other hand we believe that each professional process is bound to a capitalization process. Indeed in the design process, engineers have and share their knowledge to achieve task in a collaborative way and also develop learning issued by the capitalization process. Consequently, we attempt to identify with RIO, knowledge used by professional actors.

From experiences and observations made in the company, we define, for each organization corresponding to a stage, several roles according

Figure 1. Cycle illustrating concurrent engineering used in the SME (Gomes, 2000)

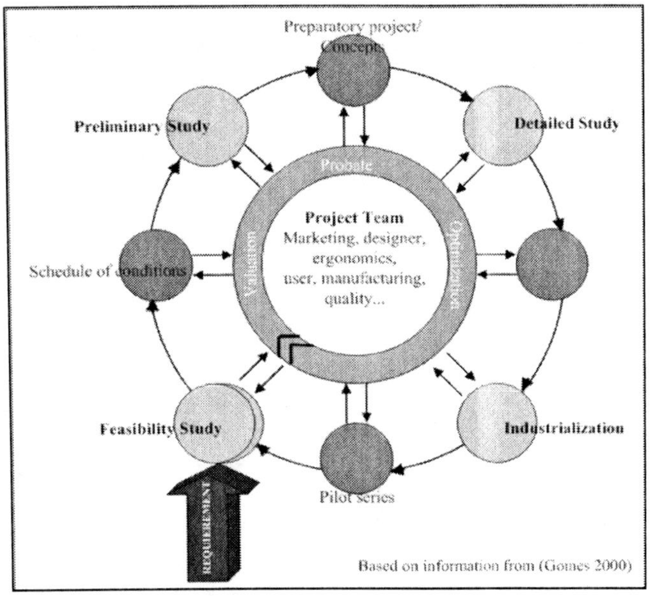

Figure 2. Organization feasability study

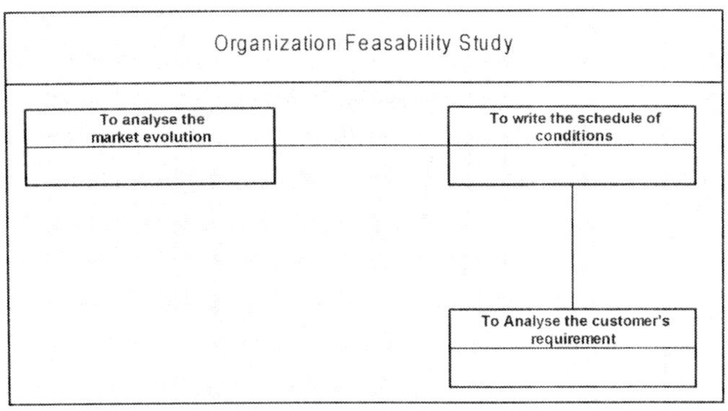

to the professional actors. We attribute to those the competences they use to fulfill tasks of the stage. The competence is defined at the individual level: "it is the capacity for an individual to implement his knowledge and to develop its know-how within a professional framework" (Kasvi, 2003). The concept of competence associated to a role allows selecting knowledge by professional fields since a role can belong to two different professional fields whereas the competence is related to a specific professional field. Table 1 presents different knowledge corresponding to two different roles belonging to different professional fields but with the same competence to a specific stage of the lifecycle. Competences are related to professional fields even if one competence can belong to two different professional fields.

Each competence is described with a set of knowledge. The interaction between several roles highlights two types of results; exchanges between professional actors and the emergence of knowledge. Thus, in an organization, a role

Table 1. Association between professional fields and competence

Prof. Fields	Competence	Role	Knowledge
Engineering and design department	To chose the good material for the product	Plastic injection mould engineer	(i) Design of the plastic injection mould, (ii)Constraints of the product to be injected
Plastic injection unit	To chose the good material for the product	Plastic injection unit technician	(i)Use of plastic material

Figure 3. RIOCK model for the professional activity "to write the schedule of condition"

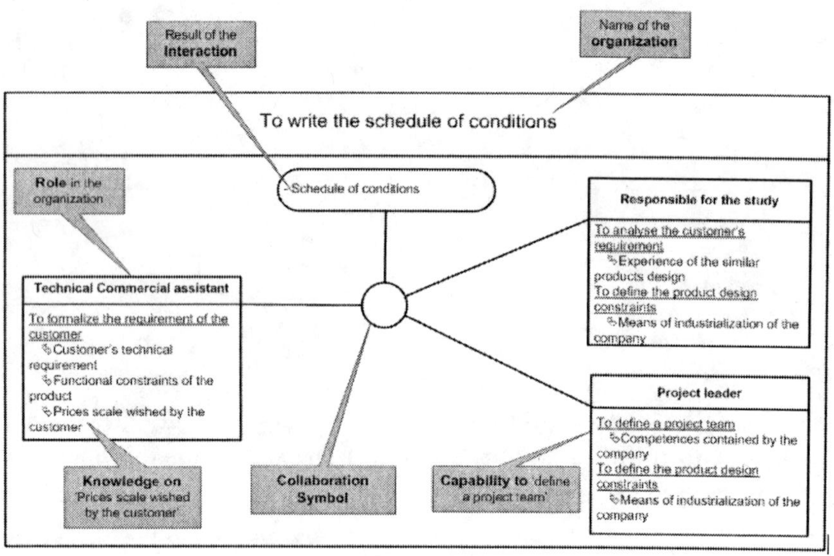

uses one or more competences which require one or more knowledge. A role interacts with other roles to achieve a task and thus develop the collaborative work and create its result. We supplement the RIO formalism to obtain the RIOCK formalism in adding the concepts of competence and knowledge.

In the activity (i.e., organization) 'to write the schedule of conditions' we observe three roles (Figure 3). The role 'technical commercial assistant' uses one of its competences; we read it like the capability to 'to formalize the requirement of the customer.' This competence requires three elements of knowledge which are used to satisfy the organization. In the RIOCK diagram the type of knowledge is read like "knowledge on," for example, the role project leader possesses the knowledge on 'means of industrialization of the company.' In addition RIOCK presents the result of the collaboration among these three roles; here this is the schedule of condition.

Knowledge Identification and Validation

We present in this section our approach to identify the emanating knowledge of the design process. We see the mechanical design process as a reference system which allows specifying for each knowledge element:

- The professional activity in which the knowledge was created;
- The roles of the professional actors in this activity;
- The competence used by the professional actor and with which the knowledge is associated.

Taking into account to all these elements, the process of design gives a precise context for each knowledge element. In order to identify and to locate all professional knowledge we use

Figure 4. Knowledge cartography from the mechanical design process in using RIOCK

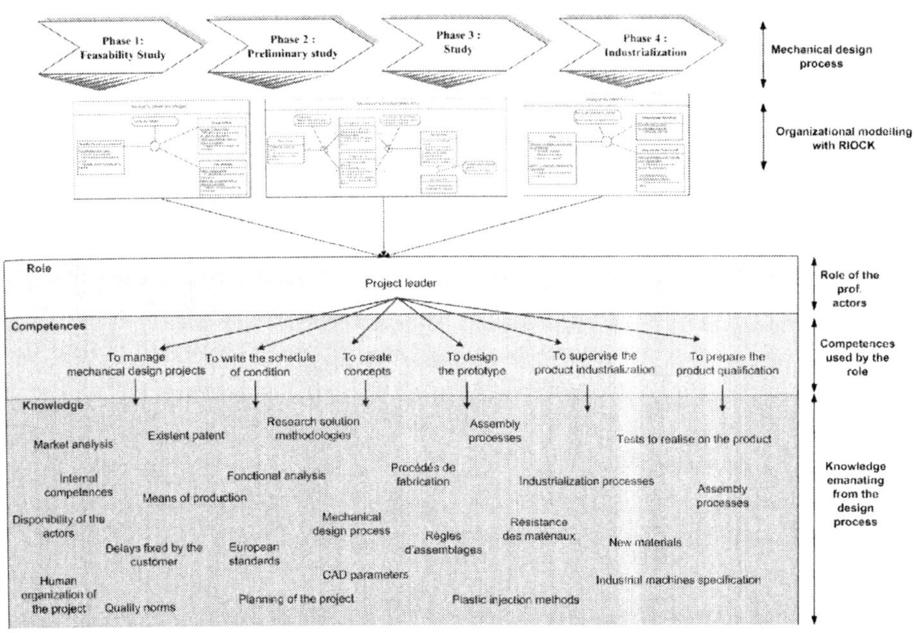

the RIOCK to model all the mechanical design process. For each professional activities organisational modelling, we identify emanating knowledge by competences and roles of the actors. Thus we can classify knowledge by competences and roles played by the professional actors. This work makes it possible to define which role has created, shared or used knowledge. Thereafter we will use this approach to capitalize knowledge according to the roles of the professional actors.

The figure below presents the project leader role. This role takes part in several professional activities throughout the mechanical design process. For each activity in which it took part, the project leader used one or more competences and one or more associated knowledge to carry out the requested tasks.

For each role we obtain the competences used to carry out activities of the design process and the associated knowledge. This list of knowledge results from the modelling of the mechanical design process.

The next step of our approach was to submit to the professional actors the identified knowledge list in order to validate it. This work was carried out with all the project teams of the company. We present each identified knowledge for each professional activity of the mechanical design project. The professional actors discussed and specified which knowledge element we have to capitalize in order to build a project memory. Thus we obtained a table with the list of knowledge to capitalize for each activity of each phase of the design process.

The mechanical design process modelling is essential in order to understand the domain and to obtain an identified knowledge list. If we had not had this result it would have been impossible to guide professional actors to validate knowledge. Actors are not able to give an exhaustive list of knowledge they create and use.

WORKING ON SEMANTIC KNOWLEDGE RESOURCES TO BUILD A PROJECT MEMORY MODEL

Typology of the Professional Knowledge

We have obtained a knowledge list from the modelling of the professional activities and its validation by the professional actors. This list contained knowledge resulting from the collaboration of the professional actors in the time of their activities. We wish to organize this knowledge in a project memory. After analysing the existent project memory model we have define six types of knowledge.

Knowledge Related to the Project Progress

The mechanical design process has the same phase (feasibility study, preliminary study, detailed study, and industrialization) for each project. On the other hand, the activities and sub activities inside the phases can be different and be treated in various orders. The professional actors and particularly the project leader define the sequence of the activities for each phase. This sequence must be capitalized, it presents the project progress and defines a reference system in which to position the professional knowledge.

To input the project progress into the project memory we present the knowledge type ***Project Context*** which contains the description of the origins, the organization, the objectives etc. of the project. Therefore for knowledge related to the project progress we organize knowledge into two sub types (Figure 5)--the project context and the project evolution. The knowledge type ***project evolution*** makes it possible to describe

Figure 5. Knowledge related to the project progress

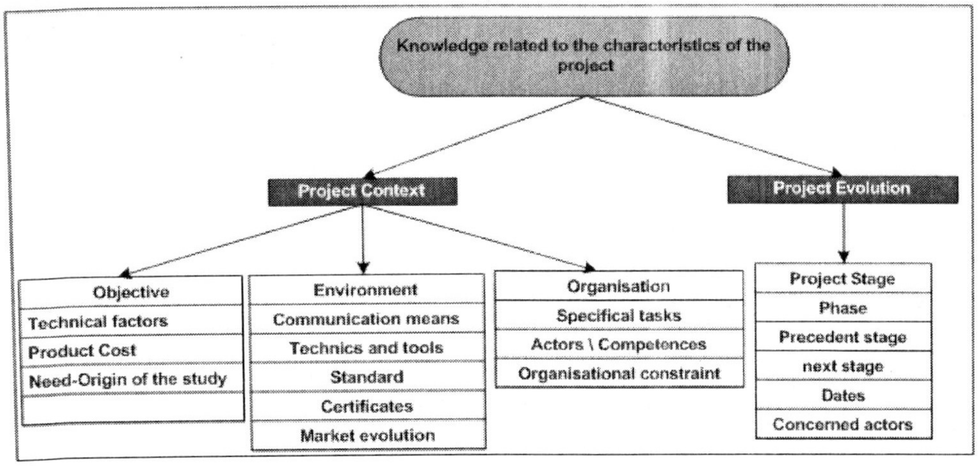

all the project stages. This knowledge aggregate defines the reference system for the knowledge storage.

Knowledge Related to the Professional Competences

The competence is built by the interaction of the professional actors working together in the same

Figure 6. Knowledge related to the professional competences

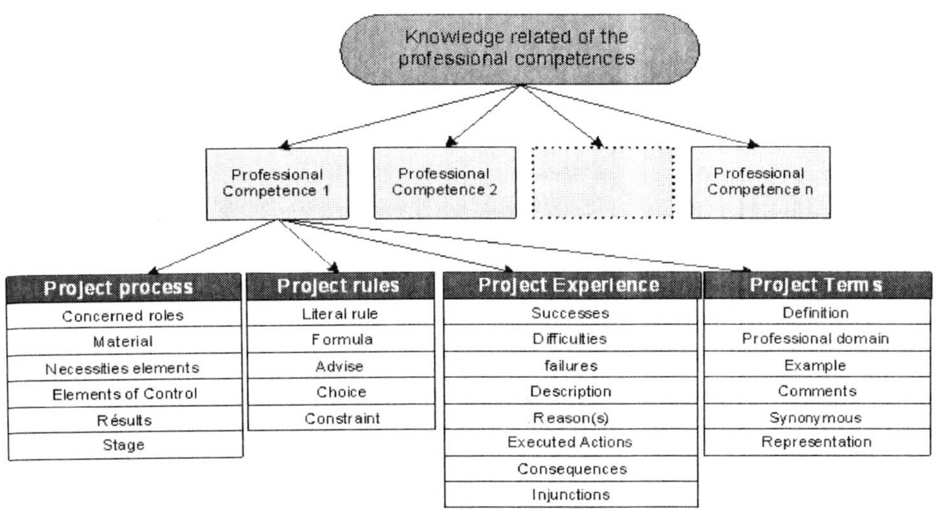

department and on the same project team towards a common goal. Our model presents a knowledge capitalization centred on human professional competences. Each role has one or several competences. The second part of the project memory describes these competences. For each of them, we define four knowledge types: the *Professional Rules* and *Professional Terms* which were used, the *Professional Process* which was employed and the *Professional Experiences* which were encountered (Figure 6).

The knowledge related to the professional process has all the elements to represent a process with a formalism like IDEF0 (Ang, 1997). The professional rule describes the precepts set up by professional actors. These rules are writ-

Figure 7. Knowledge taxonomy of MemoDesign

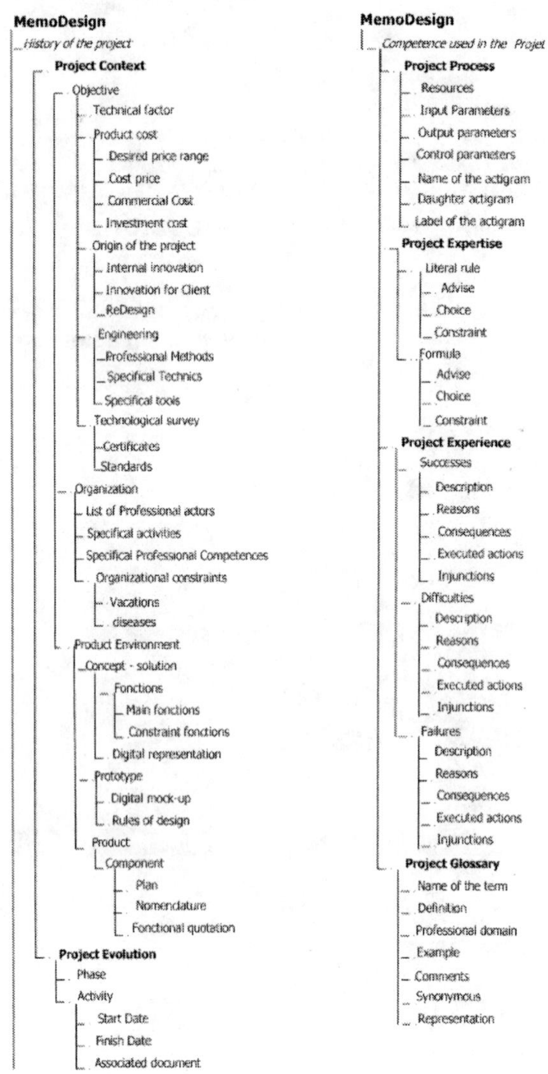

ten in a literal form or in a formula form. The professional terms allows building a glossary of all the terms used in a project. This glossary is important because we observe that actors of different departments in the company use different terms to speak about the same concept.

Taxonomy of the Professional Knowledge

In order to structure the Knowledge, we have created a taxonomy. This is a classification of information entities in the form of a hierarchy, according to the presumed relationships of the real-world entities that they represent. Furthermore the classification is based on the similarities of the information entities called concepts. This taxonomy (Figure 7) constitutes the structure of the project memory model called MemoDesign with all the elements of knowledge.

Building Knowledge Books with the Project Memory Model

The MemoDesign project memory model was used in the company to build several project memories. Based on the knowledge management methods using the experts' interviews to capitalize knowledge, we have collected, validated, and classified knowledge from past project according to MemoDesign.

A Project Memory book presents the history of the project with the knowledge related to the context and the evolution of the project. It also presents for each role (project leader, sales manager, assembly unit technician, etc.) the professional rule, the professional process, the professional terms he used and the experience (success, difficulties, failures) he encountered during the project.

However, the experiment of writing knowledge books was not satisfying. Even if the books allowed validating the project memory model, it appeared that it was very long and difficult to write a knowledge book. Indeed this work needs a high availability of the professional actors, the permanent participation of a knowledge engineer and it can be apply only on past projects. Moreover the knowledge retrieval in knowledge book is not effective and finally the actors don't use it.

Following this experiment, we have planed to design a knowledge management system to help the actors to capitalize and re-use knowledge during their projects.

DESIGNING A MULTI AGENT SYSTEM TO SUPPORT THE KNOWLEDGE MANAGEMENT PROCESS

Agents Specification from an Organisational Approach

We have seen previously that an organization is a set of entities and their interactions which are regulated by mechanisms of social order and created by autonomous actors to achieve common goals. Thus professional activities can be seen like organizations where the engineers with different professional fields work together to reach the same objective: to develop a new product. Consequently we use an organizational approach to design the MAS which support the knowledge management process all along products development projects.

The use of human organizations in computational system was suggested since 1981 (Fox, 1981). In MAS several approaches have been proposed inspired from a social metaphor, where terms like "role," "group," and "communities" represent the main concepts of the model. Organizations are used in numerous MAS specification methodologies such as GAIA (Wooldridge, 1995), MESSAGE (Caire, 2001), TROPOS (Bresciani, 2004) or PASSI (Cossentimo, 2005) and some models like AGR (Ferber, 2003), MOCA (Amiguet, 2004) or RIO (Hilaire, 2000). In this last model, the role is defined as an abstraction of a behavior in a certain context and confers a status within the organization. Indeed the role gives the playing entities the right to exercise its capacities. This corresponds exactly with our view of a role inside an organization. The modelling of the professional activities using the RIOCK notation which is based on the concepts of the RIO organisational model allows us to design a MAS taking account to the roles of the human actors. Thus agent are design according to the human roles, and build organizations when their actors interact together to carry out a professional activity. According to the role it has to monitor, an agent capitalize the knowledge used in the organization. Figure 8 describes the link between each concept of the organizational model.

Our approach consists in monitoring the human actors' activities and identifying knowledge according to the organizational model. The knowledge management process is handled by agents in order to ensure an efficient knowledge traceability, capitalization and reuse. Therefore we use the organizational model built by professional actors when they carry out a professional activity. In this model human actors interact with one another in using their competences and the associated knowledge in order to carry out the mechanical design tasks. For each role we present the competence used and the associated knowledge. The types of Knowledge are defined in a domain ontology called OntoDesign (we will describe this ontology in section 6.1).

Moreover, in this organization professional actors perform a knowledge management process to share and use their know-how. This process is composed by four stages-- location, updating, broadcasting and reuse. Our organizational model highlights this process by splitting of professional actors roles in two sub-organizations. The first sub-organization is related to the management of the knowledge by the professional role, inside the current project and the second concerns the management of knowledge resulting from all projects. Thus these two sub-organizations highlight the knowledge management process.

Consequently software agents have to monitor the professional actors' activities in playing roles

Figure 8. Organizational approach to design the MAS

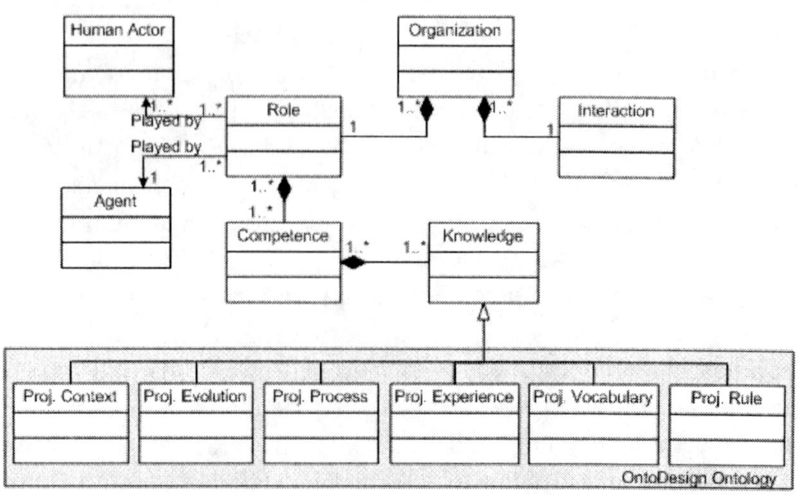

Figure 9. Agentification from the organizational model

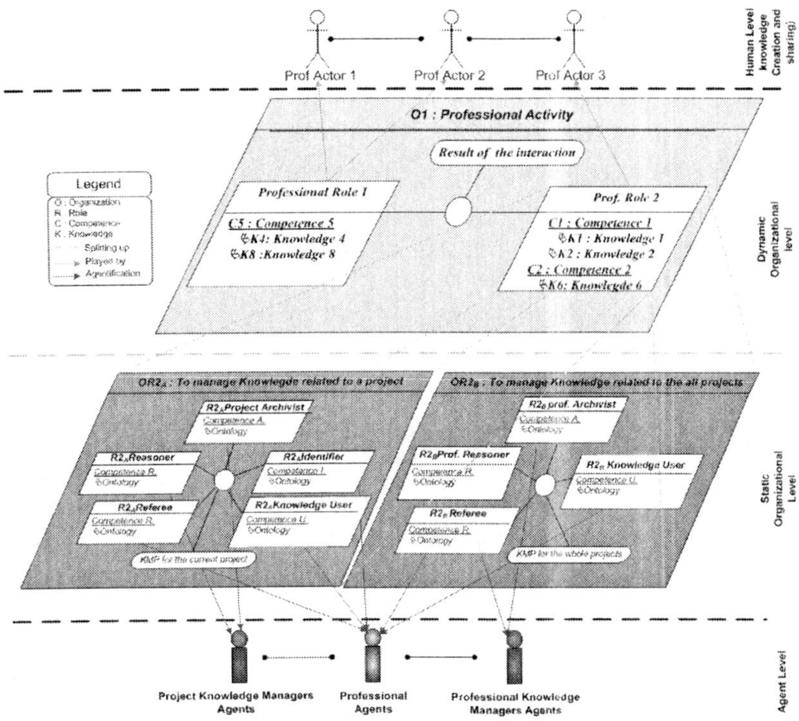

modeled in the organizational model to ensure the knowledge management process. Figure 9 shows the overview of the agentification:

- The human level where professional actors interact together to carry out mechanical design activities;
- The dynamic organizational model related to the human interactions;
- The two sub-organizations describing the properties (role, interaction, etc.) of the agents;
- The agent level specifying the type of agent which supports the knowledge management process during each professional activity.

In the agent organizations we observed five roles which ensure the knowledge management process. These five roles are played by three types of agents as described in Table 2.

The first two types, Professional Agents (PA) and Project Knowledge Managers Agents (ProjKMA), exist for each project. They have to identify, collect, validate, and reuse knowledge of the current project. On the other hand, the Professional Knowledge Managers Agents (ProfKMA) are created for all projects. They have to build a professional knowledge base, to ensure the reliability of this Knowledge and to propose solutions from knowledge capitalized during all projects.

Table 2. Agents characteristics which support the KMP

Agent	Role	Interaction	Competences	Knowledge
Professional Agent (PA)	Identifier	PA and ProjKMA	To identify and to annotate Knowledge for each prof. role	Ontology– Description of the type of Knowledge
	Knowledge User	ProjKMA and ProfKMA	To assist Professional Actor	Ontology – Project Evolution
	Referee	PA	To validate the Knowledge of the project memory	Ontology – Human organization of the project
Project Knowledge Managers Agents (ProjKMA)	Archivist	PA and ProfKMA	To build the project memory	Ontology– Relations between types of Knowledge
	Reasoner	PA	To infer with the Knowledge of the project memory	Ontology– Attributes and relations between types of Knowledge
Professional Knowledge Managers Agents (ProfKMA)	Archivist	ProfKMA	To build the professional knowledge base	Ontology– Relations between types of Knowledge
	Reasoner	PA	To infer with the Knowledge of the professional knowledge base	Ontology– Attributes and relations between types of Knowledge

Overview of the MAS

A MAS architecture describes the agents communities and their relations. We have called our MAS architecture KATRAS (Knowledge Acquisition Traceability Reused Agent System) (Figure 10). It is based on three communities of agents--the Professional Agents, the Project Knowledge Managers Agents and the Professional Knowledge Managers Agents. PA and ProjKMA communities are created for each project. PA locate and annotate knowledge in monitoring the roles of the human actors. There is as much PA as professional actors who participate to a project.

The ProjKMA community organizes knowledge and create the project memory. This community is composed by six agents. Each agent is dedicated to a type of knowledge presented in section 4.1. The ProfKMA community s created for the whole projects. It is also composed by six agents, for each type of knowledge. This community is dedicated to the management of knowledge resulting from all the projects. When a project is finish the ProfKMA integrate its project memory in a knowledge base.

Figure 10. The KATRAS architecture

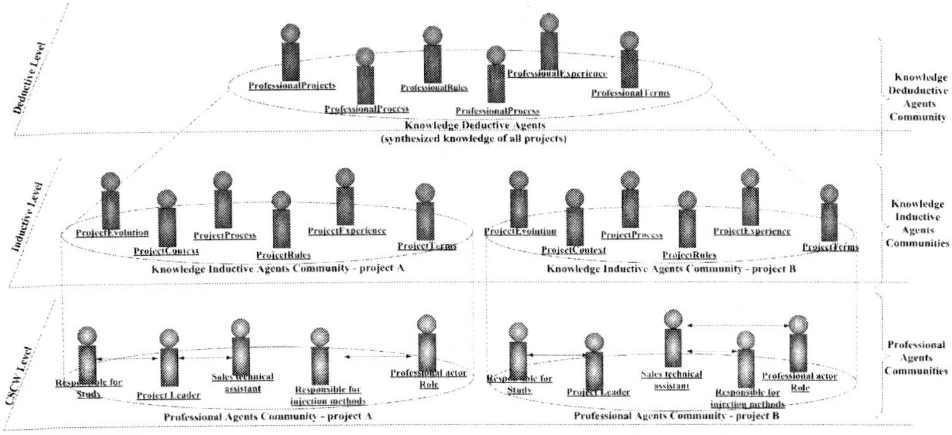

MANAGING KNOWLEDGE WITH A MULTI AGENT SYSTEM AND A DOMAIN ONTOLOGY

Engineering a Domain Ontology to Make Understandable the Knowledge Domain

The MAS is designed to identify, collect, organize knowledge to build a project memory and propose assistance to the professional actors during their activities. However agents are not able to carry out their tasks effectively if they do not understand the knowledge domain.

A domain ontology allows agents to perceive the knowledge domain. The ontology is an abstraction of a domain in terms of concepts and relations which are expressed with a standard knowledge representation language that can be reused and shared by many users (Wongthongtham, 2006). We have built the ontology OntoDesign from all the concepts encountered in the engineering projects which define the types of Knowledge of the project memory MemoDesign. Consequently the top level of this ontology is based on six classes according to the six types of Knowledge. The ontology describes the relations and the attributes of these classes and their sub classes.

We have developed this ontology with the OWL notation using the W3C recommendations. OntoDesign provides an integrated conceptual model for sharing information related to a mechanical design project.

Analyzing Existing Ontologies

Our first work, after the identification of knowledge to capitalize, was to analyze and study existing ontologies which we could re-use. Among ontologies modeling companies we can mention "Enterprise" (Uschold, 1998), "TOVE" (Fox, 2005) and "O' COMMA" (Perez, 2000). The first two ontologies are reusable at the informal level. Indeed some concepts presented guided us in the conceptualization, in particular for the activity part ("activity") of Enterprise and the part product ("part") of ontology TOVE. The ontology O' COMMA is reusable since it is developed using

RDF diagrams, technology of the semantic Web. This ontology is complete for presenting a memory for a company but its concepts do not cover the particular terms used in product design projects. Thus we have conceptualized the project memory MemoDesign and define attributes and relations between these concepts in using the study of the three ontologies presented above.

Specifying the Concepts, Their Attributes and Relations

The ontology engineering process is based on the writing of two tables to specify concepts and their relations:

- The table of concepts (see Table 3) giving: unique name of potential concepts (Term), their concept ID (ConceptID), their inheritance links (ParentID), and a natural language definition of the notion behind the concepts to try to capture their intension (Natural Language Definition)
- The table of relations (Table 4) giving: unique name of potential relations (Relation), the concepts they link (Domain and Range), and a natural language definition of the notion behind the relation to try to capture their intension (Natural Language Definition)

Nowadays the ontology, we have called OntoDesign, has 104 concepts and 32 relations. It grows as we reuse knowledge since we need to specify new relations.

OntoDesign Implementation with the Web Semantic Technologies

We have specified the project memory concepts and their relationships in the ontology OntoDe-

Table 3. Extract from the original concepts table

Concept	***ConceptID***	***ParentID***	***Natural Language Definition***
Product	Product	ProductEvolution	Result of the project
professional actor	Professional actor	ProjectOrganization	Human who takes part of a project
…	…	…	…..

Table 4. Extract from the original relations table

Relation	***RelationID***	***Domain***	***Range***	***Natural Language Definition***
Give detail Constraint function	Give detail Constraint function	Functional analysis	ConstraintFunction	Specification of a Constraint function
Is a literale rule	IsLiteraleRule	LiteraleRule	DesignRule	A literale rule is a design rule
…	…	…	…	…..

Figure 11. OntoDesign implementation using Protégé2000

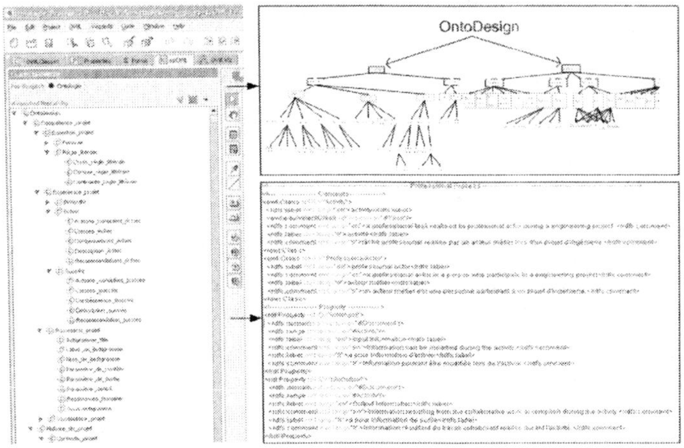

sign with Protégé 2000 (Protégé, 2000) in order to visualize, validate and build our ontology in the OWL language in conformity with the W3C recommendations. The Protégé OWL editor supports OWL-DL language except for anonymous global class axioms, which need to be given a name by the user. Thus we have developed our ontology in OWL-DL with this tool. OWL-DL is based on Description Logics (hence the suffix DL). Description Logics are a decidable fragment of First Order Logic and are therefore amenable to automated reasoning. It is therefore possible to automatically compute the classification hierarchy and check for inconsistencies in an ontology that conforms to OWL-DL.

Consequently, OntoDesign provides an integrated conceptual model for sharing information related to a mechanical design project. An OWL property (figure 11) is a binary relation to relate an OWL Class (Concept in OntoDesign) to another one, or to RDF literals and XML Schema datatypes. For example, the "infoInput" property relates the Document class to the Activity class. Described by these formal, explicit and rich semantics, the domain concept of Activity, its properties and relationships with other concepts can be queried, reasoned or mapped to support the Knowledge sharing across the mechanical design projects.

OntoDesign Integration in the MAS

The MAS is developed with the java platform Madkit which allows us to implement agents with the notion of agent, group and role (Ferber, 2003). Moreover we use the Jena java API (Seaborne, 2006) which provides to our agents the possibility to perceive the OWL ontology. Moreover Jena includes a rule-based inference engine. However, up to now, we have only used the SPARQL query engine provided with the Jena API. We used SPARQL (Seaborne, 2006) to express queries across the RDF instances of the ontology. The results of these queries are RDF graphs. Thus agents can build their queries and handle the results with the Jena API. Agents are able to create, exchange RDF instances according to the OntoDesign domain ontology.

The last column of Table 1 defines the part of the ontology needed by each role of the agents. Indeed the ontology OntoDesign defines the vocabulary with which queries and assertions are exchanged among agents. We detail the use of the domain ontology for each role of the agents:

- The *'identifier'* (role of the PA) identifies and annotates Knowledge emanating from each professional activity. This role has a research Knowledge method for every six types of Knowledge. When it detects Knowledge, it annotates it according to the OntoDesign model ontology. Thus knowledge is annotated with a RDF sequence which represents in-stances of ontology concepts and relationships.
- The *'archivist'* builds the project memory (ProjKMA) or the professional knowledge base (ProfKMA) from the RDF sequences sent by the professional agents. It needs the model ontology to organize and to gather the RDF annotations.
- The *'referee'* is a role of Professional Agents. It has to ensure the reliability of the Knowledge inside the project memory and the professional knowledge base. It uses the model ontology to identify the professional actors who are able to validate Knowledge to store.
- The *'reasoner'* has to infer with the Knowledge of the project memory (ProjKMA) or the professional knowledge base (ProfKMA) in order to propose solutions to the professional actors at the time of their project activities. Hence agents consult the OntoDesign Ontology to deduce the appropriated Knowledge inside RDF instances. The next paragraph shows an example of knowledge reuse.

Knowledge Management Example Using OntoDesign and Leads by Agents

Project teams design similar products which are gathered inside product families with similar names but referenced with the name of the project in which they were developed. During the professional activity "to realize the Tulipe prototype" engineers need to know the parameters of similar prototypes of the product called 'Tulipe.' This Knowledge corresponds to the type "Project Rule" (section III). Figure 12 shows that the Knowledge Management Process is led by the three types of agents. This process is based on seven steps:

- *Step 1*: The Professional Actor questions its Professional Agent about the capitalized Knowledge related to the 'Tulipe.'
- *Step 2*: The PA sends this request to the associated ProjKMA-ProjectRule to obtain Knowledge capitalized in the current project and to the ProfKMA-ProjectRule for the Knowledge capitalized by all projects. The message is sent to the other agents to present the concept to search for: Prototype("tulipe")
- *Step 3 and 4*: ProjKMA and ProfKMA consult the shared ontology 'OntoDesign' to identify the relations related to the concept Prototype. Hence they build a set of queries to infer Knowledge from the RDF instances:

Prototype("tulipe")^HasLiteralRule("tulipe",y) ^LiteralRule(y)
Prototype("tulipe")^HasFormulaRule("tulipe",z) ^FormulaRule(z)
Prototype("tulipe")^HasFunction("tulipe",b) ^LiteralRule(b)
Prototype("tulipe")^HasDigitalMockup("tulipe",d) ^DigitalMockup(d)

Figure 12. Knowledge management process supported by agents

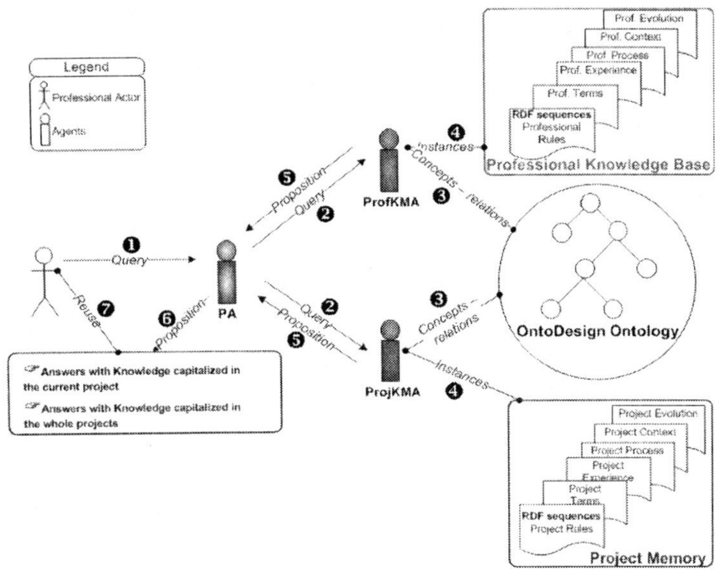

- *Step 5:* With the RDF instances and the ontology, ProjKMA and ProfKMA are able to answer queries and send a respond to PA.
- *Step 6 and 7:* The Professional Agent presents the propositions to the professional actors. In the case of the retrieve about 'tulipe,' PA is able to present the parameters (literal rules and formula rules) and the digital mock-ups related to similar prototypes capitalized in this project and in all the projects.

A INTEGRATED KNOWLEDGE MANAGEMENT MODULE IN A E-GROUPWARE

Integration of the MAS into a E-Groupware to Capture the Professional Activities Results

The professional actors in the company use an e-Groupware platform called ACSP (Atelier Cooperatif de Suivi de Projet in French) to carry out their activities. It is a Web-based collaborative engineering environment, using a multi-domain and multi-viewpoint design model. This Web-based tool was developed as a CSCW environment, in order to organize and structure the collaborative activities of designers from anywhere in the world. Thus the team project can use a synchronous communication through the ACSP chat to organize remote meeting. In addition designers can use the ACSP Forum to declare their encountered problems. The ACSP software interface, connected to a relational Database Management System, is divided into four main sub-modules managing information from project, product, process and usability design domains.

Each design domain includes various design data and files describing functional, structural and dynamic aspects of the studied domain. ACSP features are used for the design chain data management: product data and information, documents and their associated content (all types, formats and media), requirements (functional, performance, quality, cost, physical factors, interoperability, time, etc.), Product families, Product and project portfolios, plant machinery and facilities, production line equipment, and so forth.

Consequently, the e-Groupware allows capturing the professional activities results in its database including information from the project, product and process management. It offers a centralized environment with heterogeneous information (documents, data, digital mock-up, etc.).

We chose this e-Groupware environment to deploy our knowledge management system composed by the MAS and the OntoDesign ontology. There are two advantages to use the ACSP, the first is that engineers are accustomed to working with it; the second is that the agents doesn't need to treat distributive information since all the data are centralized in the database.

The Knowledge Management Process Overview

The knowledge management process in the e-Groupware is ensuring in three levels (Figure 13):

- The first level ensures the traceability of users activities inside an e-groupware platform. In this level we find the type of agents called `Professional Agents.' These agents exist for one project. They monitor roles of the professional actors throughout projects in building their own RIOCK organization to identify emanating Knowledge. Their objective is to ensure a traceability of the collaborative actions carried out by professional actors in order to capture and annotate knowledge. They consult the ontology OntoDesign to use a common vocabulary in their annotations.
- The second level gathers mechanisms of Knowledge capitalization. In this level we find the type of agents call `Project Knowledge Managers Agents' (i.e. ProjKMA). The aim of ProjKMA is to capitalize from knowledge annotations of engineering activities communicated by the PA agents. The organization of this Knowledge is done according to the ontology model OntoDesign presented in section. Communities of ProjKMA exist for each project. Therefore the ProjKMA build the project memory of the project in which they are created. They also propose solution to professional actors all along the current project.
- The third level contains the agents type 'Professional Knowledge Managers Agents' (ProfKMA). These agents exist for every projects, their aim is to synthesize the Knowledge structured according to project memories for the whole of projects. The Knowledge capitalized and reused during one project is a Project Knowledge, and the Knowledge capitalized during the whole of the projects and reused in a new project is a Professional Knowledge. Therefore ProfKMA are able to propose solution from professional Knowledge all along a new project.

KNOWLEDGE REUSE INSIDE THE E-GROUPWARE

Knowledge Consultation by Professional Actors

The integration of the knowledge management system inside the e-Groupware is materialized by the addition a "knowledge engineering module." This module makes it possible to the users to seek and consult the knowledge capitalized by the management system of knowledge. The module is composed by interfaces dedicated to the knowledge consultation. Professional actors are able to

Figure 13. Knowledge management process supported by agents

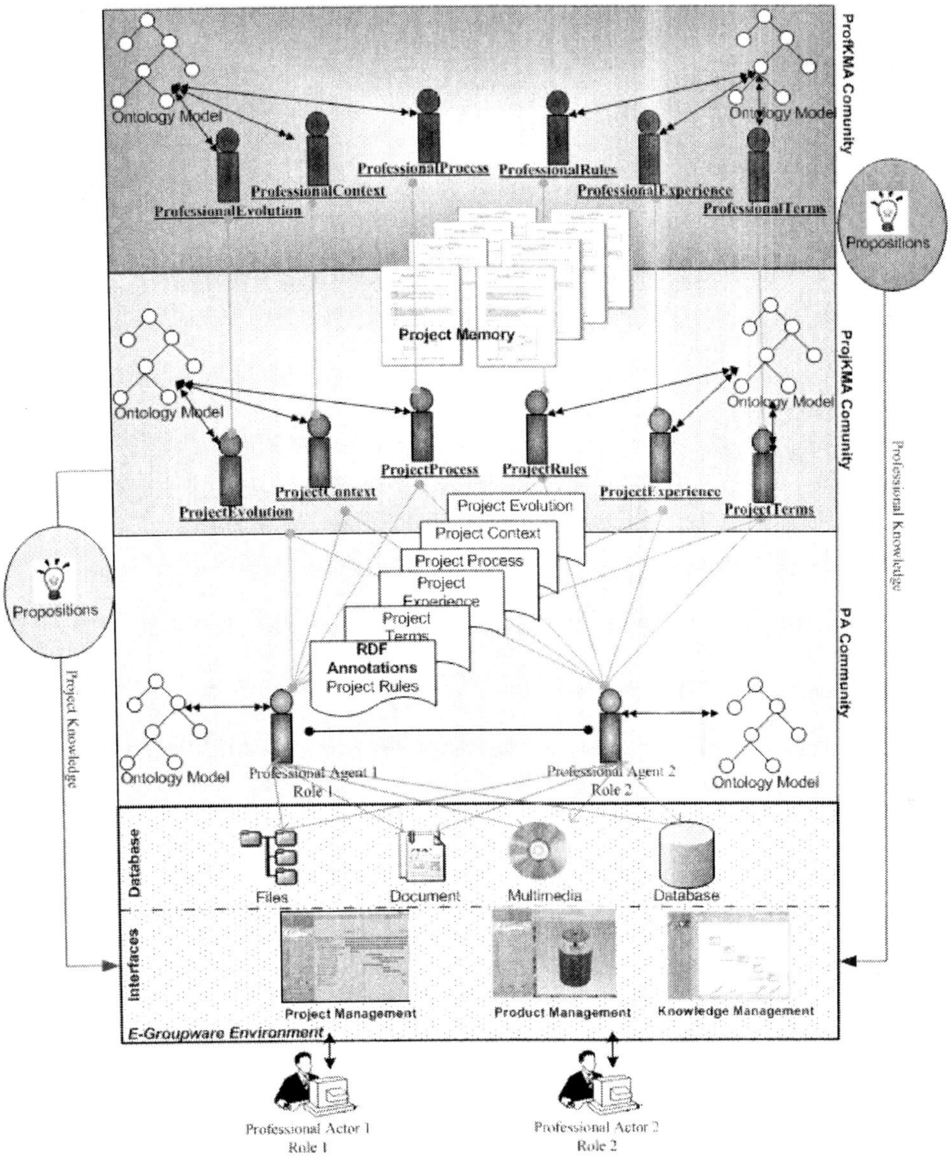

consult knowledge of the current project (i.e., its project memory) as well as knowledge of the whole projects (i.e. the whole project memories).

There is one interface for each knowledge type (Figure 14):

- The project context is represented by a form in which are described the objective, the environment and the organization of the project ;

Figure 14. Knowledge management process supported by agents

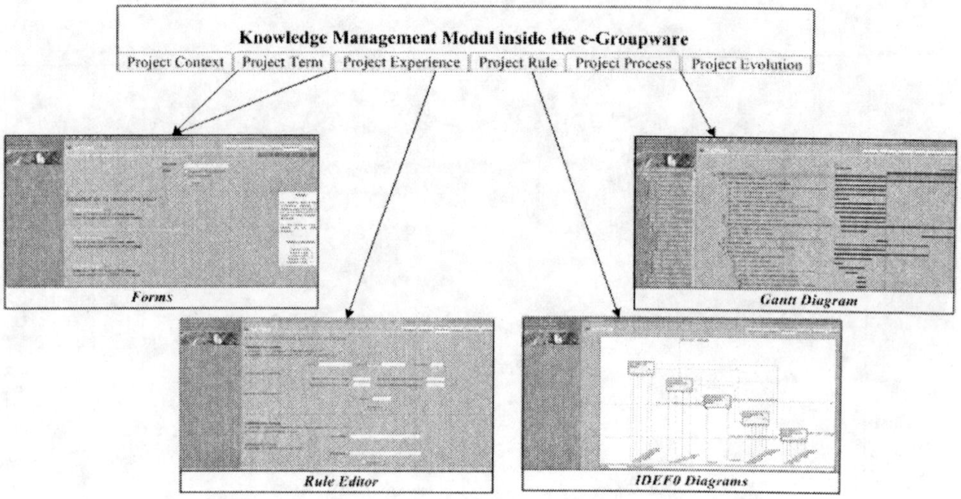

- The project evolution is described by a planning;
- The project rules is represented inside a rule editor;
- The project process is described with a idef0 diagrams;
- The project terms are represented in a glossary;
- The project experiences are represented in a form in which are mentioned the successes, difficulties and failures encountered during projects.

Proactive Assistance Providing by Agents

We use the concept of personal assistant to interact with the users. The assistant helps professional actors to reuse the knowledge of past projects. Indeed, KATRAS agents perceive the organizational context (professional activity, role and competence) where are their human actors. If agents identify knowledge capitalized in a similar organizational context (same activity and same role), they propose to their actors to consult capitalized knowledge. The assistant is just an interface in which agent active hypertext links. These links direct the actor to the knowledge management module interfaces where are described the capitalized knowledge.

CONCLUSION AND FUTURE WORK

Nowadays the MAS and the domain ontology are implemented inside the e-Groupware ACSP. They allow to capitalize, annotate, and organize knowledge according to the project memory model. In addition they help professional actors to re-use knowledge of the current project and the past projects.

Up to now the professional actors have assessed the following results:

- The project leaders use knowledge related to the 'Project Evolution' to begin a new project. This allows us to estimate the delay of a new product development from past projects in which the company has industrialized similar products;
- The production technicians use knowledge related to the 'Project process' to optimize their industrial processes. They appreciate the saving time;
- Knowledge related to the 'Project terms' are only used by novice employees. It allows them to learn about the technical terms, the product references and the technical methods used in the company;
- The most important result is about knowledge related to the 'project rule.' Indeed mechanical engineers reuse the professional rules associated to developed product parts in order to design a similar product. This functionality brings an important saving time which is estimated about twenty percent of the engineering time by the actors.

However the knowledge management system has to be improving to help more effectually engineers. Indeed nowadays the knowledge consultation is only made by keywords (project name, product name, process name, etc.). Our future work will be to perform the use of the domain ontology and allow research by concepts and their relations. In addition we actually work on the implementation of inference methods in the MAS to make effective the knowledge reuse process such as the professional process deduction and optimization from the project planning.

REFERENCES

Amiguet M., Nagy A., & Baez J. (2004). *Towards an aspect-oriented approach of multi-agent programming*, MOCA'04: 3rd Workshop on Modelling of Objects, Components, and Agents, p. 18

Ang, C. L., Gay, R. K., Khoo, L. P., & Luo, M. (1997), A knowledge-based approach to the generation of IDEF0 Models, *International Journal of Production Research*.35, 1385-1412.

Andersen, E. P. & Reenskaug, T. (1992), System design by composing structures of interacting objects, In O. L. Madsen (Ed.), *ECOOP '92, European Conference on Object-Oriented Programming*, Utrecht, The Netherlands, volume 615 of Lecture Notes in Computer Science (pp. 133–152). New York, N.Y.: Springer-Verlag.

Abecker A., Bernardi A., & Van Elst L. (2003). *Agent technology for distributed organizational memories*. In *Proceedings of the 5th International Conference on Enterprise Information Systems*, Vol. 2, pages 3–10.

Benmahamed D., Ermine J.-L. (2006). *Knowledge Management Techniques for Know-How Transfer Systems Design, The case of an Oil Company*, ICKM 2006 (International Conference on Knowledge Management), London.

Bekhti S. & Matta N. (2003). *Project memory: An approach of modelling and reusing the context and the design rationale*, In *Proceedings of IJCAI'03 (International Joint of Conferences of Artificial Intelligence) Workshop on Knowledge Management and Organisational Memory.*, Acapulco.

Belkadi F., Bonjour E., & Dulmet M. (2007) Competency characterisation by means of work situation modelling. *Computers in Industry, 58,* 164-178.

Bresciani P., Perini A., Giorgini P., Giunchiglia F., & Mylopoulos J. (2004). *Tropos: An agent-oriented software development methodology*, Autonomous Agents and Multi-Agent Systems, 8, pp. 203-236.

Buckingham Shum S., MacLean A., Bellotti V. M.E., & V. Hammond N. (1997). *Graphical argumentation and design cognition*. Rapport

Technique KMI-TR-25, The Open University, Rank Xerox Reasearch Centre, Apple Reasearch Laboratories, University of York, UK.

Caire, G., Coulier, W., Garijo, F. J., Gomez, J., Pavón, J., Leal, F., Chainho, P., Kearney, P. E., Stark, J., Evans, R., & Massonet, P. (2001). Agent oriented analysis using message/uml. In Wooldridge, M.,Weiß, G., and Ciancarini, P. Eds.), Agent-Oriented Software Engineering II, Second InternationalWorkshop, AOSE 2001, Montreal, Canada, May 29.

Castelfranchi C. (2000), *Engineering Social Order. In Engineering Societies in the Agents' World,* Lecture Notes in Artificial Intelligence. Springer Verlag, 2000.300p.

Conklin J. & Begeman (1988.) M. gIBIS: A Hypertext Tool for Exploratory Policy Discussion. ACM Transaction on O-ce Information Systems, *6*(4),303-331.

Conklin E.J.(1996), *Designing organizational memory: Preserving intellectual assets in a knowledge economy.* Electronic Publication by Corporate Memory Systems, Inc., 1996. http://www.zilker.net/business/info/pubs/desom/.

Cossentino M. (2005), *From Requirements to Code with the PASSI Methodology in Agent-Oriented Methodologies.* B. Henderson-Sellers & P. Giorgini (Eds.),Idea Group Inc., Hershey, PA, USA.

Enembreck F. & Barthès J.P. (2002). Personal assistant to improve CSCW. In *Proceedings of CSCWD,* Rio de Janeiro.

Ferber, J., Gutknecht, O., & Michel, F. (2003). *From agents to organizations: an organizational view of multi-agent systems.* In Agent-Oriented Software Engineering IV 4th InternationalWorkshop, (AOSE-2003@AAMAS 2003), volume 2935 of LNCS, pp. 214–230, Melbourne, Australia.

Fox, M. S. (1981). *An organizational view of distributed systems.* IEEE Trans. on System, Man, and Cybernetics, SMC-11(1):70–80.

Fox, M.S., & Huang, J., (2005), Knowledge provenance in enterrpriseiInformation, *International Journal of Production Research, 43*(20), 4471-4492.

Fukuda Y., (1995), *Variations of Knowledge in Information Society,* In *Proceedings of the ISMICK* 95, pp.3-8.

Gandon F., Poggi A., Rimassa G., & Turci P. (2002). *Multi-Agent Corporate Memory Management System* In Engineering Agent Systems: Best of "From Agent Theory to Agent Implementation (AT2AI)-3," *Journal of Applied Artificial Intelligence,* Volume 16, Number 9-10/October - December 2002, Taylor & Francis, p699 – 720.

Golebiowska J., Dieng-Kuntz R., Corby O., & Mousseau D. (2002). *Samovar : Using ontologies and text-mining for building an automobile project memory,* in: Knowledge Management and Organizational Memories, Kluwer Academic Publishers, July 2002, pp. 89-102.

Gomes S. & Sagot J.C. (2000). *A concurrent engineering experience based on a cooperative and object oriented design methodology,* 3rd International Conference on Integrated Design and Manufacturing in Mechanical Engineering, IDMME 2000, Montréal.

Guizzardi R., Wagner S.S., & Aroyo G. L. (2005). *Knowledge Management in Learning Communities, ICFAI Journal of Knowledge Management, 3*(3), 0-46.

Guizzardi R., Aroyo L., & Wagner Gerd (2003). *Agent-Oriented Knowledge Management in Learning Environments: A Peer-to-Peer Helpdesk Case Study,* in Agent-Mediated Knowledge Management, Springer Berlin, pp. 57-72.

Hilaire V, Koukam A, Gruer P., & Müller J-P. (2000). *Formal Specification and Prototyping of Multi-Agent Systems. Engineering Societies in the Agents* World, in Lecture Notes in Artificial Intelligence. n°1972, Springer Verlag.

Kasvi J., Vartiainen M., & Hailikari M. (2003), Managing knowledge and knowledge competences in projects and project organisations, *International Journal of Project Management, 21*(8), pp. 571-582.

Klein M. (1997) *Capturing Geometry Rationale for Collaborative Design.* In *Proceedings of the 6th IEEE Workshop on Enabling Technologies : Infrastructue for Collaborative Enterprises (WET ICE'97*), MIT, June 1997. IEEE Computer Press.

Lieberman H. (1995). *Letizia: An agent that assists web browsing.* In Chris S. Mellish, (Ed.), In *Proceedings of the 14th International Joint Conference on Artificial Intelligence (IJCAI-95),* Montreal, Quebec, Canada.

Lewkowicz, M.,& Zacklad, M., (1999, September 22-24). How a GroupWare based on a knowledge structuring method can be a collective decision-making aid: the MEMO-Net tool, in Lenca, P. (Ed.) In *Proceedings of the 10th Mini EURO Conference "Human-centered processes" (HCP'99)* (pp.175-182) Brest, France,.

Longueville B., Stal Le Cardinal J., & Bocquet J.-C. (2003). *Meydiam, a project memory for innovative product design.* In *PIAMOT03, the 12th International Conference on Management of Technology,* Nancy France.

Paraiso C. E. & Barthes J-P. (2006). *An intelligent speech interface for personal assistants in R&D projects,* in Experts Systems with applications.

Perez P., Karp K., Dieng R., Corby O., Giboin A., Gandon F., Qinqueton J., Poggi P., Rimmassa G., & Fietta Cselt C. (2000). *O'COMMA, Corporate Memory Management through Agents,* In Proceedings E-Work & E-Business, Madrid, October 17-20, pp. 383-406.

Matta N., Ribiere M., Corby O., Lewkowicz M., & Zaclad M. (2000). *Project Memory in Design, Industrial Knowledge Management - A Micro Level Approach,* Rajkumar Roy (Eds), Springer-Verlag.

Maes P. (1994). *Agents that Reduce Work and Information Overload.* In Communications of the ACM, Vol. 37, No.7, July 1994.

Protégé 2000 (2000): http://protege.stanford.edu

Rabarijaona A., Dieng R., Corby O., & Ouaddari R (2001). *Building a XML-based Corporate Memory,* IEEE Intelligent Systems, Special Issue on Knowledge Management and Internet pp. 56-64.

A. Seaborne & E. Prud'hommeaux (2006). *SPARQL Query Language for RDF.* (Tech. Rep). http://www.w3.org/TR/2006/CR-rdf-sparql-query-20060406/, W3C.

Singh, B. (1992). Interconnected Roles (IR): A Coordination Model. Technical Report CT-084-92, MCC.

Staab S. & Schnurr H.-P. (2000). Smart task support through proactive access to organizational memory. Knowledge–based Systems, 13(5):251–260.

Stuber A., Hassas S., & Mille A. (2003, June 23-26), *Combining multiagents systems and experience reuse for assisting collective task achievement.* In *Proceedings of ICCBR-2003 Workshop From structured cases to* unstructured problem solving episodes for experience-based assistance, Trondheim, Norway. Lorraine McGinty Eds.

Uschold M., King M., Moralee S., & Zorgios Y. (1998). The Enterprise Ontology, *The Knowledge Engineering Review*, Vol. 13, Special Issue on Putting Ontologies to Use (eds. Mike Uschold and Austin Tate). Also available from AIAI as AIAI-TR-195 http://www.aiai.ed.ac.uk/project/enterprise/

Van Elst L., Dignum V., & Abecker A. (2004). Towards Agent-Mediated Knowledge Management. In: L. van Elst, V. Dignum, A. Abecker (Eds.), Agent-Mediated Knowledge Management: Selected Papers, Lecture Notes in Artificial Intelligence, Springer-Verlag, Volume 2926.

Weggeman M. (1996). *Knowledge Management: The Modus Operandi for a Learning Organization*. In J. F. Schreinemakers (Ed.), Knowledge Management: Organization, Competence and Methodology, In *Proceedings of the ISMICK'96*, Rotterdam, the Netherlands, Wurzburg:Ergon Verlag, Advances in Knowledge Management, vol. 1, 21-22, p. 175-187.

Wongthongtham P., Chang E., Dillon T.S., & Sommerville I. (2006). Ontology-based multi-site software development methodology and tools, Journal of Systems Architecture.

Wooldridge, M. & Jennings, N. R. (1995). Intelligent agents: Theory and practice. *Knowledge Engineering Review, 10(2).*

Section III
Semantic-Based Applications

Chapter XII
K-link+:
A P2P Semantic Virtual Office for Organizational Knowledge Management

Carlo Mastroianni
Institute of High Performance Computing and Networking CNR-ICAR, Italy

Giuseppe Pirrò
University of Calabria, Italy

Domenico Talia
EXEURA S.r.l., Italy, & University of Calabria, Italy

ABSTRACT

This chapter introduces a distributed framework for OKM (Organizational Knowledge Management) which allows IKWs (Individual Knowledge Workers) to build virtual communities that manage and share knowledge within workspaces. The proposed framework, called K-link+, supports the emergent way of doing business of IKWs, which allows users to work at any time from everywhere, by exploiting the VO (Virtual Office) model. Moreover, since semantic aspects represent a key point in dealing with organizational knowledge, K-link+ is supported by an ontological framework composed of: (i) an UO (Upper Ontology), which defines a shared common background on organizational knowledge domains; (ii) a set of UO specializations, namely Workspace Ontologies or Personal Ontologies, that can be used to manage and search content; (iii) a set of COKE (Core Organizational Knowledge Entities) which provides a shared definition of human resources, technological resources, knowledge objects, services; and (iv) an annotation mechanism that allows users to create associations between ontology concepts and knowledge objects. K-link+ features a hybrid (partly centralized and partly distributed) protocol to guarantee the consistency of shared knowledge and a distributed voting mechanism to foster the evolution of ontologies on the basis of user needs.

INTRODUCTION

In the 1990s, Nonaka and Takeuchi proposed a new organizational paradigm (Nonaka et al., 1995). This paradigm identifies knowledge as a key resource for organizations and aims at establishing paths to be followed for better exploiting organizational knowledge. While earlier organizational models (Taylor, 1911) saw the organization as a box with the aim to maximize the output or as something that can be scientifically and rigorously managed, more recently the theme of managing knowledge has become more important (Simon, 1972) and the role of the organization in KM (Knowledge Management) processes has changed notably. The organization becomes a way to connect the knowledge of many subjects into a more complete understanding of the reality. Also the role of technologies has changed; they have become a way to increase people's rationality by enabling both knowledge management and exchange. Throughout the years, several other theories about knowledge have been proposed. A generally accepted classification proposed by Polanyi (Polanyi 1966; Polanyi 1997) and extended by Nonaka (1994) identifies on the one side "tacit knowledge" as the knowledge resulting from personal learning within an organization. On the other side, "explicit knowledge" is a generally shared and publicly accessible form of knowledge. Explicit knowledge can also be classified on the basis of the following forms: "structured" (available in databases); "semi-structured;" (generally available in Web sites: HTML pages, XML documents, etc.) and "unstructured" (available as textual documents: project documents, procedures, white papers, etc.). More recently, new importance has been given to social processes and to the CoP (Communities of Practice) as sources of knowledge. A CoP can be viewed as a group of people with shared goals and interests that employ common practices, work with the same tools, and express themselves in a common language (Lave & Wenger, 1991). In a CoP, individuals can produce and learn new concepts and processes from the community, allowing the same community to innovate and create new knowledge. This way, an organization can become a community of communities, offering space for creating autonomous sub-communities. The different types of technological solutions for managing knowledge should correspond to actual social interactions in KM processes. According to this consideration, technological systems for KM can be classified and inserted in a scheme reflecting the adopted social model. Therefore, on the one hand we have centralized systems that are practically identified with the EKP (Enterprise Knowledge Portal) and, on the other hand, we have DKM (Distributed Knowledge Management) systems. In this chapter, we will focus on the DKM approach since it naturally fits the process of creating knowledge. Following this approach, the individual is allowed to manage his/her knowledge without any superimposed schema. Therefore, he/she can share the individual knowledge by spreading it over the organization and making it an asset of the whole organization.

In particular, distributed applications for KM are based on the principle that different perspectives within complex organizations should not be viewed as an obstacle to knowledge exploitation, but rather as an opportunity to foster innovation and creativity. They are increasingly becoming popular since they permit an easy and quick creation of dynamic and collaborative groups (e.g., CoP) composed of people from a single or different organizations.

Moreover, in today's ubiquitous information society an increasing number of people work outside of the traditional office for many hours of the day. Current technologies do not properly support this new style of working and every day it is becoming harder and harder to exchange information in a labyrinth of network connections, firewalls, file systems, tools, applications, databases, voice-mails, and emails. Individual Knowledge Workers spend much of their time finding and exchanging information or reaching people, and very limited time is left to actual productive work. To cope with these issues, many companies use technological solutions that include portals, extranets, VPNs, and browser-based application strategies that, at best, have been partially successful.

We argue that IKWs need a virtual workplace where the physical office can be recreated and where everybody and everything is easily available from anywhere at anytime. The *Virtual Office* approach (Marshak, 2004) can solve most of the aforementioned issues. A VO is a work environment defined regardless of the geographic locality of employees. A VO fulfils the roles of the traditional, centralized office although employees collaborate for the most part electronically with sporadic physical contacts.

P2P (Peer-to-Peer) solutions naturally fit the DKM and VO requirements, since they offer autonomy, coordination, and scalability features (Bonifacio et al., 2002). We designed and developed a P2P system named *K-link+* (Le Coche et al., 2006) that implements the VO model and provides users with a collaborative knowledge management environment. In *K-link+,* users can integrate different applications (knowledge sharing, messaging, shared boards, agenda, etc.) within a single environment and enrich the system with new tools that can be added as new components.

In *K-link+*, peers are allowed to concurrently work on the same shared KOs (Knowledge Objects). To foster peers' autonomy, different local replicas of a KO can be created, so concurrent access can affect data consistency if adequate mechanisms are not provided. Since peers can join or leave the system at any time, synchronization is required by peers that reconnect to the network and need to be informed about recent updates made on KOs by other peers. The *K-link+* system adopts a hybrid model to guarantee content consistency and peer synchronization. This model exploits the efficiency of centralized models, but at the same time includes decentralized features that assure scalability properties when the system size increases.

The basic concept under the *K-link+* Virtual Office approach is the workspace. A *K-link+* workspace can be viewed as a work area integrating people, tools, and resources. KOs created and exchanged within a workspace are provided with a semantic meaning through ontologies. In recent years, the knowledge management community has been considering ontologies as an adequate support to harness semantics conveyed by information (Fensel, 2001). An ontology (Gruber, 1993) is an abstract representation of a knowledge domain which allows its modeling in terms of concepts, relationships among concepts, class hierarchies and properties, and permits reasoning about the represented knowledge. Ontologies also offer a way for defining a set of possible instances of concepts and relationships, thus providing links between the model and the modeled reality.

K-link+ is supported by an ontological framework that allows to:

- Give a shared definition of knowledge domains relevant for the organization through the Upper Ontology (UO). So IKWs are provided with a common and well-defined knowledge background on knowledge domains of interest for the organization.
- Provide a shared definition of typical organizational assets (e.g., human resources, knowledge objects, services) within COKE ontologies. This way the retrieval of such assets can be done more effectively.
- Deepen aspects of the organizational knowledge domain in communities through Workspace Ontologies or on a personal basis through Peer Ontologies. Therefore, IKWs are endowed with a certain degree of autonomy in defining their own conceptual schemas (i.e., ontologies).
- Annotate COKE instances and in particular KOs (i.e., textual documents, emails, Web

pages) to ontology concepts. Therefore unstructured and heterogeneous information is provided with semantically relevant metadata and can be retrieved on a semantic basis by specifying ontology concepts instead of keywords.

BACKGROUND

Most of the current architectures for content sharing and knowledge management are typically based on client/server architectures in which one or more servers act as central entities. In such architectures, knowledge handled by IKWs must be managed according to organizational guidelines. However, such centralized approaches do not reflect the social nature of knowledge (Bonifacio et al., 2002). As it is argued in (Nonaka & Takeuchi, 1995), the *seed* of new knowledge is *individual (tacit)* knowledge, but the importance of the knowledge increases when it becomes available to the whole organization. Therefore, the *externalization* of tacit knowledge is a quintessential process for creating new knowledge; this typically requires people to interact and collectively reflect on a problem or an idea. Such observations promote the demand for new technological architectures that place more emphasis on collaboration.

We argue that a P2P architecture that implements the VO model fits both the requirements of collaboration (synchronous and asynchronous) and knowledge sharing. In fact, P2P architectures naturally support the creation of communities (e.g., workspaces, peer groups) in which content and conveyed knowledge can be created, shared, exchanged, and transformed.

Content consistency is a fundamental reliability requirement for a P2P system. Current approaches depend on the scale of P2P systems. In a large-scale and dynamic system, it is complex and cumbersome to guarantee full consistency among replicas, so researchers have designed algorithms to support consistency in a best-effort way. In Datta et al. (2003), a hybrid push/pull algorithm is used to propagate updates, where flooding is substituted by rumor spreading to reduce communication overhead. SCOPE (Chen et al., 2005) is a P2P system that supports consistency among a large number of replicas at the cost of maintaining a sophisticated data structure. By building a RPT (Replica-Partition-Tree) for each key, SCOPE keeps track of the locations of replicas and then propagates update notifications.

Conversely, in a small- or medium-scale system, it is possible to adopt centralized schemes to guarantee a strong consistency model, which is often the *sequential* model (Lamport, 1979). In Wang et al. (2006), an algorithm for file consistency maintenance through virtual servers in unstructured and decentralized P2P systems is proposed. Consistency of each dynamic file is maintained by a VS (Virtual Server). A file update can only be accepted through the VS to ensure the one-copy serializability.

The *K-link+* system, which is mostly suited for small/medium enterprises, adopts a hybrid model which exploits the efficiency of centralized models, but at the same time includes decentralized features which assure scalability properties when the system size increases. This is accomplished by using: (i) a unique and stable server to maintain a limited amount of metadata information about shared objects; (ii) a number of interchangeable servers that maintain and manage the primary copy of shared objects; and (iii) a pure decentralized mechanism to allow P2P nodes to exchange up-to-date object copies when only read operations are required.

Another striking feature of *K-link+* is the use of ontologies for supporting OKM both at individual level, by Personal Ontologies, and within communities through Workspace Ontologies. Ontologies allow to "conceptualize" knowledge subjects, externalize them in terms of ontology primitives (e.g., concepts, relationships), and share knowledge through "the establishment of shared understanding" (Becerra et al., 2001). Ontologies can also be used to improve current keyword-based search techniques (Fensel, 2001), since they permit users to semantically annotate contents with respect to concepts. Conceptual search, that is, search based on meaning similarity rather than just string comparison, has been the motivation of a large body of research in the Information Retrieval field long before the Semantic Web vision emerged (Agosti et al., 1990; Järvelin et al., 2001). In the literature there are several approaches to ontology-based search (Guha et al., 2003; Vallet et al., 2005) that rely on queries expressed in formal languages, such as RDQL (Seaborne, 2004) SPARQL (Prud'hommeaux et al., 2006) or on a combination of formal queries with keyword-based queries (Castelles et al., 2007).

The approach we implemented is different from all these since we aim at creating semantic metadata associated to content (e.g., documents) by following the principle of superimposing information (Maier et al., 1999). We do not aim at explicitly populating the knowledge base of each peer with ontological knowledge, but rather at enabling users to quickly assign, by *annotations,* an immediate semantic meaning to both structured and unstructured content.

Concerning semantic-based P2P systems, there are several approaches that share common characteristics with *K-link+*. KEx (Knowledge Exchange) (Bonifacio et al., 2002) is a P2P system aimed at implementing knowledge sharing among communities of peers (called federations) that share interests. The system relies on the concept of context that peers exploit to represent their interests. KEx implements specific tools (e.g., context editors, context extractors) to extract the context of a peer from the peer knowledge (e.g., file system, mail messages). In order to discover semantic mappings among concepts belonging to different peer contexts, KEx exploits the CtxMatch algorithm. CtxMatch associates concepts with their correct meaning with respect to their context by exploiting WordNet and translates concepts in logical axioms in order to discover mappings. The algorithm implements a description logic approach in which mapping discovery is reduced to the problem of checking a set of logical relations. SWAP (Semantic Web and Peer to Peer) (Ehrig et al., 2003) aims at combining ontologies and P2P for knowledge management purposes. SWAP enables local knowledge management through a component called LR (Local node Repository), which gathers knowledge from several sources and represents it in RDF-Schema. SWAP allows searching for knowledge by using a query language called SeRQL, which is an evolution of RQL.

Different from these approaches, *K-link+* does not specifically tackle the problem of ontology mapping, since it can be time consuming thus affecting the requirement of quickness mandatory in a P2P environment. Conversely, we support a "mutual agreement" mechanism among participants since we build ontologies in a democratic way through a distributed voting mechanism.

K-LINK+ ARCHITECTURE

K-link+ is a collaborative P2P system that provides users with a Virtual Office environment in which content can be shared to enable collaborative work, and replicated, to foster peer autonomy. Different applications (document sharing, messaging, shared boards, agenda, etc.) can be integrated within a single environment (a *K-link+* workspace) and new tools can be added as new components to support emerging requirements. In this section, the system architecture is briefly presented. For a more detailed description of the *K-link+* architecture refer to the GridLab website, *http://grid.deis.unical.it/k-link.*

The *K-link+* architecture, shown in Figure 1, is based on five layers including basic grouping

Figure 1. The K-link+ architecture

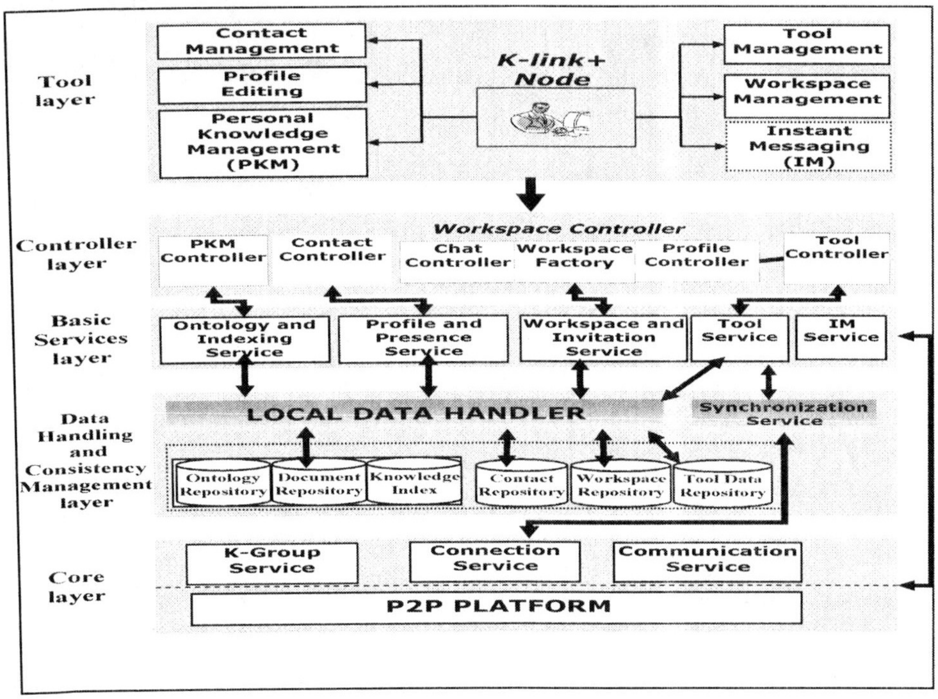

and communication services, data handling services, semantics services, workspace management services, and a set of high level tools for content sharing and user cooperation.

K-link+ Core Layer

This layer defines the *K-link+* basic services whose implementation can be based on any P2P infrastructure (for the current version of *K-link+*, we use JXTA). Services provided by the *Core Layer* are exploited by higher layers. In particular, the *K-Group Service* allows *K-link+* Nodes (KLNs) to create new *K-Groups*, for example, communities or workspaces. The *Connection Service* allows KLNs to join the *K-link+* network by contacting a *K-link+ Rendezvous*. Features used to send and receive messages are provided by the *Communication Service.*

Data Handling and Consistency Management Layer

This layer is responsible to cope with concurrent access to shared objects, object consistency, and peer synchronization. This layer includes the *Local Data Handler*, which manages a set of local repositories to store information about contacts, workspaces, objects, and so on.

K-link+ Basic Services Layer

The services of this layer manage local and remote operations performed by a *K-link+* user. The *Ontology and Indexing Service* deals with operations involving ontologies (creation, update) that *K-link+* exploits to describe resources semantically. It also copes with the indexing of documents for keyword based searches. The *Profile and Presence Service* manages state check operations and enables users to create and publish their profile within the *K-link+* network. The *Workspace and Invitation Service* handles workspace set up and population by sending invitation messages to other KLNs. The *Tool Service* is used to add new tool instances to workspaces at run time. The *IM (Instant Message) Service* allows KLNs to communicate each other via a chat-like system.

K-link+ Controller Layer

This layer contains a set of controllers through which the system interacts with the *Data Handling and Consistency Management Layer* via a set of services (provided by the *Basic Service Layer*). The *Workspace Controller* manages workspace settings through the creation of *workspace profiles* that contain information about workspace topics, sets of tools, and the IKWs that belong to the workspace. The *Contact Controller* enables IKWs to discover other IKWs on the network and add some of them to a personal *Contact List*. The *PKM Controller* is delegated to manage the *Personal Knowledge* of an IKW. Finally, the *Tool Controller* is responsible for allowing users to handle operations (add, update, remove) on private and shared tools.

K-link+ Tools Layer

This layer enables the user to choose the set of tools to include in a workspace. Basically, *K-link+* enables workspace members to choose among a set of tools (file sharing, shared calendar, contact manager, etc.). Moreover, other tools can be developed and included in the system as components. In fact, the development of a tool in the *K-link+* system can be carried out by third parties with the only requirement that the *K-link+* tool interface must be implemented.

REPLICATION AND CONSISTENCY OF DATA IN K-LINK+

In *K-link+*, several users can work concurrently on the same shared objects. To favor the autonomy of users, the system allows users to create different replicas of the same object, so that they can work on their local copies. As mentioned in the previous section, the purpose of the *Data Handling and Consistency Management* layer is to ensure data persistence, consistency management, and data synchronization. In the context of *K-link+,* we adopt the *sequential consistency* model (Lamport, 1979), which assures that all updates performed on an object are seen in the same sequence by all peers. The model is implemented by associating to each object a KLN (named *Manager*), which is responsible for authorizing object updates and putting them in a given order. In particular, each object is assigned a *VN (Version Number)*, which is incremented after each successful update. To efficiently handle the consistency problem in the P2P environment, *K-link+* defines the following roles that can be assumed by workspace nodes:

- *Creator.* This role is assumed by a KLN that creates a shared object and specifies its *ML (Manager List)*, that is, the list of KLNs that can assume the *Manager* role for this object. Managers are ordered on the basis of their degree of responsibility in managing the object.
- *Rendezvous.* For each workspace, one rendezvous node maintains metadata about

all the shared objects in a *Consistency Table* (described below) and provides such information to workspace members. The Rendezvous possesses up-to-date information about objects, in particular the identity of the node which is currently in charge of each object (i.e., the *Current Manager*) and the current VN.

- Manager. An object Manager is a KLN that manages the object life cycle and is contacted by KLNs when they want to propose an object update. An object can be assigned several Managers, but at a given time the *Current Manager*, which is the first online Manager in the ML, is actually responsible for the object. The Current Manager can decide whether or not to authorize an object update, according to the specific set of semantic rules associated to the object. KLNs are informed about the identity of the Current Manager by the Rendezvous.
- Broker. It is a KLN that maintains an updated copy of an object and can forward it to other KLNs. Whereas the Manager is a *static* role (i.e., it is assigned at object creation time), the Broker role is *dynamic*, since it is assumed by a node whenever it maintains an updated copy of the object.
- Worker. It is an ordinary KLN that can operate on an object, and possibly issue update proposals to the *Current Manager*. Workers can obtain an updated copy of an object by a *Broker*.

KLNs, as well as the *Rendezvous*, maintain information about the state of objects in a *Consistency Table*, whose structure is shown in Table 1. Each object is permanently associated to a *Consistency Entry* identified by a unique *ID* which is assigned when the object is created. Moreover, to keep trace of the object state, the Consistency Entry contains the Version Number, which is incremented at each object update, the *ID* of the Current Manager and the *Manager List*.

The definition of the mentioned roles enables three different kinds of interactions as shown in Figure 2. A *static centralized* approach is adopted when Workers interact with the unique and static Rendezvous. The aim of the Rendezvous is solely to provide information about Current Managers and object versions, but the management of each single shared object is delegated to the corresponding Current Manager. Such way of managing objects enables a *dynamic centralized* paradigm because object management can be dynamically switched among different Managers. This way,

Table 1. Consistency table

Field	**Description**
Object ID	A unique ID that identifies the shared object
VN (Version Number)	Object version number, incremented at each object update
Current Manager	The first online node contained in the ML. This node is responsible for the shared object.
Manager List	An ordered list of nodes that can assume the Current Manager role
Creator	The node that creates the object

Figure 2. The K-link approach to data consistency. Different kinds of arrows are used to show the different models of interaction among K-link+ nodes

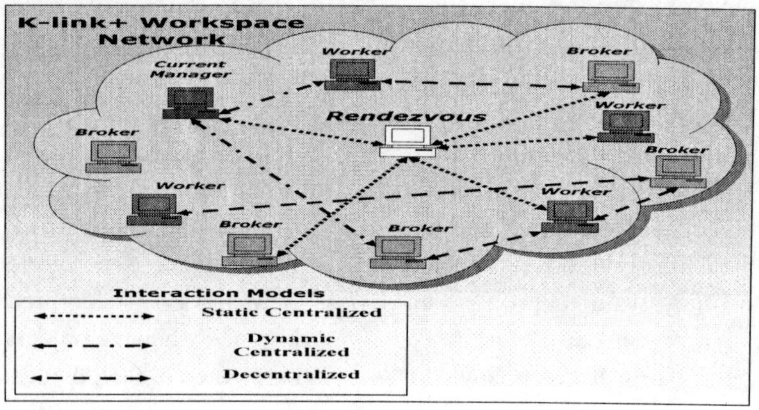

two common issues are solved: (i) we avoid the presence of a central bottleneck which would be originated if all objects were managed by a single node; (ii) we cope with the volatile nature of P2P networks, in which peers with Manager responsibilities can leave the network at any time.

A *decentralized* model is exploited by Brokers to provide updated object copies to Workers in a P2P fashion. We argue that the use of these three paradigms can represent a valid trade-off among different ways to face distributed object management. A detailed description and a performance evaluation of the consistency protocol can be found in (Mastroianni et al., 2007).

THE K-LINK+ ONTOLOGICAL FRAMEWORK

Most of the current approaches to collaborative work--while being worthwhile--do not take into account semantic aspects of knowledge management. A complete and useful collaborative system should be able to deal with both information and knowledge on a semantic basis. In recent years, the knowledge management community has been considering ontologies as an adequate support to harness semantics conveyed by information (Fensel, 2001). An ontology is an abstract representation of a knowledge domain which allows its modeling in terms of concepts, relationships between concepts, class hierarchies, and properties, and permits reasoning about the represented knowledge. Ontologies also offer a way for defining a set of possible instances of concepts and relationships, thus providing links between the model and the modeled reality. *K-link+* provides an ontology framework organized in two layers as shown in Figure 3.

The first layer contains an UO and a set of COKEs represented as ontology classes.

The UO represents a basic set of meta-concepts relevant for an organization that are defined by domain experts.

Figure 3. The user view of the K-link+ Ontology Framework. This figure shows the relationships between ontologies belonging to the two layers. The user's Personal Ontology and the Workspace Ontologies are specializations of one or more UO concepts. For example, the shown Personal Ontology specializes the UO concept Integrated Development Environment. COKE instances are annotated to Upper, Personal, and Workspace ontologies concepts.

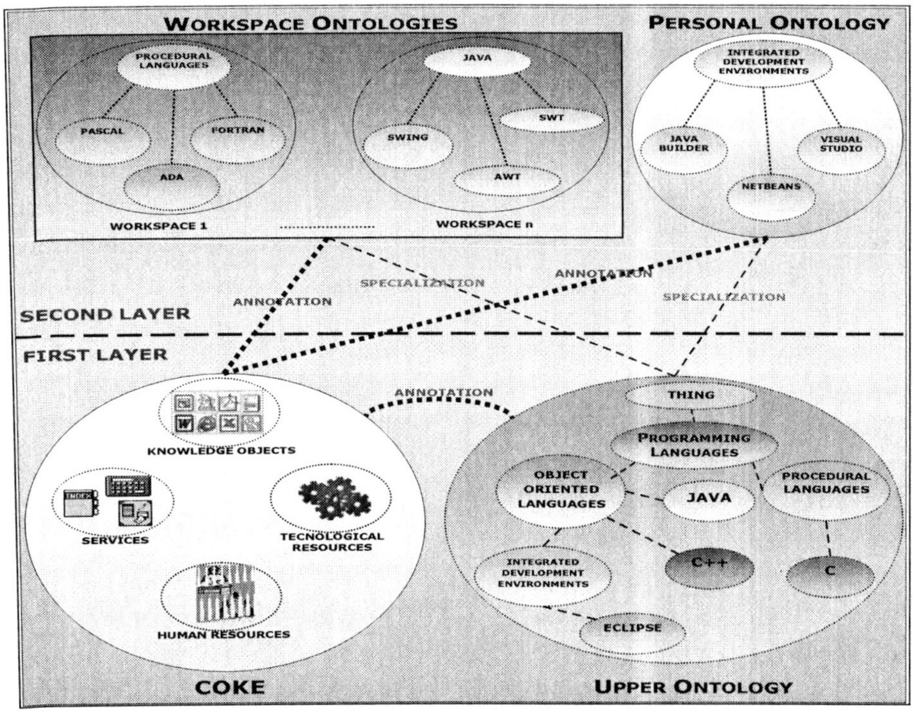

Definition 1 (UO) (Upper Ontology)

- An UO is a five-tuple of the form $UO=\langle C,\leq_C, R,\leq_R,\varphi_R\rangle$ where: C is a set of concepts, defined by domain experts, which describe knowledge domains of interest for the organization.
- $R:C\rightarrow C$ is a set of built-in relationships among concepts in C (e.g., represents, same-as, different-from, contains, associates, part-of, isa, related-to) arranged in hierarchies by means of the partial orders $\leq_C$, $\leq_R$.
- The function $\varphi R : R \rightarrow C\times C$ associates each relation $r\in R$ to its domain $dom(r)=\pi 1(\varphi R(r))$ and range $range(r)= \pi 2(\varphi R(r))$. The initial set of relationships included in the UO can be customized according to organizational needs.

The UO can be viewed as a semantic network of concepts similar to a thesaurus. For instance, the UO for a health care organization will contain concepts and relationships related to diseases, clinical practices, drugs, surgery, and so forth.

COKEs aim at giving a semantic description of some organizational sources of knowledge.

We identified four COKEs:

- *The Human Resource COKE* describes organizational groups (Community of Practices, Project Teams) and individuals. For each IKW, personal data, skills, group memberships, and topics of interest are represented. A group is described through its objectives and topics and contains information about the participant IKWs.
- The *Knowledge Object* COKE describes textual documents, database elements, emails, web pages, through metadata (e.g., data of creation, document type, author, URI). In particular, the framework exploits this COKE for enabling advanced search and retrieval capabilities in *K-link+*.
- The *Technological Resource* COKE describes tools through which knowledge objects are created, acquired, stored, and retrieved. For each tool, this kind of COKE provides information about version and features.
- The *Services* COKE describes services, provided by IKWs, in terms of provided features and access modalities.

However, each COKE has its own definition also in terms of attributes. For instance, the COKE KO, which describes different types of unstructured textual documents, contains attributes such as *name, size, author*, and so forth.

Instances of the same COKE share the same structure, so allowing for the management of implicit and explicit knowledge stored in structured, semi-structured or unstructured formats.

The *Annotation* relationships can be defined between the COKEs and the UO, which means that COKE instances can be semantically associated to the concepts of the UO by following the principle of superimposed information, that is, data or metadata "placed over" existing information sources (Maier et al., 1999). For instance, let us consider a human resource skilled in Java. An annotation relationship can specify that this human resource has a semantic annotation to the *Programming Languages/Object Oriented Languages/Java* concept contained in the UO. This way, *K-link+* can exploit this annotation to search human resources skilled or interested in Java. In general, queries can be performed using specific tools able to retrieve COKE instances, belonging to one or more of the four above mentioned classes, which are related to a specific concept.

The second layer of the ontology framework is composed of a set of UO extensions called *Workspace Ontologies*, and one or more *Personal Ontologies* for each IKW.

A PO (Personal Ontology) is the specialization of one or more UO concepts and is used to deepen a particular aspect of the knowledge domain in which an IKW is interested.

Definition 2 (PO)

A PO is a 4-tuple of the form *PO=<UO,UOC', UOP,UOR'>* where:

- UO is the UO as described in Definition 1.
- UOC' is the set of new concepts added by the peer.
- UOP is a set of attributes for concepts in UOC' added by the peer.
- UOR' is the set of relationships among concepts added by the peer.

A PO operates at individual level as semantic support for personal information management of IKWs that use the Organizational Ontology and need to extend it for their specific goals in the organizational activities. The PO can be used to annotate KOs with respect to PO concepts that describe their topics. The creation of an annotation is supposed to reflect the content of a KO and establish the foundation for its retrieval when requested by an IKW. This way unstructured information can be semantically enriched and its retrieving can be performed by specifying ontology concepts instead of keywords. However, it is expected that the annotation process can be automated to decrease the burden of the IKW. For this purpose, a method based on keyword extraction, as in (Popov et al., 2003) can be adopted. For instance, keywords extracted from the text of the KO can be viewed as descriptors of the content of the KO. Therefore, annotations between such descriptors and ontology concepts can be created.

In order to enhance social aspects of OKM, the framework allows users to create WOs (Workspace Ontologies). A WO specializes in one or more UO concepts and is used to support workspaces. IKWs can annotate COKEs instances relevant to the workspace, with respect to WO concepts, and retrieve them by specifying ontology concepts instead of keywords.

Definition 3 (WO)

A WO is a 2-tuple of the form *WO=<WB,WT>* where:

- WB has the same structure of the PO defined in Definition 2.
- WT is a set of basic concepts concerning workspace topics on which there is agreement among workspace members.

The relationships existing between the UO and the Workspace and Personal Ontologies are called *specializations* since such ontologies specialize in one or more UO concepts. For example, in Figure 3 the WO of *Workspace 1*, focused on procedural languages, specializes in the corresponding UO concept (*procedural languages*) by adding information describing further types of procedural languages.

HANDLING ONTOLOGY DRIFT IN *K-LINK+*

Although the structure of the proposed ontology framework has been designed beforehand, static or fully predefined ontologies in a dynamic distributed environment cannot satisfy the ever-changing requirements of an organization.

In *K-link+*, IKWs are allowed to propose extensions or modifications of an ontology according to their needs. Upon acceptance of such proposals, ontologies evolve in a collaborative and emerging way.

Ontology drift, that is, the evolution of an ontology, is managed in *K-link+* through a distributed voting mechanism (Ge et al., 2003). In *K-link+*, for each voting procedure, a *voting chair* is in charge of permitting or denying the voting process, collecting results and propagating them to participants. Before initiating a new voting procedure, an IKW obtains the authorization from the chair if there are no other voting procedures in progress.

An update proposal related to the UO is accepted if, within a specified amount of time, the majority of all the *K-link+* members, regardless of their workspace memberships, agree with the proposal. Similarly, to be approved, an update proposal related to a WO needs to be accepted by the majority of the workspace members.

A voting process within *K-link+* is divided into three phases:

1. *Set up phase*: in this phase the voting initiator contacts the voting chair which, if there are no pending voting procedures, forwards a "request for vote" message to all the involved IKWs. This message contains information about the update proposal along with the voting deadline.
2. *Voting phase*: IKWs vote to confirm or reject the ontology update proposed, and send their vote to the chair.

3. *Scrutiny phase*: when the deadline expires, the chair counts the votes and sends the result to the involved IKWs. If the update proposal has been accepted, the UO or WO is appropriately modified.

When IKWs, which were previously offline, reconnect while a voting procedure is in progress, they are made aware of the voting proposal by the voting chair and can join the voting process. If they reconnect when the voting procedure has terminated, they receive from the chair a notification containing information about the updated version of the ontology.

K-LINK+: A MOTIVATING EXAMPLE

As mentioned before, the Virtual Office environment provided by *K-link+* is based on the concept of *workspace*. A workspace can be viewed as a common *work area* accessible at any time from everywhere and composed by COKE instances (e.g., human resources, knowledge objects) that are annotated to WO concepts. A workspace provides a set of tools for creating and storing knowledge objects and for using services useful for the workspace members. Each KLN can be a member of a workspace under the following profiles:

- A *Workspace Manager* is a workspace administrator endowed with full capabilities for adding tools, inviting other KLNs or modifying the WO settings.
- A *Workspace Participant* is a workspace member with reduced but extensible (under Manager control) capabilities.

A workspace set-up procedure can be performed whenever a new organizational task must be carried out. For instance, let us consider a software company that must develop a graphical interface, written in Java, able to support the design of business workflows in a distributed environment. To deal with this task and fulfill the commitment requirements, the project leader can set up a proper workspace. The workspace must be associated to one or more concepts of the UO, and the WO represents a specialization of these concepts. For example, *Workspace n* of Figure 3 specializes in the *Java* concept by adding child concepts related to some available Java graphical libraries. A workspace creation is automatically followed by the creation of a group ontology instance in the COKE human resources ontology. This instance is semantically annotated to the *Java* UO concept.

Hereafter, by using the *K-link+* functionalities, the project leader:

- Chooses the existing literature and document templates concerning the project topic. In this case, it is valuable to populate the workspace document base with knowledge objects related to the concepts defined in the WO. Interesting knowledge objects can be discovered by the *K-link+ File Sharing Tool* which is able to handle keyword and semantic based searches.
- Defines an appropriate team of IKWs whose skills can be exploited to accomplish the commitments within the deadline. For the above mentioned example, the *K-link+* system should be able to find, through the ontology support, at least the following IKW profiles: experts in Java programming, experts in graphical interface development, and experts in workflow systems. People having the selected profiles become members of the workspace after receiving invitation messages sent by the workspace manager through the *K-link+ workspace and invitation service*.

- Designs an activity plan and assigns single activities to the IKWs by sending proper messages.
- Chooses a set of services for supporting the project. For example, the services ontology should contain a reference to a CVS (Concurrent Versions System) dedicated to the project. Services can be directly embedded in the *K-link+* workspace perspective that provides IKWs with a common work environment which gathers the needed applications.

Finally, the workspace manager or its delegates choose a set of tools through which the workspace members can perform the actual work. Such tools can be selected among a basic set of tools with which *K-link+* is endowed (e.g., file sharing, shared calendar, shared browser, sketch pad, etc.). Through these tools, IKWs can set project deadlines, project meetings, exchange documents, and so on. Furthermore, it is also possible to develop specific tools that can be plugged into the system as libraries at run-time. When a new tool is added to a workspace, the workspace members will automatically be informed and a local instance of the tool will be created. Afterwards, each tool update (e.g., adding a new project meeting to the shared calendar tool) will be forwarded to the workspace members that can store new information locally.

Each workspace is described by a *workspace profile* that includes the UO concept used to specialize in the WO, information about the participant IKWs and services and tools of the workspace. After creating the WO, its concepts can be used for semantically annotating new COKE instances created within the workspace. For example, a tutorial on the use of the SWT Java library can be annotated to the *SWT* WO concept.

K-link+ can be profitably used as an effective cooperative platform in organizations because:

1. It enables cooperation among IKWs by offering them an integrated and shared work environment in which they can concurrently work on the same shared objects and handle different sources of knowledge within the same environment. This way, the system avoids users to run several applications that cannot exchange data.
2. It allows providing contents (described by COKEs) with an immediate semantic meaning, by *annotations*. The principle followed by annotations is aimed at providing information with a sort of superimposed meaning. This aspect is particularly important since today information is for the most part in unstructured form and its retrieval mainly relies on statistical approaches (e.g., Information Retrieval approaches) that are not able to "interpret" its semantic meaning.
3. It fosters the retrieval of contents on a semantic basis by enabling concept based search. This is accomplished by coupling a shared representation of organizational source of knowledge (e.g., COKE ontologies) with ontologies.
4. It enables the reusability of organizational knowledge. For instance, in the described example, if the company will deal in the future with a similar commitment, such as the development of a new Java application, a search can be issued for a workspace that contains in its profile concepts like *Java, SWT, Swing* and so forth. Thereafter the project leader can select the documents, templates and human resource profiles that can profitably be reused for the new project.

The abovementioned aspects make *K-link+* a system very useful for small-medium enterprises composed of different divisions that need to cooperate, share and exchange knowledge.

CONCLUDING REMARKS

This chapter discusses how ontologies can be combined with the P2P computing paradigm to support knowledge management within organizations.

In particular, ontologies have been adopted to define an ontological framework that allows peers to conceptualize knowledge domains in which they are interested, and to semantically annotate COKE instances w.r.t. ontology concepts. The framework has been designed on two levels. Each organization can define its own UO covering the domains of interest for the organization. Moreover, the COKE ontologies aim at representing a "consensus" in defining a structure for several sources of unstructured knowledge (e.g., knowledge objects). This unified view helps managing and sharing both structured and unstructured knowledge.

The second layer represents the part of the framework which fosters the creation of new organizational knowledge since it allows users to specialize in aspects generally covered by the UO. This can be done collaboratively through WOs. Workspace Ontologies allow participants of the same group to adopt the same terminology for describing knowledge of interest. This way, aspects of a particular knowledge domain (covered by a workspace) emerge and are defined on a collaborative basis. To enable more flexibility, the framework also allows individuals to define their own ontologies. Through *Personal Ontologies*, an individual can manage its personal knowledge according to their view on a particular knowledge domain.

A very prominent feature of the defined framework is the *Annotations* mechanism. Annotations allow users to associate COKE instances to ontology concepts. They capture and harness the semantic meaning of a piece of knowledge that can be a Knowledge Object, a Service, and so forth. This feature is very striking since today the main issue related to the retrieval of information comes from the fact that information is for the most part unstructured. The framework allows users to capture and/or update implicit knowledge connected with explicit knowledge contained in unstructured content of COKE instances.

On the other side, the P2P computing paradigm has been shown to be a valuable support for today's IKWs that often work away from their usual workplace. In particular, this chapter describes how the P2P can be exploited to implement a distributed VO whose aim is to support collaborative work within *workspaces*. Within workspaces peers can autonomously manage and share knowledge without relying on any central entity thanks to a hybrid content consistency protocol that guarantees consistency of shared contents and synchronization among peers.

The combination of the two abovementioned technologies (ontologies and P2P) allows users to implement the distributed knowledge management model that naturally fits the process of creating new knowledge by allowing IKWs, on the one side to manage their knowledge without relying on any imposed schema and on the other side to exchange and retrieve knowledge on a semantic basis by exploiting ontologies.

REFERENCES

Agosti, M., Crestani, F., Gradenigo, G., &Mattiello, P. (1990). *An approach to conceptual modeling of IR auxiliary data.* Paper presented at the IEEE International Conference on Computer and Communications. Scottsdale, Arizona, USA.

Becerra-Fernandez, I., & Sabherwal, R. (2001). Organizational knowledge management: A contingency perspective. *Journal of Management Information Systems, 18* (1), 23-55.

Bonifacio, M., Bouquet, P., Mameli, G., & Nori, M. (2002). *KEEx: A Peer-to-Peer Solution for Distributed Knowledge Management.* Paper presented at the 4th International Conference on

Practical Aspects of Knowledge Management (PAKM 02), Wien, Austria.

Castelles, P., Fernández, M,, & Vallet, D. (2007). An adaptation of the vector space model for ontology-based information retrieval. IEEE Transaction on Knowledge and data Engineering (TKDE). *Journal of Management Information Systems, 19*(2), 261-272.

Chen, X., Ren, S., Wang, H., & Zhang, X. (2005). *SCOPE: scalable consistency maintenance in structured P2P systems*. Paper presented at the 6th IEEE Computer and Communications Societies Conference (INFOCOM 2005), Miami, USA, Vol. 10, pp.79–93

Datta, A., Hauswirth, M., & Aberer, K. (2003). *Updates in highly unreliable, replicated peer-to-peer systems*. Paper presented at the IEEE International Conference on Distributed Computing Systems (ICDCS '03), Providence, RI, USA, pp.76-88.

Ehrig, M., Tempich, C., Broekstra, J., Van Harmelen, F., Sabou, M., Siebes, R., Staab, S., & Stuckenschmidt, H. (2003). *SWAP: Ontology-based Knowledge Management with Peer-to-Peer Technology*. Paper presented at the 1st German Workshop on Ontology-based Knowledge Management (WOW 2003), Luzerne, Switzerland (2003).

Fensel, D. (2001). *Ontologies: Silver Bullet for Knowledge Management and Electronic Commerce*. Springer-Verlag, Berlin, Germany, 2001.

Ge, Y., Yu, Y., Zhu, X., Huang, S., & Xu, M. (2003). OntoVote: a scalable distributed vote-collecting mechanism for ontology drift on a P2P platform. *The Knowledge Engineering Review*, 18(3), 257-263.

Specifications Gruber Thomas R. A. (1993). Translation Approach to Portable Ontology. *Knowledge Acquisition* (5) 199-220.

Guha, R. V., McCool, R., & Miller, E. (2003). *Semantic search*. Paper presented at the 12th International World Wide Web Conference (WWW 2003), Budapest, Hungary, pp.700-709.

Järvelin, K., Kekäläinen, J., & Niemi, T. (2001). Expansiontool: Concept-based *query* expansion and construction. *Information Retrieval 4*(3-4), 231-255.

Lamport, L (1979). *How to Make a Multiprocessor Computer that Correctly Executes Multiprocess Programs*, IEEE Transactions on Computers, Vol. C-28(9).

Lave, S., & Wenger, E. (1991). *Situated learning: Legitimate peripheral learning*. Oxford University Press.

Le Coche, E., Mastroianni, C., Pirrò, G., Ruffolo, M., & Talia, D. (2006). *A Peer-to-Peer Virtual Office for Organizational Knowledge Management*. Paper presented at the 6th International Conference on Practical Aspects of Knowledge Management (PAKM 06), Wien, Austria.

Maier, D., & Delcambre, M. L.(1999) *Superimposed Information for the Internet*. Paper presented at the ACM SIGMOD Workshop on The Web and Databases (WebDB 1999), Philadelphia, Pennsylvania, USA (1999).

Marshak, D. S. (2004). *Groove virtual office enabling our new modes of work*. Report by Patricia Seybold Group, http://www.groove.net/pdf/backgrounder/GV0-Marshak.pdf

Mastroianni, C., Pirrò, G., & Talia, D. (2007). *Data Consistency in a P2P Knowledge Management Platform*. Paper presented at the 2nd HPDC Workshop on the Use of P2P, GRID and Agents for the Development of Content Networks (UPGRADE-CN 07), Monterey Bay, California, USA.

Nonaka I (1994). A Dynamic Theory of Organizational Knowledge Creation. *Organization Science*, 5, (1994).

Nonaka, I., & Takeuchi, H. (1995). *The Knowledge-Creating Company: How Japanese Companies Create the Dynamics of Innovation*. Oxford University Press, New York, USA, 1995.

Polanyi, M. (1966), *The tacit dimension*, Routledge & Kegan Paul, London, 1966.

Polanyi M. (1997), *Tacit Knowledge*. Chapter 7 in Knowledge in Organizations, Laurence Prusak, (Ed.),Butterworth-Heinemann, Boston, 1997.

Popov, B., Kiryakov, A., Kirilov, A., Manov, D., Ognyanoff, D., & Goranov, M. (2003). *KIM--Semantic Annotation Platform*. Paper presented at the 2nd International Semantic Web Conference (ISWC 03) (pp. 834-849) Sanibel Island, Florida, USA.

Prud'hommeaux, E., & Seaborne, A. (2006). *SPARQL Query Language for RDF*. W3C Working Draft (2006), http://www.w3.org/TR/rdfsparql-query

Seaborne, A. (2004). *RDQL - A Query Language for RDF*. W3C Working Draft (2004), http://www.w3.org/Submission/2004/SUBM-RDQL-20040109/

Simon, H.A. (1972). Theories of bounded rationality. In McGuire, C.B. e Radner R. (Eds.), Decision and organization: A volume in honor of Jacob Marschak (Chapter. 8), Amsterdam, Olanda, 1972.

Taylor, F.W. (1911), *The Principles of Scientific Management*, Harper & Row, New York, USA, 1911.

Vallet, D., Fernández, M., & Castells, P. (2005). *An Ontology-Based Information Retrieval Model*. Paper presented at the 2nd European Semantic Web Conference (ESWC 2005), Heraklion, Greece, pp.455-470.

Wang, Z., Kumar, M., Das, S. K., & Shen, H. (2006). *File Consistency Maintenance Through Virtual Servers in P2P Systems*. Paper presented at the 6th IEEE Symposium on Computers and Communications (ISCC 06), Pula-Cagliari, Italy, pp.435-441.

Chapter XIII
Formalizing and Leveraging Domain Knowledge in the K4CARE Home Care Platform

Ákos Hajnal
Computer and Automation Research Institute of the Hungarian Academy of Sciences, Hungary

Antonio Moreno
University Rovira i Virgili, Spain

Gianfranco Pedone
Computer and Automation Research Institute of the Hungarian Academy of Sciences, Hungary

David Riaño
University Rovira i Virgili, Spain

László Zsolt Varga
Computer and Automation Research Institute of the Hungarian Academy of Sciences, Hungary

ABSTRACT

This chapter proposes an agent-based architecture for home care support, whose main capability is to continuously admit and apply new medical knowledge entered into the system, capturing and codifying implicit knowledge deriving from the medical staff. Knowledge is the fundamental catalyst in all application domains, and this is particularly true especially for the medical context. Knowledge formalization, representation, exploitation, creation, and sharing are some of the most complex issues related to Knowledge Management. Moreover, Artificial Intelligence techniques and MAS (Multi-Agent System) in health care are increasingly justifying the large demand for their application, since traditional techniques are often not suitable to manage complex tasks or to adapt to unexpected events. The chapter presents also a methodology for approaching medical knowledge management from its representation symbolism to the implementation details. The codification of health care treatments, as well as the formalization of domain knowledge, serves as an explicit, a priori asset for the agent platform implementation. The system has the capability of applying new, implicit knowledge emerging from physicians.

INTRODUCTION

The work presented in this chapter is part of the K4CARE[a] (Knowledge for Care) European project, whose aim is, among the others, to provide a *Home Care Model*, and develop a prototype system based on Web technology and intelligent agents. The percentage of old and chronically ill people in European countries is putting very heavy economic and social pressure on all national health care systems. This problem can be somehow enlightened if home care services are improved and used as a valid alternative to hospitalization. In the context of the *K4CARE* project, we are targeting a software engineering method that automates the development of an agent platform for this knowledge-intensive application. The intended solution has two basic features. On the

Figure 1. Knowledge-driven architecture of the home care platform

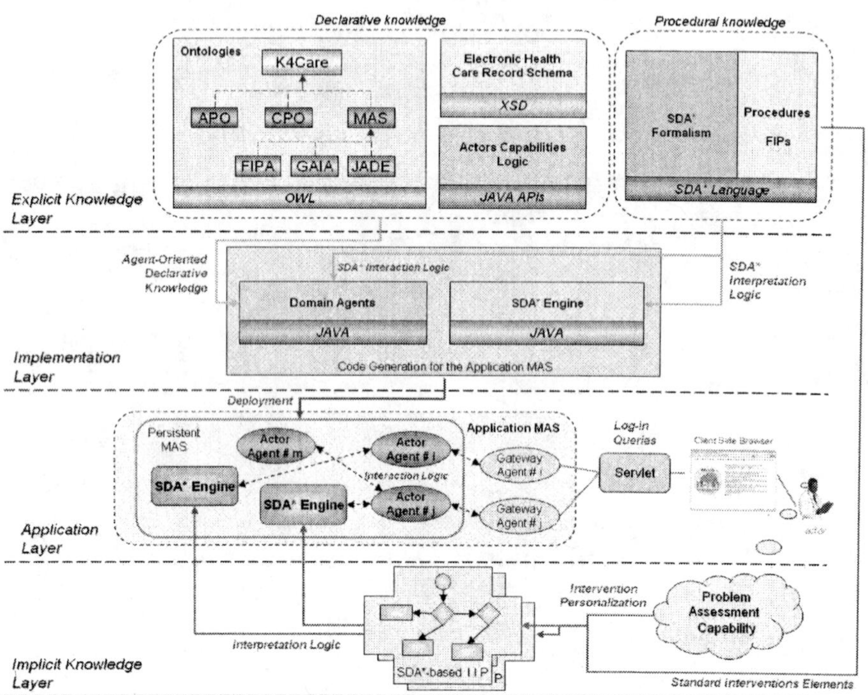

one hand, actors are members of well defined organizations. On the other hand, there is extensive domain knowledge to be considered.

Developing software for medical applications, in particular for home care, is special, since the software needs to incorporate complex and sometimes intuitive knowledge present in the mind of the medical staff. Moreover, the medical staff is organized into a well-structured model, where roles and responsibilities of each participant are well-defined. The most relevant aspect of our architecture is the separation of knowledge description from software implementation, granting a high level of interoperability and independence among elements of the system. Key elements of the architecture are shown in Figure 1 and will be described in details throughout this chapter.

The declarative and procedural knowledge form the *Explicit Knowledge Layer*, where domain entities and actor capabilities can be formally described. Agent-oriented code generation is the core function of the *Implementation Layer*. The deployment of agents and the end-user involvements are illustrated in the *Application Layer*. The *Implicit Knowledge Layer* embeds the capability of the architecture to capture implicit knowledge. This is the functional point where new medical knowledge is tacitly created and formalized by a proper description mechanism.

The agent paradigm advances the modeling of software systems by embodying a stronger notion of autonomy and control than objects, including the notion of reactive, proactive, and social behaviors, as well as assuming inherent multi-threaded control. This allows handling the complexity by powerful abstractions in engineering software systems. In order to be able to build complex and reliable systems, we need not only new models and technologies, but also an appropriate set of software engineering abstractions that can be used as a reference for system analysis, and as the basis for methodologies that enable developers to engineer software systems in a robust, reliable, and repeatable fashion.

The result of our investigations is an architecture driven by the knowledge, which is able to generate agent code from ontology and codified treatments. Moreover, the architecture enables the creation, valorization and embedment of new medical knowledge (referred to as *implicit knowledge*).

THE ACTUAL HOME CARE

In e-health it is increasingly necessary to develop tele-informatic applications to support people involved in providing basic medical care (physicians, nurses, patients, relatives, and citizens in general). The care of chronic and disabled patients involves lifelong treatments under continuous expert supervision. Moreover, healthcare workers and patients accept that being cared for in hospitals or residential facilities may be unnecessary and even counterproductive. From a global view, such patients may saturate national health services and increase health-related costs. The debate over the crisis of financing healthcare is open and is a basic political issue for old and new EU member countries and could hinder European convergence.

To face these challenges we can differentiate medical assistance in health centers from assistance in a ubiquitous way (Home Care - HC); the latter can undoubtedly benefit from the introduction of ICT. The main objective of the K4CARE project is to improve the capabilities of the new EU society to manage and respond to the needs of the increasing number of senior population requiring a personalized HC assistance.[b] In HC context there are many important factors that must be taken into account when approaching any kind of technological support:

- the need for standardization in the Sanitary Model and its ICT implementation;
- the necessary integration of different data types (e.g., text, numerical values, multi-

media parts) and documents coming from different sources (e.g., hospital services, laboratories, consultations, specialists, relatives, and patients at home);
- the integration of information coming from different countries;
- home access to clinical data stored in hospitals;
- long-term care treatments;
- the participation of non-medical staff in the care model;
- critical actors of the HC model (patients) are usually not confident with technology.

In addition to the previous ones, there are explicit technological objectives deriving from the definition of the K4CARE project, such as the work proposed in this chapter, indeed.

HOME CARE AND K4CARE

HC has been considered as a fundamental component of a network of long term care facilities (paralleled by rehabilitation units, nursing facilities), capable of reducing institutionalization, expenses and risk of death. HC is multidimensional and multidisciplinary in its nature; it is conceived as the integration of medical, social, and familiar resources addressed to the same goal of allowing the care of the patient in his own environment. Preventive home visitation programs appear to be effective (Adams, 1993), reduce mortality and admission to long term institutional care (Blair, 2001), have a significant impact on hospitalization and are cost-effective (Bernabei, 1999). Normative treatment guidelines (GLs) can provide the mechanism to link patient outcomes to the supplied care and improve quality without increasing costs (Balasubramani, 2006). However, few GLs have been developed for the homecare setting. Existing GLs for congestive heart failure, diabetes, chronic obstructive pulmonary disease, falls, osteoarthritis, depression, and medication management should be modified to be applicable in homecare (Peterson, 2004). Special issues in generating and modifying GLs in home care patients are represented by co-morbidity (several GLs have to be applied simultaneously) and reliability of GLs related to elderly patients (Gross, 1992).

According to Mary E. Tinetti,[c] *"the changed spectrum of health conditions, the complex interplay of biological and non-biological factors, the aging population, and the inter-individual variability in health priorities render medical care that is centered primarily on the diagnosis and treatment of individual diseases at best out of date and at worst harmful."*

A primary focus on disease, given the changed health needs of patients, inadvertently leads to under-treatment, over-treatment, or mistreatment. The need to ascertain and incorporate individual priorities, to address multiple contributing factors simultaneously, and to prescribe and monitor multifaceted interventions will make clinical decision making more iterative, interactive, individualized, and complex. Creative use of information technologies should facilitate the organization, presentation, and integration of this information to arrive at individualized yet systematic clinical decision making predicated on individual patient priorities.

Since no medical act can be properly performed without reliable information, appropriate sharing of patient information and patient monitoring are basic pre-requisites in delivering effective continuous care in home care facilities. The way the information system is set up in a care facility, and in particular the flow of communication, is a near replica of how the facility itself is organized; the single doctor-single patient nexus has been largely superseded in HC by a regime in which the typical patient is managed by a team of caregivers, each specializing in one aspect of care. The different nature of care sources needs to be integrated not only in terms of action (delivery of services), but also in terms of information sharing as well. In that sense, more than focusing on single pathologies,

K4CARE focuses on the patients. Information technology can thus facilitate provider practice redesign, including proactive outreach to patients, and greater involvement of non-physician health professionals. In the technological setting, the project's main contributions are:

- a proposal of an Electronic Health Care Record (the electronic and standardized form of all patient cares) for Home Care Patients;
- the production, integration, and use of 'know-what' and 'know-how' knowledge;
- all technologies required personalizing this knowledge to the professional and the patient involved in HC.

The K4CARE project is formulated under the frame of European and International standards: CEN/TC251,[d] ISO/TC215, and ASTM E31,[e] and HL7;[f] even though nowadays there is not a unified view of how to store or exchange healthcare information electronically. So, ASTM E31 is involved in the continuous development of standards for the architecture, content, storage, security, confidentiality, functionality, and communication of information, whilst HL7 is mainly concerned with protocol specifications for application level communications among health data acquisition, processing and handling systems. A model will be generated following already accepted standard recommendations (e.g., EuroRec,[g] OpenEHR[h]), languages (e.g., ACL), and terminology (e.g., OpenGALEN,[i] UMLS,[j] and SNOMED[k]) in combination with ontologies for describing both actor profiles and home care patient conditions and diseases. OWL will be taken as the ontology representation language.

With regard to the existence of realizations similar to K4CARE project we have to report that neither open source nor proprietary products are actually available in literature for the purpose of HC treatment support.

MEDICAL PROCEDURES AND TREATMENT GUIDELINES

Representation of clinical practice guidelines is a critical issue for computer-based guideline development, implementation, and evaluation. We studied eight types of computer-based guideline models. Typical primitives for these models include decisions, actions, patient states, and execution states. We also find temporal constraints and nesting to be important aspects of guideline structure representation. Integration of guidelines with electronic medical records is facilitated by the introduction of formal models of patient data. Patient states and execution states are closely related to one another. Interrelationship among data collection, decisions, patient states and interventions in a guideline's logic flow varies in different guideline representation models.

Procedures guiding health care practices are rigorously defined in HC by the different involved institutions (administrations, health system, care providers, families, social associations, etc.). Clinical Practice GLs are documents with evidence-based statements to assist clinicians to make appropriate healthcare decisions. GLs are developed to reduce inappropriate variations in practice, to improve health care quality, and to help control costs (IM, 1992). Although the importance of guidelines is widely recognized, health care organizations typically pay more attention to guideline development than to guideline implementation for routine use in clinical settings (Audet, 1990), evidently hoping that clinicians will simply familiarize themselves with written guidelines and then apply them appropriately during the care of patients. Studies have shown that computer-based clinical decision support systems can improve clinician performance and patient outcomes (Haynes, 1994).

Guideline-based clinical decision support systems have been proposed for this purpose (Audet, 1990; Hammond, 1994; McDonald, 1994;

Overhage, 1995). To implement guidelines within a computer-based clinical decision support system, guideline representation is a critical issue. A formal model for guideline representation will provide in-depth understanding of the clinical care processes addressed by guidelines, and thus will lead to (a) more rigorous methods of guideline development (for example, verification of a guideline's logical completeness and detection of ambiguity, inconsistency and redundancy (Fagan, 1987; Greenes, 1994), (b) more robust approaches for guideline implementation (for example, integration of guidelines with clinical workflow and improvements in guideline maintenance (Overhage, 1996; Zielstorff, 1998), and (c) more effective techniques for guideline evaluation (e.g., identification of variations in knowledge organization by different clinicians and resulting effects on their requirements for assistance during the process of decision making (Arocha, 2001). The concept **Computer-Interpretable Guideline** (CIG) was coined to describe GLs represented in such a form that computers can use them (not a trivial task at all). CIGs are described with languages such as PROforma (Earle, 2006), Asbru (Johnson, 1998), GLIF (Barnett, 1998), EON (Das, 1996), Arden Syntax (Hripcsak, 1994), GUIDE (Cavallini, 2000), and PRODIGY (Booth, 1997). These are languages developed by the most relevant research groups in the area: partners of the project PROTOCURE II,[1] Open Clinical organization, Stanford University School of Medicine, Harvard Medical School, and Columbia University.

METHODOLOGICAL GUIDELINES

A well-accepted approach to engineer object oriented software systems is the MDA (Model Driven Architecture), (OMG, 2001) that provides a new way of writing specifications based on a high-level platform-independent model. The complete MDA specification consists of a base UML model, platform-specific models and interface definition sets, each describing how the base model is implemented on different target platforms. In literature there are several AOSE (Agent-Oriented Software Engineering) methodologies; however they do not contain the transformations from high level models to platform-specific models in the way as the MDA approach. In this chapter we focus on the importance of the knowledge asset in providing support to home care, and particularly, on its role in different phases of the system development. We are moreover advancing agent oriented software engineering methods by applying an MDA style approach to the engineering of the agent platform of the K4CARE project.

There are two main differences from MDA. First, the high level description is completely knowledge-based compared to the object oriented model of MDA. Second, the target is a platform concerning the agent paradigm. These advancements are perceived as a considerable support when implementing software for a knowledge intensive application. MDA is mainly based on UML, which is basically a notation language and does not dedicate enough extensions to behavioral aspects (dynamism) of runtime interactions. In the actual state of the art of agent technology, there is still a lack of well-established Agent-Oriented Software Engineering (Giorgini, 2005) methodologies to support the transformation of system description to deployable agent system. Several AOSE methodologies have been proposed: (Cossentino, 2005; Dardenne, 1993; Fuentes, 2005; Fuxman, 2004).

A formal modeling technique has been provided in the K4CARE project by the GAIA methodology (Jennings, 2000), whose approach focuses on the *human organization* metaphor, which seems to be the most appropriate for highly populated domains (Demazeau, 1996; Jennings, 2001) with a required reliable behavior. Important aspects from the methodology have to be pointed out:

- *GAIA does not directly deal with particular modeling techniques.* It proposes, but does not commit to, specific techniques for modeling (e.g., roles, environment, interactions);
- *GAIA does not directly deal with implementation issues.* The result of GAIA exploitation is a detailed but technology-neutral specification that should be implemented using an appropriate agent-programming framework;
- GAIA does not explicitly deal with the activities of requirements capturing and modeling, and specifically of early requirements engineering, but it can fit and be easily integrated with modern goal-oriented approaches to requirements engineering whose abstractions closely match those of agent-oriented computing.

MASs are necessary infrastructures that support agent deployment. In this project we use JADE (Bellifemine, 1999), which is a FIPA™ compliant middleware for development of agent-based applications. In this context of methodological uncertainty, an important support can derive from the use of ontologies at modeling-time. In this chapter, we develop a complete agent-based system for the home care domain, valorizing all knowledge coming from different ontological sources, such as a domain model, project requirements, implementation standards (GAIA methodology, FIPA), and technological issues (JADE), and from medical procedure representations.

Instead of separately using an AOSE methodology to model the MAS and consequently developing the inherent code, we merged the two aspects by conceptualizing all inherent elements into ontologies and interpretable documents, and then generating the deployable agent code. Others in the literature (Battle, 2004; Eberhart, 2002) have demonstrated that the problem of deriving code from an ontology is not a trivial task because of different factors: the *higher semantics* of the OWL language in comparison with programming languages (like JAVA); the *complexity of domain* representation, the relations and knowledge contained, and the *runtime code dependencies* that must be captured and included in the automation. We can highlight key elements of the chapter as follows:

1. A general methodology is proposed in modeling an organizational domain, capturing and classifying all the explicit application knowledge, categorized into two main classes: declarative (identifying the system compositional elements) and procedural (capturing the behavioral logic governing the system).
2. The possibility to introduce ontological inference and deduction in validating the architectural model is provided.
3. The system has capability to capture the implicit knowledge deriving from physicians. The behavioral skills of agents are orchestrated by the interaction artifacts. Implicit knowledge (as well as the procedural one) is codified through elementary entities (states, decisions, actions), whose interpretation permits to capture knowledge manifested by physicians at runtime.
4. Automation in the generation of the agent-oriented code.

K4CARE MODEL DESCRIPTION

In order to better perceive the effort and the contextual background of our work we report in this section a more detailed description of the K4CARE **Home Care Model** (K4CARE Model) (Annicchiarico, 2006).

This model is the result of the analysis of several health care national systems in European Countries that was performed by the medical doctors participating in the K4CARE project (see the acknowledgments section for a complete list). In different European countries, and in different areas of the same countries, HC is structured in different ways, according to local rules, laws, and funding. The different prototypes reflect different approaches to HC, particularly referring to the kind of services provided, human resources organization and dependences.

The K4CARE Model offers a paradigm easily adoptable in any of the EU countries to project an efficient model of HC. The model proposes K4CARE services distributed by local health units and integrated with the social services of municipalities, and eventual other organizations of care or social support. It is aimed at providing the patient with the necessary sanitary and social support to be treated at home; in these terms, it is easily adaptable to those socio-sanitary systems which provide the so called "unique access" for both social and sanitary services, unifying and simplifying procedures of admission to the services.

This could represent an incentive and facilitate the shift towards such an approach. To accomplish this duty, the K4CARE Model is designed given priority to the support of the HCP (Home Care Patient), his relatives and FD (Family Doctors) as well. Because of the aim of providing a model which can be proposed as European standard, the K4CARE project recommends a *modular structure* that can be adapted to different local opportunities and needs.

The success of this model is directly related to the levels of *efficacy, effectiveness, and best practice* of the health-care services the model is able to support.

K4CARE Model is based on a nuclear structure called HCNS (Home Care Nuclear Structure) (Figure 2), which comprises the minimum number of common elements needed to provide a basic HC service. The HCNS can be extended with an optional number of accessory services that can be modularly added to the nuclear structure.

These services will respond to specialized cares, specific needs, opportunities and means, of

Figure 2. The K4CARE model architecture for HC

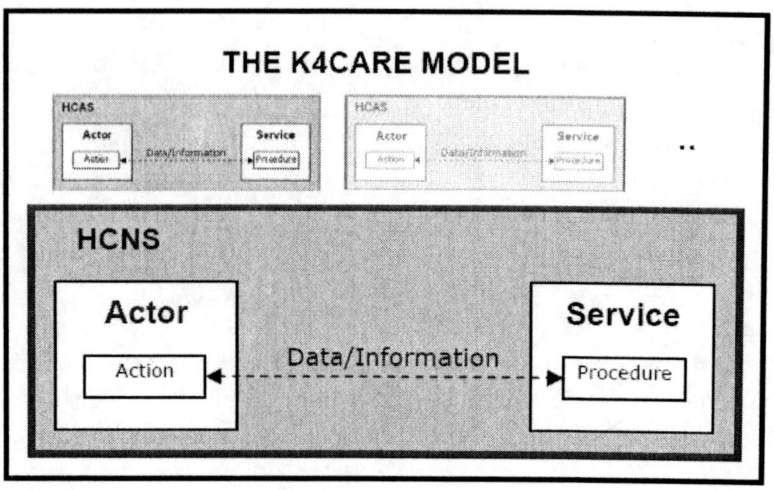

either the users of the K4Care Model or the healthcare community where the model is applied.

Going into detail, each of the HC structures consists of the same components--actors, actions, services, procedures, and documents.

Actors

In HC, there are several people interacting including patients, relatives, physicians, social assistants, nurses, rehabilitation professionals, informal care givers, citizens, social organisms, and so forth. In the HCNS, these individuals are the members of three different *groups of HC actors*.

These groups are the *patient*, the *stable members* of HCNS (the family doctor, the physician in charge of HC, the head nurse, the nurse, the social worker, and each of those defined in the HCNS), the *additional care givers* (the specialist physician, the social operator, the continuous care provider, and the informal care giver).

The family doctor, the physician in charge of HC, the head nurse, and the social worker join in a temporary structure--the Evaluation Unit--devoted to assess the patient's problems and needs.

Professional Actions and Liabilities

They represent the general actions that each of the actors in the K4Care Model performs in his duties within the HCNS service. Two lists of actions are provided for each sort of patient--the list of general actions, and the list of HCNS actions.

The list of general actions is intended to contain all the actions that actors are expected to perform in a general purpose Home Care System.

The list of HCNS actions are complementary specific actions defined for the actors involved in the HCNS. We have grouped HCNS actions as reported in Table 1.

The same action classification has been followed in the representation and definition of the K4CARE declarative knowledge.

Services

The K4Care Model provides a set of services for the care of HCP. These services are classified into *Access services*, *Patient Care services*, and *Information services*. *Access services* see the HCNS actors as elements of the K4Care Model and they address issues like patient's admission

Table 1. Professional actions and liabilities codification

P. Xx	Patient Actions
BO.xx	Back Office Actions
EU.xx	Evaluation Unit Actions
M.xx	Medical Actions
M.FM.xx	Medical Actions performed by the Family Doctor
M.SP.xx	Medical Actions performed by the Specialist Physician
N.xx	Nursing Actions
CM.xx	Case Management Actions
S.xx	Social Actions

and discharge from the HC model. *Patient Care services* are the most complex services of the HC model by considering all the levels of care of the patient as part of the HCNS. Finally, *Information services* cover the needs of information that the HCNS actors require in the K4Care Model. The chain of events that lead an actor in performing actions to provide services are called procedures and.

Information Documents

The HCNS of the K4Care Model defines a set of information units whose main purpose is to provide information about the care processes realized by the actors to accomplish a service.

Different kinds of actors are supplied with specific information that will help them to carry out their duties in the model. All these data are considered here to be part of documents, which can be classified into Documents in Access Services and Patient Care Services (These ones subdivided into *common documents*, which are used in different services, and *service specific documents*, which are specific for a definite service).

EXPLICIT KNOWLEDGE MANAGEMENT IN K4CARE

This section presents the classification of the explicit knowledge that can be formally described in the platform. First, we introduce the declarative knowledge of the Home Care domain, and then we describe how procedural knowledge can be formalized.

Declarative Knowledge

In Artificial Intelligence *ontologies* are a standard knowledge representation mechanism (Fensel, 2001). In K4CARE, they are the catalysts for the agent behavioral model as well as for the agent code generation.

We have divided *application ontologies* into different sources in relation to their application coherence. K4CARE ontologies represent the semantic description of the Multi-agent System and are described in OWL and have been developed by using the Protégé semantic tool (Crubezy, 2001). They have been classified as follows:

- **Domain ontology.** It represents the semantic domain description for HC. It is divided into APO (Actor Profile Ontology) and patient-CPO (Case Profile Ontology). APO represents the profiles of the subjects and contains their capabilities (skills, in terms of actions), services that can be initiated by them, document involved in the provision of a specific service, and so on. A simplified illustration of the APO is reported in Figure 3, in which the conceptualization of "*BO.01.ProvideInformation*" domain action is highlighted. CPO represents the relevant medical concepts (left part in Figure 4-- "*MO8.01.AlzheimerType*" disease). Domain ontology describes "know-what" knowledge about actors and pathologies.
- **FIPA ontology**. It is the general conceptualization of FIPA standards related with MAS development. It represents "know-what" knowledge of the MAS and "know-how" knowledge of interactions.
- **GAIA ontology**. It includes the description of the adopted MAS AOSE development methodology.
- **JADE ontology**. It expresses the implementation concepts complying with JADE. This ontology, together with the FIPA and the GAIA ontology, is part of higher level embodying ontology, which is called MAS Ontology (right part in Figure 4).
- **K4CARE ontology.** This ontology models the cross-ontology references. Agent capabilities, for example, are expressed in terms of "actions" in the APO; these are considered as "responsibilities" or "permissions"

Figure 3. APO partial representation in Protégé

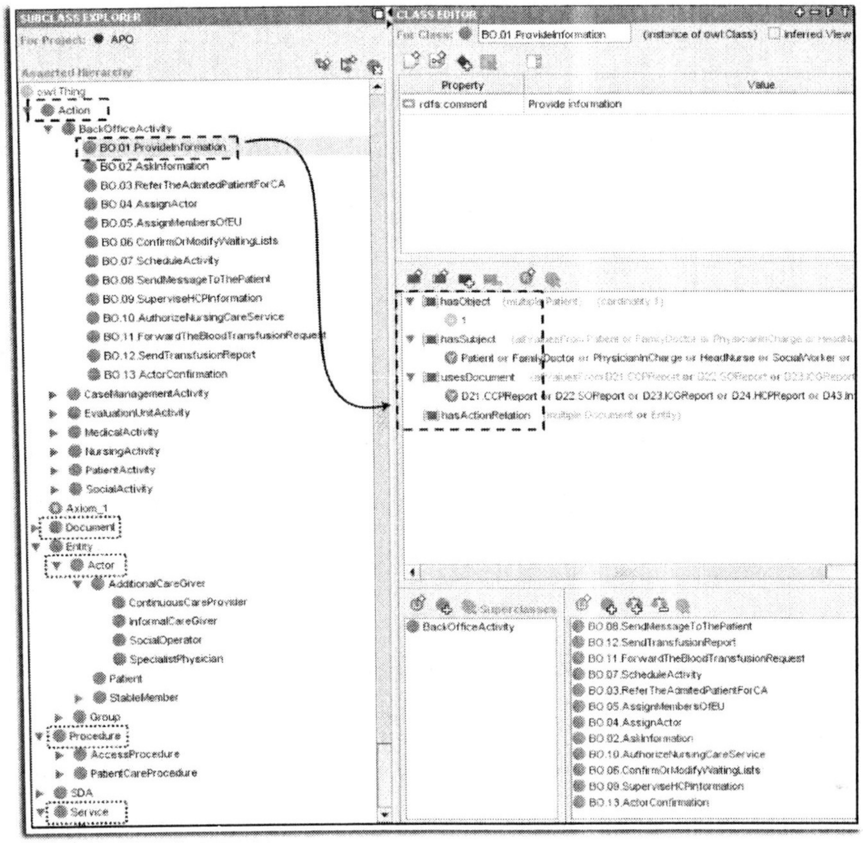

by GAIA; the behavioral logic of an agent inherent to its capabilities is expressed in JADE by "behaviors," which can contain FIPA compliant "interaction protocols."

Electronic Health Care Record represents a scheme of the patient care profile. Besides the document data, the EHCR have to store intervention plans: FIPs (Formal Intervention Plans) and IIPs (Individual Intervention Plans).

Actor Capabilities are defined by basic actions representing permanent capabilities of agents.

Procedural Knowledge

Procedural knowledge is applied in two different areas in home care:

- ***Procedures***, which are descriptions of services provided by the platform. In the K4Care Model a *procedure* represents *the way capabilities (basic actions) provided by/to the actors are combined together in order* to accomplish a service. An example of service procedure in terms of actors'

Figure 4. (From left to right) CPO and MAS ontology partial representation in Protégé

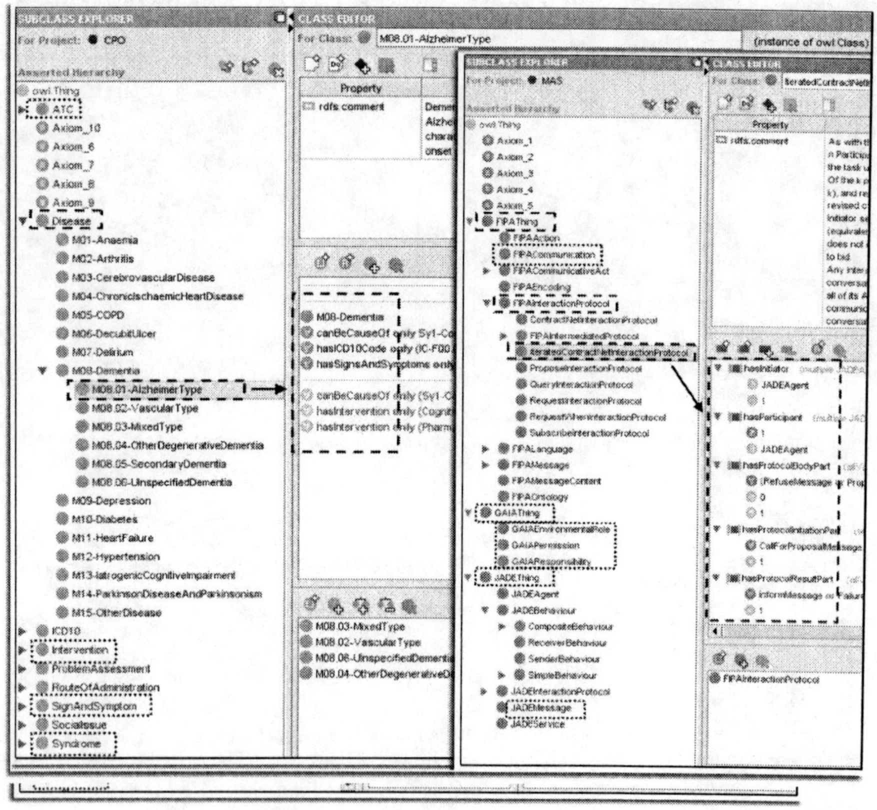

basic actions is reported in Table 2 for the "Follow-up" service;

- ***Formal Intervention Plans***, which are general descriptions of the way in which a particular pathology should be treated. This kind of intervention plan is immutable for a long time and belongs to a group of diseases, syndromes or symptoms. FIPs are usually not stored in the repository, as they are not connected to any patient. In case FIPs are stored, they may be associated to diseases, syndromes and even symptoms, described by codes proposed by medical partners.

Procedures relate to general services provided by the platform, such as patient admission. Formal intervention plans are the typical treatment procedures for specific pathologies. Both kinds of descriptions are expressed using a flowchart-based representation called SDA* Language (Riaño, 2007). SDA stands for State-Decision-Action (formalism's elementary entities). SDA* represents the repetition of States-Decisions-Actions in order to describe a FIP.

In the SDA* Language (or simply SDA*) model, *states* are used to describe patient conditions, situations, or statuses that deserve a particular

Table 2. Follow-up service procedure actions list

S3.9. Follow-up	Action		Document	
(a) The evolution of clinical and functional status of HCP is assessed according to scheduled controls and/or in case of emerging medical and social issues by the FD, SW, Nu.	EU.4	schedule controls	D26	IP
(b) The HN sends messages to the patient to make appointments.	BO.8	send message to the patient	D5	Message to the Patient
(c) The patient confirms the appointments.	P.1	confirm appointment	D6	Patient Confirmation
(d) The FD monitors parameters indicating health status and overall condition of the patient through evaluation scales, Clinical Assessment, Physical Examination, Request of Diagnostic Examination, Request of Laboratory Analysis, Consultation.	EU.1	evaluate through scales	D11	MDE Scales
	M.1	perform Clinical Assessment	D12	Clinical history
	M.2	perform Physical Examination	D13	Physical Examination Report
	M.4	request Laboratory Analysis	D15	Request of Laboratory Analysis
	M.3	request Diagnostic Procedures	D14	Request of Diagnostic Examination
	M.9	refer to SP	D16	Request of Consultation
(e) The FD fills in the medical follow-up form.	M.10	write medical follow-up	D19	Medical follow-up form
(f) The FD refers the HCP to a SP when he/she needs specific contribution from different professionals to maintain the necessary care of the patient and in order to avoid unnecessary admissions to hospital.	M.9	refer to SP	D16	Request of Consultation
(g) The Nu fills in the Nursing follow-up form during the scheduled activities.	N.26	write Nursing follow-up	D20	Nursing follow-up form
(h) The SW evaluates periodically the patient's program for social assistance and may improve it.	S.1	assess social needs and network	D18	Social Report
(i) The SW periodically supervises and improves the care providers' group.	S.3	supervise achievement of social outcomes	D18	Social Report
	S.6	write social report	D18	Social Report
(j) Trained actors can use part of the Multi-Dimensional Evaluation (one or more scales) to define special issues.	EU.1	evaluate through scales	D11	MDE Scales
(k) Other care-givers (all the actors not specified here) could provide information about HCP status.	BO.1	provide information	D21	CCP Report
		provide information	D22	SO Report
	BO.3	provide information	D23	ICG Report
	BO.4	provide information	D24	HCP Report
(l) When intervening conditions substantially modify HCP's overall status, re-evaluations can be requested by the FD, apart from the re-evaluation defined inside the IP.	M.FD.2	request of re-evaluation	D25	Request of Extra re-evaluation
(m) The HN performs Case Management's proper actions.	BO.4	assign actor	D1	Actor Assignment
	BO.13	actor confirmation	D2	Actor Confirmation
	BO.6	confirm or modify waiting lists	D3	Waiting List
	BO.7	schedule activity	D4	Daily Schedule
	BO.8	send message to the patient	D5	Message to the Patient
	P.1	confirm appointment	D6	Patient Confirmation
	P.3	give consent	D7	Patient Consent
	P.3	give consent	D8	CCP Consent

course of actions totally or partially different from the actions followed when the patient is in other state.

It provides a response to the fact that a disease, ailment, pathology or syndrome can present alternative degrees of evolution whose treatment must be distinguished. *Decisions* in the SDA* model capture the capability of FIPs to choose alternative options depending on the available information about the patient, and therefore propose a unified representation of alternative courses of action that have to be applied to patients under different conditions.

Unlike state conditions, the conditions of a decision do not attend to the degree of evolution of the disease, but to the particular characteristics of the patient. *Actions* are the proper treatment steps of the FIP which are selected according to the preceding decisions. Treatments coded in SDA* are interpreted at runtime by a special agent called SDA* Engine Agent. It provides the system with a powerful and elegant flexibility in managing and executing medical treatments.

IMPLICIT KNOWLEDGE FORMALIZATION IN K4CARE

Knowledge Management relies on the evidence of knowledge. Nevertheless, there is a type of knowledge in the medical context that cannot be explicitly codified in permanent documents. It is because of the strict relation with physicians' capability to deduct and improvise treatment solutions.

This knowledge is part of the personal skills of an actor, and it is implicitly coupled with his/her mental ability in solving emerging problems. On one side, common problems with well-patterned treatments are comprised in FIPs; on the other side, they are usually not directly applicable in most cases because of the uniqueness of patient conditions.

In the K4CARE platform, new implicit medical knowledge is captured by defining new SDA*-based IIPs, which are descriptions of the specific treatment that has to be provided to a particular patient. This kind of intervention plan is valid only for the time of the treatment. It is created on demand and based on a FIP. It is attached to the EHCR of the patient, as previously introduced.

In practice, there are two possibilities for arranging a personalized treatment: combine different standard FIPs together, or model a brand new intervention plan, respectively.

Regardless of the approach, physicians will have to model a new IIP by representing it in terms of states, decisions and actions involved in the provision of the new care service.

UNDERSTANDING IIP: A BRIEF SCENARIO

In order to better understand the complexity and the variety of elements inherent a patient's home care treatment, we report in the following a brief scenario (Figure 5).

The most difficult aspect of the whole process is that of synthesizing medical and administrative knowledge expressed in natural language and contained in procedures and intervention plans into machine-interpretable elements.

IIP MODELING SUPPORT

At the time of writing this chapter, a graphical environment for supporting SDA*-based modeling is being developed in the project. Its relevant aspects are to assist physicians and to ease the management of intervention plans (definition, maintenance and combination). An example intervention plan is illustrated in Figure 6, in which the hypertension diagnosis and treatment are emphasized.

Considering that the dynamics of an IIP are subsequently mapped to agent actions (their capabilities described in the APO), the modeling tool also provides a semantic check during the intervention definition process. This guarantees both an early avoidance of both inconsistencies in the description of domain actors' role and critical events during the treatment provision. The SDA*-based IIP execution is provided by the SDA* Engine Agent. IIPs are stored in the system, but they are usually not reusable in other circumstances, since they are unique treatments. It is still possible to elect an IIP to a FIP (and consequently consider it as the part of knowledge base of the system).

Figure 5. Scenario for home care of an old patient. Based on information from (Annicchiarico, 2006)

Scenario: the homecare of an old patient.

A Family Doctor (FD) decides to refer an 83-year old male patient for HC, since the FD needs to implement services for an adequate care.

Admission: HC is required for the patient by the FD. The patient is admitted to HC services. The Evaluation Unit (EU) team is formed and performs the Comprehensive Assessment (CA), covering medical and social issues.

Case history: the patient has been discharged from hospital after two weeks were he was admitted for a hip fracture. He underwent a successful surgical intervention (prosthesis). During hospitalization, he got a sacral pressure ulcer. His diabetes is not going well, with frequent high glucose levels. He presented also anaemia. His cognition is quite preserved. His CCP is his wife, 80 years old.

An EU defines an ***Individual Intervention Plan*** (IIP) indicating interventions to be provided. The PC prescribes a mattress overlay (to ease the cure of present ulcers and prevent the occurrence of new ones) and supportive devices to help the patient to start walking. The FD decides to ask for a series of laboratory analysis to define parameters connected with the presence of ulcers, diabetes and anaemia. The Social Worker (SW) decides to contact the municipality social service for a Social Operator (SO) to help the patient's old wife to take care of the HCP and to help her with the housework. The HCP is referred to the Cardiologist for a consultation and to the Physiatrist for rehabilitation.

Some ***interventions are scheduled***:

- a nurse (Nu) three times a week for two hours for medications of a pressure ulcer and measurement of blood pressure and glycaemia; an extra time for blood collection;
- the FD once a week for the medical follow-up;
- a SO two hours a day, five day a week to help with the HCP and the house.

The EU decides that the HCP has to be re-evaluated after two months and, if the course of care will be satisfactory, an end-treatment re-evaluation will be performed at third month. The HCP and his wife agree with the IP. The Head Nurse (HN) schedules the activity, assigns the actors. When the actors confirm their agreement, the HN confirms the daily schedule.

Follow-up: Nu, FD, SO visit the HCP in due times, while the HN (as Case Manager) controls the evolution of activity. In occasion of home visits, the Nu, FD, and SO report their follow-up observations. A cardiologist makes the consultation and suggests some variations in the therapy: the FD agrees and authorizes such variations. The Physiatrist schedules a rehabilitation treatment, in charge of the Rehabilitation Service (HCAS).

Laboratory blood tests show that the patient is recovering, so the FD decides not to intervene with regards to anaemia and diabetes.

Two months after, the EU joins again for a CA: the patient is going well. The IIP is confirmed.

At three months the patient has started to walk again inside the flat; pressure ulcers are cured. The EU decides to prolong surveillance by the FD with a twice a month access; the EU asks the Physiatrist about an extension of rehabilitation and municipality about an extension of SO support. A new re-evaluation is fixed in two months.

Two months after, the EU joins again for the ***End Treatment Evaluation***: as to regards conditions related to possible HCNS services, the HCP is cured and doesn't need any further intervention.

AGENTS OF THE K4CARE MAS

We have modeled different key agent types in the MAS of the K4CARE architecture. They are reported in the following, by emphasizing their main characteristics and role.

Gateway Agent

Gateway Agents (GAs) are a special type of agents which have ability to communicate with the MAS and the servlet. They transform the messages that are sent by the servlet to agents and vice versa. They live temporarily, created when a user logs in and deleted when he/she logs out.

Figure 6. SDA*-based IIP--CSI's hypertension diagnosis and treatment

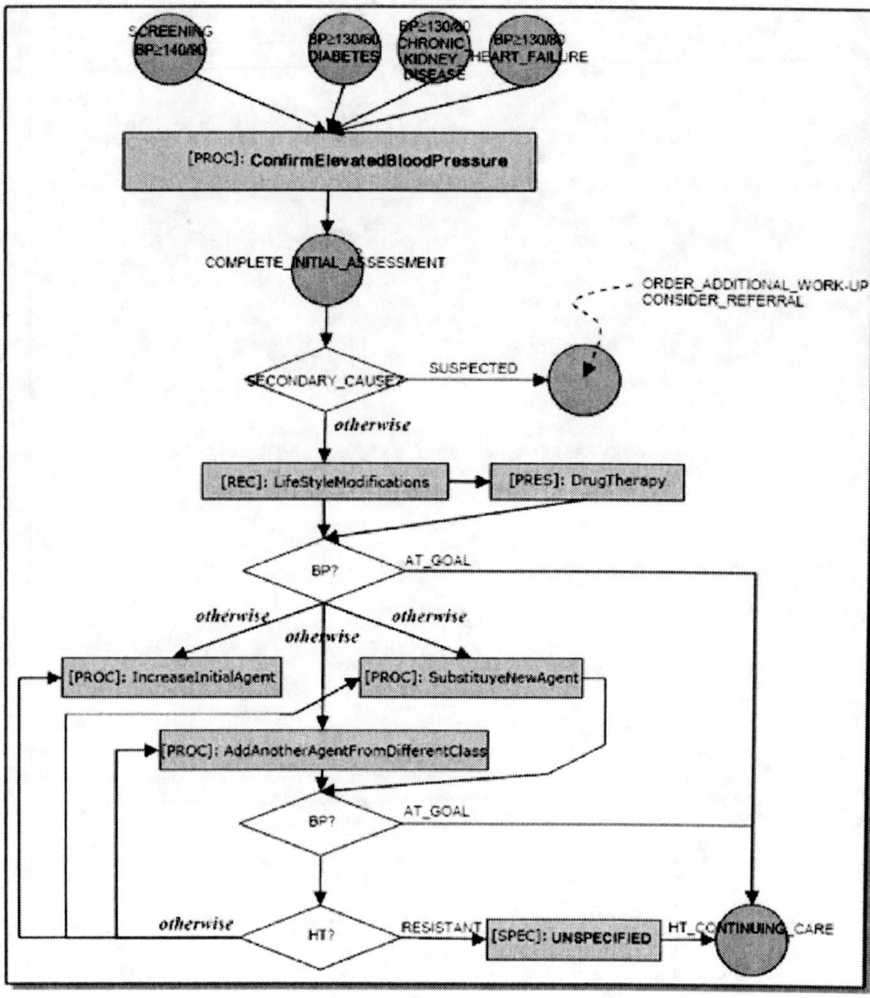

Personal Agent

Each actor in the home care model is represented by an individual (*personal* and *persistent*) agent in the platform. These agents run permanently and their states are regularly saved and restored at system restarts. An agent includes all the capabilities that the actor in the specific role (physician, nurse, patient) can perform. An agent is personal in the sense that it belongs to one actor, only.

Persistent refers to the agent characteristic to permanently run in the platform (independently of whether the user is logged in or not), as far as the actor is dismissed. Note that, due to implementation features (Java Runtime Environment), in an agent platform the executable code implementing an agent type is allocated only once, regardless of the number of agents of the same type; agents without active tasks do not consume redundant CPU time (suspended).

In addition to role-specific skills, all the agents have common behaviors to make the cooperation possible with other agents. Namely, agents can be orchestrated by SDA* Engine Agents to achieve a given goal requiring cooperate work. SDA* Engine Agents basically invoke specific actions of specific agents (according to the formal procedure or intervention plan description); however, in relation with fault-tolerant operation-sequences, agents support secure transactions. Agents are able to track different sessions, and rollback (undo) or commit the results of specific actions. Agents have also other common features that are not related to medical activities but are useful for the end-users. Such an example is a chat function that is used to allow actors sending messages among each other. Similarly, a useful agent behavior is to show the list of pending tasks (ordered by priority) to the logged-in user.

Since agents do not necessarily run permanently in the platform (option) due to performance issues, agents are able to save their status in a database (freeze, hibernate) before they are removed from the platform and recover their state when they start a useful agent ed again.

SDA* Engine Agent

The SDA* Engine Agent's goal is to separate the complex tasks of interpreting and managing medical guidelines from the other tasks assigned to Personal Agents, because these agents are not prepared to interpret and execute the SDA* medical guidelines formalism. This agent also uses a communication ontology to communicate to Persistent Agents the tasks derived from SDA* execution. All the agents interested in managing the SDA* structures (basically the agents interested in interpreting an Individual Intervention Plan or any procedure), will have to create a new SDA* Agent and using this communicative JADE-oriented ontology request him some tasks. In other words, SDA* Agent coordinates Personal Agent actions using the proper technological semantics.

This new dynamically created agent will manage and execute the SDA* structure and perform the related tasks with management and execution, relieving the invoker of these tasks. An example execution flow and message exchange within the system is described in the following, as well as a short description of the ontology used to communicate with the personal agents (numbers in the figure represent the actual step in the entire flow).

Figure 7 illustrates a possible SDA* action flow (acronyms in the picture: HN = Head Nurse agent, FD = Family Doctor agent; SW = Social Worker agent). The process starts when the Head Nurse (as the agent in charge of this execution) recovers the patient's IIP from the EHCR (step 1). After this, the execution of this IIP is started by a dynamically created SDA Agent (step 2), which is in charge of interpreting the SDA* structure, linked with the responsible HN. The latter will send action requests (using the FIPA Request Protocol) to agents implied in order to execute the SDA* (steps 3, 4). The execution ends when the agents fulfill their related document subsections, creating a final document to be saved into the EHCR of the patient (step 5).

To achieve the execution of SDA* structures, the agents have some common language formalism in order to communicate all these messages. To accomplish this objective, agents who are interested in executing an SDA* structure share concepts and actions defined in the SDA* Ontology previously described. This ontology contains all the elements needed to execute SDA* structures, like actions performed by agents, or concepts related to the execution of the concrete SDA*.

Figure 7. Individual intervention plan execution context

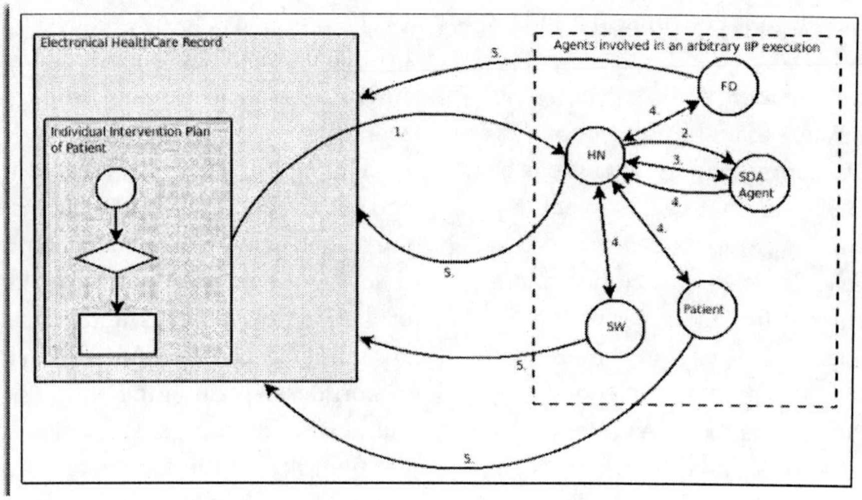

Launcher Agent

The *Launcher Agent* is responsible for deploying agents representing actors in the platform. The launcher agent is the first (and only) agent that immediately starts together with the agent platform; all other agents are started by the launcher agent in the next step.

When launching an actor agent, first the appropriate agent type is chosen according to the actor's role, and then the agent is deployed and personalized according to the identity of the actor. On agent start-up its previous state is recovered from database, and then the agent is ready to perform actions, or continue its previous activities, respectively. Each deployed agent is registered at the same time in the DF (Directory Facilitator) of the agent platform. DF registration is also among the launcher agent's tasks.

In addition to the above start-up activity, the launcher agent is used to deploy new agents when a new actor enters the system (e.g. patient admission). It first registers the new actor in the database, and then starts the agent corresponding to its role, as described above.

Similarly, the launcher agent is responsible to remove agents from the platform (e.g. patient dismissed, system shut-down). The process of stopping an agent is reverse of the start-up activity, that is, the agent is first requested to save its current state, and then take-down method is invoked. At this time the agent can be considered as unregistered from the DF.

HL7/EN13606 Translator Agent

This translator agent is responsible for transforming, standardizing and communicating data between the K4CARE system and external institutions (if such functionality is required). The agent will be active only on demand of a user that will have corresponding rights to perform such action. However, before this communication occurs, the format of data in the other system must be known.

When the translator agent is initiated, the data to be translated and communicated must be marked by the user; then the agent performs all required actions. When the agent has to import data from an external system, the corresponding translation schema is used. The pre-condition for that is that the external data structure and message structure are known and the corresponding translation schema exists. After the operation is performed the translator agent stops.

AUTOMATION IN THE IMPLEMENTATION OF THE KNOWLEDGE DRIVEN ARCHITECTURE

In this section we are going to describe the most relevant aspects and guidelines we have followed in order to automate the implementation and deployment of the presented architecture. These phases are denoted by the *Implementation* and *Application* layers in Figure 1.

The concepts of the domain knowledge were defined by medical experts. Ontologies (APO, CPO), as previously mentioned, are formalized in OWL using Protégé. Static procedural knowledge (FIPs) is represented in the form of SDA* descriptions. The construction of SDA* graphs is also supported by a graphical tool.

Elementary capabilities (actions) of actors are programmed by IT experts according to the descriptions provided by the medical experts. These capabilities are bundled in a JAVA library. Electronic Health Care Record schemes are given by international standards in XML Schema Definition Language (XSD). The general SDA* interpretation logic is implemented by SDA* experts. The application knowledge is introduced by agent experts (MAS ontology) that formalize agent technology related concepts conforming to FIPA, GAIA and JADE. The domain knowledge is then bound to application concepts in the global (K4CARE) ontology.

By formalizing the above knowledge, codes of agents in the platform can be generated automatically. For each actor in the APO an agent can be created. Capabilities of the actor (APO) are represented by JADE behaviors invoking the implementation of the corresponding action in the JAVA library. The generated SDA* Engine Agent integrates the capability of interpreting arbitrary SDA* descriptions (FIPs or IIPs) and orchestrating other agents properly during its execution. The deployment of the architecture then means the assignment of agent types to real persons in the real organization. Actors can initiate procedures, create new IIPs at runtime that are performed by SDA* Engine Agents. This solution guarantees the flexibility of the system. In this manner, when static knowledge changes, the implementation can be easily re-created. In the case of new dynamic knowledge it is applied immediately without intervening on the platform.

K4CARE MAS CODE GENERATION DETAILS

The prototype of the MAS is chosen to be based on JADE (Java Agent Development) framework. JADE is a FIPA compliant middleware that supports the implementation of multi-agent systems. The K4CARE agent code generator has been implemented both as a Protégé plug-in and as a stand-alone package within the project's over-all structure. The plug-in is a tab widget, thus the code generator tab can be added as a new tab in the opened K4CARE project ontology.

The plug-in, in this way, accesses domain ontology via Protégé's OWL API, and shows a swing-based user interface with text fields to specify deployment parameters (JADE home, JAVA home, output directories, output package names, and so forth) and facilities to generate and compile agents' source files. The plug-in, in addition to the previous features, is able to start the JADE agent platform, launch test agents for each actor type (the number of agents is parameterized), and one (or several) test engines that invoke specific actions on randomly selected agents in specified time intervals. This latter function is being used to benchmark, stress test the current configuration (hardware, software), measure performance, response times of agents at different loads.

The generated agent codes consist of a set of JADE-compliant Java classes. These classes can be grouped into three main categories: behavior classes, message ontology classes, and agent classes. Behavior classes implement different actions of agents. Message ontology defines the ontology of elements that agents can use within content of messages. Agent classes implement different agent types that start the behaviors and register the related (message) ontology. The code generator is totally knowledge-driven, valorizing the application ontology and the medical procedural formalism presented in previous sections.

There are several alternatives to define actions at different abstraction levels (e.g., using business process description language); the plug-in currently expects a Java library in which actions are implemented by simple Java methods. Method names are given by the action names in the domain ontology so that they can be derived by the code generator. Complex actions based on specific protocols (that, for example, require interaction with other agents within action body) are implemented by several methods invoked at specific states of the protocol. Activities of agents are embedded in agent behaviors.

Agents' capabilities are the actions; therefore behavior classes can be generated by iterating through all the actions in the APO. For each action a unique behavior class is created and extends a behavior schema corresponding to the protocol of the action (as declared in the domain ontology). For example, behaviors following FIPA-Request protocol extend JADE's built-in *AchieveREResponder* class (Achieve Rational-Effect Responder) that implements the FIPA-Request protocol.

The proper communicative acts of messages, the conversation-id, protocol, ontology fields are automatically set by the generated code according to the given protocol. By default, a given active (ongoing) behavior cannot be started again in JADE until its protocol finishes. To permit parallel activities of the same behavior in the same agent, each behavior is created so that on request it first registers a new (listener) behavior if all behaviors are currently active, then it starts the protocol of the activity. This way, there will always be at least one listener behavior to fulfill a new request, and the behavior pool dynamically increases according to the number parallel requests for the same behavior.

Actors are represented by agents in the system, but the code generator creates one agent class for a given actor type (the particular actor is a start-up parameter).

The capabilities of agents are determined by the actions declared for the actor type in the APO. Behaviors are registered with the appropriate message template: communicative act, protocol, ontology, that is, behaviors can be only activated by a dedicated message belonging to the action. In addition, agents are capable of handling unknown messages sent to the agent (logged), and administer its life-cycle (suspend, activate, takedown, save and recover agent state, etc.).

CONCLUSIONS

In this chapter we have presented a novel methodology and architecture for agent software development in which the role of knowledge and its description formalism are fundamental. Goal of this work is to emphasize the necessity of a formal representation for medical knowledge, in order to valorize its exploitation and incubation, through the encapsulation of implicit aspects.

The main feature of our architecture is represented by the fact that the development starts from the description of the whole explicit knowledge involved in the home care domain (divided into declarative and procedural knowledge) and then derives the agent system implementation for the K4CARE agent platform. Among others, a fundamental aspect of our approach is the capability of the platform to recognize, manage and embed new medical knowledge, expressed in terms of new SDA*-based patient treatments. This aspect extends the actor's capabilities by deriving and combining their starting behavioral model without the necessity to re-plan or re-implement the code structure of the agents. This confers to the platform a high adaptability and flexibility to domain requirements.

We have defined the architecture and implemented the knowledge layer with the help of medical staff. According to our experiences, the knowledge layer is highly flexible. Concluding we report how consulting with physicians regularly, preliminary evaluations show that the representation of the medical knowledge (including intervention plans) is also acquirable, useful and user friendly for other participants of the home care system.

ACKNOWLEDGMENTS

The authors would like to acknowledge the work of all the K4CARE partners, especially Fabio Campana, Roberta Annicchiarico, Alessia Federici, Sara Ercolani, Tiziana Caseri, Balint Eross, Luiza Spiru, Zdenek Kalvach, Dario Amici, Roy Jones, Patrizia Mecocci (K4Care Model), Aïda Valls, Karina Gibert, Joan Casals, Albert Solé, José Miguel Millán, Montserrat Batet and Francis Real (ontologies, data abstraction layer, service execution and servlet), and Viktor Kelemen (gateway agents and servlet).

REFERENCES

Adams, J., Rubinstein, L.Z., Siu, A.L., Stuck, A.E., & Wieland, G.E. (1993). Comprehensive geriatric assessment. A meta–analysis of controlled trials. *Lancet, 342*, pp. 1032–1036.

Annicchiarico, R., Campana, F., Riaño, D., & al. (2006). The K4CARE Model, *K4CARE Project Public Report D01*. Retrieved 2006, from http://www.k4care.net/fileadmin/k4care/public_website/downloads/K4C_Model_D01.rar

Arocha, J.F., How, J., Mottur–Pilson, C., & Patel, V.L. (2001).Cognitive psychological studies of representation and use of clinical guidelines. *International Journal of Medical Informatics, 63*(3), 147–167.

Audet, A., Field, M., & Greenfield, S. (1990). Medical practice guidelines: current activities and future directions. *Annals of Internal Medicine, 113*, 709–714.

Balasubramani, G.K., Biggs, M.M., Fava, M., Howland, R.H., Lebowitz, B., McGrath, P.J., Nierenberg, A.A., Norquist, G., Ritz, L., Rush, A.J., Shores–Wilson, K., Trivedi, M.H., Warden, D., & Wisniewski, S.R. (2006). Evaluation of Outcomes With Citalopram for Depression Using Measurement–Based Care in STAR*D: Implications for Clinical Practice. *American Journal of Psychiatry, 163*, 28–40.

Barnett, G.O., Gennari, J.H., Greenes, R.A., Jain, N.L., Murphy, S.N., Ohno–Machado, L., Oliver, D.E., Pattison–Gordon, E., Shortliffe, E.H., & Tu, S.W. (1998). The guideline interchange format: a model for representing guidelines. *Journal of the American Medical Informatics Association, 5*, 357–372.

Battle, S., Kalyanpur, A., Padget, J., & Pastor, D. (2004). *Automatic Mapping of OWL Ontologies into Java*. In *Proceedings of the 16th Interna-*

tional Conference on Software Engineering and Knowledge Engineering (pp. 98–103).

Bellifemine, F., Poggi, A., & Rimassa, G. (1999). *JADE – A FIPA–compliant agent framework*. In *Proceedings of the Fourth International Conference and Exhibition on the Practical Application of Intelligent Agents and Multi–Agents*, pp. 97–108.

Bernabei, R., Carbonin, P.U., Cavinato, T., Gambassi, G., Landi, F., Pola, R., & Tabaccanti, S. (1999). Impact of integrated home care services on hospital use. *Journal of American Geriatric Society*, *47*(12), 1430–1434.

Blair, M., Brummell, K., Dewey, M., Elkan, R., Hewitt, M., Kendrick, D., Robinson, J., & Williams, D. (2001). Effectiveness of home based support for older people: systematic review and meta–analysis. *British Medical Journal*, *323*(7315), 719–725.

Booth, N., Purves, I.N., Sowerby, M., & Sugden, B. (1997). The PRODIGY project – The iterative development of the release one model. *Computer Methods & Programs in Biomedicine*, *54*,59–67.

Cavallini, A., Fassino, C., Micieli, G., Mossa, C., Quaglini, S., & Stefanelli, M. (2000). Guideline–based careflow systems. *Artificial Intelligence in Medicine*, *20*, 5–22. doi: 10.1016/S0933–3657(00)00050–6.

Cossentino, M. (2005). *From requirements to code with the PASSI methodology*. In: (Giorgini, 2005), Chapter IV, pp. 79–106.

Crubezy, M., Decker, S., Fergerson, R.W., Musen, M.A., Noy, N.F., & Sintek, M. (2001). Creating Semantic Web Contents with Protégé–2000. *IEEE Intelligent Systems*, *16*(2), 60–71.

Dardenne, A., Fickas, S., & van Lamsweerde, A. (1993). Goal–directed requirements acquisition. *Science of Computer Programming*, *20*(1–2), 3–50.

Das, A.K., Musen, M.A., Shahar, Y., & Tu, S.W. (1996). EON: a component–based approach to automation of protocol–directed therapy. *Journal of the American Medical Informatics Association*, *3*, 367–388.

Demazeau, Y., & Rocha Costa, A.C. (1996). Populations and organizations in open multi–agent systems. In *Proceedings of the 1st National Symposium on Parallel and Distributed Artificial Intelligence*.

Earle, K., Sutton, D.R., & Taylor, P.(2006). Evaluation of PROforma as a language for implementing medical guidelines in a practical context. BMC Med Inform Decision Making, 6, 20.

Eberhart, A. (2002). *Automatic Generation of Java/SQL based Inference Engines from RDF Schema and RuleML*. In Hendler, J., & Horrocks, I. (Ed.). In *Proceedings of the First International Semantic Web Conference*,pp. 102–116.

Fagan, L.M., Musen, M.A., Rohn, J.A., & Shortliffe, E.H. (1987). Knowledge engineering for a clinical trial advice system: uncovering errors in protocol specification. *Bull Cancer*, *74*, 291–296.

Fensel, D. (2001). *Ontologies: A silver bullet for knowledge management and electronic commerce*. Springer, Germany.

Fuentes, R., Gomez–Sanz, J., & Pavon, J. (2005). *The INGENIAS methodology and tools*. In (Giorgini, 2005), Chapter IX, pp. 236–276.

Fuxman, A., Liu, L., Mylopoulos, J., Pistore, M., Roveri, M., & Traverso, P. (2004). Specifying and analyzing early requirements in Tropos. *Requirements Engineering*, *9*(2), 132–150.

Giorgini, P., & Henderson–Sellers, B. (Ed.). (2005). Agent–Oriented Methodologies. Hershey, United States of America: Idea Group Publishing.

Greenes, R.A., & Shiffman, R.N. (1994). Improving clinical guidelines with logic and decision table techniques: application to hepatitis immunization recommendation. *Medical Decision Making, 14*, 245–254.

Gross, C.P., Heiat, A., & Krumholz, H.M. (2002). Representation of the elderly, women and minorities in heart failure clinical trials. *Archives of Internal Medicine, 162*(15), 1682–1688.

Hammond, W.E., & Lobach, D.F. (1994). Development and evaluation of a Computer–Assisted Management Protocol (CAMP): improved compliance with care guidelines for diabetes mellitus. In *Proceedings of the Annual Symposium on Computer Applications in Medical Care*, pp. 787–791.

Haynes, R.B., Johnston, M.E., Langton, K.B., & Mathieu, A. (1994). Effects of computer–based clinical decision support systems on clinician performance and patient outcome. *Annals of Internal Medicine, 120*, 135–142.

Hripcsak, G. (1994). Writing Arden Syntax Medical Logic Modules. *Computers in Biology & Medicine, 24*, 331–363. doi: 10.1016/0010–4825(94)90002–7.

Institute of Medicine (1992). *Guidelines for clinical practice: from development to use*. Washington, DC: National Academy Press.

Jennings, N.R., Kinny, D., & Wooldridge, M. (2000). The Gaia methodology for agent–oriented analysis and design. *Autonomous Agents and Multi–Agent Systems, 3*(3), 285–312.

Jennings, N.R., Omicini, A., Wooldridge, M., & Zambonelli, F. (Ed.). (2001). *Agent–oriented software engineering for internet applications. Coordination of Internet Agents: Models, Technologies, and Applications*. Springer–Verlag, Germany: pp. 326–346.

Johnson, P., Miksch, S., & Shahar, Y. (1998). The Asgaard project: a task–specific framework for the application and critiquing of time–oriented clinical guidelines. *Artificial Intelligence in Medicine, 14*, 29–51.

McDonald, C.J., & Overhage, J.M. (1994). Guidelines you can follow and trust: an ideal and an example. *Journal of the American Medical Association, 271*, 872–873.

OMG Architecture Board ORMSC. Model driven architecture (MDA). *OMG document number ormsc/2001–07–01.* Retrieved 2001, from http://www.omg.org

Overhage, J.M., Takesue, B.Y., & Tierney, W.M., & al. (1995). Computerizing guidelines to improve care and patient outcomes: the example of heart failure. *Journal of the American Medical Informatics Association, 2*, 316–322.

Overhage, J.M., McDonald, C.J., & Tierney, W.M. (1996). Computerizing guidelines: factors for success. In *Proceedings of the AMIA Annual Fall Symposium*, pp. 459–62.

Peterson, L.E. (2004). Strengthening condition–specific evidence–based home healthcare practice. *Journal of Healthcare Quality, 26*(3), 10–18.

Riaño, D. (2007). *The SDA Model v1.0: A Set Theory Approach.* Technical Report (DEIM–RT–07–001). Retrieved 2007, from University Rovira i Virgili, http://deim.urv.es/recerca/reports/DEIM–RT–07–001.html

Zielstorff, R.D. (1998). Online practice guidelines: issues, obstacles and future prospects. *Journal of the American Medical Informatics Association, 5*, 227–236.

ENDNOTES

[a] This chapter was prepared in the context of the K4CARE project, funded under the 6th

Framework Programme of the European Community (Contract N. 026968).

[b] HC has to be properly addressed to the patients who can derive the higher benefit: the typical HC patient (HCP) is an elderly patient, with co-morbid conditions and diseases, cognitive and/or physical impairment, functional loss from multiple disabilities, impaired self-dependency. We shall refer to this "average patient" as the HCP.

[c] Professor of Medicine and Epidemiology and Public Health, Director of the Yale Hartford Foundation Center of Excellence in Aging, Director of the Yale Program on Aging, Director of the Claude D. Pepper Older Americans Independence Center.

[d] http://www.centc251.org

[e] http://www.astm.org

[f] http://www.hl7.org

[g] http://www.eurorec.org/

[h] http://www.openehr.org/home.html/

[i] http://www.opengalen.org/

[j] http://www.nlm.nih.gov/research/umls/

[k] http://www.ihtsdo.org/

[l] http://www.protocure.org/

[m] *Foundation for Intelligent Physical Agents.* Retrieved from http://www.fipa.org

Chapter XIV
Knowledge Management Implementation in a Consultancy Firm

Kuan Yew Wong
Universiti Teknologi Malaysia, Malaysia

Wai Peng Wong
Universiti Sains Malaysia, Malaysia

ABSTRACT

KM has become an important strategy for improving organisational competitiveness and performance. Organisations can certainly benefit from the lessons learnt and insights gained from those that have adopted it. This chapter presents the results of a case study conducted in a consultancy firm, and the major aim is to identify how KM has been developed and implemented. Specifically, the elements investigated in the case study include the following KM aspects: strategies and activities, leadership and coordination, systems and tools, training, culture and motivation, outcomes and measurement, and implementation approach. Hopefully, the information extracted from this study will be beneficial to other organisations that are embarking on the KM journey.

INTRODUCTION

Without doubt, the concept of knowledge has existed for ages. Likewise, researchers have widely studied and reported the backgrounds, principles, and frameworks of KM (Knowledge Management). These theoretical studies have certainly provided very useful insights into its underlying concepts. Nevertheless, a number of empirical studies have also broadened and enriched our understanding of how to design and adopt KM. However, the development and implementation of a KM initiative signifies a challenging endeavour for managers in the context of the current dynamic environment (Wong & Aspinwall, 2004a). In this respect, practical-oriented research is essential, if not more important than theoretical studies. Organisations attempting to embark on KM need information, input, examples and role models from existing adopters or practitioners to help them deal with it. To address this, this chapter is aimed to present the results of an empirical case study conducted in a consultancy company to investigate how it has implemented and is applying KM.

The initial part of this chapter will provide a brief description of the subject domain and methodology of this study. The results of the case study will then be presented. Following this, the overall key findings or lessons gathered from the study will be discussed. The chapter culminates with some future research directions and conclusions.

In order to provide a better understanding of the KM domain, a number of researchers have specifically used the case study technique to examine and explore it in practice (e.g., Claver, Zaragoza & Quer, 2007; Davenport, 1997; Forcadell & Guadamillas, 2002; Liebowitz, 2003; Ng & Ang, 2007; Pan & Scarbrough, 1998; Rubenstein-Montano, Buchwalter & Liebowitz, 2001; Skok, 2003; Smith, 2004). Their efforts have certainly helped to broaden the understanding of this field. A case study offers an approach to research by exploring and explaining a phenomenon (Yin, 2003). It is viewed not merely as a data collection technique, but as a comprehensive empirical research strategy. Essentially, a case study represents a useful method when dealing with the 'how' question of research (Yin, 2003). In retrospect, the main research question addressed in this chapter is to examine how the company implements KM or how it deals with knowledge issues. Hence, the case study method is believed to fit this purpose.

GENERAL BACKGROUND

In its broadest sense, KM can be understood as a formalised and active approach to managing knowledge resources in an organisation. It is also often viewed as comprising a series of processes such as creating, acquiring, capturing, organising, classifying, storing, transferring, sharing, and applying knowledge, to name but a few (Wong & Aspinwall, 2004b). Thus, organisations will need to manage not only their knowledge, but also the processes that act upon it. In addition, KM is concerned with the management of technological, cultural, operational, behavioural, and organisational factors that could affect its performance. Hence, as an integrative concept, it can be best defined as the optimisation and running of knowledge resources, processes, and factors (Wong, 2005).

METHODOLOGY

The company selected to participate in the case study is a consultancy firm. This is because it is a knowledge intensive organisation that develops and sells 'know-how,' and so KM is an integral part of its business function. In addition, it is an example of a thriving business, bringing demonstrable and tangible benefits to its customers through the adoption of KM. This also justifies why the company was chosen for the case study. For anonymity purposes, the company's identity is not revealed in this chapter.

Interviews with the key person responsible for KM implementation were conducted in the company. In order to minimise biased responses, no sensitive or opinion-oriented questions were asked regarding its KM initiative. Where permitted, relevant documents such as implementation plans and minutes of meetings were collected, and a direct observation of its system was made in order to achieve 'triangulation' (Gillham, 2000). Following the interviews, all transcripts were returned to the interviewee for his/her evaluation in order to check for accuracy and to avoid any undue bias in the contents.

The next section will illustrate the results of the case study. In particular, the description will cover the following themes: i) the company's background; ii) the key elements of KM implementation; and iii) its adoption approach. The first aspect is intended to capture the case company's background information such as its business activity, total number of employees and so forth, as well as general issues associated with KM such as its understanding by the company and the stimulus for practising it. The second theme is concerned with the description of the key elements of KM implementation in the company, which in this case, covers the following factors: strategies and activities, leadership and coordination, systems and tools, training, culture and motivation, and outcomes and measurement. The third aspect is about the implementation approach adopted by the company. Then, issues concerning the steps or activities for implementing KM are depicted.

CASE COMPANY

General Information

The case company is a management consultancy firm specialising in TWC (Total Working Capital) process improvement. TWC comprises three core components; supply chain, revenue, and expenditure management, which are denoted as 'forecast to fulfil,' 'customer to cash,' and 'purchase to pay' respectively by the company. Optimising TWC processes helps to improve service quality, generate cash, and reduce cost, thus enabling organisations to achieve their strategic goals. Since the company's inception in 1975, it is now a leader in its industry, and has carried out consultancy for more than 500 customers. As a whole, it employs around 160 employees and therefore is a medium sized firm.

The term KM is perceived by the company as capturing, storing, transforming, and disseminating information within the organisation. In house KM implementation began in the early 1990s. Since it is a consulting firm, its professional staff are constantly required to deliver pragmatic solutions in an increasingly complex and competitive economic landscape. Hence, one of the key stimuli for practising KM was to improve its competitive advantage. Other reasons were to promote efficiency and innovation.

Key Elements of KM Implementation

The company has a strategy for KM, that is, to build a comprehensive storage of information and knowledge that will help to deliver sustainable business advantage. Its goal is to have as much relevant information as possible including customer background, project descriptions and outcomes, best practices, reusable knowledge, and so forth. By having a comprehensive repository, consultants can use it in sales and consultation processes. As such, the primary focus of the company KM initiative is to capture and store knowledge into repositories in order to share it across the organisation.

An important element of KM implementation is the extent of commitment and support given by top management. Top level managers in the company clearly understand the KM concept, and are extremely focused and committed to it. They participate actively in KM by proposing new ideas to improve it, overseeing that employees are doing it correctly, and ensuring that knowledge is captured into repositories. The necessary budgets and resources are also provided for its implementation. This helps to send a clear message across the organisation that KM is of key importance.

The initiative was started and championed by an Internal Consultant (an employee of the company), with the help of other Managers and Directors. His main roles and responsibilities in KM are to plan the structure and content of repositories, capture, store, and disseminate organisational knowledge, and ensure the entry consistency and maintenance on a day-to-day basis. In addition, he is also responsible for the coordination and development of tools and knowledge relevant to the company's capabilities. He is assisted by the information technology department to administer and develop the software application that supports KM. There is also a GOMT (Global Organisational Management Team) in place, consisting of all Project Directors, three Operation Directors and four Practice Leaders, that oversees the KM effort. Its roles include monitoring and approving information submitted to the knowledge repositories in order to ensure that it is in line with the organisation's methodology, as well as developing new ideas. Interestingly, formal designations such as Chief Knowledge Officer and Chief Learning Officer are not used.

The company has made significant advances in building a KM system based on a Lotus Notes platform. Within it, there are two key databases called CM (Collective Memory) and CKB (Capability Knowledge Base) which were developed separately. They are password protected and can be accessed via the Internet or the company intranet. The CM acts as a repository for past project related information, such as customer data, project plans, proposals and descriptions, presentations to customers, overview of results and benefits gained by them, and so forth. On the other hand, the CKB is intended to be used as a repository for all knowledge or experience that has been developed, and which could be reused in delivering projects. This may take many different forms such as generic process maps, best practice models, templates, checklists, questionnaires, training course materials, and so forth. In addition to the internally generated materials, there is also information about, and links to, sources of knowledge beyond the company; examples of this include published books and useful Web sites.

Every employee can contribute knowledge to the repositories (and he/she is encouraged to do so). In the submission process, employees will first create a draft entry. This entails filling in templates, structuring the knowledge according to the required format, and attaching any relevant file. The knowledge will then be pending for approval. GOMT members will review it and give their comments and opinions. Once approved, its format will be checked before it is added to the repository. In order to retrieve knowledge, employees can search using the following categories: approved date, author, knowledge type, language, keyword, industrial sector, capability area, material type, and so forth.

A key premise of KM is that people themselves are important repositories of knowledge. In addition to putting knowledge into computers, providing 'pointers' to people who are knowledgeable is also crucial. The company operates both a so-called Accreditation Database and a Human Resource Portal. The former comprises a set of competency profiles, describing the skills, knowledge, and expertise of all the employees. Each of them is responsible for writing his/her own profile, posting it onto the database, and updating it. In addition, the database also displays the ratings of their performance in the following competency areas: supply chain, expenditure and revenue management, business process improvement, software, and language. A rating scale of 0 - 4 is used for this purpose (0 = No knowledge, 1 = Basic, 2 = Competent with support, 3 = Advanced knowledge, 4 = Specialist expert). On the other hand, the Human Resource Portal provides more basic details of employees, such as their extension and mobile numbers, e-mail address and location. In short, the Accreditation Database describes the topics in which people are expert, whereas the Human Resource Portal acts as a means for contacting people.

The company is trying to establish a formal and specific training programme pertaining to KM. At the moment, new employees during their induction week would be indirectly trained on how to use Lotus Notes and create an entry into databases. A supportive culture is among one of the main pillars of KM in the company. There is a high level of trust among employees, and they are not sceptical about the intentions and behaviours of others. This underlies their willingness to contribute their knowledge to databases and to share it. Employees are spurred to learn and develop new ideas. In addition, multidisciplinary team-based projects involving experienced and inexperienced people from different backgrounds also provide numerous opportunities for knowledge sharing.

An incentive scheme is an important determinant of behaviour. In this respect, the company does not operate any reward system to encourage people to practise KM. Top management however, recognises employees who add knowledge to databases, through for example, the use of simple methods such as a regular 'pat on the back.' In addition, all employees are required to set work objectives that they will achieve, which could include KM. Their performance against these goals is reviewed as part of the formal appraisal process.

Over the years, the consultancy market has become increasingly competitive, but the company has remained profitable. Although it is hard to determine causality, the company felt that KM has contributed to the minimisation of the 'reinvention of wheels' and the strengthening of its position as a niche market player. The company has yet to use systematic indicators to measure the performance of its KM initiative, but agreed that this would be done in the future. Nonetheless, regular reviews are undertaken by top management to check the quality of knowledge deposited into repositories and its dissemination within the organisation.

Implementation Approach

Formal procedures and processes are in place for implementing KM in the company. Since the main focus of its KM initiative is on capturing knowledge into repositories, its implementation approach is primarily centred on this aspect. The steps taken are best summarised through a series of phases as shown in Figure 1.

At the outset, the company identified the knowledge area that needed to be captured, and planned the structure and content of the repository. With the help of its information technology department, the repository was then designed, including its structure, its interface layout, the necessary templates, and so forth. Following this, the system draft was piloted by other employees of the company in order to obtain their feedback and to gauge its appropriateness and functionality. The test results were reviewed, and if needed, further modifications, developments, and refinements were made.

The next phase involved rolling out and formalising the use of the system. Finally, monitoring was conducted to ensure that employees added knowledge to it, and that there was consistency in the entries and maintenance of knowledge. To date, the company has been successful in operating with the CM and CKB repositories. Due to this, it is now planning to introduce another database that will capture relevant information specifically for benchmarking purposes. The interviewee pointed out that it is important not to accomplish too much at once, but rather do one thing at a time while keeping in mind the big picture and strategy.

Figure 1. Implementation approach of the company

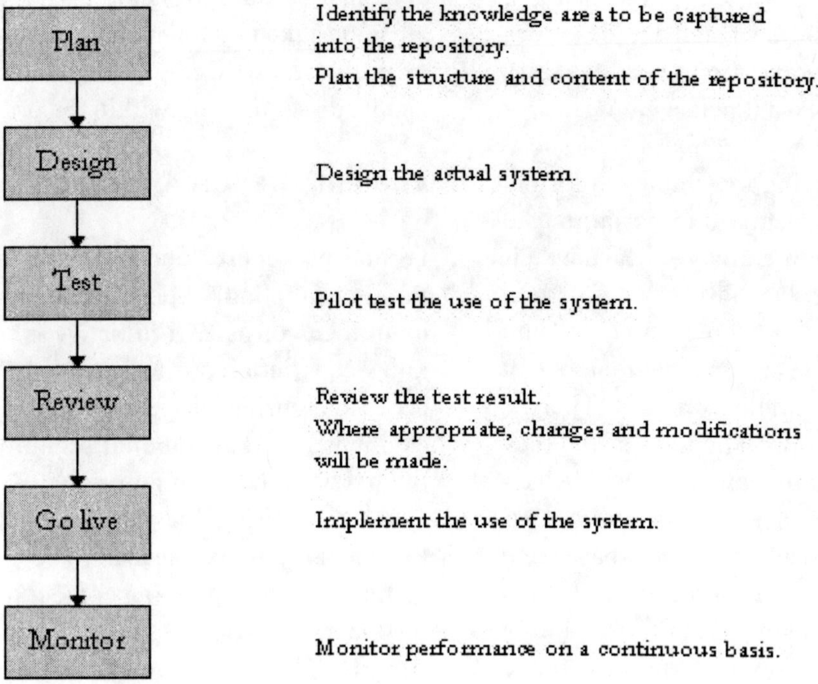

MANAGERIAL IMPLICATIONS AND LESSONS LEARNT

The analysis of this case study allows the elicitation of a number of lessons learnt that can be considered important in contributing to the effectiveness of the company's KM initiative. The first lesson is the existence of a KM champion. The champion, that is, the internal consultant is an individual who is knowledgeable in KM as well as in the operations of the company. He has spearheaded the initiative and promoted its importance to all the staff in the organisation. Although he is not designated as a chief knowledge officer or equivalent, his roles and responsibilities are clearly laid down and this enables him to carry out his tasks efficiently. Total support and commitment from top management is the second factor that provides a crucial mainstay for the KM initiative. Top-level managers participate actively in the execution of KM and they are enthusiastic about achieving its aim. Despite their participation, they do not use a top-down approach per se to implement it.

The third element is the user driven and applicable technological system. With the use of information technology, knowledge can be captured and stored easily, and subsequently, it can be accessed, retrieved and shared across the organisation. Although information technology is not a mandatory solution to KM, it is certainly a necessity. The fourth key ingredient is persistent and consistent processes in place to submit, review, store, delete, and maintain knowledge in repositories. These activities ensure that repositories will always contain useful and up-to-date knowledge, rather than junk.

Another important factor is the formalisation of KM within the company. In this respect, formal procedures are established to govern and reinforce the KM practices, and a systematic approach is followed to implement it. Formalising KM in organisations is important so that employees will treat it as an intrinsic part of their daily tasks. Otherwise, it will be perceived as an extrinsic add-on to their jobs and thus, they will take it for granted. In addition, the culture in the company offers a fertile foundation for the KM deployment. Employees are very motivated to contribute and seek knowledge because they know that it is necessary for them as a team, to deliver better work performance. It is also apparent that the company employs a hybrid hard-soft perspective towards embracing KM. Besides relying on a technological system, the importance of culture, motivation, and other organisational issues is recognised by the company. Technology excels in the capturing and organising of information, as well as rapidly disseminating it to a broad population. However, a technological system will be a waste if people do not use it. Soft organisational aspects are thus more crucial for underpinning and stimulating the right mindset and behaviour for practising KM. The interviewee has succinctly stated that the success of KM requires a harmonised balance between technology and people. Lastly, a progressive approach to implementing KM is favoured by the company. Firstly, it started its initiative with the development of the CM repository. It then proceeded to the CKB repository and it is currently working on another new database. The success of the previous databases has become a proof of concept for the company to launch a new one. Clearly, the company is accomplishing one thing at a time and progressively expanding its KM initiative. This type of gradual and continuous approach towards adopting KM is deemed crucial for its long-term success and sustainability.

FUTURE TRENDS

As a single case study, it is difficult to generalise the information presented in this chapter to other organisations. Hence, one future research avenue is to conduct multiple case studies in different organisations. This is analogous to following the logic of replicating multiple experiments, and hence the results obtained will be more convincing. In addition, future work could also focus on conducting longitudinal case studies in organisations in order to examine and probe deeper into the KM practices. Through such studies, more interesting findings could be attained.

It is strongly felt that future research should focus on the practical perspective of KM and emphasise on how to successfully develop and adopt it. Arguably, organisations need real-life examples, scenarios, and cases to help them better comprehend and implement KM. Hence, more attention and effort should be devoted to practical or empirical oriented research in this area. This will hopefully enrich the understanding and 'semantic' of KM, and provide an optimal answer to the 'how' question of adopting it.

CONCLUSIONS

This chapter has presented the results of a case study conducted to investigate the KM implementation in a consultancy company. In particular, its background, key elements of KM implementation, and adoption approach were examined. Important key points drawn from the case study were also highlighted. In essence, this chapter provides important directions and insights into how KM can be implemented in practice or reality, rather than in theory. It represents a small but crucial means to help organisations work successfully with KM. It is hoped that the information accumulated in this chapter will be beneficial and useful to other companies that would like to convert themselves into knowledge vigilant enterprises.

REFERENCES

Claver, E., Zaragoza, P., & Quer, D. (2007). Practical experiences in knowledge management processes by multinational firms: A multiple case study. *International Journal of Knowledge Management Studies, 1*(3/4), 261-275.

Davenport, T.H. (1997). Ten principles of knowledge management and four case studies. *Knowledge and Process Management, 4*(3), 187-208.

Forcadell, F.J., & Guadamillas, F. (2002). A case study on the implementation of a knowledge management strategy oriented to innovation. *Knowledge and Process Management, 9*(3), 162-171.

Gillham, B. (2000). *Case study research methods.* London: Continuum.

Liebowitz, J. (2003). A knowledge management implementation plan at a leading US technical government organization: A case study. *Knowledge and Process Management, 10*(4), 254-259.

Ng, P.T., & Ang, H.S. (2007). Managing knowledge through communities of practice: The case of the Singapore Police Force. *International Journal of Knowledge Management Studies, 1*(3/4), 356-367.

Pan, S.L., & Scarbrough, H. (1998). A sociotechnical view of knowledge-sharing at Buckman Laboratories. *Journal of Knowledge Management, 2*(1), 55-66.

Rubenstein-Montano, B., Buchwalter, J., & Liebowitz, J. (2001). Knowledge management: A U.S. Social Security Administration case study. *Government Information Quarterly, 18*(3), 223-253.

Skok, W. (2003). Knowledge management: New York city taxi cab case study. *Knowledge and Process Management, 10*(2), 127-135.

Smith, A.D. (2004). Knowledge management strategies: A multi-case study. *Journal of Knowledge Management, 8*(3), 6-16.

Wong, K.Y., & Aspinwall, E. (2004a). Knowledge management implementation frameworks: A review. *Knowledge and Process Management, 11*(2), 93-104.

Wong, K.Y., & Aspinwall, E. (2004b). A fundamental framework for knowledge management implementation in SMEs. *Journal of Information and Knowledge Management, 3*(2), 155-166.

Wong, K.Y. (2005). The potential roles of engineers in knowledge management: An overview. *Bulletin of the Institution of Engineers Malaysia,* November, 26-29.

Yin, R.K. (2003). *Case study research: Design and methods.* Thousand Oaks: Sage Publications.

Chapter XV
Financial News Analysis Using a Semantic Web Approach

Alex Micu
Erasmus University Rotterdam, The Netherlands

Laurens Mast
Erasmus University Rotterdam, The Netherlands

Viorel Milea
Erasmus University Rotterdam, The Netherlands

Flavius Frasincar
Erasmus University Rotterdam, The Netherlands

Uzay Kaymak
Erasmus University Rotterdam, The Netherlands

ABSTRACT

In this chapter we present StockWatcher, an OWL-based web application that enables the extraction of relevant news items from RSS feeds concerning the NASDAQ-100 listed companies. The application's goal is to present a customized, aggregated view of the news categorized by different topics. We distinguish between four relevant news categories: i) news regarding the company itself; ii) news regarding direct competitors of the company; iii) news regarding important people of the company; and iv) news regarding the industry in which the company is active. At the same time, the system presented in this chapter is able to rate these news items based on their relevance. We identify three possible effects that a news message can have on the company, and thus on the stock price of that company: i) positive; ii) negative; and iii) neutral. Currently, StockWatcher provides support for the NASDAQ-100 companies. The selection of the relevant news items is based on a customizable user portfolio that may consist of one or more of these companies.

INTRODUCTION

Unlike printed media or television programs, on the Web, news items can be made public as soon as they emerge. Simultaneously, Web coverage is continuously increasing. News websites provide RSS-feeds facilitating the public to remain up-to-date on nearly any topic of interest.

To better understand what the impact of the Internet is on our daily lives, we should first take a look at the main ideas behind its creation. The suggestion of social communications through networks dates from 1962, when J.C.R. Licklider, a professor at the Massachusetts Institute of Technology (MIT), suggested the "Galactic Network" theory. In this theory, he imagined a "globally interconnected set of computers through which everyone could quickly access data and programs from any site" (Licklider & Clark, 1962). The next step towards the Internet as we know it today was taken by the Defense Advanced Research Projects Agency (DARPA), which created The Advanced Research Projects Agency Network (ARPANET). This project was the first operational computer network in the world, and is seen as the ancestor of the Internet. As time progressed, different networks were created outside the ARPANET, and became eventually interconnected into one super network in 1990, creating the roots of today's modern Internet. With the presence of this technological infrastructure, the next step towards public accessibility was the foundation of the World Wide Web (WWW). This project, led by Tim Berners-Lee, included the now so popular Hypertext Markup Language (HTML) being used for the creation of web pages, and the Hypertext Transfer Protocol (HTTP) being used to access Web content.

In our technology-driven society many people have a hard time to even imagine a world without the services and benefits of the Internet. To a certain degree it is safe to assume that the society we live in is turning into an information technology society, characterized by the Internet use (Slabber, 2007). Presently more than 1.1 billion people (Miniwatts Marketing Group, 2007) make use of services provided by the Internet. Such services include e-mail messaging, file sharing, streaming media and voice communications. By making use of popular search engines such as Google, people all around the world have access to vast amounts of online information, provided by different Web sites. Simultaneously, the same people are even able to create Web content, and place information on the WWW without much effort. Eventually the success of the WWW has made it progressively more challenging to find, access, present, and maintain the information available on the Web.

In 1998 a new idea was born, under the name of Semantic Web (SW) (Berners-Lee, Hendler, & Lassila, 2001). This was supposed to be an extension to the current WWW as we know it. The SW would revolutionize the way in which data is described and presented, so that it can be read, interpreted and used by various software applications. There are three main goals that the SW seeks to achieve: i) provide common formats for integration and combination of data drawn from diverse sources; ii) record how the data relates to real world objects; and iii) semantically link documents.

Data on the Web is controlled by certain applications, and only useable by these applications. The SW tries to make this data neutral, available to all applications. One of the building stones to achieve this is the Resource Description Framework (RDF) (Brickley & Guha, 2004). RDF is a general-purpose language for representing information in the Web. Together with RDF Schema (RDFS), RDF can be used to code the data so that relations and information about the described entities get coded along (Brickley & Guha, 2004). This can be achieved by basing the representation on triples (Carroll & Stickler, 2004). The next step in the transition to the SW would thus consist of transforming all data into RDF triples.

The Semantic Web proved to be more of a challenge than expected. While it is the next logical step in the evolution of the WWW, it is still relatively unknown to the majority of Internet users. Programmers and website builders prefer to use traditional tools for data presentation, for different reasons. Another difficulty the SW is facing at the moment is converting the current available data on the Web. Because of extremely large amounts of data, automatic conversion tools will have to be developed. This is where Natural Language Processing (NLP) should play an important part. With the use of NLP, developers are trying to teach machines what we understand so easy--human language (Chowdhury, 2003). With the help of NLP, the SW can extract knowledge from different Web sources, and convert it into machine understandable formats. The role of the SW is however not different from the role of the WWW: providing access to information.

One of the domains where access to information, and implicitly news, plays a crucial role is represented by financial markets. With the introduction of new products such as click funds, the level of involvement of the general public in investment activities is on the rise. This increased involvement comes to underline the need for access to mediums which can provide relevant and reliable economical news within short time intervals. The Web comes to meet this need, while at the same time confronting users with an overwhelming amount of information. Questions such as *'Where does news appear faster?'* or *'Which news websites are trustworthy?'* have already risen.

Different companies have attempted to fill this 'technology for finance' gap, by providing different internet or desktop applications. Some popular websites already begun providing extensive financial data, allowing users to compose their own portfolio and customize the information flow. Google Finance, Microsoft Money Central and Yahoo Finance are good examples of how these major corporations attempt to implement various data sources with customized user portals for different categories of users. However, the focus of these portals is on providing raw data to users. There is no attempt made in trying to interpret the data, and give viable end solutions to users (for example: "we would advise you to buy this stock based on …"). More detailed applications for expert users are also available, in the form of databases integrated with various news sources like The Wall Street Journal. Thomson Financial DataStream is an expensive database providing reliable financial data for more then 175 countries, going back 50 years. Nevertheless, the user is presented with raw data, without any interpretation at all. In both cases it is safe to assume that companies are still reluctant in creating applications to interpret financial data.

With the emergence of the Semantic Web, languages such as RDF(S) (Brickley & Guha, 2004; Klyne & Carroll, 2004) and OWL (Patel-Schneider, Hayes, & Horrocks, 2004) help provide the basis towards speeding up this process. The goal we pursue here is related to this, and consists of creating an application that helps casual internet users with a relevant involvement in financial markets to find relevant news regarding their portfolio. This effort has resulted in StockWatcher, an application that enables the presentation of a customized, aggregated view of news items categorized by different topics, and at the same time rates these news items based on their relevance.

In the remainder of this chapter, we first provide a background of tools relevant for the current research. Next, we move on to presenting the design choices and architecture of StockWatcher. After this section, we provide a preliminary overview of the system's output. Finally, we end this chapter with some conclusions and suggestions for further research.

BACKGROUND

In this section we give an overview of projects and tools that are similar to the application presented in this chapter. We highlight the main characteristics hereof with a focus on the features offered, while placing everything in the context of the goal pursued here: the development of an application that enables the presentation of a customized, aggregated view of news items categorized by different topics, and at the same time the rating of these news items based on their relevance. Additionally, we provide an overview of current technologies that support (some of) the features envisioned for StockWatcher.

TOWL

The Time-determined Ontology Web Language (TOWL) (Milea, Frasincar, Kaymak, & di Noia, 2007) is a European 6th framework project, with the focus on content studies towards institutional equities services, investors, and businesses. The main goal of TOWL is extending the current state-of-the-art ontology language OWL with a temporal dimension. Having time available in an ontology will give the opportunity to migrate from the current static representations of the world into a more dynamic environment. Equipped with this new technology, automated approaches in knowledge extraction from text (with a focus on news) should provide the edge in making improved business decisions.

A semantic stock broker system is being developed in order to show the potential of TOWL as well as to benchmark the features of the project. This system is able to process news items and adjust the ontology employed for this purpose in order to provide better representations of the real world. Based on the extracted information, the system gives a projection of the evolution of the prices of stocks affected by this knowledge, with the final goal of generating excess returns. This last point comes to underline the similarity of this system with the goals being pursued in StockWatcher: better investment decisions based on information extracted automatically from economic news.

The stock broker application developed for TOWL has three important features. First, news items are the only input source for the prediction of the stock price. The second important feature relates to the domain ontology, which offers a great deal of background information regarding the stock markets (e.g., companies, economical events, persons of interest, and relationships between all these groups). Finally, the impact of the individual news items on the development of stock prices is assessed, enabling the composition of these impacts into an aggregated effect on stock prices.

A prototype of the stock broker application is currently available. This prototype is a pipeline based upon various plugins, from which a considerable percentage are offered by GATE (D. H. Cunningham, Maynard, Bontcheva, & Tablan, 2002):

- ANNIE Tokeniser and Orthographic Analyzer;
- TOWL Sentence Splitter;
- ANNIE POS Tagger;
- WordNet Lemmatiser;
- Cafetiere.

The first two plugins are responsible for the breakdown of the text in words, or sentences. The third plugin, ANNIE POS Tagger is responsible for identifying nouns, verbs, adjectives, and adverbs in the text. The WordNet Lemmatiser provides an interface for extracting the lemma of the words in the text (for example if the input is "running," the output would be "run"). Subsequently, Cafetiere

(Black, McNaught, Vasilakopoulos, Zervanou, & Rinaldi, 2005) is also employed for analyzing the text given the domain ontology and finding matches between the ontology and the text. Finally, the OWL Ontology Instantiator updates the ontology with the newly discovered instances.

By making use of different NLP techniques in combination with Semantic Web technologies, the TOWL stock broker shows an overlap with StockWatcher's goals. The main difference between the two applications relates to the main idea from which they stem from. While the stock broker application is intended for professional investors, StockWatcher is created for the benefit of the ordinary internet user and casual investor.

Artequakt

The Artequakt (Kim et al., 2002) project is one of the popular Semantic Web projects currently in development. One of the main factors that contribute to its popularity is the way in which it tries to bring together some of the most important advantages the Semantic Web. Artequakt's goal is to enable automated internet searches on artists and paintings, from different sources, bring that information together, and present it to different users. Furthermore, the presentation is tailored to suit the user's interest.

The project consists of three significant components. To begin with, a domain ontology describes the world of artists and paintings. Different tools are used for information extraction from Web sources. The use of NLP tools is very important at this stage. In the next phase, the focus lies on managing the information. This is done with the help of a knowledge base used to stored information. Finally, an interface allows users to query the knowledge base for information. The end-user can customize the way in which the information is presented.

The first phase in the Artequakt project is of big relevance to StockWatcher. In this phase the knowledge extraction takes place with the help of NLP tools. Right from the start there a number of differences become obvious between the TOWL stock broker and Artequakt. While the stock broker breaks down text to sentences and even words, Artequakt tries to keep the text intact, and treats paragraphs as a whole. Artequakt's approach considers that a lot of important and relevant information is overseen by breaking down the original text. The paragraphs are then processed through a syntactical analysis where verbs, nouns and other grammatical objects are identified. This is followed by a semantic analysis that consists of four parts: the text is simplified, resulting in simple sentences composed from a subject, verb and an object (also known as a triple). Then, the system attempts to identify named entities (e.g., person's name) by making use of the Apple Pie Parser (Sekine & Grishman, 1995) and GATE (D. H. Cunningham et al., 2002). Finally, the system attaches subjects inherited from the main clauses to the sentences missing one. Artequakt makes use of WordNet (Miller, 1995) to find synonyms, hypernyms, and hyponyms in order to expand the knowledge base.

Although no access to Artequakt is provided for testing purposes, a number of comments can still be made. First of all, there is a clear difference between Artequakt's aims and StockWatcher's goals. Speed is not of essence in the NLP for the knowledge acquisition phase because this process takes place before users access the Web site. StockWatcher on the other hand needs to carry out the NLP tasks on an on-demand basis, therefore making speed a relevant issue. Furthermore, the Artequakt project involves different Semantic Web tools and approaches, resulting in a wide application of NLP over several phases instead of one recognizable phase. This makes it hard to identify a similar solution for StockWatcher.

SemNews

SemNews (Java, Finin, & Nirenburg, 2006a) is a project focused on applying a complex text understanding process on the news items found on different RSS feeds. It extracts significant information and stores it in a Semantic Web environment, available for browsing and querying. The main power of SemNews is the presentation of the data, which enables complex queries on the news items, going further than simple keyword searches. SemNews also allows users to browse the stored data, so that the logic and mechanics behind the application become clear.

The SemNews workflow consists of three individual phases. Initially the news items are collected and parsed from different RSS feeds. The news items are then transferred to the NLP system where, after being processed, important information and metadata are extracted and stored in the database. The last phase relates to the fact repository interface, where users get the possibility to query and/or browse the data.

The NLP system used by SemNews is called OntoSem (Java, Finin, & Nirenburg, 2006b). With this system, the text gets processed through three stages: a syntactic, semantics, and finally a pragmatic analysis. All these result in a text meaning representation (TMR) (Java, Nirneburg et al., 2006). This is where the main difference with the two previous projects comes to light. While TOWL's stock broker and Artequakt make use of WordNet as a lexicon, SemNews utilizes an ontology as resource for fundamental text operations. The TMR does not only act as a lexicon, it goes even further, providing discourse relations, speaker attitudes, stylistic and other pragmatic factors. In this way SemNews goes beyond the normal text understanding processes, and tries to find relations between different articles. The TMR applied by OntoSem is made possible by a general-purpose ontology called Mikrokosmos, which provides over 30,000 concepts and 400,000 instances.

SemNews is available for free testing on the Web. From the first look at the Web site, it is worth mentioning that the user interface is friendly and easy to understand. There are different topics available for browsing, and there are a lot of graphical presentations, making the information look interesting. Although SemNews is a great application, the difference between the goals of this project and StockWatcher's are large. The presentation of information in SemNews is not about the meaning of individual news items, but is centered around decomposing the news item in semantically rich information.

OntoSem

OntoSem is a linguistic text processing setting, developed by the University of Maryland (UMBC). OntoSem has as input text and as output a text meaning representation (TMR). The main difference between this platform and other NLP software is that OntoSem makes use of a knowledge base for the operations needed on words.

OntoSem has the ability to perform the following tasks on any available text: preprocessing, morphological analysis, syntactic analysis and semantic analysis. The center of attention of this NLP developing platform is on finding the meaning behind words, sentences, paragraphs, and eventually create relationships between different pieces of text (McShane, Zabludowski, Nirenburg, & Beale, 2004).

GATE

GATE refers to itself as a Software Architecture for Language Engineering (H. Cunningham & Scott, 2004), a platform for developing and testing NLP software. GATE is a popular platform in the scientific world because the same results can be obtained when running the same experiment in different environments. Other benefits of GATE are the benchmarking abilities when researching various processes, and the architecture of the system. Many tools that GATE offers are used as plugins, making it possible to use them outside this platform.

GATE comes with a graphical developing interface, making it easier for users to create their own NLP applications. Another advantage for our current purpose is the Java implementation of GATE. There is also a fully documented application programming interface (API) available in Javadoc accompanied by examples available in the User Guide accessible on the website. However, GATE offers the possibility to use a Java Annotation Patterns Engine (JAPE) (H. Cunningham, 2000). This language is used to express the required items needed to be annotated in a basic text. Users involved in larger projects can create their own components for working with GATE.

At the first sight, GATE offers all the plugins necessary for StockWatcher, as discussed in the previous section of this section. To start with, it makes use of its own tokeniser, which is tuned for efficiency, so that it will not use many resources. It can also make distinctions between words, numbers, symbols, punctuations and spaces. Additionally, GATE possesses a part of speech tagger plugin, required for the identification of the place of the words in a sentence. The ANNIE POS-tagger produces a part of speech tag for every word that gets processed. Last but not least there is the morphological analyzer, which returns the lemma of each word using also its part of speech tag.

Java NLP Tools

We decided that looking at NLP developing platforms offering all the tools combined in one software package was not enough as our tool's requirements were not met. There are various tools available to fit the requirements of StockWatcher, and we discuss them here.

First, we have the Stanford part of speech tagger, a log-linear POS-tagger developed by the University of Stanford (Klein & Manning, 2003). One of the basic principles behind this tagger is the fact that unknown words need more attention and better support for the tense forms of verbs (Toutanova & Manning, 2000). The Stanford POS-tagger is easy to use in a Java environment, by making use of the Javadoc available on the Stanford website.

For the Morphology tasks of StockWatcher there are different tools available, which provide an API to the features of WordNet: JWordNet (Johar, 2004), Java WordNet Library (JWNL) (Didion, 2007), Java Interface to WordNet (JWI) (Finlayson, 2007), and WordNet Web Application (WNWA) (Bou, 2007). From the first three packages, JWNL provides the best features, giving access to the full functionality of the WordNet libraries. The JWI package can only retrieve a word's lemma, but is unable to provide synonyms, while the JWordNet package makes use of an outdated WordNet library. The last package, WNWA, offers a web interface to the libraries of WordNet, while the other tools need the WordNet dictionary installed locally.

STOCKWATCHER

The focus of this section is on the design of StockWatcher. After presenting the choice for the different building blocks of the application, the focus falls on the architecture of StockWatcher and the different processing phases.

Choosing the Right Components

At a first look, GATE seems to be the best choice for the development of the NLP component of StockWatcher. It offers the right tools for the requirements, supports Java applications, and is a popular choice in the scientific circles as far as NLP is concerned. However, a main disadvantage of the GATE plugin is the problem of a cumbersome integration with existing applications. OntoSem has a lot to offer as well, however it is not the same concept of plug and play as GATE. Moreover, OntoSem is intended to represent meaning, while StockWatcher needs a lexical reference system for synonyms. For example, "watch" returns only one synonym in OntoSem: "observe," while WordNet's dictionary has found four direct synonyms, thus recommending the latter as the more complete choice.

The Stanford POS-tagger is easy to use, works fast and reliable, and is fully designed for Java environments. For the morphology tasks, JWNL gives the best results, supporting some of the latest libraries available for WordNet, and giving access to the full functionality that the libraries have to offer. Above that it is designed for Java, making it easier to integrate when compared to the GATE morphological plugin. Finally, the Java String Tokenizer, a standard library available in Java, has the necessary functionality to fulfill the tasks concerning the division of paragraphs into sentences and words.

System Architecture

An overview of StockWatcher's architecture is depicted in Figure 1, where the workflow model has been separated in three main phases. The first phase is the Data Extraction process. This part of the model is responsible for extracting information concerning the companies supported by our application, and storing it in our local database. The first step in creating StockWatcher was to mine various Web sites for information. Once the information was found, we employed various techniques, such as HTML Wrappers, to extract this information. The main information sources were *Nasdaq.com* and *Hoovers.com*. Both websites make use of the same *id_keys*, which are used here to uniquely identify a company. Making use of these *id_keys*, we were able to query for specific HTML websites that offer the relevant company information. Furthermore, both sources provide detailed HTML information tags, making it easy to identify the required information. The first Web site, *Nasdaq.com*, has a certain amount of information on all the companies active on the technology stock market. However, this information is not always complete, so by making use of the *id_keys* found on Nasdaq.com, we queried *Hoovers.com* for additional information. This website provides company information with detailed business reports and industry profiles. For the data storage we employed the Microsoft Access database management system (DBMS). This system provides a simple and flexible solution for our data storage problems, consisting of SQL query support and easy Java integration.

Once the database has been populated, users can compose their own portfolio consisting of the NASDAQ-100 companies present in the database. After this step, an ontology corresponding to the particular user portfolio is generated automatically. All this takes place in the Ontology Creation phase. The ontology was created with the help of Protégé-OWL (Knublauch, Fergerson, Noy, & Musen, 2004), a platform with a powerful graphical user interface, facilitating easy and reliable development of ontologies. In the ontology we distinguish between three major classes: companies, industries, and persons. The first class, *Companies*, has two subclasses: companies that represent the user's portfolio and companies that represent competitors of the companies in the user's portfolio. A set of Java modules has been developed by making use of the Jena API. In this way we were able to create, edit and remove instances in our original ontology with the help of Java. With all these components in place, a user can access our website and select a portfolio. Once the selection is finished, StockWatcher produces a personalized ontology for this user. In Figure 2 we illustrate how an individual, in this case Google, is being represented in the ontology.

The search for relevant news items may start as soon as the ontology is complete and the RSS feeds are set. To filter out irrelevant matches, and make the application as reliable as possible, a ranking system has been implemented. Based hereon, the

Figure 1. StockWatcher architecture

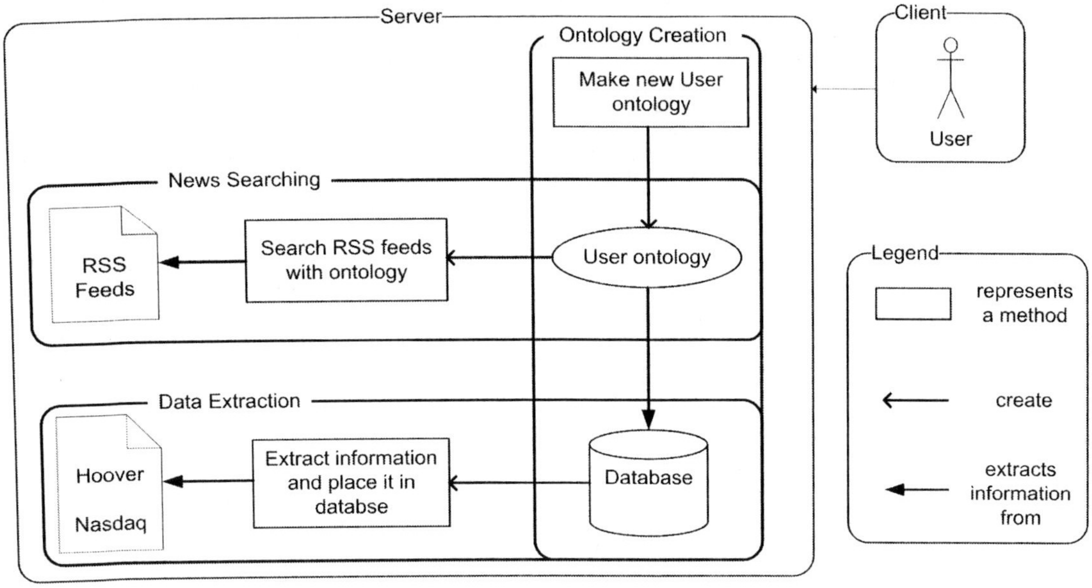

news items receive a score based on how many times a word appears in the article. In Figure 3 we present the algorithm employed by StockWatcher for finding the relevant news items for a company. As at this point we are dealing only with proper names (names of people and companies), no NLP is required. The criteria words in the algorithm represent resources like the ones displayed in Figure 2. The system also takes into account where the match is found, making distinctions between the title and the body of a news article. A match in the title receives a score of 2, while a match in the text receives a score of 1. A threshold was established, such that only news items with a score of 2 or higher are presented. This improved the relevance of the results significantly. To search the RSS feeds we employ a Java based platform--Informa (Schmuck, 2007).

Ontology Editing and Querying

For the application to be able to recognize economic events it was necessary to create a knowledge base containing this information. As an ontology is already present in the architecture of StockWatcher, the most efficient way to fulfill this objective is expanding the existing ontology with economic events. The relevant economic concepts are created and categorized in groups. Afterwards, the groups are further sorted by the effect they would normally have on the stock price.

A majority of the economic events are composed from observations gathered from news articles. Furthermore, a glossary offered by the NASDAQ site, containing key events that influence share prices, proved to be useful in further completing the knowledge base (NASDAQ). The

Figure 2. Representation of the Google individual in the ontology

```
<rdf:Description rdf:about="GOOG">
  <data:hasPrimaryIndustry rdf:resource="Internet_Search_&_Navigation_Services"/>
  <data:hasCompetitor rdf:resource="http://competitor/Yahoo!"/>
  <data:hasCompetitor rdf:resource="http://competitor/MSN"/>
  <data:hasCeo rdf:resource="http://person/George_Reyes"/>
  <data:hasCeo rdf:resource="http://person/Sergey_Brin"/>
  <data:hasCeo rdf:resource="http://person/Eric_E._Schmidt"/>
  <data:hasCompanyName>Google Inc.</data:hasCompanyName>
  <data:hasTradeName>GOOG</data:hasTradeName>
  <rdf:type rdf:resource="STOCKWATCHER.owl#CompanyPortofolio"/>
</rdf:Description>
```

following groups of events are identified and added to the ontology: (i) analyst forecasts; (ii) contracts; (iii) earnings; (iv) results; (v) sales; (vi) stocks and shares; (vii) acquisitions; (viii) collaborations; (ix) company performance; (x) new products.

Most of the events enumerated above can have a positive or a negative influence on the stock price. This gives birth to a further division of some of the existing classes in two subclasses: *PositiveEvents* and *NegativeEvents*. (e.g., *ContractsGood* and *ContractsBad* for the *Contracts* class). The groups 'acquisitions,' 'collaborations,' and 'new products' are assumed here to only have positive influences on the stock price of the company involved, and thus no further differentiations are required.

Text Mining

Making use of the economic events described in the domain ontology, StockWatcher is able to identify news items that can influence stock prices. In order to accomplish this, the NLP tools discussed in the first part of this section have been deployed in our application, creating an NLP pipeline. This consists of a tokeniser, a part of speech tagger and a morphology plugin. The first phase of this process is the categorization of the news items.

Once a user has selected his/her portfolio, StockWatcher attempts to extract all relevant news items concerning this portfolio from various RSS feeds. As soon as the news items have been properly identified and categorized, they are processed one by one by the text processor. First, the ontology is queried, extracting all economic events available in the knowledge base. This list of events, together with the list of news items corresponding to the portfolio is redirected to the text processor. The text processor is responsible for all NLP operations required by StockWatcher. Figure 4 illustrates the architectural model of our software.

Once the events have been passed on to the text processor, the application attempts to extract all the synonyms available in the WordNet dictionary. The first step in this process consists of determining the part of speech of every event. This is done by the Stanford POS-tagger that, when queried, returns whether the word is a verb, noun, adjective or adverb. With this information, the index of that word can be resolved from the WordNet dictionary. Once the index is available,

Figure 3. The search algorithm

```
FOR all criteria words available
   FOR all the news items available
      split the news item title into words
      FOR all the words in the title
         IF there is a criteria word in the title THEN
            update score with 2 points
         END IF
      END FOR
      split the news item text into words
      FOR all the words in the text
         IF there is a criteria word in the text THEN
            update score with 1 point
         END IF
      END FOR
      IF news item score > 1 THEN
         add to an array of relevant news items
      END IF
   END FOR
END FOR
```

all senses of a word can be found, resulting in a full synonym list.

The next step consists of the transformation of news articles. This transformation is required in order to identify economic events. First, the news article has to be split into words. This happens with the standard tokeniser offered by Java, which facilitates several methods for this purpose. Once the words have been separated, they are put through the Stanford POS-tagger. The words, together with their proper part of speech position, are then analyzed by the WordNet Morphological plugin (Bou, 2007). This plugin returns the lemma (canonical form of a word) for every word. This refers to the headword or heading used for words in any dictionary. Once all the words have been processed, the news article is rebuilt with the new lemmas.

The final phase of the text processing consists of finding the events in the transformed news articles. For this purpose we introduce a heuristic for the rating system, assigning scores to the news item depending on the position where the event was found. The score can be positive or negative. The positions are divided in two categories, *title* and *body* of the article. If there is a match in the title, this counts for 5 points. A match in the normal text counts for 1 point. Once the entire article has been processed, the total score is determined. This total score is important for two reasons: (i) the total score of an article reflects whether the article will be categorized as positive or negative, and (ii) articles with a total score between -1 and +1 are ignored. From extensive testing we concluded that single text hits resulting in +1 or -1 points are also not significant for our outcomes. In Figure 5 we present the heuristic for the transformation and the rating of items.

Additionally, a dynamic chart was implemented. This chart presents the company's stock price, consisting of a month prior to the user's accesses to StockWatcher. In this way the user can

Figure 4. The NLP in stockwatcher

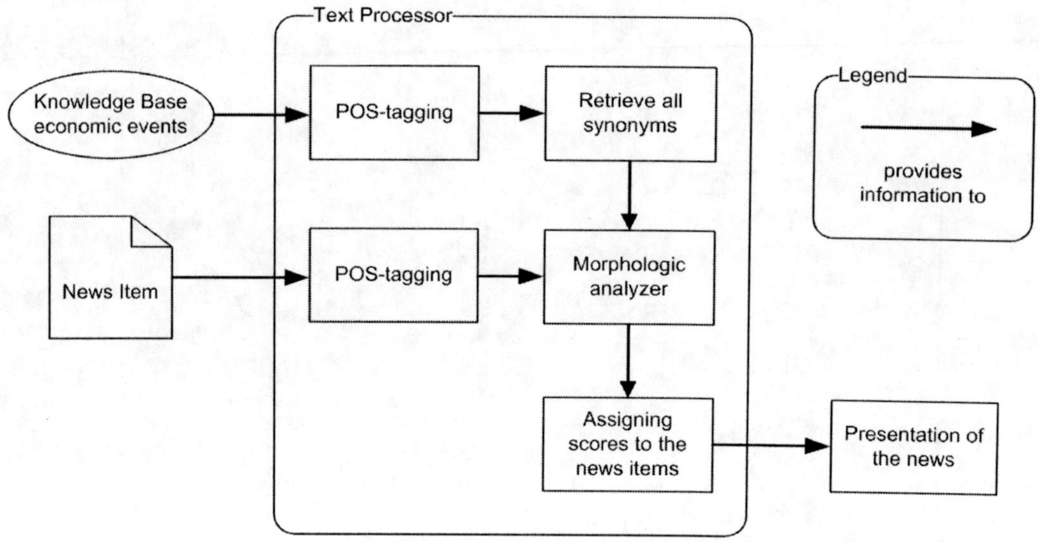

see how the price has progressed and compare it to the outcomes of the news items categorization. The chart is updated dynamically every time StockWatcher is started, and includes the latest stock price available, as shown in Figure 6.

ANALYSIS OF THE RESULTS

In this section we provide a preliminary analysis of the results produced by StockWatcher. We start off by taking a look at the reliability with which news items are categorized as being positive or negative in a concrete case.

The number of news items being categorized in a positive or negative group depends largely on whether there is an economic event identifiable within the item. After running extensive tests, we present some of the outcomes produced by StockWatcher. To start with we take a look at news about the company itself. In this case Microsoft was chosen, and eight news items were found, from which four items were categorized as being positive and the rest neutral. We discuss one of the articles categorized as positive, and evaluate whether the categorization went correctly.

Microsoft advances cited in report;
Date: Tue, Jun 12, 2007
by Paul Krill
InfoWorld
June 12, 2007

Research 2.0, in its May technology research report, found that Microsoft has made "significant advances" with .Net and Windows Vista-driven technology improvements. .Net, Research 2.0 said, has advantages compared to platforms such as the open source LAMP (Linux, Apache, MySQL, PHP) stack. "Perhaps the most striking

Figure 5. The transformation and rating of news items

```
FOR all the news items
   split the news item title into words
   FOR all the words in the title
      retrieve part of speech of the word
      retrieve lemma of the word
   END FOR
   split the news item text into words
   FOR all he words in the text
      retrieve part of speech of the word
      retrieve lemma of the word
   END FOR
   FOR all the positive events available
      FOR all the lemma words in the title
         IF there is a positive event match THEN
            update score with 5
         END IF
      END FOR
      FOR all the lemma words in the text
         IF there is a positive event match THEN
            update score with 1
         END IF
      END FOR
   END FOR
   FOR all the negative events available
      FOR all the lemma words in the title
         IF there is a negative event match THEN
            update score with -5
         END IF
      END FOR
      FOR all the lemma words in the text
         IF there is a negative event match THEN
            update score with -1
         END IF
      END FOR
   END FOR
END FOR
```

value of .Net is the efficiency it affords over other platforms. It's the ability to get to the job at hand vs. building scaffolding to get started," the report stated. Microsoft's Silverlight technology, for running multimedia applications in a browser, will fuel market gains versus Adobe Flash and AJAX, Research 2.0 said. The report also covers the latest SOA findings. Research 2.0 predicts users will keep experimenting with SOA during the next few years but that will peak in 2010 or 2011. SOA will be embraced as mainstream technology by 2015. SOA packaged applications are predicted to dominate application market revenue flows within a decade, disrupting application providers Oracle, SAP and Salesforce.com. The services industry is leading SOA adoption progress; portal- and infrastructure-based approaches to SOA developments are being explored. The Research 2.0 report, which was funded by the Research 2.0 itself, can be downloaded here. The company issues the report to entice investors and businesses to buy the company's other reports, a representative for Research 2.0 said.

This news item summarizes a report released by Microsoft in May, concerning the significant advances in their research. The most important topics were the advantages represented by own products in comparison to competitors products (.Net versus Linux, Apache, MySQL, PHP, for example). These advantages would later turn into market share, resulting in bigger profits--thus a positive effect on the stock price. In this article there were only two hits generated in the text: *buy* and *market gain*. The first one was found in the phrase "businesses to buy the" and the second one in "fuel market gains versus." Finally, this article was categorized properly as positive.

The results obtained in this particular case are further supported by the evidence obtained after performing experiments on a larger sample. For this purpose, we have analyzed a dataset of news collected over a longer period of time, stretching across 30 days, from September 1st, 2007 to September 30th, 2007. The list of companies for which the analysis was performed comprised the following entities: Apple, Dell, Google, Microsoft and Yahoo. We have limited ourselves to these companies based on the frequency of news relating to them, and considered this representative enough for the purpose of this preliminary testing. The average number of news per company per day was around four for these companies, though exceeding this number on several occasions. However,

Figure 6. StockWatcher output

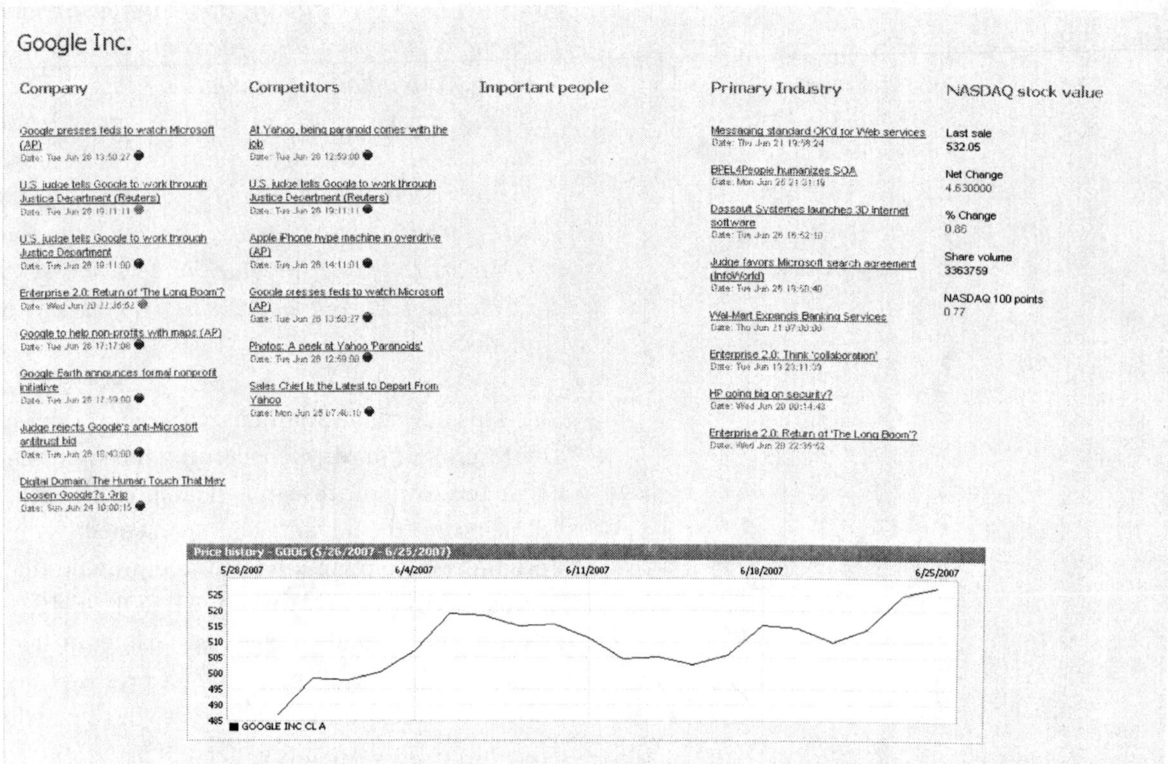

not all news messages have been categorized as positive or negative, as around half of the total sample has been categorized as neutral (meaning no effect or that the effect cannot be assessed). The other 50% that has been categorized presented interesting results. From the 'postive sample,' 30% were incorrectly categorized as positive (false positive), and thus the true-positive percentage amounted 70%. The number are similar in the case of the news with a negative effect: here, around 25% of the news were classified as being negative while they should have been classified as positive (false-negative), while 75% were correctly classified as negative (true-negative).

CONCLUSIONS AND FURTHER RESEARCH

The most important conclusion that can be drawn at the end of this chapter is that StockWatcher is able to classify news reliably. The average percentage of 72.5% correctly classified news items shows that StockWatcher may successfully be employed for the purpose of providing quick, accurate overviews about the market situation at a certain time and as relevant to specific, customizable portfolios. The uniqueness of this application in the financial trading tools landscape helps further positioning StockWatcher as a pioneer in its area. The main problem addressed by this tool relates to providing a way to keep the huge amount of news available today manageable for typical users. The focus in this case in on the financial domain, where the relevance of news items is determined based on a customizable user portfolio.

Additionally, the speed by which the impact of news messages on stock prices can be assessed by a human is negatively affected by the number of news messages available. By automating this process, a very intuitive way is provided of assessing, in one look, the general feeling of the market regarding specific companies. Additionally, less experienced investors, or investors with less experience in a particular domain, may use this tool for approaching markets still less known to them. This is all possible due to the underlying domain ontology where different aspects relevant to this issue have carefully been defined.

Placing StockWatcher in a larger context, we can regard this application as a support tool in the algorithmic trading environment. Algorithmic trading refers to the automated execution of financial trades. Despite its relevance and status as 'buzz word,' very little has been published in this domain. Trading algorithms are generally characterized by lack of transparency regarding the underlying strategy, expected costs and corresponding risks, and how the algorithm will adapt to changing market conditions such as prices and liquidity (Kissell, 2006). In this matter, StockWatcher differs from this type of algorithms through a total transparency, being freely available, and most of all because of addressing a unique problem: assessing the impact of news messages on stock prices.

Different approaches were available for StockWatcher's Natural Language Processing component. The different tools available employ different tactics to achieve the same goal: making text understandable to a machine. On the other hand, a pattern emerges: tokenizing the text first, part of speech tagging and finding the lemma for every word. This foundation was also put in practice in our application. For this purpose, several tools were selected, in order to fit our requirements. These tools are the Stanford POS-tagger and the Java WordNet Library. We used both of them in our text processing system, where news items are categorized by positive or negative influences to the stock price. At the same time a knowledge base has been developed, containing multiple economic events.

For the field of natural language processing we distinguished three different segments: speech, grammar and meaning. While speech is of no relevance to StockWatcher, and the grammar part is already implemented, meaning is the only segment that is missing from the big picture. Although the application is still reliable in correctly categorizing the news items, implementing tools to extract the meaning of the identified events would help make StockWatcher more accurate.

Points of improvement relate to the user interface which could be improved, for example by linking the news items and the price history chart (for example the charts offered by Google Finance). In this way, the user would be able to directly relate the different news items to price fluctuations. Moreover, it would function as a benchmark tool for the prediction and classification abilities of our application. If StockWatcher would identify a news item as a positive influence on the stock price, the price fluctuation on the chart should confirm or contradict this.

In addition, extending the knowledge base with new economic events would benefit the application the most. The scoring system could be improved by assigning the ratings based on the economic event, for instance an economic event involving the profits of the company has more influence on the stock price than an event concerning a collaboration. This gives the opportunity to design a more reliable system from an economic point of view.

From the results generated by StockWatcher, we can observe that matches found in the title of an article provide a high degree of certainty that the article is categorized correctly. From this we can conclude that a title match is more reliable for categorizing the news item, compared to text matches. Furthermore, the position of the match could also be of interest. For example a news article with the title "Microsoft grabs a higher market share than Linux" can get processed by StockWatcher. Based on our current algorithm, this news item would get categorized for two companies: Microsoft and Linux. However, it represents important economical news only for Microsoft. For a correct categorization, StockWatcher needs to calculate the position of the word "Microsoft" in the sentence (first in this case) and compare it to the position of "Linux" (eight), for example.

As a final point, StockWatcher could benefit from the introduction of time constraints in the ontology. The economic events could then also be described based on the moment in time the news message is referring to, how long the effect is likely to last, etc. For example, some economic events can influence the stock price only for a certain period. Based on the data stored in the time property of the economic event and the date of the news article, StockWatcher could check if the match found is still valid or the effect has already passed.

In conclusion, the Semantic Web based application StockWatcher in combination with Natural Language Processing tools has proven to be an efficient way of identifying and categorizing news items by the type of news concerned and their influence on the stock price.

ACKNOWLEDGMENT

The authors are partially supported by the EU funded IST STREP Project FP6--26896: *Time-determined ontology-based information system for realtime stock market analysis (TOWL)*. More information is available on the official Web site of the TOWL project (http://www.towl.org).

REFERENCES

Berners-Lee, T., Hendler, J., & Lassila, O. (2001). The Semantic Web. *Scientific American, 284*(5), 28-37.

Black, W., McNaught, J., Vasilakopoulos, A., Zervanou, K., & Rinaldi, F. (2005). *CAFETIERE: Conceptual Annotations for Facts, Events, Terms, Individual Entities and RElations* (Parmenides Technical Report No. TR-U4.3.1), http://www.nactem.ac.uk/files/phatfile/cafetiere-report.pdf

Bou, B. (2007). WordNet Web Application [Electronic Version]. Retrieved on June 2007 from http://wnwa.sourceforge.net/

Brickley, D., & Guha, R. V. (2004). *RDF Vocabulary Description Language 1.0: RDF Schema* (W3C Recommendation 10 February 2004).

Carroll, J. J., & Stickler, P. (2004). RDF triples in XML. *13th International World Wide Web Conference*, (412-413), ACM Press.

Chowdhury, G. G. (2003). Natural language processing. *Annual Review of Information Science and Technology, 37*(1), 51-89.

Cunningham, D. H., Maynard, D. D., Bontcheva, D. K., & Tablan, M. V. (2002). GATE: A Framework and Graphical Development Environment for Robust NLP Tools and Applications. *40th Anniversary Meeting of the Association for Computational Linguistics*, (168-175), Association for Computational Linguistics.

Cunningham, H. (2000). *JAPE - A Java Annotation Patterns Engine* (Research Memorandum CS–00–10): Department of Computer Science,

University of Sheffield, http://www.dcs.shef.ac.uk/~diana/Papers/jape.ps

Cunningham, H., & Scott, D. (2004). Software Architecture for Language Engineering. *Natural Language Engineering, 10*(3-4), 205-209.

Didion, J. (2007). The Java Wordnet Library.

Finlayson, M. A. (2007). MIT Java WordNet Interface. Retrieved on August 2007, from http://www.mit.edu/~markaf/projects/wordnet

Java, A., Finin, T., & Nirenburg, S. (2006a). SemNews: A Semantic News Framework. *Twenty-First National Conference on Artificial Intelligence*, (1939-1940), AAAI Press.

Java, A., Finin, T., & Nirenburg, S. (2006b). Text Understanding Agents and the Semantic Web. *39th Hawaii International Conference on System Sciences*, (62-71), IEEE Computer Society.

Java, A., Nirneburg, S., McShane, M., Finin, T., English, J., & Joshi, A. (2006). Using a Natural Language Understanding System to Generate Semantic Web Content. *International Journal on Semantic Web and Information Systems, 3*(4), 50-74.

Johar, K. (2004). JWordNet Browser. Retrieved on August 2007, from http://www.seas.gwu.edu/~simhaweb/software/jwordnet

Kim, S., Alani, H., Hall, W., Lewis, P. H., Millard, D. E., Shadbolt, N., et al. (2002). Artequakt: Generating Tailored Biographies with Automatically Annotated Fragments from the Web. *Workshop on Semantic Authoring, Annotation & Knowledge Markup*, (1-6), CEUR.

Kissell, R., Malamut, R. (2006). Algorithmic decision-making framework. *Journal of Trading, 1*(1), 12-21.

Klein, D., & Manning, C. D. (2003). Fast exact inference with a factored model for natural language parsing. *Advances in Neural Information Processing Systems*, (3–10), MIT Press.

Klyne, G., & Carroll, J. J. (2004). *Resource Description Framework (RDF): Concepts and Abstract Syntax* (W3C Recommendation 10 February 2004)

Knublauch, H., Fergerson, R. W., Noy, N. F., & Musen, M. A. (2004). The Protégé OWL Plugin: An Open Development Environment for Semantic Web Applications. *3rd International Semantic Web Conference*, (229–243), Springer.

Licklider, J. C. R., & Clark, W. (1962). On-Line Man-Computer Communication. *Spring Joint Computer Conference*, (113-128), National Press.

McShane, M., Zabludowski, M., Nirenburg, S., & Beale, S. (2004). OntoSem and SIMPLE: Two Multi-Lingual World Views. *ACL 2004: Second Workshop on Text Meaning and Interpretation*, (25-32), Association for Computational Linguistics.

Milea, V., Frasincar, F., Kaymak, U., & di Noia, T. (2007). An OWL-Based Approach Towards Representing Time in Web Information Systems. *Workshop on Web Information Systems Modelling (WISM2007)*, (pp. 791-802), Tapir Academic Press.

Miller, G. A. (1995). WordNet: A Lexical Database for English. *Communications of the ACM, 38*(11), 39.

Miniwatts Marketing Group. (2007). Internet World Stats [Electronic Version]. Retrieved on June 2007, from http://www.internetworldstats.com/stats.htm.

NASDAQ. NASDAQ Glossary. Retrieved on August 2007, from http://www.nasdaq.com/reference/glossary.stm

Patel-Schneider, P. F., Hayes, P., & Horrocks, I. (2004). *OWL Web Ontology Language Semantics and Abstract Syntax* (W3C Recommendation 10 February 2004)

Schmuck, N. (2007). Informa: RSS Library for JAVA. Retrieved on August 2007, from http://informa.sourceforge.net/index.html

Sekine, S., & Grishman, R. (1995). A corpus-based probabilistic grammar with only two non-terminals. *Fourth International Workshop on Parsing Technologies*, (216-223), ACL/SIGPARSE.

Slabber, N. J. (2007). The Technologies of Peace [Electronic Version]. *Harvard International Review*. Retrieved on June 2007, from http://hir.harvard.edu/articles/1336.

Toutanova, K., & Manning, C. D. (2000). Enriching the knowledge sources used in a maximum entropy part-of-speech tagger. In *Proceedings of the 2000 Joint SIGDAT conference on Empirical Methods in Natural Language Processing and Very Large Corpora*, (63-70), Association for Computational Linguistics Morristown.

Chapter XVI
Enhancing E-Business on the Semantic Web through Automatic Multimedia Representation

Manjeet Rege
Wayne State University, USA

Ming Dong
Wayne State University, USA

Farshad Fotouhi
Wayne State University, USA

ABSTRACT

With the evolution of the next generation Web—the Semantic Web—e-business can be expected to grow into a more collaborative effort in which businesses compete with each other by collaborating to provide the best product to a customer. Electronic collaboration involves data interchange with multimedia data being one of them. Digital multimedia data in various formats have increased tremendously in recent years on the Internet. An automated process that can represent multimedia data in a meaningful way for the Semantic Web is highly desired. In this chapter, we propose an automatic multimedia representation system for the Semantic Web. The proposed system learns a statistical model based on the domain specific training data and performs automatic semantic annotation of multimedia data using eXtensible Markup Language (XML) techniques. We demonstrate the advantage of annotating multimedia data using XML over the traditional keyword based approaches and discuss how it can help e-business.

INTRODUCTION

An Internet user typically conducts separate individual e-business transactions to accomplish a certain task. A tourist visiting New York might purchase airfare tickets and tickets to a concert in New York separately. With the evolution of the Semantic Web, as shown in Figure 1, the user can conduct one collaborative e-business transaction for the two purchases. Moreover, he/she can also take a virtual tour of New York city online, which actually might be a collection of all videos, images, and songs on New York appearing anywhere on the World Wide Web. With the continuing growth and reach of the Web, the multimedia data available on it continue to grow on a daily basis. For a successful collaborative e-business, in addition to other kinds of data, it is important to be able to organize and search the multimedia data for the Semantic Web.

With the Semantic Web being the future of the World Wide Web of today, there has to be an efficient way to represent the multimedia data automatically for it. Multimedia data impose a great challenge to document indexing and retrieval as it is highly unstructured and the semantics are implicit in the content of it. Moreover, most of the multimedia contents appearing on the Web have no description available with it in terms of keywords or captions. From the Semantic Web point of view, this information is crucial because it describes the content of multimedia data and would help represent it in a semantically meaningful way. Manual annotation is feasible on a small set of multimedia documents but is not scalable as the number of multimedia documents increases. Hence, performing manual annotation of all Web multimedia data while "moving" them to the Semantic Web domain is an impossible task. This we believe is a major challenge in transforming today's Web multimedia data into tomorrow's Semantic Web data.

In this chapter, we propose a generic automatic multimedia representation solution for the Semantic Web—an XML-based (Bray, Paoli, & Sperberg-McQueen, 1998) automatic multimedia representation system. The proposed system is implemented using images as an example and performs domain-specific annotation using XML. Specifically, our system "learns" from a set of

Figure 1. Collaborative e-business scenario on the Semantic Web

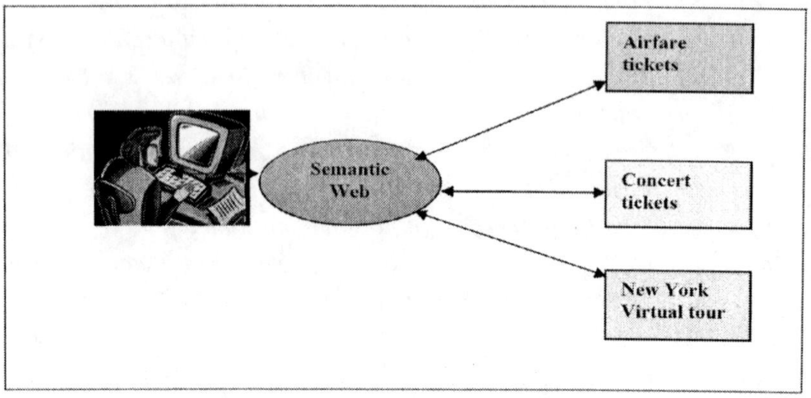

domain-specific training images made available to it a priori. Upon receiving a new image from the Web that belongs to one of the semantic categories the system has learned, the system generates appropriate XML-based annotation for the new image, making it "ready" for the Semantic Web. Although the proposed system has been described from the perspective of images, in general it is applicable to many kinds of multimedia data available on the Web today. To our best knowledge, there has been no work done on automatic multimedia representation for the Semantic Web using the semantics of XML. The proposed system is the first work in this direction.

BACKGROUND

The term *e-business* in general refers to online transactions conducted on the Internet. These are mainly classified into two categories: business-to-consumer (B2C) and business-to-business (B2B). One of the main differences between these two kinds of e-businesses is that B2C, as the name suggests, applies to companies that sell their products or offer services to consumers over the Internet. B2B on the other hand are online transactions conducted between two companies. From its initial introduction in late 1990s, e-business has grown to include services such as car rentals, health services, movie rentals, and online banking. The Web site CIO.com (2006) reports that North American consumers have spent $172 billion shopping online in 2005, up from $38.8 billion in 2000. Moreover, e-business is expected to grow even more in the coming years. By 2010, consumers are expected to spend $329 billion each year online. We expect the evolving Semantic Web to play a significant role in enhancing the way e-business is done today. However, as mentioned in the earlier section, there is a need to represent the multimedia data on the Semantic Web in an efficient way. In the following section, we review some of the related work done on the topic.

Ontology/Schema-Based Approaches

Ontology-based approaches have been frequently used for multimedia annotation and retrieval. Hyvonen, Styrman, and Saarela (2002) proposed ontology-based image retrieval and annotation of graduation ceremony images by creating hierarchical annotation. They used Protégé (n.d.) as the ontology editor for defining the ontology and annotating images. Schreiber, Dubbeldam, Wielemaker, and Wielinga (2001) also performed ontology-based annotation of ape photographs, in which they use the same ontology defining and annotation tool and use Resource Definition Framework (RDF) Schema as the output language. Nagao, Shirai, and Squire (2001) have developed a method for associating external annotations to multimedia data appearing over the Web. Particularly, they discuss video annotation by performing automatic segmentation of video, semiautomatic linking of video segments, and interactive naming of people and objects in video frames. More recently, Rege, Dong, Fotouhi, Siadat, and Zamorano (2005) proposed to annotate human brain images using XML by following the MPEG-7 (Manjunath, 2002) multimedia standard. The advantages of using XML to store meta-information (such as patient name, surgery location, etc.), as well as brain anatomical information, has been demonstrated in a neurosurgical domain. The major drawback of the approaches, mentioned previously, is that the image annotation is performed manually. There is an extra effort needed from the user's side in creating the ontology and performing the detailed annotation. It is highly desirable to have a system that performs automatic semantic annotation of multimedia data on the Internet.

Keyword-Based Annotations

Automatic image annotation using keywords has recently received extensive attention in the research community. Mori, Takahashi, and Oka (1999) developed a co-occurrence model, in which they looked at the co-occurrence of keywords with image regions. Duygulu, Barnard, Freitas, and Forsyth (2002) proposed a method to describe images using a vocabulary of blobs. First, regions are created using a segmentation algorithm. For each region, features are computed and then blobs are generated by clustering the image features for these regions across images. Finally, a translation model translates the set of blobs of an image to a set of keywords. Jeon, Lavrenko, and Manmatha (2003) introduced a cross-media relevance model that learns the joint distribution of a set of regions and a set of keywords rather than the correspondence between a single region and a single keyword. Feng, Manmatha, and Lavrenko (2004) proposed a method of automatic annotation by partitioning each image into a set of rectangular regions. The joint distribution of the keyword annotations and low-level features is computed from the training set and used to annotate testing images. High annotation accuracy has been reported. The readers are referred to Barnard, Duygulu, Freitas, and Forsyth (2003) for a comprehensive review on this topic. As we point out in the section, "XML-Based Annotation," keyword annotations do not fully express the semantic meaning embedded in the multimedia data. In this paper, we propose an Automatic Multimedia Representation System for the Semantic Web using the semantics of XML, which enables efficient multimedia annotation and retrieval based on the domain knowledge. The proposed work is the first attempt in this direction.

PROPOSED FRAMEWORK

In order to represent multimedia data for the Semantic Web, we propose to perform automatic multimedia annotation using XML techniques. Though the proposed framework is applicable to multimedia data in general, we provide details about the framework using image annotations as a case study.

XML-Based Annotation

Annotations are domain-specific semantic information assigned with the help of a domain expert to semantically enrich the data. The traditional approach practiced by image repository librarians is to annotate each image manually with keywords or captions and then search on those captions or keywords using a conventional text search engine. The rationale here is that the keywords capture the semantic content of the image and help in retrieving the images. This technique is also used by television news organizations to retrieve file footage from their videos. Such techniques allow text queries and are successful in finding the relevant pictures. The main disadvantage with manual annotations is the cost and difficulty of scaling it to large numbers of images.

MPEG-7 (Manjunath, 2002, p. 8) describes the content—"the bits about the bits"—of a multimedia file such as an image or a video clip. The MPEG-7 standard has been developed after many rounds of careful discussion. It is expected that this standard would be used in searching and retrieving for all types of media objects. It proposes to store low-level image features, annotations, and other meta-information in one XML file that contains a reference to the location of the corresponding image file. XML has brought great features and promising prospects to the future of the Semantic Web and will continue to play an important role in its development. XML keeps content, structure, and representation apart and is a much more adequate means for knowledge representation. It can represent semantic properties through its syntactic structure, that is, by the nesting or sequentially ordering relationship among elements (XML tags). The advantage of annotating multimedia using XML can best be explained with the help of an example. Suppose we have a New York image (shown in Figure 2) with keywords annotation of Statue of Liberty, Sea, Clouds, Sky. Instead of simply using keywords as annotation for this image, consider now that the same image is represented in an XML format.

Note that the XML representation of the image can conform to any domain-specific XML schema. For the sake of illustration, consider the XML schema and the corresponding XML representation of the image shown in Figure 3. This XML schema stores foreground and background object information along with other meta-information with keywords along various paths of the XML file. Compared with keyword-based approaches, the XML paths from the root node to the keywords are able to fully express the semantic meaning of the multimedia data. In the case of the New York image, semantically meaningful XML annotations would be "image/semantic/foreground/object=Statue of Liberty, image/semantic/foreground/ object = Sea, image/semantic/ background/ object = Sky, image/semantic/background /object =Clouds". The semantics in XML paths provides us with an added advantage by differentiating the objects in the foreground and background and giving more meaningful annotation.

We emphasize that the annotation performed using our approach is domain-specific knowledge. The same image can have different annotation under a different XML schema that highlights certain semantic characteristics of importance pertaining to that domain knowledge. We simply use the schema of Figure 3 that presents image foreground and background object information as a running example.

Overview of System Architecture

The goal of the proposed system is to represent multimedia data obtained from the Web in a meaningful XML format. Consequently, this data can be "moved" to the Semantic Web in an automatic and efficient way. For example, as shown in Figure 4, the system first receives an image from the Web. The image could be received by a *Web image provider* which is an independent module outside of the system that simply fetches domain-specific images from the Web and passes them onto our system. The Web image provider could also be a "Web spider" that "crawls" among domain-specific Web data sources and procures relevant images. The image is then preprocessed by two other modules, namely, *image divider* and *feature extractor*. An image usually contains several regions. Extracting low-level features from different image regions is typically the first step of automatic image annotation since regions may have different contents and represent different semantic meaning. The image regions could be determined through either image segmentation

Figure 2. Comparison of keyword annotation and XML-path-based annotation

Image	Original Annotation	XML annotation
	Statue of Liberty Sea Sky Clouds	image/semantic/foreground/object = Statue of Liberty image/semantic/foreground/object = Sea image/semantic/background/object= Sky image/semantic/background/object= Clouds

Figure 3. An example of an XML schema and the corresponding XML representation of an image

```
<!DOCTYPE image[
<!ELEMENT image(semantic, meta, features) >
<!ELEMENT semantic(category, background, foreground) >
<!ELEMENT meta(id, caption, imageOwner, dateOfCreation) >
<!ELEMENT features(color, texture ) >
<!ELEMENT background (object+)>
<!ELEMENT foreground(object+)>
<!ELEMENT color( #PCDATA )>
<!ELEMENT category(#PCDATA) >
<!ELEMENT object(#PCDATA) >
<!ELEMENT id(#PCDATA) >
<!ELEMENT caption(#PCDATA) >
<!ELEMENT imageOwner(#PCDATA) >
<!ELEMENT dateOfCr eation(#PCDATA) >
<!ELEMENT texture (#PCDATA) >
]>
```

```
<image>
  <semantic>
    <category>New York Images</category>

    <background>
      <object>sky</object>
      <object>clouds</object>
    </back ground>

    <foreground>
      <object>statue of liberty</object>
      <object>sea</object>
    </foreground>
  </semantic>

  <meta>
    <id>396003</id>
          <caption>New York</caption>
          <imageOwner>New York
                    Galleries
          </imageOwner>
          <dateOfCreation>04/10/2005</dateOfCreation>
  </meta>

  <features>
          <color> 0.65227 0.36126 0.62181.......</color>
          < texture> 0.33782 0.30867 0.31427..</texture >
  </features>
</image>
```

Figure 4. System architecture

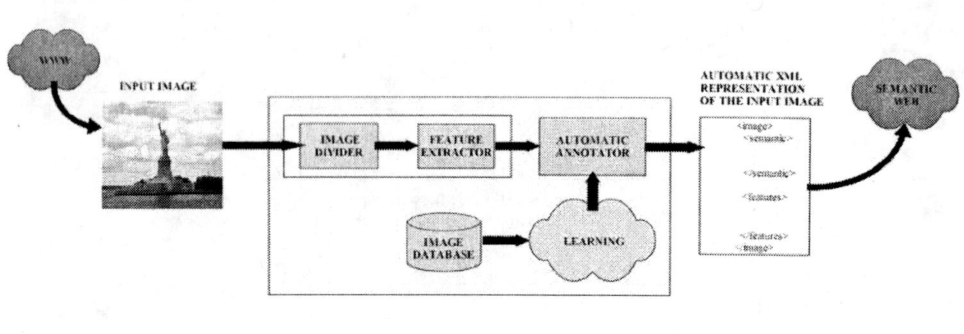

(Shi & Malik, 1997) or image cutting in the image divider. For low-level feature extraction, we used some of the features standardized by MPEG-7.

The low-level features extracted from all the regions are passed on to the *automatic annotator*. This module learns a statistical model that links image regions and XML annotation paths from a set of domain-specific training images. The training image database can contain images belonging to various semantic categories represented and annotated in XML format. The annotator learns to annotate new images that belong to at least one of the many semantic categories that the annotator has been trained on. The output of the automatic annotator is an XML representation of the image.

Statistical Model for Automatic Annotation

In general, image segmentation is a computationally expensive as well as an erroneous task (Feng et al., 2004). As an alternative simple solution, we have the image divider partition each image into a set of rectangular regions of equal sizes. The feature extractor extracts low-level features from each rectangular region of every image and constructs a feature vector. By learning the joint probability distribution of XML annotation paths and low-level image features, we perform the automatic annotation of a new image.

Let X denote the set of XML annotation paths, T denote the domain-specific training images in XML format, and let t be an image belonging to T. Let x_t be a subset of X containing the annotation paths for t. Also, assume that each image is divided into n rectangular regions of equal size.

Consider a new image q not in the training set. Let $f_q = \{f_{q1}, f_{q2}, \ldots f_{qn}\}$ denote the feature vector for q. In order to perform automatic annotation of q, we model the joint probability of f_q and any arbitrary annotation path subset x of X as follows,

$$P(x, f_q) = P(x, f_{q1}, f_{q2}, \ldots, f_{qn}) \quad (1)$$

We use the training set T of annotated images to estimate the joint probability of observing *x* and $\{f_{q1}, f_{q2, \ldots,} f_{qn}\}$ by computing the expectation over all the images in the training set.

$$P(x, f_{q1}, f_{q2}, \ldots, f_{qn}) = \sum_{t \in T} P(t)\, P(x, f_{q1}, f_{q2}, \ldots, f_{qn} \mid t) \quad (2)$$

We assume that the events of observing x and $f_{q1,}\ f_{q2,}\ f_{qn}$ are mutually independent of each other and express the joint probability in terms of P_A, P_B and P_C as follows:

$$P(x, f_{q1}, f_{q2}, \ldots f_{qn}) = \sum_{t \in T} \{ P_A(t) \prod_{a} P_B(f_a|t) \prod_{path \in x} P_C(path|t) \prod_{path \notin x} (1 - P_C(path|t)) \} \quad (3)$$

where P_A is the prior probability of selecting each training image, P_B is the density function responsible for modeling the feature vectors, and P_C is a multiple Bernoulli distribution for modeling the XML annotation paths.

In the absence of any prior knowledge of the training set, we assume that P_A follows a uniform prior and can be expressed as:

$$P_A = \frac{1}{\|T\|} \quad (4)$$

where ||T|| is the size of the training set. For the distribution P_B, we use a nonparametric, kernel-based density estimate:

$$P_B(f|t) = \frac{1}{n} \sum_i \frac{\exp\{-(f - f_i)^T \Sigma^{-1} (f - f_i)\}}{\sqrt{2^k \Pi^k |\Sigma|}} \quad (5)$$

where f_i belongs to $\{f_1, f_2, \ldots, f_n\}$ the set of all low-level features computed for each rectangular region of Σ image t. is the diagonal covariance matrix which is constructed empirically for best annotation performance.

In the XML representation of images, every annotation path can either occur or might not occur at all for an image. Moreover, as we annotate images based on object presence and not on prominence in an image, an annotation path if it occurs can occur—at most—once in the XML representation of the image. As a result, it is reasonable to assume that the density function P_C follows a multiple Bernoulli distribution as follows:

$$P_C(\text{path}|\text{t}) = \frac{(\gamma\alpha_{path,t} + N_{path})}{(\gamma + \|T\|)} \qquad (6)$$

where γ is a smoothing $\alpha_{path,t} = 1$ parameter, if the path occurs in the annotation of image *t*, else it is zero. N_{path} is the total number of training images that contain this *path* in their annotation.

EXPERIMENTAL RESULTS

Our image database contains 1,500 images obtained from the Corel data set, comprising 15 image categories with 100 images in each category. The Corel image data set contains images from different semantic categories with keyword annotations performed by Corel employees. In order to conduct our experiments, we require a training image database representing images in XML format. Each XML file should contain annotation, low-level features, and other meta-information stored along different XML paths. In the absence of such a publicly available data, we had to manually convert each image in the database to an XML format conforming to the schema shown in Figure 3. We performed our experiments on five randomly selected image categories. Each image category represents a distinct semantic concept. In the experiments, 70% of the data are randomly selected as the training set while the remaining were used for testing.

Automatic Annotation Results

Given a test image, we calculate the joint probability of the low-level feature vector and the XML annotation paths in the training set. We select the top four paths with the highest joint probability as the annotation for the image. Compared with

Figure 5. Examples of top annotation in comparison with Corel keyword annotation

Image		
Corel keyword Annotation	plane, jet, wheels, sky	sky, clouds, train, tracks
Automatic XML based Annotation	image/semantic/background/object=sky, image/semantic/foreground/object=plane, image/semantic/foreground/object=jet, image/semantic/foreground/object=wheels	image/semantic/background/object=sky, image/semantic/background/object=clouds, image/semantic/forgeround/object=train, image/semantic/forgeround/object=tracks,

Table 1. Annotation results

Number of Paths with recall > 0 is 50		
Annotation Results	**Results on all 148 paths**	**Results on top 23 paths**
Mean per-path recall	0.22	0.83
Mean per-path precision	0.21	0.73

other approaches in image annotation (Duygulu et al., 2002; Feng et al., 2004), our annotation results provide more meaningful description of a given image.

Figure 5 shows some examples of our annotation results. We can clearly see that the XML-path-based annotation contains richer semantic meaning than the original keyword provided by Corel. We evaluate the image annotation performance in terms of recall and precision. The recall and precision for every annotation path in the test set is computed as follows:

$$\text{recall} = \frac{q}{r}$$
$$\text{precision} = \frac{q}{s}$$

where q is the number of images correctly annotated by an annotation path, r is the number of images having that annotation path in the test set, and s is the number of images annotated by the same path. In Table 1 we report the results for all the 148 paths in the test set as well as the 23 best paths as in Duygulu et al. (2002) and Feng et al. (2004).

Retrieval Results

Given specific query criteria, XML representation helps in efficient retrieval of images over the Semantic Web. Suppose a user wants to find images that have an *airplane* in the background and *people* in the foreground. State-of-the-art search engines require the user to supply individual keywords such as "airplane," "people," and so forth or any combination of keywords as a query. The union of the retrieved images of all possible combinations of the aforementioned query keywords is sure to have images satisfying the user specified criteria.

However, a typical search engine user searching for images is unlikely to view beyond the first 15-20 retrievals, which may be irrelevant in this case. As a result, the user query in this scenario is unanswered in spite of images satisfying the specified criteria being present on the Web. With the proposed framework, the query could be answered in an efficient way. Since all the images on the Semantic Web are represented in an XML format, we can use XML querying technologies such as XQuery (Chamberlin, Florescu, Robie, Simeon, & Stefanascu, 2001) and XPath (Clark & DeRose, 1999) to retrieve images for the query "image/semantic/background/object = plane & image/semantic/foreground/object = people". This is unachievable with keyword-based queries and hence is a major contribution of the proposed work.

Figure 6 shows some examples of the retrieval results. In Table 2, we also report the mean aver-

Figure 6. Ranked retrieval for the query image/semantic/background/object = "sky"

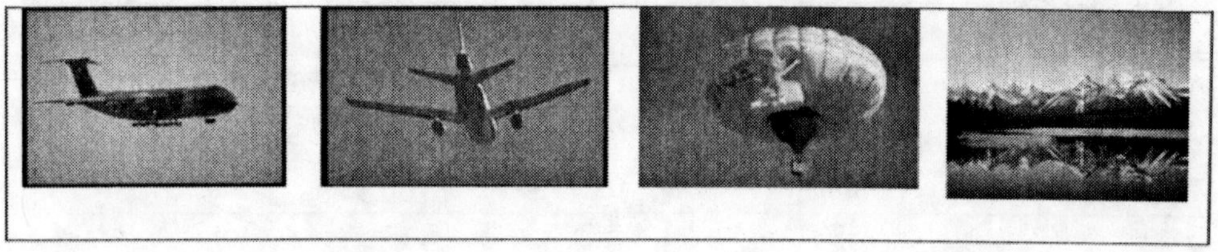

Table 2. Mean average precision results

All 148 paths	Paths with recall > 0
0.34	0.38

age precision obtained for ranked retrieval as in Feng et al. (2004).

Since the proposed work is the first one of its kind to automatically annotate images using XML paths, we were unable to make a direct comparison with any other annotation model. However, our annotation and retrieval results are comparable to the ones obtained by Duygulu et al. (2002) and Feng et al. (2004).

CONCLUSION AND DISCUSSION

With the rapid development of digital photography, more and more people are able to share their personal photographs and home videos on the Internet. Many organizations have large image and video collections in digital format available for online access. For example, film producers advertise movies through interactive preview clips. News broadcasting corporations post photographs and video clips of current events on their respective Web sites. Music companies have audio files of their music albums made available to the public online. Companies concerning the travel and tourism industry have extensive digital archives of popular tourist attractions on their Web sites. As this multimedia data is available—although scattered across the Web—an efficient use of the data resource is not being made. With the evolution of the Semantic Web, there is an immediate need for a semantic representation of these multimedia resources. Since the Web is an infinite source of multimedia data, a manual representation of the data for the Semantic Web is virtually impossible. We present the Automatic Multimedia Representation System that annotates multimedia data on the Web using state-of-the art XML technologies, thus making it "ready" for the Semantic Web.

We show that the proposed XML annotation has a more semantic meaning over the traditional keyword-based annotation. We explain the proposed work by performing a case study of images, which in general is applicable to multimedia data available on the Web.

The major contributions of the proposed work from the perspective of multimedia data sources representation can be stated as follows:

- **Multimedia annotation:** Most of the multimedia data appearing on the World Wide Web are unannotated. With the proposed system, it would be possible to annotate this data and represent it in a meaningful XML format. This we believe would enormously help in "moving" multimedia data from World Wide Web to the Semantic Web.
- **Multimedia retrieval:** Due to representation of multimedia data in XML format, the user has an advantage to perform a complex semantic query instead of the traditional keyword based.
- **Multimedia knowledge discovery:** By having multimedia data appear in an XML format, it will greatly help intelligent Web agents to perform Semantic Web mining for multimedia knowledge discovery.

From an e-business point of view, semantically represented and well-organized Web data sources can significantly help the future of a *collaborative* e-business by the aid of intelligent Web agents. For example, an agent can perform autonomous tasks such as interact with travel Web sites and obtain attractive vacation packages where the users can bid for a particular vacation package or receive the best price for a book across all the booksellers. It is important to note that in addition to multimedia data, once other data sources are also represented in accordance with the spirit of the Semantic Web, the opportunities for collaborative e-business tasks are endless.

REFERENCES

Barnard, K., Duygulu, P., Fretias, N., Forsyth, D., Blei, D., & Jordan, M. I. (2003). Matching words and pictures. *Journal of Machine Learning Research, 3,* 1107-1135.

Bray, T., Paoli, J., & Sperberg-McQueen, C. M. (1998, February 10). *Extensible markup language (XML) 1.0.* Retrieved October 15, 2006, from http://www.w3.org/TR/1998/REC-xml-19980210

Chamberlin, D., Florescu, D., Robie, J., Simeon, J., & Stefanascu, M. (2001). *XQuery: A query language for XML.* Retrieved from http://www.w3.org/TR/xquery

CIO.com. (2006). *The ABCs of e-commerce.* Retrieved October 15, 2006, from http://www.cio.com/ec/edit/b2cabc.html

Clark, J., & DeRose, S. (1999, November 16). *XML path language (XPath) Version 1.0.* Retrieved August 31, 2006, from http://www.w3.org/TR/xpath

Duygulu, P., Barnard, K., Freitas, N., & Forsyth, D. (2002). Object recognition as machine translation: Learning a lexicon for a fixed image vocabulary. In *Proceedings of European Conference on Computer Vision, 2002* (LNCS 2353, pp. 97-112). Berlin; Heidelberg: Springer.

Feng, S. L., Manmatha, R., & Lavrenko, V. (2004). Multiple Bernoulli relevance models for image and video annotation. In *Proceedings of IEEE Conference on Computer Vision Pattern Recognition, 2004* (Vol. 2, pp. 1002-1009).

Hyvonen, E., Styrman, A., & Saarela, S. (2002). Ontology-based image retrieval. In *Towards the Semantic Web and Web services, Proceedings of XML Finland Conference*, Helsinki, Finland (pp. 15-27).

Jeon, J., Lavrenko, V., & Manmatha, R. (2003). Automatic image annotation and retrieval using cross-media relevance models. In *Proceedings of the 26th Annual International ACM SIGIR Conference on Research and Development in Information Retrieval*, Toronto, Canada (pp. 119-126). New York: ACM Press.

Manjunath, B. S. (2002). *Introduction to MPEG-7: Multimedia content description interface.* John Wiley and Sons.

Mori, Y., Takahashi, H., & Oka, R. (1999). Image-to-word transformation based on dividing and vector quantizing images with words. In *Proceedings of First International Workshop on Multimedia Intelligent Storage and Retrieval Management.*

Nagao, K., Shirai, Y., & Squire, K. (2001). Semantic annotation and transcoding: Making Web content more accessible. *IEEE Multimedia Magazine, 8*(2), 69-81.

Protégé. (n.d.). (Version 3.1.1) [Computer software]. Retrieved February 19, 2006, from http://protege.stanford.edu/index.html

Rege, M., Dong, M., Fotouhi, F., Siadat, M., & Zamorano, L. (2005). Using Mpeg-7 to build a human brain image database for image-guided neurosurgery. In *Proceedings of SPIE International Symposium on Medical Imaging*, San Diego, CA (Vol. 5744, pp. 512-519).

Schreiber, A. T., Dubbeldam, B., Wielemaker, J., & Wielinga, B. (2001). Ontology based photo annotation. *IEEE Intelligent Systems, 16*(3), 66-74.

Shi, J., & Malik, J. (1997). Normalized cuts and image segmentation. In *Proceedings of 1997 IEEE Conference on Computer Vision Pattern Recognition*, San Juan (pp. 731-737).

This work was previously published in Semantic Web Technologies and E-Business: Toward the Integrated Virtual Organization and Business Process Automation, edited by A. Salam and J. Stevens, pp. 154-168, copyright 2007 by IGI Publishing, formerly known as Idea Group Publishing (an imprint of IGI Global).

Chapter XVII
Utilizing Semantic Web and Software Agents in a Travel Support System

Maria Ganzha
EUH-E and IBS Pan, Poland

Maciej Gawinecki
IBS Pan, Poland

Marcin Paprzycki
SWPS and IBS Pan, Poland

Rafał Gąsiorowski
Warsaw University of Technology, Poland

Szymon Pisarek
Warsaw University of Technology, Poland

Wawrzyniec Hyska
Warsaw University of Technology, Poland

ABSTRACT

The use of Semantic Web technologies in e-business is hampered by the lack of large, publicly-available sources of semantically-demarcated data. In this chapter, we present a number of intermediate steps on the road toward the Semantic Web. Specifically, we discuss how Semantic Web technologies can be adapted as the centerpiece of an agent-based travel support system. First, we present a complete description of the system under development. Second, we introduce ontologies developed for, and utilized in, our system. Finally, we discuss and illustrate through examples how ontologically demarcated data collected in our system is personalized for individual users. In particular, we show how the proposed ontologies can be used to create, manage, and deploy functional user profiles.

INTRODUCTION

Let us consider a business traveler who is about to leave Tulsa, Oklahoma for San Diego, California. Let us say that she went there many times in the past, but this trip is rather unexpected and she does not have time to arrange travel details. She just got a ticket from her boss' secretary and has 45 minutes to pack and catch a taxi to leave for the airport. Obviously, she could make all local arrangements after arrival, but this could mean that her personal preferences could not be observed and also that she would have to spend time at the airport in a rather unpleasant area where the courtesy phones are located or spend a long time talking on the cell phone (and listen to call-waiting music) to find a place to stay, and so forth. Yes, one could assume that she could ask her secretary to make arrangements, but this would assume that she does have a secretary (which is now a rarity in the cost-cutting corporate world) and that her secretary knows her personal preferences well.

Let us now consider another scenario. Here, a father is planning a family vacation. He is not sure where they would like to go, so he spends countless hours on the Web, going over zillions of pages, out of which only few match his preferences. Let us note here, that while he will simply skip pages about the beauty of Ozark Mountains—as his family does not like mountains, but he will "have to" go over a number of pages describing beach resorts. While doing this he is going to find out that many possible locations are too expensive, while others do not have kitchenettes that they like to have—as their daughter has special dietary requirements, and they prefer to cook most of their vacation meals themselves.

What do we learn from these two scenarios? In the first case, we have a traveler who, because of her unexpected travel, cannot engage in e-business as she does not have enough time to do it, while she could definitely utilize it. Yes, when in the near future airplanes will have Internet access, she will possibly be able to make the proper arrangements while traveling, but this is likely going to be an expensive proposition. Furthermore, the situation when a traveler is spending time on the plane to make travel arrangements is extremely similar to the second scenario, where the user is confronted with copious volumes of data within which he has to find few pertinent gems.

What is needed in both cases is the creation of a travel support system that would work as follows. In the first case, it would know personal preferences of the traveler and on their basis, while she is flying and preparing for the unexpected business meeting, would arrange accommodations in one of her preferred hotels, make a dinner reservation in one of her favorite restaurants, and negotiate a "special appetizer promotion" (knowing that she loves the shrimp cocktail that is offered there). Upon her arrival in San Diego, results would be displayed on her personal digital assistant (PDA) (or a smart cell phone) and she could go directly to the taxi or to her preferred car rental company. In the second case, the travel support system would act as an interactive advisor—mimicking the work of a travel agent—and would help select a travel destination by removing from considerations locations and accommodations that do not fit the user profile and personalizing content delivery further—by prioritizing information to be displayed and delivering one that would be predicted to be most pertinent first. Both these scenarios would represent an ideal way in which e-business should be conducted.

The aim of this chapter is to propose a system that, when mature, should be able to support the needs of travelers in exactly the previously described way. We will also argue that, and illustrate how, Semantic Web technologies combined with software agents should be used in the proposed system. We proceed as follows. In the next section we briefly discuss the current state of the art in agent systems, Semantic Web, and agent-based travel support systems. We follow with a description of the proposed system illustrated by unified modeling language (UML) diagrams of its most important functionalities. We then discuss how to work with ontologically demarcated data in the world where such resources are practically nonexistent. Finally, we show how resource description framework (RDF) demarcated data is to be used to support personal information delivery. We conclude with a description of the current state of implementation and plans for further development of the system.

BACKGROUND

There are two main themes that permeate the scenarios and the proposed solution presented previously. These are: *information overload* and need for *content personalization*. One of the seminal papers that addresses exactly these two problems was published by Maes (1994). There she suggested that it will be intelligent software agents that will solve the problem of information overload. In a way it can be claimed that it is that paper that grounded in computer science the notion of a *personal* software *agent* that acts on behalf of its user and autonomously works to deliver desired personalized services. This notion is particularly well matching with travel support, where for years human travel agents played exactly the role that *personal agents* (PAs) are expected to mimic. Unfortunately, as it can be seen, the notion of intelligent personal agent, even though extremely appealing, does not seem to materialize (while its originator has moved away from agent research into a more appealing area of ambient computing).

What can be the reason for this lack of development of intelligent personal agents? One of them seems to be the truly overwhelming amount of available information that is stored mostly in a human consumable form (demarcated using hypertext markup language (HTML) to make it look "appealing" to the viewer). Even a more recent move toward the extensible markup language (XML) as the demarcation language will not solve this problem as XML is not expressive enough. However, a possible solution to this problem has been suggested, in the form of semantic demarcation of resources or, more generally, the Semantic Web (Berners-Lee, Hendler, & Lassila, 2001; Fensel 2001). Here it is claimed that when properly applied, demarcation languages like RDF (Manola & Miller, 2005), Web ontology language (OWL) (McGuinness & Van Harmelen, 2005) or Darpa agent markup language (DAML) (DAML, 2005) will turn human-enjoyable Internet pages into machine-consumable data repositories. While there are those who question the validity of optimistic claims associated with the Semantic Web (M. Orłowska, personal communication, April 2005; A. Zaslavsky, personal communcation, August 2004) and see in it only as a new incarnation of an old problem of unification of information stored in heterogeneous databases—a problem that still remains without general solution—we are not interested in this discussion. For the purpose of this chapter we assume that the Semantic Web can deliver on its promises and focus on how to apply it in our context.

In our work we follow two additional sources of inspiration. First, it has been convincingly argued that the Semantic Web and software agents are highly interdependent and should work very well together to deliver services needed by the user (Hendler, 1999, 2001). Second, we follow the positive program put forward in the highly critical work of Nwana and Ndumu (1999). In this context we see two ways of proceeding for those interested in agent systems (and the Semantic Web). One can wait for all the necessary tools and technologies to be ready to start developing and implementing agent systems (utilize ontological demarcation of resources), or one can start to do it now (using available, however imperfect, technologies and tools)—among others, to help develop a new generation of improved tools and technologies. In our work we follow Nwana and Ndumu in believing that the latter approach is the right one. Therefore, we *do not* engage in the discussion *if* concept of a software agent is anything more but a new name for old ideas; *if* agents should be used in a travel support system; *if* agent mobility is or is not important, *if* JADE (2005), Jena (2005), and Raccoon (2005) are the best technologies to be used, and so forth.. Our goal is to use what we consider top-of-the-line technologies and approaches to develop and implement a complete skeleton of an agent-based travel support system that will utilize semantically demarcated data as its centerpiece.

Here an additional methodological comment is in order. As it was discussed in Gilbert et al. (2004); Harrington et al. (2003); and Wright, Gordon, Paprzycki, Williams, and Harrington (2003) there exists two distinct ways of managing information in an *infomediary* (Galant, Jakubczye, & Paprzycki, 2002) system like the one discussed here (with possible intermediate solutions). Information can be *indexed*—where only references to the actual information available in repositories residing outside of "the system" are stored. Or, information can be *gathered*—where actual content is brought to the central repository. In the original design of the travel support system (Angryk, Galant, Gordon, & Paprzycki, 2002; Gilbert et al., 2004; Harrington et al., 2003; Wright et al., 2003) we planned to follow the indexing path, which is more philosophically aligned with the main ideas behind the Semantic Web. It can be said metaphorically, that in the Semantic Web *everything is a resource* that is located somewhere within the Web and can be found through a generalized resource locator. In this case indexing simply links together resources of interest. Unfortunately, the current state of the Semantic Web is such that there are practically no resources that systems like ours could use. To be able to develop and implement a working system "now" we have decided to gather information. More precisely, in the central repository we will store sets of RDF triples (*tokens*) that will represent travel objects (instances of ontologies). We will also develop an agent-based data collection system that will transform Web-available information into such tokens stored in the system.

Obviously, our work is not the only one in the field of applying agents and ontologies to travel support, however, while we follow many predecessors, we have noticed that most of them have ended on a road leading nowhere. In our survey conducted in 2001 we have found a number of Web sites of agent-based travel support system projects that never made it beyond the initial stages of conceptualization (for more details see Paprzycki, Angryk, et al., 2001; Paprzycki, Kalczyński, Fiedorowicz, Abramowicz, & Cobb, 2001 and references presented there). The situation did not change much since. A typical example of the state of the art in the area is the European Union (EU) funded, CRUMPET project. During its funded existence (between approximately 1999 and 2003) it resulted in a number of publications and apparent demonstrations, but currently its original Web site is gone and it is really difficult to assess which of its promises have been truly delivered on.

Summarizing, there exists a large number of sources of inspiration for our work, but we proceed with development of a system that constitutes a rather unique combination of agents and the Semantic Web.

System Description

Before we proceed describing the system let us stress that what we describe in this chapter is the core of a much larger system that is in various stages of development. In selecting the material to be presented we have decided first, to focus on the parts under development that are finished or almost finished. This means that a number of interesting agents that are to exist in the system in the future and that were proposed and discussed in Angryk et al. (2002); Galant, Gordon, and Paprzycki (2002b); and Gordon and Paprzycki (2005) will be omitted. Furthermore, we concentrate our attention on these parts of the system that are most pertinent to the subject area of this book (Semantic Web and e-business) while practically omitting issues like, for instance, agent-world communication (addressed in Galant, Gordon, & Paprzycki, 2002a; Kaczmarek, Gordon, Paprzycki, & Gawinecki, 2005) and others.

In Figures 1 and 2 we present two distinct top level views on the system. The first one depicts basic "interactions" occurring in the system as well as its main subsystems. It also clearly places the repository of semantically demarcated data in the center of the system. More precisely, starting from right to left, we can see that *content* has been divided into (a) *verified content providers* (*VCP*) that represent sources of trusted content that are consistently available and format of which is changing rarely and not "without a notice" and (b) *other sources* that represents all of the remaining available content. Interested readers can find more information about this distinction in Angryk et al. (2002) and Gordon and Paprzycki (2005).

While the dream of the Semantic Web is a beautiful one indeed, currently (outside of a multitude of academic research projects) it is almost impossible to find within the Web large sources of clean explicitly ontologically demarcated content (in particular, travel related content). This being

Figure 1. Top level view of the system

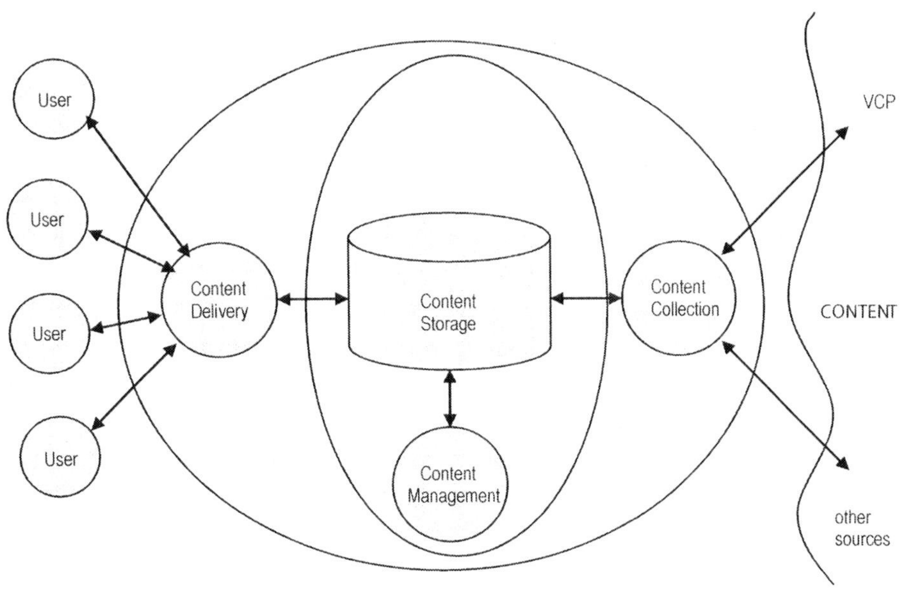

Figure 2. Top level use case diagram

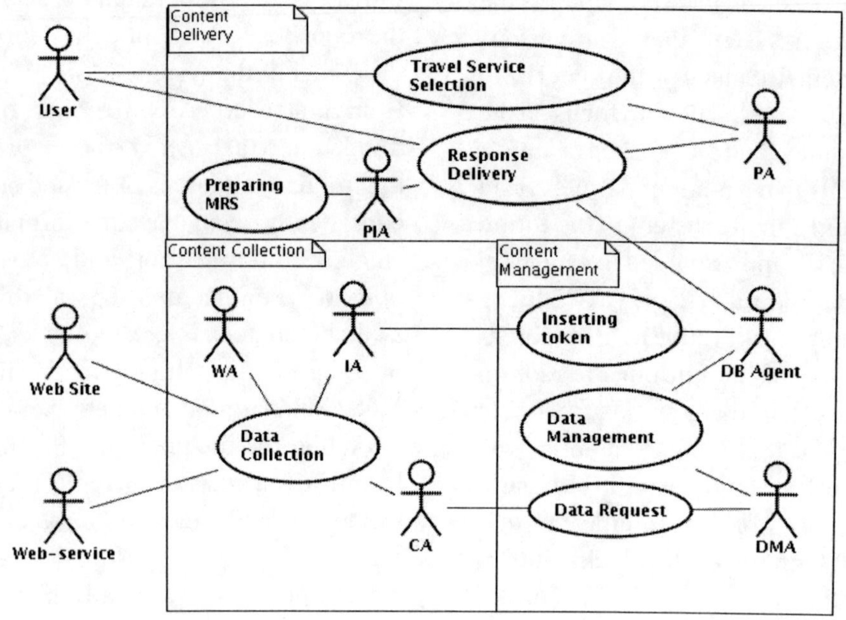

the case, it is extremely difficult to find actual data that can be used (e.g., for testing purposes) in a system like the one we are developing. Obviously, we could use some of the existing text processing techniques to classify pages as relevant to various travel topics, but this is not what we attempt to achieve here. Therefore, we will, for the time being, omit the area denoted as *other sources* that contains mostly weakly structured and highly volatile data (see also Nwana & Ndumu, 1999, for an interesting discussion of perils of dealing with dynamically changing data sources). This area will become a source of useful information when the ideas of the Semantic Web and ontological content demarcation become widespread.

Since we assume that VCPs carry content that is structured and rarely changes its format (e.g., the Web site of Hilton hotels), it is possible to extract from them information that can be transformed into a form that is to be stored in our system. More precisely, in our system, we store information about travel objects in the form of instances of ontologies, persisted in a Jena (2005) repository. To be able to do this, in the *content collection subsystem* we use *wrapper agents* (*WA*) designed to interface with specific Web sites and collect information available there (see also Figure 2). Note that currently we have no choice but to create each of the WAs manually. However, in the future, as semantic demarcation becomes standard, the only operation required to adjust our system will be to replace our current "static WAs" with "ontological WAs." This is one of the important strengths of agent-based system design, pointed to in Jennings, 2001 and Wooldridge, 2002.

As mentioned, the *content storage* is the Jena repository, which was designed to persist RDF triples (RDF is our semantic demarcation approach of choice). The *content management subsystem* encompasses a number of agents (considered jointly as a *data management agent* [*DMA*]) that work to assure that users of the system have access to the best quality of data. These agents, among others deal with: time sensitive information (such as changes of programs of movie theaters), incomplete data tokens, or inconsistent information (Angryk et al., 2002; Gordon & Paprzycki, 2005).

Content delivery subsystem has two roles. First it is responsible for the format (and syntax) of interactions between users and the system. However, this aspect of the system, as well as agents responsible for it, is mostly outside of scope of this chapter (more details can be found in Galant et al., 2002a and Kaczmarek et al., 2005). Second, it is responsible for the semantics of user-system interactions. Here two agents play crucial role. First, the *personalization infrastructure agent* (*PIA*) that consists of a number of extremely simple rule-based "RDF subagents" (each one of them is a class within the PIA) that extend the set of travel objects selected as a response to the original query to create a *maximum response set* (*MRS*) that is delivered to the PA for filtering and ordering. Second, the PA that utilizes *user profile* to filter and hierarchically organize information obtained from the PIA as the MRS. It is also the PA that is involved in gathering explicit user feedback (see section "RDF Data Utilization: Content Personalization") that is used to adjust user profile.

In Figure 2 we represent, in the form of a UML use case diagram, the aforementioned agents as well as other agents that are a part of the central system infrastructure. This diagram should be considered together with the system visualization found in Figure 1.

Since we had to abandon, hopefully temporarily, *other sources*, in Figure 2 we depict only Web sites and Web services that belong to the VCP category. They are sources of data for the function *Data Collection* that is serviced by WAs, *indexing agents* (*IA*), and a *coordinator agent* (*CA*). The IA communicates with the *DB agent (DBA)* when performing the *Inserting tokens* function. Separately, the CA receives data requests from the DMA. These data requests represent situations when data tokens were found to be potentially obsolete or incomplete (as a part of the *Data Management* function) and a new token has to be delivered by an appropriate WA to refresh/complete data available in the system. The DMA and the DBA are the only agents that have a direct access to the Jena database. In the content delivery subsystem we have three functions specified. The *Travel Service Selection* function is related to User(s) querying the system (information flow from the User to the central repository), while the *Response Delivery* function involves operations taking place between the time when the initial response to the query is obtained from Jena and when the final personalized response is delivered to the user (information flow from the central repository to the *User*). During this process the PIA performs the *Preparing MRS* function. Let us now discuss in some detail agents and their interactions. Before we proceed let us note that we omit a special situation when the system is initialized for the very first time and does not have any data stored in the Jena repository. While this situation requires agents started in a specific order, since it is only a one-time event it is not worthy of extra attention. We therefore assume that there is already data stored in the system and focus on interactions taking place in a working system.

The WA interfaces with Web sites, mapping XML- or HTML-demarcated data into RDF triples describing travel objects (according to the ontology used in our system [Gawinecki, Gordon, Nguyen, Paprzycki, & Szymczak, 2005; Gawinecki, Gordon, & Paprzycki, et al., 2005;

Gordon, Kowalski, et al., 2005]). It is created by the CA on the basis of a *configuration file*. The configuration file may be created by the system administrator and sent to the CA as a message from the *graphical user interface (GUI) agent* or may be contained in a message from the DMA that wants to update one or more tokens. Each completed token is time stamped and priority stamped and send back to the CA. Upon completion of its work the (or in the case of an error) WA sends an appropriate message to the CA and self-destructs. A new WA with the same functionality is created by the CA whenever needed. Note that to simplify agent management we create instances of WA for each "job," even though they may produce tokens describing the same travel resource. For instance, when one WA is working on finding information about *all* Westin Hotels in Central Europe (task assigned by the system administrator), another WA may be asked to find information about Westin Hotel in Warszawa (job requested by the DMA). It is the role of the IA to assure that the most current available token is stored in the repository (see Figure 3). An UML statechart of the WA is contained in Figure 3.

CA manages all activities of the content collection subsystem. When started, it creates a certain number of IA (specified by the system administrator—*Servicing agent management request* function in Figure 4) and enters a listening state. There are six types of messages that may be received: (1) a self-destruction order received from the GUI Agent (send by the system administrator)—resulting in the CA killing all existing WAs and IAs first, and then self-destructing; (2) message from the WA that it encountered an error or that it has completed its work and will self-destruct—resulting in appropriate information being recorded; (3) message from the WA containing a token—to be inserted into the priority queue within the CA; (4) message from one of the IAs requesting a new token to be inserted into the repository—which results in the highest priority token being removed from the priority queue and send to the requesting IA. When the queue is empty, a message is send to the IA informing about this fact (as seen in Figure 5, IA will retry requesting token after some delay); (5) message from the DMA containing a request (in the form of a configuration file) to provide one or more

Figure 3. Statechart of the WA

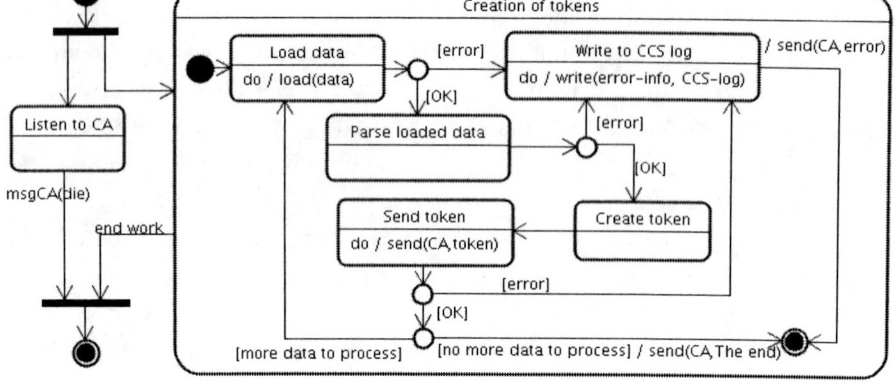

tokens—resulting in creation of an appropriate WA (or a number of WAs); and, finally, (6) message from the GUI Agent ordering adjustment of the number of IAs in the system. A complete statechart of the CA is depicted in Figure 4.

IA is responsible for inserting tokens into the central repository as well as initial pre-processing of tokens to facilitate cleanness of data stored in the system. For the time being the IA performs the following simple checks: (1) time consistency of tokens to be inserted—since it is possible that multiple WAs generate tokens describing the same travel resource (see above), the IA compares time stamps of the token to be inserted with that in the repository and inserts its token only when it is newer; (2) data consistency—token to be used to update/append information has to be consistent with the token in the repository (e.g., the same hotel has to have the same address); and (3) inconsistent tokens are marked as such and they are to be deconflicted (Angryk et al., 2002). In the case when the priority queue is empty, request will be repeated after delay *T.* The statechart of the IA is represented in Figure 5 (top panel presents the overall process flow, while the bottom panel specifies processes involved in servicing tokens).

Let us now briefly describe the next three agents visible in Figure 2. The DBA represents interface between the database (in our case the Jena repository) and the agent system. It is created to separate an agent system from an "outside technology" in such a way that in case of changes in the repository all other changes will be localized to that agent, while the remaining parts of the system stay unchanged.

In the current system the DMA is a simple one. A number of agents of this type, responsible for different travel objects, are created upon system

Figure 4. Statechart of the CA

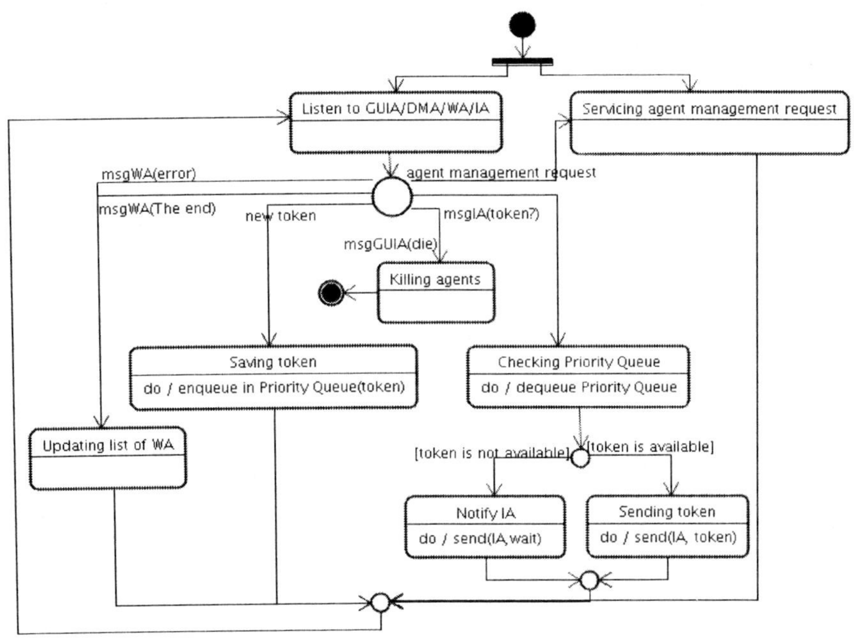

Figure 5. Statechart of the IA

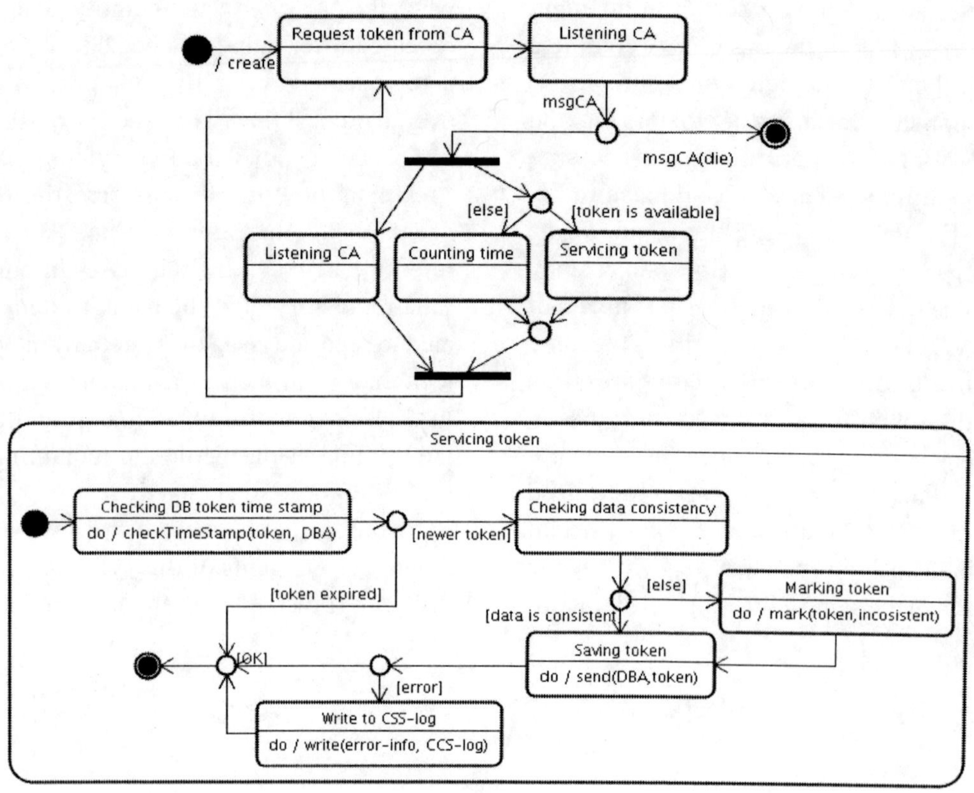

startup. Their role is to "traverse" the repository to find outdated and incomplete tokens and request new/additional ones to be generated to update/complete information stored in the repository. To achieve this goal DMAs generate a configuration file of an appropriate WA and send them to the CA for processing. In the future DMAs will be responsible for complete management of tokens stored in the repository to assure their completeness, consistency, and freshness.

The PIA consists of a manager and a number of "RDF subagents" (*PIA workers* in Figure 6). Each of these subagents represents one or more of simple rules of the type "Irish pub is also a pub" or "Japanese food is Oriental food." These rules are applied to the set of RDF triples returned by the initial query. Rule application involves querying the repository and is expected to expand the result set (e.g., if the user is asking for a Korean restaurant then other Oriental restaurants are likely to be included). The PIA subagents operate as a team passing the result set from one to the next (in our current implementation they are organized in a ring), and since their role is to maximize the set of responses to be delivered to the user no potential response is removed from the set. Final result of their operation is the MRS that is operated on by the PA. Action diagram of the PIA is depicted in Figure 6.

Figure 6. Action diagram of the PIA

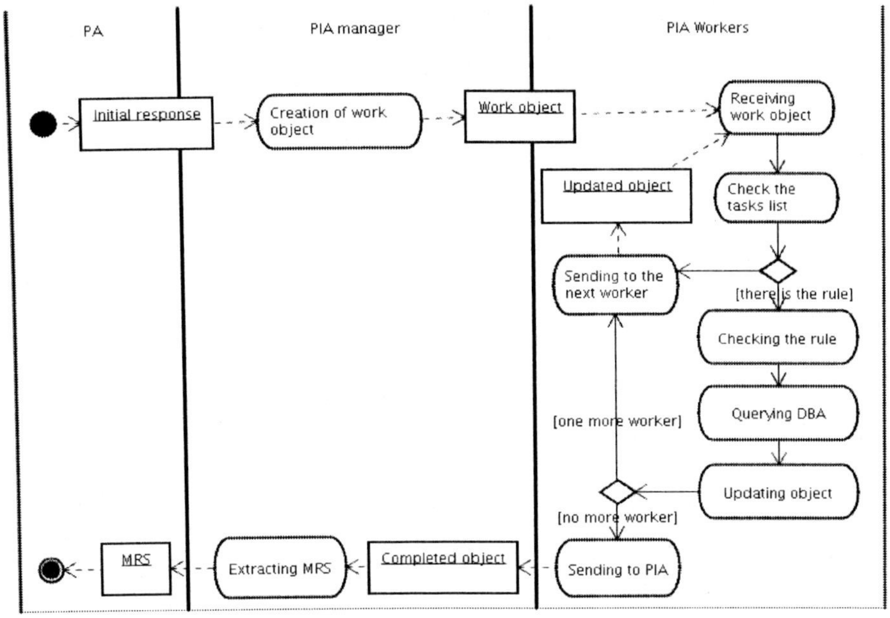

A separate PA will be created for each user and will play two roles in the content delivery subsystem. First, it is the central coordinator—for each user query it directs it from one agent to the next, constantly monitoring processing progress. Second, it utilizes user profile to filter and order responses that are to be sent to the user. More precisely, the user query, after being pre-processed and transformed into an RDQL query (see Kaczmarek et al., 2005 for more details), is being sent to the DBA. What is returned is the initial response consisting of a number of tokens that satisfy the query. This response is being redirected (by the PA) to the PIA to obtain the MRS. Then the PA utilizes the user profile to: (1) remove from the set responses that do not belong there (e.g., user is known to be adversely inclined toward Italian food, and pizza in particular, and thus all of the Italian food serving restaurants have to be excluded); (2) order the remaining selections in such a way that those that are believed to be of most interest to the user will be displayed first (e.g., if user is known to stay in Hilton hotels, they will be displayed first). The statechart diagram of the PA is contained in Figure 7.

As we can see the PA behaves differently depending if the user is using the system for the first time or if it is a returning user. In the latter case, the PA will attempt at gathering explicit feedback related to the information delivered to the user during the previous session. This will be done through a generation of a questionnaire that will be shown to the user, who may decide to ignore it (see also Galant & Paprzycki, 2002). Obtained responses will be used to adjust the user profile. We can also see how the PA plays the role of response preparation orchestrator by always receiving responses from other agents and

Figure 7. Statechart of the PA

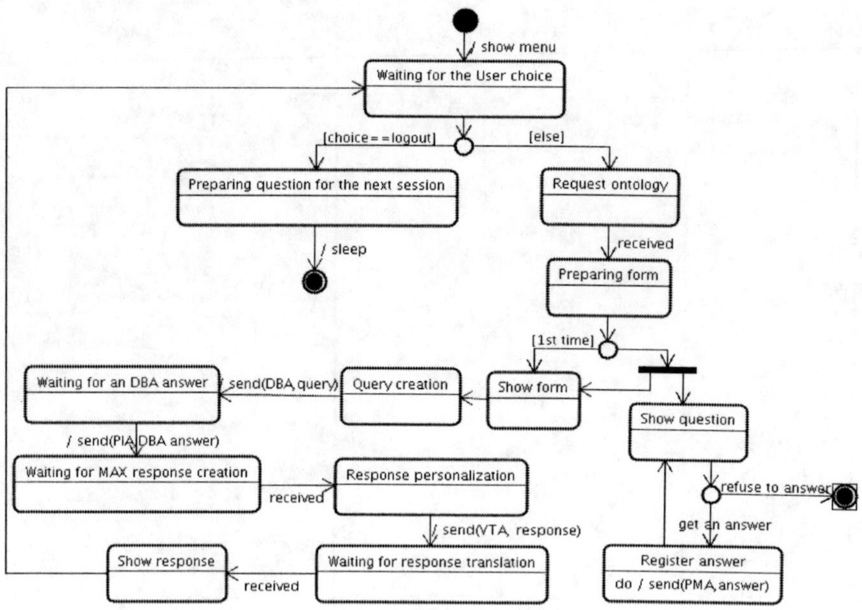

forwarding them to the next agent in the processing chain. We have selected this model of information processing so that "worker agents" like the DBA or the PIA know only one agent to interact with (the PA). Otherwise, an unnecessary set of dependencies would be introduced to the system making it substantially more difficult to manage (any change to one of these agents would have to be propagated to all agents that interact with it—while in our case only a single agent needs to be adjusted).

Replacing Semantic Web with a Semantic Database

As noted before, currently the Semantic Web is an attractive idea that lacks its main component—large repositories of semantically demarcated (in particular travel-related) data. This was one of the important reasons to change the design of our systems from data indexing into data gathering. As a result we are able to create our own "mini Semantic Web" (in the form of a semantic database) and store there information that in the future will allow us to extend our system beyond the basic skeleton described here, and start experimenting with its true projected functionalities—like content personalization.

Let us describe how the HTML-demarcated information available on the Web is turned into semantic tokens representing travel objects in our repository. Before proceeding let us discuss briefly ontologies utilized in the system. As reported in Gawinecki, Gordon, Nguyen, et al., 2005; Gawinecki, Gordon, Paprzycki, et al., 2005; and Gordon, Kowalski, et al., 2005, while there exists a large number of attempts at designing ontologies depicting various aspects of the world, we were not able to locate a complete ontology of the most basic objects in the "world of travel" such as a *hotel* and a *restaurant*. More precisely, there exists an implicit ontology of restaurants utilized by the ChefMoz project (ChefMoz, 2005), but it cannot be used directly as a Semantic Web resource, due to the fact that data stored there is infested with bugs that make its automatic utilization impossible without pre-processing that also involves manual operations (see Gawinecki, Gordon, Paprzycki, et al., 2005 and Gordon, Kowalski, et al., 2005 for more details).

This being the case we have proceeded in two directions. First, as reported in Gawinecki, Gordon, and Paprzycki, et al. (2005) and Gordon, Kowalski, et al. (2005) we have reverse engineered the restaurant ontology underlying the ChefMoz project and cleaned data related to Polish restaurants. Separately we have proceeded with designing hotel ontology using a pragmatic approach. Our hotel ontology is to be used to represent, manipulate, and manage hotel information actually appearing within Web-based repositories (in context of travel; i.e., not hotels as landmarks, or sites of historical events). Therefore we have studied content of the 10 largest Internet travel agencies and found out that most of them describe hotels using very similar vocabulary. Therefore we used these common terms to shape our hotel ontology and the results of this process have

Figure 8. Hilton Sao Paulo Morumbi main page

been reported in Gawinecki, Gordon, Nguyen, et al. (2005); Gawinecki, Gordon, Paprzycki, et al. (2005); and Gordon, Kowalski, et al. (2005). As an outcome we have two fully functional, complete ontologies (of a hotel and of a restaurant) that are used to shape data stored in our Jena repository.

In this context, let us illustrate how we transform the VCP featured data into travel tokens. As an example we will utilize the Web site belonging to Hilton hotels (www.hilton.com). More precisely, let us look at some of the information that is available at the Web site of Hilton Sao Paulo Morumbi depicted in Figure 8.

As clearly seen, from this page we can extract information such as the hotel name, address, and phone numbers. This page would also have to be interacted with, in case we planned to utilize our travel support system to make an actual reservation (which is only in very long-term plans and out of scope of this chapter). To find the remaining information defined by the hotel ontology requires traversing the Web site deeper. Therefore, for instance, the WA has to go to the page contained in Figure 9, to find information about hotel amenities.

As a result the following set of RDF triples (in XML-based notation) will be generated:

Figure 9. Hilton Sao Paulo Morumbi amenities page

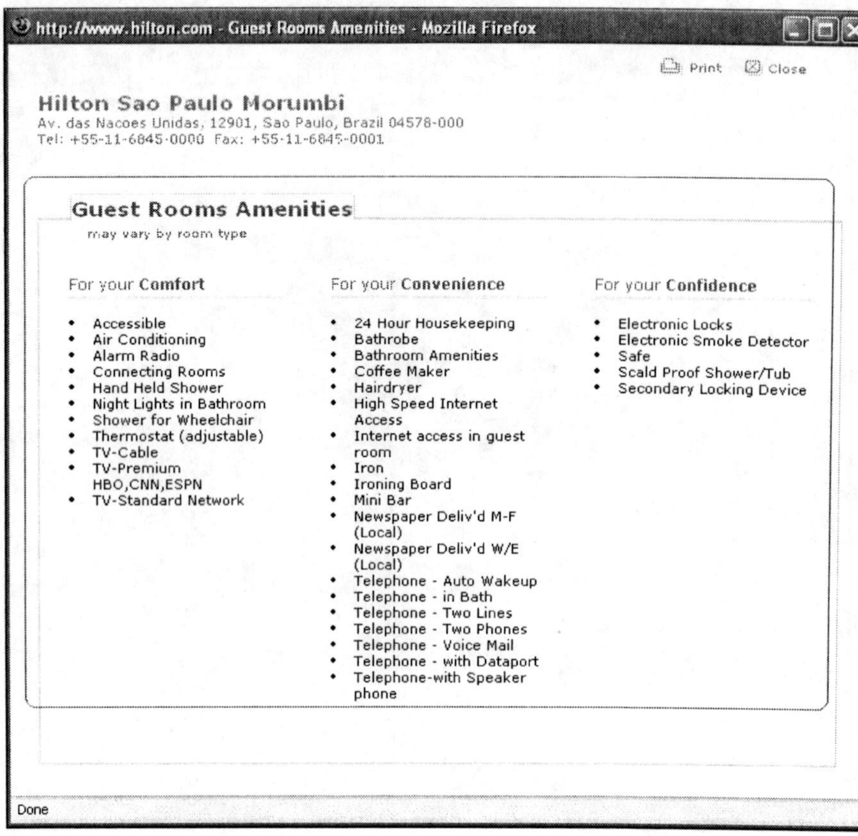

```
<rdf:Description
rdf:about="http://www.agentlab.net/travel/hotels/Hilton/
      SAOMOHI">
   <j.1:roomAmenit rdf:resource="http://.../hotel.
      rdf#AccessibleRoom"/>
   <j.1:roomAmenity rdf:resource="http://.../hotel.
      rdf#AirConditioning"/>
   <j.1:roomAmenity rdf:resource="http://.../hotel.
      rdf#ConnectingRooms"/>
   <j.1:roomAmenity rdf:resource="http://.../hotel.
      rdf#Shower"/>
   <j.1:roomAmenity rdf:resource="http://.../hotel.
      rdf#CableTelevision"/>
   <j.1:roomAmenity rdf:resource="http://.../hotel.
      rdf#CNNavailable"/>
   <j.1:roomAmenity rdf:resource="http://.../hotel.
      rdf#Bathrobe"/>
   <j.1:roomAmenity rdf:resource="http://.../hotel.rdf#Bathro
      omAmenities"/>
   <j.1:roomAmenity rdf:resource="http://.../hotel.rdf#Coffee_
      TeaMaker"/>
   <j.1:roomAmenity rdf:resource="http://.../hotel.
      rdf#Hairdryer"/>
   <j.1:roomAmenity
      rdf:resource="http://.../hotel.rdf#HighSpeedInternetC
      onnection"/>
   <j.1:roomAmenity rdf:resource="http://.../hotel.
      rdf#InternetAccess"/>
   <j.1:roomAmenity rdf:resource="http://.../hotel.rdf#Iron"/>
   <j.1:roomAmenity rdf:resource="http://.../hotel.
      rdf#IroningBoard"/>
   <j.1:roomAmenity rdf:resource="http://.../hotel.
      rdf#Minibar"/>
   <j.1:roomAmenity rdf:resource="http://.../hotel.
      rdf#Newspaper"/>
   <j.1:roomAmenity rdf:resource="http://.../hotel.rdf#Wake-
      upCalls"/>
   <j.1:roomAmenity rdf:resource="http://.../hotel.rdf#Two-
      linePhone"/>
   <j.1:roomAmenity rdf:resource="http://.../hotel.
      rdf#VoiceMail"/>
   <j.1:roomAmenity
      rdf:resource="http://.../hotel.rdf#TelephoneWithData
      Ports"/>
   <j.1:roomAmenity rdf:resource="http://.../hotel.
      rdf#SpeakerPhone"/>
   <j.1:roomAmenity rdf:resource="http://.../hotel.
      rdf#SmokeDetektors"/>
   <j.1:roomAmenity rdf:resource="http://.../hotel.
      rdf#Safe"/>
</rdf:Description>
```

These RDF triples represent a part of our hotel ontology, but this time they became its instance representing a given Hilton hotel (values of various aspects of the hotel are filled-in). Our WA will then continue traversing the hotel site to find, for instance, information about fitness and recreation as well as check-in and check-out times. An appropriate page belonging to the same hotel is depicted in Figure 10 while the resulting set of RDF triples follows.

```
<rdf:Description
rdf:about="http://www.agentlab.net/travel/hotels/Hilton/
      SAOMOHI">
   <j.1:recreationService
      rdf:resource="http://.../hotel.rdf#FitnessCenterOnsit
      e"/>
   <j.1:recreationService
rdf:resource="http://.../hotel.rdf#IndoorOrOutdoorConnec
      tingPool"/>
      <j.1:petsPolicy rdf:resource="http://.../hotel.
      rdf#NoPetsAlowed"/>
   <j.1:additionalDetail
rdf:resource="http://www.agentlab.net/travel/hotels/Hilton/
      SAOMOHI/CheckIn-CheckOut"/>
</rdf:Description>

<rdf:Description
rdf:about="http://www.agentlab.net/travel/hotels/Hilton/
      SAOMOHI/CheckIn-CheckOut">
   <j.1:detail>Check-in: 2:00PM, Check-out: 12:00PM</j.1:
      detail>
</rdf:Description>
```

In this way the WA processes all necessary pages belonging to the Hilton Sao Paulo Morumbi

Figure 10. Hilton Sao Paulo Morumbi fitness and recreation and check-in and check-out information

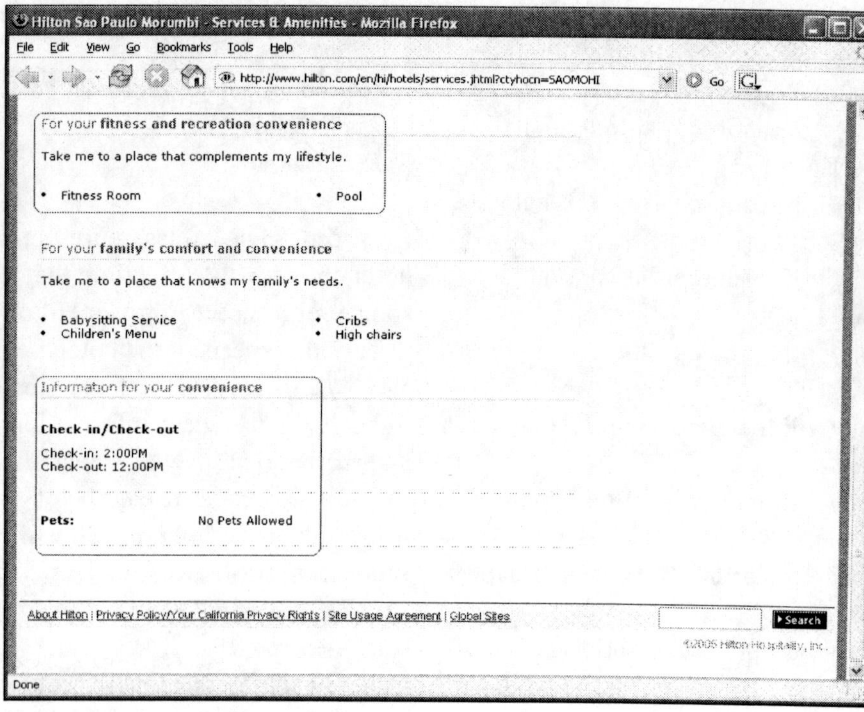

and as a result obtains a set of RDF triples that constitute its complete definition (from the point of view of ontology utilized in our system). This set of RDF triples is then time and priority level stamped, packed into an ACL message and send to the CA that inserts it into the priority queue—to be later inserted, by the IA, to the semantic database. Depending on the assignment the WA may continue producing tokens of other Hilton hotels or, if work is completed, it informs the CA about this fact and self-destructs. In this way in our system, by manually creating WAs for a variety of travel information sources, we can collect real-life data representing actual travel objects.

RDF Data Utilization: Content Personalization

Let us now discuss how the data stored in the system is used to deliver personalized responses to the user. While our approach to user profile construction and utilization is based on ideas presented in Burke (2002); Fink and Kobsa (2002); Galant and Paprzycki (2002); Kobsa, Koenemann, and Pohl (2001); Montaner, López, and De La Rosa (2003); Rich (1979) and Sołtysiak and Crabtree (1998), however utilization of these methods in the context of ontologically demarcated information is novel and was proposed originally in Gawinecki, Vetulani, Gordon, and Paprzycki (2005).

Figure 11. Overlay model utilized to represent user profile

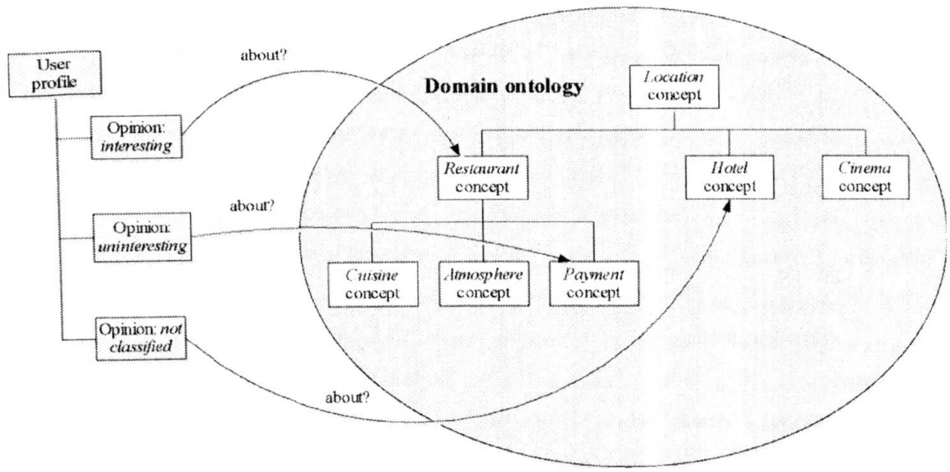

To be able to deliver personalized content to the user of the system, we have to be able to represent the user in the system first—define user profile. Furthermore, the proposed user profile has to be created in such a way to simplify interactions in the system. Since our system is oriented toward processing of ontologically demarcated data, it is very natural to represent user preferences in the same way. Thus we adapted an *overlay model* of user profile, where opinions are "connected" with appropriate concepts in the domain ontology. This approach is also called a *student model*, since it has been found useful to describe knowledge of the student about specific topics of the domain (Greer & McCalla, 1994). Basic tenets of the overlay model are depicted in Figure 11.

For instance, let us consider our hotel ontology and assume that the user likes to stay in hotels that have both a *pool* and *fitness center*. Both these features are subclasses of the concept *amenities*. We can represent user interest by assigning weight to each amenity (the larger the weight the more important the given feature is to the user). In case of our hypothetical customer, both pool and exercise room will be assigned large weights, while features that user is not particularly interested in (e.g., availability of ironing board—see Figure 9) will be assigned small weight—the lesser the interest is the closer to 0 the value will be. In the case of features about which we do not know anything about users' preferences, no value will be assigned (see Figure 11). Let us observe that in this approach we are mimicking the notion of probability—all assigned values are from the interval (0, 1). This means that even in the case of strong counter preference towards a given feature we will assign value 0 (there are no negative values available). Proceeding in this described way, we will create a special instance of hotel ontology, one that represents *user-hotel-profile*. The following fragment of an instance of hotel ontology (this time represented in an N3 notation) depicts user (Karol) profile as it is represented in our system:

```
:KarolOpinions    a sys:OpinionsSet;
 sys:containsOpinion
  [sys:about hotel:Pool;
   sys:hasClassification sys:Interesting;
   sys:hasNormalizedProbability 0.89].
  [sys:about hotel:ExerciseRoom;
   sys:hasClassification sys:Interesting;
   sys:hasNormalizedProbability 0.84].
  [sys:about res:AirConditioning;
   sys:hasClassification sys:Interesting;
   sys:hasNormalizedProbability 0.89].
  [sys:about hotel:BathroomAmenities;
   sys:hasClassification sys:Interesting;
   sys:hasNormalizedProbability 0.73].
  [sys:about hotel:IroningBoard;
   sys:hasClassification sys:NotInteresting;
   sys:hasNormalizedProbability 0.11].
  [sys:about hotel:Iron,
   sys:hasClassification sys:NotInteresting;
   sys:hasNormalizedProbability 0.15].
```

The previous hotel profile of Karol, tells us that he likes to stay in hotels with swimming pool and exercise room, while the availability of an iron and ironing board is inconsequential to him.

Obviously, somewhere in the system we have to store, in some form, information about the user. To assure consistency across the system, this is done in the form of a simplistic user ontology. Next, we present a fragment of such ontology:

```
:hasDress a rdf:Property ;
      rdfs:range :Dress ;
      rdfs:domain :UserProfileData.

:hasAge a rdf:Property ;
      rdfs:range :Age ;
      rdfs:domain :UserProfileData .

:hasWealth a rdf:Property ;
      rdfs:range :Wealth ;
      rdfs:domain :UserProfileData .

:hasProfession a rdf:Property ;
      rdfs:range :Profession ;
      rdfs:domain :UserProfileData .
```

Let us now assume that Karol is a 24-year-old painter, who has enough money to feel rich and whose dressing style is a natural one, then his profile would be represented as:

```
:KarolProfile a sys:UserProfile;
      sys:hasUserID 14-32-61-3456;
      sys:hasUserProfileData :KarolProfileData;
      sys:hasOpinionsSet :KarolOpinions.

:KarolProfileData a sys:UserProfileData;
      sys:hasAge 24;
      sys:hasWealth sys:Rich;
      sys:hasDress sys:NaturalDress;
      sys:hasProfession sys:SpecialistFreeLancer.
```

Rather than keeping them separate, we combine instances of user ontology with the previously described user profile into a complete ontological description—a comprehensive user profile. This user profile is then to be stored in the Jena repository.

One of the important questions that all recommender systems have to address is, how to "introduce" new users to the system (Galant & Paprzycki, 2002). In our system we use stereotyping (Rich, 1979). Obviously, we represent stereotypes the same way we used to represent user profiles, with the difference that instead of specific values representing preferences of a given user, we use sets of variables of nominal (to represent categories—e.g., profession), ordinal (e.g., low income, medium income, high income), and interval (e.g., age between 16 and 22) types. For values of nominal and ordinal types we have established sets of possible values, while for the values of interval types, we defined borders of intervals considered in the system. Using results of a survey and expert knowledge, we were able to create restaurant-related stereotypes (one instance of restaurant ontology of each identified stereotype). To illustrate such a case, here is a fragment of artistic profile in the area of restaurants:

```
:ArtistStereotypeOpinions    a sys:OpinionsSet;
  sys:containsOpinion
   [sys:about res:CafeCoffeeShopCuisine;
    sys:hasClassification sys:Interesting;
    sys:hasNormalizedProbability 1.0].
   [sys:about res:CafeteriaCuisine;
    sys:hasClassification sys:Interesting;
    sys:hasNormalizedProbability 0.75].
   [sys:about res:TeaHouseCuisine;
    sys:hasClassification sys:Interesting;
    sys:hasNormalizedProbability 0.9].
   [sys:about res:WineBeer;
    sys:hasClassification sys:Interesting;
    sys:hasNormalizedProbability 0.8].
   [sys:about res:WineList;
    sys:hasClassification sys:Interesting;
    sys:hasNormalizedProbability 1.0].
   [sys:about res:HotDogsCuisine;
    sys:hasClassification sys:NotInteresting;
    sys:hasNormalizedProbability 0.0].
```

In this stereotype we can see, among others, that an *artist* has been conceptualized as a person who likes *coffee houses* a bit more than *tea houses* and is willing to eat in a *cafeteria*, likes *wine* (a bit more than *beer*), but does not like *hot dogs* (*fast food*). Other stereotypes have been conceptualized similarly and their complete list and a detailed description of their utilization can be found in Gawinecki, Kruszyk, and Paprzycki (2005).

When a new user logs onto the system he/she will be requested to fill out a short questionnaire about age, gender, income level, occupation, address (matching user features defined by the user ontology), as well as questions about travel preferences. While the basic user ontology-based data will be required, answering questions about travel preferences will be voluntary. Personal data collected through the questionnaire will be used to match a person to a stereotype. More precisely, we will calculate a distance measure between user-specified characteristics and these appearing in stereotypes defined in the system and find one that matches his/her profile the closest. To achieve this we will use the following formula:

$$d\left(\hat{S},\hat{u}\right) = \frac{\sum_{f=1}^{k} w^f \delta^f_{\hat{S}\hat{u}} d^f_{\hat{S}\hat{u}}}{\sum_{f=1}^{k} w^f \delta^f_{\hat{S}\hat{u}}}$$

where: w^f – weight of attribute, $d^f_{S,u}$ – distance between values of the attribute in the stereotype S and user's data u, $\delta^f_{S,u}$ – Boolean flag that informs whether attribute f appears in both: stereotype's data (S) and user's data (u).

To illustrate this, let us consider Karol, the painter, again. In the Table 1 we present Karol's data and the artist stereotype data and show how the closeness between Karol and that stereotype is calculated.

The same process is then repeated comparing Karol's data against all other stereotypes to find the one that fits him the best. In the next step this stereotype is joined with his user data to become his *initial profile*. In the case when he answers any domain-specific questions (recall, that he may omit them), this data will be used to modify his user profile. For example, let us assume that he has been identified as student stereotype, but he has also specified that he does not like coffee houses (while in the student stereotype coffee houses have been assigned a substantial positive weight). Obviously, in his profile, this positive value will be replaced by zero—as explicit personal preferences outweigh these specified in the stereotype (see also Nistor, Oprea, Paprzycki, & Parakh, 2002):

Table 1. Calculating closeness between user profile (Karol) and a stereotype (artist)

Attribute (*f*)	Attribute weight (w^f)	Data of artist stereotype (comma means OR relation): (*S*)	Karol's Data: (*u*)	Distance between value of attribute: ($d^f_{S,u}$)	Weighted distance: ($w^{f*} d^f_{S,u}$)
Age	2	20-50	24	0.00	0.00
Wealth	4	Not Rich, Average Rich	Rich	0.33	1.33
Dress	1	Naturally, Elegantly	Naturally	0.00	0.00
Profession	2	Student/Pupil, Scientist/Teacher, Specialist/FreeLancer Unemployed/ WorkSeeker	Specialist/ FreeLancer	0.00	0.00
			COMBINED		1.3(3) / (2+4+1+2)= 0.14(6)

```
:KarolOpinions a sys:OpinionsSet;
 sys:containsOpinion
  [sys:about res:CafeCoffeeShopCuisine;
   sys:hasClassification sys:Interesting;
   sys:hasNormalizedProbability 0.0].
```

Observe that as soon as the system is operational we will be able to store information about user behaviors (Angryk et al., 2003; Galant & Paprzycki, 2002; Gordon & Paprzycki, 2005). These data will be then used not only to modify individual user profiles, but also mined (e.g., clustered) to obtain information about various group behaviors taking place in the system. This information can be used to verify, update, or completely replace our initial stereotypes. Such processes are based on the so-called implicit relevance feedback (Fink & Kobsa, 2002; Kobsa et al., 2001). As described earlier (see Figure 7) we will also utilize explicit feedback based on user responses to subsequent questionnaires. Currently as explicit feedback we utilize only a single question: "Did you like our main suggestion presented last time?" but a more intricate questionnaire could also be used. Specifically, at the end of each user system interaction, on the basis of what was recommended to the user, a set of questions about these recommendations could be prepared. When the user returns to the system, these questions would be then asked to give him/her opportunity to express his/her direct opinion. Both implicit and explicit feedbacks are used to adjust user profile (see also Gawinecki, Vetulani, et al., 2005). Note here, that in most recommender systems stereotyping is *the* method of information filtering (demographic filtering); thus making such systems rather rigid—in this case individual user preferences cannot be properly modeled and modified (Kobsa et al., 2001). In our system we use stereotyping only to solve the cold-start problem—and modify them over time—and thus avoid the rigidity trap.

User profile is utilized by the PA to rank and filter travel objects. Let us assume that after the query, the response preparation process has passed all stages and in the last one the PIA agent has completed its work and the MRS has been delivered to the PA. The PA has now to compute a *temperature* of each travel object that is included in the MRS. The temperature represents the "probability" that a given object is a "favorite" of the user. This way of calculating the importance of selected objects was one of the reasons for the way that we have assigned importance measures to individual features (as belonging to the interval [0,1]). Recall here that the DBA and the PIA know nothing about user preferences and that the PIA uses a variety of general rules to increase the response set beyond that provided as a response to the original query.

To calculate the temperature of a travel object (let us name it an *active object*) three aspects of the situation have to be taken into account. First, features of the active object. Second, user interests represented in the user profile—if a given feature has no preference specified then it cannot be used. In other words, for each token in the MRS we will crop its ontological graph to represent only these features that are defined in user profile. Third, features requested in user query. More specifically, if given keywords appear in the query (representing explicit wishes of the user), for example, if the query was about a restaurant in Las Vegas, then such restaurants should be presented to the user first. Interactions between these three aspects are represented in Figure 12.

Figure 12. Construction of final response: Interactions between features

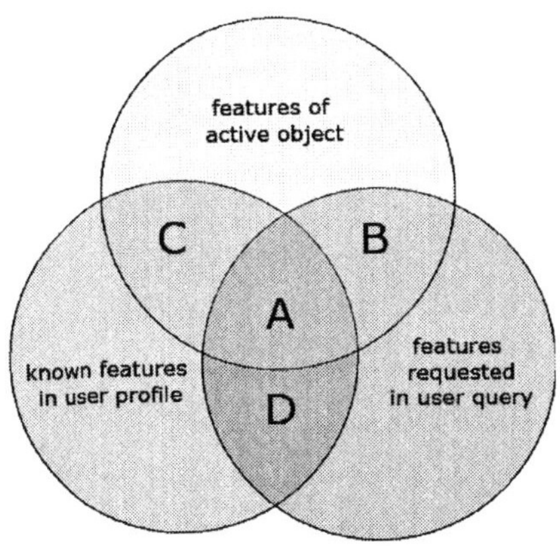

Here we can distinguish the following situations:

A. Features explicitly requested by the user that appear in the active object as well as in the user-profile;
B. Features requested by the user and appearing in the active object;
C. Features not requested that are a part of the user profile and that appeared in the active object; and
D. Features that do not appear in the active object (we are not interested in them).

Ratings obtained for each token in the MRS represent what the system believes are user preferences and are used to filter out these objects temperatures of which are below a certain threshold and rank the remaining ones (objects with highest scores will be displayed first). We will omit discussion of a special case when there is no object above the threshold. The MRS is processed in the following way:

1. Travel objects are to be returned to the user in two groups (buckets)
   a. Objects requested explicitly by the user (via the query form) – Group I
   b. Objects not requested explicitly by the user but predicted by the system to be of potential interest to the user – Group II

   Thus, for each active object we divide features according to the areas depicted in Figure 11. Objects for which at least one feature is inside of either area A or B belong to Group I, objects with all features inside area C belong to Group II, while the remaining objects are discarded.

2. Inside of each bucket travel objects are sorted according to their temperature computed in the following way: for a given object *O* its temperature

$$temp(0) = \sum_{f \in O} temp(f)$$

where $temp(f) = 1$ if $f \in A \cup B$, or $p_n(f)$ if $f \in C$, while $temp(f)=temp(f) - 0.5$. This latter calculation is performed to implicate that these features that are not of interest to the user (their individual temperatures are less than 0.5) reduce the overall temperature of the object. Function $p_n(f)$ is a normalized probability of feature *f*, based on the user profile.

Let us consider Karol, who is interested in selecting a restaurant. In his query he specified that this restaurant has to serve Italian cuisine and has to allow smoking. Additionally, we know, from Karol's profile, that he does not like *coffee* (weight 0.1) and *outdoor dining* (weight 0.05). Thus for the restaurant X:

```
:RestaurantX a res:Restaurant;
    res:cuisine res:ItalianCuisine;
    res:cuisine res:PizzaCuisine;
    res:cuisine res:CafeCoffeeShopCuisine;
    res:feature res:Outdoor.
```

the overall score will be decreased due to the influence of *Outdoor* and *CafeCoffeeShopCuisine* features, but will receive a "temperature boost" because of the *ItalianCuisine* feature (explicitly specified feature). However, the restaurant X it won't be rated as high as the restaurant Y:

Table 2. Computing temperature of a restaurant

Restaurant N3 descriptions (bold – requested by the user, underlined – in the user profile; could be conjunctive)	Calculations
:RestaurantX a res:Restaurant; res:cuisine res:ItalianCuisine; res:cuisine res:PizzaCuisine; res:cuisine res:CafeCoffeeShopCuisine; res:feature res:Outdoor.	+0.5 (=1-0.5) requested; B +0 -0.49 (=0.01-0.5) profile -0.45 (=0.05-0.5) profile = -0.44
:RestaurantY a res:Restaurant; res:cuisine res:ItalianCuisine; res:smoking res:PermittedSmoking.	+0.5 (=1-0.5) requested; B +0.5 (=1-0.5) requested; B = 1
:RestaurantZ a res:Restaurant; res:cuisine res:WineBeer; res:smoking res:PermittedSmoking.	+0.3 (=0.8-0.5) not requested; profile; C +0.5 (=1-0.5) not requested; profile; C = 0.8

```
:RestaurantY a res:Restaurant;
    res:cuisine res:ItalianCuisine;
    res:smoking res:PermittedSmoking.
```

which serves *ItalianCuisine*, where smoking is also permitted. To be more specific, let us consider these two restaurants and the third one described by the following features:

```
:RestaurantZ a res:Restaurant;
    res:cuisine res:WineBeer;
    res:smoking res:PermittedSmoking.
```

Then Table 2 represents the way that temperatures of each restaurant will be computed.

As a result, restaurants X and Y belong to the first bucket (to be displayed to the user as they both have features that belong to area B). However, while restaurant Y has high temperature (1) and definitely should be displayed, restaurant X has very low temperature (-0.44) and thus will not likely be displayed at all. Interestingly, restaurant Z, which belongs to the second bucket (belongs to area C), has an overall score of 0.8 and is likely to be displayed. This example shows also the potential adverse effect of lack of information (e.g., in the ChefMoz repository; but more generally, within the Web) on the quality of content-based filtering (at least done in a way similar to that proposed previously). Simply said, what we do not know cannot decrease the score, and thus a restaurant for which we know only address and cuisine may be displayed as we do not know that it allows smoking on the premises (which would make it totally unacceptable to a given user).

RDF Data Utilization: Content Delivery

Let us now present in more detail how the delivery of content to the user is implemented as an agent system. To be able to do this we need to briefly introduce additional agents (beyond these presented in Figure 2) and their roles (using Prometheus methodology [Prometheus, 2005])—as represented in Figure 13.

In addition to the PA (described in details in Figure 7) and the DBA, we have also: (1) *view transforming agent* (*VTA*) responsible for delivering response in the form that matches the user I/O device; (2) *proxy agent* (*PrA*) that is responsible for facilitating interactions between

Figure 13. Content delivery agents and their roles

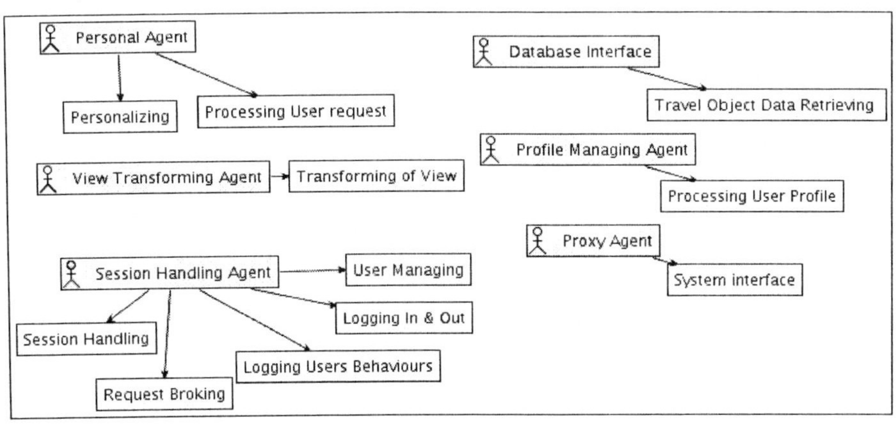

the agent system and the outside world (need for these agents as well as a detailed description of their implementation can be found in Kaczmarek et al. (2005); (3) *session handling agent (SHA)*, which is responsible for complete management and monitoring of functional aspects of user interactions with the system; and (4) *profile managing agent (PMA)* which is responsible for (a) creating profiles for new users, (b) retrieving profiles of returning users and (c) updating user-profiles, based on implicit and explicit relevance feedback. Let us now summarize processes involved in content delivery through a UML action diagram. While rather complex, descriptions contained in Figure 14 represent a complete conceptualization of actions involved in servicing user request from the moment that the user logs on to the system, to the moment when he/she obtains response to their query.

State of the System

As indicated earlier in this chapter, we have concentrated on these features of our system that are currently being implemented and close to being ready, while omitting the features that we would like to see developed in the future. While the interface to the system is still under construction, it is possible to connect to it from a browser. Furthermore, we have emulated WAP-based connectivity. As of the day this chapter is being written, we have implemented a function-complete content collection subsystem consisting of: (1) a number of hotel wrappers (WA) that allow us to feed hotel data into the system; (2) CA and IA agents that collaborate with the WAs to insert data into Jena-based repository; and (3) an initial version of the DMA and the PIA. For the CCS we have semi-automatically cleaned-up subsets of ChefMoz data, describing selected restaurants. We have also a relatively complete content delivery subsystem. In particular, (1) the PrA, the SHA, and the VTA that facilitate user-system interactions

Figure 14. Content delivery action diagram

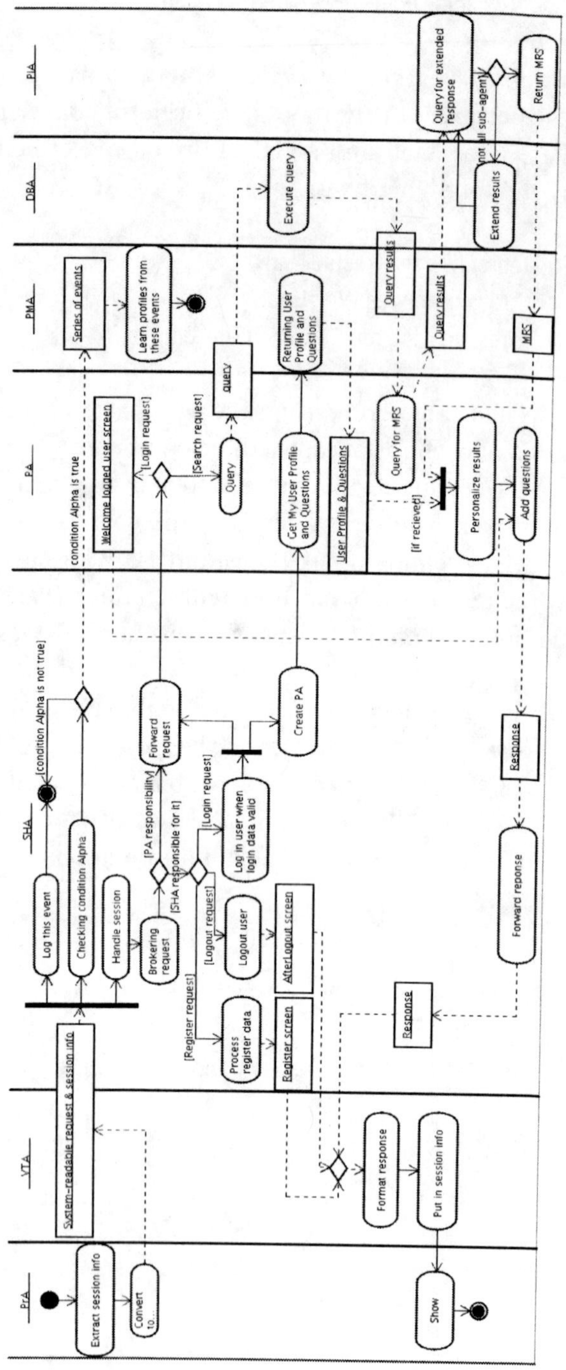

Figure 15. System query screenshot

have been implemented and tested; (2) the PA is working as described in this chapter (with the PIA working in the case of restaurants only); (3) the PMA has only limited capacity, it is capable of creating and managing a single user profile; (4) while the existing set of stereotypes involves only restaurants. Let us briefly illustrate the work of the system, by screen-shots of the query (Figure 15) and the response (Figure 16). The query was a general query about restaurants in Greensboro, NC; note the box that attempts at asking a question about *Bistro Sophia* that was suggested to the user in the previous session (Figure 16).

One of the biggest problems related to testing our system is the fact that, being realistic, no user would be interested in a system that only provides a few hotel chains and restaurants (e.g., in Poland). This being the case we can ourselves test features

Figure 16. System response screenshot

of the system like: (1) is the user query handled correctly, that is, do the returned results represent the correct answer taking into account the current state of the system; (2) do the WAs correctly deliver and the CA and IAs accurately insert tokens into the system; and (3) are agent communication and interactions proceeding without deadlocks and does the system scale. Unfortunately, it is practically impossible to truly test adaptive features of the system. Without actual users utilizing the system to satisfy their real travel needs, all the work that we have done implementing the system cannot be practice verified.

This is a more general problem of the chicken-and-egg type that is facing most of Semantic Web research (regardless of its application area). Without real systems doing real work and utilizing actual ontologically demarcated data on a large scale (to deliver what users need) it is practically impossible to assess if the Semantic Web, the way it was conceptualized, is the way that we will be able to deal with information overload, or is it just another pipe dream like so many in the past of computer science.

FUTURE DEVELOPMENTS

As described previously, it seems to be clear what the future of the development of Semantic Web technologies applied in context of e-business (or in any other context) has to be. It has to follow the positive program put forward by Nwana and Ndumu (1999). The same way as agent systems and a large number of systems utilizing Semantic Web technologies have to be implemented and experimented with. Furthermore, it is necessary to develop tools that are going to speed up ontological demarcation of Web content. Here, both the content that is about to be put on the Web as well as tools supporting demarcation of legacy content need to be improved and popularized. Only then, we will be able to truly assess the value proposition of the Semantic Web. Furthermore, since software agents and the Semantic Web are truly intertwined, the development of the Semantic Web should stimulate development of agent systems, while development of agent systems is likely to stimulate development of the Semantic Web.

To facilitate these processes we plan to continue development of our agent-based travel support system. The first step will be to complete integration and testing of the aforementioned described system skeleton. We will proceed further by: (1) developing ontologies of other important travel objects, for example, movie theaters, museums, operas, and so forth; (2) fully developing and implementing the PIA and the DMA infrastructures—according to the previously presented description; (3) continuing implementing WAs to increase the total volume of data available in the system; (4) adding a geographic information system (GIS) component to the system, to allow answering queries like: which restaurant is the closest one to that hotel?; (5) developing and implementing an agent-based collaborative filtering infrastructure; and (6) investigating the potential of utilizing text processing technologies for developing new generation of adaptive WAs.

REFERENCES

Angryk, R., Galant, V., Gordon, M., & Paprzycki, M. (2002). Travel support system: An agent based framework. In H. R. Arabnia & Y. Mun (Eds.), *Proceedings of the International Conference on Internet Computing (IC'02)* (pp. 719-725). Las Vegas, NV: CSREA Press.

Berners-Lee, T., Hendler, J., Lassila, O. (2001). The Semantic Web. *Scientific American*. Retrieved May, 2001, from http://www.sciam.com/article.cfm?articleID=00048144-10D2-1C70-84A9809EC588EF21

Burke, R. (2002). Hybrid recommender systems: Survey and experiments. *User Modeling and User-Adapted Interaction, 12*(4), 331-370.

ChefMoz. (2005). *ChefMoz dining guide*. Retrieved November, 2004, from http://chefdmoz.org

Darpa Agent Markup Language (DAML). (2005). *Language overview*. Retrieved October, 2005, from http://www.daml.org/

Fensel, D. (2001). *Ontologies: A silver bullet for knowledge management and electronic commerce*. Berlin: Springer.

Fink, J., & Kobsa, A. (2002). User modeling for personalized city tours. *Artificial Intelligence Review, 18*, 33-74.

Galant, V., Gordon, M., & Paprzycki, M. (2002a). Agent-client interaction in a Web-based e-commerce system. In D. Grigoras (Ed.), *Proceedings of the International Symposium on Parallel and Distributed Computing* (pp. 1-10). Iasi, Romania: University of Iaşi Press.

Galant, V., Gordon, M., & Paprzycki, M. (2002b). Knowledge management in an Internet travel support system. In B. Wiszniewski (Ed.), *Proceedings of ECON2002, ACTEN* (pp. 97-104). Wejcherowo: ACTEN.

Galant, V., Jakubczyc, J., & Paprzycki, M. (2002). Infrastructure for e-commerce. In M. Nycz & M. L. Owoc (Eds.), *Proceedings of the 10th Conference Extracting Knowledge from Databases* (pp. 32-47). Poland: Wrocław University of Economics Press.

Galant, V., & Paprzycki, M. (2002, April). Information personalization in an Internet based travel support system. In *Proceedings of the BIS'2002 Conference* (pp. 191-202). Poznań, Poland: Poznań University of Economics Press.

Gawinecki, M., Gordon, M., Nguyen, N., Paprzycki, M., & Szymczak, M. (2005). RDF demarcated resources in an agent based travel support system. In M. Golinski et al. (Eds.), *Informatics and effectiveness of systems* (pp. 303-310). Katowice: PTI Press.

Gawinecki, M., Gordon, M., Paprzycki, M., Szymczak, M., Vetulani, Z., & Wright, J. (2005). Enabling semantic referencing of selected travel related resources. In W. Abramowicz (Ed.), *Proceedings of the BIS'2005 Conference* (pp. 271-290). Poland: PoznaD University of Economics Press.

Gawinecki, M., Kruszyk, M., & Paprzycki, M. (2005). Ontology-based stereotyping in a travel support system. In *Proceedings of the XXI Fall Meeting of Polish Information Processing Society* (pp. 73-85). PTI Press.

Gawinecki, M., Vetulani, Z., Gordon, M., & Paprzycki, M. (2005). Representing users in a travel support system. In H. Kwaśnicka et al. (Eds.), *Proceedings of the ISDA 2005 Conference* (pp. 393-398). Los Alamitos, CA: IEEE Press.

Gilbert, A., Gordon, M., Nauli, A., Paprzycki, M., Williams, S., & Wright, J. (2004). Indexing agent for data gathering in an e-travel system. *Informatica, 28*(1), 69-78.

Gordon, M., Kowalski, A., Paprzycki, N., Pełech, T., Szymczak, M., & Wasowicz, T. (2005). Ontologies in a travel support system. In D. J. Bem et al. (Eds.), *Internet 2005* (pp. 285-300). Poland: Technical University of Wrocław Press.

Gordon, M., & Paprzycki, M. (2005). Designing agent based travel support system. In *Proceedings of the ISPDC 2005 Conference* (pp. 207-214). Los Alamitos, CA: IEEE Computer Society Press.

Greer, J., & McCalla, G. (1994). *Student modeling: The key to individualized knowledge based instruction* (pp. 3-35). NATO ASI Series. Springer-Verlag.

Harrington, P., Gordon, M., Nauli, A., Paprzycki, M., Williams, S., & Wright, J. (2003). Using software agents to index data in an e-travel system. In N. Callaos (Ed.), *Electronic Proceedings of the 7th SCI Conference* [CD-ROM, file: 001428].

Hendler, J. (1999, March 11). Is there an intelligent agent in your future? *Nature.* Retrieved March, 2004, from http://www.nature.com/nature/webmatters/agents/agents.html

Hendler, J. (2001). Agents and Semantic Web. *IEEE Intelligent Systems Journal, 16*(2), 30-37.

JADE. (2005). (Version 3.4) [Computer software]. Retrieved from http://jade.tilab.com/

Jena. (2005, March). *A Semantic Web framework* (Version 2.4) [Computer software]. Retrieved from http://www.hpl.hp.com/semweb/jena2.htm

Jennings, N. R. (2001). An agent-based approach for building complex software systems. *Communications of the ACM, 44*(4), 35-41.

Kaczmarek, P., Gordon, M., Paprzycki, M., & Gawinecki, M. (2005). The problem of agent-client communication on the Internet. *Scalable Computing: Practice and Experience, 6*(1), 111-123.

Kobsa, A., Koenemann, J., & Pohl, W. (2001). Personalized hypermedia presentation techniques for improving online customer relationships. *The Knowledge Engineering Review, 16*(2), 111-155.

Maes, P. (1994). Agents that reduce work and information overload. *Communications of the ACM, 37*(7), 31-40.

Manola, F., & Miller, E. (Eds.). (2005). *RDF primer.* Retrieved from http://www.w3.org/TR/rdf-primer .

McGuinness, D. L., & Van Harmelen, F. (Eds.). (2005, February 10). *OWL Web ontology language overview.* Retrieved December, 2004, from http://www.w3.org/TR/owl-features/

Montaner, M., López, B., & De La Rosa, J. L. (2003). A taxonomy of recommender agents on the Internet. *Artificial Intelligence Review, 19,* 285-330.

Nistor, C. E., Oprea, R., Paprzycki, M., & Parakh, G. (2002). The role of a psychologist in e-commerce personalization. In *Proceedings of the 3rd European E-COMM-LINE 2002 Conference* (pp. 227-231). Bucharest, Romania: IPA S. A.

Nwana, H., & Ndumu, D. (1999). A perspective on software agents research. *The Knowledge Engineering Review, 14*(2), 1-18.

Paprzycki, M., Angryk, R., Kołodziej, K., Fiedorowicz, I., Cobb, M., Ali, D., et al. (2001) Development of a travel support system based on intelligent agent technology. In S. Niwiński (Ed.), *Proceedings of the PIONIER 2001 Conference* (pp. 243-255). Poland: University of PoznaD Press.

Paprzycki, M., Kalczyński, P. J., Fiedorowicz, I., Abramowicz, W., & Cobb, M. (2001) Personalized traveler information system. In B. F. Kubiak & A. Korowicki (Eds.), *Proceedings of the 5th International Conference Human-Computer Interaction* (pp. 445-456). Gdańsk, Poland: Akwila Press.

Raccoon. (2005). (0.5.1) [Computer software]. Retrieved November 2005, from http://rx4rdf.liminalzone.org/Raccoon

Rich, E. (1979). User modeling via stereotypes. *Cognitive Science, 3,* 329-354.

Prometheus. (2005). *Prometheus methodology.* Retrieved from http://www.cs.rmit.edu.au/agents/prometheus/

Sołtysiak, S., & Crabtree, B. (1998). Automatic learning of user profiles—towards the personalization of agent service. *BT Technological Journal, 16*(3), 110-117.

Wooldridge, M. (2002). *An introduction to multiAgent systems.* John Wiley & Sons.

Wright, J., Gordon, M., Paprzycki, M., Williams, S., & Harrington, P. (2003). Using the ebXML registry repository to manage information in an Internet travel support system. In W. Abramowicz & G. Klein (Eds.), *Proceedings of the BIS2003 Conference* (pp. 81-89). Poland: Poznań University of Economics Press.

This work was previously published in Semantic Web Technologies and E-Business: Toward the Integrated Virtual Organization and Business Process Automation, edited by A. Salam and J. Stevens, pp. 325-359, copyright 2007 by IGI Publishing, formerly known as Idea Group Publishing (an imprint of IGI Global).

Chapter XVIII
Personalized Information Retrieval in a Semantic-Based Learning Environment

Antonella Carbonaro
University of Bologna, Italy

Rodolfo Ferrini
University of Bologna, Italy

ABSTRACT

Active learning is the ability of learners to carry out learning activities in such a way that they will be able to effectively and efficiently construct knowledge from information sources. Personalized and customizable access on digital materials collected from the Web according to one's own personal requirements and interests is an example of active learning. Moreover, it is also necessary to provide techniques to locate suitable materials. In this chapter, we introduce a personalized learning environment providing intelligent support to achieve the expectations of active learning. The system exploits collaborative and semantic approaches to extract concepts from documents, and maintaining user and resources profiles based on domain ontologies. In such a way, the retrieval phase takes advantage of the common knowledge base used to extract useful knowledge and produces personalized views of the learning system.

INTRODUCTION

Most of the modern applications of computing technology and information systems are concerned with information-rich environments, the modern, open, large-scale environments with autonomous heterogeneous information resources (Huhns & Singh, 1998; Cooley, Mobasher, & Srivastava, 1997). The effective and efficient management of the large amounts and varieties of information they include is the key to the above applications.

The Web inherits most of the typical characteristic of an information-rich environment: information resources can be added or removed in a loosely structured manner, and it lacks global control of the content accuracy of those resources. Furthermore, it includes heterogeneous components with mutual complex interdependencies; it includes not just text and relational data, but varieties of multimedia, forms, and executable code. As a result, old methods for manipulating information sources are no longer efficient or even appropriate. Mechanisms are needed in order to allow efficient querying and retrieving on a great variety of information sources which support structured as well as unstructured information.

In order to foster the development of Web-based information access and management, it is relevant to be able to obtain a user-based view of available information. The exponential increase of the size and the formats of remotely accessible data allows us to find suitable solutions to the problem. Often, information access tools are not able to provide the right answers for a user query, but rather, they provide large supersets thereof (e.g., in Web search engines). The search for documents uses queries containing words or describing concepts that are desired in the returned documents. Most content retrieval methodologies use some type of similarity score to match a query describing the content, and then they present the user with a ranked list of suggestions (Belkin & Croft, 1992). Designing applications for supporting the user in accessing and retrieving Web information sources is one of the current challenges for the artificial intelligence community.

In a distributed learning environment, there is likely to be large number of educational resources (Web pages, lectures, journal papers, learning objects, etc.) stored in many distributed and differing repositories on the Internet. Without any guidance, students will probably have great difficulty finding the reading material that is relevant for a particular learning task. The metadata descriptions concerning a learning object (LO) representation provide information about properties of the learning objects. However, the sole metadata does not provide qualitative information about different objects nor provide information for customized views. This problem is becoming particularly important in Web-based education where the variety of learners taking the same course is much greater. In contrast, the courses produced using adaptive hypermedia or intelligent tutoring system technologies are able to dynamically select the most relevant learning material from their knowledge bases for each individual student. Nevertheless, generally these systems cannot directly benefit from existing repositories of learning material (Brusilovsky & Nijhavan, 2002).

In educational settings learning objects can be of different kinds, from being files having static content (like HTML, PDF, or PowerPoint presentation format) or in sophisticated interactive format (like HTML pages loaded with JavaScript or Java applet, etc.). Audio files, video clips, or Flash animations could also constitute learning objects. An LO comprises a chunk of content material, which can be re-used or shared in different learning situations. Such a re-use of content from one system to another makes LO standardized so that it can be adopted across different computer platforms and learning systems. The IEEE Standard for Learning Object Metadata (LOM)[1] is the first accredited standard for learning object technology.[2]

Presently there are countless LOs available for commercial and academic use. Because of time and capability constraints, however, it is almost impossible both for a learner and a teacher to go through all available LOs to find the most suitable one. In particular, learning object metadata tags may facilitate rapid updating, searching, and management of content by filtering and selecting only the relevant content for a given purpose (Carbonaro, 2004). Searchers can use a standard set of retrieval techniques to maximize their chances of finding the resources via a search engine (Recker, Walker, & Lawless, 2003). Nevertheless, the value searching and browsing results depend on the information and organizational structure of the repository. Moreover, searching for LOs within heterogeneous repositories may become a more complicated problem. What we are arguing in this chapter is that one can alleviate such difficulties by using suitable representations of both available information sources and a user's interests in order to match as appropriately as possible user information needs, as expressed in his or her query and in any available information. The representation we propose is based on ontologies representing the learning domain by means of its concepts, the possible relations between them and other properties, the conditions, or regulations of the domain. In the digital library community, a flat list of attribute/value pairs is often assumed to be available. In the Semantic Web community, annotations are often assumed to be an instance of an ontology. Through the ontologies the system will express hierarchical links among entities and will guarantee interoperability of educational resources. Recent researches on ontologies have shown the important role they can play in the e-learning domain (Dzbor, Motta, & Stutt, 2005).

In this context, standard keyword search is of very limited effectiveness. For example, it does not allow users and the system to search, handle, or read concepts of interest, and it does not consider synonymy and hyponymy that could reveal hidden similarities potentially leading to better retrieval. The advantages of a concept-based document and user representations can be summarized as follows: (i) ambiguous terms inside a resource are disambiguated, allowing their correct interpretation and, consequently, a better precision in the user model construction (e.g., if a user is interested in computer science resources, a document containing the word 'bank' as it is meant in the financial context could not be relevant); (ii) synonymous words belonging to the same meaning can contribute to the resource model definition (for example, both 'mouse' and 'display' bring evidence for computer science documents, improving the coverage of the document retrieval); (iii) synonymous words belonging to the same meaning can contribute to the user model matching, which is required in recommendation process (for example, if two users have the same interests, but these are expressed using different terms, they will considered overlapping); and (iv) classification, recommendation, and sharing phases take advantage of the word senses in order to classify, retrieve, and suggest documents with high semantic relevance with respect to the user and resource models.

For example, the system could support computer science last-year students during their activities in courseware like bio computing, internet programming, or machine learning. In fact, for these kinds of courses, it is necessary to have the active involvement of the student in the acquisition of the didactical material that should integrate the lecture notes specified and released by the teacher. Basically, the level of integration depends both on the student's prior knowledge in that particular subject and on the comprehension level he wants to acquire. Furthermore, for the mentioned courses, it is necessary to continuously update the acquired knowledge by integrating recent information available from any remote digital library.

The rest of the chapter is organized as follows. The next section describes background and literature review proposing significant examples of semantic-based e-learning systems. We then illustrate our personalized learning retrieval framework detailing proposed system requirements and architecture. We propose a concept-based semantic approach to model resource and user profiles providing word sense disambiguation process and resource representation, and provide some notes about test implementation and experimental sessions. Some final considerations and comments about future developments conclude the chapter.

BACKGROUND AND LITERATURE REVIEW

The research on e-learning and Web-based educational systems traditionally combines research interests and efforts from various fields, in order to tailor the growing amount of information to the needs, goals, and tasks of the specific individual users. Semantic Web technologies may achieve improved adaptation and flexibility for users, and new methods and types of courseware which will be compliant with the semantic Web vision. In the following sections we will describe some examples of existing projects thanks to which we will be able to outline what the current research on these fields offers. They are based on ontologies and standards that have an important role in the representation of LOs. Heflin (2004) defined an ontology as a structure in which defined terms are used to describe and represent an area of knowledge. Moreover, ontologies include computer-usable definitions of basic concepts in the domain and the relationships among them. Ontologies could be used to share domain information in order to make that knowledge reusable. The W3C standard language for ontology creation is OWL. More detailed review on ontology-based applications in education can be found in Kanellopoulos, Kotsiantis, and Pintelas (2006).

Edutella

Edutella (*http://edutella.jxta.org/*) is defined as a multi-staged effort to scope, specify, architect, and implement an RDF-based[3] metadata infrastructure for P2P-networks for exchanging information about learning objects. Edutella P2P architecture is essentially based on JXTA and RDF. JXTA (*http://www.jxta.org/*) is an open source technology that provides a set of XML-based protocols supporting different kinds of P2P applications.

According to Mendes and Sacks (2004), three types of services that a peer can offer are defined in an Edutella network:

- **Edutella query service:** This is the basic service in the framework. It presents a common, RDF-based query interface (the Query Exchange Language–RDF-QEL) for metadata providing and consuming through the Edutella network.
- **Edutella replication:** This provides replication of data within additional peers to ensure data persistence
- **Edutella mapping, mediation, clustering:** This kind of service manages metadata allowing semantic functionality of the global infrastructure.

An important point to underline is that Edutella does not share resource content but only metadata.

Smart Space for Learning

Smart Space for Learning is the result of the Elena project work (*http://www.elena-project.org*). According to Stojanovic, Stojanovic, and Volz (2002), a Smart Space for Learning can be defined as a set of service mediators which support the personalized consumption of heterogeneous educational services provided by different management systems. Learning services are entities designed to satisfy a specific purpose (e.g., the delivery of a course). They may use resources as learning objects (e.g., exercises and exams) and Web services to interface the formers with learners. WSDL and WSDL-S are languages to syntactically and semantically describe a Web service.

The system architecture of a Smart Space for Learning is essentially composed of two building blocks: an Edutella network and a set of ontologies. In a Smart Space for Learning, providers of learning services are connected to a learning management system that is based on Edutella. Ontology has to describe the learning domains using concepts and relations that may be referred to in the annotations of the learning services.

HyCo

HyCo (García, Berlanga, Moreno, García, & Carabias, 2004) stands for Hypermedia Composer; it is a multiplatform tool that supports the creation of learning materials. HyCo is the result of the development of an authoring tool created in order to define ALDs.

According to Berlanga and García (2005), ALDs are learning units that contain personalized behavior in order to provide each student with a learning flow which is to be adequate to his or her characteristics. ALDs are semantically structured in order to allow reusability.

The last version of HyCo also manages a kind of resource named SLO. An SLO is a learning object compliant with IMS metadata (*http://www.imsglobal.org/metadata/index.cfm*). Every resource created with HyCo is turned into an SLO. Whenever the conversion process is finished, an XML file is generated for the new SLO and stored in a repository.

Magpie

Magpie (*http://kmi.open.ac.uk/projects/magpie/*) provides automatic access to complementary Web sources of knowledge by associating a semantic layer to a Web page. This layer depends on one of a number of ontologies, which the user can select. When an ontology is selected, the user can also decide which classes are to be highlighted on the Web page. Clicking on an instance of a class from the selected ontology gives access to a number of semantic services. Magpie is proposed in a learning context to help students of a course in climate science understand the subject. The provided semantic services are integrated into the browsing navigation both in active and passive user involvement.

Ontology Mapping

The *ontology space* holds all the ontologies used by the system. The distributed nature of ontology development has led to a large number of different ontologies covering the same or overlapping domains. In this scenario it is possible that a particular sub-domain can be modeled by using different ontologies and, in general, if the ontology space contains n elements, the same sub-domain can be modeled n times, one for each ontology maintained by the system. This could be very useful in ontology mapping. *Ontology mapping* is the process whereby two ontologies are semantically related at the conceptual level, and the source ontology instances are transformed into the target ontology entities according to those semantic relations. Ontology mapping though is not an easy task; it has been widely treated in literature, and some crucial problems are listed below:

1. **The lack of a universally recognized standard for ontology:** On the Web a number of ontologies are available, but they are developed using different languages.
2. **The difficulty of commonly modeling the knowledge domain:** Different developers could have different visions of the domain, and they could give most weight to some aspect rather than other one.
3. **The granularity of the domain to be represented may be different in different communities:** Different communities may have overlapping sub-domains, but concepts and relations could have been developed with a different granularity.

While the first point represents a technical problem, the last two are related to the physical ontology design and development. In particular, the second case represents a fixed domain in which different developers produce different ontologies, while the third case refers to different communities having the same domain but with a different perspective of the involved semantics.

In the literature, one can distinguish three different approaches for ontology mapping. For each of them we propose an example application:

Automatic Mapping

- **MAFRA** (Maedche, Motik, Silva, & Volz, 2002) aims to automatically detect similarities between entities belonging to source and target ontologies. The overall process is composed of five steps. First, data are normalized; second, similarity between entities are calculated according to a previously proposed algorithm, then the mapping is obtained through the semantic bridging phase, and finally transformation of instances and checking of the achieved results are executed.
- **IF-Map** (Kalfoglou, 2003) is a semi-automatic method for ontology mapping. The authors make the assumption that if two communities want to share their knowledge, they must refer their local ontologies to a reference ontology. The overall process is obtained by composing the following four major steps: ontology harvesting, in which ontologies are acquired; translation, as the IF-Map method is specified in Horn logic, the data are translated in prolog clauses; IF-Map, the main mapping mechanism; and, finally, the display result step.

Manual Mapping

- **SKOS** (SKOS Core Vocabulary specification, *http://www.w3.org/TR/swbp-skos-core-spec/ 2005*; SKOS Mapping Vocabulary specification, *http://www.w3.org/2004/02/skos/ mapping/spec/ 2005*) is a group of RDF-based vocabularies developed to support the interoperability between different types of knowledge organization systems. In particular, SKOS consists of three RDF vocabularies:
  - *SKOS Core:* Provides a model for expressing contents and structures of different kind of concept schemas.
  - *SKOS Mapping:* Provides vocabularies for describing mappings between concept schemas.
  - *SKOS Extension:* Contains extensions to the SKOS Core useful for specialized applications.

  For example one could use SKOS Core to translate knowledge structures like taxonomies or thesauri into a common format, and subsequently he can create a mapping between them by using SKOS Mapping.

Semi-Automatic Mapping

As an example of semi-automatic tool for ontology mapping, we would like to illustrate the one proposed in Ehrig and Sure (2004). The implemented approach is based on manually encoded mapping rules. The rules are then combined to achieve better mapping results compared to one obtained using only one at a time. In order to learn how to combine the methods, both manual and automatic approaches are introduced.

PERSONALIZED LEARNING RETRIEVAL FRAMEWORK

System Requirements

Traditional approaches to personalization include both content-based and user-based techniques (Dai & Mobasher, 2004). If, on one hand, a content-based approach allows the definition and maintenance of an accurate user profile (for example, the user may provide the system with a list of keywords reflecting his or her initial interests, and the profiles could be stored in form of weighted keyword vectors and updated on the basis of explicit relevance feedback), which is particularly valuable whenever a user encounters new content, on the other hand it has the limitation of concerning only the significant features describing the content of an item. Differently, in a user-based approach, resources are processed according to the rating of other users of the system with similar interests. Since there is no analysis of the item content, these information management techniques can deal with any kind of item, being not just limited to textual content. In such a way, users can receive items with content that are different from those received in the past. On the other hand, since a user-based technique works well if several users evaluate each item, new items cannot be handled until some users have taken the time to evaluate them, and new users cannot receive references until the system has acquired some information about the new user in order to make personalized predictions. These limitations are often referred to as sparsity and start-up problems (Melville et al., 2002). By adopting a hybrid approach, a personalization system is able to effectively filter relevant resources from a wide heterogeneous environment like the Web, taking advantage of common interests of the users and also maintaining the benefits provided by content analysis.

A hybrid approach maintains another drawback: the difficulty of capturing semantic knowledge of the application domain—that is, concepts, relationships among different concepts, inherent properties associated with the concepts, axioms or other rules, and so forth.

A semantic-based approach to retrieving relevant LOs can be useful to address issues like trying to determine the type or the quality of the information suggested from a personalized learning environment. In this context, standard keyword search has a very limited effectiveness. For example, it cannot filter for the type of information (tutorial, applet or demo, review questions, etc.), the level of information (aimed to secondary school students, graduate students, etc.), the prerequisites for understanding information, or the quality of information. Some examples of semantic-based e-learning systems can be found in Mendes and Sacks (2004), in Lytras and Naeve (2005), and in the last paragraph of this chapter.

The aim of this chapter is to present our personalized learning retrieval framework based on both collaborative and semantic approaches. The collaborative approach is exploited both in retrieving tasks (to cover recommendation and resource sharing tasks) and in semantic coverage of the involved domain. The semantic approach is exploited introducing an ontology space covering domain knowledge and resource models based on word sense representation. The ontologies are updated as time goes on to reflect changes in the research domain and user interests. Also the ontology level exploits system collaborative aspect.

In Carbonaro (2005), we introduced the InLinx (Intelligent Links) system, a Web application that provides an online bookmarking service. InLinx is the result of three filtering components integration, corresponding to the following functionalities:

1. **Bookmark Classification (content-based filtering):** The system suggests the more suitable category that the user can save the bookmark in, based on the document content; the user can accept the suggestion or change the classification by selecting another category he considers the best for such a given item.
2. **Bookmark Sharing (collaborative filtering):** The system checks for newly classified bookmarks and recommends them to other

users with similar interests. Recipient users can either accept or reject the recommendation once they receive the notification.

3. **Paper Recommendation (content-based recommendation):** The system periodically checks if a new issue of some online journal has been released; then, it recommends the plausible appealing documents, according to the user profiles.

Over the years we have designed and implemented several extensions of the original architecture such as personalized category organization and mobile services (Andronico, Carbonaro, Colazzo, & Molinari, 2004). Most recently, we have introduced concepts for classification, recommendation, and document sharing in order to provide a better personalized semantic-based resource management. Generally, recommender systems use keywords to represent both the users and the resources. Another way to handle such data is by using hierarchical concept categories. This issue will enable users and the system to search, handle, or read only concepts of interest in a more general manner, providing a semantic possibility. For example, synonymy and hyponymy can reveal hidden similarities, potentially leading to better classification and recommendation. We called the extended architecture EasyInfo.

In this chapter we present the introduction of an ontology layer in our e-learning domain to describe the content and the relations between the various resources. It will formulate an exhaustive representation of the domain by specifying all of its concepts and the existing relations. Through the ontologies the system will express hierarchical links between entities and will guarantee interoperability of educational resources. We decide to maintain the several existing ontologies that each user knows. This approach allows us to easily compare the knowledge of a user with his or her personal ontologies without having a single consensual ontology that will accommodate all his or her needs. In this section we describe our approach to support personalization retrieval of relevant learning resources in a given Web-based learning system. This framework distinguishes between the generic user and the system administrator points of view.

Marco: A User Seeking Resources

Web technologies will continue to mature, and learning through the World Wide Web will become increasingly popular, particularly in distance education systems. Teachers can distribute lecture notes and other required materials via the Web, so Marco gets the opportunity to freely and autonomously use learning materials by collecting other related materials on the Web as well.

Active learning is the ability of learners to carry out learning activities in such a way that they will be able to effectively and efficiently construct knowledge from information sources. That is, Marco should be able to acquire, apply, and create knowledge and skills in the context of personal requirements and interests (Lee, 1999). Marco expects more than being able to filter, retrieve, and refer to learning materials. He prefers to have personalized access to library materials that he can customize according to his personal requirements and interests.

Therefore, new tools should allow the learners to integrate their selections from digital information sources and create their own reference sources. Moreover, in order to give intelligent support to achieve the expectations of active learning, it is also necessary to provide techniques to locate suitable materials. These mechanisms should extend beyond the traditional facilities of browsing and searching, by supporting active learning and by integrating the user's personal library and remote digital libraries. The user will be able to carry out learning activities when browsing both the personal and the remote digital libraries, therefore he can build personalized views on those materials while turning them into an accessible reference collection.

Because of the complexity of the system as well as the heterogeneity and amount of data, the use of semantics is crucial in this setting. For example, semantic description of resources and student profiles can be used to cluster students or resources with similar content or interests.

From a functional point of view, Marco needs a procedure to submit new material integrating the existing personal and remote libraries which consist of the following two phases:

1. An interface to submit new resources to the system, and
2. An interface to propose the mapping between the submitted resource and the ontology concepts.

Francesco: Learning System Administrator

Francesco wants to offer a personalized e-learning system that is able to respond to the effective user needs and modifiable user behavior and interests. The keyword profiling approach suffers because of a polysemy problem (the presence of multiple meanings for one term) and a synonymy problem (the presence of multiple words having the same meaning). If user and resource profiles do not share the same exact keywords, relevant information can be missed or wrong documents could be considered as relevant. Francesco wants an alternative method that is able to learn semantic profiles capturing key concepts, and which represents user and resource contents. The concepts should be defined in some ontologies. Moreover, Francesco wants to offer a procedure to map resources with respect to an ontology by creating an open and flexible ontology space describing the learning domain, in order to avoid specialized retrieving.

From a functional point of view, Francesco needs a procedure to organize the ontology space consisting of the following three phases:

1. An interface to add, remove, and modify ontologies belonging to the ontology space;
2. An interface to execute ontology mapping; and
3. An interface to propose the mapping between resources submitted by users and the ontology concepts.

System Architecture

As shown in Figure 1, the proposed architecture is divided into five different layers:

- **Search layer:** In this layer the user can specify his or her query and subscribe new resources to the system.
- **Ontology space layer:** In this the layer the system logically maintains the system ontologies.
- **Mapping layer:** This layer organizes the structure in which the mapping between resources and ontology concepts.
- **DB layer:** In this layer are stored all the meta-information about the resources—that is, information like title, author, physical location, and so on.
- **Resource layer:** This layer stores the different learning resources.

The following sections describe in more detail each layer.

Search Layer

This is the layer where the user can query the system for resources and propose new ones. Through the GUI the user composes his or her query by using the *Query Composition* module (see Figure 2). A simple query specifying only keyword is not enough for a semantic search. The query composer interacts with the ontology management middleware in order to navigate the ontology and

Figure 1. System architecture

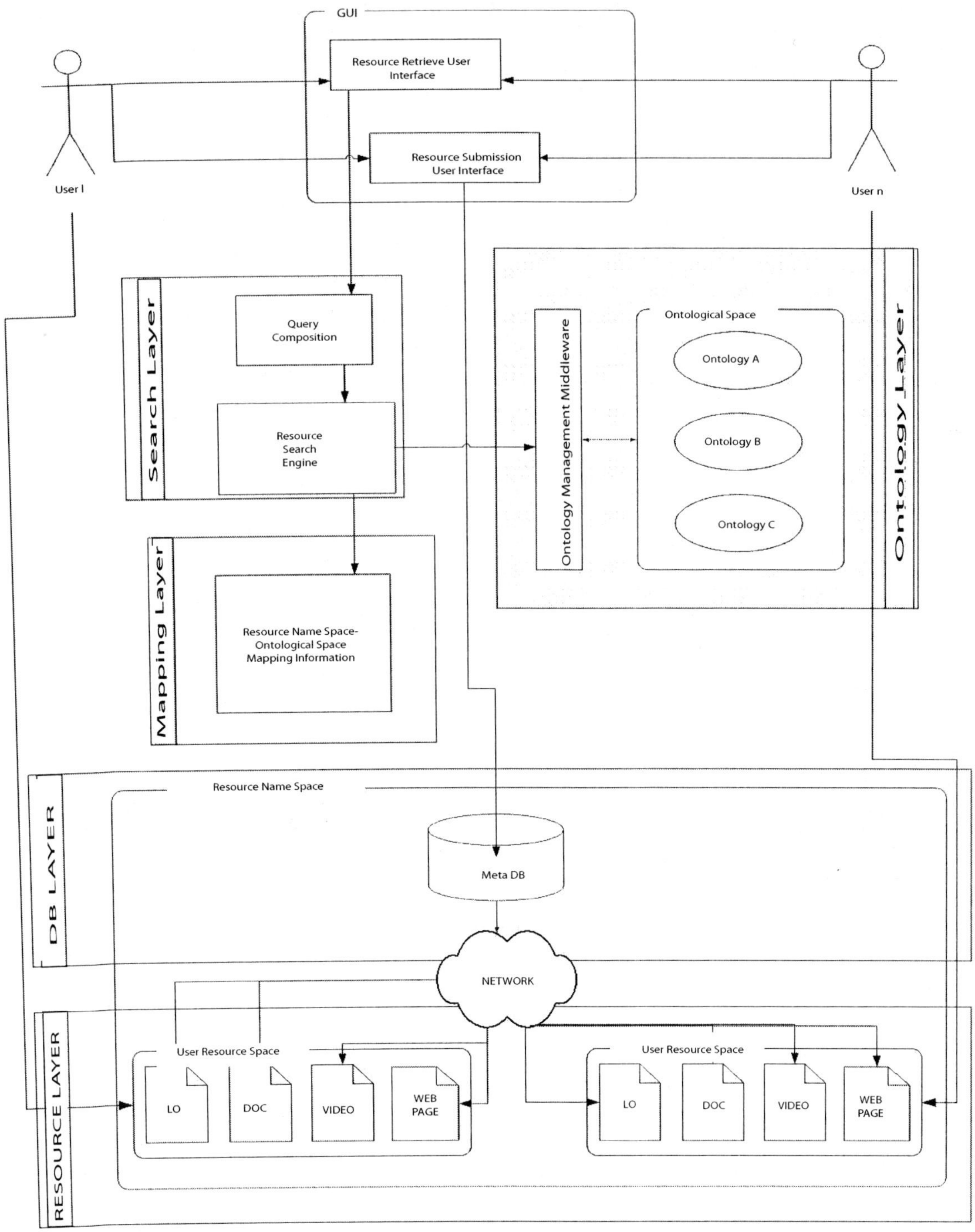

Figure 2. Query composition GUI

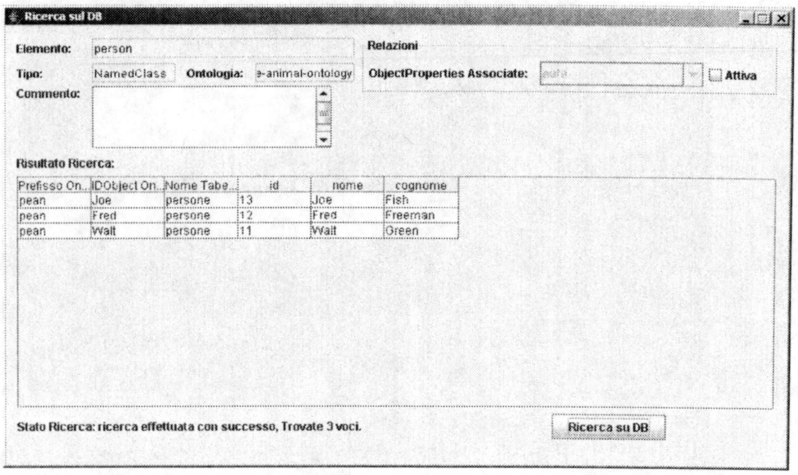

allows the user to choose not only the concept, but also a property associated with it.

Once the query has been composed, the Query Composition module passes the query to the Resource Search Engine. This module interacts with the ontology space and queries the mapping layer retrieving a list, eventually empty, of resources to be proposed to the user.

Ontology Space Layer

In this section we would like to center our discussion on the kind of ontology needed for the description of a semantic-based system domain. In particular, the ontology has to be:

- **From the system perspective:** large enough to describe all the resources that the system must manage; and
- **From the user perspective**: descriptive enough to efficiently satisfy user requirements.

The emergence of the semantic Web made it possible to publish and access a large number of ontologies; their widespread use by different communities represents the backbone for semantically rich information sharing. The sharing of ontology, though, is not a solved problem. With the proposed domain requirements in mind, we need to maintain the view of each system user on the personal ontology without altering its original schema, while assuming that the different communities desire to share knowledge to infer the relationships among their concepts and to amplify the effectiveness of the system response. For example, let us consider an example taken from Kalfoglou and Schorlemmer (2003) that shows the issues one has to take into account when attempting to align specified English and French concepts. We argue that promoting services to support group collaboration among users involved in the learning process could be a useful approach to solve such problems.

According to Stutt and Motta(2004), there are a lot of 'knowledge neighborhoods' built around some topic by handling different learning resources, ontologies, and users. It is necessary to create an ontology space comprising more than one global ontology, even partially overlapping, belonging to different knowledge neighborhoods. So doing, it is possible to propose to a huge user-maintained repository, and also create links and automatic search to another community.

At this point we need to outline a crucial aspect: the ontology space analysis phase. We can think that Francesco has built the perfect system, but the performance—that is, the accuracy in the query reply—will strongly depend on the ontology used to describe the knowledge domain. The ontology space analysis is not a trivial task; not only must the designer perfectly know the domain he wants to describe, but he must also have an excellent knowledge both of the living ontologies in the various communities and the kind of users that the system must serve. For example, if the target of Francesco's system is an user with an in-depth knowledge about a particular domain, the ontology space must be as detailed as possible. On the contrary, if the expected user is at a more scholastic level, the domain will be more general and with less detailed information. These choices are related to the design phase of the system, but they cannot be a binding obstacle for future improvements. Communities and their domains evolve in time, and as a consequence, the representation of the overall system domain must evolve.

Ontology mapping is not a trivial task. If, at first glance, the biggest problem seems to be related to highly time-consuming aspects of the subsequent process, it is easy to verify that matching of concepts belonging to different ontologies can be considered the hardest part of the work. Initially, the purpose of manually mapping different ontologies can seem a titanic effort, so the first idea is the development of an automatic tool able to solve the task. Unfortunately, this approach has problems with accuracy of matching. An automatic tool such as MAFRA could solve the mapping process in little time and certainly the results are not prone to classical human errors. But other errors may occur and we think that they can be even more dangerous. An automatic tool, for example, will find it difficult to detect semantic differences between concepts belonging to different and complex ontologies. Moreover, the accuracy of algorithms and rules used for automatic semantic relationship deduction between different schemas could not be satisfactory.

In particular, a human error could be related to the absent-mindedness of the mapper and can be categorized as syntactical mistakes. These kinds of errors, or a big percentage of them, can be detected through the help of a parser. On the contrary, an accuracy problem is a semantical error and is much more difficult to identify. This kind of error could reduce the expected performance improvement deriving from ontology use.

A manual process is necessary because the semantic relationships that can occur between ontologies are too complex to be directly learned by machines. For this reason, in order to avoid semantic errors, one can adopt a manual mapping approach; however, it could be unacceptably expensive.

At the time of writing, the mapping process is an open problem in our architecture. For our test cases we used a manual mapping, but a semi-automatic ontology mapping tool is in development.

Mapping Layer

Another crucial aspect of the proposed system is the resource mapping phase. The resource representation may be accomplished using two different strategies:

1. **By using a list containing ontology concepts**: this solution represents a good resource representation and it is easily practicable;

2. **By using a subgraph of the ontology space**: this solution could represent in more detail the learning resources, but it is more difficult to implement.

The main difference between the two mentioned strategies is related to concept properties. Without the properties the subgraph can be conformed to the concept list; nevertheless, the properties allow differentiation between similar resources.

Generally, the choice depends on the domain one has to manage. If the resource space is composed of resources made up of generic domain topics, then the first solution may be the best one. On the contrary, if the resources are extremely detailed, the graph model may be the best choice. We have chosen the first proposed model; our choice is limited by the interaction with the resource representation produced by the disambiguation module of EasyInfo, which is similar to a concept list expressed in an XML-based language. In future works we intend to go through this limitation also supporting the graph model.

In the last part of this section, we describe the resource ontology mapping task. As shown in Figure 1, all the information about resources are maintained within the DB; through the DB layer it provides a Resource Name Space to other system modules. More precisely, the Resource Name Space is the set of logical names of the resources managed by the system. For this reason, the list of ontology concepts is mapped with a record of the database.

Most of the efforts in the field of mapping between ontologies and databases have been spent in the directions of heterogeneous database integration. The purpose of such an approach is to map a database record to a list of ontology concepts in order to give a semantical representation of the data they represent.

In our architecture the database maintains all the meta information about the learning resources such as title, author, physical location, and so on. Through the DB, the system provides a Resource Name Space in which each element represents a single resource. Both system and users can refer to resources by using their logical name and all the other information handled within the Database Layer. In order to give an ontological–logical–resource representation, we have to create an ontological–physical–database mapping. In the rest of this section, we refer to some existing techniques of mapping between databases and ontologies.

- *Kaon reverse* (Stojanovic et al., 2002) is a KAON plug-in for semi-automatically mapping relational database to ontologies. In the first step of this approach, the relational database model is transformed into an ontology structure expressed in F-Logic (Kifer, 1995). In the second step, the database content is migrated into the created ontology. If needed, the F-Logic structure can be translated in RDF.
- *D2R* (Bizer, 2003) is defined as a declarative XML-based language used to describe mappings between relational database schemas and OWL[4] ontologies without changing the database schema. The D2R mapping process comprises the following steps:
    - selection of a record set from the database,
    - grouping of the record set by the d2r: group By attribute,
    - creation of class instances, and
    - mapping of the grouped record set data to instance properties.
- *Deep annotation* (Handschuh, Staab, & Volz, 2003) is defined as a manual annotation process that uses information properties, information structures, and information context in order to derive mapping between database schema and ontologies. This approach proposes the annotation of Web pages maintaining DB content by using information about the database schema. In

this way, a client can map the public mark up of the Web page to its own ontology.

Our first approach was inspired by the ones proposed in Kaon Reverse. We studied a two-step process for the semi-automatic mapping between database schemas and ontologies. We had taken into consideration the approach proposed in D2R, and we have developed an XML-based language to express the resulting mapping (see Figure 3). In order to improve the accuracy of the mapping process, we have adopted the idea of manual mapping proposed in Deep Annotation. Although the resource manual mapping can be considered time consuming, we have preferred the accuracy of the resource representation rather than the quickness of the overall process.

Figure 3. XML-based language to express the resource mapping process

```
<?xml version="1.0" encoding="UTF-8" ?>
<!DOCTYPE Map (View Source for full doctype...)>
- <Map>
  - <DBConnection>
      <NameDB>testDB</NameDB>
      <Login>root</Login>
      <Password />
    </DBConnection>
  - <Ontologies>
    + <Ontology>
    + <Ontology>
    + <Ontology>
    + <Ontology>
    </Ontologies>
  - <ClassesMap>
    + <ClassMap type="Inferred">
    + <ClassMap type="Asserted">
    - <ClassMap type="Inferred">
        <TableName>animali</TableName>
      + <IDRow>
        <PrefixOntology>pean</PrefixOntology>
        <IDObject>animal</IDObject>
      </ClassMap>
    - <ClassMap type="Asserted">
        <TableName>animali</TableName>
      - <IDRow>
          <KeyValue>2</KeyValue>
        </IDRow>
        <PrefixOntology>pean</PrefixOntology>
        <IDObject>duck</IDObject>
      </ClassMap>
    </ClassesMap>
  </Map>
```

Figure 4. A screenshot of the GUI for the mapping phase

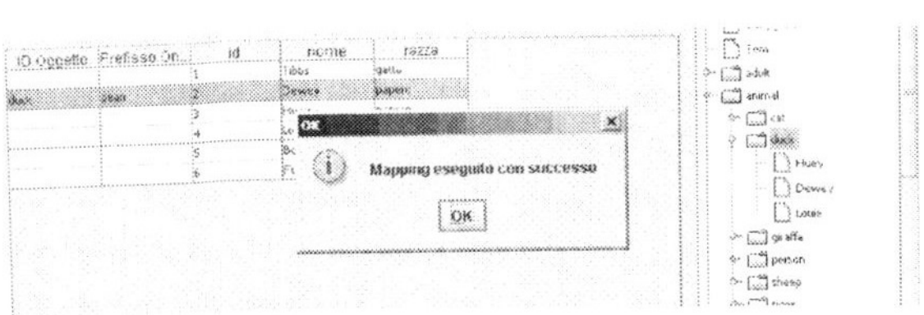

DB Layer

In the DB layer we maintain all the meta-information about the resources, information like title, author, physical location, and so on. As previously described, this layer provides the Resource Name Space, which is the set of resource logical names managed by the system.

Resource Layer

This is the layer of resources. A resource can be maintained both on the same machine in which the system is running and in a remote accessible machine. All the information about resources are stored in the DB layer.

CONCEPT-BASED SEMANTIC APPROACH TO MODEL RESOURCE AND USER PROFILES

Word Sense Disambiguation Process

In order to substitute keywords with univocal concepts into user and resource profiles, we must build a process called Word Sense Disambiguation (WSD). Given a sentence, a WSD process identifies the syntactical categories of words and interacts with an ontology both to retrieve the exact concept definition and to adopt some techniques for semantic similarity evaluation among words. We use GATE (Cunningham, Maynard, Bontcheva, & Tablan, 2002) to identify the syntactic class of the words and WordNet (Fellbaum, 1998), which is one of the most used reference lexicons in the Word Sense Disambiguation task.

The use of the described Word Sense Disambiguation step reduces classification errors due to ambiguous words, thus allowing better precision in the succeeding recommendation and sharing phases. For example, if the terms "procedure," "subprogram," and "routine" appear in the same resource, we consider three occurrences of the same sysnset "{06494814}: routine, subroutine, subprogram, procedure, function (a set sequence of steps, part of larger computer program)" and not one occurrence for each word.

Moreover, the implemented WSD procedure allows more accurate document representation. For example, let us process two sentences containing the "mouse" polysemous word. The disambiguation process applied to the first sentence "The white cat is hunting the mouse" produces the following WordNet definition:

{2244530}: mouse (any of numerous small rodents typically resembling diminutive rats having pointed snouts and small ears on elongated bodies with slender usually hairless tails), while the same process applied to the second sentence "The mouse is near the pc" produces the following result:

{3651364}: mouse, computer mouse (a hand-operated electronic device that controls the coordinates of a cursor on your computer screen as you move it around on a pad; on the bottom of the mouse is a ball that rolls on the surface of the pad; "a mouse takes much more room than a trackball").

To the best of our knowledge, no systems use a concept-based semantic approach to model resource and user profiles in a learning environment.

Resource Representation

Many systems build document and user representations by taking into account some word properties in the document, such as their frequency and their co-occurrence. Nevertheless, we described how a purely word-based model is often not adequate when the interest is strictly related to the resource semantic content. We now describe how the novice user and resource semantic profiles differ from the old ones in taking into account word senses representing user and resource contents.

In the early version of our system, we adopted a representation based on the Vector Space Model (VSM), the most frequently used model in information retrieval (IR) and text learning. Since the resources of the system are Web pages, it was necessary to apply a sequence of contextual processing to the source code of the pages in order to obtain a vector representation. To filter information resources according to user interests, we must have a common representation both for the users and the resources. This knowledge representation model must be expressive enough to synthetically and significantly describe the information content. The use of the VSM allows updates of the user profile in accordance with consulted information resources (Salton, 1989).

To guarantee a customizable architecture, the system needs to construct and maintain user profiles. For a particular user, it is reasonable to think that processing a set of correctly classified relevant and inappropriate documents from a certain domain of interest may lead to identifying the set of relevant keywords for such a domain at a certain time. Thus, the user domain-specific sets of relevant features, called prototypes, may be used to learn how to classify documents. In particular, in order to consider the peculiarity of positive and negative examples, we define positive prototype for a class c_j, a user u_i at time t, as a finite set of unique indexing terms, chosen to be relevant for c_j, up to time t. Then we define a negative prototype as a subset of the corresponding positive one, whereas each element can be found at least once in the set of documents classified as negative examples for class c_j. Positive examples for a specific user u_i and for a class c_j are represented by the explicitly registered documents or accepted by u_i in c_j, while negative examples are either deleted bookmarks, misclassified bookmarks, or rejected bookmarks that happen to be classified into c_j.

After the WSD, our resources are represented by using a list of WordNet concepts obtained by the described architecture from the words in the documents and their related occurrence. Our hypothesis is that concept-based document and user representations produce retrieved documents with high semantic relevance with respect to the user and resource models.

EXPERIMENTAL DOMAIN

The following paragraphs describe how we consider the resource content to propose a fitted technique in a personalized information retrieval framework. The automatic retrieval of relevant learning objects is obtained by considering students and learning material profiles, and by adopting filtering criteria based on the value of selected metadata fields. Our experiments are based on SCORM[5]-compliant LOs. For example, we use the student's knowledge of domain concept to avoid recommendation of highly technical papers to a beginner student or popular magazine articles to a senior graduate student. For each student, the system evaluates and updates his or her skill and technical expertise levels.

We use artificial learners to get a flavor of how the system works. We created SCORM-compliant learning material using the abstract of several papers in .html version from scientific journals published on the Web. We linked an imsmanifest SCORM file to each paper. Then, we simulated 10 users with different initial profiles (based on the field of interest and on the skill level) and saved, in four turns, 10 learning resources for each user, obtaining 400 LOs. The main advantage of the described approach is the semantic accuracy growth. To give a quantitative estimation of the improvement induced by a concept-based approach, we are executing a comparative experiment between word-based user and resource models on one side and concept-based user and resource models on the other one. In particular, in order to evaluate the collaborative approach, we have considered different initial student profiles. The several components influencing the choice of recommendation receivers are:

- **User interest in the category of recommended resource:** The system maintains a user vs. category matrix that, for a specific user, stores the number of times he or she shows interest for a certain class, saving a bookmark in that class.
- **Confidence level between users:** We use a matrix maintaining the user's confidence factor, ranging from 0.1 to 1, to represent how many documents recommended by a specific user are accepted or rejected by another one. The confidence factor is not bi-directional.
- **Relation between the class prototype of recommended resource and the class prototype of other categories:** To obtain a fitting recommendation, we apply the Pearson-r correlation measure to a weighted user-category matrix in which classes related to the class of the recommended bookmark are enhanced.

To verify the effectiveness of the EasyInfo module on the recommendation process, we considered a certain snapshot of the user/category matrix and of the confidence factor matrix. Then, we observed the behavior of the system while performing the same recommendation task both using and without using the EasyInfo extension.

For simplicity, we have considered three users, user1, user2 and user3, and three resources, r1, r2, and r3. In the first case, whenever user1 saves (or accepts) r1, the system will recommend it to user2 who has a high interest in that topic (independent of similarity among user profiles). The same resource will not be recommended to user3 because the system is not able to discover similarity between two students by simply using word-based user and resource models. In the second case, the same resource could also be recommended to user3 who is conceptually similar to user1, even if the similarity is not evident in a simple word matching system. Moreover, the system is able to discover word sense similarities between r1 and r3 and to propose r3 both to user2 and user3, thus allowing better personalization.

CONSIDERATIONS

This chapter addresses key limitations with existing courseware on the Internet. Humans want immediate access to relevant and accurate information. There has been some progress in combining learning with information retrieval, however, these advances are rarely implemented in e-learning courseware. With this objective in mind, we described how to propose a personalized information retrieval framework, considering student and learning material profiles, adopting filtering criteria based on the value of selected metadata fields, and capturing not only structural but also semantics information. We showed how the semantic technologies can enhance the traditional keyword approach by adding semantic information in the resource and user profiles.

Summarizing, the key elements of the described system could be highlighted as follows. The system provides immediate portability and visibility from different user locations, enabling access to a personal bookmark repository just by using a Web browser. The system assists students in finding relevant reading material providing personalized learning object recommendations. The system directly benefits from existing repositories of learning material by providing access to large amounts of digital information. The system reflects continuous ongoing changes of the practices of its members, as required by a cooperative framework. The system proposes resource and student models based on word senses rather than simply on words exploiting a word sense-based document representation.

REFERENCES

Andronico, A., Carbonaro, A., Colazzo, L., & Molinari, A. (2004). Personalisation services for learning management systems in mobile settings. *International Journal of Continuing Engineering Education and Lifelong Learning.*

Belkin, N.J., & Croft, W.B. (1992). Information filtering and information retrieval: Two sides of the same coin. *Communications of the ACM, 35*(12), 29-38.

Berlanga, A.J., & García, F.J. (2005). IMS LD reusable elements for adaptive learning designs. *Journal of Interactive Media in Education,* 11(Special Issue).

Bizer, C. (2003). D2R MAP□a database to RDF mapping language. *Proceedings of the 12th International World Wide Web Conference.*

Brusilovsky, P., & Nijhavan, H. (2002). A framework for adaptive e-learning based on distributed re-usable learning activities. *Proceedings of the World Conference on E-Learning* (E-Learn 2002), Montreal, Canada.

Budanitsky, A., & Hirst, G. (2001). Semantic distance in WordNet: An experimental, application-oriented evaluation of five measures. *Proceedings of Workshop on WordNet and Other Lexical Resources of the 2nd Meeting of the North American Chapter of the Association for Computational Linguistics,* Pittsburgh, PA.

Carbonaro A. (2004). Learning objects recommendation in a collaborative information management system. *IEEE Learning Technology Newsletter, 6*(4).

Carbonaro, A. (2005). Defining personalized learning views of relevant learning objects in a collaborative bookmark management system. In *Web-based intelligent e-learning systems: Technologies and applications.* Hershey, PA: Idea Group.

Cooley R., Mobasher, B., & Srivastava, J. (1997). Web mining: Information and pattern discovery on the World Wide Web. Proceedings of the 9th International Conference on Tools with Artificial Intelligence (ICTAI '97).

Cunningham, H., Maynard, D., Bontcheva, K., & Tablan, V. (2002). GATE: A framework and graphical development environment for robust NLP tools and applications. *Proceedings of the 40th Anniversary Meeting of the Association for Computational Linguistics,* Budapest.

Dai, H., & Mobasher, B. (2004). Integrating semantic knowledge with Web usage mining for personalization. In A. Scime (Ed.), *Web mining: Applications and techniques* (pp. 276-306). Hershey, PA: Idea Group.

Dzbor, M., Motta, E., & Stutt, A. (2005). Achieving higher-level learning through adaptable semantic Web applications. *International Journal of Knowledge and Learning, 1*(1/2).

Ehrig, M., & Sure, Y. (2004, May). Ontology mapping—an integrated approach. In C. Bussler, J. Davis, D. Fensel, & R. Studer (Eds.), *Proceedings of the 1st European Semantic Web Symposium* (pp. 76-91), Heraklion, Greece. Berlin: Springer-Verlag (LNCS 3053).

Fellbaum, C. (Ed.). (1998). *WordNet: An electronic lexical database.* Cambridge, MA: MIT Press.

García, F.J., Berlanga, A.J., Moreno, M.N., García, J., & Carabias, J. (2004). *HyCo—an authoring tool to create semantic learning objects for Web-based e-learning systems* (pp. 344-348). Berlin: Springer-Verlag (LNCS 3140).

Handschuh, S., Staab, S., & Volz, R. (2003). On deep annotation. *Proceedings of the 12th International World Wide Web Conference.*

Heflin, J. (2004, February). OWL Web Ontology Language use cases and requirements. Retrieved from http://www.w3.org/TR/Webont-req/

Huhns, M.N., & Singh, M.P. (1998). *Multiagent systems in information-rich environments. Cooperative information agents II* (pp. 79-93). (LNAI 1435).

Kalfoglou, Y., & Schorlemmer, M. (2003). IF-Map: An ontology mapping method based on information-flow theory. In S. Spaccapietra et al. (Eds.), *Journal on data semantics.* (LNCS 2800).

Kanellopoulos, D., Kotsiantis, S., & Pintelas, P. (2006, February). Ontology-based learning applications: A development methodology. *Proceedings of the 24th Iasted International Multi-Conference Software Engineering,* Austria.

Kifer, M., Lausen, G., & Wu, J. (1995). Logical foundations of object-oriented and frame-based languages. *Journal of the ACM, 42*(4), 741-843.

Koivunen, M., & Miller, E. (2002). W3C semantic Web activity. In E. Hyvonen (Ed.), *Semantic Web kick-off in Finland* (pp. 27-44). Helsinki: HIIT.

Leacock, C., & Chodorow, M. (1998). Combining local context and WordNet similarity for word sense identification. In C. Fellbaum (Ed.), *Word-*

Net: An electronic lexical database (pp. 265-283). Cambridge, MA: MIT Press.

Lee, J. (1999). Interactive learning with a Web-based digital library system. *Proceedings of the 9th DELOS Workshop on Digital Libraries for Distance Learning.* Retrieved from *http://courses.cs.vt.edu/~cs3604/DELOS.html*

Lytras, M.D., & Naeve, A. (Eds.). (2005). *Intelligent learning infrastructure for knowledge intensive organizations.* London: Information Science.

Maedche, A., Motik, B., Silva, N., & Volz, R. (2002). MAFRA—a mapping framework for distributed ontologies. *Proceedings of EKAW (Knowledge Engineering and Knowledge Management) 2002.* Berlin: Springer-Verlag (LNCS 2473).

Mendes, M.E.S., & Sacks, L. (2004). Dynamic knowledge representation for e-learning applications. In M. Nikravesh, L.A. Zadeh, B. Azvin, & R. Yager (Eds.), *Enhancing the power of the Internet—studies in fuzziness and soft computing* (vol. 139, pp. 255-278). Berlin/London: Springer-Verlag.

Nagarajan, R. (2002). Content-boosted collaborative filtering for improved recommendations. *Proceedings of the 18th National Conference on Artificial Intelligence,* Canada.

Recker, M., Walker, A., & Lawless, K. (2003). What do you recommend? Implementation and analyses of collaborative filtering of Web resources for education. *Instructional Science, 31,* 229-316.

Resnik, P. (1995). *Disambiguating noun groupings with respect to WordNet senses.* Chelmsford, MA: Sun Microsystems Laboratories.

Salton, G. (1989). *Automatic text processing: The transformation, analysis and retrieval of information by computer.* Reading, MA: Addison-Wesley.

Stojanovic, L., Stojanovic, N., & Volz, R. (2002). Migrating data-intensive Web sites into the semantic Web. *Proceedings of the 17th ACM Symposium on Applied Computing* (pp. 1100-1107).

Stutt, A., & Motta, E. (2004). Semantic learning Webs. *Journal of Interactive Media in Education,* (10).

Tang, T., & McCalla, G. (2005). Smart recommendation for an evolving e-learning system: Architecture and experiment. *International Journal on E-Learning, 4*(1), 105-129.

ENDNOTES

1 *http://grouper.ieee.org/p1484/wg12/files/LOM_1484_12_1_v1_Final_Draft.pdf*

2 *http://ltsc.ieee.org*

3 RDF is the W3C recommendation for the creation of metadata about resources. With RDF, one can make statements about a resource in the form of a subject–predicate–object expression. The described resource is the subject of the statement, the predicate is a specified relation that links the subject, and the object is the value assigned to the subject through the predicate.

4 OWL is the W3C recommendation for the creation of new ontology optimized for the Web. The Web Ontology Language OWL is a semantic markup language for publishing and sharing ontologies on the World Wide Web. OWL is developed as a vocabulary extension of RDF, and it is derived from the DAML+OIL Web Ontology Language. For these reasons it provides a greater machine interpretability of Web content than the one supported by its predecessors. Essentially, with OWL one can describe a specific domain in terms of class, properties, and individuals. It has three increasingly expressive sublanguages: OWL Lite, OWL DL, and OWL Full.

5 SCORM (Sharable Courseware Object Reference Model) is a suite of technical standards that enable Web-based learning systems to find, import, share, reuse, and export learning content in a standardized way. It is a specification of the Advanced Distributed Learning Initiative (*http://www.adlnet.org/*).

This work was previously published in Social Information Retrieval Systems: Emerging Technologies and Applications for Searching the Web Effectively, edited by D. Goh and S. Foo, pp. 270-288, copyright 2008 by Information Science Reference, formerly known as Idea Group Reference (an imprint of IGI Global).

Compilation of References

Abdul-Rahman, A., & Hailes, S. (2000). Supporting trust in virtual communities. In *Hicss '00: Proceedings of the 33rd hawaii international conference on system sciences-volume 6* (p. 6007). Washington, DC, USA: IEEE Computer Society.

Abecker A., Bernardi A., & Van Elst L. (2003). *Agent technology for distributed organizational memories.* In *Proceedings of the 5th International Conference on Enterprise Information Systems*, Vol. 2, pages 3–10.

Aberer, K., & Despotovic, Z. (2001). Managing trust in a peer-2-peer information system. In *Cikm '01: Proceedings of the tenth international conference on information and knowledge management* (pp. 310-317). New York, NY, USA: ACM Press.

Abiteboul, S., Hull, R., & Vianu, V. (1995). Foundations of Databases. Addison-Wesley.

Acciarri, A., Calvanese, D., De Giacomo, G., Lembo, D., Lenzerini, M., Palmieri, M., et al., (2005). Quonto: Querying ontologies. In *Proceedings of the 20th National Conference on Artificial Intelligence* (aaai 2005) (pp. 1670-1671).

Adams, J., Rubinstein, L.Z., Siu, A.L., Stuck, A.E., & Wieland, G.E. (1993). Comprehensive geriatric assessment. A meta–analysis of controlled trials. *Lancet, 342*, pp. 1032–1036.

Adelsberger, H., Bick, M., Körner, F., & Pawlowski, J.M. (2001). Virtual education in business information systems (VAWI)--Facilitating collaborative development processes using the Essen learning model. In H. Hoyer (Ed.), *20th ICDE World Conference on Open Learning and Distance Education. The Future of Learning – Learning for the Future: Shaping the Transition.*

Adomavicius, G., & Tuzhilin, A. (2005, June). Toward the next generation of recommender systems: A survey of the state-of-the-art and possible extensions. *IEEE Transactions on Knowledge and Data Engineering, 17* (6), 734-749.

Afuah, A. (2002). *Innovation management: Strategies, implementation, and profits.* Oxford University Press, USA.

Agosti, M., Crestani, F., Gradenigo, G., &Mattiello, P. (1990). *An approach to conceptual modeling of IR auxiliary data.* Paper presented at the IEEE International Conference on Computer and Communications. Scottsdale, Arizona, USA.

Alavi, M., & Leidner, D. E. (2001). Review: Knowledge management and knowledge management systems: Conceptual foundations and research issues. *MIS Quarterly*, 25(1), 107-136.

Al-Rawas, A. & Easterbrook, S. (1996, February 1-2). Communications problems in requirements engineering: A field study.In *Proceedings of the 1st Westminster Conference on Professional Awareness in Software Engineering*, London, The Royal Society.

Amiguet M., Nagy A., & Baez J. (2004). *Towards an aspect-oriented approach of multi-agent programming,* MOCA'04: 3rd Workshop on Modelling of Objects, Components, and Agents, p. 18

An, A. (2005). Classification methods. In J. Wang (Ed.), *Encyclopedia of Data Warehousing and Mining* (pp. 144-149). New York: Idea Group Inc.

Andersen, E. P. & Reenskaug, T. (1992), System design by composing structures of interacting objects, In O. L. Madsen (Ed.), *ECOOP '92, European Conference on Object-Oriented Programming*, Utrecht, The Netherlands, volume 615 of Lecture Notes in Computer Science (pp. 133–152). New York, N.Y.: Springer-Verlag.

Anderson, P. (2007). What is Web 2.0? Ideas, technologies and implications for education. *JISC Technology and Standards Watch*, Feb. 2007.

Andronico, A., Carbonaro, A., Colazzo, L., & Molinari, A. (2004). Personalisation services for learning management systems in mobile settings. *International Journal of Continuing Engineering Education and Lifelong Learning.*

Ang, C. L., Gay, R. K., Khoo, L. P., & Luo, M. (1997), A knowledge-based approach to the generation of IDEF0 Models, *International Journal of Production Research.*35, 1385-1412.

Angehrn, A.A. (2004). Designing intelligent agents for virtual communities. INSEAD CALT Report 11-2004.

Angryk, R., Galant, V., Gordon, M., & Paprzycki, M. (2002). Travel support system: An agent based framework. In H. R. Arabnia & Y. Mun (Eds.), *Proceedings of the International Conference on Internet Computing (IC '02)* (pp. 719-725). Las Vegas, NV: CSREA Press.

Annicchiarico, R., Campana, F., Riaño, D., & al. (2006). The K4CARE Model, *K4CARE Project Public Report D01*. Retrieved 2006, from http://www.k4care.net/fileadmin/k4care/public_website/downloads/K4C_Model_D01.rar

Arbib, M. A., & Hanson, A. R. (Eds.). (1987). Vision, brain, and cooperative computation. Cambridge, MA, USA: MIT Press.

Aringhieri, R., Damiani, E., De Capitani di Vimercati, S., Paraboschi, S., & Samarati, P. (2006). Fuzzy techniques for trust and reputation management in anonymous peer-to-peer systems: Special topic section on soft approaches to information retrieval and information access on the web. *Journal of the American Society for Information Science and Technology (JASIST), 57* (4), 528-537.

Arkin A., Askary S., Bloch B., Curbera F., Goland Y., Kartha N., Liu C., Thatte S., Yendluri P., Yiu A., editors, (2005). Web services business process execution language version 2.0. Working Draft, WS-BPEL TC OASIS.

Arocha, J.F., How, J., Mottur–Pilson, C., & Patel, V.L. (2001). Cognitive psychological studies of representation and use of clinical guidelines. *International Journal of Medical Informatics, 63*(3), 147–167.

Artz, D., & Gil, Y. (2007). *A survey of trust in computer science and the semantic web.* (To appear in Journal of Web Semantics, 2007).

Audet, A., Field, M., & Greenfield, S. (1990). Medical practice guidelines: current activities and future directions. *Annals of Internal Medicine, 113*, 709–714.

Baader, F., Calvanese, D., McGuinness, D., Nardi, D., & Patel-Schneider, P. F. (Eds.). (2003). Description logic handbook: Theory, implementation and applications. Cambridge University Press.

Balakrishnan, H., Kaashoek, F. M., Karger, D., Morris, R., & Stoica, I. (2003, February). Looking up data in P2P systems. *Commun. ACM, 46* (2), 43-48.

Balasubramani, G.K., Biggs, M.M., Fava, M., Howland, R.H., Lebowitz, B., McGrath, P.J., Nierenberg, A.A., Norquist, G., Ritz, L., Rush, A.J., Shores–Wilson, K., Trivedi, M.H., Warden, D., & Wisniewski, S.R. (2006). Evaluation of Outcomes With Citalopram for Depression Using Measurement–Based Care in STAR*D: Implications for Clinical Practice. *American Journal of Psychiatry, 163*, 28–40.

Balkenius, C. (1993). Some properties of neural representations. In M. Bodn & L. Niklasson, (Eds.), Selected readings of the Swedish conference on connectionism.

Balkenius, C., & Gärdenfors, P. (1991). Nonmonotonic inferences in neural networks. In Kr (pp. 32-39).

Barnard, K., Duygulu, P., Fretias, N., Forsyth, D., Blei, D., & Jordan, M. I. (2003). Matching words and pictures. *Journal of Machine Learning Research, 3,* 1107-1135.

Barnes-Lee, T. (1998), Semantic Web Roadmap. *W3C Design Issues.* Retrieved on April 12, 2005, from http://www.w3.org/DesignIssues/Semantic.html

Barnes-Lee, T. (2000). What the Semantic Web can represent. Retrieved on September 22, 2006, from http://www.w3.org/DesignIssues/RDFnot.html

Barnett, G.O., Gennari, J.H., Greenes, R.A., Jain, N.L., Murphy, S.N., Ohno–Machado, L., Oliver, D.E., Pattison–Gordon, E., Shortliffe, E.H., & Tu, S.W. (1998). The guideline interchange format: a model for representing guidelines. *Journal of the American Medical Informatics Association, 5,* 357–372.

Battle, S., Kalyanpur, A., Padget, J., & Pastor, D. (2004). *Automatic Mapping of OWL Ontologies into Java.* In *Proceedings of the 16th International Conference on Software Engineering and Knowledge Engineering* (pp. 98–103).

Becerra-Fernandez, I., & Sabherwal, R. (2001). Organizational knowledge management: A contingency perspective. *Journal of Management Information Systems, 18* (1), 23-55.

Beckett, D. (2004). RDF/XML Syntax Specification, Retrieved on January, 2007, from http://www.w3.org/TR/rdf-syntax-grammar/

Bekhti S. & Matta N. (2003). *Project memory: An approach of modelling and reusing the context and the design rationale*, In *Proceedings of IJCAI'03 (International Joint of Conferences of Artificial Intelligence) Workshop on Knowledge Management and Organisational Memory.,* Accapulco.

Belkadi F., Bonjour E., & Dulmet M. (2007) Competency characterisation by means of work situation modelling. *Computers in Industry, 58,* 164-178.

Belkin, N.J., & Croft, W.B. (1992). Information filtering and information retrieval: Two sides of the same coin. *Communications of the ACM, 35*(12), 29-38.

Bellifemine, F., Poggi, A., & Rimassa, G. (1999). *JADE – A FIPA–compliant agent framework.* In *Proceedings of the Fourth International Conference and Exhibition on the Practical Application of Intelligent Agents and Multi–Agents*, pp. 97–108.

Benmahamed D., Ermine J.-L. (2006). *Knowledge Management Techniques for Know-How Transfer Systems Design, The case of an Oil Company,* ICKM 2006 (International Conference on Knowledge Management), London.

Bennett, B. & Fellbaum, C. (Eds.), (2006). *Formal ontology in information systems.* In *Proceedings of the4th International Conference* (FOIS 2006), Volume 150, Frontiers in Artificial Intelligence and Applications. IOS Press.

Berlanga, A.J., & García, F.J. (2005). IMS LD reusable elements for adaptive learning designs. *Journal of Interactive Media in Education,* 11(Special Issue).

Bernabei, R., Carbonin, P.U., Cavinato, T., Gambassi, G., Landi, F., Pola, R., & Tabaccanti, S. (1999). Impact of integrated home care services on hospital use. *Journal of American Geriatric Society, 47*(12), 1430–1434.

Berners-Lee, T., (1996). Www: past, present, and future, *Computer,* 29(10), 69-77.

Berners-Lee, T., Hendler, J., & Lassila, O. (2001). The Semantic Web. *Scientific American, 284*(5), 28-37.

Bertelsen, O.W. (2000). *Scandinavian Journal of Information Systems 12,* pp. 15-27.

Bestavros, A., & Mehrotra, S. (2001). *DNS-based internet client clustering and characterization* (Tech. Rep.). Boston, MA, USA: Boston University.

Bieber, M., Engelbart, D., Furata, R., Hiltz, S. R., Noll, J., Preece, J., Stohr, E. A., Turoff, M., & Walle, B.V.D. (2002). Toward virtual community knowledge evolution. *Journal of Management Information Systems*, 18(4), 11-35.

Bizer, C. (2003). D2R MAP-a database to RDF mapping language. *Proceedings of the 12th International World Wide Web Conference.*

Black, W., McNaught, J., Vasilakopoulos, A., Zervanou, K., & Rinaldi, F. (2005). *CAFETIERE: Conceptual Annotations for Facts, Events, Terms, Individual Entities and RElations* (Parmenides Technical Report No. TR-U4.3.1), http://www.nactem.ac.uk/files/phatfile/cafetiere-report.pdf

Blackler, F. (1993). Knowledge and the theory of organisation: Organisation as activity systems and reframing of management. *Journal of Management studies 30(6)*, 863-885.

Blair, M., Brummell, K., Dewey, M., Elkan, R., Hewitt, M., Kendrick, D., Robinson, J., & Williams, D. (2001). Effectiveness of home based support for older people: systematic review and meta–analysis. *British Medical Journal, 323*(7315), 719–725.

Blumberg, R., & Atre S. (2003). Automatic classification: Moving to the mainstream. *DR Review Magazine 13*(4), 12-19.

Boer, N.I., van Baalen, P.J., & Kumar, K. (2002). An activity theory approach for studying the situatedness of knowledge sharing. In *Proceedings of the 35th Annual Hawaii International Conference on System Sciences* (HICSS 35.02)

Boley, H., Dean, M., Grosof, B., Horrocks, I., Patel-Schneider, P. F., & Tabet, S. (2004). SWRL: A Semantic Web rule language combining OWL and RuleML.

Bonatti, P., & Olmedilla, D. (2005). Driving and monitoring provisional trust negotiation with metapolicies. In *Proceedings of the 6th IEEE International Workshop on Policies for Distributed Systems and Networks (POLICY'05)* (pp. 14-23). Washington, DC, USA: IEEE Computer Society.

Bonifacio, M., Bouquet, P., Mameli, G., & Nori, M. (2002). *KEEx: A Peer-to-Peer Solution for Distributed Knowledge Management*. Paper presented at the 4th International Conference on Practical Aspects of Knowledge Management (PAKM 02), Wien, Austria.

Bonino, D., Corno, F., Farinetti, L., & Bosca A. (2004). Ontology driven semantic search. *WSEAS Transaction on Information Science and Application, 1*(6), 1597-1605.

Booth, N., Purves, I.N., Sowerby, M., & Sugden, B. (1997). The PRODIGY project – The iterative development of the release one model. *Computer Methods & Programs in Biomedicine, 54*,59–67.

Bosc, P., & Damiani E. (2001). Fuzzy service selection in a distributed object-oriented environment, *IEEE Transactions on Fussy Systems, 9* (5), 682-698.

Bou, B. (2007). WordNet Web Application [Electronic Version]. Retrieved on June 2007 from http://wnwa.sourceforge.net/

Bouchon-Meunier, B., Rifqi, M., Bothorel S. (1996). Towards general measures of comparison of objects, *Fuzzy Sets and Systems, 84*, 143-153.

Bouras, C., Igglesis, V., Kapoulas, V., & Tsiatsos, T. (2005). A Web-based virtual community. *Inernational. Journal of Web Based Communities, 1*(2), 127–139.

Brachman, R.J. (1983). *What IS-A is and isn't: An analysis of taxonomiclLinks in semantic networks.*

Bray, T., Paoli, J., & Sperberg-McQueen, C. M. (1998, February 10). *Extensible markup language (XML) 1.0.* Retrieved October 15, 2006, from http://www.w3.org/TR/1998/REC-xml-19980210

Brennan, M., Funke, S., & Andersen, C. (2001). The learning content management system--a new e-Learning market segment emerges. *IDC White Paper.*, Retrieved on September 25, 2006, from http://www.internettime.com/Learning/lcms/IDCLCMSWhitePaper.pdf

Bresciani P., Perini A., Giorgini P., Giunchiglia F., & Mylopoulos J. (2004). *Tropos: An agent-oriented software development methodology*, Autonomous Agents and Multi-Agent Systems, 8, pp. 203-236.

Brickley, D., & Guha, R. V. (2004). *RDF Vocabulary Description Language 1.0: RDF Schema* (W3C Recommendation 10 February 2004).

Brin, S., & Page, L. (1998). The anatomy of a large-scale hypertextual web search engine. In *Proceedings of the 7th linternational Conference on World Wide Web 7 (Www7)* (pp. 107-117). Amsterdam, The Netherlands: Elsevier Science Publishers B. V.

Broder, A. (2002). A taxonomy of Web search. In *ACM SIGIR Forum* (pp. 3-10). New York, USA: ACM.

Broekstra, J., Kampman, A., van Harmelen, F. (2002). Sesame: A generic architecture for storing and querying rdf and rdf schema, pp. 54+.

Brooks, F. P. (1995). The mythical man-month: Essays on software engineering (anniversary ed.). Reading, MA: Addison-Wesley.

Brown, J. & Isaacs, D. (1996). Conversation as a core business process. *The Systems Thinker*, 7(10), 1-6.

Brusilovsky, P., & Nijhavan, H. (2002). A framework for adaptive e-learning based on distributed re-usable learning activities. *Proceedings of the World Conference on E-Learning* (E-Learn 2002), Montreal, Canada.

Buckingham Shum S., MacLean A., Bellotti V. M.E., & V. Hammond N. (1997). *Graphical argumentation and design cognition.* Rapport Technique KMI-TR-25, The Open University, Rank Xerox Reasearch Centre, Apple Reasearch Laboratories, University of York, UK.

Budanitsky, A., & Hirst, G. (2001). Semantic distance in WordNet: An experimental, application-oriented evaluation of five measures. *Proceedings of Workshop on WordNet and Other Lexical Resources of the 2nd Meeting of the North American Chapter of the Association for Computational Linguistics,* Pittsburgh, PA.

Burke, R. (2002). Hybrid recommender systems: Survey and experiments. *User Modeling and User-Adapted Interaction, 12*(4), 331-370.

Caire, G., Coulier, W., Garijo, F. J., Gomez, J., Pavón, J., Leal, F., Chainho, P., Kearney, P. E., Stark, J., Evans, R., & Massonet, P. (2001). Agent oriented analysis using message/uml. In Wooldridge, M.,Weiß, G., and Ciancarini, P. Eds.), Agent-Oriented Software Engineering II, Second InternationalWorkshop, AOSE 2001, Montreal, Canada, May 29.

Calvanese, D., De Giacomo, G., Lembo, D., Lenzerini, M., & Rosati, R. (2005). Tailoring OWL for data intensive ontologies. In *Proceedings of the Workshop on owl: Experiences and directions* (owled 2005).

Carbonaro A. (2004). Learning objects recommendation in a collaborative information management system. *IEEE Learning Technology Newsletter, 6*(4).

Carbonaro, A. (2005). Defining personalized learning views of relevant learning objects in a collaborative bookmark management system. In *Web-based intelligent e-learning systems: Technologies and applications.* Hershey, PA: Idea Group.

Carcagnì, A., *Metodologia e sviluppo di un workflow per la definizione di ontologie.* Unpublished degree dissertation, University of Salento, Italy.

Carroll, J. J., & Stickler, P. (2004). RDF triples in XML. *13th International World Wide Web Conference*, (412-413), ACM Press.

Castelfranchi C. (2000), *Engineering Social Order. In Engineering Societies in the Agents' World,* Lecture Notes in Artificial Intelligence. Springer Verlag, 2000.300p.

Castelles, P., Fernández, M,, & Vallet, D. (2007). An adaptation of the vector space model for ontology-based information retrieval. IEEE Transaction on Knowledge and data Engineering (TKDE). *Journal of Management Information Systems, 19*(2), 261-272.

Castro, M., Druschel, P., Hu, Y. C., & Rowstron, A. (2002). *Topology-aware routing in structured peer-to-peer overlay networks* (Tech. Rep. No. MSR-TR-2002-82). Microsoft Research, One Microsoft Way.

Cavallini, A., Fassino, C., Micieli, G., Mossa, C., Quaglini, S., & Stefanelli, M. (2000). Guideline–based careflow systems. *Artificial Intelligence in Medicine, 20,* 5–22. doi: 10.1016/S0933–3657(00)00050–6.

Ceravolo, P., Corallo, A., Damiani, E., Elia, E., Viviani, M., & Zilli, A. (2006). Bottom-up extraction and maintenance of ontology-based metadata, *Fuzzy Logic and the Semantic Web*, Computer Intelligence, Elsevier.

Ceravolo, P., Corallo, A., Elia, G., and Zilli, A. (2004). Managing ontology evolution via relational constraints. In Mircea, Howlett, R. J., Jain, L. C., Mircea, Howlett, R. J., and Jain, L. C., (Eds.), KES, volume 3215 of Lecture Notes in Computer Science, pp. 335-341. Springer.

Ceravolo, P., Damiani, E., & Viviani, M. (2006). Adding a trust layer to Semantic Web metadata. In F. C. Enrique Herrera-Viedma Gabriella Pasi (Ed.), *Soft computing in web information retrieval: models and applications* (Vol. 197). New York, NY, USA: Springer.

Ceravolo, P., Nocerino, M. C., & Viviani, M. (2004). Knowledge extraction from semi-structured data based on fuzzy techniques, *Knowledge-Based Intelligent Information and Engineering Systems*, In *Proceedings of the 8th International Conference,* KES 2004, Part III, pp. 328-334.

Chamberlin, D., Florescu, D., Robie, J., Simeon, J., & Stefanascu, M. (2001). *XQuery: A query language for XML.* Retrieved from http://www.w3.org/TR/xquery

ChefMoz. (2005). *ChefMoz dining guide.* Retrieved November, 2004, from http://chefdmoz.org

Chekuri C., Goldwasser, M., Ragavan, P., & Upfal, E. (1997). *Web search using automatic classification.* Paper presented at 6th International World Wide Web Conference, Santa Clara, California USA.

Chen, L., Cox, S.J., Goble, C., Keane, A.J., Roberts, A., Shadbolt, N.R., Smart, P., & Tao, F. (2002). Engineering knowledge for engineering grid applications. In *Proceedings of the Euroweb 2002 Conference, The Web and the GRID: from e-science to e-business*, Oxford, UK, pp12-25.

Chen, P. P. (1976). The entity-relationship model--toward a unified view of data. ACM Trans. Database Syst., 1(1), pp.9-36.

Chen, X., Ren, S., Wang, H., & Zhang, X. (2005). *SCOPE: scalable consistency maintenance in structured P2P systems.* Paper presented at the 6th IEEE Computer and Communications Societies Conference (INFOCOM 2005), Miami, USA, Vol. 10, pp.79–93

Chinowsky, P. S. & Rojas, E. M. (2003). Virtual teams: Guide to successful implementation. *Journal of Management in Engineering*, July 2003, pp. 98-106.

Chowdhury, G. G. (2003). Natural language processing. *Annual Review of Information Science and Technology, 37*(1), 51-89.

Chung, C. Y., Lieu, R., Liu, J., Mao, J., & Raghavan, P. (2002). Thematic mapping--From unstructured documents to taxonomies. In *Proceedings of the 11th Iinternational Conference on Information and Knowledge Management 2002* (pp. 608-610). Virginia, USA: ACM.

CIO.com. (2006). *The ABCs of e-commerce.* Retrieved October 15, 2006, from http://www.cio.com/ec/edit/b2cabc.html

Clark, J., & DeRose, S. (1999, November 16). *XML path language (XPath) Version 1.0.* Retrieved August 31, 2006, from http://www.w3.org/TR/xpath

Claver, E., Zaragoza, P., & Quer, D. (2007). Practical experiences in knowledge management processes by multinational firms: A multiple case study. *International Journal of Knowledge Management Studies, 1*(3/4), 261-275.

Clegg, C. (1994). Psychology and information technology: The study of cognition in organisations. *British Journal of Psyschology, 85*, 449-477.

Codd, E. F. (1990). The relational model for database management: version 2. Boston, MA, USA: Addison-Wesley Longman Publishing Co., Inc.

Cole, H. & Engeström, Y. (1993). A cultural historical approach to distributed cognition. In G. Solomon (Ed.) *Psychological and educational considerations* (pp. 1-46). Cambridge, UK: Cambridge University Press

Collins, P., Shukla, S. & Redmiles, D. (2002). Activity theory and system design: A view from the trenches, Special Issue of CSCW on Activity Theory and the Practice of Design, Introduction to the Special Issue on Activity Theory and the Practice of Design , Computer Supported Cooperative Work (CSCW), Vol. 11, No 1-2/March , Springer, Netherlands.

Comito, C., Patarin, S., & Talia, D. (2006). A semantic overlay network for p2p schema-based data integration. In *Proceedings of the 11th IEEE symposium on computers and communications (ISCC '06)* (pp. 88-94). Washington, DC, USA: IEEE Computer Society.

Conklin E.J.(1996), *Designing organizational memory: Preserving intellectual assets in a knowledge economy.* Electronic Publication by Corporate Memory Systems, Inc., 1996. http://www.zilker.net/business/info/pubs/desom/.

Conklin J. & Begeman (1988.) M. gIBIS: A Hypertext Tool for Exploratory Policy Discussion. ACM Transaction on O-ce Information Systems, *6*(4),303-331.

Cooley R., Mobasher, B., & Srivastava, J. (1997). Web mining: Information and pattern discovery on the World Wide Web. Proceedings of the 9th International Conference on Tools with Artificial Intelligence (ICTAI '97).

Cooper, J. (2003). Educational MUVES: Virtual learning communities. *Journal of Education, Community and Values*, Volume 3, Issue 9.

Corallo, A., Elia, G., & Zilli, A. (2005). *Enhancing communities of practice: an ontological approach.* Paper presented at 11th International Conference on Industrial Engineering and Engineering Management, Shenyang, China.

Corallo, A., Ingraffia, N., Vicari, C., & Zilli, A. (2007). *SIMS: An ontology-based multi-source knowledge management system*. Paper presented at the 11th Multi-Conference on Systemics, Cybernetics and Informatics (MSCI 2007), Orlando, Florida, USA.

Corcho, O., & Lopez, M. F., Perez, A. G., (2003). Methodologies, tools and languages for building ontologies. Where is their meeting point? *Data & Knowledge Engineering*, 46 (2003), 41–64.

Cornelli, F., Damiani, E., Vimercati, S. D. C. di, Paraboschi, S., & Samarati, P. (2002). Choosing reputable servents in a p2p network. In*: Proceedings of the 11th international conference on world wide web (Www '02)* (pp. 376-386). New York, NY, USA: ACM Press.

Cossentino M. (2005), *From Requirements to Code with the PASSI Methodology in Agent-Oriented Methodologies*. B. Henderson-Sellers & P. Giorgini (Eds.),Idea Group Inc., Hershey, PA, USA.

Coulouris, G. F., & Dollimore, J. (1988). *Distributed systems: concepts and design.* Boston, MA, USA: Addison-Wesley Longman Publishing Co., Inc.

Crawford, K. & Hasan. H. (2006). Demonstrations of the activity theory framework for research in information systems. *Australasian Journal of Information Systems Volume 13 Number 2, May 2006.*

Crespo, A., & Garcia-Molina, H. (2002). *Semantic overlay networks for P2P systems* (Tech. Rep.). Computer Science Department, Stanford University.

Crubezy, M., Decker, S., Fergerson, R.W., Musen, M.A., Noy, N.F., & Sintek, M. (2001). Creating Semantic Web Contents with Protégé–2000. *IEEE Intelligent Systems*, *16*(2), 60–71.

Cui, Z., Damiani, E., Leida, M., & Viviani M.(2005). OntoExtractor: A fuzzy-based approach in clustering semi-structured data sources and metadata generation, *Knowledge-Based Intelligent Information and Engineering Systems, 9th International Conference, KES 2005*, Melbourne, Australia, September 14-16, 2005, Proceedings, Part I, ser. Lecture Notes in Computer Science, vol. 3681. Springer, pp. 112-118.

Cunningham, H. (2000). *JAPE - A Java Annotation Patterns Engine* (Research Memorandum CS–00–10): Department of Computer Science, University of Sheffield, http://www.dcs.shef.ac.uk/~diana/Papers/jape.ps

Cunningham, H., & Scott, D. (2004). Software Architecture for Language Engineering. *Natural Language Engineering, 10*(3-4), 205-209.

Cunningham, H., Maynard, D., Bontcheva, K., & Tablan, V. (2002). GATE: A framework and graphical development environment for robust NLP tools and applications. *Proceedings of the 40th Anniversary Meeting of the Association for Computational Linguistics,* Budapest.

Dai, H., & Mobasher, B. (2004). Integrating semantic knowledge with Web usage mining for personalization. In A. Scime (Ed.), *Web mining: Applications and techniques* (pp. 276-306). Hershey, PA: Idea Group.

Damásio, C. V., Analytu, A., Antoniou, G., & Wagner, G. (2005, September 11-16). Supporting open and closed world reasoning on the Web. In *Proceedings of the Principles and Practice ofSemantic Web Reasoning, 3rd International Workshop*, ppswr 2005, Dagstuhl castle, Germany. (Vol. 4187). Springer.

Damiani, E., Ceravolo, P., & Viviani, M. (2007). Bottom-up extraction and trust-based refinement of ontology metadata. *IEEE Transactions on Knowledge and Data Engineering, 19* (2), 149-163.

Damiani, E., Corallo, A., Elia, G., & Ceravolo, P. (2002, November). *Standard per i learning objects: Interoperabilità ed integrazione nella didattica a distanza.* Paper presented at the International Workshop eLearning: una sfida per l'Università - Strategie Metodi Prospettive, Milan, Italy.

Damiani, E., De Capitani di Vimercati, S., Paraboschi, S., & Samarati, P. (2003). Managing and sharing servents' reputations in p2p systems. *IEEE Transactions on Knowledge and Data Engineering, 15* (4), 840-854.

Damiani, E., De Capitani di Vimercati, S., Samarati, P., & Viviani, M. (2006). A WOWA-based aggregation technique on trust values connected to metadata. *Electronic Notes in Theoretical Computer Science, 157* (3), 131-142.

Damiani, E., Nocerino, M. C., & Viviani, M. (2004). Knowledge extraction from an XML data flow: building a taxonomy based on clustering technique, *Current Issues in Data and Knowledge Engineering*, In *Proceedings of EUROFUSE 2004: 8th Meeting of the EURO Working Group on Fuzzy Sets*, 133-142.

Damiani, E., Vimercati, De Capitani di Vimercati, S, Paraboschi, S., Samarati, P., & Violante, F. (2002). A reputation-based approach for choosing reliable resources in peer-to-peer networks. In *Proceedings of the 9th ACM conference on computer and communications security* (*CCS '02)* (pp. 207-216). New York, NY, USA: ACM Press.

Dardenne, A., Fickas, S., & van Lamsweerde, A. (1993). Goal–directed requirements acquisition. *Science of Computer Programming, 20*(1–2), 3–50.

Darpa Agent Markup Language (DAML). (2005). *Language overview.* Retrieved October, 2005, from http://www.daml.org/

Das, A.K., Musen, M.A., Shahar, Y., & Tu, S.W. (1996). EON: a component–based approach to automation of protocol–directed therapy. *Journal of the American Medical Informatics Association, 3,* 367–388.

Datta, A., Hauswirth, M., & Aberer, K. (2003). *Updates in highly unreliable, replicated peer-to-peer systems.* Paper presented at the IEEE International Conference on Distributed Computing Systems (ICDCS '03), Providence, RI, USA, pp.76-88.

Davenport, T.H. (1997). Ten principles of knowledge management and four case studies. *Knowledge and Process Management, 4*(3), 187-208.

Davenport, T.H., DeLong, D.W. & Beeres, M.C. (1998). Successful knowledge management Projects. *Sloan Management Review, Winter 1998,* pp 43-57.

Davies, J., Duke, A., & Sure Y. (2003). OntoShare: A knowledge management environment for virtual communities of practice. In *Proceedings of the 2nd International Conference on Knowledge Capture (K-CAP 2003)*, 20-27.

De Giacomo, G., Lenzerini, M., Poggi, A., & Rosati, R. (2006). On the update of description logic ontologies at the Instance Level. In Aaai 2006.

Debowski, S. (2006). Knowledge management. John Wiley & Son, Australia.

Delphi Group. (2002). *Taxonomy & content classification,* Retrieved on March, 2007, from http://lsdis.cs.uga.edu/SemanticEnterprise/Delphi_LingoMotorfinal.pdf

Demazeau, Y., & Rocha Costa, A.C. (1996). Populations and organizations in open multi–agent systems. In *Proceedings of the 1st National Symposium on Parallel and Distributed Artificial Intelligence.*

Dennis, S., & Bruza, P., McArtur, R. (2002). Web searching: A process-oriented experimental study of three interactive search paradigms. *Journal of the American Society for Information Science and Technology, 53*(2),120-133.

Denoue, L., & Vignollet, L. (2001, January). *Personal Information Organization using Web Annotation*. Paper presented at the *WebNet 2001 World Conference on the WWW and Internet, Orlando, FL.*

Desilets, A., Paquet, S. & Vinson, N. (2005, October 16-18). Are wikis usable?. *WikiSym 2005 Conference*. San Diego CA USA.

Didion, J. (2007). The Java Wordnet Library.

Dieberger, A., Hook, K., Svensson, M., &Lonnqvist, P. (2001). *Social navigation researchagenda. In: CHI '01 extended abstracts on Human factors in computing systems, ACM Press (2001).* pp.107–108.

Donini, F. M., Lenzerini, M., Nardi, D., & Schaerf, A. (1998). AL-log: Integrating datalog and description logics. J. of Intelligent Information Systems, 10(3), 227-252.

Dourish, P. & Chalmers, M. (1994). Running out of space: Models of information navigation. (short paper). *HCI'94 (British Computer Society)*. Retrieved on from ftp://parcftp.xerox.com/pub/europarc/jpd/hci94-navigation.ps.

Drucker, P. (2000). Need to know: Integrating e-learning with high velocity value chains. *Delphi Group White Paper*. Retrieved on September 22, 2006, from www.delphigroup.com

Drucker, P. F. (1994). *Post-capitalist society*. Collins.

Dubin, R., (1978). *Theory Building*. Free Press, New York.

Dublin Core Metadata Initiative (2006). Dublin Core Metadata Terms., Retrieved on May 26, 2003, from http://dublincore.org

Duygulu, P., Barnard, K., Freitas, N., & Forsyth, D. (2002). Object recognition as machine translation: Learning a lexicon for a fixed image vocabulary. In *Proceedings of European Conference on Computer Vision, 2002* (LNCS 2353, pp. 97-112). Berlin; Heidelberg: Springer.

Dzbor, M., Motta, E., & Stutt, A. (2005). Achieving higher-level learning through adaptable semantic Web applications. *International Journal of Knowledge and Learning, 1*(1/2).

Earle, K., Sutton, D.R., & Taylor, P.(2006). Evaluation of PROforma as a language for implementing medical guidelines in a practical context. BMC Med Inform Decision Making, 6, 20.

Eberhart, A. (2002). *Automatic Generation of Java/SQL based Inference Engines from RDF Schema and RuleML*. In Hendler, J., & Horrocks, I. (Ed.). In *Proceedings of the First International Semantic Web Conference*,pp. 102–116.

eBMS. (2005). *KIWI--Application Context* (Project Deliverable). Lecce, Italy: University of Lecce

eBMS. (2005). *KIWI--Ontology for knowledge mapping* (Project Deliverable). Lecce, Italy: University of Lecce

eBMS. (2006). *Test Verity in the Virtual eBMS project* (Project Deliverable). Lecce, Italy: University of Lecce

Edvinsson, L. & Malone, M. S. (1997). *Intellectual capital: Realizing your company's true value by finding its hidden brainpower*. Collins.

Ehrig, M., & Sure, Y. (2004, May). Ontology mapping—an integrated approach. In C. Bussler, J. Davis, D. Fensel, & R. Studer (Eds.), *Proceedings of the 1st European Semantic Web Symposium* (pp. 76-91), Heraklion, Greece. Berlin: Springer-Verlag (LNCS 3053).

Ehrig, M., Tempich, C., Broekstra, J., Van Harmelen, F., Sabou, M., Siebes, R., Staab, S., & Stuckenschmidt, H. (2003). *SWAP: Ontology-based Knowledge Management with Peer-to-Peer Technology*. Paper presented at the 1st German Workshop on Ontology-based Knowledge Management (WOW 2003), Luzerne, Switzerland (2003).

Elia , G., Secundo, G., and Taurino, C. (2006), Towards unstructured and just-in-time learning: The "Virtual eBMS" e-Learning system. In A Méndez-Vilas, A. Solano-Martin, J. Mesa González, & J.A. Mesa González (Eds.), *m-ICTE2006: Vol. 2. Current Developments in Technology-Assisted Education* (pp. 1067-1072). FORMATEX, Badajoz, Spain.

Elia, G., Secundo, G. & Taurino, C. (2006). A process-oriented and technology-based model of virtual communities of practices: Evidence from a case study in higher education. *m-ICTE2006--IV International Conference on Multimedia and Information and Communication Technologies in Education.*

Enembreck F. & Barthès J.P. (2002). Personal assistant to improve CSCW. In *Proceedings of CSCWD*, Rio de Janeiro.

Engeström, Y. (1987). Learning by expanding: An activity-theoretical approach to developmental research. Helsinki: Orienta-Konsultit, OY. Finland.

Engeström, Y. (1990). Developmental work: Research as activity theory in practice: Analysisng the work of general practitioners. In Y. Engeström, Learning, Working and Imaging: Twelve studies in activity theory, Orienta-Konsultit OY, Helsinki.

Engeström, Y. (1999). Innovative learning in work teams: analysing knowledge creation in practice. In Y. Engeström, R. Miettinen, & R-L Punamaki (Eds.), *Perspectives on activity theory: Learning in doing: Social, cognitive and computational perspectives.* (pp, 377-404) Cambridge University Press, UK.

Engeström, Y. (2005). Developmental work research: Expanding activity theory in practice, Vol. 12, ICHS, Berlin, 2005.

Etzioni, O., & Weld, D. S. (1995). Intelligent agents on the Internet: Fact, fiction, and forecast. IEEE Expert, pp. 44-49.

Euzenat, J. (2001). An infrastructure for formally ensuring interoperability in a heterogeneous Semantic Web, In *Proceeding of 1stlinternationalConference on Semantic Web Working Symposium (SWWS'01)* (pp. 345-360) Stanford, CA, USA.

Ezzy, E. (2006). Search 2.0 vs Traditional search. Retrieved on September, 2007, from http://www.readwriteweb.com/archives/search_20_vs_tr.php

Fagan, L.M., Musen, M.A., Rohn, J.A., & Shortliffe, E.H. (1987). Knowledge engineering for a clinical trial advice system: uncovering errors in protocol specification. *Bull Cancer, 74,* 291–296.

Fagin, R. (1998). Fuzzy Queries in Multimedia Database Systems, *ACM Sigact Sigmod Sigart Symposium on Principles of Database Systems*, 17, pp. 1-10.

Fagin, R. (1999). Combining fuzzy information from multiple systems. *Journal of Computer and System Sciences, 58* (1), 83-99.

Fagin, R. (2002). Combining fuzzy information: An overview, *Sigmod Record, 31* (2),109-118.

Falcone, R., & Castelfranchi, C. (2001). Social trust: A cognitive approach. In *Trust and deception in virtual societies* (pp. 55-90). Norwell, MA, USA: Kluwer Academic Publishers.

Fedotova, N., Bertucci, M., & Veltri, L. (2007). Reputation management techniques in dht-based peer-to-peer networks. *Second International Conference on Internet and Web Applications and Services (ICIW'07).*

Fellbaum, C. (Ed.). (1998). *WordNet: An electronic lexical database.* Cambridge, MA: MIT Press.

Feng, S. L., Manmatha, R., & Lavrenko, V. (2004). Multiple Bernoulli relevance models for image and video annotation. In *Proceedings of IEEE Conference on Computer Vision Pattern Recognition, 2004* (Vol. 2, pp. 1002-1009).

Fensel, D. (2001). *Ontologies: A silver bullet for knowledge management and electronic commerce.* Berlin: Springer.

Ferber, J., Gutknecht, O., & Michel, F. (2003). *From agents to organizations: an organizational view of multi-agent systems.* In Agent-Oriented Software Engineering IV 4th InternationalWorkshop, (AOSE-2003@AAMAS 2003), volume 2935 of LNCS, pp. 214–230, Melbourne, Australia.

Fernandez, M., Gomez-Perez, A., & Juristo, N. (1997). Meta-ontology. *From ontological art toward ontological engineering. In Spring Symposium Series, Stanford University. Stanford, CA.*

Fielden, (1975) G. D. R., *Engineering Design.* London: HMSO

Fink, J., & Kobsa, A. (2002). User modeling for personalized city tours. *Artificial Intelligence Review, 18,* 33-74.

Finlayson, M. A. (2007). MIT Java WordNet Interface. Retrieved on August 2007, from http://www.mit.edu/~markaf/projects/wordnet

Fodor,J., Marichal, J. L. & Roubens, M. (1995). Characterization of the ordered weighted averaging operators, *IEEE Trans. on Fuzzy Systems, 3* (2), 236-240.

Foot, K.A. (2001). Cultural historical activity theory as practical theory: Illuminating the development of a conflict monitoring network. *Communication Theory Vol.0 No.1. Feb 2001,* 56-83.

Forcadell, F.J., & Guadamillas, F. (2002). A case study on the implementation of a knowledge management strategy oriented to innovation. *Knowledge and Process Management, 9*(3), 162-171.

Forman, G. (2002). Incremental machine learning to reduce biochemistry lab costs in the search for drug discovery. In *Proceedings of the 2nd ACM SIGKDD Workshop on Data Mining in Bioinformatics.* Edmonton, Alberta, Canada.

Foster, I., & Kesselman, C. (1998). *The grid: Blueprint for a new computing infrastructure.* San Francisco, CA, USA: Morgan Kaufmann Publishers Inc.

Fowler, M. & Scott, K. (Eds.). (1999). *UML Distilled Second Edition--A Brief Guide to the Standard Object Modelling Language.* A. Wesley.

Fox, M. S. (1981). *An organizational view of distributed systems.* IEEE Trans. on System, Man, and Cybernetics, SMC-11(1):70–80.

Fox, M.S., & Huang, J., (2005), Knowledge provenance in enterrpriseiInformation, *International Journal of Production Research, 43*(20), 4471-4492.

Frege, G. (1918). Der Gedanke: Eine logische Untersuchung. Beiträge zur Philosophie des Deutschen Idealismus, I, pp.58-77.

Fuentes, R., Gomez–Sanz, J., & Pavon, J. (2005). *The INGENIAS methodology and tools.* In (Giorgini, 2005), Chapter IX, pp. 236–276.

Fukuda Y., (1995), *Variations of Knowledge in Information Society,* In *Proceedings of the ISMICK* 95, pp.3-8.

Fuxman, A., Liu, L., Mylopoulos, J., Pistore, M., Roveri, M., & Traverso, P. (2004). Specifying and analyzing early requirements in Tropos. *Requirements Engineering, 9*(2), 132–150.

Galant, V., & Paprzycki, M. (2002, April). Information personalization in an Internet based travel support system. In *Proceedings of the BIS'2002 Conference* (pp. 191-202). Poznań, Poland: Poznań University of Economics Press.

Galant, V., Gordon, M., & Paprzycki, M. (2002). Agent-client interaction in a Web-based e-commerce system. In D. Grigoras (Ed.), *Proceedings of the International Symposium on Parallel and Distributed Computing* (pp. 1-10). Iasi, Romania: University of Iaşi Press.

Galant, V., Gordon, M., & Paprzycki, M. (2002). Knowledge management in an Internet travel support system. In B. Wiszniewski (Ed.), *Proceedings of ECON2002, ACTEN* (pp. 97-104). Wejcherowo: ACTEN.

Galant, V., Jakubczyc, J., & Paprzycki, M. (2002). Infrastructure for e-commerce. In M. Nycz & M. L. Owoc (Eds.), *Proceedings of the 10th Conference Extracting Knowledge from Databases* (pp. 32-47). Poland: Wrocław University of Economics Press.

Gambetta, D. (1988). Can we trust trust? In *Trust: Making and breaking cooperative relations.* Basil Blackwell. (Reprinted in electronic edition from Department of Sociology, University of Oxford, chapter 13, pp. 213-237).

Gandon F., Poggi A., Rimassa G., & Turci P. (2002). *Multi-Agent Corporate Memory Management System* In Engineering Agent Systems: Best of "From Agent Theory to Agent Implementation (AT2AI)-3," *Journal of Applied Artificial Intelligence*, Volume 16, Number 9-10/October - December 2002, Taylor & Francis, p699 – 720.

Ganter, B., & Wille, R. (1999). *Formal concept analysis: Mathematical foundations* (translated from B. Ganter, R. Wille: Formale Begriffsanalyse - Mathematische Grundlagen. Springer, Heidelberg 1996) Springer-Verlag, Berlin-Heidelberg.

García, F.J., Berlanga, A.J., Moreno, M.N., García, J., & Carabias, J. (2004). *HyCo—an authoring tool to create semantic learning objects for Web-based e-learning systems* (pp. 344-348). Berlin: Springer-Verlag (LNCS 3140).

Gasson, S. (Working Paper) (2004). Organisational 'problem solving' and theories of social cognition. Available from http://www.cis.drexel.edu/faculty/gasson/research/problem-solving.html

Gawinecki, M., Gordon, M., Nguyen, N., Paprzycki, M., & Szymczak, M. (2005). RDF demarcated resources in an agent based travel support system. In M. Golinski et al. (Eds.), *Informatics and effectiveness of systems* (pp. 303-310). Katowice: PTI Press.

Gawinecki, M., Gordon, M., Paprzycki, M., Szymczak, M., Vetulani, Z., & Wright, J. (2005). Enabling semantic referencing of selected travel related resources. In W. Abramowicz (Ed.), *Proceedings of the BIS'2005 Conference* (pp. 271-290). Poland: PoznaD University of Economics Press.

Gawinecki, M., Kruszyk, M., & Paprzycki, M. (2005). Ontology-based stereotyping in a travel support system. In *Proceedings of the XXI Fall Meeting of Polish Information Processing Society* (pp. 73-85). PTI Press.

Gawinecki, M., Vetulani, Z., Gordon, M., & Paprzycki, M. (2005). Representing users in a travel support system. In H. Kwaśnicka et al. (Eds.), *Proceedings of the ISDA 2005 Conference* (pp. 393-398). Los Alamitos, CA: IEEE Press.

Ge, Y., Yu, Y., Zhu, X., Huang, S., & Xu, M. (2003). OntoVote: a scalable distributed vote-collecting mechanism for ontology drift on a P2P platform. *The Knowledge Engineering Review*, 18(3), 257-263.

Gilbert, A., Gordon, M., Nauli, A., Paprzycki, M., Williams, S., & Wright, J. (2004). Indexing agent for data gathering in an e-travel system. *Informatica, 28*(1), 69-78.

Gillham, B. (2000). *Case study research methods*. London: Continuum.

Giorgini, P., & Henderson–Sellers, B. (Ed.). (2005). Agent–Oriented Methodologies. Hershey, United States of America: Idea Group Publishing.

Glasser, L. (1986). The Integration of Computing and Routine Work. *ACM Translation on Office Information Systems Vol. 4.* pp. 205-252.

Gloor, P. A. (2006). *Swarm creativity : Competitive advantage through collaborative innovation networks.* Oxford University Press, USA.

Golebiowska J., Dieng-Kuntz R., Corby O., & Mousseau D. (2002). *Samovar : Using ontologies and text-mining for building an automobile project memory*, in: Knowledge Management and Organizational Memories, Kluwer Academic Publishers, July 2002, pp. 89-102.

Gomes S. & Sagot J.C. (2000). *A concurrent engineering experience based on a cooperative and object oriented design methodology*, 3rd International Conference on Integrated Design and Manufacturing in Mechanical Engineering, IDMME 2000, Montréal.

Gordon, M., & Paprzycki, M. (2005). Designing agent based travel support system. In *Proceedings of the ISPDC 2005 Conference* (pp. 207-214). Los Alamitos, CA: IEEE Computer Society Press.

Gordon, M., Kowalski, A., Paprzycki, N., Pełech, T., Szymczak, M., & Wasowicz, T. (2005). Ontologies in a travel support system. In D. J. Bem et al. (Eds.), *Internet 2005* (pp. 285-300). Poland: Technical University of Wrocław Press.

Gordon, M., Pathak, P. (1999). Finding information on the World Wide Web: The retrieval effectiveness of search engines *Information Processing & Management*, 35(2), 141-180.

Grandison, T., & Sloman, M. (2000, September). A Survey of Trust in Internet Applications. *IEEE Communications Surveys and Tutorials, 3* (4). (http://www.comsoc.org/livepubs/surveys/public/2000/dec/index.html)

Greenberg, L. (2002). LMS and LCMS: What's the Difference? *Learning Circuits, ASTD.* Retrieved September on 25, 2006, from http://www.learningcircuits.org/2002/dec2002/greenberg.htm

Greenes, R.A., & Shiffman, R.N. (1994). Improving clinical guidelines with logic and decision table techniques: application to hepatitis immunization recommendation. *Medical Decision Making, 14*, 245–254.

Greer, J., & McCalla, G. (1994). *Student modeling: The key to individualized knowledge based instruction* (pp. 3-35). NATO ASI Series. Springer-Verlag.

Griffiths, N. (2005). Trust: Challenges and opportunities. In *Agentlink News, 19*, 9-11.

Griffiths, N. (2006, September 11-13). A fuzzy approach to reasoning with trust, distrust and insufficient trust. In M. Klusch, M. Rovatsos, & T. R. Payne (Eds.), In *Proceedings of the Cooperative information agents x, 10th International Workshop, cia2006,* Edinburgh, UK (p. pp. 360-374). Springer.

Grosof, B. N., Horrocks, I., Volz, R., & Decker, S. (2003). Description logic programs: Combining logic programs with description logic. In *Proceedings of the 12th International. World Wide Web Conference* (www 2003) (pp. 48–57). ACM.

Gross, C.P., Heiat, A., & Krumholz, H.M. (2002). Representation of the elderly, women and minorities in heart failure clinical trials. *Archives of Internal Medicine, 162*(15), 1682–1688.

Gross, T. (2004). Design, specification, and implementation of a distributed virtual community system. In *Proceedings of the Workshop on Parallel, Distributed and Network-Based Processing (PDP 2004)*, pp. 225-232.

Gruber, T. R. (1993). Towards principles for the design of ontologies used for knowledge sharing. In Guarino, N. and Poli, R., (Eds.), *Formal ontology in conceptual analysis and knowledge representation*, Deventer, The Netherlands. Kluwer Academic Publishers.

Gruber, T. R. (1993). *What is an ontology?* Retrieved on July 2007, from http://www-ksl.stanford.edu/kst/what-is-an-ontology.html

Gruber, T.R. (1995). *Toward principles for the design of ontologies used for knowledge sharing.* Int. J. Hum. Comput. Stud *43,* (5/6), 907–928.

Gruniger, M. & Lee J. (2002). *Ontology applications anddDesign.* Comm. of the ACM, *45*(2), 39-41.

Grüninger, M., Fox, M. (1995, April 13).Methodology for the design and evaluation of ontologies, In IJCAI'95, Workshop on Basic Ontological Issues in Knowledge Sharing.

Guha, R. V., McCool, R., & Miller, E. (2003). *Semantic search.* Paper presented at the 12th International World Wide Web Conference (WWW 2003), Budapest, Hungary, pp.700-709.

Guizzardi R., Aroyo L., & Wagner Gerd (2003). *Agent-Oriented Knowledge Management in Learning Environments: A Peer-to-Peer Helpdesk Case Study,* in Agent-Mediated Knowledge Management, Springer Berlin, pp. 57-72.

Guizzardi R., Wagner S.S., & Aroyo G. L. (2005). *Knowledge Management in Learning Communities, ICFAI Journal of Knowledge Management, 3*(3), 0-46.

Guozhen, F., Xueqi, C., & Shuo, B. (2001). SAInSE: An intelligent search engine based on WWW structure analysis. In *Proceedings of the 15th International Parallel & Distributed Processing Symposium* (p. 168*)*. Washington, DC, USA: IEEE Computer Society.

Haase, P., & Stojanovic, L. (2005). Consistent evolution of OWL ontologies. In ESWC (pp. 182-197).

Hafeez, K. & Alghatas, F. (2007). Knowledge management in a virtual community of practice using discourse analysis. *The Electronic Journal of Knowledge Management, 5*(1), 29-42.

Hammond, W.E., & Lobach, D.F. (1994). Development and evaluation of a Computer–Assisted Management Protocol (CAMP): improved compliance with care guidelines for diabetes mellitus. In *Proceedings of the Annual Symposium on Computer Applications in Medical Care*, pp. 787–791.

Handschuh, S., Staab, S., & Volz, R. (2003). On deep annotation. *Proceedings of the 12th International World Wide Web Conference.*

Handy, C. (2005). Understanding Organisation. (4th Ed.) Penguin Global, 2005.

Harren, M., Hellerstein, J. M., Huebsch, R., Loo, B. T., Shenker, S., & Stoica, I. (2002). Complex queries in DHT-based Peer-to-Peer Networks. In *Revised papers from the first international workshop on peer-to-peer systems (Iptps '01)* (pp. 242-259). London, UK: Springer-Verlag.

Harrington, P., Gordon, M., Nauli, A., Paprzycki, M., Williams, S., & Wright, J. (2003). Using software agents to index data in an e-travel system. In N. Callaos (Ed.), *Electronic Proceedings of the 7th SCI Conference* [CD-ROM, file: 001428].

Harris K., Fleming M., Hunter R., Rosser B. & Cushman A. (1998). The knowledge management scenario: Trends and directions for 1998-2003. (Tech. Rep.*)* *Gartner Group.*

Hasan, H. (2000). The mediating role of technology in making sense of information in a knowledge intensive industry. *Knowledge and Process Management 6*(2) 72-82.

Haynes, R.B., Johnston, M.E., Langton, K.B., & Mathieu, A. (1994). Effects of computer–based clinical decision support systems on clinician performance and patient outcome. *Annals of Internal Medicine, 120*, 135–142.

Healy, M. J., & Caudell, T. P.(2006). Ontologies and worlds in category theory: Implications for neural systems. Axiomathes, 16(1-2), 165-214.

Heflin, J. (2004, February). OWL Web Ontology Language use cases and requirements. Retrieved from http://www.w3.org/TR/Webont-req/

Hendler, J. (1999, March 11). Is there an intelligent agent in your future? *Nature.* Retrieved March, 2004, from http://www.nature.com/nature/webmatters/agents/agents.html

Hendler, J. (2001). Agents and Semantic Web. *IEEE Intelligent Systems Journal, 16*(2), 30-37.

Hevner, A.R.., March, S.T., & Park, J. (2004) Design research in information systems research, *Mis Quarterly 28*(1), 75-105.

Hilaire V, Koukam A, Gruer P., & Müller J-P. (2000). *Formal Specification and Prototyping of Multi-Agent Systems. Engineering Societies in the Agents* World, in Lecture Notes in Artificial Intelligence. n°1972, Springer Verlag.

Holsapple C. W. & Joshi K. D. (2001). *A collaborative approach to ontology design.* Communications of the ACM. *45* (2), Welbourne, M. Knowledge, Acumen Publishing.

Holsapple, C.W. (2003). Handbook on knowledge management. Heidelberg: Springer.

Horrocks, I., Kutz, O., & Sattler, U. (2006). The even more irresistible SROIQ. In *Proceedings of the 10th International Conference on Principles of Knowledge Representation and Reasoning* (kr 2006) (pp. 57–67). AAAI Press.

Horrocks, I., Sattler, U., & Tobies S. (1999). Practical reasoning for expressive description logics. In *Proceedings of the 6th International Conference on Logic Programming and Automated Reasoning LPAR '99*, , (pp. 161-180). London, UK: Springer-Verlag

Hossain, L. & Wigand, R. T. (2004). ICT enabled virtual collaboration through trust. *Journal of Computer-Mediated Communication JCMC, 10* (1), Article 8.

Hripcsak, G. (1994). Writing Arden Syntax Medical Logic Modules. *Computers in Biology & Medicine, 24,* 331–363. doi: 10.1016/0010–4825(94)90002–7.

Hu, T. H. ting, Ardon, S., & Sereviratne, A. (2004). Semantic-laden peer-to-peer service directory. In *Proceedings of the 4th International Conference on Peer-toPpeer Computing (P2p '04)* (pp. 184-191). Washington, DC, USA: IEEE Computer Society.

Huang, X.-M., & Chang, C.-Y. (2006). PeerCluster: A cluster-based peer-to-peer system. *IEEE Trans. Parallel Distrib. Syst., 17* (10), 1110-1123.

Huberman, B. A., & Adamic, L. A. (1999). *Internet: Growth dynamics of the world-wide web. Nature,* 401(6749):131-131.

Huhns, M.N., & Singh, M.P. (1998). *Multiagent systems in information-rich environments. Cooperative information agents II* (pp. 79-93). (LNAI 1435).

Huysman, M. & Wulf, V. (2006). IT to support knowledge sharing in communities, towards a social capital analysis. *Journal of InformationTechnology 2* (1),. 40 – 51.

Hyvonen, E., Styrman, A., & Saarela, S. (2002). Ontology-based image retrieval. In *Towards the Semantic Web and Web services, Proceedings of XML Finland Conference*, Helsinki, Finland (pp. 15-27).

Institute of Medicine (1992). *Guidelines for clinical practice: from development to use.* Washington, DC: National Academy Press.

ISO (1999). ISO 13407. Human centred design processes for interactive systems. International Standards Organisation.

JADE. (2005). (Version 3.4) [Computer software]. Retrieved from http://jade.tilab.com/

Jafari, A. (2002). Conceptualizing intelligent agents for teaching and learning. *Educause Quarterly, 3,* 28-34.

Järvelin, K., Kekäläinen, J., & Niemi, T. (2001). Expansiontool: Concept-based *query* expansion and construction. *Information Retrieval 4*(3-4), 231-255.

Java, A., Finin, T., & Nirenburg, S. (2006). SemNews: A Semantic News Framework. *Twenty-First National Conference on Artificial Intelligence,* (1939-1940), AAAI Press.

Java, A., Finin, T., & Nirenburg, S. (2006). Text Understanding Agents and the Semantic Web. *39th Hawaii International Conference on System Sciences,* (62-71), IEEE Computer Society.

Java, A., Nirneburg, S., McShane, M., Finin, T., English, J., & Joshi, A. (2006). Using a Natural Language Understanding System to Generate Semantic Web Content. *International Journal on Semantic Web and Information Systems, 3*(4), 50-74.

Jena. (2005, March). *A Semantic Web framework* (Version 2.4) [Computer software]. Retrieved from http://www.hpl.hp.com/semweb/jena2.htm

Jennings, N. R. (2001). An agent-based approach for building complex software systems. *Communications of the ACM, 44*(4), 35-41.

Jennings, N.R., Kinny, D., & Wooldridge, M. (2000). The Gaia methodology for agent–oriented analysis and design. *Autonomous Agents and Multi–Agent Systems, 3*(3), 285–312.

Jennings, N.R., Omicini, A., Wooldridge, M., & Zambonelli, F. (Ed.). (2001). *Agent–oriented software engineering for internet applications. Coordination of Internet Agents: Models, Technologies, and Applications.* Springer–Verlag, Germany: pp. 326–346.

Jeon, J., Lavrenko, V., & Manmatha, R. (2003). Automatic image annotation and retrieval using cross-media relevance models. In *Proceedings of the 26th Annual International ACM SIGIR Conference on Research and Development in Information Retrieval*, Toronto, Canada (pp. 119-126). New York: ACM Press.

Jin, S., Park, C., Choi, D., Chung, K., & Yoon, H. (2005). Cluster-based trust evaluation scheme in an ad hoc network. *ETRI Journal, 27* (4), 465-468.

Johar, K. (2004). J WordNet Browser. Retrieved on August 2007, from http://www.seas.gwu.edu/~simhaweb/software/jwordnet

Johnson, P., Miksch, S., & Shahar, Y. (1998). The Asgaard project: a task–specific framework for the application and critiquing of time–oriented clinical guidelines. *Artificial Intelligence in Medicine, 14*, 29–51.

Jösang, A., & Pope, S. (2005). Semantic constraints for trust transitivity. In *Proceedings of the 2nd asia-pacific conference on conceptual modelling (Apccm '05):* (pp. 59-68). Darlinghurst, Australia: Australian Computer Society, Inc.

Jösang, A., Ismail, R., & Boyd, C. (2007). A survey of trust and reputation systems for online service provision. *Decis. Support Syst., 43* (2), 618-644.

Kacimi, M., Yetongnon, K., Ma, Y., & Chbeir, R. (2005). HON-P2P: A Cluster-based Hybrid Overlay Network for Multimedia Object Management. In *Proceedings of the 11th international conference on parallel and distributed systems (Icpads'05)* (pp. 578-584). Washington, DC, USA: IEEE Computer Society.

Kaczmarek, P., Gordon, M., Paprzycki, M., & Gawinecki, M. (2005). The problem of agent-client communication on the Internet. *Scalable Computing: Practice and Experience, 6*(1), 111-123.

Kalfoglou, Y., & Schorlemmer, M. (2003). IF-Map: An ontology mapping method based on information-flow theory. In S. Spaccapietra et al. (Eds.), *Journal on data semantics.* (LNCS 2800).

Kamvar, S. D., Schlosser, M. T., & Garcia-Molina, H. (2003). The EigenTrust algorithm for reputation management in P2P networks. In *Proceedings of the 12th international conference on world wide web (Www'03)* (pp. 640-651). New York, NY, USA: ACM Press.

Kanellopoulos, D., Kotsiantis, S., & Pintelas, P. (2006, February). Ontology-based learning applications: A development methodology. *Proceedings of the 24th Iasted International Multi-Conference Software Engineering,* Austria.

Kashyap, V., Ramakrishnan, C., Thomas, C., Bassu, D., Rindflesch, T.C., & Sheth, A. (2005). TaxaMiner: An experiment framework for automated taxonomy bootstrapping. *International Journal of Web and Grid Services, Special Issue on Semantic Web and Mining Reasoning.*

Kasvi J., Vartiainen M., & Hailikari M. (2003), Managing knowledge and knowledge competences in projects and project organisations, *International Journal of Project Management, 21*(8), pp. 571-582.

Keegan, M. (Ed.). (2000). *e-Learning, The engine of the knowledge economy.* Morgan Keegan & Co.

Kelly, J. J. (1997). The essence of logic. Upper Saddle River, NJ, USA: Prentice-Hall, Inc.

Keong Lua, E., Crowcroft, J., Pias, M., Sharma, R., & Lim, S. (2005). A survey and comparison of peer-to-peer overlay network schemes. *Communications Surveys & Tutorials, IEEE*, 72-93.

Khushalani, A., Smith. R. & Howard, S. (1994). What happens when designers don't play by the rules: towards a model of opportunistic behavior in design. *Australian Journal of Information Systems, May,* 13-31.

Kifer, M., Lausen, G., & Wu, J. (1995). Logical foundations of object-oriented and frame-based languages. *Journal of the ACM, 42*(4), 741-843.

Kim, S., Alani, H., Hall, W., Lewis, P. H., Millard, D. E., Shadbolt, N., et al. (2002). Artequakt: Generating Tailored Biographies with Automatically Annotated Fragments from the Web. *Workshop on Semantic Authoring, Annotation & Knowledge Markup*, (1-6), CEUR.

Kinshuk & Lin, T. (2004). Cognitive profiling towards formal adaptive technologies in Web-based learning communities, *International Journal of WWW-based Communities, 1,* 103-108.

Kissell, R., Malamut, R. (2006). Algorithmic decision-making framework. *Journal of Trading, 1*(1), 12-21.

Klein M. (1997) *Capturing Geometry Rationale for Collaborative Design*. In *Proceedings of the 6th IEEE Workshop on Enabling Technologies : Infrastructue for Collaborative Enterprises (WET ICE'97)*, MIT, June 1997. IEEE Computer Press.

Klein, D., & Manning, C. D. (2003). Fast exact inference with a factored model for natural language parsing. *Advances in Neural Information Processing Systems*, (3–10), MIT Press.

Klyne, G., & Carroll, J. J. (2004). *Resource Description Framework (RDF): Concepts and Abstract Syntax* (W3C Recommendation 10 February 2004)

Knublauch, H., Fergerson, R. W., Noy, N. F., & Musen, M. A.(2004). The protégé owl plugin: An open development environment for Semantic Web applications. In International Semantic Web Conference (pp. 229-243).

Kobsa, A., Koenemann, J., & Pohl, W. (2001). Personalized hypermedia presentation techniques for improving online customer relationships. *The Knowledge Engineering Review, 16*(2), 111-155.

Koenig, J. (2004), JBoss jBPM White Paper.

Kohonen, T. (2000). Self-organizing maps. Springer.

Koivunen, M., & Miller, E. (2002). W3C semantic Web activity. In E. Hyvonen (Ed.), *Semantic Web kick-off in Finland* (pp. 27-44). Helsinki: HIIT.

Kolovski, V., & Galletly, J. (2003). Towards e-learning via the Semantic Web. In B. Rachev, & A. Smrikarov (Eds.), In *Proceedings of the 4th International Conference on Computer Systems and Technologies--CompSysTech'2003* (pp. 591 - 596). ACM New York, NY, USA.

Koper R. (2004). Use of the Semantic Web to solve some basic problems in education. *Journal of Interactive Media in Education*. 2004(6), pp.1-23.

Korpela, M., Soriyan, H. A., & Olufokunbi, K. C. (2000). Activity analysis as a method for information systems development: General introduction and experiments from Nigeria and Finland. *Scandinavian Journal of Information Systems, 12,* 191-210.

Kosko, B. (1986). Fuzzy Cognitive Maps. *International Journal of Man-Machine Studies, 24* (1), 65-75.

Kraft, A., Vetter, M., & Pitsch, S.. (2000, January 4-7). Agent-driven online business in virtual communities. In *Proceedings of the 33rd Hawaii International Conference on System Sciences*, Volume 8, p.8033.

Krishnamurthy, B., Wang, J., & Xie, Y. (2001). Early measurements of a cluster-based architecture for p2p systems. In *Proceedings of the 1st acm sigcomm workshop on internet measurement (Imw '01)* (pp. 105-109). New York, NY, USA: ACM Press.

Kurabayashi, N., Yamazaki, T., Yuasa, T., & Hasuike, K. (2002). Proactive information supply for activating conversational interaction in virtual communities. *In the IEEE International Workshop on Knowledge Media Networking (KMN'02)* (pp.167-170).

Kurfess, F. J. (1999). Neural networks and structured knowledge: Knowledge representation and reasoning. *Applied intelligence*, 11(1), 5-13.

Kuutti, K. & Vikkunen, J. (1995). Organisational memory and learning network organisation: The case of Finnish Labour Protection Inspectors. In *Proceedings of HICSS 28.*

Kuutti, K. (1996). Activity theory as a potential framework for human-computer interaction. In B. Nardi (Ed.), *Context and Consciousness* (pp.17-44). MIT Press.

Kuutti, K. (1999). Activity theory, transformation of work, and information system design. In Y. Engeström, R. Miettinen, & R-L Punamaki (Eds.), *Perspectives on activity theory: Learning in doing: Social, cognitive and computational perspectives.* (pp, 360-376). Cambridge University Press, UK.

Lamport, L (1979). *How to Make a Multiprocessor Computer that Correctly Executes Multiprocess Programs,* IEEE Transactions on Computers, Vol. C-28(9).

Landauer, T. K., Foltz, P. W., & Laham, D. (1998). Introduction to latent semantic analysis. *Discourse Processes, 25,* 259-284.

Lanzara, G.F. (1983). The design process: Frames, metaphors and games. In U. Brefs, C. Ciborra, & L. Schneider (Eds), *System Design for, with and by The User*. North-Holland Publishing Company.

Lave, J., & Wenger, E. (1991). *Situated learning: Legitimate peripheral participation*, Cambridge University Press.

Le Coche, E., Mastroianni, C., Pirrò, G., Ruffolo, M., & Talia, D. (2006). *A Peer-to-Peer Virtual Office for Organizational Knowledge Management*. Paper presented at the 6th International Conference on Practical Aspects of Knowledge Management (PAKM 06), Wien, Austria.

Leacock, C., & Chodorow, M. (1998). Combining local context and WordNet similarity for word sense identification. In C. Fellbaum (Ed.), *WordNet: An electronic lexical database* (pp. 265-283). Cambridge, MA: MIT Press.

Leal, W. L. M., & Coello Baêta, A. M. (2006). The contribution of communities of practice in an innovative enterprise. *Journal of Technology Management & Innovation, 1* (4).

Lee, J. (1999). Interactive learning with a Web-based digital library system. *Proceedings of the 9th DELOS Workshop on Digital Libraries for Distance Learning*. Retrieved from *http:// courses.cs.vt.edu/~cs3604/DELOS.html*

Lee, S. Y., Kwon, O.-H., Kim, J., & Hong, S. J. (2005). A reputation management system in structured peer-to-peer networks. In *Proceedings of the 14th IEEE international workshops on enabling technologies: Infrastructure for collaborative enterprise* (*Wetice'05)* (pp. 362-367). Washington, DC, USA: IEEE Computer Society.

Leont'ev, A.N. (1978). Problems of the development of the mind. Moscow, Progress.

Levien, R. L. (1995). *Attack resistant trust metrics*. Unpublished doctoral dissertation, University of California at Berkeley.

Lewkowicz, M.,& Zacklad, M., (1999, September 22-24). How a GroupWare based on a knowledge structuring method can be a collective decision-making aid: the MEMO-Net tool, in Lenca, P. (Ed.) In *Proceedings of the 10th Mini EURO Conference "Human-centered processes" (HCP'99)* (pp.175-182) Brest, France,.

Li, M., Lee, W.-C., & Sivasubramaniam, A. (2004). Semantic small world: An overlay network for peer-to-peer search. In *Proceedings of the Network Protocols, 12th IEEE international conference on (Icnp'04)* (pp. 228{238). Washington, DC, USA: IEEE Computer Society.

Licklider, J. C. R., & Clark, W. (1962). On-Line Man-Computer Communication. *Spring Joint Computer Conference*, (113-128), National Press.

Lieberman H. (1995). *Letizia: An agent that assists web browsing*. In Chris S. Mellish, (Ed.), In *Proceedings of the 14th International Joint Conference on Artificial Intelligence (IJCAI-95)*, Montreal, Quebec, Canada.

Liebowitz, J. (2003). A knowledge management implementation plan at a leading US technical government organization: A case study. *Knowledge and Process Management, 10*(4), 254-259.

Lin, F.-R., & Hsueh, C.-M. (2003). Knowledge map creation and maintenance for virtual communities of practice. In *Proceedings of the 36th Hawaii International Conference on System Sciences (HICSS'03)* (pp. 11-10) Big Island, Hawaii.

Ling, K., Beenen, G., Ludford, P., Wang, X., Chang, K., Cosley, D., Frankowski, D., Terveen, L., Rashid, A. M., Resnick, P., & Kraut, R. (2005). Using social psychology to motivate contributions to online communities. *Journal of Computer-Mediated Communication*, 10(4), article 10.

Liu, H., Lutz, C., Milicic, M., & Wolter, F. (2006). Updating Description Logic ABoxes. In Kr (pp. 46-56).

Lloyd, J. W. (1987). Foundations of logic programming; (2nd extended ed.). New York, NY, USA: Springer-Verlag New York, Inc.

Lockwood, F., & Gooley, A. (Eds.). (2001). *Innovation in open and distance learning - successful development of online and Web-based learning*. London, Kogan Page.

Longueville B., Stal Le Cardinal J., & Bocquet J.-C. (2003). *Meydiam, a project memory for innovative product design*. In *PIAMOT03, the 12th International Conference on Management of Technology*, Nancy France.

Löser, A., Naumann, F., Siberski, W., Nejdl, W., & Thaden, U. (2003). Semantic overlay clusters within super-peer networks. In K. Aberer, V. Kalogeraki, & M. Koubarakis (Eds.), *Databases, information systems, and peer-to-peer computing, first international workshop, dbisp2p, Berlin, Germany, September 7-8, 2003, revised papers* (p. 33-47). Springer.

Löser, A., Siberski, W., Wolpers, M., & Nejdl, W. (2003). Information integration in schema-based peer-to-peer networks. In J. Eder & M. Missiko® (Eds.), In *Proceedings of the Conference on Advanced Information Systems Engineering* (Vol. 2681, p. 258-272). Springer.

Loucopoulos, P. & Karakostas, V. (1995). *Systems Engineering*. MCGraw-Hill, Maidenhead, UK,

Lytras, M.D., & Naeve, A. (Eds.). (2005). *Intelligent learning infrastructure for knowledge intensive organizations*. London: Information Science.

MacGrath, M. & Uden, L. (2000, January) Modelling softer aspects of the software development process: An activity theory based approach. Thirty-third Hawaii International Conference on System Sciences. (HICSS-33) Wailea, Maui, Hawaii, USA - Software Process Improvement. IEEE Computer Society Press.

Maedche, A., Motik, B., Silva, N., & Volz, R. (2002). MAFRA—a mapping framework for distributed ontologies. *Proceedings of EKAW (Knowledge Engineering and Knowledge Management) 2002*. Berlin: Springer-Verlag (LNCS 2473).

Maedche, A., Staab, S. (2001). Ontology learning for the Semantic Web. Intelligent Systems, IEEE [see also IEEE Intelligent Systems and Their Applications], 16(2), 72-79.

Maes, P. (1994). Agents that reduce work and information overload. *Communications of the ACM, 37*(7), 31-40.

Maguire, M. (2000). Context with usability Actions. *International Journal of Human-Computer Studies 55*, 453-483.

Maier, D., & Delcambre, M. L.(1999) *Superimposed Information for the Internet*. Paper presented at the ACM SIGMOD Workshop on The Web and Databases (WebDB 1999), Philadelphia, Pennsylvania, USA (1999).

Malone, T. W. (2004). *The future of work: How the new order of business will shape your organization, your managementsStyle and yourlLife*. Harvard Business School Press.

Manjunath, B. S. (2002). *Introduction to MPEG-7: Multimedia content description interface*. John Wiley and Sons.

Manola, F., & Miller, E. (Eds.). (2005). *RDF primer*. Retrieved from http://www.w3.org/TR/rdf-primer

Markus, M.L., Majchrzak, A., & Gasser, L. (2002). A design theory for systems that support emergent knowledge processes. *MIS Quarterly, 26*(3) 179-212.

Marsh, S. P. (1994). *Formalising trust as a computational concept*. Unpublished doctoral dissertation, Department of Computing Science and Mathematics, University of Stirling.

Marshak, D. S. (2004). *Groove virtual office enabling our new modes of work*. Report by Patricia Seybold Group, http://www.groove.net/pdf/backgrounder/GV0-Marshak.pdf

Martin, T. P., & Azvine, B. (2003). Acquisition of soft taxonomies for intelligent personal hierarchies and the soft Semantic Web. *BT Technology Journal, 21*, 113-122.

Masini G., Napoli A., Colnet D. & Leonard D. (1991). *Object-Oriented Languages*. A.P.I.C. Series, No. 34.

Mastroianni, C., Pirrò, G., & Talia, D. (2007). *Data Consistency in a P2P Knowledge Management Platform*. Paper presented at the 2nd HPDC Workshop on the Use of P2P, GRID and Agents for the Development of Content Networks (UPGRADE-CN 07), Monterey Bay, California, USA.

Matta N., Ribiere M., Corby O., Lewkowicz M., & Zaclad M. (2000). *Project Memory in Design, Industrial Knowledge Management - A Micro Level Approach*, Rajkumar Roy (Eds), Springer-Verlag.

Mayer, R. J., et al., (1992), IDEF Family of Methods for Concurrent Engineering and Business Re-engineering Applications, Knowledge-Based Systems, Inc.

Maymounkov, P., & Mazières, D. (2002). Kademlia: A peer-to-peer information system based on the XOR Metric. In *Revised papers from the1stt International Workshop onPpeer-to-Peer Systems (Iptps '01)* (pp. 53-65). London, UK: Springer-Verlag.

Maynard, D., Peters, W., & Li, Y. (2006, May). *Metrics for evaluation of ontology-based information extraction*. Paper presented at WWW2006, Edinburgh, UK.

McCrea, F., Gay, R. K., & Bacon, R. (2000). *Riding the big waves: a white paper on the B2B e-Learning Industry*. San Francisco/Boston/New York/London: Thomas Weisel Partners LLC.

McDonald, C.J., & Overhage, J.M. (1994). Guidelines you can follow and trust: an ideal and an example. *Journal of the American Medical Association, 271*, 872–873.

McGuinness, D. L., & Van Harmelen, F. (Eds.). (2005, February 10). *OWL Web ontology language overview*. Retrieved December, 2004, from http://www.w3.org/TR/owl-features/

McKnight, D. H., & Chervany, N. L. (1996). *The meanings of trust* (Tech. Rep. No. WP 96-04). University of Minnesota, Carlson School of Management.

McMichael, H. (1999). An activity based perspective for information system research. In *Proceedings of the 10th Amsterdam Conference on Information Systems.*

McShane, M., Zabludowski, M., Nirenburg, S., & Beale, S. (2004). OntoSem and SIMPLE: Two Multi-Lingual World Views. *ACL 2004: Second Workshop on Text Meaning and Interpretation*, (25-32), Association for Computational Linguistics.

Mendes, M.E.S., & Sacks, L. (2004). Dynamic knowledge representation for e-learning applications. In M. Nikravesh, L.A. Zadeh, B. Azvin, & R. Yager (Eds.), *Enhancing the power of the Internet—studies in fuzziness and soft computing* (vol. 139, pp. 255-278). Berlin/London: Springer-Verlag.

Milea, V., Frasincar, F., Kaymak, U., & di Noia, T. (2007). An OWL-Based Approach Towards Representing Time in Web Information Systems. *Workshop on Web Information Systems Modelling (WISM 2007)*, (pp. 791-802), Tapir Academic Press.

Miller, G. A. (1995). WordNet: A Lexical Database for English. *Communications of the ACM, 38*(11), 39.

Milojicic, D. S., Kalogeraki, V., Lukose, R., Nagaraja, K., Pruyne, J., Richard, B., et al., (2003, July). *Peer-to-peer computing* (Tech. Rep. No. HPL-2002-57R1). Hewlett Packard Laboratories.

Miniwatts Marketing Group. (2007). Internet World Stats [Electronic Version]. Retrieved on June 2007, from http://www.internetworldstats.com/stats.htm.

Minsky, M. (1986). The society of mind. New York, NY, USA: Simon & Schuster, Inc.

Mizoguchi, R. (2000). IT revolution in learning technology, In *Proceedings of SchoolNet 2000*, Pusan, Korea (pp. 46-55).

Montague, R. (1974). Formal philosophy: Selected papers of Richard Montague. New Haven, Connecticut: Yale University Press. (Edited, with an introduction, by Richmond H. Thomason)

Montaner, M., López, B., & De La Rosa, J. L. (2003). A taxonomy of recommender agents on the Internet. *Artificial Intelligence Review, 19,* 285-330.

Moore, A. (2005, July 22-27) Towards a design theory for community information systems. In *Proceedings of the 11th International Conference on Human-Computer Interaction (HCII 2005)* Las Vegas, NV. Lawrence Erlbaum Associates, Mahwah, NJ.

Mori, Y., Takahashi, H., & Oka, R. (1999). Image-to-word transformation based on dividing and vector quantizing images with words. In *Proceedings of First International Workshop on Multimedia Intelligent Storage and Retrieval Management.*

Motik, B., Sattler, U., & Studer, R. (2005). Query answering for OWL-DL with rules. *Journal of Web Semantics,* 3(1), pp.41-60.

Muehlen, M. Z., Becker, J. (1999). Workflow process definition language - development and directions of a meta-language for wokflow processes, In Bading, L. et al., (Eds.) In *Proceedings of the 1st KnowTech Forum*, Potsdam.

Mui, L., Mohtashemi, M., & Halberstadt, A. (2002). Notions of reputation in multi-agents systems: a review. In *Proceedings of the1stt International Joint Conference on Autonomous Agents and Multiagent Systems (Aamas '02)* (pp. 280-287). New York, NY, USA: ACM Press.

Musser, J. & Oreilly, T. (2006). Web 2.0 Report. O'Reilly Media.

Nabeth, T., Angehrn, A.A., Mittal, P.K., & Roda, C. (2005). Using artificial agents to stimulate participation in virtual communities. CELDA 2005: 391-394.

Naeve, A., Nilsson, M., & Palmer, M. (2001), E-learning in the semantic age. CID, Centre For User Oriented It Design. Stockhom, Sweden. Retrieved on September 30, 2006

Nagao, K., Shirai, Y., & Squire, K. (2001). Semantic annotation and transcoding: Making Web content more accessible. *IEEE Multimedia Magazine, 8*(2), 69-81.

Nagarajan, R. (2002). Content-boosted collaborative filtering for improved recommendations. *Proceedings of the 18th National Conference on Artificial Intelligence,* Canada.

NASDAQ. NASDAQ Glossary. Retrieved on August 2007, from http://www.nasdaq.com/reference/glossary.stm

Naughton, J. (2000). A brief history of the future: Origins of the internet, Phoenix mass market p/bk.

Nejdl, W. (2001). Learning repositories--Technology and context. In A. Risk (Ed.), *ED-Media 2001 World Conference on education multimedia, Hypermedia and Telecommunications: Vol. 2001, N. 1.*

Nejdl, W., Wolpers, M., Siberski, W., Schmitz, C., Schlosser, M., Brunkhorst, I., et al. (2003). Super-peer-based routing and clustering strategies for rdf-based peer-to-peer networks. In *Proceedings of the 12th International Conference on World Wide Web (Www '03)* (pp. 536-543). New York, NY, USA: ACM Press.

Netcraft (2007). September 2007 Web Server Survey, Retrieved on September 2007, from http://news.netcraft.com/archives/web_server_survey.html

Ng, P.T., & Ang, H.S. (2007). Managing knowledge through communities of practice: The case of the Singapore Police Force. *International Journal of Knowledge Management Studies, 1*(3/4), 356-367.

Nistor, C. E., Oprea, R., Paprzycki, M., & Parakh, G. (2002). The role of a psychologist in e-commerce personalization. In *Proceedings of the 3rd European E-COMM-LINE 2002 Conference* (pp. 227-231). Bucharest, Romania: IPA S. A.

Nonaka I (1994). A Dynamic Theory of Organizational Knowledge Creation. *Organization Science*, 5, (1994).

Nonaka, I. & Konno, N. (1998). The concept of 'Ba': Building a foundation for knowledge creation. *California Management Review. 40*(3) Spring.

Nonaka, I., & Takeuchi, H. (1995). *The knowledge-creating Company : How Japanese companies create the dynamics of innovation.* Oxford University Press.

Novak, J. & Wurst, M. (2004). Supporting knowledge creation and sharing in communities based on mapping implicit knowledge. *Journal of Universal Computer Science, Special Issue on Communities of Practice, 10*(3), 235-251.

Noy N. F., Sintek M., Decker S., Crubezy M., Fergerson R. W., & Musen M. A. (2001). *Creating Semantic Webc-Contents with Protégé 2000.* IEEE Intelligent Systems 16(2), 60-71.

Noy, N. F., & Klein, M. (2002). *Ontology evolution: Not the same as schema evolution.* (Tech. Rep. SMI-2002-0926). Stanford University.

Ntoulas, A., Chao, G. & Cho, J. (2005). *The infocious Web search engine: Improving Web searching through linguistic analysis.* Paper presented at International World Wide Web Conference Committee (IW3C2), Beijing, China.

Nwana, H., & Ndumu, D. (1999). A perspective on software agents research. *The Knowledge Engineering Review, 14*(2), 1-18.

Obrst, L., Ceusters, W., Mani, I., Ray, S., & Smith, B. (2007). The evaluation of ontologies, pp. 139-158.

Ogden, C. K. & Richards, I. A. (1923). *The meaning of meaning.* 8th Ed. New York, Harcourt, Brace & World, Inc.

Olmedilla, D., Rana, O. F., Matthews, B., & Nejdl, W. (2006). Security and trust issues in semantic grids. In C. Goble, C. Kesselman, & Y. Sure (Eds.), *Semantic grid: The convergence of technologies.* Internationales Begegnungs- und Forschungszentrum fuer Informatik (IBFI), Schloss Dagstuhl, Germany.

OMG Architecture Board ORMSC. Model driven architecture (MDA). *OMG document number ormsc/2001–07–01.* Retrieved 2001, from http://www.omg.org

Oram, A. (2001). *Peer-to-Peer: Harnessing the Power of Disruptive Technologies.* Sebastopol, CA, USA: O'Reilly & Associates, Inc.

Overhage, J.M., McDonald, C.J., & Tierney, W.M. (1996). Computerizing guidelines: factors for success. In *Proceedings of the AMIA Annual Fall Symposium*, pp. 459–62.

Overhage, J.M., Takesue, B.Y., & Tierney, W.M., & al. (1995). Computerizing guidelines to improve care and patient outcomes: the example of heart failure. *Journal of the American Medical Informatics Association, 2*, 316–322.

Pan, S.L., & Scarbrough, H. (1998). A socio-technical view of knowledge-sharing at Buckman Laboratories. *Journal of Knowledge Management, 2*(1), 55-66.

Paprzycki, M., Angryk, R., Kołodziej, K., Fiedorowicz, I., Cobb, M., Ali, D., et al. (2001) Development of a travel support system based on intelligent agent technology. In S. Niwiński (Ed.), *Proceedings of the PIONIER 2001 Conference* (pp. 243-255). Poland: University of PoznaD Press.

Paprzycki, M., Kalczyński, P. J., Fiedorowicz, I., Abramowicz, W., & Cobb, M. (2001) Personalized traveler information system. In B. F. Kubiak & A. Korowicki (Eds.), *Proceedings of the 5th International Conference Human-Computer Interaction* (pp. 445-456). Gdańsk, Poland: Akwila Press.

Paraiso C. E. & Barthes J-P. (2006). *An intelligent speech interface for personal assistants in R&D projects*, in Experts Systems with applications.

Patel-Schneider, P. F., Hayes, P., & Horrocks, I. (2004). *OWL Web Ontology Language Semantics and Abstract Syntax* (W3C Recommendation 10 February 2004)

Perez P., Karp K., Dieng R., Corby O., Giboin A., Gandon F., Qinqueton J., Poggi P., Rimmassa G., & Fietta Cselt C. (2000). *O'COMMA, Corporate Memory Management through Agents*, In Proceedings E-Work & E-Business, Madrid, October 17-20, pp. 383-406.

Perkins, C. E. (2001). Ad hoc networking: An introduction. In *Ad hoc networking* (pp. 1-28). Boston, MA, USA: Addison-Wesley Longman Publishing Co., Inc.

Peterson, L.E. (2004). Strengthening condition–specific evidence–based home healthcare practice. *Journal of Healthcare Quality, 26*(3), 10–18.

Pettigrew, A. M. (1990). Longitudinal field research on change: Theory and practice. *Organization Science* 1(3), 267-292.

Piaget, J. (1952). The origins of intelligence in children. New York, NY: Norton.

Piaget, J., & Inhelder, B.(1973). Memory and intelligence. Basic Books.

Pinch, T. J. & W. E. Bijker (1984). The social construction of facts and artifacts: Or how the sociology of science and the sociology of technology might benefit each other. In W. Bijker, T. Hughes and T. Pinch (Eds.), *The Social Construction of Technological Systems*. Cambridge, MA: MIT Press.

Polanyi M. (1997), *Tacit Knowledge*. Chapter 7 in Knowledge in Organizations, Laurence Prusak, (Ed.),Butterworth-Heinemann, Boston, 1997.

Polanyi, M. (1966). *The tacit dimension*. London: Routledge & Kegan Paul.

Popov, B., Kiryakov, A., Kirilov, A., Manov, D., Ognyanoff, D., & Goranov, M. (2003). *KIM-- Semantic Annotation Platform*. Paper presented at the 2nd International Semantic Web Conference (ISWC 03) (pp. 834-849) Sanibel Island, Florida, USA.

Probert, S.K. Requirements engineering, soft system methodology and workforce empowerment. *Requirements Engineering, 4,* (1999), Springer-Verlag, London, pp. 85-91.

Probst, G., Raub, S. & Romhardt, K. (2003). Managing knowledge: Building blocks for Success. John Wiley & Son, Chichester, UK.

Prometheus. (2005). *Prometheus methodology.* Retrieved from http://www.cs.rmit.edu.au/agents/prometheus/

Protégé 2000 (2000): http://protege.stanford.edu

Protégé. (n.d.). (Version 3.1.1) [Computer software]. Retrieved February 19, 2006, from http://protege.stanford.edu/index.html

Prud'hommeaux, E., & Seaborne, A. (2006). *SPARQL Query Language for RDF.* W3C Working Draft (2006), http://www.w3.org/TR/rdfsparql-query

Rabarijaona A., Dieng R., Corby O., & Ouaddari R (2001). *Building a XML-based Corporate Memory*, IEEE Intelligent Systems, Special Issue on Knowledge Management and Internet pp. 56-64.

Raccoon. (2005). (0.5.1) [Computer software]. Retrieved November 2005, from http://rx4rdf.liminalzone.org/Raccoon

Ramchurn, S. D., Huynh, D., & Jennings, N. R. (2004). Trust in multi-agent systems. *Knowl. Eng. Rev., 19* (1), 1-25.

Rasmusson, L., & Jansson, S. (1996). Simulated social control for secure internet commerce. In *Nspw '96: Proceedings of the 1996 workshop on new security paradigms* (pp. 18-25). New York, NY, USA: ACM Press.

Ratnasamy, S., Francis, P., Handley, M., Karp, R., & Schenker, S. (2001, October). A scalable content-addressable network. In *Proceedings of the 2001 Conference on Applications, Technologies, Architectures, and Protocols for Computer Communications (Sigcomm '01)* (pp. 161-172). New York, NY, USA: ACM Press.

Recker, M., Walker, A., & Lawless, K. (2003). What do you recommend? Implementation and analyses of collaborative filtering of Web resources for education. *Instructional Science, 31,* 229-316.

Rege, M., Dong, M., Fotouhi, F., Siadat, M., & Zamorano, L. (2005). Using Mpeg-7 to build a human brain image database for image-guided neurosurgery. In *Proceedings of SPIE International Symposium on Medical Imaging,* San Diego, CA (Vol. 5744, pp. 512-519).

Reid, E.M. (1991). Electropolis: Communication and community on Internet relay chat, electronic document of a B.A. Honors Thesis, University of Melbourne, Australia, also published in Intertek 3(3) (1992), pp. 7-15.

Resnik, P. (1995). *Disambiguating noun groupings with respect to WordNet senses.* Chelmsford, MA: Sun Microsystems Laboratories.

Riaño, D. (2007). *The SDA Model v1.0: A Set Theory Approach.* Technical Report (DEIM–RT–07–001). Retrieved 2007, from University Rovira i Virgili, http://deim.urv.es/recerca/reports/DEIM–RT–07–001.html

Rich, E. (1979). User modeling via stereotypes. *Cognitive Science, 3,* 329-354.

Roberts, T. (1998). Are newsgroups virtual communities? *In the SIGCHI conference on Human factors in computing systems,* ACM Press/Addison-Wesley Publishing Co. 360–367.

Roda, C., Angehrn, A., Nabeth, T. & Razmerita L. (2003). Using conversational agents to support the adoption of knowledge sharing Practices. Interacting with computers, elsevier, *15*(1), 57-89.

Rosenberg, M. J. (Ed.). (2006). *Beyond E-Learning: Approaches and technologies to enhance knowledge, learning and performance.* Pfeiffer.

Rowstron, A., & Druschel, P. (2001, November). Pastry: Scalable, distributed object location and routing for large-scale peer-to-peer systems. In *Proceedings of the 18th ifip/acm International Conference on Distributed Systems Platforms (middleware 2001)* (p. 329-350).

Rubenstein-Mantano B., Liebowitz J., Buchwalter J., McCaw D., Newman B., & Rebeck K. (2001). SMART-Vision: a knowledge-management methodology. *Journal of Knowledge Management, 5*(4), 300-310. MCB University Press.

Rubenstein-Montano, B., Buchwalter, J., & Liebowitz, J. (2001). Knowledge management: A U.S. Social Security Administration case study. *Government Information Quarterly, 18*(3), 223-253.

Rumelhart, D. E., & McClelland, J. L. (1986). Parallel distributed processing. Cambridge, MA, USA: MIT Press.

Russell, B.(1908). Mathematical logic as based on the theory of types. *American Journal of Mathematics, 30,* 222-262.

Sabater, J., & Sierra, C. (2001). REGRET: reputation in gregarious societies. In *Proceedings of the fifth international conference on autonomous agents* (*Agents '01*) (pp. 194-195). New York, NY, USA: ACM Press.

Sabater, J., & Sierra, C. (2002). Reputation and social network analysis in multi-agent systems. In *Proceedings of the first international joint conference on autonomous agents and multi-agent systems* (*Aamas '02*) (pp. 475-482). New York, NY, USA: ACM Press.

Safi, S.M., & Rather, R.A. (2005). Precision and recall of five search engines for retrieval of scholarly information in the field of biotechnology. *Webology,* 2(2), Article 12.

Salton, G. (1989). *Automatic text processing: The transformation, analysis and retrieval of information by computer.* Reading, MA: Addison-Wesley.

Salton, G., & Buckley, C. (1987). *Term weighting approaches in automatic text retrieval* (Tech. Rep. UMI Order Number: TR87-881). Cornell University.

Salton, G., , Singhal, A., Buckley, C., & Mitra M. (1996). Automatic Text Decomposition Using Text Segments and Text Themes, *Conference on Hypertext*, pp.53-65.

Schank, R. C., & Abelson, R. P. (1977). Scripts, plans, goals and understanding: an inquiry into human knowledge structures. Hillsdale, NJ: L. Erlbaum.

Schmuck, N. (2007). Informa: RSS Library for JAVA. Retrieved on August 2007, from http://informa.sourceforge.net/index.html

Schreiber G., Akkermaus H., Anjewierden A., de Hoog R., Shadbolt N., van der Velde W., & Wielinga B. (1999). Knowledge engineering and management--The common KAD methodology. MIT press, Cambridge, MA.

Schreiber, A. T., Dubbeldam, B., Wielemaker, J., & Wielinga, B. (2001). Ontology based photo annotation. *IEEE Intelligent Systems, 16*(3), 66-74.

Schwier, R. A. (2001). Catalysts, emphases, and elements of virtual learning communities. Implication for research. *The Quarterly Review of Distance Education,* 2(1), 5-18.

Seaborne, A. & E. Prud'hommeaux (2006). *SPARQL Query Language for RDF.* (Tech. Rep). http://www.w3.org/TR/2006/CR-rdf-sparql-query-20060406/, W3C.

Seaborne, A. (2004). *RDQL - A Query Language for RDF.* W3C Working Draft (2004), http://www.w3.org/Submission/2004/SUBM-RDQL-20040109/

Secundo, G., Corallo, A., Elia, G., & Passiante G. (2004). *An e-learning system based on Semantic Web supporting a learning in doing environment,* Paper presented at the International Conference on Information Technology Based Higher Education and Training, Istanbul, Turkey.

Secundo, G., Corallo, A., Elia, G., and Passiante, G. (2004). An e-Learning system based on semantic Web supporting a Learning in Doing Environment. In *Proceedings of International Conference on Information Technology Based Higher Education and Training--ITHET 2004.* IEEE XPlore, available at http://ieeexplore.ieee.org/iel5/9391/29802/01358145.pdf

Sekine, S., & Grishman, R. (1995). A corpus-based probabilistic grammar with only two non-terminals. *Fourth International Workshop on Parsing Technologies*, (216-223), ACL/SIGPARSE.

Selker, T. (1994). COACH: A teaching agent that learns. Communications of the ACM, Vol. 37, No. 7, ACM Press. 92 – 99.

Sheth, A., Ramakrishnan, C., & Thomas, C. (2005). Semantics for the Semantic Web: The implicit, the formal and the powerful. *International Journal on Semantic Web & Information Systems*, *1*(1), 1-18.

Shi, J., & Malik, J. (1997). Normalized cuts and image segmentation. In *Proceedings of 1997 IEEE Conference on Computer Vision Pattern Recognition*, San Juan (pp. 731-737).

Simon, H.A. (1972). Theories of bounded rationality. In McGuire, C.B. e Radner R. (Eds.), Decision and organization: A volume in honor of Jacob Marschak (Chapter. 8), Amsterdam, Olanda, 1972.

Sinclair, J. & Cardew-Hall, M. (2007). The folksonomy tag cloud: When is it useful? Journal of Information Science, pp. 0165551506078083v1.

Singh, B. (1992). Interconnected Roles (IR): A Coordination Model. Technical Report CT-084-92, MCC.

Skok, W. (2003). Knowledge management: New York city taxi cab case study. *Knowledge and Process Management, 10*(2), 127-135.

Slabber, N. J. (2007). The Technologies of Peace [Electronic Version]. *Harvard International Review.* Retrieved on June 2007, from http://hir.harvard.edu/articles/1336.

Smith, A.D. (2004). Knowledge management strategies: A multi-case study. *Journal of Knowledge Management, 8*(3), 6-16.

Smith, M. K., Welty, C., McGuinness, & Deborah L. (2004). *OWL Web ontology language guide*, Retrieved on January 2007, from http://www.w3.org/TR/owl-guide/

Smolensky, P. (1993). On the proper treatment of connectionism. In Readings in philosophy and cognitive science (pp.769–799). Cambridge, MA, USA: MIT Press.

Snowden, S. (1999). The paradox of story. *Scenario and Strategy Planning,* 1(5).

Sole, D. & Wilson, D.G. (2002). Storytelling in organizations: The power and traps of using stories to share knowledge in organizations. *LILA Harvard University.*

Sołtysiak, S., & Crabtree, B. (1998). Automatic learning of user profiles—towards the personalization of agent service. *BT Technological Journal, 16*(3), 110-117.

Song, M., Lim, S., Park, S., Kang, D., & Lee, S. (2005). Automatic classification of Web pages based on the concept of domain ontology. In *Proceedings of the 12th Asia-Pacific Software Engineering Conference (APSEC'05)* (pp. 645-651). IEEE.

Specia, L., & Motta, E. (2007). Integrating folksonomies with the Semantic Web, in The Semantic Web: Research and Applications, volume (4519/2007), pp. 624--639.

Specifications Gruber Thomas R. A. (1993). Translation Approach to Portable Ontology. *Knowledge Acquisition* (5) 199-220.

Srinivasan, P. (1992). Thesaurus construction, pp. 161-218.

Staab S. & Schnurr H.-P. (2000). Smart task support through proactive access to organizational memory. Knowledge–based Systems, 13(5):251–260.

Stoica, I., Morris, R., Karger, D., Kaashoek, F., & Balakrishnan, H. (2001). Chord: A scalable peer-to-peer lookup service for internet applications. In *Proceedings of the 2001 acm Sigcomm Conference* (pp. 149-160).

Stojanovic, L., Staab, S., & Studer, R. (2001,October 23-27). eLearning based on the Semantic Web. In W. A. Lawrence-Fowler & J. Hasebrook (Eds.), In *Proceedings of WebNet 2001--World Conference on the WWW and Internet,* Orlando, Florida. (pp.1174-1183). AACE.

Stojanovic, L., Stojanovic, N., & Volz, R. (2002). Migrating data-intensive Web sites into the semantic Web. *Proceedings of the 17th ACM Symposium on Applied Computing* (pp. 1100-1107).

Storelli, D. (2006). *Una piattaforma basata sulle ontologie per la gestione integrata di sorgenti di conoscenza eterogenee*. Unpublished degree dissertation, University of Salento, Italy.

Stuber A., Hassas S., & Mille A. (2003, June 23-26), *Combining multiagents systems and experience reuse for assisting collective task achievement.* In *Proceedings of ICCBR-2003 Workshop From structured cases to* unstructured problem solving episodes for experience-based assistance, Trondheim, Norway. Lorraine McGinty Eds.

Stutt, A., & Motta, E. (2004). Semantic learning Webs. *Journal of Interactive Media in Education,* (10).

Sun Microsystems, Inc. (2002). Java Blueprints--Model-view-controller. Retrieved on July 15, 2003, from http://dublincore.org http://java.sun.com/blueprints/patterns/MVC-detailed.html

Sure, Y., & Studer, R., (1999). *On-to-knowledge methodology* (Final Version, Project Deliverable D18). Germany: University of Karlsruhe.

Tang, T., & McCalla, G. (2005). Smart recommendation for an evolving e-learning system: Architecture and experiment. *International Journal on E-Learning, 4*(1), 105-129.

Tapscott, D. & Williams, A. D. (2006). *Wikinomics: How mass collaboration changes everything.* Portfolio Hardcover.

Tatarinov, I., Ives, Z., Madhavan, J., Halevy, A., Suciu, D., Dalvi, N., et al. (2003). The piazza peer data management project. *SIGMOD Rec., 32* (3), 47-52.

Taylor, F.W. (1911), *The Principles of Scientific Management*, Harper & Row, New York, USA, 1911.

Thaiupathump, C., Bourne, J., & Campbell, J. (1999). Intelligent agents for online learning. *Journal of Asynchronous Learning Networks, 3*(2). Retrieved on May 17, 2004, from http://www.sloan-c.org/publications/jaln/v3n2/pdf/v3n2_choon.pdf

The Apache Software Foundation, (2006). Apache Struts. Retrieved on September 22, 2006, from http://struts.apache.org/

Thomas, J.C., Kellogg, W.A., & Erickson, T. (2001). The knowledge management puzzle: Human and social factors in knowledge management. *IBM Systems Journal, 40*(4), 863-884.

Thomson Scientific. (2004). *Getting just what you need: strategies for search, taxonomy and classification*". Retrieved on July, 2007, from http://scientific.thomson.com/free/ipmatters/infosearch/8228762/search_tax_class.pdf

Torra, V. (1997). The weighted owa operator. *International Journal of Intelligent Systems, 12* (2), 153-166.

Toutanova, K., & Manning, C. D. (2000). Enriching the knowledge sources used in a maximum entropy part-of-speech tagger. In *Proceedings of the 2000 Joint SIGDAT conference on Empirical Methods in Natural Language Processing and Very Large Corpora*, (63-70), Association for Computational Linguistics Morristown.

University of Washington, *XML Data Repository*, Retrieved on from, http://www.cs.washington.edu/research/xmldatasets, 2005.

Uschold M., King M., Moralee S., & Zorgios Y. (1998). The Enterprise Ontology, *The Knowledge Engineering Review*, Vol. 13, Special Issue on Putting Ontologies to Use (eds. Mike Uschold and Austin Tate). Also available from AIAI as AIAI-TR-195 http://www.aiai.ed.ac.uk/project/enterprise/

Uschold, M. (1996). Building ontologies: Towards a unified methodology. In *Proceedings of the16th Annual Conference of the British Computer Society Specialist Group on Expert Systems,* Cambridge, UK.

Uschold, M., & Gruninger, M. (1996). *Ontologies: Principles, methods and applications*. Scotland, United Kingdom: University of Edinburgh.

Uschold, M., & Grüninger, M. (1996). Ontologies: principles, methods, and applications, *Knowledge Engineering Review*, 11(2), 93-155.

Vallet, D., Fernández, M., & Castells, P. (2005). *An Ontology-Based Information Retrieval Model*. Paper presented at the 2nd European Semantic Web Conference (ESWC 2005), Heraklion, Greece, pp.455-470.

Van Elst L., Dignum V., & Abecker A. (2004). Towards Agent-Mediated Knowledge Management. In: L. van Elst, V. Dignum, A. Abecker (Eds.), Agent-Mediated Knowledge Management: Selected Papers, Lecture Notes in Artificial Intelligence, Springer-Verlag, Volume 2926.

Vanderaalst, W., & Vanhee, K. (2004). Workflow management: Models, methods, and systems, (Cooperative Information Systems), The MIT Press.

Varlamis, I., & Apostolakis, I. (2006). A framework for building virtual communities for education. *EC-TEL 2006 Workshops Proceedings*, pp. 165-172.

Verity Inc. (2004). *Verity Collaborative Classifier*. Verity Inc.

Verity Inc. (2004). *Verity Intelligent Classification Guide*. Verity Inc.

Viller, S. & Sommerville, I. (1999). Social analysis in the requirement engineering process: From ethnology to method. *4th IEEE International Symposium on Requirement Engineering,* Limerick, Ireland. IEEE Computer Society Press, Los Alamitos, pp. 6-13.

Vygotsky, L. (1962). *Thought and language*. Cambridge, MA. MIT Press.

Vygotsky, L.S. (1978). *Mind in society*. Harvard University Press, Cambridge, MA

Walls, J., Widmeyer, G., & El Sawy, O. (1992). Building an information system design theory for vigilant EIS, Information Systems Research **3**(1), 36 - 59.

Wang, Z., Kumar, M., Das, S. K., & Shen, H. (2006). *File Consistency Maintenance Through Virtual Servers in P2P Systems*. Paper presented at the 6th IEEE Symposium on Computers and Communications (ISCC 06), Pula-Cagliari, Italy, pp.435-441.

Weggeman M. (1996). *Knowledge Management: The Modus Operandi for a Learning Organization*. In J. F. Schreinemakers (Ed.), Knowledge Management: Organization, Competence and Methodology, In *Proceedings of the ISMICK'96*, Rotterdam, the Netherlands, Wurzburg: Ergon Verlag, Advances in Knowledge Management, vol. 1, 21-22, p. 175-187.

Wenger, E. (1999). *Communities of practice: Learning, meaning, and identity*. Cambridge University Press.

Wenger, E., McDermott, R., & Snyder, W. (2002). Cultivating communities of practice. Cambridge, MA: Harvard Business School Press.

WfMC (1996). The workflow management coalition specification (Feb 99), workflow management coalition terminology and glossary, Document Number WFMC-TC-1011, Document Status--Issue 3.0.

WfMC (1998). The workflow management coalition specification workflow management application programming interface (Interface 2&3) Specification, Document Number WFMC-TC-1009.

WfMC (2002). Workflow management coalition workflow standard: Workflow process definition interface-

-XML Process Definition Language (XPDL)--Document Number WFMC-TC-1025, Document Status –1.0 Final Draft October 25, 2002, Version 1.0, (WFMCTC-1025).

White, S. A. (2004). Business process modeling notation (BPMN) Version 1.0. Business Process Management Initiative, BPMI.org.

Wiig, K. (1999). Establish, govern and renew the enterprise's knowledge practices. Schema Press, Arlington, TX.

Winograd, T. (1995). From programming environments to environments for designing. *Communications of the ACM*, 38(6), 65-74.

Wong, K.Y. (2005). The potential roles of engineers in knowledge management: An overview. *Bulletin of the Institution of Engineers Malaysia*, November, 26-29.

Wong, K.Y., & Aspinwall, E. (2004a). Knowledge management implementation frameworks: A review. *Knowledge and Process Management, 11*(2), 93-104.

Wong, K.Y., & Aspinwall, E. (2004b). A fundamental framework for knowledge management implementation in SMEs. *Journal of Information and Knowledge Management, 3*(2), 155-166.

Wongthongtham P., Chang E., Dillon T.S., & Sommerville I. (2006). Ontology-based multi-site software development methodology and tools, Journal of Systems Architecture.

Wooldridge, M. & Jennings, N. R. (1995). Intelligent agents: Theory and practice. *Knowledge Engineering Review, 10(2).*

Wooldridge, M. (2002). *An introduction to multiAgent systems.* John Wiley & Sons.

World Wide Web Consourtium. *OWL Web Ontology Language*--Overview, December 2003. http://www.w3.org/TR/owl-features/

Wright, J., Gordon, M., Paprzycki, M., Williams, S., & Harrington, P. (2003). Using the ebXML registry repository to manage information in an Internet travel support system. In W. Abramowicz & G. Klein (Eds.), *Proceedings of the BIS2003 Conference* (pp. 81-89). Poland: Poznań University of Economics Press.

Wynne-Jones, M. (1991). Constructive algorithms and pruning: Improving the multi layer perceptron. In Vichnevetsky, R. & Miller, J.J. (Ed.), 13th imacs world congress on computation and applied mathematics, (Vol. 2, pp. 747-750).

Xu, W., Kreijns, K., & Hu, J.. (2006). Designing social navigation for a virtual community of practice. In Z. Pan, R. Aylett, H.Diener, & X. Jin, (Eds.), Edutainment: Technology and Application, proceedings of Edutainment 2006, *International Conference on E-learning and Games.* LNCS 3942, pp.27-38.

Yang, B., & Garcia-Molina, H. (2003, March 5-8). Designing a Super-Peer Network. In U. Dayal, K. Ramamritham, & T. M. Vijayaraman (Eds.), In *Proceedings of the 19t International Conference on Data Engineering,* Bangalore, India (p. 49-). IEEE Computer Society.

Yin, R.K. (2003). *Case study research: Design and methods.* Thousand Oaks: Sage Publications.

Yu, B., & Singh, M. P. (2002). An evidential model of distributed reputation management. In *Proceedings of the first international joint conference on autonomous agents and multiagent systems (Aamas '02)* (pp. 294-301). New York, NY, USA: ACM Press.

Za, D. (2004). *Una piattaforma basata sulle ontologie per la gestione integrata di sorgenti di conoscenza eterogenee.* Unpublished degree dissertation, University of Lecce, Italy.

Zacharia, G., Moukas, A., & Maes, P. (2000). Collaborative reputation mechanisms for electronic marketplaces. *Decis. Support Syst., 29* (4), 371-388.

Zappen J. P., & Harrison, M (2005). Intention and motive in information-system design: Towards a Theory and Method for Assessing Users' Needs. P. van den Basselaar & S. Koizumi (Eds.), Digital Cities 2003, LNCS 3081 pp. 354-368. Springer-Verlag, Berlin, Heidelberg, 2005.

Zhao, B. Y., Huang, L., Stribling, J., Rhea, S. C., Joseph, A. D., & Kubiatowicz, J. D. (2004). Tapestry: A resilient global-scale overlay for service deployment. *Selected Areas in Communications, IEEE Journal on, 22* (1), 41-53.

Zhou, R., & Hwang, K. (2006). Trust overlay networks for global reputation aggregation in p2p grid computing. In *20th international parallel and distributed processing symposium (ipdps 2006), proceedings, 25-29 April 2006, Rhodes island, Greece.* IEEE.

Zielstorff, R.D. (1998). Online practice guidelines: issues, obstacles and future prospects. *Journal of the American Medical Informatics Association, 5,* 227–236.

About the Contributors

Antonio Zilli graduated in phisics. He is a research fellow at e-business management section at the Scuola Superiore Isufi--Univeristy of Salento (Lecce, Italy). His research interests regard the technologies that enable powerful virtual collaboration in communities and organizations. He participated in research projects on Semantic Web studying how to represent and use ontologies and semantic descriptions, and participated at the design of technologies and tools for managing ontologies, semantic metadata and semantically annotated documents (semantic search engine). He participated in research projects on knowledge management in economic districts composed of organization and public administration. He participated on research projects on social network analysis as a strategy for monitoring and improving collaboration in wide teams and with a particular focus on the changes brought by the technological innovations. He is in the program board of the international conference on knowledge management in organization.

Ernesto Damiani is a full professor at the department of information technology of the University of Milan, Italy. He has held visiting positions at several international institutions, including George Mason University, VA (USA), and is an adjunct professor at the University of Technology, Sydney, Australia. Prof. Damiani coordinates several research projects funded by the Italian Ministry of Research, the European Commission and by a number of private companies including Cisco, st microelectronics, Siemens mobile and bt exact. His research interests include knowledge extraction and metadata design, advanced software architectures and soft computing. On these topics he has filed international patents and published more than 200 refereed papers in international journals and conferences. Ernesto Damiani is the vice-chair of the ifip wg on Web Semantics (wg 2.12) and the secretary of the ifip wg on open source systems (wg 2.13). He is the author, together with W. Grosky and R. Khosla, of the book "Human-centered e-Business" (Kluwer 2003). In 2000, he was the recipient of acm sigapp outstanding service award.

Paolo Ceravolo (born October 13, 1977) holds a degree of laurea in philosophy from the philosophy department of the Catholic University of Milan, Italy and a PhD in computer science from the department of information technologies of the University of Milan, Italy. Currently, he is an assistant professor at the same department. His research interests include ontology-based knowledge extraction and management, process measurement, Semantic Web technologies, emergent process applied to semantics, uncertain knowledge and soft computing. On these topics he has published several scientific papers and book chapters. He is involved in the organization of different conferences such as innovation in knowledge-based & intelligent engineering systems (kes), ieee/ies conference on digital ecosystems and technologies (ieee-dest), knowledge management in organizations (kmo). Since 2008 he has been the secretary of the ifip 2.6 working group on database semantics.

Angelo Corallo is researcher in the department of innovation engineering at the University of Lecce. He graduated in physics at the University of Lecce. He has been researcher at the osservatorio astronomico di capodimonte. He teaches within the master and PhD programs of Scuola Superiore Isufi (University of Lecce) and PhD program in complex industrial systems. His research interests encompass mainly the co-evolution of technological and organizational innovation, with a specific focus on business ecosystem, extended enterprise and on knowledge management and collaborative working environment in project based organizations. He has been and is currently involved in many research projects related to technological and organizational issues both at the Italian and European levels (knowledge hub, technological system for tourism and cultural heritage, multichannel adaptive information system, digital business ecosystem). Angelo collaborates with the Massachusetts Institute of Technology in projects related to enterprise process modeling enabling business to e-business transition, and social network analysis in community of innovation. He collaborates with the business enterprise integration domain task force of omg in order to define an organizational metamodel supporting the architecture of business modelling framework.

Gianluca Elia is a researcher in knowledge and learning networks in the faculty of engineering--department of innovation engineering, University of Salento (Italy) and at the e-business management section (ebms) of the Scuola Superiore Isufi--University of Salento (Italy). After his degree in computer science engineering, he completed the master studies in e-business management at the e-business management section (ebms) of the Scuola Superiore Isufi. His research field concerns the methodological and technological aspect of knowledge management and Web learning processes and platforms. Moreover, he is responsible for some research projects involving Mediterranean countries in experimenting innovative approaches of human capital creation through the usage of internet based technologies.

* * * * *

Alex Brojba-micu received his BSC degree at Erasmus University Rotterdam, The Netherlands, in 2007. He is currently working towards the MSC degree in informatics & economics at the same university. His research interests include the Semantic Web, natural language processing, artificial intelligence, and stock price prediction.

Eliana Campi has a degree in computer science engineering from the University of Lecce. My thesis concerns the modelling and the implementing of ontology to support the local development. Currently, I am a research fellow at e-business management school and my field of research focuses mainly on ontology application for knowledge management, innovative technologies, and methodologies to organize a knowledge base, to index and search information with metadata, innovative approaches based on the vision of the semantic web. I am involved in the "knowledge warehousing" project that aims to define a knowledge management system able to manage documents about the process of new product development this project intends to represent the knowledge of these documents in a structured away to render easy its storage and reuse.

Alessandra Carcagnì graduated in computer engineering at University of Salento with a thesis in "organizational systems" entitled "methodology and workflow definition for ontology developing;" the research activity deals with logic modelling and implementation of process for ontology development for sharing and reusing knowledge in an information domain; the application field of this research is knowledge management, Semantic Web and organizational contexts. Currently she is attending an high training course at e-business management section of Scuola Superiore Isufi, Università of Salento on "engineers of e-business solutions for sme district" for production of ict platform directed to new processes and technologies for industrial districts; the course is connected with discorso project ("distributed information systems for coordinated service oriented interoperability") organized by the Italian minister of scientific research.

Maria Chiara Caschera received her degree in informatic engineering at the University of Rome 'la sapienza.' She is doctoral researcher in computer science at the 'roma tre' university sponsored by the multimedia & modal laboratory (m3l) of the National Research Council of Italy. She is mainly interested in human-computer interaction, multimodal interaction, visual languages, visual interfaces, and sketch-based interfaces.

Arianna d'Ulizia received her degree in informatic engineering at the University of Rome 'La Sapienza'. She is a doctoral researcher in computer science at the 'roma tre' university sponsored by the multi media & modal laboratory (m3l) of the National Research Council of Italy. She is mainly interested in human computer interaction, multimodal interaction, visual languages, visual interfaces, and geographical query languages.

Stefano David was born in Bressanone, bz, Italy in August 1972. He received his MSC Degree in computer science from the Universidad Politécnica de Madrid (spain) and the Free University of Bolzano (italy) in 2006. His research interests are in knowledge representation, ontology design patterns, description logics, and the Semantic Web. He is currently a PhD student at the Università Politecnica delle Marche, where he joined the 3medialabs group.

Fernando Ferri received the degrees in electronic engineering in 1990 and the PhD in medical informatics at the University of Rome "la sapienza" in 1993. He is senior researcher of the National Research Council of Italy. He was an adjunct professor from 1993 to 2000 of "sistemi di elaborazione" at the University of Macerata. He is the author of more than 100 papers on international journal, books, and conferences. His main research areas of interest are geographic information systems, human-computer interaction, user modelling, visual interfaces, and sketch based interfaces.

Flavius Frasincar obtained the MSC degree in computer science from "Politehnica" University Bucharest, Romania, in 1998. In 2000, he received the pdeng in software engineering from Eindhoven University of Technology, The Netherlands. He got the PhD degree in computer science from Eindhoven University of Technology, The Netherlands, in 2005. Since 2005, he has been Assistant Professor in information systems at Erasmus University Rotterdam, The Netherlands. He has published in numerous conferences and journals in the areas of databases, Web information systems, personalization, and the Semantic Web.

Cristiano Fugazza was born in Milan, Italy, in July 1971. He graduated in computer science by the dept. of information science, Università Degli Studi di Milano. He obtained the PhD in computer science from the dept. of information technologies, Università Degli Studi di Milano. He is primarily committed to knowledge management techniques, which he applies to context modelling, particularly in the field of business intelligence.

Samuel Gomes received his PhD in mechanical engineering from Belfort-Montbéliard University of Technology (France) in 1999. He is currently Assistant Professor in the department of mechanical engineering in the same university. His current research interest includes product lifecycle management, collaborative engineering, and knowledge engineering.

Patrizia Grifoni received the degrees in electronic engineering at the University of Rome "La Sapienza." She is a researcher at the National Research Council of Italy. From 1994 to 1999 she was an adjunct professor of "elaborazione digitale delle immagini" at the University of Macerata. She is the author of more than 70 papers in journal, books, and conferences. Her main research interests are in human computer interaction, visual interfaces, sketch based interfaces, accessing web information, and geographc information systems.

Ákos Hajnal was born in 1972. He studied electrical engineering at Budapest Technical University, 1991-96. He got his diploma in electrical engineering at Budapest Technical University in 1996. He was a PhD student at Eötvös Lóránd University of Cciences, Budapest, between 1997-2000. Currently, he is working on his PhD thesis. Since 1996, he has a research fellow at the computer and automation research institute of the Hungarian Academy of Sciences (mta sztaki).

Associate Prof. **Vincent Hilaire** got his PhD in computer science and his position in the University of Technology of Belfort Montbéliard in 2000. The main focus of the PhD was formal specification and methodologies for engineering of multi-agent systems. Since then his research follows axes : multi-agent systems organizational theories and holonic systems, languages for formal specification prototyping and proofs of mas, agent architectures and agent mediated knowledge management.

Nunzio Ingraffia graduated cum laude in eletronics engineering with major in computer electronic in 1997. After working in diverse software companies, he started working in engineering from 2000, participating in business software teams. Since 2003, he has been employed in r&d, where he has acquired expertise in project management and coordination of several national research projects. The main results are related on human-computer interaction (specification of a user presentation language based on visual and verbal design pattern paradigm), Semantic Web-based systems (design of information management framework on ontology-based search engine), information extraction area (studies on latent semantic analysis over databases), business process modelling (specification of an editor to integrate business process modelling notation and xml process definition language). During his research activities, he has been author of some scientific international publications. Currently, he is head of a unit, dealing topics on business processes modelling and semantics-based information systems.

Uzay Kaymak received the MSC degree in electrical engineering, the pdeng in information technology, and the PhD degree in control engineering from Delft University of Technology, The Netherlands, in 1992, 1995, and 1998, respectively. From 1997 to 2000, he was a reservoir engineer with Shell international exploration and production. He is currently associate professor of economics and computer science with the econometric institute, Erasmus University Rotterdam, The Netherlands. Dr. Kaymak is an associate editor of the ieee transactions on fuzzy systems and is a member of the editorial board of fuzzy sets and systems.

Prof. **Abder Koukam** received the PhD In computer science from University of Nancy (France) in 1990, where he served as an assistant professor from 1986 to 1989 and researcher in "centre de recherche en informatique de nancy (crin)" from 1985 to 1990. In 1999, he received the enabling to direct researches in computer science from University of Bourgogne . Presently, he is professor of computer science at "Université de Technologie de Belfort-Montbeliard utbm". He heads research activities at systems and transportation (set) laboratory on modeling and analysis of complex systems, including software engineering, multi-agent systems and optimization, and he is authors or co-authors of over 80 scientific publications.

Marcello Leida was born the 29th of July 1977 in Romano di Lombardia (bg), Italy. He graduated in information technology at the Università Degli Studi of Milan in 2004. From October 2004 to November 2005 he has worked as a research collaborator at the department of information technologies of Università Degli Studi of Milan doing research work on knowledge management. Since November 2005 he has been a PhD student in the department of information technologies of Università Degli Studi of Milan doing research work on data integration, matching operators and ontology reasoning. He is the author of several articles appearing in international science publications about knowledge management, data integration and query, and business process modelling. Marcello Leida is involved in several research projects, partly funded by public institutions and industrial partners regarding data integration, knowledge management and development of systems for data integration and query of knowledge bases.

Gianluca Lorenzo is a software engineer. I took my degree in computer science engineering at University of Lecce (Italy), with a thesis concerning the analysis of electronic distribution channels in travel industry, design and implementation of a prototype of "last minute multi-channel booking system." I am a research fellow at e-business management school. My fields of interest are distributed computing systems, soa and roa architectures and web technologies.

Laurens Mast received his BSC degree at Erasmus University of Rotterdam, The Netherlands in 2007. He is currently working towards the MSC degree in informatics & economics at the same university. His research interests include the Semantic Web, project management, and intelligent systems.

Carlo Mastroianni has been a researcher at the institute of high performance computing and networks of the Italian National Research Council (icar-cnr) in Cosenza, Italy, since 2002. He received his PhD in computer engineering from the University of Calabria in 1999. His research interests focus on distributed systems and networks, in particular on grid computing, peer-to-peer networks, content distribution networks, multi agent systems. He has published more than 60 scientific papers in international journals and conferences. He currently lectures on computer networks at the University of Calabria.

Viorel Milea obtained the MSC degree in informatics & economics from Erasmus University Rotterdam, The Netherlands in 2006. Currently, he is working towards his PhD degree at Erasmus University in Rotterdam, The Netherlands. The focus of his PhD is on employing Semantic Web technologies for enhancing the current state-of-the-art in automated trading with a focus on processing information contained in economic news messages and assessing its impact on stock prices. His research interests cover areas such as semantic web theory and applications, intelligent systems in finance, and nature-inspired classification and optimization techniques.

Anna Montesanto was born in Fermo (ap), Italy, in June 1969. She received the laurea degree in psychology from the university of Rome "la sapienza" (Italy) in 1995, the MSC degree in "cognitive psychology and neural networks" in 1996, and the PhD Degree in "artificial intelligent systems" from the University of Ancona (Italy) in 2001. She was a visiting scientist at the robotic lab, department of computer science University of Manchester in 2000. Currently she works in the department of electronics, artificial intelligence and telecommunications (deit), Università Politecnica delle Marche. Her current interests are connectionistic methods applied to biometrics.

Mr. **Davy Monticolo** is currently the project leader of the knowledge management project in the Zurfluh-feller company. He is also a PhD student of computer science at Belfort-Montbéliard University of Technology (France). His research focuses on multi-agent system, methods and tools for knowledge modeling.

Antonio Moreno is a lecturer at the University Rovira i virgili's computer science and mathematics department. He is the founder and head of the itaka research group (intelligent technologies for advanced knowledge acquisition). His main research interests are the application of agent technology to health care problems and ontology learning from the Web. He received a PhD on artificial intelligence from UPC (Technical University of Catalonia) in 2000. He is the academic coordinator of the master on computer engineering and security (urv) and the master on artificial intelligence (upc-urv-ub).

Giuseppina Passiante is full professor at the Department of Innovation Engineering, Faculty of Engineering, University of Lecce, (Italy) and at the eBMS- ISUFI. Currently her research fields concern the e-Business management, and more specifically the management of learning Organizations and learning processes in the Net-Economy. Her focus is mainly on the development of Intellectual Capital, both in the entrepreneurial and in the academic organizations. She is also expert in development of local systems versus information and communications technologies, ICTs and clusters approach, complexity in economic systems: in these research fields she has realized programs and projects, and published several papers.

Gianfranco Pedone was born in 1975 in Casarano, Italy. He studied information technology and management at the University of studies in lecce where he got his it engineering diploma in 2004. He is a PhD student at the Eötvös Lóránd University of Sciences in Budapest. Currently, he is working on his PhD thesis. Since 2006 he has been a research fellow at computer and automation research institute of the Hungarian Academy of Sciences (mta sztaki) in the system development department. His main research interests include agent, languages and Web computing for semantic interoperability in scientific and business applications.

Giuseppe Pirrò is a PhD student at university of calabria, italy. He received his laurea degree from the same university in 2005. His research interests include semantic Web technologies, ontology mapping in open environments and peer-to-peer systems.

David Riaño is a lecturer of the department of computer sciences and mathematics at the Rovira i Virgili University. He is the head of the research group on artificial intelligence at this university. During the last decade he has been working in the areas of medical informatics, knowledge management, and knowledge discovery in medicine. During 2005 he was invited researcher of the Stanford Medical Informatics Group. He is the general coordinator of the fp6 european k4care project (ist-2004-026968) and the Spanish national project higia (tin2006-15453-c04-01).

Cesare Rocchi is a PhD student at Università Politecnica delle Marche and a research consultant at Fondazione Bruno Kessler. He received a degree in philosphy at Università di Bologna. He has been working in the areas of adaptive hypermedia, intelligent user interface, user modelling. He is currently researching on tabletop interfaces and multi-modality, with a particular attention to semantic issues involved in these fields.

Giustina Secundo is a researcher in management education at the e-business management section (ebms) of the Scuola Superiore isufi– University of Salento (Italy). After a degree in mathematics, she completed her master studies in e-business management at the ebms. Her research field concerns the emerging trends in management education and the human capital creation process in business schools, with a special interest to the learning processes supported by the information and communication technologies. These research fields are strictly connected to her activities related to the management of the advanced education programs of the ebms.

Silvio Sorace graduated from the University of Palermo in 2002 with a bachelors degree in it engineering. His dissertation, entitled "Projection and Realization of an Agent-based Software System for a Mobile Robot with Surveillance Components" allowed him to study agent-based platforms in great depth. In 2003, as a result of his dissertation studies, he published the article "Patterns Reuse in the Passi Methodology," at the esaw'03 workshop. Since 2003, he has worked in the laboratories of ricerca & sviluppo di engineering ingegneria informatica s.p.a. At present he deals with business process management systems, with particular focus on the processes execution into workflow engines.

Domenico Talia is a professor of computer engineering at the University of Calabria, Italy, and a research associate at icar-cnr in rende, italy. He received the laurea degree in physics from the University of Calabria. His research interests include grid computing, distributed knowledge discovery, parallel data mining, parallel programming languages, and peer-to-peer systems. Talia has published four books and more than 200 papers in international journals and conference proceedings. He is a member of the editorial boards of ieee tkde, the future generation computer systems journal, the international journal on web and grid services, the parallel and distributed practices journal, and the web intelligence and agent systems international journal. He is a member of the executive committee of the coregrid network of excellence. He is serving as a program committee member of several conferences and is a member of the acm and the ieee computer society.

Cesare Taurino is research fellow in Web learning at the e-business management section (ebms) of the Scuola Superiore Isufi--University of Salento (Italy). After a degree in computer science engineering, he started his professional experience at the ebms. His research field concerns the emerging trends, methodologies and technologies for Web learning, as well as the implication of Semantic Web on Web learning. Actually he is responsible of the Web learning lab of the ebms and he is involved in managing, customizing and administrating a Web learning platform and in creating Web learning contents.

Dr. **Lorna Uden** is a senior lecturer in the faculty of computing, engineering and technology at Staffordshire University in the UK. She has published over 120 papers in conferences, journals, chapters of books, and workshops. She co-authored the book "Technology and problem - based larning", published by ideal publishers. Dr. Uden is program committee member for many international conferences and workshops. She is on the editorial board of several international journals. She is visiting professor and research scientist to several countries. She has been keynote speaker at several international conferences. She collaborates widely with colleagues from Australia, Finland, Italy, Slovenia, Spain, South Africa, Taiwan and the USA.

László Zsolt Varga is a senior scientific associate and head of the system development department at mta sztaki. He was visiting researcher in cern and in the department of electronic engineering at Queen Mary & Westfield College, University of London where his research focused on basic and applied research into the development of multi-agent systems. His current research interests include agent, grid and Web computing for semantic interoperability in scientific and business applications. He has PhD in informatics from the electronic engineering and informatics faculty of the Technical University of udapest.

Marco Viviani holds a degree of laurea in computer science from the department of information technologies of the University of Milan, Italy. Currently, he is a research collaborator and a PhD student at the same department. His research interests include knowledge extraction and management, semantic Web technologies, data mining techniques, pattern recognition and clustering, trust/reputation and fuzzy logic. On these topics he has published several scientific papers and book chapters.

Kuan Yew Wong, PhD, Is a senior lecturer at the Universiti Teknologi Malaysia (utm), Malaysia. He has published numerous km articles in various international journals, for example the Journal of knowledge management, knowledge and process management, industrial management & data systems, journal of information & knowledge management, international journal of information technology and management, expert systems with applications, international journal of business information systems etc. He is currently the regional editor--Asia Pacific for international journal of knowledge management studies, and associate editor for vine: the journal of information and knowledge management systems. In addition, he has successfully completed a number of research projects funded by the Malaysian government and Intel Corporation.

Wai Peng Wong, PhD, is a lecturer at the Universiti Sains Malaysia (usm), Malaysia. Her publications have appeared in industrial management & data systems, benchmarking: an international journal and international journal of applied systemic studies, to name but a few. Her research interests are centred on supply chain management and knowledge management.

Index

D

E

P

Q

R

S

T